WORLD

PEACE

EFFORTS

Since Gandhi

This book is dedicated
to all who work
for peace and justice
with love, joy, and integrity.

Books by Sanderson Beck
from World Peace Communications:

HISTORY OF PEACE:

1. Guides to Peace and Justice
     from Ancient Sages to the Suffragettes
2. World Peace Efforts Since Gandhi

ETHICS OF CIVILIZATION:

1. Middle East & Africa to 1875
2. India & Southeast Asia to 1875
3. China, Korea & Japan to 1875
4. Greece & Rome to 30 BC
5. Roman Empire 30 BC to 610
6. Medieval Europe 610-1300

Wisdom Bible (editor)

Nonviolent Action Handbook

The Art of Gentle Living

BEST FOR ALL: How We Can Save the World

History of Peace
Volume 2

WORLD
PEACE
EFFORTS
Since Gandhi

by Sanderson Beck

Second Edition

World Peace Communications

Goleta, California

World Peace Communications was founded September 1,
2001 as a non-profit corporation for educational, literary,
and charitable purposes.

For more information please contact:

World Peace Communications
495 Whitman St. #A
Goleta, CA 93117
USA
1worldpeace.org
san@beck.org

Publishers Cataloging-in-Publication Data

Beck, Sanderson, 1947-
    History of Peace, Volume 2: World Peace Efforts Since
Gandhi
— 2nd ed.
Goleta, California: World Peace Communications, 2006
x, 624 p. 21 cm.
Includes bibliography, chronological index of events, and
    alphabetical index of names.
ISBN 0-9762210-6-3
1. Nonviolence.
2. Peaceful Change.
3. Peace movements.
4. Peace: international law.
5. Pacific settlement of international disputes.
6. Peace and disarmament.
7. Peace—History.
I. Title.
II. Series.
JZ 5548 .B42   341.73–dc21   LCCN: 2005929408

Contents

1. Gandhi's Nonviolent Revolution   **1**

2. Wilson and the League of Nations   **28**

3. United Nations and Human Rights   **70**

4. United Nations Peacekeeping   **99**

5. Einstein & Schweitzer on Peace in the Atomic Age   **130**

6. Pacifism of Bertrand Russell and A. J. Muste   **150**

7. Clark-Sohn Plan for World Law and Disarmament   **174**

8. King and the Civil Rights Movement   **193**

9. Lessons of the Vietnam War   **233**

10. Women for Peace   **254**

11. Anti-Nuclear Protests   **301**

12. Resisting Wars in Central America   **324**

13. Gorbachev and Ending the Cold War   **363**

14. Mandela and Freeing South Africa   **391**

15. Chomsky and Zinn on US Imperialism   **431**

16. Protesting the Bush-Iraq Wars   **476**

17. Nonviolent Revolution for Global Justice   **514**

Appendix: My Efforts for World Peace   **532**

Bibliography   **565**

Chronological Index of Events   **593**

Alphabetical Index of Names   **600**

Topics

1. Gandhi's Nonviolent Revolution   1
Gandhi's Experiments in South Africa   2
Nonviolent Campaign for Indian Independence   8
Soul Force and Nonviolence   20

2. Wilson and the League of Nations   28
The Hague Peace Conferences   29
Wilson and a League for Peace   32
Versailles Peace Treaty   42
United States' Rejection of the League   50
League of Nations Progress 1920-29   52
League of Nations Failures After 1930   58

3. United Nations and Human Rights   70
Roosevelt and the United Nations Alliance   71
United Nations Charter   81
Nuremberg Trials and Geneva Conventions   84
Universal Declaration of Human Rights   89

4. United Nations Peacekeeping   99
UN Peacekeeping During the Cold War   99
UN Peacekeeping After the Cold War   117

5. Einstein & Schweitzer on Peace in the Atomic Age   130
Einstein on Peace and World Government   131
Schweitzer's Reverence for Life   141

6. Pacifism of Bertrand Russell and A. J. Muste   150
Bertrand Russell and the World Wars   151
Bertrand Russell in the Nuclear Age   157
Nonviolent Activism of A. J. Muste   166

7. Clark-Sohn Plan for World Law and Disarmament   174
Nuclear Weapons and World Government   174
Grenville Clark's Peace Plan   178
Clark-Sohn Proposal for World Law   181

McCloy-Zorin Disarmament Effort   187

8. King and the Civil Rights Movement   **193**
NAACP, CORE, and Desegregation   194
King and the Montgomery Bus Boycott   196
King and SCLC Campaigns   202
Student Nonviolent Coordinating Committee   210
King Challenges Poverty and War   217
Chavez and the United Farm Workers   222

9. Lessons of the Vietnam War   **233**
French Colonial Vietnam   234
American Vietnam War   238
American Lessons from Vietnam   249

10. Women for Peace   **254**
Suttner, Courtney, Royden, and Weil   256
Addams, Woman's Peace Party, and WILPF   264
Dorothy Day and the Catholic Worker   275
Women Strike for Peace   280
Feminism and Nonviolence   283
Aung San Suu Kyi in Burma   290
Medea Benjamin and Code Pink   296

11. Anti-Nuclear Protests   **301**
Protesting Nuclear Testing   301
Protesting Nuclear Power   306
Protesting Nuclear Weapons   308
Nuclear Weapons Freeze Campaign   316

12. Resisting Wars in Central America   **324**
Central American History   325
El Salvador's Civil War   328
Nicaragua's Sandinistas and Contras   336
Resisting Reagan's Proxy Wars   342
Costa Rica and Arias   350
Bush's Panama Invasion   356
School of the Americas Protests   360

13. **Gorbachev and Ending the Cold War**   363
      Nonviolently Resisting Tyranny   364
      Rebelling Against Soviet Domination   367
      Gorbachev's Reforms and Arms Race Reversal   373
      Liberation of Eastern Europe 1989-91   379
      Gorbachev and the Earth Charter   387

14. **Mandela and Freeing South Africa**   391
      Luthuli, Mandela, and the ANC 1943-61   393
      Mandela's Sabotage and Imprisonment   403
      Biko and Black Consciousness   407
      Mandela's ANC Negotiation with South Africa   412
      Mandela's Presidency of South Africa   419
      Truth and Reconciliation Commission   424

15. **Chomsky and Zinn on US Imperialism**   431
      Chomsky's Analysis of US Foreign Policy   432
      Chomsky on Propaganda and Profits   444
      Zinn on US History and Wars   450
      Yugoslavia War   457
      George W. Bush's War on Terrorism   463
      Chomsky on US Hegemony   467

16. **Protesting the Bush-Iraq Wars**   476
      Clark on the 1991 Iraq War   477
      Sanctions Against Iraq   488
      Kelly on the Sanctions and War   494
      Bush II's War on Iraq   500
      Millions Protest the War Against Iraq   505

17. **Nonviolent Revolution for Global Justice**   514
      Global Emergency   514
      Nonviolent Strategies   518
      Democratic Revolution   526
      Disarmament and World Justice   528
      Sustainable Civilization   529

Appendix: My Efforts for World Peace   **532**
    My Path to the World Peace Movement   533
    Protesting the MX and Cruise Missiles   539
    Networking for Peace   542
    Nuremberg Actions at Concord   550
    Protesting the Trident Missiles   553
    2003 Peace Campaign   556

Bibliography   **565**

Chronological Index of Events   **593**

Alphabetical Index of Names   **600**

1

Gandhi's Nonviolent Revolution

Gandhi continues what the Buddha began.
In the Buddha the spirit of love set itself the task
of creating different spiritual conditions in the world;
in Gandhi it undertakes to transform *all* worldly conditions.
Albert Schweitzer, *Indian Thought and Its Development*

If man will only realize
that it is unmanly to obey laws that are unjust,
no man's tyranny will enslave him.
Mohandas Gandhi, *Hind Swaraj*

Nonviolence is the law of our species
as violence is the law of the brute.
The spirit lies dormant in the brute,
and he knows no law but that of physical might.
The dignity of man requires obedience to a higher law—
to the strength of the spirit.
Mohandas Gandhi, *Young India* August 11, 1920

For self-defense, I would restore the spiritual culture.
The best and most lasting self-defense is self-purification.
Mohandas Gandhi, 1924

Those who say that religion has nothing to do with politics
do not know what religion means.
Mohandas Gandhi, *Autobiography*

A nonviolent revolution is not a program of seizure of power.
It is a program of transformation of relationships
ending in a peaceful transfer of power.
Mohandas Gandhi, 1942

Mohandas Karamchand Gandhi was born on October 2, 1869 at Porbandar in western India. His father was prime minister of the very small state, and his mother was a religious Vaishnavite. At the age of 13 Mohandas was married to a girl his own age and began an active sex life. In his autobiography he admitted that as a boy he secretly ate meat with his friends so that they could become strong like the English. After some local education it was decided that he should go to England to study law. He gained his mother's permission by promising to refrain from wine, women, and meat, but he defied his caste's regulations which forbade travel to England. He joined the Inner Temple law college in London. In searching for a vegetarian restaurant he discovered its philosophy in Henry Salt's A *Plea for Vegetarianism* and became convinced. He organized a vegetarian club and met people with theosophical and altruistic interests. He discovered the *Bhagavad-Gita* in Edwin Arnold's poetic translation, *The Song Celestial,* and offered his limited knowledge of Sanskrit to others. This Hindu scripture and the Sermon on the Mount later became his bibles and spiritual guidebooks. He memorized the *Gita* during his daily tooth brushing and often recited its original Sanskrit at his prayer meetings.

Gandhi's Experiments in South Africa

By the time Gandhi returned to India in 1891, his mother had died. He was not successful at breaking into the legal profession because of his shyness. So he took the opportunity of representing an Indian firm in Natal, South Africa for a year. South Africa, which was notorious for racial discrimination, gave Gandhi the insults which awakened his social conscience. He refused to remove his turban in court; he was thrown out of a first-class railway compartment; he was beaten for refusing to move to the footboard of a stage-coach for the sake of a European passenger; and he was pushed and kicked off a footpath by a policeman. As a lawyer Gandhi did his best to discover the facts and get the parties to accept arbitration and compromise in order to settle out of court. After solving a difficult case in this way he was elated and commented, "I had learned to find out the better side of human nature and to enter men's hearts. I realized that the true function of a lawyer was to unite parties riven asunder."[1] He also insisted on receiving the truth from his clients; if he found out that they had lied, he dropped their cases. He believed that the lawyer's duty is to help the court discover the truth, not to try to prove the guilty innocent.

At the end of the year during a farewell party before he was to sail for India, Gandhi noticed in the newspaper that a bill was being proposed that would deprive Indians of the vote. His friends urged him to stay and lead the fight for their rights in South Africa. He founded the Natal Indian Congress in 1894, and their efforts were given considerable notice by the press. While he was visiting India, Gandhi wrote a green pamphlet entitled *The Grievances of the British Indians in South Africa*. When he returned from fetching his family from India in January 1897, the South Africans tried to stop him from landing by bribing and threatening the ship-owner Dada Abdulla Sheth; but Dada Abdulla was Gandhi's client, and finally after a long quarantine period Gandhi was allowed to disembark. The waiting mob recognized Gandhi, and some whites began to hit his face and body until the Police Superintendent's wife came to his rescue. The mob threatened to lynch him, but Gandhi escaped in a disguise and remained in protective police custody for a few days. Later he refused to prosecute anyone, holding to the principle of self-restraint in regard to a personal wrong; besides, it had been the community leaders and the Natal government who caused the problem.

Gandhi felt it was his duty to support the British during the Boer War; so he organized and led an Indian Ambulance Corps to nurse the wounded on the battlefield. Even this effort was somewhat delayed by race prejudice; but when three hundred free Indians and eight hundred indentured servants volunteered, the whites were impressed. Gandhi was given a medal for his service in the Boer War. In 1902 he traveled in India, and with Gokhale's support his resolution for the Indians in South Africa was passed by the Indian Congress in Calcutta.

Gandhi served the Indian community in Johannesburg, and during the plague of 1904 he got Indian money sterilized so that they could get nursing services. He was instrumental in publishing *Indian Opinion* weekly in English, Gujarati, Hindi, and Tamil from the hundred-acre Phoenix Farm community he founded. Attracted to the simple agricultural life, Gandhi was influenced by John Ruskin's *Unto This Last*, which he translated into Gujarati. He readily agreed with Ruskin's idea that the good of the individual is contained in the good of all; but the value of labor in tilling the soil or in handicrafts was a revelation to Gandhi. He recruited another Indian ambulance unit during the Zulu Rebellion and was made a sergeant major. Gandhi experimented with celibacy during his thirties, and in 1906 he took the Brahmacharya vow for the rest of his life. That year Gandhi led a delegation to London and met with the Secretary of State for India, John Morley, to present the case for Indians' rights in South Africa. Gandhi also met with Winston Churchill, who promised to help.

His first use of civil disobedience on a mass scale began in September 1906 when the Transvaal government wanted to register the entire Indian population and passed what the Indians called the "Black Act." In response they held a mass meeting in the Imperial Theatre of Johannesburg; some were so angry at the humiliating ordinance that they threatened a violent response if put to the test. However, with Gandhi's advice they all decided as a group to refuse to comply with the registration provisions. Gandhi suggested that they take a pledge in the name of God; even though they were Hindus and Muslims, they all believed in one and the same God. Every one of the nearly three thousand Indians present took the solemn pledge. Gandhi decided to call this technique of refusing to submit to injustice *satyagraha*, which means literally "holding to the truth." One week after the pledge, Asiatic women were excused from having to register.

When the Transvaal government finally put the Asiatic Registration Act into effect in 1907, only 511 out of 13,000

Indians registered. Gandhi and several other Indians were arrested. He was given two months without hard labor, and he spent the time reading. During his life Gandhi would spend a total of 249 days in South African jails and 2,089 days in Indian jails. Gandhi declared to his followers that a *satyagrahi* must be fearless and always trust his opponent, "for an implicit trust in human nature is the very essence of his creed."[2] *Satyagraha* thus by its honest purity appeals to the best in the adversary and exposes the true situation for all to see.

It uncovers concealed motives and reveals the truth.
It puts the best possible interpretation
on the opponent's intentions and thereby
gives him another chance to discard baser impulses.
If he fails to do so,
his victims see more clearly and feel more intensely,
while outsiders realize who is wrong.[3]

On February 3, 1908 General Jan Christiaan Smuts promised Gandhi that he would repeal the Transvaal Asiatic Registration Act if they would accept the compromise and register. Gandhi explained the agreement to a meeting, and a majority agreed to register. However, Gandhi's former client Mir Alam Khan accused him of selling out to General Smuts and swore he would kill any man who gave his fingerprints. A week later Gandhi went to register, and the tall Mir Alam knocked him out. Gandhi was kicked and beat by Mir Alam and his companions until he was rescued by passing Europeans. Gandhi was taken to the home of Baptist minister Joseph Doke, where he gave his fingerprints and recovered from his injuries.

General Smuts then introduced a bill to validate the voluntary certificates but not to repeal the Black Act. So on August 16, 1908 three thousand Indians gathered outside the Hamida Mosque in Johannesburg to hear Gandhi make a speech before they burned about two thousand registration certificates. Mir Alam apologized to Gandhi, and they shook hands. Some Chinese burned their certificates too.

Two days later the government started deporting new Asiatic immigrants for not knowing a European language. On October 7 Gandhi was arrested for not having his certificate and for refusing to be fingerprinted. He asked for the maximum punishment and was sentenced to a fine or two months hard labor; he chose the latter.

While reading in jail, Gandhi discovered Thoreau's "Civil Disobedience." He was already familiar with the works of Tolstoy and was "overwhelmed" by *The Kingdom of God is Within You* as he "began to realize more and more the infinite possibilities of universal love."[4] Gandhi distinguished *satyagraha* from "passive resistance," which had been used by religious Non-conformists and suffragettes in England and sometimes inflicted injuries and damage. In *Satyagraha in South Africa* Gandhi wrote that passive resistance had been used along with the use of arms; but *satyagraha* is the negation of brute force and avoids any injury to the opponent while being willing to suffer in one's own person. As other examples of *satyagraha* he gave Jesus Christ, the early Christians, and the Russian Dukhobors cited by Tolstoy.

The protest movement for Indian rights in South Africa continued to grow; at one point out of the 13,000 Indians in the province 2,500 were in jail, while 6,000 had fled Transvaal. In being civil to the opponents during the disobedience, Gandhi developed the use of *ahimsa*, which means "non-hurting" and is usually translated "nonviolence." Gandhi followed the precept, "Hate the sin and not the sinner." Since we are all one spiritually, to hurt or attack another person is to attack oneself. Though we may attack an unjust system, we must always love the persons involved. Thus *ahimsa* became his method in the search for truth. People said that Gandhi was a saint who was losing himself in politics, but he considered himself a politician trying his hardest to be a saint.

Gandhi was sent to London again in 1909, but he felt that suffering in jail did more good than spending money in England seeing politicians and journalists. After meeting extremists who insisted that India could never win its independence without violence, on his return voyage Gandhi wrote the dialog *Hind Swaraj*, which means "Indian Self-Rule." Based on the conversations he had in London, in this diatribe against the corruption of Western civilization Gandhi suggested that India could gain its independence by nonviolent means and self-reliance. He rejected brute force and its oppression and declared that soul force or love is what keeps people together in peace and harmony. History ignores the peaceful qualities but notices the interruptions and violations which disrupt civilization. He concluded the dialog by declaring that his life was henceforth dedicated to attaining Indian self-rule.

Aided by a donation of 1500 pounds and the 1,100-acre farm bought and built by architect Hermann Kallenbach, Gandhi named this ashram Tolstoy Farm. He exchanged a few letters with the great Russian novelist before he died and continued to write and edit the journal *Indian Opinion* in order to elucidate the principles and practice of *satyagraha*.

Three issues brought the quest for Indian rights in South Africa to a crisis—there was a three-pound annual tax on former indentured servants; Asian immigration was banned; and in March 1913 a law went into effect invalidating all but Christian marriages. When Gandhi explained the new law to his wife Kasturbai, she and others crossing the border into Transvaal in protest were arrested on September 15, 1913. Gandhi could not figure out how to feed the striking miners that gathered around him at Newcastle; so after warning them about the horrors of European-run jails, at the end of October he led them from Natal into Transvaal so that they could be "safely deposited in jail." He was followed by 2,037 men, 127 women, and 57 children. After they crossed the border, they were not arrested. Gandhi was arrested and paid bail to return to his army; he was arrested again and released and arrested once more, all within four days. The pilgrims headed toward Tolstoy Farm but were deported back to the Newcastle mines, where they were imprisoned. Gandhi was sentenced to three months' hard labor, but the strikes and demonstrations went on with about 50,000 indentured laborers on strike and thousands of free Indians in prison. The Christian missionary Charles F. Andrews donated all his money to the movement. Gandhi and the other leaders were released and announced another march. However, Gandhi refused to take advantage of a railway strike by white employees and called off the march in spite of Smuts' broken pledge in 1908. Gandhi explained, "Forgiveness is the ornament of the brave."[5] After six months of negotiation the issues were finally resolved by Smuts and Gandhi at the end of June in 1914, and the Indian Relief Act went into effect in July. All marriages regardless of religion were valid; the tax on indentured laborers was canceled including arrears; and Indians were allowed to move more freely. General Smuts expressed his respect for Gandhi and his gentle but powerful methods, which had made him realize which laws had to be repealed. Gandhi summarized in *Indian Opinion* the power of the *satyagraha* method and prophesied how it could transform modern civilization.

It is a force which, if it became universal,
would revolutionize social ideals
and do away with despotisms
and the ever-growing militarism
under which the nations of the West are groaning
and are being almost crushed to death,
and which fairly promises to overwhelm
even the nations of the East.[6]

Nonviolent Campaign for Indian Independence

Meanwhile India was still suffering under British colonial rule. Gandhi arrived in England during the first week of the World War, and again he supported the British by raising and leading an ambulance corps; but he became ill and returned to India in January 1915. The great poet

Rabindranath Tagore gave Gandhi the title "Mahatma," meaning "Great Soul," and in May 1915 Gandhi founded the Satyagraha Ashram for his family and co-workers near the textile city of Ahmedabad in Gujarat. When a family of untouchables asked to live in the ashram, Gandhi admitted them. Orthodox Hindus believed this polluted them. Funds ran out, and Gandhi was ready to live in the untouchable slums if necessary; but an anonymous benefactor donated enough money to last a year. To help change people's attitudes about these unfortunate pariahs, Gandhi renamed them "Harijans" or "Children of God." Later he called his weekly magazine *Harijan* also. In a speech at the opening of Benares University on February 6, 1916 Gandhi said he was ashamed to be speaking in English but questioned whether the anarchists' use of assassination and bomb-throwing was honorable. Yet he agreed that Indians must take power into their hands to gain self-government. Actually Gandhi had not planned to say these things but did so after he was interrupted by the opposition of Theosophist Annie Besant.

Gandhi began wearing home-spun *khadi* in order to encourage self-sufficient village industries and thus help alleviate poverty in India. In April 1917 Gandhi went to Bihar to learn how suffering indigo workers in Champaran were being exploited by exorbitant fees of landlords. He was arrested and ordered to leave; but as he insisted on staying, he was put in jail. However, the officials soon realized that the Mahatma was the only one who could control the crowds. Assistants helped by carefully documenting the grievances of several thousand peasants, and reforms were won again by civil disobedience. The textile workers of Ahmedabad were also economically oppressed. Gandhi suggested a strike; when the workers were weakening in their resolve, he went on a fast to encourage them to continue the strike. Gandhi explained that he did not fast to coerce the opponent but to strengthen or reform those who loved him. He did not believe in fasting for higher wages, but he fasted so that the workers would accept the system of arbitration to resolve the conflict, which they did.

In the spring of 1918 Gandhi was persuaded by the British to help raise soldiers for a final victory effort in the war. Charlie Andrews criticized Gandhi for recruiting Indians to fight for the British. Gandhi spoke to large audiences but gained hardly any recruits. He was experimenting with a limited raw-food diet and became sick. Even after the war the Rowlatt Act continued the strict laws against sedition. Despite India's cooperation with Britain during the war, they did not receive Dominion Status, and civil liberties were being curtailed.

Guided by a dream or inner experience, Gandhi decided to call for a one-day *hartal* or general strike on all economic activity. Many signed the *satyagraha* pledge, and Gandhi suggested making "a continuous and persistent effort to return good for evil."[7] Before that day in Old Delhi, Gurka troops opened fire on a march and killed five Hindus and four Muslims. On April 6, 1919 all Indians stopped working. Gandhi spoke and said that machine-guns would no longer afflict them. Two days later he was arrested trying to go to Delhi. News of his arrest led to civil disobedience. Gandhi was allowed to return to Ahmedabad, which he found under martial law because mill workers had killed a British officer, burned government buildings, extorted money, captured weapons, plundered shops, and attacked private houses. Gandhi realized that now he must protest the behavior of his own people, and he announced a penitential fast for three days, calling off the campaign and declaring he had made a "Himalayan miscalculation."

In an infamous incident at Amritsar on April 13, 1919 Brigadier General Reginald Dyer, reacted to the killing of three Englishmen by an Indian mob by prohibiting public meetings and then ordering his soldiers to fire into the crowd at an outdoor gathering, killing 379 and wounding 1,137 with only 1,650 bullets. The Hunter Report quoted Dyer's own report that he was less concerned with dispersing the crowd and more intent on "producing a sufficient moral effect from a military point of view."[8]

General Drake-Brockman of Delhi also made the statement, "Force is the only thing that an Asiatic has any respect for."[9] The Hunter Report concluded that the moral effect was quite opposite from the one intended; General Dyer was censured and later relieved of his command.

Gandhi was given editorial control over two weeklies without advertisements—*Young India* in English and *Navajivan* in Gujarati and later Hindi. More than seven thousand delegates attended the Amritsar Congress the last week of 1919. Gandhi agreed to support the Muslim Khilafat movement without requiring them to stop slaughtering cows. Instead of civil disobedience, he proposed a nation-wide campaign of nonviolent noncooperation with the British government. For the peasant this meant not paying taxes and not buying liquor because the government gained revenue from its sale. Gandhi wrote to the Viceroy, returning his war medals. In October 1920 at the annual Indian Congress 14,000 delegates enthusiastically agreed on noncooperation with the British and to end untouchability. Gandhi promised that noncooperation would bring about self-government in one year. At the beginning of 1921 Motilal Nehru, D. R. Das, Vallabhbhai Patel, and thousands of others abandoned their law practices and British courts as students, teachers, and professionals went into the villages to teach literacy and noncooperation.

Gandhi traveled throughout India addressing mass meetings, and imported fabrics were burned. He urged people to spin and weave their own cloth while boycotting British products, and he designed a Congress flag with a spinning wheel in the center. When the Prince of Wales (Edward VIII) visited Bombay in November 1921, protests degenerated into mob violence with looting. Some policemen were beaten to death; in three days of riots 58 Bombay citizens were killed, and four hundred were injured. Gandhi went on a fast to end the violence. In December the arrests began. By the time Congress met in the last week of 1921 there were 20,000 in jail. Some nationalist patriots urged rebellion. Although Gandhi believed that cowardice is worse than violence, he still believed that nonviolent action is better than both. Six thousand delegates approved Gandhi's resolution for civil disobedience of all government laws, especially those banning public meetings.

Gandhi planned a massive nonviolent campaign in Bardoli, a county of 87,000; but news of how an Indian mob had murdered 23 constables by burning their police station reached him on February 8, 1922, the day it was to begin. Although this incident occurred 800 miles from Bardoli, he once again canceled the campaign, this time before it had started; instead, he fasted for five days in penance. Yet the British Viceroy ordered Gandhi's arrest, and on March 10, 1922 Gandhi was given his only judicial trial by the British. He made no apology for his noncooperation, which he admitted was legally seditious. To Justice Robert Broomfield he said,

I do not ask for mercy.
I do not plead any extenuating act.
I am here, therefore, to invite and cheerfully submit to
the highest penalty that can be inflicted upon me
for what in law is a deliberate crime
and what appears to me to be
the highest duty of a citizen.[10]

He explained, "In my opinion, non-cooperation with evil is as much a duty as is cooperation with good."[11] Broomfield sentenced him to six years and hoped the government would reduce the term. Gandhi was in fact released after 22 months after he had an appendectomy.

Perhaps the greatest block to Indian unity and self government was the religious conflict between Hindus and Muslims. In 1924 an anti-Muslim book led to riots and the murder of its author. After 36 Hindus were killed at Kohat, Gandhi fasted for three weeks. He pleaded for unity in diversity, religious tolerance, and love for one another. After he approved of killing stray dogs, Gandhi was accused of abandoning *ahimsa*. He was blamed for killing a maimed calf that was suffering from an incurable disease at his ashram; but he considered that action nonviolent because the unselfish purpose was to relieve the pain of the calf.

During the late 1920s Gandhi wrote *An Autobiography,* which he subtitled "The Story of My Experiments with Truth." This book is quite candid and humble in the way he examined his faults and his efforts to overcome them. In the preface he indicated that his goal was spiritual liberation *(moksha).* In his speeches he pointed out his five-point program on the fingers of his hand: equality for untouchables, spinning, no alcohol or opium, Hindu-Muslim friendship, and equality for women. They were all connected to the wrist, which stood for nonviolence. Finally in 1928 he announced a *satyagraha* campaign in Bardoli against a 22% increase in British-imposed taxes. Refusing to pay taxes, the people had their possessions confiscated, and some were driven off their land; but they remained nonviolent. It lasted several months, and hundreds were arrested. Finally the government gave in and agreed to cancel the tax increase, release all prisoners, and return confiscated land and property; the peasants agreed to pay their taxes at the previous rate.

The Indian Congress wanted self-government and considered war for independence. Gandhi naturally refused to support a war but declared that if India was not free under Dominion Status by the end of 1929, then he would demand independence. Consequently on January 26, 1930 he asked people to celebrate Independence Day, and he proclaimed a manifesto that India must sever its connection with Britain and attain complete independence. Gandhi announced an eleven-point program that included reducing land revenue by fifty percent, abolishing the salt tax, prohibiting alcohol, passing a tariff to protect against foreign cloth, enacting a coastal reservation bill to help Indian shipping, revaluating the *rupee,* reducing military expenditures by at least fifty percent, reducing salaries of civil servants by half, releasing all political prisoners except for murder, abolishing or controlling the Criminal Investigation Department that was targeting Congress, and issuing firearms for self-defense under popular control. Then on March 2, 1930 Gandhi wrote a long letter to Viceroy Irwin informing him that civil disobedience would begin on March 11. He noted how ruinously expensive was the British military administration that was exploiting them. Even the salt from the sea was taxed. He believed that nothing but organized nonviolence could stop the organized violence of the British government. Civil disobedience would begin with a few people from his Satyagraha Ashram, but others might choose to join. Gandhi explained, "My ambition is no less than to convert the British people through nonviolence, and thus make them see the wrong they have done to India. I do not seek to harm your people."[12] Gandhi decided to disobey the Salt Laws, which forbade Indians from making their own salt, because this British monopoly especially struck at the poor.

Beginning with 78 members of his ashram, Gandhi led a 240-mile march to the sea that took 24 days. Thousands had gathered at the start, and several thousand joined them on the march. First Gandhi and then others all along the seacoast gathered some salt water in pans to dry it. In Bombay the Congress had pans on the roof; 60,000 people assembled, and hundreds were arrested. At Karachi, where 50,000 watched the salt being made, the crowd was so thick that the police could make no arrests. The jails were filled with at least 60,000 offenders. Amazingly enough there was practically no violence at all; the people did not want Gandhi to cancel the movement. Gandhi was arrested before he could invade the Dharasana Salt Works, but the poet Sarojini Naidu led 2,500 volunteers and warned them not to resist the blows of the police. According to an eyewitness account by the United Press reporter Webb Miller, they continued to march in hour after hour and were beaten down with steel-shod lathis by the 400 police; but they did not try to fight back, and the injured were dragged away by women. The poet Tagore declared that Europe had lost her moral prestige in Asia. Soon more than 100,000 Indians were in prison, including almost all the leaders. Gandhi was called to meet with Viceroy Irwin eight times. Lord Irwin wanted the civil disobedience ended, but Gandhi demanded an inquiry into the police brutality. Finally on March 5, 1931 they signed the Delhi Pact that treated India as an equal with England and provided for constitutional issues to be discussed at a Round Table Conference in London. Civil disobedience was called off; prisoners were released; and salt manufacture was permitted on the coast.

Gandhi traveled to London, where he met Charlie Chaplin, George Bernard Shaw, and Maria Montessori among others. Not having seen a movie, Gandhi did not know who Chaplin was; but his criticisms of modern civilization may have influenced his film *Modern Times*. Gandhi spoke for a half hour on radio to the United States about a nonviolent way better than brute force to fight for freedom that is more consistent with human dignity. He appealed to the conscience of the world to rescue his people, who were dying in order to regain liberty. In discussing relations with the British he said he did not want isolated independence but voluntary interdependence based on love. However, the British Labour Party had been replaced by a coalition led by Ramsay MacDonald, and they used the Indian minorities problems to divide the Indian Congress. In his final speech at the Conference on November 30, 1931 Gandhi said he still wanted complete independence and warned, "Today you have to fight the school of terrorists which is there with your disciplined and organized terrorism, because you will be blind to the facts or the writing on the wall."[13]

Back in India at the beginning of 1932, communication with the Viceroy broke down over the threat of civil disobedience, and Gandhi was arrested. As during the salt campaign, the old Regulation XXV of 1827 was used to detain him indefinitely without a trial. While in the Yeravda jail Gandhi fasted on behalf of the Harijans because they had been given a separate electorate. It was to be a "fast unto death" unless he could awaken the Hindu conscience. On September 21, 1932 millions of Indians fasted with him for 24 hours. Three days later the Yeravda Pact was signed, and it was ratified the next day. After an overwhelming vote in favor of it, Hindu temples were opened to untouchables for the first time. Gandhi replaced *Young India* with the weekly *Harijan*. Still concerned about the Harijans, he fasted for three weeks in May 1933; British officials, afraid he might die, released him from prison. In August 1933 he was arrested again and was sentenced to one year. On the seventh day of his fast he was released unconditionally in a very precarious condition. After he recovered, Gandhi went on a speaking tour and raised money for the Harijans (untouchables), traveling more than 12,000 miles. In May 1934 the All-India Congress endorsed Gandhi's proposal to call off the civil disobedience campaign except for specific grievances.

By the time the second world war was approaching, Gandhi had been confirmed in his pacifist principles. He pointed out how Abyssinia could have used nonviolence against Mussolini, and he recommended it to the Czechs and China. He suggested, "If it is brave, as it is, to die to a man fighting against odds, it is braver still to refuse to fight and yet to refuse to yield to the usurper."[14] As early as 1938 he exhorted the Jews to stand up for their rights and die if necessary as martyrs so that a degrading manhunt could be turned into a calm and determined stand. Gandhi even recommended the British use nonviolent methods to fight Hitler; no longer could he support any kind of war or killing. On December 24, 1938 he wrote,

How can nonviolence combat aerial warfare,
seeing that there are no personal contacts?
The reply to this is that behind the death-dealing bomb
there is the human hand that releases it,
and behind that still is the human heart
that sets the hand in motion.
And at the back of the policy of terrorism

is the assumption that terrorism
if applied in a sufficient measure
will produce the desired result,
namely, bend the adversary to the tyrant's will.
But supposing a people make up their mind
that they will never do the tyrant's will,
nor retaliate with the tyrant's own methods,
the tyrant will not find it worth his while
to go on with this terrorism.[15]

He even wrote an open letter to Hitler himself, asking him not to go to war. In April 1939 Gandhi prophesied that before the war ended, the democracies would have adopted the tactics of the Fascists and Nazis, including conscription and methods of force to compel and exact obedience.

Calling for mass *satyagraha* in defiance of the ban on propaganda against the war, Gandhi promised Congress he would stay out of jail; but his disciple Vinoba Bhave was arrested in October 1940, and about 15,000 were in prison by May 1941. The next year Gandhi wrote, "Supposing that the women and the children of Europe became fired with the love of humanity, they would take the men by storm and reduce militarism to nothingness in an incredibly short time."[16] He suggested ways to resist the Japanese nonviolently, though he also said that if India had a national government, it should ally itself with the United Nations against the Fascist powers. He criticized the Japanese for attacking China and predicted that their ambition would fail and might prevent the "world federation and brotherhood without which there can be no hope for humanity."[17]

Gandhi was concerned that the British presence would invite the Japanese to invade India. So on July 14, 1942 the Congress Working Committee adopted the famous "Quit India" resolution, and on August 7 the massive nonviolent struggle began under the leadership of Gandhi. Two days later he and the other leaders were arrested, and Congress was declared illegal. The paper *Harijan* was put under a ban and was not allowed to publish again until 1946. Thus for three and a half years we have little or no writing from Gandhi. While he was detained at the Aga Khan palace, he complained that the government was spreading rumors that he was encouraging violent activities. He announced a three-week fast to seek justice from God because the government had denied him justice. Although the Viceroy warned him that he would consider a fast by Gandhi "political blackmail" and would let him die, Gandhi disagreed and began fasting on February 10, 1943. If he had not taken some lime juice with his water, he probably would have died. Gandhi's release from prison on May 5, 1944 has been called the end of the Gandhian era.

When the war ended, Gandhi hoped for a real peace based on freedom and equality for all races and nations. He contrasted nonviolence to the horrible violence of the atomic bomb, and he called the use of this weapon on Japan cowardice. In his last years he became more of a socialist, because he believed that inequality breeds violence while equality produces nonviolence. He went on a pilgrimage to Noakhali to help the poor. Independence for India was now imminent, but the Muslim leader Jinnah was holding out for the creation of a separate state of Pakistan. In a last-ditch effort to salvage Indian unity, on April 1, 1947 Gandhi proposed that Jinnah and his Muslim League control the new government; but this was considered impractical as partition became inevitable. Two weeks later the last viceroy Mountbatten and Gandhi did get Jinnah to sign with them the following statement:

We denounce for all time
the use of force to achieve political ends,
and we call upon all the communities of India,
to whatever persuasion they may belong,
not only to refrain from all acts of violence and disorder,
but also to avoid both in speech and writing,
any word which might be construed
as an incitement of such acts.[18]

Gandhi prayed for unity and tolerance, and he even

read from the *Qur'an* at his prayer meetings. Hindus attacked him because they thought he was partial to Muslims; but Muslims demanded he let them have Pakistan.

Gandhi went to Calcutta to calm the Hindu-Muslim strife and violence, and on August 15, 1947, the long-awaited independence day for India, he fasted and prayed there instead of going to the ceremonies at Delhi. On the first of September he fasted again, and he only broke it three days later after municipal officials assured him that there had been no violence for 24 hours. The princely state of Kashmir was invaded by Muslim tribesmen and Pakistani troops. The Hindu maharajah asked to join the Indian Union and said he intended to appoint the Muslim Sheikh Abdulla prime minister, whose National Conference party also appealed to India to repel the invaders. On October 29, 1947 India announced the accession of Kashmir and sent in troops. Gandhi was criticized for approving this action; but he believed it was justified in these circumstances because not to stand one's ground to defend oneself against an aggressor would be cowardice. Although he may not help one retaliate, Gandhi believed that he must not let a coward find shelter behind the guise of nonviolence.

His last fast began on January 13, 1948, and on the third day the Indian cabinet followed Gandhi's advice and agreed to pay the forty million pounds from united India's assets that they had withheld from Pakistan because of Kashmir. Gandhi's kidneys were not functioning well, and on January 18 Congress got the Hindus, Muslims, Sikhs, Christians, Jews, and other religious groups to sign a peace agreement; on that day he ended his fast. Although this religious hatred saddened Gandhi, India had gained her independence, accomplishing the greatest nonviolent revolution in the history of the world. Finally Gandhi was assassinated by a small Hindu conspiracy on January 30, 1948 at a prayer meeting; with his last breath the Mahatma chanted the name of God.

Soul Force and Nonviolence

Albert Einstein considered Gandhi to be the most enlightened statesman of the age and declared,

> Gandhi had demonstrated that a powerful human following
> can be assembled not only through the cunning game
> of the usual political maneuvers and trickeries
> but through the cogent example
> of a morally superior conduct of life.[19]

Einstein also predicted, "The problem of bringing peace to the world on a supranational basis will be solved only by employing Gandhi's method on a large scale."[20] The *Encyclopedia Britannica* summarizes Gandhi's significance with the statement, "He was the catalyst if not the initiator of three of the major revolutions of the 20th century: the revolutions against colonialism, racism, and violence."[21] What was his philosophy of nonviolent soul-force, and what instructions did he give in the use of these methods?

Satyagraha means literally holding on to the truth. The Hindu understanding of *Sat* is more than conceptual truth but means also being, existence, reality; ultimately we realize that our spiritual beingness is the essence of truth as a reality greater than any concept of the mind. Thus the term "soul-force" conveys the idea of employing our spiritual energies. For Gandhi this truth or spiritual reality is the goal, and the means to the goal must be as pure and loving as possible. He noted that we may always control the means but never the ends. Thus the means must be as good as the goal. *Ahimsa* therefore is the way of acting without hurting anyone or inflicting oneself against another spiritual being. We may hate an injustice for the harm that it brings to people, but we must always love all the people involved out of respect for human dignity. *Satyagraha* attempts to awaken an awareness of the truth about the injustice in the perpetrators, and by *ahimsa* this is done without hurting them. Since humans are subject to error and we cannot be sure we are judging accurately, we must refrain from punishing. Thus *ahimsa* is an essential safe-guard in the quest for truth and justice.

Gandhi explained that *satyagraha* is not a method of the weak, like passive resistance, but it is a tool for the strong that excludes the use of violence in any shape or form. *Satyagraha* is insisting on the truth and can be offered in relation to one's family, rulers, fellow citizens, or even the whole world. Gandhi elucidated three necessary conditions for its success:

1. The *satyagrahi* should not have any hatred in his heart against the opponent.
2. The issue must be true and substantial.
3. The *satyagrahi* must be prepared to suffer till the end for his cause.[22]

Gandhi emphasized self-suffering rather than inflicting suffering on others. By undergoing suffering to reveal the injustice the *satyagrahi* strives to reach the consciences of people. *Satyagraha* does not try to coerce anyone but rather to convert by persuasion, to reach the reason through the heart. *Satyagraha* appeals to intelligent public opinion for reform. In the political field the struggle on behalf of the people leads to the challenging of unjust governments or laws by means of noncooperation or civil disobedience. When petitions and other remedies fail, then a *satyagrahi* may break an unjust law and willingly suffer the penalty in order to call attention to the injustice. However, one does not hide or try to escape from the law like a criminal, rather one openly and civilly disobeys the law as a protest, fully expecting to be punished. In *Hind Swaraj* Gandhi wrote, "It is contrary to our manhood if we obey laws repugnant to our conscience."[23] By eliminating violence *satyagraha* gives the opponent the same rights and liberties.

Satyagraha requires self-discipline, self-control, and self-purification, and *satyagrahis* must always make the distinction between the evil and the evil-doer. They must overcome evil with good, hatred with love, anger with patience, falsehood with truth, and violence with *ahimsa*. This takes a perfect person for complete success, and therefore training and education are essential to even make it workable. Gandhi emphasized that every child should know about the soul, truth, love, and the powers latent in the soul. Both men and women and even children may participate, and it demands the courage that comes from spiritual strength and the power of love. Surely it takes more courage to face the weapons of death without fighting than it does to fight and kill. From his experience Gandhi believed that those who wished to serve their country through *satyagraha* should observe chastity, adopt poverty, follow truth, and cultivate fearlessness. It is through fearlessness that we can have the courage to renounce all harmful weapons, filling and surrounding ourselves with the spiritual protection of a loving and peaceful consciousness.

Gandhi listed detailed rules to guide the *satyagrahi*. One should harbor no anger but suffer the anger of the opponent, putting up with assaults without retaliating but not submitting out of fear of punishment nor to any order given in anger. One should not resist arrest by a person in authority nor resist confiscation of property; but if one is the trustee for the property of another, one may refuse to surrender it. One should not swear or curse or insult the opponent nor join cries that are contrary to the spirit of nonviolence. Civil resisters may not salute the Union Jack (a flag), but they should not insult it nor officials. If officials are being assaulted, one should protect them by risking one's life. In prison one should behave with decorum and observe discipline that is not contrary to self-respect; one should not consider oneself superior to other prisoners nor observe any distinction. One should not fast to gain conveniences. Gandhi believed that civil resisters who have chosen to join the corps should obey all orders of the leader. One should trust the care of dependents to God. One should not cause communal quarrels; but in the event of a disagreement should support the party clearly in the right.

Noncooperation is a comprehensive policy used by people when they can no longer in good conscience participate in or support a government that has become oppressive, unjust, and violent. Although *satyagrahis* do not attack the wrong-doer, it is their responsibility not to promote or support the wrong actions. Thus noncooperators withdraw from government positions, renounce government programs and services, and refuse to pay taxes to the offending government. While challenging the power of the state in this way noncooperators have the opportunity to learn greater self-reliance. Gandhi held that noncooperation with an unjust government was not only an inherent right but as much a duty as is cooperation with a just government.

Most of the time Gandhi and his followers were involved in constructive programs, and he considered these the most important part of nonviolent action. For Gandhi they included Hindu-Muslim friendship or communal unity, removing untouchability or racial discrimination, abstaining from alcohol and drugs, practicing spinning, weaving, and other village industries, sanitation, schooling and adult education, uplift of women, education in hygiene and health, cultivating one's language, working for economic equality, forming labor unions, helping the poor, rural people and lepers, and improving the education and lives of students.

Ahimsa or nonviolence is absolutely essential to Gandhi's civil disobedience. *Satyagrahis* are expected to give their lives in efforts to quell violence if it erupts. Gandhi interpreted *ahimsa* broadly as refraining from anything at all harmful. This principle can be hurt by every evil thought, by undue haste, by lying, by hatred, by wishing ill to anybody, or by our holding on to what the world needs. Thus even greed and avarice can violate *ahimsa*. Nonviolence has a great spiritual power, but the slightest use of violence can taint a just cause. The strength is not physical but comes from the spiritual will. Nonviolence implies self-purification, and the spiritual power the nonviolent person has is always greater than one would have by using violence. The end of violence is always defeat, but nonviolence is endless and is never defeated. The following is Gandhi's summary of the implications of nonviolence:

1. Nonviolence is the law of the human race
   and is infinitely greater than and superior to brute force.
2. In the last resort it does not avail to those
   who do not possess a living faith in the God of Love.
3. Nonviolence affords the fullest protection
   to one's self-respect and sense of honor,
   but not always to possession of land or movable property,
   though its habitual practice does prove a better bulwark
   than the possession of armed men to defend them.
   Nonviolence, in the very nature of things,
   is of no assistance in the defense of ill-gotten gains
   and immoral acts.
4. Individuals or nations who would practice nonviolence
   must be prepared to sacrifice (nations to the last man)
   their all except honor.
   It is, therefore, inconsistent with the possession
   of other people's countries, i.e., modern imperialism,
   which is frankly based on force for its defense.
5. Nonviolence is a power
   which can be wielded equally by all—
   children, young men and women or grown-up people,
   provided they have a living faith in the God of Love
   and have therefore equal love for all mankind.
   When nonviolence is accepted as the law of life
   it must pervade the whole being
   and not be applied to isolated acts.
6. It is a profound error to suppose that
   while the law is good enough for individuals
   it is not for masses of mankind.[24]

Gandhi's struggle was so overwhelming and significant, because he challenged the institutional violence of the modern state. He not only recommended refusing military service but also refusing to pay taxes to a militarized state. In addition to citizens' not cooperating with an evil government, a neutral country also has the obligation to refuse to support or assist a military state or aggressor.

Gandhi suggested a nonviolent army that could engage in constructive activities, lessen tensions, and sacrifice their lives to calm mobs and end riots. He described the qualifications for such a peace brigade in 1938. One must have a living faith in nonviolence and the courage to die without anger, fear, or retaliation. The peace messenger must have equal respect for all religions. This work for peace is done locally alone or in groups. Peace messengers will cultivate contacts with people through personal service. One must have integrity and be strictly impartial. Peace brigades should be aware of brooding conflicts and anticipate conflicts before they break out into conflagrations. Volunteers can be drawn from various walks of life. A distinctive dress would enable the brigade to be recognized without difficulty. The cost of training and equipping such a peace brigade or even an army of *satyagrahis* would be insignificant compared to the huge expenses of the modern military establishment.

Gandhi envisioned a nonviolent state which would protect itself by not cooperating with any aggressor. He was concerned that the democracies would adopt the forceful methods of the Fascists; but true democracy must ultimately be nonviolent, for violence is an obvious restriction of liberty. He observed that the science of war leads to dictatorship, but the science of nonviolence leads to democracy. In 1946 Gandhi asserted that a true democracy will not rely on an army. It is a poor democracy that depends on military assistance because military force interferes with the free growth of the mind and smothers the soul.

Gandhi criticized America for its treatment of the Negro. He observed that armaments are used for greedy exploitation and that the competition and desire for material possessions and the great power's imperialistic designs are the biggest blocks to world peace. Also they must shed their fear of destruction; then by disarmament peace can be attained. Gandhi warned that if the mad arms race continued, it would result in unprecedented slaughter. If a victor remains, the victory will be a living death for that nation. The only escape from this impending doom is by boldly and unconditionally accepting nonviolence with all its glorious implications. His concept of *sarvodaya* urged us to go beyond family and country to consider the good of all, and he recommended a world governing body which would recognize the equal independence of each nation. He believed that religion means being friendly to one's opponents because being friendly to friends is just business. Gandhi said that the golden way is to be friends with the world and regard the whole human family as one.

Notes

1. *An Autobiography* by M. K. Gandhi, p. 100.
2. *The Life of Mahatma Gandhi* by Louis Fischer, p. 81.
3. *Ibid.*, p. 84.
4. *An Autobiography* by M. K. Gandhi, p. 119.
5. *The Life of Mahatma Gandhi* by Louis Fischer, p. 115.
6. *Ibid.*, p. 117.
7. *Ibid.*, p. 177.
8. *Ibid.*, p. 182.
9. *Ibid.*, p. 183.
10. *Ibid.*, p. 202.
11. *Ibid.*, p. 203.
12. *Speeches and Writings of Mahatma Gandhi*, p. 744.
13. *Ibid.*, p. 891.
14. *The Life of Mahatma Gandhi* by Louis Fischer, p. 344-345.
15. M. K. Gandhi in *Harijan*, December 24, 1938 quoted in *The Gandhi Reader* ed. Homer A. Jack, p. 339.
16. *Women and Social Justice*, p. 100 quoted in Verma, M. M., *Gandhi's Technique of Mass Mobilization*, p. 135.
17. *The Life of Mahatma Gandhi* by Louis Fischer, p. 383.
18. *Mahatma: Life of Mohandas Karamchand Gandhi*, Volume 7 by D. G. Tendulkar, p. 377.
19. *Gandhi: A Life* by Yogesh Chadha, p. 467.
20. *Einstein on Peace* ed. Otto Nathan and Heinz Norden, p. 543.
21. *The New Encyclopedia Britannica*, 1975, Vol. 7, p. 878.
22. M. K. Gandhi in *Harijan*, 31 March 1946 quoted in *Non-*

Violent Resistance (Satyagraha), p. 382.
23. *Hind Swaraj or Indian Home Rule* by Mahatma Gandhi, p. 80.
24. M. K. Gandhi in *Harijan*, 5 November 1936, vol. IV, p. 236 in *Non-Violence in Peace & War*, Volume 1, p. 127-128.

2

Wilson and the League of Nations

Friendship is the only cement
that will ever hold the world together.
Woodrow Wilson

Interest does not bind men together:
interest separates men.
There is only one thing that can bind men together,
and that is common devotion to right.
Woodrow Wilson

What we seek is the reign of law,
based upon the consent of the governed,
and sustained by the organized opinion of mankind.
Woodrow Wilson

Political liberty can exist only when there is peace.
Social reform can take place only when there is peace.
Woodrow Wilson

President Wilson had come to Europe
with a program of peace for all men.
His ideal was a very high one,
but it involved great difficulties,
owing to these century-old hatreds between some races.
Georges Clemenceau

The High Contracting Parties,
In order to promote international cooperation
and to achieve international peace and security
by the acceptance of obligations not to resort to war,
by the prescription of open, just and honorable
relations between nations,
by the firm establishment
of the understandings of international law
as the actual rule of conduct among Governments,
and by the maintenance of justice
and a scrupulous respect for all treaty obligations

in the dealings of organized peoples with one another,
Agree to this Covenant of the League of Nations.
Covenant of the League of Nations, Preamble

At the close of the Napoleonic wars in 1815 the
Congress of Vienna established a balance of power they
called the "Concert of Europe." With some popular support
from peace societies, which were founded at that time, and
with a concern for international law, national leaders were
able to solve many of their differences by means of arbitration. Between 1815 and 1900, of the two hundred cases in
which states agreed to arbitration, not a single case led to a
war. However, the states had not pledged that they would
submit to arbitration in every international conflict. The
Swiss humanitarian Henri Dunant initiated a movement
that led to a conference at Geneva in 1864 that protected the
sick and wounded in land warfare with the Red Cross
convention. Four years later another Geneva conference
added more articles for a convention on the sea, but these
articles were not ratified.

Also in 1868 Czar Alexander II invited European diplomats to meet at St. Petersburg to outlaw especially cruel
weapons. Another conference initiated by the Russian Czar
led to a meeting at Brussels six years later in which representatives of fifteen European nations formulated laws of
land warfare. These were influenced by the General Orders
for the United States Army that President Lincoln had
issued during the Civil War based on the ideas of the
German-born Francis Lieber, who wrote *A Code for the
Government of Armies*. However, British diplomats refused
to consider naval issues at this 1874 conference. In 1890 the
United States and ten other American republics signed a
Pan American Treaty of Arbitration, but it was not ratified.

The Hague Peace Conferences

In 1899 Czar Nicholas II, concerned that Russia was at a
financial disadvantage in the armaments competition,
proposed a conference to discuss limitation of arms, the

laws of war, and arbitration to settle international disputes. Peace advocates championed the second Russian circular by calling for a "Peace Conference," and the Dutch government offered The Hague as a meeting place. Quaker Dr. Benjamin Trueblood for years had been writing essays in the American Peace Society's journal, *The Peace Advocate*, on plans by Kant, Ladd, and others for international organization. Quaker Alfred K. Smiley had been inviting peace leaders and prominent politicians to his hotel retreat in New York annually since 1895. The Polish Jew, Ivan Bloch, attended the 1899 conference and gave delegates copies of his six-volume *The Future of War*, which showed how war had become so economically ruinous.

The first Hague Conference that began on May 18, 1899 included 26 states and is considered the first international assembly that met in peace time in order to preserve peace instead of to conclude a war. The diplomats' meetings went on for ten weeks, and their official Act agreed on the following conventions and declarations:

I. Convention for the peaceful adjustment
   of international differences.
II. Convention regarding the laws
   and customs of war by land.
III. Convention for the adaptation to maritime warfare
   of the principles of the Geneva Convention
   of the 22nd August, 1864.
IV. Three Declarations:
   1. To prohibit the launching of projectiles and explosives
      from balloons or by other similar new methods.
   2. To prohibit the use of projectiles
      the only object of which is the diffusion
      of asphyxiating or deleterious gases.
   3. To prohibit the use of bullets
      which expand or flatten easily in the human body,
      such as bullets with a hard envelope,
      of which the envelope does not entirely cover the core,
      or is pierced with incisions.[1]

Although recognizing the regulation of the rules of war

for those nations agreeing to them, the Kaiser declared most of the goals utopian because not a single country was willing to submit all questions to arbitration. The "Permanent Court of Arbitration" that was established could be used voluntarily to resolve differences. The first convention on the Pacific Settlement of International Disputes provided an instrument for a permanent panel of commissioners. Each party to the dispute would select two commissioners, and the fifth commissioner was to be named by the other four. In September 1900 ministers of the ratifying countries met to establish the administrative council of the Permanent Court. They included the eight great powers—Russia, Germany, Austria-Hungary, Italy, France, Great Britain, United States, and Japan, plus Belgium, the Netherlands, Spain, Portugal, Romania, and Siam.

A Pan-American Conference began in October 1901 and agreed to all three Hague conventions. Delegates from Argentina, Bolivia, Paraguay, Peru, Uruguay, El Salvador, Guatemala, Dominican Republic, and the host Mexico even agreed to a treaty of compulsory arbitration. United States president Theodore Roosevelt submitted a dispute about a Pious Fund going back to 1697, and on October 14, 1901 the five arbitrators awarded payments to Catholic bishops in California. In 1902 Argentina and Chile agreed to a Convention on Limitation of Naval Armaments. Britain and France signed an arbitration treaty in 1903. Roosevelt followed their example and signed arbitration treaties with France, Germany, Portugal, and Switzerland. He was negotiating with Great Britain, Italy, Mexico, Russia, Japan, and others when the Senate led by Henry Cabot Lodge insisted on approving each treaty. T. R. felt this undercut his efforts and therefore abandoned them. An attack by Russian warships on British fishing vessels while on their way to fight the Japanese in 1904 was judged a violation in the *Dogger Bank* case. Russia accepted the decision and paid Britain 65,000 pounds.

Theodore Roosevelt supported arbitration and arms

limitation at the second Hague Conference in the summer of 1907 when 44 nations attended, including 24 from beyond Europe. A Korean delegation was turned away because they had not been invited. Japan forced the Korean monarch to abdicate and later took over the country. After much debate the Conference had to announce that they could not agree on how to choose judges for the World Court. The French favored an obligatory arbitration treaty, but the Germans opposed this. As in 1899, the 1907 Conference failed to limit armaments, and many nations pushed ahead with their naval construction of large battleships despite the efforts of the London Naval Conference, though the Declaration of London in January 1909 did clarify issues of international law.

Ten of the 1907 Hague Conference's eleven conventions were ratified and are still in force for those nations. These include such legal issues as the opening of hostilities, laws and customs of war on land, rights and duties of neutral powers, status of enemy merchant ships, conversion of merchant ships into warships, laying of automatic submarine contact mines, bombardment by naval forces, maritime warfare, and restrictions on the right of capture in naval war. At this conference three neutrals were added to each commission of inquiry. Between 1909 and 1914 the Permanent Court of Arbitration made judgments in ten cases. This method was used in 1910 to settle a dispute over the Newfoundland Fisheries between the United States and Britain. Under President Taft the United States negotiated arbitration treaties with the British and French, but the Germans declined; in 1912 Taft complained that the Senate had truncated the treaties with its amendments. A third Hague Peace Conference was planned for 1915; but because of the World War it was not held.

Wilson and a League for Peace

Several years after being awarded the Nobel Peace Prize, in 1910 Theodore Roosevelt spoke to the Nobel Prize Committee about a League of Peace, which the great powers could form "not only to keep the peace among themselves, but to prevent by force if necessary, its being broken by others."[2] The problem with The Hague approach, he believed, was that it lacked an effective executive police power. Until that was achieved, he suggested that peace could be assured by a combination of powerful nations which sincerely want peace and have no intention of committing aggression. Roosevelt concluded that the statesman who could bring this about would have the gratitude of all mankind.

In 1909 Norman Angell published a pamphlet that was enlarged to a book and went through several editions by 1913 as *The Great Illusion*. In this work he endeavored to show that the development of industry and commerce had made the use of military power economically and socially futile because nations no longer gain by trying to take over territories beyond their borders. To tamper with credit and commerce by confiscation is self-injurious to powers that attempt this, as small nations are able to compete with them for trade effectively without having expensive military power. Neither do nations impose their moral ideals on other nations by means of war because all of the moral and ideological struggles are occurring within nations and across political boundaries, not between nations. Thus he prophesied that armaments are obsolete and that the current arms race between European powers, such as Germany and England, were self-destructive. He lamented the failure of the Hague Conferences to bring about any disarmament and appealed to public opinion to see through the current political illusions.

The tragic story of the League of Nations begins with the man who conceived it and offered it to the world, who developed its charter and bore the pains of its formulation at the Peace Conference in France, and who broke down in exhaustion when his own nation, the United States, refused to ratify it in the Senate.

Thomas Woodrow Wilson was born December 28, 1856 in Staunton, Virginia. His father was a Presbyterian minister, and Woodrow was a deeply religious man throughout his life. He was fascinated by politics and longed to be a statesman like England's Prime Minister Gladstone. He wrote several books on government and taught political economy at Princeton University. As an educational reformer he was unanimously chosen president of Princeton in 1902. Wilson emphasized broad liberal studies more than specialization and mere preparation for a career. In 1910 the Democratic Party nominated him for governor of New Jersey, and his persuasive expression of progressive principles swept him to victory. His liberal reforms were successful, and in 1912 he won the Democratic Presidential nomination and then a popular plurality over the divided Republicans and Theodore Roosevelt's Progressive Party. He offered "New Freedom" and set out to break up the privileges of trusts and tariffs; he championed the worker's right to overtime pay beyond an eight-hour day. However, his greatest challenges were to be in foreign policy after the outbreak of the World War in 1914.

In the spring of 1914 President Wilson sent his close friend and advisor, Colonel Edward M. House, to Europe as an unofficial ambassador for peace. House met with German officials and the Kaiser explaining that with the community of interests between England, Germany, and the United States they could together maintain the peace of the world. However, England was concerned about Germany's growing navy. House went to Paris and then London, where he conferred with Edward Grey about negotiating with Germany. Even after the assassination of Archduke Ferdinand, the event which precipitated the war, House returned to Berlin and appealed to the Kaiser through a letter that England, France, and Germany could settle their differences peacefully. Many years later the Kaiser admitted that the mediation offer by Wilson and House had almost prevented the war. However, the German militarists were intent on fighting, and the war broke out with Austria leading the way. President Wilson on August 19 declared that the United States was neutral, and he requested that the American people be impartial. He tried to mediate peace between the European powers through his pacifist Secretary of State William Jennings Bryan, and in January 1915 Wilson again sent House to Europe on a peace mission; but both efforts failed.

Hamilton Holt and William B. Howland initiated a meeting of American professors at the Century Club in New York on January 25, 1915 to discuss a future League that could guarantee two principles—friendly settlement of disputes between nations and protection of the territorial integrity and sovereignty of nations against outside aggression. On April 9 at Independence Hall in Philadelphia the League to Enforce Peace was organized, and former President William Howard Taft became its founding president. In England a League of Nations Society was founded in May 1915, and the idea was supported publicly by Edward Grey and Herbert Asquith. In the United States numerous branches of the League to Enforce Peace sprang up around the country. On May 27, 1916 the League to Enforce Peace heard speeches by President Wilson and Republican Senator Henry Cabot Lodge. Lodge was wary of forming permanent alliances, about which George Washington had warned America, but this he felt should not preclude joining with other civilized nations to diminish war and encourage peace. In fact Senator Lodge stated strongly that they must find some way "in which the united forces of the nations could be put behind the cause of peace and law."[3]

In his speech President Wilson called for a new and more wholesome diplomacy and a way for the nations of the world to band themselves together so that right may prevail against any selfish aggression. Civilization is not yet firmly established until nations are governed by the same code of conduct that we demand of individuals. He outlined three fundamental principles: first, that every people has the right to choose their sovereignty; second, that small nations as well as large ones ought to have the guarantee of territorial integrity; and third, that the world and the rights of its people and nations ought to be

protected from disturbing aggression. He proposed that the
United States initiate a movement for peace calling for a

> universal association of the nations to maintain
> the inviolate security of the highway of the seas
> for the common and unhindered use
> of all the nations of the world,
> and to prevent any war
> begun either contrary to treaty covenants
> or without warning and full submission of the causes
> to the opinion of the world
> a virtual guarantee of territorial integrity
> and political independence.[4]

While speaking to West Point graduates in 1916 Wilson
contrasted the spirit of militarism to the citizen spirit, and
he asserted that in the United States the civilian spirit is
intended to dominate the military, which is why the President, a civilian authority, is commander-in-chief of all
forces. In September, Wilson was renominated by the
Democratic Party, and in his acceptance speech he
discussed world peace. America must contribute to a just
and settled peace because no longer can any nation remain
wholly apart from world turmoil. Again he appealed to
world opinion to establish joint guarantees for peace and
justice in a spirit of friendship. President Wilson's re-election was promoted under the slogan "He kept us out of
war," and he managed to win a narrow victory.

In January 1917 the Germans decided to pursue unre-
stricted submarine warfare. Wilson was trying to get the
western allies and central powers to negotiate peace with
each other, and he was not informed of the Germans'
change in policy when he delivered his "Peace without
Victory" speech on January 22. This was the first time a
President had appeared alone before the Senate since
George Washington vowed never to return there. Wilson
expressed his hope that peace could be negotiated soon,
and he was convinced that after the war an international
concert of power must prevent war. He offered the United

States Government in its tradition of upholding liberty to serve in using its authority and power to guarantee peace and justice throughout the world by means of a League for Peace.

The President wanted to indicate the conditions upon which the United States could enter into this process. First, the war must be ended and by a treaty of peace that will be universally approved and guaranteed by a universal covenant, which must include the peoples of the New World. The organized force of mankind protecting the peace must be greater than any nation or probable combination of nations. Wilson did not believe that the war should end in a new balance of power but rather in a just and organized common peace, for no one can guarantee the stability of a balance of power. Neither side really intends to crush the other; therefore it must be a peace without victory so that the victor will not impose intolerable sacrifices, which result in resentment and probably future hostilities. Equality of nations is the right attitude for a lasting peace as well as a just settlement regarding territory and national allegiance. Equality of nations means a respect for the rights of small nations based upon the common strength of the concert of nations, not upon individual strength. A deeper principle yet is

Governments derive all their just powers
from the consent of the governed,
and that no right anywhere exists
to hand peoples about from sovereignty to sovereignty
as if they were property....
That henceforth inviolable security of life,
of worship, and of industrial and social development
should be guaranteed to all peoples.[5]

Peace can only be stable with justice and freedom; otherwise the spirit rebels. Wilson asserted the importance of freedom of the seas and also the need to limit navies and armies. He felt that he was speaking "for liberals and friends of humanity in every nation ... for the silent mass of mankind everywhere."[6] He suggested that the American principles of the Monroe Doctrine should be extended throughout the world so that "every people should be left free to determine its own polity, its own way of development, unhindered, unthreatened, unafraid."[7] These principles of self-determination, freedom, and protection from aggression are the principles of humanity and must prevail.

Wilson struggled to keep America out of the war; but when the Germans announced submarine warfare even against neutral shipping, he immediately broke diplomatic relations with Germany. American intelligence reports indicated that Germany was trying to form an alliance with Mexico against the United States. Wilson had considered entry into the war a crime against civilization, and he loathed the implications. Privately he told the reporter Frank Cobb,

It would mean that we would lose our heads
along with the rest and stop weighing right and wrong.
It would mean that a majority of people in this hemisphere
would go war mad, quit thinking
and devote their energies to destruction.[8]

However, in March 1917 several US ships were attacked, and the President decided to propose a declaration of war to the Congress on April 2. He appealed to international law and the freedom of the seas. Because of the loss of noncombatants' lives he interpreted the German submarine warfare against commerce as "warfare against mankind." He did not recommend revenge or the victorious assertion of physical might as motives for action but rather the vindication of human right and a refusal to submit to wrongs. Therefore since the Imperial German Government was at war with the United States, they must accept the belligerent status thrust upon them. Wilson clearly stated that the purpose of America's role

is to vindicate the principles of peace and justice

in the life of the world
as against selfish and autocratic power
and to set up amongst the really free
and self-governed peoples of the world
such a concert of purpose and of action
as will henceforth insure the observance of those principles.[9]

He declared that a new age was beginning in which nations and governments must be held to the same standards of conduct and responsibility as the individual citizens of civilized states. He indicated that America had no animosity toward the German people, and he explained that small groups of ambitious men were using those people as pawns under the veil of the private courts of a privileged class. Wilson believed that peace could only be maintained by a partnership of democratic nations; autocratic governments cannot be trusted. Therefore Americans must fight for the liberation of the world's people, including the German peoples. "The world must be made safe for democracy."[10] Peace must be founded on political liberty. President Wilson disavowed any desire for conquest or dominion; America was to be merely one of the champions of humanity's rights. Wilson's speech was greeted with wildly enthusiastic applause; later he thought how strange it was to hear applause for a message that meant death for many young men.

The United States was involved in the World War, but it would be six months before many soldiers would be fighting in France. That summer President Wilson appointed an Inquiry of several distinguished experts to gather information on Europe's oppressed peoples, international business, international law, proposals for a peace-keeping organization, and ideas on repairing the war damage in Belgium and France. He said he wanted a basis to decide what would be fair for all and prophetically warned that seeds of jealousy, discontent, and restrained development could breed future wars.

Utilizing this research by experts, Wilson formulated the war aims and peace suggestions of the United States and presented them before Congress on January 8, 1918 as his famous Fourteen Points. He reiterated that the United States was seeking only a peaceful world that is safe for self-governing nations. His specific points may be summarized as follows:

1. "Open covenants of peace, openly arrived at"—
   no secret treaties.
2. Free navigation of the seas outside territorial waters.
3. Equality of trade and removal of economic barriers.
4. "Adequate guarantees given and taken
   that national armaments will be reduced
   to the lowest point consistent with domestic safety."
5. Impartial adjustment of all colonial claims
   weighing equally the interests of the populations
   with the claims of governments.
6. Evacuation of Russian territory and the opportunity
   for Russians to choose their own institutions,
   and aid according to their needs and desires.
7. Evacuation and restoration of Belgium
   under her own sovereignty.
8. Liberation and restoration of invaded French territory
   and the return of Alsace-Lorraine to France,
   correcting the wrong of 1871.
9. "A readjustment of the frontiers of Italy
   should be effected along clearly recognizable lines
   of nationality."
10. The peoples of Austria-Hungary
    should be freely allowed autonomous development.
11. Romania, Serbia, and Montenegro
    should be evacuated and restored,
    and the Balkan states ought to be established
    along lines of allegiance and nationality
    with international guarantees of independence
    and territorial integrity,
    with access to the sea for Serbia.
12. Turkey itself should have secure sovereignty;
    but other nationalities should be freed of Turkish rule
    and be assured of autonomous development,
    and the Dardanelles should be open to all ships
    and commerce under international guarantees.

13. An independent Poland
    should include territories of Polish populations,
    have access to the sea and guaranteed territorial integrity.
14. "A general association of nations must be formed
    under specific covenants for the purpose of affording
    mutual guarantees of political independence
    and territorial integrity to great and small states alike."[11]

The President then declared that the United States was willing to fight for these principles to secure liberty and safety for all peoples under international justice. Germany was to be allowed her fair and equal place among the nations, and Wilson requested negotiation with representatives of the majority of German people rather than the military party and imperialists.

These Fourteen Points were adopted by the Allied statesmen as a basis for the peace. Responses to this speech soon came from representatives of Germany and Austria. These replies by Count von Hertling and Count Czernin were answered by Wilson in a speech on February 11; he was especially critical of the German Chancellor von Hertling. Peace must be established justly in view of world opinion and not involving militarily only the separate states that are most powerful. Wilson also pointed out that there were to be no annexations, no punitive damages, no arbitrary handing of people about by antagonists, but respect for national aspirations and self-determination.

Wilson again summarized the great ideals America was fighting for in a 4th of July speech at Mount Vernon. Over a million American men had already been shipped to France. The four goals he stated were:

1) destruction of every arbitrary power that disturbs the world's peace;
2) settlement of political and economic questions with the consent of those involved, not according to the material interests of other nations;
3) consent of all nations to live under common law and mutual respect for justice; and

4) establishment of a peace organization of the free
nations' combined power to check violations of
peace and justice according to the tribunal of
international opinion to which all must submit.

By the end of summer 1918 the Central Powers were
breaking up, and on September 27 Wilson appealed to the
peoples of those countries by suggesting more specific
peace proposals. Once more he emphasized that right must
be made superior to might. The idea of a League of Nations
was beginning to take a more definite shape. Each government must be willing to pay the price necessary to achieve
impartial justice, to be made effective by the instrumen-
tality of a League of Nations. The constitution of the
League of Nations must be a part of the peace settlement;
for if it preceded peace it would be confined to the nations
allied against a common enemy; and if it followed the
peace settlement, it could not guarantee the peace terms.
Wilson then outlined five particulars:

1. Impartial justice means no discrimination
   or favoritism between peoples.
2. No special interest of a single nation
   should infringe upon the common interest of all.
3. "There can be no leagues or alliances
   or special covenants and understandings
   within the general and common family
   of the League of Nations."
4. There can be no selfish economic combinations or boycotts
   except as "may be vested in the League of Nations itself
   as a means of discipline and control."
5. "All international agreements and treaties of every kind
   must be made known in their entirety
   to the rest of the world."[12]

Versailles Peace Treaty

On October 6 the German government requested an
armistice; President Wilson sent a reply declaring that the
armies of the Central Powers must withdraw immediately

from all invaded territory. A German response dodged the
issue of evacuation, and therefore another message clari-
fying the military situation was sent through the Secretary
of State. On October 25 Wilson made perhaps one of his
worst political mistakes when he requested the election of a
Democratic majority in Congress in order to indicate to the
world American support of the President's leadership. This
intrusion of party politics into non-partisan foreign affairs
was deeply resented by Republicans and in fact backfired
against Wilson, as the Republicans won both houses.

Meanwhile the Germans agreed to disarm and relinquish the monarchical military leadership and wanted a
peace according to the points made in Wilson's speeches.
Austria-Hungary also accepted the President's declarations
and recognized the rights of the Czecho-Slovaks and the
Jugo-Slavs. The Allied Governments agreed to accept the
Fourteen Points and the subsequent addresses with one
reservation by Great Britain on freedom of the seas. Poland
and Germany each announced themselves as republics.
Finally on November 11 German representatives signed the
Armistice Agreement at Marshall Foch's headquarters. The
Germans agreed to an almost total surrender and to the
payment of reparations. The German Navy was to be
dismantled, and its Army was to be reduced to 100,000
men. Conscription was abolished, and weapons were
strictly limited, allowing no tanks or military aircraft as
well as no submarines. However, the German General Staff,
which was supposed to be abolished, merely changed its
name. If these disarmament conditions had been maintained, the second world war in Europe could never have
occurred as it did.

On the same day President Wilson read the Armistice
Agreement to Congress and promised food and relief to a
suffering Europe. He pointed out the disorder in Russia
and the folly of attempting conquest by the force of arms.
He also asserted,

The nations that have learned the discipline of freedom
and that have settled with self-possession

to its ordered practice
are now about to make conquest of the world
by the sheer power of example of friendly helpfulness.[13]

America must hold the lamp of liberty for the peoples who were just then coming into their freedom. A peace must be established that will define their places among the nations and protect their security.

Wilson decided to attend the Peace Conference in France with a select group of experts, such as geographers, ethnologists, and economists, whom he told, "Tell me what is right, and I'll fight for it."[14] Unfortunately he did not invite anyone to attend from the Senate, which later was to cause irreconcilable problems. In Europe, Wilson was enthusiastically greeted by thousands of cheering people almost as a messiah. After arriving in France in December, he visited England and said that never before in the history of the world had there been such a keen international consciousness. On the same day in Manchester he spoke of America's desire for peace in the world, not merely a balance of power or peace in Europe. At Rome on January 3, 1919 President Wilson explained how military force is unable to hold people together, that only friendship and good will can bind nations together.

Therefore, our task at Paris is
to organize the friendship of the world,
to see to it that all the moral forces
that make for right and justice and liberty are united
and are given a vital organization to which
the peoples of the world will readily and gladly respond.[15]

The idealistic American President, who wanted only permanent peace under universal justice with no special rewards for his country, faced an awesome challenge among the European old-school diplomats, who were determined to gain all they could for their own national interests. Lloyd George had just been re-elected British prime minister under the slogan "Be tough on Germany," and Clemenceau of France was even more adamant about making Germany pay all she could and leaving her as weak as possible. The Italians represented by Prime Minister Vittorio E. Orlando and the Japanese wanted control of specific territories, and secret treaties made between the Allies during the war were to emerge and confound several of Wilson's points. Against Wilson's protests the conference news was censored, and what did leak out to the press tended to be through the French newspapers controlled by their government.

Meanwhile most of Europe was in turmoil, and many military leaders wanted to grab what they could get. For this reason on January 24 Wilson published a statement warning those who would take possession of territory by force that they would be prejudicing their cause, because they were placing in doubt the justice of their claims which the Peace Conference must determine. The next day he addressed the Peace Conference, which he felt had two purposes—not only the settlements required by the war but also the secure establishment of a means for the maintaining of world peace. Wilson believed the League of Nations was necessary for both purposes. He argued that settlements may be temporary, but their actions as nations for peace and justice must be permanent. Although they could not make permanent decisions, they could set up permanent processes. Therefore the League of Nations must be made vital and continuous so that it may be ever watchful and effective. The idea for a League as an essential part of the Treaty was adopted unanimously by the representatives of the 32 states present on January 25, and a subcommittee for the drafting of a League of Nations Covenant was selected with President Wilson as chairman.

On January 27 Wilson suggested a solution to the problem of what to do about the German colonies. Because he felt world opinion was against annexations, the League of Nations could mandate that districts be administered by a mandatory power for the improvement of the inhabitants' conditions and without discriminatory economic access.

General Jan Christiaan Smuts, the leader from South Africa who had confronted Gandhi, had published a pamphlet, *The League of Nations: A Practical Suggestion,* calling for a strong and active League, which would not only prevent wars but also be a living and working organ of peaceful civilization. It must have general control of international affairs involving commerce, communications, and social, industrial, and labor relations. Smuts proposed the mandate system by which powerful nations would be assigned to oversee temporarily the former colonies of Germany and the non-Turkish portions of the former Ottoman empire that needed assistance. Wilson and Colonel House, the American members of the committee, managed to get together with the British delegates Smuts and Lord Cecil, who also had his own draft, to hammer out what was called Wilson's second draft, which was revised into an Anglo-American version. Although the French and Italians submitted drafts, this version was accepted as the basis for discussion. Working every night, the committee of fourteen members turned out its Draft Agreement after eleven days. Wilson announced that a living thing had been born.

A proud President Wilson presented the League of Nations draft to the Peace Conference with an address on February 14. The League was to consist of a body of delegates, an executive council, and a permanent secretariat. Any issue of international relationship would have free discussion because that is the moral force of public opinion. Nevertheless if moral force did not suffice, armed force was to be in the background, but only as a last resort. The League was designed to be simple and flexible, yet a definite guarantee of peace, at least in words. Securing peace was not the only purpose of the League; it could be used for cooperation in any international matter, such as ameliorating labor conditions. All international agreements must be registered with the secretary-general and openly published. Wilson believed the mandate policy of aiding development was a great advance over annexation and exploitation. All in all, Wilson felt that they had created a document that was both practical and humane, that could serve the conscience of the world. The day after the draft was accepted by the plenary session, the President departed for the United States.

In Washington, Wilson met with Congressional representatives to discuss the League. By the time he returned to France in March 1919 American public opinion was insisting on four alterations. First, the Monroe Doctrine must be explicitly protected. Second, there must be a way nations could withdraw from the League. Third, domestic disputes must be exempt from League interference, including tariffs and immigration quotas. Fourth, a nation must have the right to refuse a mandate for a territory. Wilson felt that these provisions were not necessary, but he was willing to get them put into the covenant for the sake of its acceptance. However, he had to compromise in order to do so, and thus his position on other issues was weakened.

Colonel House had been compromising on every side at the peace talks, such that when Wilson returned to Paris, he felt he had to start all over again. This caused an irreparable breach between the President and his close friend and advisor. The Allies were forcing unbearable reparations and indemnities on Germany and the defeated nations. Wilson did not consider it wise for England to retain naval supremacy or for the American and British navies to patrol the world together. Militarism on the sea is the same as on the land. He felt that power must not be vested in a single nation or combination of nations; the sea is a free highway and should be protected by a league of all the nations under international law.

Wilson developed a comprehensive plan for disarmament to fulfill one of his most important points. Armaments were only to be used to preserve domestic safety and to maintain international order according to the League. Compulsory military service and the private manufacture of munitions must be abolished. Disarmament policies must be worked out after the peace settlement, be unanimously agreed upon, and have publicity to assure compliance. Although disarmament was temporarily forced upon Germany, these policies were never universally carried out. Wilson persistently argued for a new attitude of mind and an organization of cooperation for peace which considered moral force above armed force.

Returning to the negotiations of the peace settlement, Wilson faced intransigent obstacles to his principles. Several territorial arrangements had already been agreed upon by the major powers during the war in such secret agreements as the Sykes-Picot Treaty and the Treaty of London. Wilson spoke up for self-determination, and at his suggestion a commission of inquiry was sent to the Middle East to discover what the peoples' wishes were. The other powers verbally agreed but never did send their representatives. By the time the Americans went and returned with their information, the issues had been settled. The French wanted not only Alsace-Lorraine but also the coal mining district of Saar and a buffer state in the Rhineland. Italy wanted not only the opposite coast of the Adriatic including Trieste, which had been promised in the Treaty of London, but they also demanded the port of Fiume, which represented Yugoslavia's only hope for a commercial port. England and Japan had divided up the German colonies in the Pacific Ocean, giving Japan those north of the equator and Britain those south of the equator, but Japan also wanted Shandong (Shantung) on the mainland.

In early April 1919 Wilson became ill. He had reached the limit of his patience and requested that the ocean-liner *George Washington* be prepared to take him home. The President decided to take his stand on the issue of Fiume; it had not been included in the Pact of London, because it naturally belonged to the new Jugo-Slav state. Wilson consequently went to the public with his arguments, and the Italian delegation withdrew from the Conference. With the Italians already turning their back on the League, the Japanese saw their chance to push for control of the Shandong Province in China. Wilson backed China's rights and lectured the nations on their duties toward each other. However, he did not want Japan to leave also and perhaps form an alliance with Russia and Germany; neither England nor America was willing to go to war with Japan over Shandong. Therefore it was agreed that Japan would control Shandong temporarily, and Wilson hoped that the League of Nations would later rectify the situation for China. Above all, Wilson struggled to save the League itself. The Italians never did get Fiume, but they did return to sign the final Treaty. By preventing an unjust decision, a war between the Jugo-Slavs and the Italians was made less likely. Wilson also compromised with the French on the Saar and Rhineland districts, and annexations were modified into temporary mandate agreements.

Germany had been suffering greatly; a food blockade by the Allies had been maintained against them for four months after the Armistice. Finally at the instigation of Herbert Hoover, President Wilson convinced the Allied leaders that the blockade must be lifted for humanitarian reasons. The Treaty agreed upon by the Allies and neutral nations was presented to the Germans on May 7. Their response on May 29 repeatedly complained of failures of the Treaty to adhere to the "Fourteen Points and subsequent addresses." They felt unnecessarily humiliated by the severe provisions the French had demanded. However, facing the threat of Marshal Foch moving the French army in on them, the Germans decided to sign the Treaty. On June 28, 1919 the Treaty of Versailles was signed by Clemenceau, Lloyd George, Wilson, and other representatives of the nations. When Austria signed the peace treaty in September 1919, the major powers and several other nations signed the Convention for the Control of the Trade in Arms and Ammunition, which prohibited arms sales in most of Africa and part of Asia. The Central American States adopted a Convention on Arms Limitation on February 7, 1923.

United States' Rejection of the League

Wilson was greeted by ten thousand people when he returned to New York. However, in the Senate there were strong isolationist sentiments against the Treaty. Presenting it to the Senate on July 10, President Wilson wondered forebodingly, "Dare we reject it and break the heart of the world?"[16] A few "irreconcilables" were completely against the League. Many senators favored it, but ratification of a treaty required two-thirds of the Senate. A third group led by Senator Lodge demanded reservations, particularly to Article 10 of the League Covenant which read:

> The Members of the League undertake to respect and
> preserve as against external aggression
> the territorial integrity and existing political independence
> of all Members of the League.
> In case of any such aggression
> or in case of any threat or danger of such aggression
> the Council shall advise upon the means
> by which this obligation shall be fulfilled.[17]

For Wilson this was the key article; it was the Monroe Doctrine applied to the world and protected by all. The President explained to the senators that this was a moral obligation but not necessarily a legal obligation. Senator Warren Harding asked what good it would do if it was only a moral obligation which a nation could ignore since it was not legally bound. Wilson pointed out that because it was not legally binding, the nation would have the right to exercise its moral judgment in each case. Lloyd George had explained that the Covenant did not necessarily imply "military action in support of the imperiled nation" but mainly economic pressure and sanctions against the aggressing nation. Former President Taft favored ratifying the League Covenant and agreed that the chance of getting involved in a war was small because of the universal boycott, which in most cases would be effective; only a world conspiracy would require the members of the

League to unite against it, and in that case the sooner the better. Taft, a Republican, believed the United States could not be forced into a war against its will, and to think so was a narrow and reactionary viewpoint.

Nevertheless opposition in the Senate was growing. Therefore President Wilson decided to take his case to the people with a busy speaking tour across the whole country. Young Americans had fought and died in France, and he would not give up the struggle for a world of peace without giving all he could. Wilson argued that the League of Nations was founded according to the American principles of self-government, open discussion and arbitration instead of war, a universal boycott of an offending nation, disarmament, rehabilitation of oppressed peoples, no annexations but trusteeships, abolition of forced labor especially of women and children, rejection of secret treaties, protection of dependent peoples, high standards of labor, the Red Cross, international regulation of drugs and alcohol, and prohibition of arms sales. He warned against violent revolutions such as had occurred in Russia rather than revolution by vote. The United States could be isolated no more, for it has become a determining factor in human history and in the development of civilization. He declared that peace of the world could not be established without America. Seven and a half million men had been killed in the war; this was more than all the wars from 1793 to 1914. He spoke of the children who would have to die in a worse war if the League of Nations was not established.

Wilson pushed himself to the limit, traveling 8,000 miles in 22 days and giving 38 speeches. He had increasingly bad headaches which became constant until he finally collapsed in Pueblo, Colorado. The train took him straight back to Washington, where he suffered a stroke that left the left side of his face and body paralyzed. His wife Edith coordinated his Presidential responsibilities. The push in the Senate for reservations to the Treaty was strong; but Wilson refused to give in because it would be repudiating what each nation had signed. If the United States demanded changes, then why could not the Germans also? Thus the President asked those who supported the Treaty to vote against ratification with the reservations, and consequently the Treaty was never ratified by the United States. Wilson hoped, perhaps, to be nominated again for President in 1920, but he was a broken man. The Republican Harding declared nebulously that he favored some sort of association of nations, and he was elected for a "return to normalcy." In Wilson's last public statement on Armistice Day, November 11, 1923 he lamented, "I have seen fools resist Providence before, and I have seen their destruction."[18] He still believed that his principles would eventually prevail. He died on February 3, 1924.

League of Nations Progress 1920-29

On January 16, 1920 President Wilson formally convoked the Council in accordance with the League provision for the summoning of the first Council and Assembly by the President of the United States. It was to be the last official participation by the United States in the entire history of the League of Nations. The League became a dead issue in American politics, and even Herbert Hoover and Franklin Roosevelt, who both had been early League supporters, could not get the United States involved during their presidencies. The League, which the United States was expected to lead, lost much of its universal acceptance and credibility without the American power. Yet almost every other nation in the world joined the League. In addition to the 32 original members, thirteen neutral states were named in the annex. Any self-governing state, dominion or colony could be admitted to membership by a two-thirds vote of the Assembly. States could leave the organization but were required to give two years' notice. A member-state violating the Covenant could be expelled by a unanimous vote of all the other member states.

The Assembly was composed of three delegates from each member-state. The League Council was to be made up of the five Allied Powers that won the war; but without the

United States this became Britain, France, Italy, and Japan. Four other nations were to be elected from time to time to serve on the Council. Initially Belgium, Brazil, Spain, and Greece were selected. Any member could go to the Council with a concern and was allowed a vote at the Council on that issue. At the top of the Secretariat administration was the Secretary-General, and the British diplomat James Eric Drummond was selected for that position before the League went into effect. He served as Secretary-General until June 1933, when he was replaced by Joseph Avenol. League decisions were recommendations for the states to follow, but those who refused were subject to the voluntary sanctions of the nations. No state could be legally bound against its consent and thus maintained sovereignty over its own decisions. In September 1921 the Permanent Court of International Justice (PCIJ) with nine judges was established at The Hague, as the League Covenant was amended.

The four strategies that could be used by the League to prevent wars were 1) reducing armaments, 2) settling disputes peacefully with sanctions against any state refusing to do so, 3) guaranteeing current boundaries and agreements, although they could be legally modified, and 4) settling international conflicts before they lead to war. Article 8 required the "reduction of national armaments to the lowest point consistent with national safety and the enforcement of common action of international obligations."[19] The Council was supposed to formulate plans for reduction which were to be revised at least every ten years. The League Covenant acknowledged the problem of private manufacturing of arms, and the Council was to advise how to limit it to what members needed for their safety. However, a naval arms race between Britain and the United States occurred and was dealt with independently of the League at the Washington naval conference of 1922.

Disputes were to be settled peacefully by using arbitration, the International Court (PCIJ), or by an inquiry before the Council, which would make a report. Article 12 prohibited member-states from going to war until at least three months after a decision by the arbitrators, the Court, or the Council. If a dispute was not submitted to any of these, Article 15 authorized the Council to make recommendations, and states were not to go to war with other states that complied with its report. Article 16 declared that a state disregarding Articles 12, 13, or 15 was to be deemed to have committed an act of war against all other members of the League, which would then sever all trade or financial relations with the Covenant-breaking state. Article 11 authorized the Council to meet and act in regard to any threat to peace or possible war as follows:

1. Any war or threat of war,
whether immediately affecting
any of the Members of the League or not,
is hereby declared a matter of concern to the whole League,
and the League shall take any action that may be deemed
wise and effectual to safeguard the peace of nations.
In case any such emergency should arise,
the Secretary-General shall on the request of any Member
of the League forthwith summon a meeting of the Council.
2. It is also declared to be the friendly right
of each Member of the League to bring to the attention
of the Assembly or of the Council
any circumstance whatever affecting international relations
which threatens to disturb international peace
or the good understanding between nations
upon which peace depends.[20]

Without the power of the United States the strong guarantees of Article 10 were left mostly to the British to enforce, and after the war they were in no mood to undertake such a burden alone. Article 18 called for all treaties to be registered with the Secretariat, and those that were not so registered could not be cited at the International Court (PCIJ). In the next decade 2,330 treaties were registered with the League, which published them in English and French.

Article 22 explained how the former colonies and territories of Germany and Turkey were to have their peoples treated as a "sacred trust of civilization" by the mandatory powers responsible for their administration, and annual reports were to be submitted to the Council. A permanent commission of experts was delegated to examine the reports and advise the Council. The war victors of the Supreme Allied Council in April 1920 at San Remo actually selected Britain, France, Japan, Belgium, South Africa, Australia, and New Zealand as the mandatories. The secret Sykes-Picot agreement of May 1916 resulted in Iraq, Transjordan, and Palestine being assigned to Britain, as Syria and Lebanon were put under France.

Article 23 urged all member nations to "maintain fair and humane conditions of labor for men, women, and children, both in their own countries and in all countries to which their commercial and industrial relations extended."[21] It also entrusted the League to supervise agreements regarding traffic in women, children, drugs, and arms, to provide for the freedom of communication, transit, and equitable commerce, and to take steps to prevent and control disease.

The coal mines of the Saar had been ceded to France in 1919 to compensate for their mines in the Nord and Pas-de-Calais that had been destroyed in the war. Most of the people in the Saar region spoke German, and in the French mandate it was stipulated that after fifteen years a plebiscite would determine who governed it. In 1920 the League Council appointed a High Commissioner for the free city of Danzig. In June 1921 the Council suggested that the Aaland islands should belong to Finland, and with guarantees protecting the islanders Sweden accepted that decision. British power focused by Lloyd George and the League Council persuaded Yugoslavia to withdraw from Albania by December 1921; Italy was authorized to protect the political and economic independence of Albania. Lithuania objected to Poland's occupation of Vilna, but this dispute was not so easily solved. In October 1922 the League confirmed the independence of Austria, and the British, French, and Italian governments offered loan guarantees for reconstruction. That year it became clear that nations were not willing to disarm until they could trust an alternative system of security. Resolution 14 of the League Assembly elucidated this principle that led a commission to draft a treaty of mutual assistance.

When Germany got behind on its reparation payments, French and Belgian armies invaded the Ruhr in January 1923; but a London conference the next August sponsored by the MacDonald government led to the Dawes plan for German reconstruction. However, unwilling to commit itself to enforcement, in March 1925 the British refused to accept the Geneva Protocol for the Pacific Settlement of International Disputes. This Protocol proposed that all disputes related to international law be submitted to the world court at The Hague and be binding on the parties. Instead, Britain's Austen Chamberlain proposed "special arrangements" for special needs. Political negotiation between the principal powers of western Europe led in October 1925 to the Rhineland Pact that came to be known as the Treaty of Locarno between Britain, France, Germany, Italy, and Belgium. Germany accepted the borders imposed by the Versailles Treaty and the demilitarization of the west bank of the Rhine. Germany also agreed to Arbitration Conventions with Belgium, France, Poland, and Czechoslovakia. Germany was then admitted into the League of Nations in 1926 and was given a permanent seat on its Council.

At Geneva on June 17, 1925 representatives of 42 nations and the British empire signed the Protocol for the Prohibition of Poisonous Gases and Bacteriological Methods of Warfare, although the United States never ratified the treaty. Violence broke out between Bulgarian and Greek troops on the border on October 19, 1925. The Bulgarian government appealed to the League, and on October 23 the Council's presiding Briand sent a telegram urging both sides to withdraw from the battlefield. After the Council repeated its appeal three days later, first the Bulgarians and then the Greeks complied. After an inquiry the Council recommended that Greece pay Bulgaria 45,000 pounds indemnity, and two officers from a neutral country were appointed to watch the border. The Kurds wanted independence from Iraq; but in December 1925 the League Council voted unanimously to give Iraq a 25-year mandate over Mosul; Iraq's mandatory Britain was supposed to make sure that the Kurdish minority was protected. France withdrew its garrison from the Saar in 1927.

By then France had alliances with Belgium, Poland, Czechoslovakia, Romania, and Yugoslavia. Informal League of Nations support groups existed in many countries, and the peace movement was particularly enthusiastic in the United States. They urged the Coolidge Administration to sign a friendship treaty with France. Wary of a specific alliance, they came up with the idea for a multi-lateral treaty renouncing war. This Pact of Perpetual Friendship was negotiated by US Secretary of State Frank Kellogg and France's minister Aristide Briand, who was persuaded to accept it with a reservation for self-defense. This famous Kellogg-Briand Pact or Treaty of Paris was signed on August 27, 1928 by them and representatives of Germany, Belgium, Italy, Japan, Poland, Czechoslovakia, and Great Britain with its Dominions in Canada, Australia, New Zealand, South Africa, Ireland, and India. This treaty had only three articles, the third of which established the ratification procedure. The first two articles of the Kellogg-Briand Pact read as follows:

1. The High Contracting Parties solemnly declare
   in the names of their respective peoples
   that they condemn recourse to war
   for the solution of international controversies,
   and renounce it as an instrument of national policy
   in their relations with one another.
2. The High Contracting Parties agree that the settlement
   or solution of all disputes or conflicts of whatever nature
   or of whatever origin they may be,

which may arise among them,
shall never be sought except by pacific means.[22]

The United States Senate did ratify this treaty as did all the other signatories. An additional 31 nations adhered to the Treaty of Paris by the time it was proclaimed on July 24, 1929. Within seven months fourteen more nations had joined. Brazil did so two years after that, but Argentina, Bolivia, El Salvador, and Uruguay never did. Thus for nearly every nation in the world this treaty renouncing war became a landmark in international law, and it can be argued that any politician since that time, who has used war as an instrument of national policy, has violated this Treaty and committed a crime against international law.

League of Nations Failures After 1930

Japan had given up Shandong (Shantung) at the Washington naval conference in 1922, but on September 18, 1931 they invaded Manchuria, claiming that Japanese troops guarding the South Manchuria Railway had been fired upon by the Chinese, though a subsequent investigation denied this. China appealed to the League Council, which on September 22 requested that the fighting stop. Japanese delegate Kenkichi Yoshizawa assured the Council that Japan had "no territorial designs" on Manchuria. The Chinese authority withdrew to Jinzhou (Chinchow), which the Japanese bombed on October 8. The League Council met five days later, and US Secretary of State Henry Stimson indicated that the United States "would endeavor to reinforce what the League does."[23] However, the American Consul-General to Switzerland, Prentiss Gilbert, who attended the Council, did little more than offer moral support. On October 24 Yoshizawa vetoed a Council resolution calling for Japanese withdrawal. On January 7, 1932 Stimson announced that the United States would not recognize any change in Manchuria that violated the Kellogg-Briand Pact.

Although the Chinese mayor of Shanghai accepted a

Japanese ultimatum, on January 27 Admiral Koichi Shiozawa ordered Japanese occupation of the Chapei district. When the Chinese resisted, Japan bombed Chapei. On January 29 China appealed to Articles 10 and 15 by taking their case to the League Assembly. A commission headed by Victor Lytton began investigating the situation. Meanwhile the Council did no more than adopt Stimson's non-recognition policy. By March 1932 Japan had set up a puppet government in Manchuria called Manchukuo under the last emperor of China, Pu Yi, using the name Kangde. By the time Japan agreed to a cease-fire in May they had devastated Chapei, and several thousand Chinese and Japanese had been killed or wounded. In September 1932 the Lytton Commission concluded that Manchukuo was not established by the will of the native Chinese but was a result of Japanese imperialism. Japan managed to delay League action for several months; but on February 24, 1933 the Assembly passed a resolution agreeing with the Lytton Commission's judgment. This was opposed only by the Japanese delegation, and Yosuke Matsuoka dramatically walked out. The following month Japan gave formal notice that it was withdrawing from the League. By then the Japanese army had also occupied Jehol, a border province between Manchuria and China.

In the London Naval Treaty of April 1930 Britain, the United States, and Japan had extended their 1922 Washington arms-limit agreement to include cruisers, destroyers, and submarines. The 1922 Naval Treaty had set limits the same for Britain and the United States with Japan allowed 60% and Italy and France one-third as much. After five years of study the League Council's Preparatory Commission scheduled a Disarmament Conference for February 1932 in Geneva. Fifty-nine nations were represented, and Soviet foreign minister Maxim Litvinov came to the Disarmament Conference with a proposal for a substantial reduction of offensive weapons. Germany wanted other powers to reduce their arms to the levels to which they had been restricted by the Versailles Treaty, and they quoted that document's call for "a general limitation of the armaments of all nations."[24] They reminded the French officials that they had been given assurances that these limitations would be "the first steps toward the general reduction of armaments."[24] The French, lacking support from Britain and the United States to protect their national security, were unwilling to make concessions to Germany. France proposed that all major offensive weapons be controlled by the League and an international force under Council authority. German Chancellor Heinrich Bruening demanded equality for Germany by having the other powers reduce their arms.

On April 10, 1932 Germans re-elected President Paul von Hindenburg, but Adolf Hitler got more than thirteen million votes. Bruening suggested that Germany be allowed to double its army to 200,000. On June 2 Franz von Papen replaced Bruening and harshly criticized the Versailles Treaty. That month United States president Herbert Hoover proposed abolishing offensive weapons and reducing all others by a third, but neither Britain nor Japan would accept the abolition of armored forces and bombers. The Germans announced that they would withdraw until they were given equality. On December 11 envoys of France, Germany, Britain, and the United States declared equal rights in a system to provide security for all nations. On January 30, 1933 President Hindenburg appointed Hitler chancellor of Germany. On March 5 the Nazi party won the election, and with the nationalists they held a majority in the recently burned Reichstag. On March 16 British prime minister Ramsay MacDonald proposed parity in troops between France, Germany, Italy, and Poland at 200,000 each while allowing Russia 500,000, France 200,000 more in her empire, and Italy 50,000 more; every power would be limited to 500 military aircraft. MacDonald then left to consult in Rome with Benito Mussolini, who proposed a four-power pact between France, Germany, Britain, and Italy outside of the League. On May 16, 1933 US president Franklin D. Roosevelt declared his support for the British plan. The next day Hitler made a speech calling war "unlimited madness" and offered to disband Germany's entire military establishment if its neighbors would do the same. He complained that Germany was being treated unjustly by the Versailles Treaty; he threatened that if Germany was not given equality, it would withdraw from the Disarmament Conference and from the League. The example of Japanese aggression in Manchuria persuaded most diplomats that disarmament would be foolish, and Britain insisted on keeping its strategic bombing capability. France proposed amending MacDonald's plan, delaying German rearmament for four years and its equality for eight years. A four-power power pact was signed by Britain, France, Germany, and Italy at Rome on July 15, but this did little but agree to consider the revision of treaties. On October 14, 1933 Hitler announced that Germany was withdrawing from the Disarmament Conference and from the League of Nations. When Hitler put this to a national referendum on November 12, about 95% of the German people voted in favor of his decision. Although the French and British intelligence agencies were aware that Germany had been secretly rearming since the 1920s in violation of the Versailles Treaty, no sanctions were proposed.

In October 1932 the mandate for Iraq had been declared terminated, and that nation was unanimously admitted into the League. On July 1, 1933 the French diplomat, Deputy Secretary-General Joseph Avenol, replaced Secretary-General Eric Drummond. In March 1934 the German budget for the next fiscal year revealed a 90% increase in military expenditures, persuading France to end negotiations. In July 1934 Mussolini used four divisions to keep the Nazis from taking over Austria after they murdered Chancellor Engelbert Dollfuss. Despite opposition to admitting a Communist country by Switzerland, the Netherlands, and Portugal, the Soviet Union was voted into the League of Nations on September 18, 1934 and was given a permanent seat on the Council. Nazi threats regarding the impending plebiscite in the Saar prompted Geoffrey Knox of the Governing Commission to request troops from the League Council, and 1,500 soldiers, mostly Italian, were sent. In the 1935 Saar election 90% voted for reunion with Germany; less than 50,000 wanted to remain under the League; and only 2,214 voted to unite with France.

An undeclared border war had been going on at the Gran Chaco between Bolivia and Paraguay since December 1928 over rich oil deposits. On December 19 that year those governments had informed Secretary-General Drummond that they had chosen Pan-American arbitration; 52,000 Bolivians and 36,000 Paraguayans were killed in the conflict. When the Washington Commission of Neutrals failed in 1933, Bolivia appealed to the League, which sent a Commission of Inquiry. An arms embargo was recommended, and 28 nations agreed to it in May 1934. The arms embargo was lifted from Bolivia after they accepted the cease-fire proposal, but Paraguay did not accept it and resigned from the League in February 1935. In May the League gave the Gran Chaco dispute back to a South American mediation conference that included the United States, and on June 12, 1935 Bolivia and Paraguay signed protocols ending the dispute. In January 1935 the United States Senate had defeated an effort by the Roosevelt administration to become a member of the Permanent Court of International Justice (PCIJ).

During the 1920s Italy had used troops to suppress native resistance in Somaliland, and from 1929 to 1932 the Fascists conducted a brutal campaign in Libya, destroying villages, hanging leaders, and putting civilians in concentration camps. On December 5, 1934 a clash at the Wal Wal oasis killed over a hundred Ethiopians (Abyssinians) and about thirty native soldiers under Italian authority. Italy had been planning war to gain Ethiopia's coal, oil, gold, and platinum and so rejected arbitration under the treaty they had signed in 1928. On January 3, 1935 Ethiopian emperor Haile Selassie asked the League to intervene to protect his nation as stated in Article 11. Mussolini agreed to arbitration in order to postpone the Council's consideration. Then he disregarded its decision by building up Italian forces in Somaliland and Eritrea. On March 17 Ethiopia appealed to Article 15; but two days before that, Hitler had announced compulsory conscription and an increase in the German army from 10 to 36 divisions. On April 17, 1935 the League Council condemned German rearmament as a violation of the Versailles Treaty. In June Stanley Baldwin became prime minister, and a special poll of British voters called the "Peace Ballot" showed that they overwhelmingly supported the League, favoring economic sanctions 15-1 and military sanctions 3-1.

On October 3, 1935 the Italian army invaded Ethiopia, and within a week both the League Council and its Assembly had condemned Italy for violating the Covenant, though Albania, Austria, and Hungary opposed the resolution. After France's Pierre Laval and England's Samuel Hoare endorsed a sanctions regime that capitulated to Mussolini, it was so unpopular that both foreign ministers had to resign, Hoare on December 19 and Laval on January 22, 1936. Ethiopians submitted evidence that the Italians were using mustard gas in violation of the Geneva Protocol they signed in 1925. After the French Chamber of Deputies ratified a mutual aid pact with the Soviet Union in February 1936, Hitler ordered German troops to occupy the Rhineland on March 7 in violation of the Locarno Pact as well as the Versailles Treaty. French and Belgian diplomats asked the League for sanctions and military force, but the British opposed. On May 6 the Italians captured Addis Ababa, and Mussolini proclaimed his "African victory." When the Ethiopian delegate attended the League Council on May 11, the Italian delegate walked out; but Secretary-General Avenol negotiated with Mussolini and criticized Selassie.

A month later the British government advised lifting the sanctions against Italy. This decision was bitterly criticized in the House of Commons as opposition leader Clement Attlee accused them of destroying the League of

Nations. However, this policy of Anthony Eden was also adopted by France. Selassie was allowed to speak to the League Assembly on June 30 and warned them that "the very existence of the League" was in danger, saying "God and history will remember your judgment."[25] Four days later the Assembly voted to end the sanctions as Ethiopia cast the only opposing vote. After the Ethiopian delegates were allowed to be seated in September 1936, the Italians no longer attended any meetings. On November 1, 1936 Mussolini announced the Rome-Berlin Axis.

In July 1936 General Francisco Franco and military officers tried to take over the government of Spain by force from the Popular Front led by Manuel Azaña, who had been elected on May 8. Azaña asked for military aid from France and England while appealing to the League. France's socialist prime minister Leon Blum was sympathetic, but the French parliament feared war with Italy and Germany, who were already supplying Franco with aircraft; thus the French government prohibited selling arms to the Spanish republic. On September 9, 1936 in London 26 European nations met as the International Committee for the Application of the Agreement for Non-Intervention in Spain. Attempting to mollify Italy and Germany, the League's Secretary-General Avenol blocked the effort of Spain's foreign minister, Julio Alvarez del Vayo, to bring up the issue in the League Assembly. Although they all accepted the Non-Intervention Agreement, Italy and Germany continued to aid Franco's war; in response the USSR sent supplies to the Spanish government. Avenol invited the countries involved in the crisis to the Council for a mediation effort but removed consideration of possible aggression against Spain. After the Axis powers recognized Franco on November 18, Avenol began blocking League aid to the Spanish republic.

In December 1936 Alvarez del Vayo accused the Fascist powers of violating the Agreement, and in February 1937 the Non-Intervention Committee decided to police Spanish borders and ports to prevent outside aid and volunteers to

Spain with naval patrols from Britain, France, Germany, Italy, Portugal, and Russia. The next month Italian troops were captured in the battle of Guadalajara, proving that four Italian divisions were fighting. On April 26 German aircraft destroyed the city of Guernica. The Spanish foreign minister accused Italy again at the League Council on May 28, and the next day the Council unanimously passed a resolution for all non-Spanish forces to withdraw from the Civil War. The day after that, 22 of the crew on the *Deutschland* were killed in an air attack, prompting the German navy to blast the port of Almeria and to withdraw from the interdiction patrols. In September 1937 the Mediterranean powers met to stop submarine warfare, and on the 16th Spanish prime minister Juan Negrin went to the League and asked them to protect Spanish ships and condemn Italy for the losses. Despite Avenol's continuing efforts to conciliate Italy, on December 11 Mussolini announced Italy's resignation from the League.

In May 1938 Alvarez del Vayo asked the League to end the sham of non-intervention, but only the USSR voted with Spain. In October 1938 the international brigades fighting for the Loyalist government were disbanded; but Franco kept bombing, and a British report to the League Council in January 1939 called it "contrary to the conscience of mankind and to the principles of international law."[26] The League did arrange aid for the refugees as Franco's offensive captured Barcelona, Catalonia, and finally Madrid before the republican armies surrendered on April 1. On May 9, 1939 Franco announced that Spain was withdrawing from the League of Nations. Avenol's concessions to try to keep the Fascist powers in the League had failed.

Fighting broke out between Chinese and Japanese troops at the Marco Polo Bridge west of Beijing on July 7, 1937 and spread in the north and to Shanghai the next month. On September 12 China asked the League to help; but British consul Edmond in Geneva, Secretary-General Avenol, and French foreign minister Delbos persuaded the

Chinese delegate Wellington Koo that League action would prevent President Roosevelt from assisting because of America's neutrality law. So Koo agreed to an advisory committee, and on September 27 he did not ask for sanctions but only requested a review of the bombing issue. Britain's delegate Robert Cecil modified Koo's proposal for collective support from the League for China and deleted the motion to bar aid to Japan. Britain over Koo's objections also got the issue given to the nations of the Nine Power Treaty of 1922 that had limited Japanese armaments. No war had been declared, but in December 1937 *Time* magazine estimated that the Japanese had killed 20,000 Chinese prisoners of war and civilians in Nanjing (Nanking). In January 1938 Koo again got the run-around that the League could not act without the United States, which was waiting for the League. Koo appealed to the League again in February, May, and in the autumn of 1938 but still could not get even an embargo against aiding Japan with arms or loans.

Although he had pledged to respect Austrian sovereignty in a 1936 treaty, Hitler announced it would be unified with Germany on March 12, 1938. Austria's Chancellor Kurt von Schuschnigg capitulated but scheduled a plebiscite for March 13. Fearing a defeat at the polls, Hitler ordered his army to invade, and to avoid carnage Schuschnigg cancelled the plebiscite on March 11. British officials advised against the League trying to pass any ineffective resolutions. Next Hitler campaigned for the Sudetanland to be returned to Germany; but on September 22, 1938 Czechoslovakia began mobilizing and appealed to France to fulfill its treaty obligation. At the end of the month British Prime Minister Neville Chamberlain and French Premier Edouard Daladier met with Hitler at Munich as Czech officials were excluded. Chamberlain accepted Germany's terms and was given a paper by Hitler saying that it was "the desire of our two peoples never to go to war with one another again."[27] In March 1939 German troops occupied Bohemia, Moravia, and Slovakia as Hitler let Hungary take over the Ruthenian region of what had been Czechoslovakia. When its former President Benes appealed to the League, Secretary-General Avenol dismissed his request and began admitting that the League could no longer make political pronouncements or maneuvers. Instead, he hoped that the League could expand its social and economic services.

On April 7, 1939 the Italian army invaded Albania, and Mussolini forced its government to resign from the League. On August 23 the new Soviet foreign minister Molotov and Germany's Ribbentrop announced a Nazi-Soviet non-aggression pact. As German troops invaded Poland on September 1, it became clear that Poland had been divided between them. Britain and France gave Hitler an ultimatum and then declared war on Germany. Avenol and the League did nothing until the USSR invaded Finland on November 30, 1939. On December 14 the League Assembly expelled the Soviet Union for violating its Covenant. Technical assistance was offered to Finland; but it was over-run by Soviet armies by March 1940. During World War II the League survived at Geneva, though Avenol resigned on July 25 and was replaced by Irish Sean Lester. Finally the League of Nations itself was replaced and its remaining functions were taken over by the United Nations Organization in April 1946.

Perhaps the League had helped to prevent small wars and through cooperation brought more collective consciousness into international affairs, but its failure had become overwhelmingly obvious when the aggressions of Japan, Italy, and Germany brought on a second world war that many had feared.

Notes

1. *The Hague Peace Conferences of 1899 and 1907*, Volume 2 by James Brown Scott, p. 77.
2. *Advocate of Peace*, LXXII (1910), 147 quoted by Calvin De Armond Davis in *The United States and the Second Hague Peace Conference*, p. 319.
3. Quoted by Page Smith in *America Enters the World*, p. 615.
4. *The Messages and Papers of Woodrow Wilson*. Volume 1, p. 275.
5. *Ibid.*, p. 353.
6. *Ibid.*, p. 355.
7. *Ibid.*, p. 355.
8. Quoted by Arthur S. Link in *Wilson: Campaigns for Progressivism and Peace 1916-1917*, p. 398.
9. *The Messages and Papers of Woodrow Wilson*. Volume 1, p. 378.
10. *Ibid.*, p. 381.
11. *Ibid.*, p. 468-470.
12. *Ibid.*, p. 524.
13. *Ibid.*, p. 556.
14. Baker, Ray Stannard, *Woodrow Wilson and World Settlement*, Volume 1, p. 10.
15. *The Messages and Papers of Woodrow Wilson*. Volume 1, p. 597.
16. *The Messages and Papers of Woodrow Wilson*. Volume 2, p. 709.
17. *The Law of War: A Documentary History* ed. Leon Friedman, Volume 1, p. 424.
18. *Woodrow Wilson and the Great Betrayal* by Thomas A. Bailey, p. 350.
19. *The Law of War: A Documentary History* ed. Leon Friedman, Volume 1, p. 423.
20. *Ibid.*, p. 424.
21. *Ibid.*, p. 429.
22. *Peace in Their Time: The Origins of the Kellogg-Briand Pact* by Robert Ferrell, p. 266.
23. *The League of Nations: its life and times 1920-1946* by F. S. Northedge, p. 147.

24. *The League of Nations from 1929 to 1946* by George Gill, p. 9.
25. *Ibid.*, p. 46.
26. *Ibid.*, p. 64.
27. *Ibid.*, p. 80.

3
United Nations and Human Rights

Truly if the genius of mankind
that has invented the weapons of death
cannot discover the means of preserving peace,
civilization as we know it lives in an evil day.
Franklin Roosevelt

Freedom means the supremacy of human rights everywhere.
Franklin Roosevelt

We the peoples of the United Nations determined
to save succeeding generations from the scourge of war,
which twice in our lifetime
has brought untold sorrow to mankind,
and to reaffirm faith in fundamental human rights,
in the dignity and worth of the human person,
in the equal rights of men and women
and of nations large and small,
and to establish conditions under which justice
and respect for the obligations arising from treaties
and other sources of international law can be maintained,
and to promote social progress
and better standards of life in larger freedom,
and for these ends to practice tolerance
and live together in peace with one another as good neighbors,
and to unite our strength
to maintain international peace and security,
and to ensure, by the acceptance of principles
and the institution of methods,
that armed force shall not be used,
save in the common interest,
and to employ international machinery for the promotion
of the economic and social advancement of all peoples,
have resolved to combine our efforts to accomplish these aims.
Charter of the United Nations

Recognition of the inherent dignity
and of the equal and inalienable rights

of all members of the human family
is the foundation of freedom, justice, and peace in the world.
Universal Declaration of Human Rights

Roosevelt and the United Nations Alliance

As with Woodrow Wilson and the League of Nations, the primary initiator of the United Nations was an American president, Franklin Roosevelt. However, Roosevelt, the United States, and the world had learned from failures with the League. Roosevelt was not as closely identified with the United Nations as Wilson had been with the League, and he died shortly before the United Nations' founding conference and the termination of the second world war.

Franklin Delano Roosevelt was born on January 30, 1882 at Hyde Park, New York. At Harvard young Franklin was not particularly studious, but he excelled in extracurricular activities. He admired the progressive policies of President Theodore Roosevelt, who was his distant cousin, and he married TR's niece Eleanor Roosevelt. Eleanor was his lifelong partner in political work, and after his death she was a leading promoter of the United Nations. Franklin became a lawyer and was elected state senator in 1910 as a progressive Democrat. Roosevelt supported Woodrow Wilson for President, and he was appointed assistant secretary of the Navy in 1913.

In July 1919 when the League of Nations was being debated, Roosevelt argued that the League was necessary for a successful peace settlement. He concluded hopefully, "If the League of Nations, with its future benefits to the world, is adopted, the future generations will look to us and call us blessed."[1] In 1920 FDR was selected by the Democratic convention as their candidate for Vice President and running mate of James Cox. Roosevelt campaigned in favor of the League of Nations, saying that for the first time in history nations were being placed on the same basis as the relations between individuals. He asked,

Why should one outlaw nation be able to run amuck

and murder or maim a brother nation
without being called to account for it,
without being prevented from further misdeeds
in the community of nations?[2]

Roosevelt believed that the United States loves peace but loves honor more and so threw its nation into the war. Then he prophetically warned his country,

If you want the repetition of another war against civilization,
then let us go back to the conditions of 1914.
If you want the possibility of sending once more
our troops and navies to foreign lands,
then stay out of the League.[3]

In a speech on September 24, 1920 candidate Roosevelt explained how Republican party leaders decided to sabotage the League in order to prevent a Republican defeat in the Presidential election, even after President Wilson had met with Republican leaders and gotten the Monroe Doctrine incorporated into the League Covenant. FDR described how Will Hays, chairman of the Republican National Committee, secretly met with Senators Lodge, Borah, Brandegee and others and convinced them to follow

a deliberate and carefully planned campaign
to throw over the treaty of peace
and to discredit the President of the United States,
in order to secure a victory for the Republican Party.
The choice was made at that time.
Partisan advantage was placed first,
and the restoration of peace to civilization
was thrown into the discard.
As a result of that determination of more than one year ago,
the restoration of peace still hangs in the balance.
This is recognized not only here but throughout the world.[4]

In the closing days of the campaign Roosevelt raised the moral question of the League versus the banking interests: he pointed out how educators, religious leaders, lawyers, organizations of mothers, and soldiers who fought in France favored the League because they were aware of the issues. He warned voters,

> Those who are not "up" on the League,
> who have not read it,
> who do not comprehend it in an intelligent sense
> will cast the majority of the votes in favor of
> the Republican nominees for President and Vice President.
> Lined up with them are
> most of the financiers and moneyed interests,
> also about eighty percent of the newspapers
> of the United States.[5]

The Republicans won the election.

Suddenly in August 1921 Franklin Roosevelt was struck with polio and was almost completely paralyzed. He regained the use of everything except his legs, but he remained physically crippled in the legs for the rest of his life. However, he refused to retire, as his mother suggested, and he stayed active in politics with Eleanor's help. In 1924 he proposed a new international organization to replace the League, and at the Democratic convention he nominated his fellow New Yorker, Governor Al Smith, for President. Smith urged him to run for governor in 1928, and Roosevelt was elected and re-elected in 1930.

In 1932 Roosevelt wrestled the Presidential nomination away from Smith and won a big victory over Hoover during the depth of the Depression. As President, Roosevelt took immediate action to meet the crisis with his various New Deal programs of recovery for a blighted economy. He was overwhelmingly re-elected in 1936, but he had difficulty with the Supreme Court and a recession in 1937. Roosevelt had brought a creative and dynamic activity to government to deal with massive economic problems based on his real concern for the poor, the unemployed, and the destitute. His programs attempted to establish economic and social security for all Americans.

His first major foreign policy speech was on Woodrow

Wilson's birthday at the end of 1933. He clearly defined United States policy as being opposed to armed intervention. In an unusual statement for a politician, he admitted, "The blame for the danger to world peace lies not in the world population but in the political leaders."[6] He recalled how the masses of people had enthusiastically responded to Wilson's gallant appeal and how political profit, personal prestige, and national aggrandizement had handicapped the League's inception. Roosevelt believed

that the old policies, alliances,
combinations and balances of power
have proved themselves inadequate
for the preservation of world peace.
The League of Nations, encouraging as it does
the extension of non-aggression pacts,
of reduction of armament agreements,
is a prop in the world peace structure.[7]

Perhaps the same is true of the United Nations today, and the same challenge that Wilson and Roosevelt faced we still face today, which is, as FDR stated, "whether people themselves could not some day prevent governments from making war."[8]

Although it was politically impossible for the American President to get the United States involved in the League, Roosevelt did encourage cooperation with the non-political and humanitarian work of League agencies. In his "Quarantine" speech on October 5, 1937 Roosevelt spoke out against the worsening world situation caused by violations of treaties and undeclared acts of war that killed innocent civilians. He warned that America would not be safe from the contagion of war. He asserted that peace-loving nations must attempt to uphold laws and treaties, because in international anarchy there is no escape through isolation.

Those who cherish their freedom
and recognize and respect the equal right
of their neighbors to be free and live in peace,

must work together for the triumph
of law and moral principles
in order that peace, justice and confidence
may prevail in the world.[9]

He pointed out how much of the world's economy was being spent on armaments. The President believed that America must actively engage in the search for peace, and he suggested a quarantine against the epidemic of aggressor nations. Thus the policy of the United States was no longer isolation, and shortly a League committee declared that Japan was the aggressor against China.

A year later Roosevelt pleaded with Hitler to settle the differences between Germany and Czechoslovakia by peaceful means, but Hitler marched his troops into that country. In April 1939 Roosevelt again appealed to Hitler and Mussolini to prevent the disaster of war. Speaking from strength and human friendship, he asked these dictators not to invade thirty independent nations he named; he proposed negotiations to reduce the crushing economic burdens of armaments and to open international trade. Finally one week before the war broke out, FDR sent an appeal to Hitler, King Victor Emmanuel of Italy, and President Moscicki of Poland; but only the Polish leader was interested in averting war. When war was declared, President Roosevelt sent messages to Britain, France, Italy, Germany, and Poland requesting that they not bomb civilians. In a fireside chat to the nation on September 3, 1939 he declared that the policy of the United States was neutrality, but he did not expect people to be neutral in their minds and consciences. He hoped that America would be able to stay out of the war.

After winning an unprecedented third term as President, at the end of 1940 Roosevelt declared that America must become "the great arsenal democracy" to aid economically the Allies against the Fascists' warfare. Then he gave his famous "four freedoms" speech on January 6, 1941. America had been founded on the first two freedoms of religion and speech. Roosevelt's response to the Depression and World War II was to call for freedom from want and freedom from fear. Not only did he believe that all Americans deserved these rights, but also everyone in the world. Roosevelt said that freedom from want "means economic understandings which will secure to every nation a healthy peace time life for its inhabitants—everywhere in the world,"[10] and freedom from fear "means a world-wide reduction of armaments to such a point and in such a thorough fashion that no nation will be in a position to commit an act of physical aggression against any neighbor— anywhere in the world."[11] On March 11 President Roosevelt signed the Lend-Lease bill that allowed military and economic aid to the countries that were fighting Germany and Japan.

In August 1941 Roosevelt and Winston Churchill, the prime minister for the United Kingdom, agreed on the Atlantic Charter, which declared their nations' principles and intentions in regard to the circumstances of the war. First, they sought no territorial aggrandizement. Second, they wanted no territorial changes that would not be in "accord with the freely expressed wishes of the peoples concerned."[12] Third, they respected the right of all peoples to self-government. Fourth, they supported states' equal access to trade and the raw materials of the world. Fifth, they wished to promote economic cooperation, "improved labor standards, economic advancement, and social security."[13] Sixth, after destroying the Nazi tyranny they hoped to establish a peace that would be secure to all nations and peoples in freedom from fear and want. Seventh, this peace would include freedom of the seas. Eighth and last, they declared,

All of the nations of the world,
for realistic as well as spiritual reasons,
must come to the abandonment of the use of force.
Since no future peace can be maintained
if land, sea, or air armaments continue to be employed
by nations which threaten, or may threaten,

aggression outside of their frontiers,
they believe, pending the establishment
of a wider and permanent system of general security,
that the disarmament of such nations is essential.
They will likewise aid and encourage
all other practicable measures
which will lighten for peace-loving peoples
the crushing burden of armaments.[14]

The "they" refers to the two signers, Franklin D. Roosevelt and Winston S. Churchill.

With the surprise attack on the United States naval base at Pearl Harbor by the Japanese on December 7, 1941 America was drawn fully into the war. When Churchill and the Soviet ambassador Litvinov met with Roosevelt in Washington to confirm the new alliance against the Axis powers, FDR suggested the name "United Nations." On January 1, 1942 these representatives along with Soong of China signed the Declaration of the United Nations "to defend life, liberty, independence and religious freedom, and to preserve human rights and justice in their own lands as well as in other lands."[15] The pact was later signed by the other twenty-two nations named in the declaration. More than three years later when the name of the new international organization was being discussed in San Francisco, the name "United Nations" was selected as a tribute to Roosevelt.

Roosevelt conceived the organization as world-wide in scope, although important decisions would be made by the United States, Britain, Russia, and China, who would have the responsibility of policing the world. This is what he told the British foreign minister Anthony Eden and Churchill in March 1943. On November 1, Secretary of State Cordell Hull, Eden, Soviet foreign minister Molotov, and the Chinese ambassador to Moscow signed the Moscow Declaration in which the four powers agreed to maintain international peace after the war, stating,

That they recognize the necessity of establishing

at the earliest practicable date
a general international organization,
based on the principle of the sovereign equality
of all peace loving states,
and open to membership by all such states, large and small,
for the maintenance of international peace and security.[16]

This statement was incorporated into the Connally Resolution and was passed by the United States Senate on November 6, 1943. Already Congress was on record in favor of a world organization. On November 9, representatives of forty-four nations met at the White House and established the United Nations Relief and Rehabilitation Administration (UNRRA).

At the end of November 1943 Roosevelt met with Churchill and Stalin at Tehran, and FDR began to share his outline of the organization for the preservation of world peace. The Assembly would include all members of the United Nations and would be world-wide in scope; they would discuss world problems and recommend solutions. The Executive Committee would be composed of the USSR, the US, the UK, and China along with representatives of two European nations, one South American, one Middle Eastern, one Far Eastern, and one British Dominion. They would deal with all non-military questions such as economy, food, health, etc., but both Stalin and Roosevelt were reluctant to give them any binding power. The third group would be the "Four Policemen" (USSR, US, UK, and China). They would have the power to use force against any threat to the peace. Both Stalin and Churchill suggested regional committees, but Roosevelt did not expect the forces of China or the US to be needed in Europe. Apparently the possibility of one of the Four Policemen being an aggressor was not discussed. The conference concluded amicably with Roosevelt saying how nations with different customs and philosophies could blend in harmony like the colors of a rainbow for the common good.

In his annual message to Congress in January 1944 Roosevelt proposed an "economic Bill of Rights." He said that security means not only safety from attacks by aggressors but also "economic security, social security, moral security—in a family of nations."[17] He felt that these rights should include earning enough from a job for food, clothing, and recreation, buying and selling products, a decent home, medical care, and education.

In August 1944 representatives of the Big Four met at the Dumbarton Oaks Conference in Washington. The Russians insisted that the Chinese be excluded until the major decisions were made by the other three powers. The tentative American plan had two broad purposes for the international organization: 1) to preserve peace and security, and 2) to promote international cooperation on economic and social problems. The plan now had five functional divisions; in addition to a General Assembly and Executive Council, there would be an International Court, a Secretariat, and subsidiary agencies. Security questions were to be solely vested in the Executive Council, which now would include France as a fifth permanent member and six rotating members. Any one of the five permanent members would be able to block an action in regard to disputes, settlements, sanctions, and uses of force.

There was still a question whether one of the five powers could use this veto if that nation was itself involved in the dispute. The Americans went along with the British in proposing that a veto not be allowed by a power who was a party to a dispute. The Soviet representative Gromyko responded to this by requesting that all sixteen Soviet republics be included as charter members of the United Nations. Roosevelt felt that this would make it very difficult for him to get the international organization accepted by the United States Senate. With the abeyance of these two questions, the American tentative proposals were generally accepted. A compromise on the veto issue was suggested on September 13 and was later adopted in the United Nations Charter. A permanent member could veto any use of force even if it was a party to a dispute; but it could not veto a decision which came under "Pacific Settlement of Disputes" if it was a party to that dispute.

Roosevelt was elected to a fourth term as President, and in his Inaugural Address on January 20, 1945 he spoke of the lessons the United States had gained from the war.

> We have learned that we cannot live alone, at peace;
> that our own well-being is dependent on
> the well-being of other nations—far away.
> We have learned that we must live as men,
> not as ostriches, nor as dogs in the manger.
> We have learned to be citizens of the world,
> members of the human community.
> We have learned the simple truth.
> Emerson said that
> "the only way to have a friend is to be one."
> We can gain no lasting peace if we approach it
> with suspicion and mistrust—and with fear.
> We can gain it only if we proceed with the understanding
> and confidence and courage which flow from conviction.[18]

Roosevelt met again with Churchill and Stalin at Yalta in February 1945. Stalin agreed to the veto solution but insisted on at least two extra votes for the Ukraine and Byelorussia in the General Assembly. Since it would not affect the Executive Council and as a gesture of goodwill toward the Russians, who had lost twenty million killed fighting the Nazis, Roosevelt accepted this proposal, if the UN conference they scheduled to begin in San Francisco on April 25 would also accept the two additional Russian republics after discussion and a free vote. Roosevelt considered the Crimean Conference more successful than the peace efforts made a quarter of a century earlier. He believed that a universal organization of all peace-loving nations should mark the end of methods such as unilateral action, exclusive alliances, spheres of influence, and balances of power which had failed for centuries.

On March 1 President Roosevelt reported to the Congress about the Crimean Conference, saying how the Senate was being advised of the new international security organization and declaring, "World peace is not a party question."[19] World peace cannot depend upon the work of one man, one party, or one nation, or even the large nations or the small nations. "It must be a peace which rests on the cooperative effort of the whole world."[20] In a press conference on April 5 Roosevelt expressed the view that for the Soviet Union to have three votes in the General Assembly was not that significant because it was only an investigative body that really would not decide important issues.

Franklin Roosevelt died on April 12, 1945. On that day he wrote a speech to be given in honor of Thomas Jefferson's birthday the next day. He looked past the conquest of the malignant Nazi state toward the conquest of the root causes—doubts, fears, ignorance, and greed. He asked us to face the fact that

if civilization is to survive,
we must cultivate the science of human relationships—
the ability of all peoples, of all kinds, to live together
and work together in the same world, at peace....
The work, my friends, is peace,
more than an end of this war—
an end to the beginning of all wars, yes, an end, forever,
to this impractical, unrealistic settlement of the differences
between governments by the mass killing of peoples.[21]

In his last words he appealed to people to dedicate themselves to peace and act with faith. "The only limit to our realization of tomorrow will be our doubts of today. Let us move forward with strong and active faith."[22]

United Nations Charter

Delegates of fifty nations met in San Francisco on April 25 for the United Nations Conference on International Organization. Using the Dumbarton Oaks proposals as a basis, they worked in committees and plenary sessions to draw up the 111-article Charter, which was adopted unanimously on June 25, 1945. The Charter became effective the following October 24 after China, France, the Soviet Union, the United Kingdom, the United States, and a majority of the signing nations had ratified the document.

The first article of the *United Nations Charter* reads as follows:

> The Purposes of the United Nations are:
> 1. To maintain international peace and security, and to that end: to take effective collective measures for the prevention and removal of threats to peace, and for the suppression of acts of aggression or other breaches of the peace, and to bring about by peaceful means, and in conformity with the principles of justice and international law, adjustment or settlement of international disputes or situations which might lead to a breach of the peace:
> 2. To develop friendly relations among nations based on respect for the principle of equal rights and self-determination of peoples, and to take other appropriate measures to strengthen universal peace;
> 3. To achieve international cooperation in solving international problems of an economic, social, cultural, or humanitarian character, and in promoting and encouraging respect for human rights and for fundamental freedoms for all without distinction as to race, sex, language, or religion; and
> 4. To be a center for harmonizing the actions of nations in the attainment of these common ends.[23]

In the second article the Members agree to act in accordance with the following principles:

> 1) the sovereign equality of all Members,
> 2) fulfillment of Charter obligations,
> 3) settlement of "international disputes by peaceful means and in such a manner that international peace and security, and justice, are not endangered,"
> 4) refraining "from the threat or use of force against the territorial integrity

or political independence of any state."
5) assistance of the United Nations
   and refraining from assisting "any state
   against which the United Nations
   is taking preventive or enforcement action."
6) ensuring that states that are not Members
   act in accordance with the Principles, and
7) the United Nations is not authorized "to intervene
   within the domestic jurisdiction of any state."[24]

The second chapter describes Membership. The third chapter lists the Organs as a General Assembly, a Security Council, an Economic and Social Council, a Trusteeship Council, an International Court of Justice, and a Secretariat. The fourth chapter describes the General Assembly in which each member shall have one vote. The fifth chapter defines the Security Council, naming China, France, the Soviet Union, the United Kingdom, and the United States as permanent members. Article 26 begins, "In order to promote the establishment and maintenance of international peace and security with the least diversion for armaments of the world's human and economic resources," and it sets up a committee to work to establish "a system for the regulation of armaments."[25]

Chapter VI entitled "Pacific Settlement of Disputes" begins with Article 33:

The parties to any dispute,
the continuance of which is likely to endanger
the maintenance of international peace and security,
shall, first of all, seek a solution by negotiation, enquiry,
mediation, conciliation, arbitration, judicial settlement,
resort to regional agencies or arrangements,
or other peaceful means of their own choice.[26]

The Security Council may request parties to use such means, may investigate disputes, and may make recommendations. Chapter VII discusses actions which may be taken to maintain or restore international peace when there are threats to the peace, breaches of the peace, and acts of aggression. The Security Council may decide to use force or economic sanctions and call upon member nations to make available armed forces, assistance, and facilities. Chapter VIII states that regional arrangements for maintaining peace are not precluded by the Charter.

When Harry Truman became President and the atomic bomb was developed, the relations of the United States toward the Soviet Union and the United Nations began to change into the Cold War. Lend-Lease aid to Russia was ended on May 12, 1945, while Britain was granted a low-interest loan. Soviet fears of an international bloc against them were also fed by America's support for regional blocs' use of collective self-defense, which reversed the US position at Dumbarton Oaks. Truman also decided to use the atomic bomb as a bargaining factor in dealing with the Russians, and he attempted to negate Roosevelt's abandonment of control over Eastern Europe. In October 1945 Truman saw the UN as the only alternative to "a bitter armament race with the Russians."

Nuremberg Trials and Geneva Conventions

After the first world war the Allied powers had accused 896 persons of war crimes; but only twelve were tried before the German Supreme Court at Leipzig in 1921; six were convicted, and the longest sentence was four years in prison.

On August 8, 1945 the governments of the United States, France, Britain, and the Soviet Union announced their agreement to prosecute and punish the major war criminals of the European Axis. In the Charter of the International Military Tribunal they defined crimes against peace, war crimes, and crimes against humanity, and they noted that the defendants' official positions or the fact that they were following orders of their governments did not free them of responsibility. President Harry S. Truman designated US Supreme Court Justice Robert H. Jackson, who became the chief prosecutor for the United States. He suggested Nuremberg as the best site for the Military Tribunal, which began there on October 18. Jackson observed that no trial in history ever had such a comprehensive scope. German organizations such as the Nazi party, the SS, the SA, the SD, the General Staff and OKW, and the Gestapo were also tried.

Some argued that the crimes charged in the Nuremberg Principles were *ex post facto* and therefore invalid; but they were also accused of violating the Hague Conventions, Versailles Treaty, Locarno Treaty, Kellogg-Briand Pact, and other recognized principles of international law. Defense attorneys argued that if these men were guilty, then many of the Allies were also. The first trial lasted nearly a year. The final judgment found a "common plan or conspiracy and aggressive war" based on meetings that took place as early as November 5, 1937, aggression against Poland, aggressive war against the Soviet Union, war against the United States, murder and ill-treatment of prisoners of war and civilian population, slave-labor policy, persecution of the Jews, and other crimes. Of the 22 men first indicted, Schacht, von Papen, and Fritzsche were acquitted; Goering, von Ribbentrop, Keitel, Kaltenbrunner, Rosenberg, Frank, Frick, Streicher, Sauckel, Jodl, and Seyss-Inquart were hanged; Bormann was probably killed trying to escape; Hess, Funk, and Raeder were put in prison for life; and Doenitz was sentenced to ten years, von Neurath to fifteen years, and von Schirach and Speer to twenty years.

The international Military Tribunal for the Far East began in Tokyo on June 4, 1946, but the judgment was not given until November 4, 1948. Of the 28 Japanese indicted Class A war criminals, two died during the trial; seven were hanged; one was sent to a psychiatric ward and was released in 1948; one was sentenced to twenty years; and the rest were sentenced to life imprisonment, though fourteen had been paroled by 1956. By November 1948 military courts had charged 7,109 defendants with war crimes that had resulted in 3,686 convictions and 924 acquittals; 1,019 were given death sentences, and 33 committed suicide; and

2,667 were sentenced to prison. By 1958 the Western Allies had convicted 5,025 Germans, sentenced 806 to death, and executed 486. The Soviet Union had convicted about ten thousand. More trials were held for many years. On December 11, 1946 the United Nations General Assembly unanimously passed Resolution 95 affirming the principles of international law recognized by the charter and judgment of the Nuremberg Tribunal. These Principles of International Law were formulated and published by the International Law Commission on July 29, 1950:

Principle I. Any person who commits an act which constitutes a crime under international law is responsible therefore and liable to punishment.

Principle II. The fact that internal law does not impose a penalty for an act which constitutes a crime under international law does not relieve the person who committed the act from responsibility under international law.

Principle III. The fact that a person committed an act which constitutes a crime under international law acted as Head of State or responsible Government official does not relieve him from responsibility under international law.

Principle IV. The fact that a person acted pursuant to order of his Government or of a superior does not relieve him from responsibility under international law, provided a moral choice was in fact possible to him.

Principle V. Any person charged with a crime under international law has the right to a fair trial on the facts and law.

Principle VI. The crimes hereinafter set out are punishable as crimes under international law:

a. Crimes against peace:
i. Planning, preparation, initiation or waging
of a war of aggression or a war in violation
of international treaties, agreements or assurances;

ii. Participation in a common plan or conspiracy
for the accomplishment of any of the acts
mentioned under (i).

b. War crimes:
Violations of the laws or customs of war which include,
but are not limited to, murder, ill-treatment
or deportation to slave-labor or for any other purpose
of civilian population of or in occupied territory,
murder or ill-treatment of prisoners of war
or persons on the seas, killing of hostages,
plunder of public or private property,
wanton destruction of cities, towns, or villages,
or devastation not justified by military necessity.

c. Crimes against humanity:
Murder, extermination, enslavement, deportation
and other inhuman acts done
against any civilian population,
or persecutions on political, racial or religious grounds,
when such acts are done
or such persecutions are carried on
in execution of or in connection with
any crime against peace or any war crime.

Principle VII. Complicity in the commission of a crime
against peace, a war crime, or a crime against humanity
as set forth in Principle VI
is a crime under international law.[27]

On December 9, 1948 the United Nations General
Assembly passed Resolution 260 adopting the Convention
on the Prevention and Punishment of the Crime of Genocide and invited the International Law Commission to
study the issue of International Criminal Jurisdiction.
Genocide was defined as an act intended to destroy all or

part of a national, ethnic, racial, or religious group and may include killing or harming members of the group or attempting to prevent or remove children of the group. The Convention was ratified by enough nations to become effective in 1951.

Four Geneva Conventions, also called the Red Cross Conventions, were signed by representatives of 58 nations on August 12, 1949 to update and protect the rights of the wounded and sick, prisoners of war, and civilians in time of war. The fourth Geneva Convention Relative to the Protection of Civilian Persons in Time of War was ratified by the United States and went into force February 2, 1956; it includes the following:

Article 27. Protected persons are entitled,
in all circumstances, to respect for their persons, their honor,
their family rights, their religious convictions and practices,
and their manners and customs.
They shall at all times be humanely treated,
and shall be protected specifically
against all acts of violence or threats thereof
and against insults and public curiosity.
    Women shall be especially protected
against any attack on their honor, in particular against rape,
enforced prostitution, or any form of indecent assault.
    Without prejudice to the provisions
relating to their state of health, age and sex,
all protected persons shall be treated
with the same consideration by the Party to the conflict
in whose power they are, without any adverse distinction
based, in particular, on race, religion or political opinion.

Article 30. The High Contracting Parties specifically agree
that each of them is prohibited from taking any measure
of such character as to cause physical suffering
or extermination of protected persons in their lands.
This prohibition applies not only to murder, torture,
corporal punishment, mutilation
and medical or scientific experiments not necessitated
by the medical treatment of a protected person,
but also to any other measures of brutality

whether applied by civilian or military agents.

Article 31. No protected person may be punished for an offense he or she has not personally committed. Collective penalties and likewise all measures of intimidation or of terrorism are prohibited.
  Pillage is prohibited.
  Reprisals against protected persons and their property are prohibited.

Article 32. The taking of hostages is prohibited.[28]

Universal Declaration of Human Rights

In February 1946 the United Nations General Assembly and the Economic and Social Council established a Commission on Human Rights to work on an international bill of human rights. In January 1947 the Commission representing eighteen nations met for the first time and chose Eleanor Roosevelt chairman by acclamation. The other officers were Dr. Peng-Chun Chang, who spoke up for Confucian values, and Dr. Charles H. Malik from Lebanon, who emphasized Christian humanism and Thomas Aquinas. They decided on a three-step process. First, they worked on a Declaration that could be passed by the General Assembly; but Mrs. Roosevelt explained in her autobiography *On My Own* that since the United Nations was not a world parliament, two more steps were needed. A Covenant could take the form of a binding treaty that could be ratified by nations, and the third step then would be to implement and enforce the rights.

The Universal Declaration of Human Rights was adopted unanimously by the General Assembly on December 10, 1948. In its resolution the UN called upon all countries to publicize the text of the Declaration and "to cause it to be disseminated, displayed, read and expounded principally in schools and other educational institutions." Eleanor Roosevelt reported why eight members abstained from the unanimous vote. The Soviets and their satellites asserted that the Declaration emphasized mainly the 18th-century political rights more than the new economic and social rights of the 20th century; South Africa felt the opposite—that the rights granted were too modern; and Saudi Arabia objected to an individual's right to change his religion or belief because this was forbidden to Muslims in the *Qur'an.*

Because the political and civil rights were already a part of many nations' constitutions and laws, the Human Rights Commission decided to draft a separate Covenant for these and another for the more modern economic and social rights that would need to be adopted by most nations. The Soviets opposed this because they feared that the latter would be delayed for many years; but they were outvoted. The Commission submitted both the International Covenant on Civil and Political Rights and the International Covenant on Economic, Social, and Cultural Rights to the General Assembly in 1954; but they were not passed by the General Assembly until 1966. Both Covenants had been ratified by 35 states and entered into force by 1976. By 1995 both Covenants had been ratified by 132 nations including the United States but not China. The legal language of the Covenants makes them much longer than the Declaration, which is included here in its entirety because of its importance in elucidating an ideal modern standard of freedoms, rights, and responsibilities for all people and nations.

UNIVERSAL DECLARATION OF HUMAN RIGHTS

Preamble
Whereas recognition of the inherent dignity
and of the equal and inalienable rights
of all members of the human family
is the foundation of freedom, justice and peace in the world,
Whereas disregard and contempt for human rights
have resulted in barbarous acts
which have outraged the conscience of mankind,
and the advent of a world in which human beings
shall enjoy freedom of speech and belief
and freedom from fear and want
has been proclaimed

as the highest aspiration of the common people,
Whereas it is essential,
if man is not to be compelled to have recourse,
as a last resort, to rebellion against tyranny and oppression,
that human rights should be protected by the rule of law,
Whereas it is essential to promote the development
of friendly relations between nations,
Whereas the peoples of the United Nations
have in the Charter
reaffirmed their faith in fundamental human rights,
in the dignity and worth of the human person
and in the equal rights of men and women
and have determined to promote social progress
and better standards of life in larger freedom,
Whereas Member States have pledged themselves
to achieve, in co-operation with the United Nations,
the promotion of universal respect for and observance of
human rights and fundamental freedoms,
Whereas a common understanding of these rights
and freedoms is of the greatest importance
for the full realization of this pledge,

Now, Therefore,
THE GENERAL ASSEMBLY
proclaims
THIS UNIVERSAL DECLARATION OF HUMAN RIGHTS
as a common standard of achievement
for all peoples and all nations,
to the end that every individual and every organ of society,
keeping this Declaration constantly in mind,
shall strive by teaching and education to promote respect
for these rights and freedoms and by progressive measures,
national and international, to secure
their universal and effective recognition and observance,
both among the peoples of Member States themselves
and among the peoples of territories under their jurisdiction.

Article 1.
All human beings are born free
and equal in dignity and rights.
They are endowed with reason and conscience
and should act towards one another

in a spirit of brotherhood.

Article 2.
Everyone is entitled to all the rights and freedoms
set forth in this Declaration, without distinction of any kind,
such as race, color, sex, language, religion,
political or other opinion, national or social origin,
property, birth or other status.
Furthermore, no distinction shall be made on the basis of
the political, jurisdictional or international status
of the country or territory to which a person belongs,
whether it be independent, trust, non-self-governing
or under any other limitation of sovereignty.

Article 3.
Everyone has the right to life, liberty and security of person.

Article 4.
No one shall be held in slavery or servitude;
slavery and the slave trade shall be prohibited
in all their forms.

Article 5.
No one shall be subjected to torture
or to cruel, inhuman or degrading treatment or punishment.

Article 6.
Everyone has the right to recognition everywhere
as a person before the law.

Article 7.
All are equal before the law and are entitled
without any discrimination to equal protection of the law.
All are entitled to equal protection
against any discrimination in violation of this Declaration
and against any incitement to such discrimination.

Article 8.
Everyone has the right to an effective remedy
by the competent national tribunals
for acts violating the fundamental rights
granted him by the constitution or by law.

Article 9.
No one shall be subjected to arbitrary arrest,
detention or exile.

Article 10.
Everyone is entitled in full equality
to a fair and public hearing
by an independent and impartial tribunal,
in the determination of his rights and obligations
and of any criminal charge against him.

Article 11.
(1) Everyone charged with a penal offense
has the right to be presumed innocent
until proved guilty according to law in a public trial
at which he has had all the guarantees
necessary to his defense.
(2) No one shall be held guilty of any penal offense
on account of any act or omission
which did not constitute a penal offense,
under national or international law,
at the time when it was committed.
Nor shall a heavier penalty be imposed
than the one that was applicable
at the time the penal offense was committed.

Article 12.
No one shall be subjected to arbitrary interference
with his privacy, family, home or correspondence,
nor to attacks upon his honor and reputation.
Everyone has the right to the protection of the law
against such interference or attacks.

Article 13.
(1) Everyone has the right to freedom of movement
and residence within the borders of each state.
(2) Everyone has the right to leave any country,
including his own, and to return to his country.

Article 14.
(1) Everyone has the right to seek and to enjoy
in other countries asylum from persecution.

(2) This right may not be invoked in the case of prosecutions genuinely arising from non-political crimes or from acts contrary to the purposes and principles of the United Nations.

Article 15.
(1) Everyone has the right to a nationality.
(2) No one shall be arbitrarily deprived of his nationality nor denied the right to change his nationality.

Article 16.
(1) Men and women of full age,
without any limitation due to race, nationality or religion,
have the right to marry and to found a family.
They are entitled to equal rights as to marriage,
during marriage and at its dissolution.
(2) Marriage shall be entered into only with the free
and full consent of the intending spouses.
(3) The family is the natural
and fundamental group unit of society
and is entitled to protection by society and the State.

Article 17.
(1) Everyone has the right to own property alone
as well as in association with others.
(2) No one shall be arbitrarily deprived of his property.

Article 18.
Everyone has the right to freedom of thought,
conscience and religion;
this right includes freedom to change his religion or belief,
and freedom, either alone or in community with others
and in public or private, to manifest his religion or belief
in teaching, practice, worship and observance.

Article 19.
Everyone has the right to freedom of opinion and expression;
this right includes freedom to hold opinions
without interference
and to seek, receive and impart information and ideas
through any media and regardless of frontiers.

Article 20.
(1) Everyone has the right to freedom of peaceful assembly and association.
(2) No one may be compelled to belong to an association.

Article 21.
(1) Everyone has the right to take part
in the government of his country,
directly or through freely chosen representatives.
(2) Everyone has the right of equal access
to public service in his country.
(3) The will of the people shall be the basis
of the authority of government;
this will shall be expressed in periodic and genuine elections
which shall be held by secret vote
or by equivalent free voting procedures.

Article 22.
Everyone, as a member of society,
has the right to social security
and is entitled to realization,
through national effort and international co-operation
and in accordance with the organization
and resources of each State,
of the economic, social and cultural rights indispensable
for his dignity and the free development of his personality.

Article 23.
(1) Everyone has the right to work,
to free choice of employment,
to just and favorable conditions of work
and to protection against unemployment.
(2) Everyone, without any discrimination,
has the right to equal pay for equal work.
(3) Everyone who works has the right
to just and favorable remuneration
ensuring for himself and his family
an existence worthy of human dignity,
and supplemented, if necessary,
by other means of social protection.
(4) Everyone has the right to form and to join trade unions
for the protection of his interests.

Article 24.
Everyone has the right to rest and leisure,
including reasonable limitation of working hours
and periodic holidays with pay.

Article 25.
(1) Everyone has the right to a standard of living
adequate for the health and well-being of himself
and of his family,
including food, clothing, housing and medical care
and necessary social services,
and the right to security in the event of unemployment,
sickness, disability, widowhood, old age
or other lack of livelihood
in circumstances beyond his control.
(2) Motherhood and childhood are entitled to special care
and assistance.
All children, whether born in or out of wedlock,
shall enjoy the same social protection.

Article 26.
(1) Everyone has the right to education.
Education shall be free,
at least in the elementary and fundamental stages.
Elementary education shall be compulsory.
Technical and professional education
shall be made generally available,
and higher education shall be equally accessible to all
on the basis of merit.
(2) Education shall be directed
to the full development of the human personality
and to the strengthening of respect
for human rights and fundamental freedoms.
It shall promote understanding, tolerance and friendship
among all nations, racial or religious groups,
and shall further the activities of the United Nations
for the maintenance of peace.
(3) Parents have a prior right
to choose the kind of education
that shall be given to their children.

Article 27.
(1) Everyone has the right freely to participate
in the cultural life of the community, to enjoy the arts
and to share in scientific advancement and its benefits.
(2) Everyone has the right to the protection of the moral
and material interests resulting from any scientific,
literary or artistic production of which he is the author.

Article 28.
Everyone is entitled to a social and international order
in which the rights and freedoms
set forth in this Declaration can be fully realized.

Article 29.
(1) Everyone has duties to the community in which alone
the free and full development of his personality is possible.
(2) In the exercise of his rights and freedoms,
everyone shall be subject only to such limitations
as are determined by law solely for the purpose of securing
due recognition and respect
for the rights and freedoms of others
and of meeting the just requirements of morality,
public order and the general welfare in a democratic society.
(3) These rights and freedoms may in no case be exercised
contrary to the purposes and principles of the United Nations.

Article 30.
Nothing in this Declaration may be interpreted
as implying for any State, group or person
any right to engage in any activity or to perform any act
aimed at the destruction of any of the rights and freedoms
set forth herein.[29]

Notes

1. *Franklin D. Roosevelt's Own Story,* p. 51.
2. *Ibid.,* p. 57.
3. *Ibid.,* p. 57.
4. *Ibid.,* p. 61.
5. *Ibid.,* p. 66.
6. *Ibid.,* p. 198.
7. *Ibid.,* p. 198.

8. *Ibid.*, p. 199.
9. *Nothing to Fear: The Selected Addresses of Franklin Delano Roosevelt 1932-1945*, p. 112.
10. *Ibid.*, p. 266.
11. *Ibid.*, p. 266.
12. *Ibid.*, p. 285.
13. *Ibid.*, p. 285.
14. *Ibid.*, p. 286.
15. *A History of the United Nations Charter* by Ruth B. Russell, p. 976.
16. *Ibid.*, p. 977.
17. *Nothing to Fear: The Selected Addresses of Franklin Delano Roosevelt 1932-1945*, p. 389.
18. *Ibid.*, p. 439.
19. *Ibid.*, p. 447.
20. *Ibid.*, p. 448.
21. *Ibid.*, p. 455-456.
22. *Ibid.*, p. p. 456.
23. *A History of the United Nations Charter* by Ruth B. Russell, p. 1036,
24. *Ibid.*, p. 1036.
25. *Ibid.*, p. 1040
26. *Ibid.*, p. 1041.
27. *Report of the International Law Commission*, General Assembly Official Records: fifth session supplement No. 12 (A/1316) in *An International Criminal Court* by Benjamin B. Ferencz, Volume 2, p. 236-239.
28. *The Law of War: A Documentary History* ed. Leon Friedman, Volume 1, p. 650-652.
29. *The United Nations and Human Rights*, p. 193-197.

4
United Nations Peacekeeping

It is not by suppressing his views,
but by forming his views on an independent basis
and by consistently maintaining them
that a Secretary-General can gain and maintain
the confidence on which he is dependent.
Dag Hammarskjold

My country has steadfastly pursued
over the years a policy of nonalignment,
and friendship for all other nations whatever their ideologies.
In my new role, I shall continue
to maintain this attitude of objectivity,
and to pursue the ideal of universal friendship.
U Thant, November 3, 1961

UN Peacekeeping During the Cold War

In addition to the five permanent members with veto power on the Security Council—Britain, China, France, Soviet Union, and United States—the first elected members of the Security Council were Australia, Brazil, Egypt, Mexico, Netherlands, and Poland. Iranians complained that the Soviet troops had not withdrawn from Iran by March 2, 1946 as agreed in the 1942 Tripartite Treaty; but after the Soviets promised that they would evacuate by May 6, the Iranians withdrew their complaint.

Although the Ukrainian representative of the Soviet Union raised the issue of violence on the Greece-Albania border on August 24, 1946, when the United States proposed a commission to investigate, it was vetoed by the Soviet Union. On December 2 Greece complained to the Security Council that Communist guerrillas in northern Greece were being assisted by Albania, Yugoslavia, and Bulgaria. The Soviet Union did not block the Commission that was sent at the beginning of 1947, though they disagreed with its reports and vetoed resolutions. So the

United States took the case to the General Assembly, which on October 21, 1947 by majority vote established the United Nations Special Committee on the Balkans (UNSCOB) to be composed from all eleven nations of the Security Council, though the USSR and Poland did not participate. After Yugoslavia became more independent and left the Cominform organization in 1948, the Greek Communists received little support; UNSCOB was terminated in 1951.

After Japan surrendered, Indonesia declared its independence on August 17, 1945; but the Netherlands, its former colonial overlord, tried to regain control, and the issue was brought to the Security Council, which on August 1, 1947 called upon both sides to cease hostilities and accept arbitration. A Consular Commission drawn from Australia, Belgium, France, the United Kingdom, and the United States went to observe the cease-fire. After fighting began again in late 1948, the Security Council again requested a cease-fire and on January 28, 1949 asked the Consular Commission to provide military observers (Milobs). With no more than 63 persons at any time they were able to mark the cease-fire lines, supervise troop withdrawals, stop infiltration between lines, and investigate violations and damages to rubber plantations. By the end of 1949 the disputed territory had been transferred to the sovereignty of Indonesia.

By 1947 the failure of the Security Council to organize the forces necessary for the collective security framework in which disarmament could have been established allowed the Cold War arms race to dominate the international scene. Meanwhile the permanent members of the Security Council were getting around their partial ban of the veto if they were a party to a dispute simply by not calling it a "dispute."

In April 1947 British diplomats brought the issue of the League mandate over Palestine to the United Nations, and the Assembly appointed a Special Committee, which proposed partition in November; but the plan was rejected by Palestinians and Arab States. In the last month of 1947 and the first month of 1948 the UN reported 2,778 casualties in Palestine (1,462 Arabs, 1,106 Jews, and 181 British). After repeated calls for a cease-fire in April, on the 23rd the Security Council established a Truce Commission for Palestine from representatives of Belgium, France, and the United States to supervise the requested cease-fire. On May 14, 1948 the General Assembly terminated the Palestine Commission and appointed a UN Mediator. The next day the United Kingdom relinquished its Mandate, and on that same day the Jewish Agency proclaimed the state of Israel. As the British withdrew their forces, Arabs invaded. On May 22 the Security Council called for a cease-fire within 36 hours and ordered the truce commission to report on compliance. A week later the Security Council authorized military advisors to supervise observance. As the war continued, the number of military advisors grew to 572 and became known as the United Nations Truce Supervision Organization (UNTSO).

A four-week truce expired on July 9, and Arab governments refused to extend it. As fighting erupted again, the Security Council ordered a cease-fire and threatened Chapter VII action; both sides complied. On September 17, 1948 the UN Mediator, Count Bernadotte, and a senior French observer were assassinated in Jerusalem by the Jewish terrorist Stern organization, and Ralph Bunche became acting Mediator. On November 16 the Security Council ordered an armistice, and all agreed except Egypt, which accepted it in January. Between February and July 1949 Israel made separate bilateral agreements with Egypt, Lebanon, Jordan, and Syria. The area of the partition that was to be Palestine was divided between Israel and Jordan, which got the West Bank, while Egypt gained the Gaza strip. Israel was admitted into the United Nations on May 11, 1949. The Mediator role was ended in August, but the UNTSO continued.

India and Pakistan gained their independence from Britain on August 15, 1947, but Kashmir was unsure which nation to join. When Muslims from Pakistan invaded in October, Kashmir's Maharaja asked India for troops and agreed to join India. On the first day of 1948 India went to the Security Council and accused Pakistan of threatening international peace. Pakistan argued that Kashmir's accession to India was illegal and requested a plebiscite under United Nations supervision. India agreed, but only if peace was restored. On January 20 the Security Council established the United Nations Commission on India and Pakistan (UNCIP), but they did not arrive in Kashmir for six months. In August UNCIP proposed a cease-fire and submitted new proposals in December. On the first day of 1949 both India and Pakistan agreed on a cease-fire, and it was formalized two weeks later. The United Nations Military Observers Group in India and Pakistan (UNMOGIP) was implemented in February. On July 27, 1949 the Karachi Agreement established the cease-fire line, and any disputes were to be decided by the Commission's Military Adviser. The Commission was terminated in 1950, but UNMOGIP was still there in 1965 when hostilities broke out again.

After Mao Zedong's Communists took over the Chinese mainland and proclaimed the People's Republic of China on October 1, 1949, Soviet delegates walked out of most UN bodies as a protest against China still being represented by the Nationalist regime that held only Taiwan. Norwegian Secretary-General Trygve Lie tried to get the Beijing regime seated, but the United States refused to recognize them as the government of China. During the spring of 1950 Secretary-General Lie traveled to the capitals of the big four powers on a peace mission to improve the effectiveness of the United Nations. He proposed the following ten points: veto limitation on the Security Council pacific settlement procedures, international control of atomic energy, arms limitation, a UN armed force, universal membership in the UN, private and intergovernmental technical and economic development, more use of the UN's specialized agencies, human rights development, peaceful decolonization, and accelerated development of enforceable world law. Unfortunately these ideals soon gave way to the crisis in Korea.

The armies of the United States and Soviet Union had occupied Korea in 1945 to accept the surrender of Japanese troops on each side of the 38th parallel. The United Nations Temporary Commission on Korea (UNTCOK) was established in November 1947. The next year UNTCOK failed to persuade the Soviet Union to withdraw its troops from northern Korea, and North Koreans refused to cooperate with UNTCOK. Thus they did not participate in the elections that took place in South Korea on May 10, 1948. The next year the UN General Assembly established UNCOK to continue the work of UNTCOK, and their peace-observation function reported that on June 25, 1950 North Koreans using Russian T-34 tanks invaded South Korea. The United States also reported the attack by North Korea. Secretary-General Lie considered this attack a violation of the UN Charter and asked the Security Council to take steps to reestablish peace. Since Soviet delegates were boycotting the Council because of China, it was able to vote nine to zero with Yugoslavia abstaining to direct North Korea to withdraw its troops north of the 38th parallel, requesting states to assist the UN and refrain from helping North Korea. North Korea ignored the resolution, and President Truman sent US troops to South Korea.

On July 7 the Security Council established a Unified Command under the United States, and Truman appointed General Douglas MacArthur as UN Commander. Fourteen other nations also sent troops to support South Korea. The UN forces were on the defensive in South Korea until Gen. MacArthur led a landing at Inchon on September 15, 1950. UN forces retook Seoul and by September 30 they crossed north of the 38th parallel. On that day Secretary-General Lie suggested settlement terms; but these were ignored by MacArthur, and on October 7 the United States got the General Assembly to adopt a resolution supporting UN forces moving north of the 38th parallel. The next day

MacArthur sent North Korea an ultimatum to cooperate in establishing a unified government. As South Korea's forces neared the Yalu River and the borders with China and the Soviet Union, Chinese "volunteer" forces aiding North Koreans began pushing them back south. On October 24 MacArthur started using non-Korean troops, but they were driven back south of the 38th parallel.

In November 1950 the western powers also took advantage of Russia's absence from the Security Council to pass the "Uniting for Peace" resolution, which enables the General Assembly to recommend collective measures for maintaining peace if the Security Council does not fulfill its peacekeeping responsibility because of lack of unanimity among its permanent members. The USSR returned to the Security Council so that it could make effective use of its veto. Lie contacted the Chinese to negotiate a cease-fire, but the Chinese delegation left New York in December. By the end of 1950 the North Korean and Chinese forces had regained Pyongyang and Seoul. UN forces fought back, and by March 14, 1951 they had retaken Seoul once again. In the spring see-saw battles were fought along the 38th parallel as Secretary-General Lie and the Security Council called for a cease-fire.

On June 23, 1951 the Soviet Union's UN ambassador Jacob Malik suggested discussions for an armistice, and two days later the *People's Daily* of Beijing endorsed the idea. On June 27 Soviet foreign minister Gromyko declared that the ceasefire should be separate from political problems. Armistice talks began on July 10. Amid continued fighting in a military stale-mate, negotiations dragged on for two years as Americans were accused of war crimes, and controversy whether prisoners of war were to be repatriated voluntarily or not delayed agreement. Guerrilla warfare was countered with aerial bombing of North Korea. In 1953 US President Eisenhower's threat to use tactical nuclear weapons eventually stimulated agreement, and the POW issue was settled on June 8. Ten days later South Korean president Syngman Rhee allowed 27,000

North Korean prisoners to escape. North Koreans complained, and the United States agreed to enforce the armistice that was signed on July 27, 1953. In the three-year Korean War about three million Koreans died; about one million Chinese were killed; and 54,246 Americans lost their lives. This bloodiest of the hot wars during the Cold War alienated both superpowers from Secretary-General Trygve Lie, and he was replaced by Swedish Dag Hammarskjold on April 10, 1953. As of 2003 the United States still had about 37,000 troops at the 38th parallel enforcing the armistice, but in the next two years many forces were removed to support the military occupation of Iraq.

On July 19, 1956 Secretary of State John Foster Dulles announced that the United States would not finance Egypt's Aswan Dam, and a week later President Gamal Abdel Nasser nationalized the Suez Canal Company. France and the United Kingdom took their case to the Security Council on September 23, and the next day Egypt accused Britain and France of endangering the peace. Most of the canal's shareholders were British and French, and English prime minister Anthony Eden ordered an Anglo-French invasion of Egypt while the foreign ministers of the three nations were negotiating a six-point agreement mediated by Secretary-General Hammarskjold. President Dwight Eisenhower rejected the use of force, but on October 29 Israel began the attack by parachuting a battalion into Sinai. The next day the United States requested a Security Council meeting. Then according to their plan, the British and French called upon both Egypt and Israel to retreat ten miles from the canal or they would send troops, although Israel's forces were still more than ten miles from the canal. Egypt rejected the ultimatum, claiming it was defending its sovereign territory. Two days later Anglo-French air forces attacked Egyptian air bases.

On November 2, 1956 the UN General Assembly passed the resolution proposed by Dulles ordering the parties to withdraw to the 1949 armistice boundaries and cease fire so that the canal could reopen. On the 5th the UN General Assembly established the United Nations Emergency Force (UNEF). By November 7 British forces had landed at Port Said, and French troops had occupied Port Fouad; but the British government agreed to the cease-fire that started that day. On November 24 the General Assembly called for the withdrawal of all British and French forces, and their governments agreed to remove them by December 22. The United States pressured compliance from Israel, which delayed withdrawing from the Gaza strip and Sharm el Shaikh at the strategic Strait of Tiran. Israel would not allow UN troops on their territory, and thus they were all deployed on the Egyptian side of the border. UNEF was drawn from ten countries and ranged from three to six thousand during its mission for ten and a half years.

During the Suez crisis police fired on a crowd of peaceful demonstrators at a Budapest radio station on October 23, 1956. Soviet tanks and troops soon entered Budapest, but ferocious Hungarian resistance caused them to withdraw on October 29. However, a massive Soviet invasion began on November 4, and within four days the uprising had been brutally suppressed. The UN Security Council met on the 4th, but the Soviet delegate vetoed an American resolution condemning the intervention. The General Assembly also condemned the invasion, but the Secretary-General could do little in this sphere of influence dominated by a superpower.

In February 1958 Egypt and Syria formed the United Arab Republic (UAR). In May the murder of a dissident Christian newspaper editor provoked a civil war in Lebanon between those supporting pro-western President Camille Chamoun and the mostly Muslims who opposed him. Armed resistance to the government stimulated Chamoun to ask for military assistance from the United States on May 13. President Eisenhower agreed but said he would not support an unconstitutional second term for Chamoun. On May 22 Lebanon's UN delegate asked the Security Council to look into infiltration from Syria. After a pause to see if the Arab League could solve the problem, on June 10 the Security Council created the United Nations Observation Group in Lebanon (UNOGIL). The Soviet Union was opposed but abstained.

After the pro-western King Faisal of Iraq was overthrown by a military coup on July 14, 1958 Chamoun asked for American military support; at the same time Jordan's King Hussein likewise asked for British help. US Marines landed in Beirut the next day. Two days later British troops flew into Jordan, and the US proposed transforming UNOGIL into an armed peacekeeping force; but the Soviet Union vetoed it. In August the United States and United Kingdom both recognized the new government of Iraq and sent identical letters to the UN General Assembly offering to withdraw their troops. By December 1958 UNOGIL had withdrawn from Lebanon.

In May 1960 Patrice Lumumba's party won a majority in both houses of the Congo, and the king of Belgium invited him to form a government. On June 30 the Republic of the Congo became independent, but a few days later an army mutiny occurred. On July 10 Belgian troops were deployed, and Lumumba appealed to Under Secretary-General Ralph Bunche. The next day pro-western Moishe Tshombé declared the secession of the rich mineral province of Katanga. Congo government ministers asked the US ambassador to provide American troops to restore order. By the 14th the Security Council had authorized Secretary-General Hammarskjold to provide military assistance as needed and called upon Belgium to withdraw its troops, but by July 19 ten thousand Belgian troops had returned to the Congo, ostensibly to protect Belgian lives and property. While Lumumba was traveling in November, he was arrested and apparently killed while in custody. The Soviets then called for the dismissal of Hammarskjold and a withdrawal of UN forces, but they gained no support.

Secretary-General Hammarskjold sought a tougher mandate and went to the Congo himself, but on September 17, 1961 he was killed in a plane crash while going to meet with Tshombé. On November 3 U Thant of Burma became acting Secretary-General, reflecting the sharp increase of new nations from Asia and Africa that expanded UN membership from 50 states to 103. That month the United Nations Operation in the Congo (ONUC) was further expanded by the Security Council to support the Central Government of the Republic of the Congo while condemning the illegal secessionist activities of the Katanga revolt. A year later U Thant was nominated by the Security Council and elected by the General Assembly to a regular five-year term. U Thant developed a plan for drafting a federal constitution for the Congo, and US President John Kennedy and Belgian foreign minister Paul-Henri Spaak threatened Katanga with severe economic sanctions if progress was not made toward unification.

The next month in December 1962 U Thant asked for a boycott of key minerals purchased from Katanga unless duties were paid to the Adoula government at Leopold-ville. When fighting broke out that Tshombé could not stop, UN troops occupied Elisabethville and Kaminaville on January 3, 1963 with little resistance and few casualties. The UN continued to have military success, and withdrawal of its troops was debated. The United States and other western interests asked that the UN remain while Congolese troops were retrained; they were finally withdrawn in June 1964 as the Congo became an independent nation. ONUC was the most complex UN peacekeeping operation so far, employing nearly 20,000 troops, lasting four years, and costing about $400,000,000. The Soviet Union, as with UNEF, refused to pay its share. The United Nations was nearly bankrupted, and the United States threatened a resolution to deny the Soviet Union voting rights; but they promised to pay their dues.

Another decolonization effort in Indonesia was not as controversial. In October 1961 the Netherlands asked the UN General Assembly to administer West New Guinea during its transition to independence, but there was no acting Secretary-General at that time. In December, Indonesia's Sukarno began infiltrating forces into the region and proclaimed that "West Irian" would join Indonesia in 1962. Pressure from the United States and a United Nations buffer enabled the Dutch to make a graceful withdrawal. In September 1962 the UN General Assembly endorsed the Dutch-Indonesian accord of the previous month. By November the Dutch forces had withdrawn, and on the last day of 1962 the Dutch flag was replaced by the Indonesian flag. The UN Temporary Executive Authority (UNTEA) transferred administrative control to the Indonesian government on May 1, 1963. Almost all of the 1608 troops used in the UN Security Force (UNSF) were from Pakistan. However, the vote in 1969 that brought West New Guinea formally into Indonesia was dominated by Indonesian authorities.

During the Cuban missile crisis Secretary-General U Thant sent identical letters to US President Kennedy and Soviet Chairman Khrushchev on October 24, 1962. Khrushchev accepted his proposal the next day. U Thant then asked him to keep Soviet ships away from the blockade, and again Khrushchev agreed, criticizing the United States for its "piratical measures." U Thant mediated the understanding that the Soviets would withdraw their missiles from Cuba if the United States gave assurances not to invade nor support an invasion of the island. After this dangerous crisis, both superpower leaders thanked the Secretary-General for his mediation.

After Yemen's Imam Ahmed bin Yahya died on September 19, 1962, a civil war broke out in Yemen; as the military tried to take control with Egyptian support for republicans, Saudi Arabia and Jordan assisted the royalists. In November, President Kennedy proposed a phased withdrawal of the Egyptian, Saudi, and Jordanian forces, but neither Nasser nor the Saudis would agree. Yemen's royalist diplomats at the United Nations sent a letter to Secretary-General U Thant on November 27 asking for an investigation to see if Cairo had instigated the military coup. In February 1963 U Thant sent Ralph Bunche on a fact-finding mission. On April 29 U Thant announced that Yemen, Saudi Arabia, and Egypt had all asked for UN intervention, and on June 11 the Security Council established the United Nations Yemen Observation Mission (UNYOM). However, the civil war continued after UNYOM ended its mission in September 1964; the royalists were still powerful while about 40,000 Egyptian troops were in Yemen and were increasing.

Cyprus gained its independence from Britain in August 1960; but on November 30, 1963 President Makarios, the Greek archbishop, proposed constitutional amendments that would reduce the influence of the minority Turks. Three weeks later fighting broke out in Nicosia, and Turkey mobilized military forces to aid Turkish Cypriots. Within three days the governments of Britain, Greece, and Turkey had organized peacekeeping forces under British command and began to negotiate in January. Cyprus appealed to the UN Security Council in January and was joined in this by Britain the next month. On March 4, 1964 the Security Council established the United Nations Peacekeeping Force in Cyprus (UNFICYP). However, on July 15 the Greek military dictatorship sponsored a take-over by the Cypriot National Guard to replace President Makarios, and five days later the Turkish military intervened also, citing the 1960 Treaty of Guarantees. The UN Security Council met and called for a cease-fire to begin on July 22, though the fighting around the Nicosia airport did not stop until the 24th. UNFICYP continues to monitor the cease-fire, though additional crises occurred in 1967 and 1974.

After thirty years of a Trujillo dynasty, Juan Bosch was elected President of the Dominican Republic in December 1962, but he was removed by a military coup the following September. In April 1965 Bosch and others led an uprising to overthrow the military junta, causing a civil war. On April 25 the United States began sending in 22,500 military officers, claiming they were to protect US citizens and property, but actually they were preventing the radical

Bosch from returning to power. The Organization of American States (OAS) justified the intervention after it occurred. The Soviet Union complained at the UN Security Council, which called for a cease-fire on May 14. However, the US made the UN mission difficult, showing once again that the UN could do little within the sphere of a superpower.

In Kashmir fighting broke out again when armed civilians from Pakistan crossed the cease-fire line in August 1965. The UN Security Council passed five resolutions to try to stop the fighting, and U Thant made several appeals. On September 17 he suggested invoking Chapter VII of the UN Charter, declaring a failure to comply with the cease-fire order a breach of the peace. Five days later a cease-fire became mostly effective, though sporadic battles continued until January 1966. UNMOGIP was increased from 45 to 102 officers, and 90 more were sent in by October 14 as the United Nations India-Pakistan Observation Mission (UNIPOM). Pakistan and India agreed to withdraw their troops by February 25; UNIPOM was disbanded in March, and UNMOGIP was reduced back to 44 observers along the cease-fire line. UNMOGIP had to stop a conflict again in 1971, and as of 2005 it is still monitoring the tense cease-fire line between Pakistan and India.

In November 1966 troops from Israel raided Jordanian villages, and in April 1967 they bombarded Syrians in the demilitarized zone south of the Sea of Galilee. Further incidents were blamed on Syria by Israel prime minister Levi Eshkol on May 11. Two days later the Soviet Union advised the Egyptian government to anticipate an Israeli invasion of Syria, though later it was recognized that this was a false alarm. On May 16 Egypt's chief of staff Fawzi asked the UNEF commander to withdraw his troops. Recognizing Egypt's right to make this request, Secretary-General U Thant agreed, and after being there more than ten years, the UNEF troops began leaving the Sinai on May 29. While they were still withdrawing, on June 5, 1967 Israel launched a surprise attack on airfields in several Arab countries, destroying most of these air forces while they were still on the ground. Then within a week Israel's army invaded its neighbors, capturing all the West Bank by the Jordan River and Jerusalem from Jordan, occupying the Golan Heights in Syria, and taking the Gaza Strip, the Sinai peninsula, and Sharm el-Sheikh from Egypt. UN Security Council demands for a cease-fire had been ignored, and the United States was not willing to cooperate in a settlement. Fifteen United Nations officers were killed before they were able to evacuate Egypt by June 17.

The UN General Assembly in July declared Israel's unification of Jerusalem illegal. On November 22 the UN Security Council passed Resolution 242 calling for the "withdrawal of Israeli armed forces from territories occupied in the recent conflict" and for

Termination of all claims or states of belligerency
and respect for and acknowledgement of the sovereignty,
territorial integrity and political independence
of every State in the area and their right to live in peace
within secure and recognized boundaries
free from threats or acts of force.[1]

The landmark resolution also affirmed the necessity of guaranteeing the freedom of navigation in international waters, "achieving a just settlement of the refugee problem," and gaining territorial inviolability by establishing demilitarized zones.

On October 6, 1973 on the Jewish holiday of Yom Kippur the Egyptian army attacked Israeli forces on the east bank of the Suez Canal while Syrian forces attacked Israeli positions on the Golan Heights. The Egyptian army broke through the Bar Lev line the next day, and neither side was willing to consider a cease-fire. The United States requested a UN Security Council meeting on the 8th. Jordan entered the war; but Israel, aided by US supplies of ammunition, had surrounded the Egyptian army by October 15, and in the north their army was approaching Damascus. On October 20 Saudi king Faisal announced the first oil embargo against the United States and the Netherlands. US Secretary of State Henry Kissinger flew to Moscow to negotiate, and the two superpowers took their resolution to the UN Security Council on October 21. The next day the Council adopted Resolution 338 calling for a cease-fire and immediate termination of all military activity.

Fighting continued, and two days later Soviet leader Brezhnev sent US President Nixon a letter threatening unilateral action if the United States did not agree to a joint US-Soviet force to implement the cease-fire. Washington leaders put American forces on a higher stage of alert and warned Egypt's Sadat they would pull out of the peace talks with Israel if Soviet forces intervened. Sadat then changed his request from US-Soviet forces to a UN peacekeeping force. On October 25 the Security Council Resolution 340 demanded an immediate cease-fire and that the parties return to the positions held as of October 22. Kissinger mediated an agreement between the military leaders of Israel and Egypt that was signed on November 11, and UNEF II began its peacekeeping operations four days later. Syria and Israel signed an agreement on May 31, 1974 that created three zones monitored by the United Nations Disengagement Observer Force (UNDOF). US President Jimmy Carter mediated a peace treaty between Israel and Egypt that resulted in Israeli forces withdrawing from the Sinai on May 23, 1979, and UNEF II's mandate ended two months later. However, UNDOF is still supervising the Golan Heights as of 2005.

The Cairo Agreement signed by Palestinian Liberation Organization (PLO) chairman Yasser Arafat and Lebanon's chief of staff on November 3, 1969 was supposed to regulate the armed Palestinians in Lebanon, but the PLO conducted raids across the Israeli border. On June 1, 1976 Syria broke a tacit agreement with Israel when they invaded Lebanon with troops to intervene in the civil war on the side of the Christians. On March 11, 1978 PLO forces seized a bus near Haifa and in a battle with Israeli security forces killed 37 Israelis. Three days later Prime Minister Menachem Begin retaliated by ordering the Israel Defense Forces (IDF) to invade southern Lebanon. US ambassador Andrew Young sponsored a UN Security Council resolution calling for a cease-fire, withdrawal of Israeli forces, and a UN peacekeeping force to supervise this. Resolution 425 was adopted on March 19, establishing the United Nations Interim Force in Lebanon (UNIFIL) with 4,000 troops that were increased to 6,000 in May.

On April 13, 1982 Israel's representative at the United Nations complained to the Security Council that two PLO terrorists had tried to bring large quantities of explosives into Israel. Eight days later Israeli aircraft began attacking PLO targets in Lebanon. On the same day Secretary-General Pérez de Cuellar appealed for a cessation of hostilities. On May 9 Israel's air force again attacked the PLO in Lebanon. On June 6 IDF Chief of Staff Eitan gave UNIFIL General Callaghan thirty minutes warning that Israel was going to invade Lebanon. UNIFIL troops were ordered to stop the invading army but were overrun within 24 hours. The next evening Arafat informed the Secretary-General that the Lebanese-Palestinian command would comply with the Security Council resolution. UNIFIL attempted to fulfill its mission despite the Israeli occupation. The IDF withdrew from Beirut in September 1983 and began to withdraw from Lebanon in February 1985. UNIFIL is still in operation.

After its third war with Britain in 1919 Afghanistan became an independent kingdom, which was replaced by a republic in 1973. The Marxist People's Democratic Party (PDPA) seized power in Afghanistan five years later. Reforms of old religious and social institutions were resisted in the countryside. After Prime Minister Hafizullah Amin had the Afghanistan President murdered, the Soviet army invaded on December 27, 1979 and installed Babrak Karmal as prime minister. The UN Security Council met in January 1980 but could not pass a resolution. The General

Assembly recognized the Karmal government in Kabul but condemned the invasion by a vote of 104 to 18. On May 14 the Kabul regime proposed the four points that eventually became the basis of the Geneva accords, namely, withdrawal of foreign troops, noninterference in domestic politics, international guarantees, and the return of refugees to Afghanistan. UN Secretary-General Kurt Waldheim sent Pérez de Cuellar to Afghanistan in 1981, and he got the governments of Afghanistan and Pakistan to accept the four-point plan.

However, Islamic *mujahideen* continued to fight the Soviet army from the countryside. Resistance bases in Pakistan directed the guerrilla campaign which was supported by American weapons, especially after the Soviets started using special forces in the spring of 1985. Finally, three years after Mikhail Gorbachev became the leader of the Soviet Union, the Geneva Accords were signed on April 14, 1988 and were implemented a month later by the United Nations Good Offices Mission to Afghanistan and Pakistan (UNGOMAP). The Soviet Union still had 103,000 troops at 18 garrisons in 17 of Afghanistan's thirty provinces, and with the Afghan army of 50,000 they held all the major cities and towns in Afghanistan. The fourth Geneva Accord resulted in the withdrawal of half the Soviet troops by August and the remainder by February 1989. After the attempted coup of 1991 in the Soviet Union, the Russians and the Americans agreed to end their military assistance to forces in Afghanistan in 1992.

The Shah of Iran and Vice President Saddam Hussein of Iraq signed the Algiers Treaty in March 1975, agreeing to settle border disputes and allowing Iranians the Shatt al-Arab waterway. As a gesture of good faith to the Shah, in 1978 Iraq deported the exiled Ayatollah Khomeini to France. After the Shah was overthrown on February 11, 1979, Khomeini came to power in Iran and still resented Saddam Hussein for having deported him. Iraq complained that Iran had not withdrawn from the disputed territory according to the Algiers Treaty. On September 10,

1980 Iraqi forces moved into the disputed territories in Khuzistan and a week later abrogated the Algiers Treaty. The day after notifying UN Secretary-General Waldheim on September 21, Iraq attacked Iran with its air force and invaded with a large army. On the 28th the UN Security Council called for an end to the use of force; but Iran rejected the resolution because Iraq was not named as the aggressor. The Soviet Union stopped supplying arms to Baghdad, and by July 1982, when the Security Council passed two resolutions for a cease-fire, the larger Iranian army had pushed the battle-lines back into Iraqi territory. Concerned about the fundamentalist Shi'i Iranians, Gulf Arabs began supporting Iraq. France loaned Iraq money to buy billions of dollars worth of arms from them; Moscow resumed selling Iraq weapons; and the United States allowed arms sales and provided military intelligence to Iraq even after Iraq used poison gas in 1983 to overcome the Iranian superiority in numbers. Washington resumed diplomatic relations with Iraq in 1984. The next year the United States with Israeli help secretly sold weapons to Iran in order to free American hostages and used the profits to provide weapons illegally to the Contras fighting the Sandinista government of Nicaragua. Both the Soviet Union and the United States tried to protect Kuwaiti oil tankers. The UN Security Council passed Resolution 598 to try to stop the war on July 20, 1987. A year later the US cruiser *Vincennes* mistakenly shot down an Iranian Airbus, killing 290 civilians, but unpopular Iran could not get the UN to condemn the United States for this crime. However, Iran then accepted Resolution 598, and the Security Council began implementing it with the United Nations Iran-Iraq Military Observer Group (UNIIMOG) in August 1988.

Even if the veto could be circumvented, the capabilities of nuclear weapons made action against an offending superpower too risky, as the reluctance to intervene in Hungary in 1956 and Czechoslovakia in 1968 made clear. Yet UN Secretary-General U Thant criticized Russian intervention in Czechoslovakia and American involvement in

Vietnam. The deterrence of nuclear weapons essentially replaced the collective system of deterrence if the nuclear powers were involved. After the Korean War fiasco, the Cold War prevented the use of the large powers' forces as United Nations police, which was the original intention, because of mutual fear. Instead the forces of small countries were usually employed to stop small wars and hostilities in such places as Palestine, Pakistan-India, Indonesia, Congo, Cyprus, Israel and the Sinai, Syria, and Lebanon. The UN supported decolonization, and economic sanctions were imposed on Rhodesia and South Africa because of their flagrant violations of human rights.

UN Peacekeeping After the Cold War

The United Nations was powerless to mediate the conflicts in Central America until the Cold War declined in the late 1980s. In August 1989 Nicaragua's Sandinista government agreed to conditions for national elections in exchange for demobilization of the Contra rebels. The United Nations Observer Group in Central America (ONUCA) was established on November 7. Honduras and the other Central American countries also wanted the Contras demobilized, and on April 19, 1990 they signed the Managua Agreements. Contras surrendered their weapons, uniforms, and ammunition to the ONUCA and received a demobilization certificate, designer jeans and a shirt, and a food ration from an organization co-sponsored by the United Nations and the Organization of American States (OAS). By June 22,000 Contras had been demobilized, and the UN's security zones were abolished.

On July 26, 1990 the government of El Salvador and the resistance group Frente Farabundo Marti para la Liberacion Nacional (FMLN) signed the Agreement on Human Rights at San Jose, Costa Rica, and on April 27, 1991 both sides signed an agreement for constitutional reforms to be presented in the Legislative Assembly of El Salvador. The United Nations Observer Mission in El Salvador (ONUSAL) began its work on July 26, and on January 16,

1992 the two sides signed a Peace Agreement at Chapultepec Castle in Mexico City. ONUSAL supervised the elections of March and April 1994.

After 36 years of conflict a Guatemala peace agreement was finally signed in December 1996, and the United Nations Verification Mission in Guatemala (MINUGUA) verified the human rights agreement and the cease-fire as the Unidad Revolucionaria Nacional Guatemalteca (URNG) combatants were demobilized.

During World War I South Africa occupied the German colony of South West Africa and was given the League mandate over it; but after World War II, South Africa refused to accept UN authority and tried to annex the territory. Efforts began for independence, but the United Nations did not revoke South Africa's mandate until 1966, and five years later the International Court of Justice ruled that South Africa's occupation was illegal. After the Caetano regime of Portugal fell in 1974, its former colonies became independent as Angola and Mozambique with Marxist governments. A civil war broke out in Angola the next year as Portugal withdrew; the government was supported militarily by Cuba and the Soviet Union, while the United States and South Africa aided rebel groups.

Meanwhile South Africa tried and failed to impose a non-Marxist apartheid government in Namibia (South West Africa). In 1976 the five western nations of Canada, France, Britain, United States, and West Germany formed the Contact Group to negotiate a settlement that was proposed to the UN Security Council two years later. Although the Council adopted the plan in a resolution that year, more than a decade of negotiation passed before the United Nations Transition Assistance Group (UNTAG) was implemented in April 1989. Elections were held in independent Namibia on November 1, and a week later half of Cuba's 50,000 troops had left with those remaining north of the 13th parallel.

The United Nations Angola Verification Mission

(UNAVEM) also began with the signing of peace accords by South Africa, Angola, and Cuba on December 22, 1988, and its mission ended when the last Cuban troops were withdrawn two months early in May 1991. UNAVEM II was deployed the next month and was to last until November 1992, but it was extended. In Mozambique, President Chissano, who was elected in 1986, and Afonso Dhlakama signed the General Peace Agreement in Rome on October 4, 1992, and the United Nations Operation in Mozambique (ONUMOZ) began monitoring it in 1993. Elections were held in Mozambique the next year and were declared free and fair by ONUMOZ, which left Mozambique before the end of 1994. In Angola signing of the Lusaka Protocol on November 20, 1994 brought about a cease-fire two days later, and UNAVEM III was implemented in February 1995. Its mandate ended in 1997, and it was replaced by the United Nations Observer Mission in Angola (MONUA) until February 1999.

After Spain withdrew from the Western Sahara in 1976, Morocco was given two-thirds of the territory and Mauretania one-third. That year a Popular Front (POLISARIO) declared independence as the Saharan Arab Democratic Republic (SADR) with support from Algeria, Libya, and Cuba and began fighting Mauretania, which relinquished its territory in the Algiers Agreement of August 1979; but Morocco then annexed that territory. That year the Organization of African Unity (OAU) called for a cease-fire and a referendum in the Western Sahara, establishing a committee to work with the United Nations. When the OAU seated the SADR in 1985, Morocco resigned in protest. Libya supported Morocco, and in October 1985 SADR's foreign minister Hassan declared a unilateral cease-fire. On August 11, 1988 UN Secretary-General Pérez de Cuellar suggested a joint UN-OAU plan for a ceasefire and a referendum conducted by the UN; representatives of Morocco and POLISARIO agreed. Diplomatic relations improved, and by February 1989 the region founded the Arab Mahgreb Union, modeled after Europe's common market. However, talks made little progress, though King Hassan declared a universal truce when the Secretary-General visited in February 1990. The United Nations Mission for the Referendum in Western Sahara (MINURSO) was established on April 29, 1991, and a cease-fire went into effect on September 6. However, the referendum was delayed, and the MINURSO mandate had to be extended several times and is still in effect.

Chad and Libya submitted a border dispute to the International Court of Justice in September 1990, and in the spring of 1994 the United Nations Aouzou Strip Observer Group (UNASOG) monitored Libya's withdrawal.

Somalia became independent of Italy and Britain in 1960 but began fighting with Ethiopia and was taken over by the Soviet-trained army led by General Siad Barre in October 1969. Ethiopia's Emperor Haile Selassie was deposed in 1975, and the Soviet Union and Cuba provided military aid to the new government. In 1991 General Aidid toppled President Siad Barre. So much fighting occurred that in 1992 more than four million people were threatened by starvation, and about 300,000 died. In February UN Secretary-General Boutros-Ghali sponsored talks between General Aidid and his rival Ali Mahdi, and they agreed to a cease-fire on March 3. The United Nations Operation in Somalia (UNOSOM) was deployed to monitor the cease-fire in July. In December 1992 the UN Security Council authorized States to provide military forces to secure the delivery of humanitarian aid, and in 1993 the Council expanded the force, implementing UNOSOM II. On March 24, 1994 Ali Mahdi and General Aidid signed a declaration of national reconciliation, agreeing to a cease-fire and voluntary disarmament. Although some district and regional courts were established, after a while it was determined that the UN presence was no longer aiding national reconciliation. UNOSOM was completely withdrawn by March 2, 1995.

After two years of fighting over the border, mediation by Algeria and the Organization of African Unity (OAU) helped Ethiopia and Eritrea sign an agreement in June 2000 to cease hostilities. In July the UN Security Council set up the United Nations Mission in Ethiopia and Eritrea (UNMEE) to be a liaison and to verify the ceasefire. In September the Council authorized deployment of military personnel to monitor the peace and the redeployment of troops and to assist in ensuring observance of security and a temporary security zone, and it is still in operation.

The United Nations Observer Mission Uganda-Rwanda (UNOMUR) began in August 1993, and this led two months later to the creation of the United Nations Assistance Mission in Rwanda (UNAMIR). After an airplane crash killed the presidents of Rwanda and Burundi on April 6, 1994, a civil war turned into mass murder as Hutus killed between 500,000 and one million Tutsis and "moderate" Hutus in one of the worst cases of genocide in history. Ten Belgian UN peacekeepers were killed trying to protect Prime Minister Agathe Uwilingiyimana. Amid the civil war Belgium decided to withdraw its battalion from UNAMIR. On April 30 the UN Security Council demanded that the interim government of Rwanda and the Rwandese Patriotic Front (RPF) prevent attacks on civilians. On May 13 UN Secretary-General Boutros-Ghali suggested adding 5,500 troops to UNAMIR, and four days later the Security Council imposed an arms embargo on Rwanda, expanding UNAMIR's mandate. On July 14 the Security Council demanded an immediate cease-fire. After the RPF took Gisenyi on July 17, they declared a unilateral cease-fire the next day. On July 19 a broad-based government of national unity formed and began controlling all of Rwanda. UNAMIR helped refugees to return safely and ended its mission in March 1996.

A civil war began in Liberia in 1989 that led to the death of more than 100,000 civilians, making 700,000 refugees. The Economic Community of West African States (ECOWAS) created the ECOWAS Monitoring Group (ECOMOG) in 1990 with 4,000 troops from Gambia, Ghana, Guinea, Nigeria, and Sierra Leone. On November 19, 1992 the UN Security Council imposed an arms embargo on deliveries to Liberia except for those going to the peace-keeping forces of ECOWAS. The Cotonou Peace Agreement was signed on July 25, 1993, and in September the UN Security Council established the United Nations Observer Mission in Liberia (UNOMIL) to cooperate with ECOWAS in implementing the Cotonou agreement. UNOMIL helped ECOWAS and the OAU monitor elections in Liberia and ended its mission in September 1997. In the multi-party elections Charles Taylor was elected president of Liberia, but several factions were not absorbed into the security forces.

In May 2003 President Taylor agreed to a joint assess-ment mission by the United Nations, African Union, and ECOWAS. By then two rebel movements controlled nearly two-thirds of Liberia, and they decided the hostilities were not conducive to holding elections in October. A cease-fire agreement was signed on June 17, and in July ECOWAS leaders decided to send a vanguard force to facilitate Taylor's handing over of power, and the United States posi-tioned a military force off the coast. On August first the UN Security Council authorized a multinational force in Liberia that began three days later with the ECOWAS Mission in Liberia (ECOMIL). The United Nations Mission in Liberia (UNMIL) was established by the Security Council in September 2003 to support the implementation of the ceasefire agreement and the peace process, and its mission continues.

After mutinies in the army of the Central African Republic, in January 1997 four African Presidents mediated a truce as parties signed the Bangui Agreements. An inter-African force (MISAB) was deployed to monitor implemen-tation. The United Nations Mission in the Central African Republic (MINURCA) helped maintain security and monitor the disarmament, restructuring of the national police, and election plans, ending its mission in February 2000.

In May 1997 a military coup overthrew the democratically elected government in Sierra Leone; but the Economic Community of West African States (ECOWAS) and its peacekeeping force restored the elected government in March 1998. The United Nations Observer Mission in Sierra Leone (UNOMSIL) was established to monitor the military situation, disarmament, and demobilization. In October 1999 it was replaced as the UN Security Council established the United Nations Mission in Sierra Leone (UNAMSIL) to help implement the peace plan and assist the government with disarmament, demobilization, and law and order.

Also in 1999 six regional States and two Congolese rebel movements signed a Ceasefire Agreement to stop hostilities between the belligerent forces in the Democratic Republic of Congo. The United Nations Organization Mission in Democratic Republic of the Congo (MONUC) was established to be a liaison between the parties. In February 2000 MONUC began monitoring the implementation of the ceasefire and prepared an action plan to implement the Agreement and verify disengagement and the redeployment of the parties' forces. MONUC is still in the Congo.

In May 2004 the United Nations Operation in Burundi (ONUB) was authorized to support the Arusha Peace and Reconciliation Agreement for Burundi that had been signed at Arusha on 28 August 2000. Parties in the Ivory Coast region signed a peace agreement in January 2003, and the UN Security Council set up the United Nations Mission in Côte d'Ivoire (MINUCI) in May 2003. This was replaced by the United Nations Operation in Côte d'Ivoire (UNOCI) in April 2004. The Government of Sudan and the Sudan People's Liberation Movement/Army signed the Comprehensive Peace Agreement in January 2005, and on March 24 the UN Security Council decided to establish the United Nations Mission in the Sudan (UNMIS) to support its implementation.

After four factions signed the Agreements on a Comprehensive Political Settlement of the Cambodia

Conflict on October 23, 1991 in Paris, the United Nations Transitional Authority in Cambodia (UNTAC) helped to disarm and demobilize the armed forces, promote human rights, repatriate refugees, supervise elections, clear mines, and generally rehabilitate the country. Although the Party of Democratic Kampuchea (PDK) did not participate in the elections in late 1992 and early 1993, they were considered successful. After the new Constitution was adopted on September 21, 1993, UNTAC ended its mandate.

On August 2, 1990 the Iraqi army invaded Kuwait, and the same day the UN Security Council condemned it and demanded that Iraq withdraw unconditionally. After ten more similar resolutions that added naval and air embargos, the Security Council passed Resolution 678 on November 29, warning that if Iraq did not implement the resolutions by January 15, 1991, Member States would be authorized "to use all necessary means to uphold and implement" the resolutions and restore peace in the region.[2] On January 16 a coalition of forces led by the United States launched air attacks on Iraq. Ground forces moved into southern Iraq and Kuwait on February 24 and soon captured Iraqi forces remaining there. The US decision to stop the ground war after one hundred hours allowed divisions of the Iraqi Republican Guard to escape to northern Iraq, where they later suppressed rebellions by the Shi'a and Kurdish majority, causing refugees to flee toward Turkey and Iran. On April 3 the Security Council passed Resolution 687 detailing the terms of the cease-fire that Iraq accepted three days later. The United Nations Iraq-Kuwait Observer Mission (UNIKOM) was established to deter boundary violations and for surveillance of the demilitarized zone. Resolution 687 also created the following:

The United Nations Special Commission to oversee the destruction, removal or rendering harmless of all Iraq's chemical and biological weapons and related capabilities and facilities, and its ballistic missiles with a range

greater than 150 kilometers.
The Commission has also assisted
the International Atomic Energy Agency (IAEA)
in the destruction, removal, or rendering harmless
as appropriate of Iraq's nuclear capabilities.[3]

UNIKOM became operational as the last US Army unit left Iraq on May 7, 1991.

On December 16, 1990 Jean-Bertrand Aristide was elected president of Haiti with two-thirds of the vote. On September 30, 1991 he was forced into exile by a *coup d'état* led by Lt. General Raoul Cédras of the High Command of the Haitian Armed Forces (FADH). The UN General Assembly condemned this and the violation of human rights in Haiti in a resolution on October 11. Acting under Chapter VII of the UN Charter on June 16, 1993 the Security Council imposed an oil and arms embargo against Haiti. A month later a pact was signed in New York to guarantee a peaceful transition, and on August 25 the Haitian Parliament ratified Aristide's appointment of Robert Malval as designated prime minister. A month after that, the Security Council authorized the United Nations Mission in Haiti (UNMIH). Non-compliance by FADH resulted in Secretary-General Boutros-Ghali reimposing the sanctions in October.

On July 31, 1994 the UN Security Council authorized Member States to form a multinational force to remove the military leadership and restore Haiti's elected President. In a final diplomatic effort former US President Jimmy Carter led a delegation that got the Haitian military to cooperate with the military mission led by the United States, and on September 19 the 28-nation multinational force entered Haiti without opposition. Ten days later the UN Security Council authorized the Secretary-General to send in the UNMIH advance team. Lt. General Cédras resigned on October 10, and five days later President Aristide returned to Haiti. UNMIH helped support professionalization of the national police and ended its mission in June 1996. The UN Security Council established the United Nations Support

Mission in Haiti (UNSMIH) in June 1996 to help train police; after being extended, the mission was ended in July 1997. For the next four months the United Nations Transition Mission in Haiti (UNTMIH) bridged the gap until it was replaced by the United Nations Civilian Police Mission in Haiti (MIPONUH), which completed its mandate in March 2000.

On February 29, 2004 United States forces abducted and removed President Jean-Bertrand Aristide from Haiti. Believing that Aristide had resigned, a few hours later the UN Security Council authorized the Multinational Interim Force (MIF). The United States and France blocked the UN Security Council or the 15-member Caribbean Community (CARICOM) from investigating the abduction of Aristide which international law professor, Francis Boyle, called a violation of the United Nations Charter. The UN Security Council transferred authority from MIF to the United Nations Stabilization Mission in Haiti (MINUSTAH) on April 30, 2004 and in November renewed it for 2005.

After Abkhaz separatists began fighting the government of Georgia in 1992, the United Nations Observer Mission in Georgia (UNOMIG) was established to verify a cease-fire in 1993. In May 1994 the Commonwealth of Independent States (CIS) deployed a peacekeeping force in Georgia, and an expanded UNOMIG still observes their operation.

The United Nations offered its good offices to help resolve a civil war in Tajikistan in 1992, and starting in December 1994 the United Nations Mission of Observers in Tajikistan (UNMOT) began monitoring a cease-fire and the deployed peacekeeping force of the Commonwealth of Independent States (CIS). A peace agreement was signed in June 1997, and UNMOT helped implement it before pulling out in May 2000.

After turmoil in Yugoslavia in the 1980s popular referenda in Croatia and Slovenia led to their declaring independence in June 1991. That month Serbs living in Croatia began fighting with support from the Yugoslav People's Army (JNA), though in Slovenia the JNA withdrew after the European Community mediated an agreement. On September 25 the UN Security Council called upon all States to implement a complete embargo on all weapons to Yugoslavia and commended the efforts of the Conference on Security and Cooperation in Europe (CSCE). In February 1992 the UN Security Council established the United Nations Protection Force (UNPROFOR). On May 22 the General Assembly admitted into the United Nations the Republic of Slovenia, the Republic of Bosnia and Herzegovina, and the Republic of Croatia. On May 30 the Security Council invoked Chapter VII of the UN Charter to impose sanctions on the Federal Republic of Yugoslavia (Serbia and Montenegro) in order to stimulate peaceful settlement of conflicts.

In 1993 US Secretary of State Cyrus Vance and European Community mediator Lord Owen proposed a peace plan through the International Conference on the Former Yugoslavia (ICFY), and in 1994 Croatia and Bosnia and Herzegovina formed the Bosniac-Croat Federation as territory was divided between these groups and the Bosnian Serbs. The United Nations Confidence Restoration Operation in Croatia (UNCRO) helped implement a ceasefire and demilitarization in the Prevlaka peninsula. Croatia used force to reintegrate Western Slavonia and Krajina from May to August 1995 as the UN withdrew from those areas. On October 5, 1995 the United States secured a cease-fire of the fighting that was raging in Bosnia and Herzegovina, and on November 22 the UN Security Council suspended the sanctions against Yugoslavia. UNCRO ended its mission in January 1996. That month the United Nations Transitional Administration for Eastern Slavonia, Baranja and Western Sirmium (UNTAES) oversaw the Basic Agreement of November 1995 that provided for the peaceful integration of Croatia, supervising demilitarization, voluntary return of refugees, and the April 1997 elections.

The United Nations Preventive Deployment Force

(UNPREDEP) replaced UNPROFOR in March 1995 in Macedonia and monitored the borders between Yugoslavia and Albania until February 1999. As the international force (IFOR) led by the North Atlantic Treaty Organization (NATO) was deployed, the United Nations Mission in Bosnia and Herzegovina (UNMIBH) helped implement the General Framework Agreement by coordinating humanitarian relief, demining, human rights, elections, and rehabilitation of infrastructure. UNMIBH's Police Task Force continues to monitor law enforcement. In January 1996 the United Nations Mission of Observers in Prevlaka (UNMOP) took over from UNCRO the monitoring of the demilitarization of the Prevlaka peninsula in southern Croatia on the border of Yugoslavia.

After the United States and NATO took it upon themselves to bomb Yugoslavia in the spring of 1999 for its oppression of Kosovo, in June the UN Security Council authorized NATO to lead a security presence (KFOR) to demilitarize Kosovo and maintain law and order. The United Nations Interim Administration Mission in Kosovo (UNMIK) was established to operate as peacekeepers and to exercise administrative and executive authority, administering justice, rehabilitating the territory and preparing Kosovo for elections as an autonomous province within the Federal Republic of Yugoslavia.

In August 1999 the United Nations conducted a poll in which East Timorese chose to separate from Indonesia; but anti-independence forces reacted with a campaign of terror. The UN Security Council authorized an international force (INTERFET) to restore order and in October established the United Nations Transitional Administration in East Timor (UNTAET) to help the East Timorese to become independent, administer the Territory, organize elections and assure the rule of law and human rights. On May 20, 2002 East Timor became an independent nation with the name Timor-Leste, and UNTAET was replaced by the United Nations Mission of Support in East Timor (UNMISET) to provide assistance to the newly elected Timor-Leste government for three years.

The United Nations has difficulty keeping states in line against their will, but the veto has at least kept the super-powers talking together in the Security Council, even though they were not always able to agree. The General Assembly became a great public forum for the debate of international issues, and the developments of the economic and social functions made progress in dealing with many of the root causes of war. In 1992 the new Secretary-General Boutros Boutros-Ghali wrote *Agenda for Peace* and suggested that the United Nations become more active in peacekeeping, peacemaking, and what he called "peace-building." With the Cold War over, this has meant the use of many more military forces, especially by the United States. In 1992 there were about 12,000 military and police personnel functioning as UN peacekeepers, but by the end of 1994 the number had increased to nearly 80,000, not counting the 10,000 US troops in Haiti. In 2004 United Nations peace operations rotated 120,000 military and civilian police personnel. In 2005 United Nations peace-keeping was spending an annual budget of five billion dollars for operations with about 67,000 military personnel and civilian police. The United Nations is far from perfect and complete as a world organization, but it has enabled humanity to take many important steps on the path of social evolution.

Notes

1. Security Council Res. 131, 22 November, 1967 in *View from the UN: The Memoirs of U Thant*, p. 492.
2. Quoted in *The Evolution of UN Peacekeeping* ed. William J. Durch, p. 259.
3. *The Blue Helmets: A Review of United Nations Peacekeeping*, Third edition, p. 682-683.

5

Einstein and Schweitzer
on Peace in the Atomic Age

Every thoughtful, well-meaning
and conscientious human being
should assume, in time of peace,
the solemn and unconditional obligation
not to participate in any war, for any reason,
or to lend support of any kind, whether direct or indirect.
Albert Einstein to War Resisters' International, 1928

Mankind's desire for peace can be realized
only by the creation of a world government.
Albert Einstein, January 1946

Our world faces a crisis as yet unperceived
by those possessing the power
to make great decisions for good and evil.
The unleashed power of the atom has changed everything
save our modes of thinking,
and thus we drift toward unparalleled catastrophe.
Albert Einstein, May 1946

What can we do in the prevailing situation
to bring about peaceful coexistence among all nations?
The first goal must be
to do away with mutual fear and distrust.
Solemn renunciation of the policy of violence,
not only with respect to weapons of mass destruction,
is without doubt necessary.
Such renunciation, however, will be effective
only if a supranational judicial and executive agency
is established at the same time,
with power to settle questions of immediate concern
to the security of nations.
Albert Einstein, February 1950

Strengthening the United Nations

requires admission of all nations,
irrespective of their internal organization;
for averting the danger of war
is the supreme and most immediate interest of all.
Albert Einstein, June 1953

The highest insight man can attain is the yearning for peace,
for the union of his will with an infinite will,
his human will with God's will.
Albert Schweitzer

The peace of God is pulsating power, not quietude.
Albert Schweitzer, Sermon October 13, 1918

The laying down of the commandment not to kill
and not to damage is one of the greatest events
in the spiritual history of mankind.
Albert Schweitzer, *Indian Thought and Its Development*

Only a humanity which is striving after ethical ends
can in full measure share in the blessings
brought by material progress
and become master of the dangers which accompany it.
Albert Schweitzer

Only such thinking as establishes the sway
of the mental attitude of reverence for life
can bring to mankind perpetual peace.
Albert Schweitzer, *Civilization and Ethics*

The renunciation of nuclear weapons is vital to peace.
Albert Schweitzer, *Peace or Atomic War?*

Einstein on Peace and World Government

Albert Einstein, the renowned scientist whose theories
of relativity led to the development of atomic energy and
weapons, was a dedicated pacifist and advocate of world
government. He was born March 14, 1879 in Ulm,
Germany. He grew up in Munich, where he attended strict
schools in which he performed poorly. His mother insisted
he take violin lessons, and his uncles introduced him to

mathematics and science. At the age of five he wondered why a compass always pointed north, and at twelve he began a quest to understand the mystery of the "huge world." He continued to have difficulty in school until he moved to Switzerland, where in 1900 he graduated in physics from the reputable Polytechnic Academy in Zurich. He gained Swiss citizenship and got a job in the patent office in Bern examining inventions.

In 1905 Einstein began to publish important papers in theoretical physics, particularly on the special theory of relativity, which synthesized the law of the conservation of the mass with the law of the conservation of energy into an equivalence in terms of the speed of light squared: $E=mc^2$. The three-dimensional coordinates of space and the one of time were also joined into the four-dimensional continuum of space-time. Einstein gained some recognition from eminent physicists and began teaching at universities in Switzerland and Germany. He moved his family to Berlin in April 1914 to accept a position with the Prussian Academy. His wife and two sons were vacationing in Switzerland when the war broke out, and the enforced separation foreshadowed a later divorce. Einstein hated the war and criticized German militarism, but he devoted himself to his scientific work. He published "The Foundation of the General Theory of Relativity" in 1916. Using the space-time continuum concept, he postulated that gravity is not a force as much as a field shaped by bodies of mass. His theory was proved correct when he accurately predicted that even light from stars would bend when passing near the sun; this was measured and verified by Arthur Eddington during a total eclipse in 1919.

Einstein was now internationally acclaimed as perhaps the greatest scientist of the twentieth century. In 1921 he was awarded the Nobel Prize for Physics. Einstein spent the rest of his scientific career working on his unified field theory, attempting to find the mathematical relationship between the electromagnetic field and the gravitational field. However, quantum theory and the uncertainty principle thwarted his efforts to find a formula which could predict subatomic events. Einstein clung to his belief that the universe is comprehensible, saying that God does not play dice with the world.

As a world-famous celebrity, Einstein's statements on peace were given considerable publicity. When the First World War began, Einstein and two others signed a statement by Georg Friedrich Nicholai, the "Manifesto to Europeans," which challenged the "Manifesto to the Civilized World," which was a blatant promotion of German militarism that had been signed by ninety-three prominent Germans. Nicholai's statement warned that every nation in the war would pay a heavy price, and he suggested a League of Europeans to achieve unity. During the war Einstein was a founder and supporter of the New Fatherland League, which sought to establish after the war a supranational organization to prevent future wars. He gleefully smuggled pacifist literature to his friend Nicholai in prison. In 1915 he signed a declaration by this League criticizing annexationist policies of the Chancellor. In a letter to the French pacifist writer, Romain Rolland, Einstein compared the "insanity of nationalism" to the religious fanaticism of three centuries earlier which had caused so many useless wars. In 1917 he wrote again to Rolland, suggesting a military arbitration pact involving the United States, Britain, France and Russia, which any democratic nation could join.

Although Einstein was not religious in the traditional sense, he was proud of being a Jew. Within the war atmosphere that swept up so many around him, on February 24, 1918 he wrote to an academic,

I prefer to string along with my compatriot, Jesus Christ, whose doctrines you and your kind consider to be obsolete. Suffering is indeed more acceptable to me than resort to violence.[1]

Late in 1918 when Germany was undergoing revolution, Einstein gave a speech at the Reichstag, suggesting to the revolutionary committees, "Our common goal is democracy, the rule of the people," but warning them,

Do not be lured by feelings of vengeance to the fateful view
that violence must be fought with violence,
that a dictatorship of the proletariat is temporarily needed
in order to hammer the concept of freedom
into the heads of our fellow countrymen.
Force breeds only bitterness, hatred and reaction.[2]

After the war Einstein favored the publication of the war crimes committed by the German High Command in Belgium and France to communicate to Germans how the others felt in order to "prevent the emergence of a spirit of vengefulness."[3] In 1922 he made a trip to Paris to discuss with political figures methods of preventing wars, and after returning to Germany, he spoke again in the Reichstag at a meeting of the German Peace Federation, calling for good-will between peoples of different languages and cultures. In a German pacifist publication Einstein explained how war blocks international cooperation and culture by destroying intellectual freedom, chaining the energies of the young to the engines of destruction, and causing economic depression.

Einstein supported the League of Nations, but he resigned from the League Committee on Intellectual Cooperation in 1923 when France did not agree to arbitration concerning Germany's war-reparations payment. He felt that the League was merely a tool of the dominant nations. In 1924 he was re-elected to that Committee and decided to "let bygones be bygones" and accept the position, hoping that the League would "live up to its great mission of creating a world of peace."[4]

In 1928 Einstein began recommending that individuals refuse military service and any participation in war activities. During this period Einstein's pacifism was absolute, and he believed that any killing of a human being, even during war, is murder. He saw how science and technology were changing warfare, and he believed that international conventions to limit the applications of science did not solve the real problem, which was how to end war by establishing international justice. In pleading for disarmament, Einstein felt that its risks and sacrifices were less than the risks and sacrifices of war. People ought to refuse to kill other innocent people. In a letter to a friend Einstein warned,

In a Europe which is systematically preparing for war,
both morally and materially,
an impotent League of Nations will not be able to command
even moral authority in the hour of nationalist madness.[5]

He suggested that a country could assume the risk of not defending itself as a sacrifice for human progress. Surely it would not suffer as much damage as Germany did in four years of war. Otherwise the preparations for war along with fear, distrust, and selfish ambitions would lead again to war. He believed we could not wait until the governing classes give up their sovereign power. Public personalities can influence people. He asked how can decent and self-respecting people wage war, knowing that innocent people will be killed? Finally, the welfare of humanity must take precedence over one's country.

Einstein believed that the production of armaments was damaging not only economically but also spiritually. In 1930 he signed a manifesto for world disarmament sponsored by the Women's International League for Peace and Freedom (WILPF). The same year Einstein warned the Zionist movement that he would not continue to support them unless they made peace with the Arabs. On December 14, 1930 Einstein made his famous statement in New York that if two percent of those called for military service were to refuse to fight and were to urge peaceful means of settling international conflicts, then governments would become powerless since they could not imprison that many people. He struggled against compulsory military service and urged international protection of conscientious objectors. He concluded that peace, freedom for individuals, and security for societies depended on disarmament; otherwise, "slavery of the individual and the annihilation of civilization threaten us."[6] As part of his work for intellectual cooperation, Einstein wrote an open letter to Sigmund Freud in 1932, asking him to discuss the causes and cures of war. In his letter Einstein suggested that an international legislative and judicial body was needed to solve conflicts and maintain security. In his carefully reasoned response Freud came to the same conclusion that Einstein had intuitively grasped. Later that year Einstein supported the French Premier Herriot's proposal for "a police force which would be subject to the authority of international organs."[7] Early in 1933 Einstein warned that powerful industrial interests, which produce arms, were trying to sabotage efforts to settle international disputes peacefully.

When Hitler and the Nazi Party came to power in 1933, Einstein left Germany for good and settled at Princeton, where he joined the Institute for Advanced Study. He saw that Germany was "secretly arming at a great pace," and noticing "the desire for revenge among the educated," he predicted "the sacrifice of a terrifying number of human lives and untold destruction."[8] Being realistic about this danger, he ceased to be an absolute pacifist; although he still recommended a supranational organization of force, in its absence he felt that the democracies ought to prepare to defend themselves. He was criticized by some pacifists, but Einstein felt that it would be foolish to close one's eyes to the Nazi menace. He tried to communicate the dreadfulness of Fascism and the Nazis' fanatical drive toward war. He encouraged the United States to join the League of Nations and to make it an effective instrument of international security. By 1935 he estimated that war would come in two or three years. He reiterated the need for world government:

First, create the idea of supersovereignty:

men must be taught to think in world terms;
every country will have to surrender a portion
of its sovereignty through international cooperation.
If we want to avoid war,
we must try to make aggression impossible
through the creation of an international tribunal
having real authority.[9]

Second, Einstein believed we must understand the economic causes of war, the selfish desires that put profit before humanity. In 1937 he declared that true pacifism works for international law, while neutrality and isolation practiced by a great power contribute to international anarchy and consequently to war.

Einstein's famous formula $E=mc^2$ indicates that a very small amount of matter may be converted into a tremendous amount of energy. In July 1939 Leo Szilard told Einstein about the work under way which showed that through nuclear fission a chain reaction might be started. This was a shock to Einstein. Four and a half years earlier he had discounted the likelihood of releasing energy from a molecule, saying, "It is something like shooting birds in the dark in a country where there are only a few birds."[10] Now he immediately realized the danger if Germany were to get uranium from the Belgian Congo, and he agreed to contact the Belgium government through his friend, Queen Elizabeth.

Alexander Sachs, one of President Roosevelt's unofficial advisors, suggested to Einstein that he address a letter directly to the President. On August 2, 1939 Einstein wrote to President Roosevelt explaining how nuclear chain reactions in a large mass of uranium could generate large amounts of power and radium-like elements. In fact, in the immediate future, a powerful enough bomb could be built to destroy an entire port. He pointed out that the best uranium is found in Canada, the former Czechoslovakia, and especially the Belgian Congo, and he had heard that Germany had stopped the sale of uranium from the Czechoslovakian mines. He added that the son of the German Under-Secretary of State was attached to the Kaiser Wilhelm Institut in Berlin, and they were repeating some of the American work on uranium. The letter, with a memorandum by Szilard, actually was not delivered to the President by Sachs until October 11. President Roosevelt immediately appointed an Advisory Committee on Uranium. Later Einstein considered the writing of this letter the one great mistake of his life; at the time he felt justified because of the danger that the Germans would make atom bombs. This was the extent of Einstein's role in nuclear energy; he did not know an atomic bomb had been developed by the United States until he heard of the Hiroshima blast.

For the rest of his life Einstein emphasized the need for a supranational organization with the authority and power to maintain international security. With the unleashing of the atomic bomb in 1945 his pleas became even more fervent. As a knowledgeable scientist he felt that it was his responsibility to inform the public of the enormity of the danger. The United Nations was a step in the right direction, but from the beginning Einstein believed that it was "a tragic illusion unless we are ready to take the further steps necessary to organize peace."[11] There must be effective world law with a federal constitution and a permanent world court to restrain the executive branch of the world government from going beyond peacekeeping. National military power must be abandoned in favor of the supranational authority. Otherwise war preparations inevitably lead to war, and in the atomic age there is the danger of pre-emptive war and the possibility of total annihilation. Einstein supported efforts to strengthen the United Nations and give it the powers it needs. Survival, he felt, must be the first priority, and survival depends on world government. There is no defense against nuclear weapons. Einstein evaluated every nation's foreign policy by one criterion: "Does it lead us to a world of law and order or does it lead us back toward anarchy and death?"[12] He said,

"We need a great chain reaction of awareness and communication."[13]

Einstein criticized as political exploitation the policy of stockpiling atomic bombs without promising not to initiate their use. In 1947 only the United States had atomic weapons. However, the cold war had already begun, and the Soviet Union was developing them also. Both sides refused to consider supranational control, and Einstein lamented that the victors of the second world war had degraded themselves to the low ethics of their enemy and remained at that level after the war. In 1948 Einstein predicted that the arms race would increase tension between the United States and the Soviet Union, undermine the democratic spirit in America, impose heavy and unnecessary economic burdens because of the unproductive work, and generate that militaristic spirit which Toynbee said is fatal to civilizations. For Einstein, the problem of peace and security was far more important than the conflict between socialism and capitalism.

Einstein worked with the Emergency Committee of Atomic Scientists to educate people about the dangers of atomic war and the necessity of effective world government. By 1949 the Soviet Union had atomic weapons, and the United States had begun working on the hydrogen bomb. Einstein's prophecy that the cold war would threaten democratic principles in the United States came to pass with the operations of the House Un-American Activities Committee (HUAC). He recommended that intellectuals use Gandhi's method of non-cooperation by refusing to testify. Einstein believed that Gandhi held the most enlightened political views and that his method of nonviolent revolution is the only way of bringing peace to the world on a supranational basis. With this method the small countries together could become a decisive factor in the world. Nevertheless he felt that a responsible statesman would not use Gandhi's methods unilaterally until there had been a period of transition.

In the last week of his life Einstein collaborated with

Bertrand Russell on a manifesto that concluded with a resolution to be presented to a world convention of scientists
which read:

> In view of the fact that in any future world war
> nuclear weapons will certainly be employed,
> and that such weapons threaten
> the continued existence of mankind,
> we urge the governments of the world to realize,
> and to acknowledge publicly,
> that their purposes cannot be furthered by a world war,
> and we urge them, consequently,
> to find peaceful means for the settlement
> of all matters of dispute between them.[14]

When Einstein died on April 18, 1955, he left a piece of
writing ending in an unfinished sentence. These were his
last words:

> In essence, the conflict that exists today is
> no more than an old-style struggle for power,
> once again presented to mankind
> in semi-religious trappings.
> The difference is that, this time,
> the development of atomic power
> has imbued the struggle with a ghostly character;
> for both parties know and admit that,
> should the quarrel deteriorate into actual war,
> mankind is doomed.
> Despite this knowledge,
> statesmen in responsible positions on both sides
> continue to employ the well-known technique
> of seeking to intimidate and demoralize the opponent
> by marshaling superior military strength.
> They do so even though such a policy
> entails the risk of war and doom.
> Not one statesman in a position of responsibility
> has dared to pursue the only course
> that holds out any promise of peace,
> the course of supranational security,
> since for a statesman to follow such a course

would be tantamount to political suicide.
Political passions, once they have been fanned into flame,
exact their victims[15]

Schweitzer's Reverence for Life

After Einstein's death, Albert Schweitzer wrote to
Einstein's niece that he and the great physicist understood
each other and that they had the same ideals. Schweitzer
was born four years before Einstein on January 14, 1875 in
Alsace, which at that time was part of Germany but now is
part of France. His father was a Lutheran pastor, and Albert
studied and gained doctorate degrees in both philosophy
and theology. He was an accomplished organist, and he
wrote a comprehensive book on Johann Sebastian Bach and
later edited Bach's complete works. His theological books
combined his deep religious convictions with a scholarly
search for historical truth. Beyond the historical considerations he found the essence of Jesus' teachings to be love
and preparing the heart for the sovereignty of God. He
concluded *Quest of the Historical Jesus* with Jesus' call for
people to follow him.

He commands. And to those who obey Him,
whether they be wise or simple,
He will reveal Himself in the toils, the conflicts,
the sufferings which they shall pass through
in His fellowship, and, as an ineffable mystery,
they shall learn in their own experience Who He is.[16]

At the age of thirty Schweitzer decided to become a
physician so that he could dedicate himself to practical
missionary work. He resigned from his university teaching
position and attended medical school full-time. His theological views were considered controversial by the mission
officials. However, by making personal contacts with each
of them to assure them he was going as a doctor rather than
a preacher, he was granted the opportunity to serve in
French Equatorial Africa at Lambaréné. His wife trained as
a nurse, and by 1913 they were prepared. His farewell

sermon was on "The Peace of God," which comes when our will is absorbed in the infinite. This, he said, must be our active search, and those who experience God's peace can face any eventuality. Sensing a coming war, he had their money converted into coins before they left.

Schweitzer quickly gained the trust of the Africans in his medical practice; but when the World War began, Schweitzer, as a German, became a prisoner of the French authorities. The native Africans could not understand such a terrible war. One old man, hearing that as many as ten people had died, wondered why they did not negotiate a settlement since such great losses could not be paid back. According to their tribal customs they reimbursed the opposing tribe for those they killed. Also as cannibals they felt that the Europeans must kill out of cruelty if they have no desire to eat the dead. Schweitzer was a prisoner for three years, although much of the time he was allowed to continue his work at the hospital. He began working on his *Philosophy of Civilization,* and while paddling down the Ogowe River in the midst of a herd of hippopotami the concept "reverence for life" suddenly occurred to him. He was taken to France, and while imprisoned at Saint Remy he realized that he was in a room that Van Gogh had painted.

At the end of the war Schweitzer's first sermon at St. Nicholai's Church in Strasbourg was again on peace and also on the future of mankind. He repeated that we must place our will in God's infinite will and look for that, not only in individual affairs but also in the concerns of nations and mankind. The will of God is a spiritual intention toward perfection, and people as a whole must be united by spiritual goals. In another sermon on December 1, 1918 he said,

Those millions who were made to kill,
forced to do it in self-defense or under military orders,
must impress the horror of what they had to endure
on all future generations
so that none will ever expose itself to such fate again.

Reverence for human suffering and human life,
for the smallest and most insignificant,
must be the inviolable law to rule the world from now on.[17]

The huge waste of life during the war terribly grieved Schweitzer, and he was deeply depressed for several years. The war, he believed, was proof that religion was not a real force in the spiritual life of the age. Looking back on his first visit to Africa, he considered his work there not benevolence but rather atonement for a tiny part of the guilt the white race bears for all it has done to the colored races. Schweitzer hailed the League of Nations but was afraid that it would fail; he remained apolitical.

In *The Decay and the Restoration of Civilization* Schweitzer examined the problems of civilization and their solution through ethics. Nationalism has helped to bring about the decay of civilization because of the spirit of barbarism. Even the economic difficulties can be solved only "by an inner change of character."[18] Revolutionary change is needed without revolutionary action. When the collective body dominates the individual's spiritual and moral worthiness, the constriction causes deterioration. The individuals must rise to a higher conception of their capabilities and produce new spiritual-ethical ideas. A new public opinion must be created to counteract the press, which is under the influence of political and financial forces. This requires independent and strong personalities, who are free of the prevalent conditions. Nationalistic patriotism must be replaced by the noble "patriotism which aims at ends that are worthy of the whole of mankind."[19] This idealism encourages people to focus on the values of civilization even amid the increasing absorption in material concerns. Nothing less than a reconstruction of the world-view can bring about such changes. The lack of a positive and life-affirming world-view is pathological to societies as well as individuals, because there is no true self-direction. Schweitzer declared,

From the ethical comes ability to develop
the purposive state of mind
necessary to produce action on the world and society
and to cause the co-operation of all our achievements
to secure the spiritual and moral perfection of the individual
which is the final end of civilization.[20]

The second book in his Philosophy of Civilization, *Civilization and Ethics*, reviews the history of ethics and its relation to civilization. For Schweitzer ethics is the key to peace.

All those who in any way
help forward our thought about ethics
are working for the coming of peace
and prosperity in the world.
They are engaged in the higher politics,
and the higher national economics.[21]

His ethical philosophy is based on reverence for life and the will-to-live, which affirm both life and the world and through activity then produce values. The thinking person feels the need to revere every will-to-live and experience that other life as one's own. Being good is preserving life, promoting life, and raising life to the highest value it is capable of developing. Being evil is destroying life, injuring life, and repressing life that is capable of development. This universal ethic widens to include all that lives, and it seeks to relieve all suffering. One joins in the mysterious infinite will of all Being which acts for life through the person, giving meaning to existence from within outwards. To attain peace the ethic of reverence for life must be applied to the state so that collective interests will not overshadow the human feelings of empathy and cause interpersonal conflicts. The illusions of national interests must be criticized and replaced by moral and spiritual values, by concern for humanity as a whole.

Schweitzer advised people to put an end to the illusions that the modern state cherishes about itself. He believed that things would not get better until a majority took up a critical attitude. The spirit of the state must become quite different. Progress will come when we demand that the state become more ethical. He suggested that we must look beyond peoples and states to humanity as a whole. He criticized the well intentioned Kant for believing that rules for treaties could bring lasting peace. Schweitzer believed that only the mental attitude of reverence for life could bring peace to humanity.

In a world of violence Schweitzer still had faith that truth, love, peacefulness, meekness, and kindness could overcome all violence. When a sufficient number with purity of heart, strength and perseverance think and live out the thoughts of love, truth, and peace, then the world will be theirs. Violence produces its own limitations, but kindness works simply and effectively without straining relations. A question Schweitzer posed was whether the spiritual will be strong and create world history or be weak and suffer world history. He believed that we will either realize the sovereignty of God or perish, and the sovereignty of God begins in our hearts.

Schweitzer returned to Africa in 1924 and spent most of the next four decades working there. Occasionally he visited Europe, and in 1934 he vowed never to enter Nazi Germany. He was in Lambaréné throughout World War II. Hearing of V-E Day, he quoted Lao-zi's teaching that the victors ought not to rejoice in the murder of war but rather mourn as at a funeral. Following the war, Schweitzer expressed concerns about the danger of nuclear war. He said that Africans could solve their own problems if the "civilized" nations of Europe and America did not blow up themselves and Africa first. In 1953 he was given the Nobel Peace Prize; he used the money for a building at the Leper Village he had established in Lambaréné.

In 1955 Schweitzer corresponded with Albert Einstein concerning atomic weapons and the hazardous tests of atomic bombs. He also conferred with Bertrand Russell on the same problem. In April 1954 Schweitzer had suggested that the protest against the H-bomb should be initiated by scientists.

Hoping for a statement by the renowned Schweitzer on the nuclear weapons issue, Norman Cousins traveled to Lambaréné to discuss the idea with the aging but vital doctor. Schweitzer said he was always reluctant to make public statements, preferring instead to make his life his argument. However, because of the overwhelming importance of the issue, Schweitzer agreed to consider it. The result was a series of three radio broadcasts from Oslo, Norway in 1958 and a letter to President Eisenhower.

In the first broadcast Schweitzer called for the renunciation of nuclear tests. He explained to the general public the harmful medical effects of radiation in the bones and blood and how this continues for generations, causing birth defects. He referred to the declaration that was signed by 9,235 scientists throughout the world and given to the Secretary-General of the United Nations by Linus Pauling in January 1958. This, he stated, refutes the propaganda that scientists do not agree on the dangers of radiation. He criticized the concept of "a permissible amount of radiation." He asked who permitted it and if they had any right to permit it. He appealed especially to women to raise their voices against the nuclear tests that cause deformed babies. He asked why international law and the United Nations have not done anything about this. He cited the Soviet tests in Siberia and the American tests at Bikini Atoll that contaminated the Pacific Ocean and Japan. Humanity is imperiled by the tests. "Mankind insists that they stop, and has every right to do so."[22]

The second talk discussed the danger of an atomic war. Schweitzer recounted the first decade of the nuclear arms race and concluded that as a result of the arms buildup neither side could be victorious in an atomic war.

Those who conduct an atomic war for freedom will die, or end their lives miserably.
Instead of freedom they will find destruction.
Radioactive clouds resulting

from a war between East and West
would imperil humanity everywhere.[23]

Missiles equipped with H-bombs have radically changed the situation. The United States and the Soviet Union threaten each other from a distance, and there is the danger of their war occurring on European soil. The United States is arming countries, which may use the weapons for defense against the Soviet Union, which in turn might defend itself. These countries include Turkey and key nations in the Middle East, where both the US and USSR seek alliances by giving financial and military aid. Conflicts between these smaller countries could endanger the peace of the world. The technology required and the short time intervals involved mean that war could originate from a mere incident or even an error. He pointed out that these quick decisions are being "entrusted to an electronic brain" which may become faulty. He criticized America for terrifying her opponent "to maintain peace" and for attempting to pressure NATO countries into acquiring weapons in spite of adverse public opinion. "The theory of peace through terrifying an opponent by a greater armament can now only heighten the danger of war."[24] He supported the recent proposal to establish an atom-free zone in Europe and re-affirmed the public opinion in Europe "that under no circumstances is Europe to become a battlefield for an atomic war between the Soviet Union and the United States."[25]

In the third broadcast Schweitzer proposed negotiations at the highest level for complete nuclear disarmament with international verification. There is no justification for nuclear weapons or tests because they threaten the health and very existence of mankind. He suggested that America withdraw its forces from Europe, for the Europeans, east and west, must learn to get along with each other. The Soviet Union should also agree to reduce her army and agree not to attack Germany. We must rid ourselves of the paralyzing mistrust of our adversaries and approach each other "in the spirit that we are human beings, all of us."[26] He saw two choices: one is a mad atomic-arms race with the danger of an unavoidable atomic war; the other is a mutual renunciation of nuclear weapons in the hope that we can manage to live in peace. Because the first is hopeless, we must risk the second.

Albert Schweitzer continued his medical work until he died at the age of ninety. Even in 1965, his last year, he was deeply upset about the Vietnam War, the tensions in the Middle East, and relations between the United States, Russia, and China. He died in Africa among the people he had served.

Notes

1. *Einstein on Peace*, p. 22.
2. *Ibid.*, p. 25.
3. *Ibid.*, p. 32.
4. *Ibid.*, p. 68.
5. *Ibid.*, p. 100.
6. *Ibid.*, p. 164.
7. *Ibid.*, p. 205.
8. *Ibid.*, p. 224.
9. *Ibid.*, p. 260.
10. *Ibid.*, p. 290.
11. *Ibid.*, p. 340.
12. *Ibid.*, p. 385.
13. *Ibid.*, p. 387.
14. *Ibid.*, p. 635.
15. *Ibid.*, p. 639-640.
16. *The Quest for the Historical Jesus* by Albert Schweitzer, tr. W. Montgomery, p. 403.
17. *Reverence for Life* by Albert Schweitzer, p. 104.
18. *The Philosophy of Civilization* by Albert Schweitzer, tr. C. T. Campion, p. 36.
19. *Ibid.*, p. 47.
20. *Ibid.*, p. 58.
21. *Ibid.*, p. 104.
22. *Peace or Atomic War?* by Albert Schweitzer, p. 19.

23. *Ibid.*, p. 27.
24. *Ibid.*, p. 32.
25. *Ibid.*, p. 32-33.
26. *Ibid.*, p. 44.

6

Pacifism of Bertrand Russell and A. J. Muste

Life and hope for the world
are to be found only in the deeds of love.
Bertrand Russell

If war no longer occupied men's thoughts and energies,
we would, within a generation,
put an end to all serious poverty throughout the world.
Bertrand Russell, *The Future of Mankind*

Either man will abolish war, or war will abolish man.
Bertrand Russell

War can only be abolished
by the establishment of a world government.
Bertrand Russell

I favor the complete prohibition of all nuclear weapons.
Bertrand Russell, *Common Sense and Nuclear Warfare*

The time has come, or is about to come,
when only large-scale civil disobedience,
which should be nonviolent,
can save the populations from the universal death
which their governments are preparing for them.
Bertrand Russell

For love of domination we must substitute equality;
for love of victory we must substitute justice;
for brutality we must substitute intelligence;
for competition we must substitute cooperation.
We must learn to think of the human race as one family.
Bertrand Russell

Only the nonviolent can apply therapy to the violent.
A. J. Muste

The survival of democracy

depends on the renunciation of violence
and the development of nonviolent means
to combat evil and advance the good.
A. J. Muste

There is no way to peace; peace is the way.
A. J. Muste

Bertrand Russell and the World Wars

One of the greatest philosophers of the twentieth century, Bertrand Russell, was an active pacifist, who spent considerable energy working for world peace, especially in his eighties and nineties. Bertrand Russell was born in England on May 18, 1872, and he died on February 2, 1970. Both of his parents died while he was a small child, and he was raised by his grandmother Russell. Bertrand was well educated and was an outstanding student at Trinity College, Cambridge. In addition to his expertise in mathematics and philosophy he studied and lectured on economics and political science. Although he believed that the intellect maintained his sanity, he considered the emotions and passions fundamental in human life. He married four times. His skeptical attitudes and questioning of authority and popular tradition made him seem scandalous to many people.

Russell earned his reputation as a distinguished thinker by his work in mathematics and logic. In 1903 he published *The Principles of Mathematics* and by 1913 he and Alfred North Whitehead had published the three volumes of *Principia Mathematica*. Although Russell was an analytic rationalist all of his life, he did have a significant mystical experience in 1901 which influenced his values for the rest of his life. In his *Autobiography* he described what happened.

Suddenly the ground seemed to give way beneath me,
and I found myself in quite another region.
Within five minutes I went through
some such reflections as the following:

the loneliness of the human soul is unendurable;
nothing can penetrate it except the highest intensity
of the sort of love that religious teachers have preached;
whatever does not spring from this motive is harmful,
or at best useless;
it follows that war is wrong,
that a public school education is abominable,
that the use of force is to be deprecated,
and that in human relations one should penetrate
to the core of loneliness in each person and speak to that.[1]

The usually skeptical Russell called it a "mystical illumination;" for a while he felt he could sense people's inmost thoughts; he became closer to his friends; he changed from an imperialist to a pacifist and sided with the Boers against Britain; for a time his analytic mind was swept away by ecstatic feelings about beauty, an intense interest in children, and the desire to found a philosophy, as the Buddha had done, to make human life more endurable.

During the First World War Russell's pacifism challenged British society. In July 1914 he collected signatures from fellow professors for a statement urging England to remain neutral in the imminent war. When the British were swept into the war and 90% of the population favored the fighting and killing, Russell was horrified and reassessed his views of human nature. In a letter to the London *Nation* for August 15 he criticized the pride of patriotism which promotes mass murder. Bertrand Russell was not an absolute pacifist. He explained that the use of force is justifiable when it is ordered according to law by a neutral authority for the general good but not when it is primarily for the interest of one of the parties in the quarrel. One solution, then, was for an international organization backed up by force to keep the peace. Another solution he suggested was passive resistance. If this was intelligently adopted by the whole nation with as much courage and discipline as was being shown in the war, then the national life could be better protected with far less carnage and waste.

In 1916 Russell began to work for the No Conscription Fellowship; he became its chairman when all of the original committee had gone to prison. He wrote a leaflet to defend the case of Ernest Everett, who had refused military service. When six men were arrested for distributing the leaflet, Russell wrote to *The Times* declaring he was its author. Russell was accused of hampering recruiting, and as his own attorney he explained that the case of a conscientious objector could hardly influence someone who is considering volunteering. He cited the English tradition of liberty, but he was convicted nonetheless. When he refused to pay the fine, the authorities preferred confiscating some of his possessions to putting him in prison. This conviction, however, prevented him from getting a passport to visit America. Russell felt that the more policemen and officials they could occupy with the innocent work of monitoring their pacifist activities, the less men would be available for the "official business of killing each other."

After Wilson's re-election in 1916, Russell wrote an open letter to the President which Katherine Dudley smuggled across the Atlantic. He appealed to the United States Government to make peace between the European governments. He wrote,

If the German Government, as now seems likely,
would not only restore conquered territory,
but also give its adherence to the League to Enforce Peace
or some similar method of settling disputes without war,
fear would be allayed,
and it is almost certain that an offer of mediation from you
would give rise to an irresistible movement
in favour of negotiations.[2]

Russell's speeches to munitions workers in South Wales were inaccurately reported by detectives, and the War Office forbade Russell from entering prohibited areas. In January 1918 an article by Russell appeared in a little weekly newspaper called *The Tribunal* suggesting that American soldiers were likely to be used as strike-breakers in England, because they had been employed in that way in the United States. This statement was backed up by a Senate Report. For this, Russell was sentenced to prison for six months. He spent the uninterrupted time cheerfully writing.

During the war Russell published several books on politics, war, and peace. *Principles of Social Reconstruction* was released in America as *Why Men Fight.* In this work Russell began with the idea that the passions of war must be controlled, not by thought alone, but by the passion and desire to think clearly. Reason by itself is too lifeless. Wars can be prevented by a positive life of passion. Impulse must not be weakened but directed "towards life and growth rather than towards death and decay." Russell suggested that the excessive discipline of impulse not only exhausts vitality but often results in impulses of cruelty and destruction; this is why militarism is bad for national character. He recommended therefore active pacifism with the impulse and passion to overcome the impulses of war. Great courage and passion are necessary to face the onslaught of the hostile public opinion of a nation. Three forces for life are love, constructiveness, and joy.

Russell believed that there must be strong action to assure international justice by a "Parliament of the nations." War can be prevented if the great powers firmly determine that peace shall be preserved. They could establish diplomatic methods to settle disputes and educational systems to teach the horrors of killing rather than admiration for war. Peace can only be permanently maintained by a world federation with the civil functions of a state—legislative, administrative, and judicial—and an international military force. This authority would legislate, adjudicate, and enforce international laws, but would not interfere with the internal affairs of nations. Pragmatically he suggested that at any given time we ought to support the best direction of movement available in the situation. This direction can be determined by applying the two principles of liberty and reverence. In other words, the freedom of individuals and communities ought to be encouraged, but not at the expense of others.

Russell replied to the War Office's restriction of his movement in the book *Justice in War Time*. He refused to surrender his spiritual liberty and declared that they could not prevent him from discussing political subjects, although they could imprison him under the Defense of the Realm Act. In the book he delineated the evils of war—the young men killed and maimed, the atrocities to non-combatants, the poverty of economic and social conditions, and the spiritual evils of hatred, injustice, falsehood, and conflict. He traced the theory of nonresistance held by Quakers and Tolstoy, and he imagined what might happen if England used nonresistance and noncooperation with the invaders as a means of defense. First there would be no justification at all for aggression. England would be giving up its empire and therefore could not be accused of oppressing anyone. Even if Germans did invade, what could they do if all the officials refused to cooperate? Would they really shoot or imprison them all? If the population refused to obey any German orders, they would not learn German nor serve in the army nor even work to pay taxes or supply products. Russell noted that this would require courage and discipline. The most the Germans could do would be to take away the empire and withhold food while demanding tribute.

For Russell, the empire was not a source of pride, and its self-governing parts could do the same thing. Demanding tribute is like the highwayman who says, "Your money or your life." Just as a reasonable man would hand over his money rather than be shot, a reasonable nation ought to give tribute rather than resist by force of arms. Primarily the rich would lose by this because the poor would have to retain enough to be able to work and supply the means of tribute. It is unlikely that this tribute would be more than the cost of fighting the war. Many deaths and the moral degradation of war would be avoided. Russell suggested that it takes more courage and discipline to practice nonresistance than it does to kill out of fear. Thus militarism is caused by "cowardice, love of dominion, and lust for blood." Even though nonresistance is a better defense than fighting, the more likely solution to the threat of war is the establishment of world government. In *Political Ideals* Russell discussed the need for an international government to secure peace in the world by means of effective international law. Just as police are needed to protect private citizens from the use of force, so an international police can prevent the lawless use of force by states. The benefit of having law rather than international anarchy will give the international government a respected authority so that states will no longer feel free to use aggression. Then a large international force will become unnecessary.

Roads to Freedom includes a section where Russell pointed out the capitalistic factors which promote war. First is the desire of finance to exploit the resources of undeveloped countries. Second, large newspapers require capital and promote capitalistic interests. Third, capitalists like power and expect to command others. Nevertheless, Russell did not recommend abolishing capitalism as a means to peace. However, he did recommend abolishing the private ownership of land and capital as one necessary step toward peace. Writing in 1918, he supported the idea of the League of Nations and international cooperation. He asserted that no idea is as practical as the brotherhood of man. Again he emphasized the need for a world government and national disarmament.

While visiting China in 1920, Russell fell ill and was treated by John Dewey. Dewey was moved by a statement that Russell made while he was delirious—"We must make a plan for peace."[3] In 1922 Russell was intending to go to a Congress in Italy, but Mussolini informed the organizers of the Congress that, while no harm was to be done to Russell, any Italian who spoke to him was to be assassinated. Naturally Russell decided to avoid the country he felt Mussolini was defiling. In 1923 Russell prophesied that without a world government it would be impossible to preserve civilization for another century. He declared the fundamental principle that the rights of a nation against humanity are no more absolute than the rights of an individual against the community. In 1931 Russell applauded Einstein's statement recommending that pacifists refuse military service. Like Einstein, Russell decided not to adhere to absolute pacifism in the face of the Nazi threat.

Russell published *Which Way to Peace?* in 1936. He criticized isolationism and encouraged international law and government with an international armed force to prevent war. He could not imagine Hitler, Mussolini, or Stalin voluntarily renouncing national power. He also felt that England would not consent until after the disaster of war and that the United States would be reluctant unless Washington was in control. He cited Denmark as a successful example of national pacifism. Russell indicated that the three obstacles to disarmament are fear, pride, and greed. In 1937 he wrote a mock obituary of himself and described how he escaped to a neutral country before the Second World War broke out, because he thought sensible people stay out of the way while lunatics are employed in killing each other. However, when the war came, Russell believed that Nazi Germany had to be fought for human life to remain tolerable.

Bertrand Russell in the Nuclear Age

The development of nuclear weapons caused Bertrand Russell deep concern. In November 1945 he gave a speech in the House of Lords warning that atomic weapons were going to be made more destructive and cheaper. Understanding nuclear physics, he explained how a hydrogen bomb with much more explosive force could work. He predicted that soon the Russians would have bombs as destructive as those of the United States. He recommended that nuclear weapons be under international control, and he supported the Baruch Plan for an International Atomic Development Authority. Such great danger did he see if

Russia and other nations developed atomic weapons that during this period when the United States was the only nuclear power he advocated that the US ought to force the Russians to accept a world government under American leadership, even by going to war against Russia if necessary. He believed that the only cause worth fighting for was world government. He compared this policy to the alternative of waiting until the Russians had atomic bombs and choosing between a nuclear war and submission. Russell never liked Communism, but his anti-Communism was moderated with the death of Stalin. McCarthyism's restriction of civil liberties and the Bikini test in 1954 gradually led Russell to consider the United States a greater threat to unleash nuclear war than the Russians.

In 1950 Bertrand Russell was given the Nobel Prize for Literature. The last twenty years of his life were primarily devoted to warnings about the nuclear danger, advocacy of world government, and the active work of peacemaking and protesting about policies of war. He believed that world government was the only alternative to the disaster of nuclear war. People and nations must become willing to submit to international law. *New Hopes for a Changing World* is an optimistic view of how to solve world problems. He suggested that happiness depends on harmony with other people. The problem in forming a world government is that the nations are not yet willing to give it enough power to be effective. Yet war is inevitable as long as different sovereign states try to settle their disagreements by the use of armed force. Russell expressed the hope that if the west with its superior strength does not go to war, after a while the Russians may become less suspicious and begin to have friendly relations, which eventually could open the way to world government. Then both countries could be spared the expense of armaments, could benefit from reciprocal trade, and could escape the threat of nuclear destruction.

On March 1, 1954 the Bikini test of the H-bomb made it clear that this weapon is about one thousand times more powerful than the A-bomb. The radioactive fallout also proved to be deadly. Russell suggested that all fissionable raw material be owned by an international authority. International inspectors ought to make sure that no nation or individual has access to fissionable raw material. On December 23, 1954 Russell made a broadcast over the BBC on "Man's Peril." He spoke not as a Briton or European but as a human being. He recommended that some neutral countries form a commission of experts to report on the destructive effects of a war using hydrogen bombs and that they submit this report to the governments of the great powers so that they could agree that a world war could not serve the purpose of any of them. Russell pleaded,

There lies before us, if we choose,
continued progress in happiness, knowledge and wisdom.
Shall we instead choose death
because we can not forget our quarrels?
I appeal as a human being to human beings.
Remember your humanity and forget the rest.
If you can do so the way lies open to a new Paradise;
if you cannot, nothing lies before you but universal death.[4]

Russell followed this address by drafting a statement for scientists to sign. He sent it to Einstein and was disappointed when he heard the news of Einstein's death. However, as one of his last acts, the great scientist had sent Russell a letter agreeing to sign. This Russell-Einstein Manifesto was also signed by a Communist scientist and several Nobel Prize winners.

The Parliamentary Association for World Government in August 1955, invited representatives from every country, including four from the Soviet Union. Russell moved a resolution that urged the world's governments to realize and to acknowledge publicly that their purposes cannot be advanced by world war. Russell addressed an open letter to Eisenhower and Khrushchev in November 1957, asking that they make an agreement with each other on some points in which the interests of Russia and America are the same. Russell proposed the following: first, since the continued existence of the human race is paramount, neither side should incite war by trying for world dominion; second, the diffusion of nuclear weapons to other countries must be stopped; third, lessening hostility could lead to immense savings on armament expenditures; and fourth, by respecting each other's rights and using argument instead of force, fears of collective death could be diminished.

Bertrand Russell was one of the main organizers of the Pugwash Conferences of Scientists. At the first meeting in 1957 three committees were formed—one on the hazards of atomic energy, one on the control of nuclear weapons, and one on the social responsibilities of scientists. One of the achievements of the Pugwash movement was the eventual agreement on at least a partial Test-ban Treaty. Russell considered this only a slight mitigation of the dangers. Russell was also the President of the Campaign for Nuclear Disarmament (CND), which worked for the unilateral disarmament of Britain and the expulsion of US bases from her soil.

Russell was also expressing his views on television in 1959 and in the books *Common Sense and Nuclear Warfare* and *Has Man a Future?* Nuclear warfare imperils mankind as a whole and therefore is to be treated like an epidemic and not be entangled in the conflicts of power politics. As a mathematician, Russell knew that as long as nuclear war is a possibility, its probability over time is increased. He quoted Linus Pauling's estimates of the hundreds of thousands of birth defects and embryonic and neo-natal deaths likely if tests were continued. The steps toward peace include the abolition of nuclear tests, the solving of differences without the threat of war, complete disarmament of nuclear weapons and a reduction of conventional forces, appointment of a Conciliation Committee with representatives from the powers and neutrals, the prohibition of foreign troops on any territory, and the establishment of a Federal International Authority with armed force to prevent war. Russell cautioned that the armed force should be in units of mixed nationalities and under the command of officers from neutral countries. A federal constitution would leave the nations autonomous in regard to their own internal affairs. The international court must have the same authority as national courts. To those who fear the tyranny of a world government, Russell responded that there would be more real freedom in the world under effective law and that in large modern governments it is fairly easy to maintain civilian control over the military. Technical advances have not only made international anarchy infinitely more dangerous, but also the facility of world cooperation is now more available. Eventually, for the sake of a stable world, greater economic equality and opportunity must be granted to the poorer peoples of the world. Education ought to be global in scope and perspective. Also the increase of population must be brought under control. Peace movements in every country ought to work together in spite of minor differences.

At the age of 88 Russell came to believe that a more radical strategy was needed, and he resigned from the CND to plan actions of civil disobedience through the Committee of 100. A sit-down demonstration took place at a US Polaris Base in which 20,000 people attended a rally and 5,000 sat down and risked arrest. On August 6, 1961 ("Hiroshima Day") they met at Hyde Park, and Russell illegally used a microphone. He was arrested and convicted of inciting the public to civil disobedience; his sentence was commuted to one week. Russell wrote eloquent leaflets and gave speeches for these and other demonstrations urging that the seriousness of nuclear peril justified nonviolent civil disobedience against the offending governments which are "organizing the massacre of the whole of mankind."

In October and November of 1962 Bertrand Russell acted as a peacemaker in two very serious international crises, even though he was only a private citizen. When President Kennedy ordered the naval blockade of Cuba to stop any Russian ship from carrying missiles to the island, Russell issued a press statement, which began, "It seems likely that within a week you will all be dead to please American madmen."[5] Russell hoped there would be large demonstrations of protest, and he noted that the most impressive was in New York, where Michael Scott and A. J. Muste spoke to ten thousand. On October 23 Russell sent a telegram to Kennedy, calling his action "desperate" and a "threat to human survival" without justification and pleading that he end the madness. To Khrushchev he telegraphed an appeal that he not be provoked but seek condemnation of US action through the United Nations. On the next day Premier Khrushchev publicized a long letter in reply to Mr. Russell assuring him that the Soviet government would not be reckless as the Americans had been in their pre-election excitement. Russell then telegraphed Khrushchev thanking him for his "courageous stand for sanity" and asking him to hold back the ships so that the Americans could come to an agreement. He also telegraphed Kennedy to urge him to negotiate.

Khrushchev ordered some ships to turn away and allowed others to be inspected; Russell praised the Soviet Premier for this magnanimous, unilateral act. In another press statement Russell argued that the US blockade was illegal and immoral even though he believed nuclear bases to be intolerable in Cuba or anywhere. How would America respond if the Russians or Chinese blockaded Formosa? Khrushchev offered to dismantle the nuclear bases in Cuba if the United States would guarantee that it would not invade Cuba. This Cuban fear was obviously valid, since the US had already tried to invade once at the Bay of Pigs. When Kennedy cabled Russell about the "secret Soviet missiles" and the Russian "burglars," Russell pointed out that they had not been secret, that even if they had been long-range, which they were not, the US and USSR already had enough long-range missiles and submarines to destroy each other, and that the Russians were not burglars any more than Americans in Britain and western

Europe; actually the Americans were contemplating "burglary."

Russell wired Kennedy, asking him to accept inspection by the United Nations and to remove US missiles in Turkey as an exchange. This would show America's stand for peace. He cabled Dr. Castro, requesting that he accept the dismantling and UN inspection in exchange for the pledge not to be invaded. Russell sent a long letter to Khrushchev, suggesting further steps toward peace, such as the abandonment of the Warsaw Pact. He telegraphed UN Secretary General U Thant, asking him if he would arbitrate and inspect bases. Castro wanted U Thant to mediate in Cuba, but the US refused to discuss the Guantanamo base or accept UN inspectors of Florida camps. In the face of US intransigence to trading bases in Turkey, Russell telegraphed Castro and Khrushchev, urging them to dismantle the bases, since even the insane American blackmail is preferable to catastrophe. Although he was no lover of Communism, in this instance Russell commended Khrushchev for his wisdom and courage but criticized Kennedy for violating the UN Charter and perverting the Monroe Doctrine into the idea that if the US does not like the form of government of a western hemisphere state and is threatening to attack it, then no outside power ought to try to help it.

In November 1962 Russell was similarly involved in mediating the border dispute between China and India in Kashmir. In numerous telegrams to Nehru and Zhou Enlai, Russell urged a cease-fire and withdrawal so that negotiation and arbitration could settle the conflict. He also urged President Sukarno of Indonesia and U Thant to help mediate. In this situation India, which as a neutral nation, had so often pleaded for peaceful relations, seemed to be overcome by war hysteria, and thus Russell found that the nation for which he had the most sympathy again was being the most unreasonable. This time Zhou Enlai exercised wisdom and thanked Russell for his peacemaking efforts.

Reflecting on these two crises, Russell reiterated the danger of brinkmanship and the need for nuclear disarmament, since nuclear weapons only offer the options of complete submission or annihilation. The value of an unarmed and reasonable mediator made it easier for Khrushchev and others to make concessions without damaging their pride as much. Russell hoped that these crises might help discredit the western belief that all Communists are wicked and all anti-Communists are virtuous. These situations and many others indicate the need for world government and strong international law so that disputes can be peacefully decided in courts.

The Bertrand Russell Peace Foundation was formed in 1963. He worked to free political prisoners in over forty countries. Russell began publishing articles criticizing the unofficial war in Vietnam. He explained how the French, Japanese, British, and Americans had prevented the Vietnamese people from obtaining their independence for the sake of imperialism and capitalistic exploitation. He described the atrocities that had been perpetrated by puppet governments of the west and American "advisors." By mid-1963 there were already about 160,000 dead, 700,000 tortured and injured, 400,000 imprisoned, 31,000 raped, and 1,000 temples destroyed; 46 villages had been attacked with poisonous chemicals, and 8,000,000 villagers were in 6,000 concentration camps. He felt the time for protest was overdue. By 1965 the numbers had increased and in a speech criticizing the British Labor Party's foreign policy, Russell tore up his Labor Party membership card. He complained that visas the Peace Foundation had requested for three members of the National Liberation Front (NLF) had been refused.

In January 1966 Bertrand Russell wrote "Peace Through Resistance to US Imperialism," in which he warned that peace could not be obtained merely by requesting the United States to behave better, because a powerful system is based on continued exploitation and an increasing scale of military production. He suggested,

A united and co-ordinate resistance
to this exploitation and domination must be forged.
The popular struggle of oppressed people will remove
the resources from the control of US imperialism
and in so doing,
strengthen the people of the United States itself,
who are striving first to understand
and second to overcome the cruel rulers
who have usurped their revolution and their government.
This, in my view, is the way to create a secure peace,
rather than a tenuous and immoral
acquiescence in US domination,
which can neither work nor be tolerated by humane men.[6]

Russell backed up his vituperative criticism of US policies with numerous facts and figures. He gave four reasons
why the United States must be compelled to withdraw
from Vietnam. First, the US war crimes in Vietnam had
been amply documented. Second, the US had no right to be
there; only a puppet ruler and a few ambitious Vietnamese
generals wanted them there. Third, US claims of "halting
aggression" were absurd since the Geneva agreements had
arranged for unification of Vietnam through election,
which the US had blocked. Fourth, the US must not be
encouraged to think that aggression pays. On May 24, 1966
Bertrand Russell spoke over NLF radio to American
soldiers to explain to them the injustice of their involvement. Since the US was continuing to drop three million
pounds of bombs daily on North Vietnam, Russell called
for an international War Crimes Tribunal in keeping with
the principles of the Nuremberg trials. The Tribunal
convened in November 1966 to announce that it would
prepare evidence of crimes in the following five areas:

1) aggression violating international treaties;
2) using gas and chemicals as experimental
   weapons;
3) bombing hospitals, sanatoria, schools, dikes and
   other civilian areas;

4) torturing and mutilating prisoners;
5) pursuing genocidal policies, such as forced labor
   camps, mass burials, and other techniques of
   extermination in South Vietnam.

Distinguished individuals from various countries agreed to join the Tribunal. The War Crimes Tribunal met in Sweden and Denmark and became independent of the Bertrand Russell Peace Foundation. The proceedings of the Tribunal were published in *Against the Crime of Silence,* and in the introduction Russell wrote

War crimes are the actions of powers
whose arrogance leads them to believe
that they are above the law.
Might, they argue, is right.
The world needs to establish and apply certain criteria
in considering inhuman actions by great powers.
These should not be the criteria convenient to the victor,
as at Nuremberg, but those which enable
private citizens to make compelling judgments
on the injustices committed by any great power.[7]

Russell was now 95. He continued to work for peace to the end, and his last political statement was a condemnation of Israel's aggression sent to the International Conference of Parliamentarians in Cairo in February 1970.

Nonviolent Activism of A. J. Muste

Abraham Johannes Muste was born in Zeeland of the Netherlands on January 8, 1885; his family brought him to the United States at the age of six and raised him in Michigan as a Calvinist. He graduated from Union Theological Seminary in New York in 1909 and married that year. He was ordained a minister, but during World War I his pacifist convictions and ideas led to his resignation.

Moving to Boston in 1918, Muste formed a Comradeship of pacifists and began to observe the labor situation at the Lawrence textile mills. He felt that during the war the pacifists had not risked their lives, but the strike was an opportunity to see if nonviolence really works. Muste raised money for the strikers and was soon made the executive secretary of the strike committee for 30,000 strikers. A. J. placed himself at the head of the picket line and was beat to exhaustion by the police and arrested. Several weeks into the strike, the police tried to provoke violence by lining up machine guns and having a labor spy urge the strikers to overcome them. Muste suggested that the strikers take the following courageous action:

> I told them, in line with the strike committee's decision,
> that to permit ourselves to be provoked into violence
> would mean defeating ourselves;
> that our real power was in our solidarity
> and our capacity to endure suffering
> rather than to give up the fight for the right to organize;
> that no one could "weave wool with machine guns;"
> that cheerfulness was better for morale than bitterness
> and that therefore we would smile
> as we passed the machine guns and the police
> on the way from the hall to the picket lines around the mills.
> I told the spies, who were sure to be in the audience,
> to go and tell the police and the mill managements
> that this was our policy.[8]

This speech was greeted by cheers, and they went out, laughing and singing. Later Muste's room was broken into by a strong-arm squad, but he was not there. A colleague of his was taken out into the country, beat terribly, and left senseless in a ditch. After fifteen weeks the workers were weakening. Muste and the leaders successfully urged them to stay out for a week longer, but they decided they would not pressure them after that. Muste was leaving town to report their failure to the union headquarters when he was contacted by management to arrange a settlement granting the strikers' demands.

Muste served as general secretary of the Amalgamated Textile Workers for over two years. Strikes occurred somewhere almost every week. From 1921 to 1933 he was the educational director of Brookwood Labor College. During the Depression he worked with the labor movement, the Unemployed Leagues, the Workers Party, the sit-down strikes, and the forming of the Congress of Industrial Organizations (CIO). Muste helped start the Conference for Progressive Labor Action (CPLA), which offered a radical alternative to the Communist Party. In 1936 he helped organize a strike of the Goodyear Tire workers in Akron, Ohio; this was the first time the sit-in tactic was used in the American labor movement. Also in 1936 A. J. gave up his Trotskyism and returned to Christian pacifism for the rest of his life, saying that God is love, and "Love is the central thing in the universe."[9] Love, he felt, must be carried into every aspect of family life, race relations, labor movement, political activity, and international relations.

In 1940 A. J. Muste published *Non-violence in an Aggressive World* outlining a Christian pacifist approach to revolution in a war-torn world. He described the interrelationships of the three revolutionary reform movements to which he was committed in the fields of religion, economics, and politics—namely Christianity, socialism, and democracy. He urged a pacifist revolution, which will enlighten minds and redirect wills. With unity and solidarity among the workers and using nonviolent methods, Muste predicted there will be less economic and social dislocation than in most revolutions. He criticized the totalitarian repression, terrorism, and conformity of some post-revolutionary regimes, and he called instead for democratic and brotherly life. Although he considered struggling against injustice by any means to be nobler than cowardice, Muste's experience in the labor movement led him to believe that violence was always self-defeating, whether it was resorted to by workers or by employers using open or covert violence or by agents of the state.

The oppressed will make surer and faster progress
if they eschew violence and depend,

as they do mainly depend
in their organizing and strike activities,
on their solidarity, courage,
capacity for suffering and sacrifice,
and on non-cooperation
where injustice becomes extreme.[10]

Instead of using national armies, Muste saw the need for an international police force. A political federation built on fair economic arrangements will be held together by mutual benefits, making armies unnecessary. He pointed out that there is a necessary connection between democracy and nonviolence; when external force is used, freedom is lost. Racism and nationalism, which promote war, are destructive to democracy, corrupting the external and internal relations of a country. Imperialism in foreign policy likewise causes injustice and oppression at home as well as abroad through the "crushing burden of militarism and totalitarian war." Muste advocated unilateral disarmament, pointing out how reluctant people are to fight and kill in a war. How could they be led to slaughter a helpless population? "With much less effort than is required to put a nation on a war-basis, it could be organized to meet, confuse, and rout an invader with nonviolent noncooperation."[11] He concluded that pacifism is based on love and fellowship and treating one's neighbor as oneself; our resources for living this life of love have hardly been tapped at all so far.

In an essay on "The World Task of Pacifism" in 1941 Muste declared that as long as people believe that war is a solution to social problems, then human resources will be devoted to "forging diabolically effective instruments of slaughter and destruction."[12] Once this delusion has been dispelled, then a new order will be built. He noted that Gandhi's campaigns in India were giving the world an example of how nonviolence could be used on a massive scale. In another essay that year Muste suggested the following:

Christian realism would lead us to renounce
war preparation and war as obviously suicidal;
to offer to surrender our own special privileges;
to participate in lowering tariff walls,
in providing access to basic resources
on equitable terms to all peoples;
to spend the billions we shall otherwise squander
on war preparations, and war,
for the economic rehabilitation of Europe and Asia,
for carrying a great "offensive" of food, medicine,
and clothing to the stricken peoples of the world;
and to take our full share of responsibility
for building an effective federal world government.[13]

In 1942 Muste suggested that the United States enter into negotiations with all the nations in the war with the following proposals:

1) The US will help build a federal world government;
2) the US will invest billions for the economic rehabilitation of Europe and Asia;
3) "no attempt shall be made to fasten *sole* war guilt on any nation or group of nations;"
4) subject nations such as India, Philippines, Puerto Rico, Denmark, Norway, France, Belgium, and Holland must be granted full self-determination;
5) "all peoples should be assured of equitable access to markets and to essential raw materials;"
6) to further democracy the US should provide decent housing, adequate medical and hospital service, and equal educational facilities for all its people, "including Negroes and Orientals;"
7) the US must repudiate racism and call on Germany and other countries to do the same; and
8) drastic reduction of armaments by all nations should move all rapidly to an economy of peace.

As early as 1943 Muste recommended the use of nonviolent methods to bring an end to Jim Crow practices of racial discrimination. He was Executive Secretary of the Fellowship of Reconciliation (FOR) from 1940 until 1953, and he influenced civil rights leaders such as James Farmer and Bayard Rustin, who were FOR staff members. In 1942 they founded the Congress of Racial Equality (CORE). Martin Luther King, Jr. and others were also influenced by Muste's nonviolence philosophy and tactics. During the war he gave moral support to conscientious objectors, and in 1947 he sponsored a session of draft-card burning. He responded to Einstein's "Emergency Appeal" in 1946 by urging scientists to become conscientious objectors by refusing to work on military projects. Einstein accepted this view and later said, "Noncooperation in military matters should be an essential moral principle for all true scientists."[14] Muste refused to pay Federal income tax from 1948 on. After the war he completely rejected Communism, but during the McCarthy period Muste spoke out for the civil rights of Communists. He called for the cessation of hostilities in Korea, urged the United Nations to stop acting as a war agency, advocated that the US abandon war and adopt nonviolence, and promoted the spirit of pacifism.

Muste helped organize and participated in many direct action campaigns. In 1955 he joined Dorothy Day and others in refusing to take cover in a New York civil defense drill. On August 7, 1957 he participated in a vigil protesting nuclear weapons tests near Las Vegas, Nevada. The following year he was an advisor in the project of sailing the *Golden Rule* into a bomb-test area. He chaired the "Walk for Peace Committee" which included the American Friends Service Committee (AFSC), the *Catholic Worker*, the Fellowship of Reconciliation, Peacemakers, the War Resisters League (WRL), and the Women's International League for Peace and Freedom (WILPF). For the Committee for Nonviolent Action (CNVA) Muste coordinated the Omaha Action project and was arrested as one of the trespassers at the Mead Missile Base. He considered nuclear war politically irrational, morally indefensible, and a hideous atrocity. Even preparation for such a war is a degradation of mankind. Neither the aims of Communism nor those of Christian democracy can be advanced or even salvaged after a nuclear war. He referred to threatening the obliteration of an enemy people as an extreme mental sickness. The real enemy is war.

In December 1959 Muste traveled to Africa to help coordinate a protest against French nuclear bomb tests in the Sahara. Meanwhile the Peace Walk had gone from San Francisco to Moscow. About 80,000 leaflets were distributed in the Soviet Union; the demonstrators spoke to meetings of several hundred people every night. Muste felt national barriers had been transcended in favor of a common humanity. In 1961 an experimental World Peace Brigade was formed at a conference in Beirut, Lebanon, under the direction of Muste, Michael Scott, and Jayaprakash Narayan. A training center for nonviolent action was established in Dar es Salaam, Tanzania. Muste hoped this was a beginning toward realizing Gandhi's concept of a world peace army *(Shanti sena)*. In the summer of 1962 the World Peace Brigade and others, such as the CNVA, CND, and the Committee of 100, sponsored the voyage of *Everyman III* to Leningrad to protest Soviet nuclear testing.

In the early Vietnam War era Muste was able to help bring together a broad-based coalition of groups to protest. He helped to establish the policy of refusing to accept the co-sponsorship of organizations that support war, military build-up, or violence, although any individual accepting nonviolent discipline could participate. In 1965 over 50,000 people paraded down Fifth Avenue in New York. Again in this war he suggested that the United States withdraw its forces and disarm. To young men facing conscription he always recommended "holy disobedience." In 1966 Muste met with anti-war Buddhist and Catholic leaders in Saigon. In January 1967 he met with Ho Chi Minh in Hanoi to try to find ways to end the war. Muste died seventeen days later. He was honored in New York at the march of the Spring

Mobilization to End the War in Vietnam.

Notes

1. *The Autobiography of Bertrand Russell 1872-1914*, p. 234.
2. *The Autobiography of Bertrand Russell 1914-1944*, p. 24.
3. *Ibid.*, p. 181.
4. Quoted in "Bertrand Russell and the Peace Movement" by Ralph Schoenman in *Bertrand's Russell's Philosophy*, p. 239.
5. *The Life of Bertrand Russell* by Ronald W. Clark, p. 596.6. *War Crimes in Vietnam*, p. 99-100.
7. Quoted in "Bertrand Russell and the Peace Movement: Liberal Consistency of Radical Change?" by Edward F. Sherman in *Bertrand's Russell's Philosophy*, p. 262-263.
8. "Sketches for an Autobiography" in *The Essays of A. J. Muste*, p. 70.
9. "Return to Pacifism" in *The Essays of A. J. Muste*, p. 201.
10. *Non-violence in an Aggressive World* by A. J. Muste, p. 118.11. *Ibid.*, p. 159.
12. "The World Task of Pacifism" in *The Essays of A. J. Muste*, p. 223.
13. "Where Are We Going?" in *The Essays of A. J. Muste*, p. 250.
14. Quoted in *Ban the Bomb: A History of SANE* by Milton Katz, p. 8.

7

Clark-Sohn Plan
for World Law and Disarmament

What can fairly be called peace
is the result only of enforceable law;
under modern conditions,
general disarmament is the precondition
of enforceable world law.
Grenville Clark

The proposition "no peace without law"
also embodies the conception that
peace cannot be ensured by a continued arms race,
nor by an indefinite "balance of terror,"
nor by diplomatic maneuver,
but only by universal and complete national disarmament
together with the establishment of institutions
corresponding in the world field
to those which maintain law and order
within local communities and nations.
Clark and Sohn

Either world problems will be settled
through real world organization, meaning world law,
or they will be settled by world war.
Norman Cousins

Nuclear Weapons and World Government

In 1913 the prophetic H. G. Wells wrote the novel *The World Set Free* in which he described a war that was fought with "atomic bombs." This war was so catastrophic that the survivors initiated a world government to end the war and use science for beneficial purposes. Nuclear physicist Leo Szilard read this book in 1932 and could not forget it. Four years later he realized that nuclear fission was so dangerous that scientists must work together to prevent a disaster. After conducting an experiment proving fission in

1939, Szilard urged his colleagues to be careful not to let the Nazis become aware of this. In September 1942 Szilard warned in a memo,

We cannot have peace in a world in which
various sovereign nations have atomic bombs
in the possession of their armies
and any of these armies could win a war
within twenty-four hours after it starts one.[1]

By early 1945 Szilard realized that Germany was losing the war and that the only likely use of the atomic bomb would be offensively against Japan. On March 25 Albert Einstein gave Szilard a letter of introduction so that he could meet with President Roosevelt. In his memo Szilard cautioned that using atomic bombs would "precipitate a race in the production of these devices between the United States and Russia."[2] After Roosevelt died, President Truman had his new Secretary of State, James F. Byrnes, meet with Szilard. Byrnes argued that using the bomb would justify the great expense of the Manhattan Project and that it would make it easier to manage the Russians in eastern Europe. General Groves assured Byrnes that the Russians did not have uranium, though Szilard tried to contradict this. In June 1945 Szilard met with the Committee on Social and Political Implications of Atomic Energy, and their report written by Eugene Rabinowitch and Szilard argued against using the bomb in combat against Japan, warning,

If the United States were to be the first to release
this new weapon of indiscriminate destruction upon mankind,
she would sacrifice public support throughout the world,
precipitate the race of armaments,
and prejudice the possibility of reaching
an international agreement on the future control
of such weapons.[3]

They recommended demonstrating the weapon in an

uninhabited area. However, Secretary of War Henry Stimson told his assistant John J. McCloy that the bomb would help the US regain the lead from the Soviet Union, and he was intent on using it for military victory and to enhance postwar power.

In July Szilard circulated a petition that collected 68 signatures of scientists, mostly from the Chicago Metallurgical Laboratory. A more moderate petition to warn the Japanese was supported by 67 scientists at the Oak Ridge Lab in Tennessee. General Groves kept the petitions for a week and gave them to Stimson on the first of August, but he did not show them to President Truman until after the bombs were dropped. On August 6 the first uranium bomb killed about 100,000 people in Hiroshima immediately, and nearly that many would die later from burns and radiation sickness. Three days later the first plutonium bomb killed about 75,000 people in Nagasaki, and again about that many would die later.

This experience resulted in millions of Japanese becoming critics of military force and especially nuclear weapons. Several hundred thousand people joined the War Resisters International (WRI) that had been founded after the First World War, while many religious people became members of the International Fellowship of Reconciliation (IFOR) that had been initiated in 1913 by Quaker Henry Hodgkin and German pastor Friedrich Siegmund-Schultze, who was arrested 27 times during the First World War and was in exile during the Second. The first annual Memorial Day was held at Hiroshima on August 6, 1946. A campaign to make August 6 World Peace Day spread around the world. Norman Cousins returned from the 1949 memorial ceremony with a peace petition signed by 110,000 Hiroshima residents, but President Truman refused to accept it. The US military was still occupying Japan when the Soviet Union exploded its first atomic weapon on August 29, 1949, and they made sure that news was censored from Japanese newspapers. They also tried to suppress Japanese post-war novels such as *City of Corpses* by Yoko Ota and *Summer Flower* by Tamiki Hara. John Hersey's powerful novel *Hiroshima* was published in 1946, but it was not allowed into Japan until the Authors' League of America protested in 1949. On September 1, 1951 in Tokyo 20,000 people gathered for a peace rally.

H. G. Wells had also portrayed the need for world government in his 1933 novel, *The Shape of Things to Come*, which was made into a successful film with Raymond Massey in 1936. Republican Wendell Wilkie, who had lost the presidential election in 1940 to Roosevelt, published *One World* in 1943; this book was serialized in a hundred newspapers and sold two million copies in two years. Perhaps the most effective advocacy of world government was *The Anatomy of Peace* by Emery Reves that came out in June 1945 and was translated into twenty languages by 1950. Soon after the Hiroshima bomb exploded, Norman Cousins wrote his famous editorial for *Saturday Review* that "modern man is obsolete," arguing that the need for world government could no longer be ignored. By 1949 the United World Federalists (UWF) had 720 chapters in the US with 46,775 members.

By early 1946 the new Federation of American Scientists (FAS) had 3,000 members, and Rabinowitch started the *Bulletin of Atomic Scientists* with its "doomsday clock," which they set at seven minutes to midnight and still revise periodically. The FAS published the book *One World or None*, which included articles by Einstein, Bohr, Urey, Bethe, Oppenheimer, and Szilard. They supported the Baruch Plan for the international control of atomic weapons, but this effort failed. When President Truman announced in February 1950 a program to develop the hydrogen bomb, the FAS warned that the Russians would build them too. On November 1, 1952 the United States tested a thermonuclear device (H-bomb) that was a thousand times more powerful than an atomic bomb. Less than a year later the Soviet Union tested their first hydrogen bomb. The Communists around the world supported the World Peace Council (WPC); but in most countries it had little influence over non-Communists because the WPC refused to criticize the policies of the Soviet Union.

Many philosophers and proponents of world peace have expressed ideas similar to the credo of the World Federalists, that world peace depends upon world justice, which depends upon enforceable world law, which depends upon world government. Probably the most discussed plan for effective world law is the comprehensive proposal to strengthen the United Nations delineated by Grenville Clark and Louis B. Sohn in their book *World Peace Through World Law.*

Grenville Clark's Peace Plan

Grenville Clark graduated from Harvard Law School in 1906. Foreseeing the likelihood of American involvement in the First World War, he put forward the "Plattsburgh Idea," which led to the recruitment of 60,000 line officers between 1915 and 1917. During the First World War he served in the United States Army. He supported the New Deal, helping to draft the Economy Act of 1933. Yet he opposed FDR's scheme to pack the US Supreme Court in 1937.

At the beginning of World War II when the Nazis had occupied Norway, Clark initiated the Selective Service Act of 1940 to prepare the US for the war. He served as a consultant to Secretary of War Stimson for the next four years. He was aware of the A-bomb development, but in June 1944 he left that position "in order to devote myself to efforts to prevent future wars, the appalling results of which on the assumption of nuclear weapons were already apparent in 1944."[4] He wrote a letter to the *New York Times* that was published on October 14, 1944 in which he criticized the Dumbarton Oaks proposals for repeating the basic errors of the League of Nations. He complained that by giving each nation only one vote in the General Assembly it was bound to be only a subordinate organ because it would not be fair to the large nations. When Bernard Baruch proposed on June 12, 1946 that the United States transfer its monopoly on nuclear weapons to an international authority, Clark strongly supported the idea.

In 1950 Clark published *A Plan for Peace*, asserting that disarmament of all arms by all nations is the only real hope for enduring peace, and this "disarmament must be supported by institutions of world law through a world federation of universal membership."[5] He recommended a federal structure in which all powers, not expressly delegated to war prevention, be reserved to the nations and their peoples. In the promotion of economic and social welfare the powers of United Nations agencies to *inquire* and *recommend* should be strengthened. Written from an American perspective, Clark's plan was submitted to the United States Congress. Five essential points of the plan are to:

1) encourage discussion of the shocking implications of a third world war;
2) recognize that complete disarmament is necessary to a stable and peaceful world, and that disarmament requires effective world law and government;
3) urge the United States to explore proposals for disarmament and revision of the United Nations;
4) maintain military resistance to Communist expansion while working toward an overall settlement; and
5) realize that executive officials need new ideas from the people and help from Congress.

Clark explained why the "peace by strength" doctrine of deterrence is so insecure and leads to a continuous arms race. In deterring Russia the United States had also alarmed her, resulting in a vicious circle in which each side accused the other of aggression and imperialism, while each increased its armaments, engendering more suspicion and fear, and thus more armaments, etc. A Pax Americana achieved through conquest, like the Pax Romana, could never last. A constructive plan for general disarmament and enforceable world law is needed.

Clark faced the obstacles to his plan and also looked at the counter forces working in its favor. The nations' reluctance to modify their claims to unlimited sovereignty is a major problem. People must overcome their fear of "foreigners" and develop a world consciousness. Conflicts of religion, particularly between Christians and Communists, could be a stumbling block, but with some tolerance it should not prevent a solution. Recriminations between the east and west were a great psychological handicap, but this atmosphere could be improved with effort. Pessimism that such a new system could ever be instituted in a short time could be a negative self-fulfilling prophecy; but again, working for a realistic solution could dissolve that attitude. Skepticism about the Russians' willingness to negotiate in reasonable terms is a common attitude in America. Yet a plan that is in everyone's interest would be beneficial to Russians as well as Americans.

Most of the counter forces to these obstacles are steadily increasing in strength. The severity of modern war is becoming worse rapidly. A world war is becoming more likely to be instant mass suicide. Self-interest is enhanced with world order. The crushing economic burden of armaments would be drastically reduced, and the psychological relief could be euphoric. Besides the problem of the superpower rivalry, there is a general need for peace to prevent the various small wars and to use resources to improve the general welfare. The federal principle of government is being understood by more people because of political evolution in various countries and regions. New generations are producing new leaders with new ideas that are more appropriate to our new problems. Clark had great vision, and he prophetically remarked that a crisis often gets worse until the proud opponents look down into the dark abyss that awaits them if they do not change. The closer we get to the brink of disaster, the more likely we are to find a solution.

Clark-Sohn Proposal for World Law

Louis B. Sohn was born in Lwow, Poland the year World War I began. He earned his first law degree at John Casimir University in Lwow. He participated in the San Francisco Conference that established the United Nations, and he was a legal officer in the United Nations Secretariat for two years. In 1951 he joined the faculty at Harvard Law School. He also worked on the Law of the Sea Treaty.

Clark and Sohn collaborated in suggesting a Revised United Nations Charter in their book *World Peace Through World Law,* which was first published in 1958. They refined their ideas in a second, revised edition in 1960. Subsequent revisions in 1966 and 1973 offered an additional alternative to a revised UN Charter by suggesting a new world security and development organization to supplement current UN functions. This discussion will focus on the proposed UN Charter Revision.

The basic premise agreed with President Eisenhower's statement in 1956, "There can be no peace without law."[6] Thus for world peace, enforceable world law is required. By presenting a detailed plan Clark and Sohn hoped to stimulate world-wide discussion of the needed world institutions. World law is essential because of the increasing number and destructive power of modern weapons, because more nations are acquiring nuclear weapons, and because of the resources wasted on the arms race; in 1973 Sohn added the concern about protecting the environment and natural resources. They proposed revising the United Nations because of the UN's established functions and purpose of preventing war. However, they admitted that forming a new institution could also serve the same principles. In fact, in 1962 Clark and Sohn formulated their proposals in the form of a comprehensive Draft Treaty between the US and USSR, which would not require revision of the UN Charter.

The Clark-Sohn Plan is based on these principles. First, genuine peace depends on an effective system of world law which can ensure complete disarmament with institutions to state clearly the law, courts to apply the law, and police to enforce the law. Second, world law must be formulated in a constitution and statutes forbidding nations to use violence, except in self-defense, and must be applicable to all nations and individuals. Third, world judicial tribunals and organs of mediation and conciliation must be established in order to use peaceful means of adjudication instead of violence or the threat of violence in the solving of all international disputes. Fourth, a permanent world police force must be maintained, with careful safeguards against abuse, in order to suppress any violation of the world law that prohibits international violence. Fifth, complete disarmament of all nations must be "accomplished in a simultaneous and proportionate manner by carefully verified stages and subject to a well-organized system of inspection."[7] Sixth, the tremendous disparities in the economic conditions of different regions of the world must be mitigated by world institutions in order to resolve conflicts and instability. Seventh, humanity's common resources and environment must be managed and protected equitably.

Supplementary principles suggested that the world law must apply to all nations and individuals, and nearly all nations must be participating actively in the institutions. Also, the basic rights and duties of all nations should be clearly defined in the constitutional document with the world body's powers limited primarily to the area of war prevention, while all other powers are reserved to the nations and their peoples.

Now let us briefly outline the features of the Clark-Sohn Plan for a Revised Charter of the United Nations. For the plan to go into effect, nearly every major nation must agree to become a member. Every independent state in the world would be eligible for membership, and ratification would require at least five-sixths of all nations, nations combining at least five-sixths of the world population, plus all four of the largest nations and at least six of the ten next largest nations in population. The few remaining nonmember nations would be required to comply with the disarmament plan and world law.

Voting in the General Assembly would be adjusted according to a nation's population, and the Assembly would be given adequate powers to maintain peace and enforce the disarmament process. The 1973 Clark-Sohn voting proposal suggested the following: the four largest nations would have thirty representatives each; the next ten largest nations would have twelve each; the next fifteen nations would have eight each; the next twenty nations six each; the next thirty nations four each; the next forty nations three each; and the smallest nations, those with under one million inhabitants, would have one representative each. This particular scheme of weighted voting is perhaps one of the weakest elements of their plan, but they admit that they are not dogmatic about its specifics. Certainly, if the General Assembly is going to be given greater powers, some system which takes into account the population differences among nations must be devised. Clark and Sohn suggested stages eventually leading to the election of representatives by popular vote, although at first some nations would probably insist on choosing them in their national legislatures.

An Executive Council would replace the Security Council, and the veto power would be abolished. The four largest nations (China, India, USSR, and US) would be permanent members. Five of the next ten largest nations would alternate with the other five as members, and the remaining eight members would be chosen by the Assembly. "Important" matters would require a vote of twelve of the seventeen members, a majority of the nine larger nations, and a majority of the eight other members. The Economic and Social Council and the Trusteeship Council would be continued and enlarged for greater responsibilities subject to the General Assembly.

Disarmament is carefully worked out by Clark and Sohn to eliminate national military forces in a step-by-step process. Complete disarmament down to the level of local police is required because of the destructive power of modern weapons. Even a small number of nuclear weapons or biological and chemical weapons would leave the world very insecure, and they would make it difficult for the world police force to deter or suppress international violence. Besides, nations would not need armies if the world police force is protecting every nation and their people from international aggression. Each nation would need only enough police forces and weapons to quell internal disruptions and the violence of criminals.

The original Clark-Sohn Plan scheduled the verified disarmament process over twelve years, but the Draft Treaty cut that time in half. Nevertheless, the process was essentially the same. The first two years (or one in the Draft Treaty) would stop further military build-up, establish the UN Inspection Service to make a detailed arms census for every nation, and allow time to verify those facts. Then each nation would disarm ten percent of their forces each year (or six months) for the next ten years (or five years). Each step would be carefully verified by the Inspection Service, and if necessary the process would be delayed until compliance was achieved. A Nuclear Energy Authority would become responsible for all nuclear materials. An Outer Space Agency would also be created to ensure the peaceful use of space. Some of the national armaments would be given to the UN Peace Force, which would come up to its full strength by the end of the disarmament process. Every nation in the world would be bound by the disarmament and at its conclusion would be reduced to lightly armed police.

A World Police Force would be the only military force permitted in the world, once disarmament was completed. Clark and Sohn devised various safeguards to prevent any nation from taking control of the World Force. Thus major roles are given to people from the smaller countries. This force would be under the direction of the General Assembly and would have between 200,000 and 400,000 professional soldiers, drawn mostly from the smaller nations. No more than three percent of the force could be from any one nation, and the forces would be scattered around the globe in various regions with no permanent military bases in any of the larger countries. A Peace Force Reserve would have between 300,000 and 600,000 volunteers on call in case of an emergency. The Peace Force would be equipped with the most modern weapons; but biological, chemical, and nuclear weapons would be forbidden. If nuclear weapons somehow were illegally produced and became a threat, the General Assembly could order the Nuclear Energy Authority to release nuclear weapons to the Peace Force. Otherwise nuclear weapons would be forever banned. A Military Staff Committee of five persons drawn from the smaller nations would direct the Peace Force under the civilian authority of the Executive Council and ultimately the General Assembly.

The Revised Charter required every nation to settle all international disputes by peaceful means such as negotiation, inquiry, mediation, conciliation, arbitration, judicial settlement, etc. All nations would be obligated to submit any "legal question," which in the opinion of the General Assembly (or the Executive Council) endangers the peace of the world, to the International Court of Justice for a final and binding decision. Those disputes which are not of a legal nature would be brought to the World Conciliation Board for a voluntary agreement or would be referred to the World Equity Tribunal for a solution, which could be made binding by the General Assembly. The International Court of Justice would have compulsory jurisdiction on all cases submitted to it by the Assembly as well as disputes over treaties, international agreements, and the UN Charter. Individuals responsible for violations of the disarmament provisions could also be prosecuted. A civil police force of less than 10,000 would aid the Inspection Service in detecting such violators.

A World Development Authority would aid the underdeveloped areas of the world in improving their economic conditions in order to alleviate the immense disparities between their circumstances and those of the industrialized nations. A United Nations Ocean Authority would manage the resources of the seas. A UN Environmental Protection Authority would coordinate environmental programs, collect data, and monitor and assess services. As of 1973 Sohn suggested $75 billion for world development, $12 billion for the Peace Forces, and $3 billion for the other agencies. This budget of $90 billion represented less than half of the world's military expenditures for the year 1970. Obviously the world economy would be greatly enhanced by such a plan. They also suggested an over-all limit of three percent of the gross world product for the UN budget. Each nation would be taxed by the General Assembly according to its gross domestic product with a "per capita deduction" for the poorest nations. No nation could be taxed more than four percent of its GDP, and each nation would collect its own taxes for the UN fiscal office in the nation. Once the Revised UN Charter was ratified, no nation would be allowed to withdraw.

A Bill of Rights is annexed to the Revised Charter to protect individual rights such as freedom of religion, communication, assembly and petition, and a fair trial without double jeopardy, *ex post facto* laws, excessive bail, cruel and unusual punishments, unlawful detention, or unreasonable searches and seizures. The many useful organs of the United Nations would be continued, such as the Food and Agriculture Organization (FAO), the United Nations Educational, Scientific and Cultural Organization (UNESCO), the International Labor Organization (ILO), and the World Health Organization (WHO). The purpose of the Clark-Sohn Plan was not to delete any of these useful functions but to strengthen the UN's ability to prevent war by making the General Assembly and Security Council more representative and filling the major lacks of the UN, namely the lack of effective disarmament, the lack of a standing world police force, the lack of a judicial system with compulsory jurisdiction over international disputes, and the lack of a reliable revenue system.

To the obstacles Clark saw in 1950, Sohn added the resistance of the vested interests in armament, both in the military and industry, as well as the vested interests in traditional diplomacy. However, the advanced "delivery systems" of nuclear weapons had made the problem much more urgent. In addition, pollution of the environment is becoming more critical as is the disparity between the developed northern hemisphere and the underdeveloped southern hemisphere.

McCloy-Zorin Disarmament Effort

The year after the Clark-Sohn Plan was first proposed, Soviet Premier Khrushchev visited the United Nations and on September 19, 1959 suggested in a speech that general and complete disarmament could be the best approach to peace. The next day the "Declaration of the Soviet Government on General and Complete Disarmament" was filed with the United Nations. On December 1, 1959 the United States, the Soviet Union, and ten other major countries agreed to the Antarctic Treaty, which banned all weapons and military activities from Antarctica. The next year the two superpowers negotiated reduction of forces and limiting nuclear testing.

Although he had campaigned on an erroneous contention that the United States was behind the Soviets in a "missile gap," President Kennedy fulfilled another campaign pledge to create the US Arms Control and Disarmament Agency; he was greatly aided in this by Republican John McCloy. On September 25, 1961 President Kennedy spoke before the United Nations General Assembly and said, "Mankind must put an end to war—or war will put an end to mankind."[8] The goal of disarmament must no longer be a dream but had become a practical question of life or death; its risks were small compared to the costs of an unlimited arms race. Kennedy presented the American plan and asked that negotiations continue "without interruption until an entire program for general and complete disarmament has not only been agreed but has been actually achieved."[9] He suggested that the logical place to begin was with a test-ban treaty.

In this speech at the UN Kennedy also said that it was not enough to destroy arms, they must also create world-wide law with enforcement as they outlaw world-wide war and weapons, saying, "We prefer world law, in the age of self-determination, to world war, in the age of mass extermination."[10] He suggested that UN machinery be improved to provide for "the peaceful settlement of disputes, for on-the-spot fact-finding, mediation and adjudication, for extending the rule of international law." He concluded that his generation would be remembered either for destroying the planet or for saving future generations from war. Never before did the world have so much to gain and so much to lose. "Together we shall save our planet, or together we shall perish in its flames."[11]

On September 20, 1961 the Soviet Union and the United States issued a "Joint Statement of Agreed Principles for Disarmament Negotiations" known as the McCloy-Zorin Agreement. This agreement declared,

> The United States and the U.S.S.R. have agreed
> to recommend the following principles as the basis
> for future multilateral negotiations on disarmament
> and to call upon other States to cooperate in reaching
> early agreement on general and complete disarmament
> in a peaceful world in accordance with these principles.
>
> 1. The goal of negotiations is to achieve agreement
> on a program which will ensure that
>
> (a) disarmament is general and complete
> and war is no longer an instrument
> for settling international problems, and
>
> (b) such disarmament is accompanied
> by the establishment of reliable procedures
> for the peaceful settlement of disputes
> and effective arrangements for the maintenance of peace

in accordance with the principles
of the United Nations Charter.

2. The program for general and complete disarmament
shall ensure that States will have at their disposal
only such non-nuclear armaments, forces, facilities
and establishments as are agreed to be necessary
to maintain internal order
and protect the personal security of citizens;
and that States shall support and provide agreed manpower
for a United Nations peace force.

3. To this end,
the program for general and complete disarmament
shall contain the necessary provisions,
with respect to the military establishment of every nation,
for:

(a) Disbanding of armed forces,
dismantling of military establishments, including bases,
cessation of the production of armaments
as well as their liquidation or conversion to peaceful uses.

(b) Elimination of all stockpiles of nuclear, chemical,
bacteriological, and other weapons of mass destruction
and cessation of the production of such weapons;

(c) Elimination of all means of delivery
of weapons of mass destruction;

(d) Abolishment of the organization and institutions
designed to organize the military effort of States,
cessation of military training,
and closing of all military training institutions;

(e) Discontinuance of military expdenditures.[12]

The Joint Statement also suggested that disarmament
be implemented in stages with adequate verification for
each stage by effective international control. Soviet Deputy
Foreign Minister Vasily Zorin would not agree on the veri-

fication terms recommended by McCloy because the Soviets suspected they could be used as "legalized espionage." McCloy put the US position on record by including the following statement in a letter the same day to Zorin: "Such verification should ensure that not only agreed limitations or reductions take place but also that retained armed forces and armaments do not exceed agreed levels at any stage."[13] The McCloy-Zorin Statement is considered a high point in disarmament efforts during the Cold War. An 18-nation committee on disarmament was formed in December 1961. The Soviet Union presented a draft treaty for general and complete disarmament on March 15, 1962 and proposed a nuclear-free zone in Europe on March 28. The United States presented their draft treaty for disarmament on April 18, and by August both superpowers were negotiating a draft treaty to present to the 18-nation disarmament committee.

In May 1962 Clark and Sohn recast their proposals as a "Proposed Treaty Establishing a World Disarmament and World Development Organization within the Framework of the United Nations." The US proposal gave the International Court jurisdiction over disputes on the disarmament during the first stage, while the Soviet version did not mention the International Court at all. The Clark-Sohn Plan offered incentives to most people in the world with its development provisions, but the Soviet and US proposals ignored this need. The Soviets were reluctant to give up their veto in the Security Council, and the American proposal was vague on how the UN would enforce disarmament. However, the Clark-Sohn treaty gave the new disarmament organization enforcement authority. The Soviet Treaty would have led to a disarmed world, but it would not have provided a workable system for settling international disputes. The US treaty would have begun to try to deal with international conflicts only after the first stage of disarmament.

Both the US and Soviet plans would have resulted in a balance of national power instead of the world-based enforceable world law of the Clark-Sohn approach. The Clark-Sohn Plan had the advantage of solving unanswered questions prior to agreement and implementation so that confidence in the future could be gained. Obviously none of these proposals were implemented. After the Cuban missile crisis in October 1962, the Soviets decided to catch up with the US in the nuclear arms race.

The Clark-Sohn proposals were presented as a useful basis for discussion of these questions, and they did stimulate much thought. Saul Mendlovitz and Richard Falk used *World Peace Through World Law* as a foundation upon which to build elaborate teaching materials for discussions on world order. The Institute for World Order developed outstanding educational materials from experts around the world in their World Order Models Project (WOMP). Such notables as Herman Kahn and Andrei Sakharov recommended careful study of the Clark-Sohn proposals. As early as 1973 these materials had been studied in about 500 colleges and universities in the United States.

Why have these ideas not yet succeeded? Richard Falk pointed out in a *Study of Future Worlds* that change-oriented groups have not been responsive to law-based appeals, which are at the same time both radical and conservative. Law and order is a conservative approach, while giving up national sovereignty to world institutions is a radical change. Amitai Etzioni in *The Hard Way to Peace* asked what could be done to accelerate the historical processes that would lead to these solutions. He suggested the formation of supranational communities and also economic and political development around the world. Falk and Mendlovitz credited the Clark-Sohn Plan with providing a framework of international law within which the widest possible shaping and sharing of human values could take place.

Notes

1. Quoted in *One World or None: A History of the World Nuclear Disarmament Movement Through 1953* by Lawrence S. Wittner, p. 20.

2. *Ibid.*, p. 24.
3. *Ibid.*, p. 25-26.
4. *Grenville Clark: Public Citizen* by Gerald T. Dunne, p. 141.
5. *A Plan for Peace* by Grenville Clark, p. ix.
6. *World Peace Through World Law* by Grenville Clark and Louis B. Sohn, p. xv.
7. *Ibid.*, p. xvi.
8. *A Thousand Days: John F. Kennedy in the White House* by Arthur M. Schlesinger, Jr., p. 484.
9. *Ibid.*
10. *Kennedy* by Theodore C. Sorensen, p. 521-522.
11. *A Thousand Days: John F. Kennedy in the White House* by Arthur M. Schlesinger, Jr., p. 484.
12. *Documentary History of Arms Control and Disarmament*, p. 470-471.
13. *Ibid.*, p. 469.

8
King and the Civil Rights Movement

True peace is not merely the absence of tension;
it is the presence of justice.
Martin Luther King, Jr., *Stride Toward Freedom*

With nonviolent resistance,
no individual or group need submit to any wrong,
nor need anyone resort to violence in order to right a wrong.
Martin Luther King, Jr.

I submit that an individual who breaks a law
that conscience tells him is unjust,
and who willingly accepts the penalty of imprisonment
in order to arouse the conscience
of the community over its injustice,
is in reality expressing the highest respect for law.
Martin Luther King, Jr., "Letter from Birmingham Jail"

Unearned suffering is redemptive.
Suffering, the nonviolent resister realizes,
has tremendous educational and transforming possibilities.
Martin Luther King, Jr., *Stride Toward Freedom*

Today the choice is no longer
between violence and nonviolence.
It is either nonviolence or nonexistence.
Martin Luther King, Jr., *Stride Toward Freedom*

The aftermath of nonviolence is reconciliation
and the creation of the beloved community,
while the aftermath of violence is tragic bitterness.
Martin Luther King, Jr., *Stride Toward Freedom*

We Mexicans here in the United States,
as well as all other farm laborers,
are engaged in another struggle
for the freedom and dignity which poverty denies us.
But it must not be a violent struggle,

even if violence is used against us.
Cesar Chavez, September 16, 1965

History will judge societies and governments—
and their institutions—not by how big they are
or how well they serve the rich and the powerful,
but by how effectively they respond
to the needs of the poor and the helpless.
Cesar Chavez

NAACP, CORE, and Desegregation

In 1909 William Lloyd Garrison's grandson, Oswald Garrison Villard, wrote a call for a national conference to renew the struggle for civil liberty. Supported by Jane Addams, William Dean Howells, Ida B. Wells, John Dewey, W. E. B. Du Bois, and others, they formed the National Association for the Advancement of Colored People (NAACP). Du Bois became director of publicity and research and begin editing and writing for the *Crisis* magazine. Arthur B. Spingarn led the legal effort and got the grandfather clauses that blocked descendants of non-voters (slaves) from voting declared unconstitutional. By 1921 the NAACP had more than 400 branches in the United States. Howard University law school dean Charles Houston worked for the NAACP and in 1935 launched a campaign to remedy educational inequalities. He was assisted by young Thurgood Marshall and in 1938 argued before the US Supreme Court that Lloyd Lionel Gaines had a right to attend the University of Missouri School of Law.

In 1941 A. Philip Randolph, who was president of the Brotherhood of Sleeping Car Porters, called upon African Americans to march on Washington to demand an end to racial discrimination in government hiring and an end to the segregation in the US armed forces. Randolph and NAACP executive secretary Walter White met with President Franklin Roosevelt before the march, and on June 25 Roosevelt issued an executive order prohibiting racial discrimination in federal hiring and establishing the Fair Employment Practice Committee (FEPC).

In 1942 Bayard Rustin and students led by white George Houser and black James Farmer in the Chicago chapter of the Fellowship of Reconciliation (FOR) formed a committee that later became known as the Congress of Racial Equality (CORE). They and A. J. Muste were strongly influenced by the book *War Without Violence* by Krishnalal Shridharani, a former associate of Gandhi. That year Rustin was beaten and arrested for sitting at the front of buses going from Louisville to Nashville. Asserting the power of love, he stood up to the injustice and found that his nonviolent action was supported by some witnesses. In 1943 CORE activists protested by sitting in segregated Chicago restaurants. In *Morgan v. Virginia* the US Supreme Court in June 1946 declared unconstitutional the Virginia law requiring segregated seating on interstate buses. The next year sixteen people from FOR and CORE undertook a Journey of Reconciliation to test the judgment, and four riders arrested in North Carolina were sentenced to thirty days on a chain gang.

Meanwhile the FEPC was not too effective because it lacked the power to enforce the law, and Congress ended its funding in 1946. In 1944 Swedish sociologist Gunnar Myrdal published a massive study on race relations called *An American Dilemma: The Negro Problem and Modern Democracy*, describing the conflict between the American creed of equal rights with the actual discrimination against Negroes. In December 1946 President Harry Truman appointed a Committee on Civil Rights that filed a scathing report on the crimes of lynching, police brutality, discrimination in public accommodations, and the lack of justice in the courts. They found that "separate but equal" had failed and that the rights to voting and education had not yet been secured. They recommended magnifying the civil rights section in the Justice department, establishing a Commission on Civil Rights under the President, making state and local police forces more professional, and action by Congress to protect voting rights and equal access to employment, education, and public services. In March 1948

Randolph warned President Truman that he would lead a civil disobedience campaign to protest segregation in the military. In July, Truman issued an executive order for equal opportunity in the armed services, and Randolph ended his call for civil disobedience.

Thurgood Marshall became chief counsel for the NAACP in 1940, and in 1946 he set up the NAACP's Legal Defense Fund. At an NAACP conference in New York in 1950 he argued that the "separate but equal" doctrine of *Plessy v. Ferguson* from 1896 was unconstitutional by the 14th amendment because separate schools could not be equal. In 1951 Marshall and NAACP attorneys challenged school segregation in South Carolina, Kansas, and Delaware. On May 17, 1954 the new US chief justice Earl Warren announced a unanimous decision in *Brown v. Board of Education of Topeka* overturning *Plessy v. Ferguson* and accepting the plaintiffs' argument by the NAACP lawyers that segregation has a detrimental effect on colored children, making separate educational facilities inherently unequal. Implementation was delayed by another hearing, but a year later the Supreme Court decided that educational authorities have the primary responsibility to solve these problems and must admit students "on a racially nondiscriminatory basis with all deliberate speed." The first major challenge came in September 1957 when Arkansas governor Orval Faubus used the National Guard to deny nine Negro children admission to Central High School in Little Rock. A district court ordered him to remove the Guard, and he did so; but the black students were assaulted by an angry mob. President Eisenhower then ordered the mob blocking the students to disperse and made a speech announcing that he was sending in a thousand paratroopers to enforce the law by protecting the minority students.

King and the Montgomery Bus Boycott

From 1956 until his tragic assassination in 1968 Martin Luther King, Jr. was the foremost leader in African Americans' nonviolent quest for civil rights and a better life. He was born on January 15, 1929 in Atlanta, Georgia and was named after his father, who was a successful Baptist preacher. His father taught him self-respect in the face of racial discrimination. Martin started at Morehouse College in Atlanta when he was only 15, and he graduated four years later. Choosing the ministry over medicine and law, he attended Crozer Theological Seminary in Pennsylvania for three years. While there he heard A. J. Muste lecture, and after hearing Mordecai Johnson lecture on Gandhi he went out and bought every book he could find on Gandhi and nonviolence. Martin had already read Thoreau's "Essay on Civil Disobedience" at Morehouse; he was so moved by the idea of refusing to cooperate with an evil system that he reread it several times. In his theological studies he leaned toward the social gospel of Walter Rauschenbusch. He read Marx and rejected his materialism and deprecation of individual freedom; however, he also questioned the materialism and injustices of capitalism.

In reading Gandhi, King realized that the love ethic of Jesus could go beyond individuals and be applied to the conflicts of racial groups and nations. He discovered the method for social reform in Gandhi's soul force (*satyagraha*) and nonviolence (*ahimsa*). After being elected student body president and graduating first in his class at Crozer, King moved on to Boston University, where he earned his Ph.D. in Theology. In 1953 he married Coretta Scott, a bright student of music, and they eventually had four children. Believing in the guidance of a personal God and equipped with the techniques of nonviolence, King accepted a pastorate in Montgomery, Alabama, hoping he could help his people achieve social justice.

King had only recently completed his doctoral dissertation and gotten settled in the Dexter Avenue Baptist Church when the issue of racial segregation on the public buses erupted in Montgomery. On May 17, 1954 the United States Supreme Court had declared, "Separate educational facilities are inherently unequal,"[1] and in 1955 the same Court ordered all public schools to be desegregated "with all deliberate speed." In Montgomery, King had become active in the National Association for the Advancement of Colored People (NAACP) and in the integrated Alabama Council on Human Relations. In March 1955 a fifteen-year-old girl had been arrested for refusing to give up her seat to a white passenger on the bus. King was on the committee that protested this, but no action was taken.

On December 1, 1955 Mrs. Rosa Parks felt her feet were too tired for her to stand up for a white man, who had boarded after her. The bus driver ordered her to stand up and give her seat to the white man, but she refused. She was arrested and taken to the courthouse. From there she called E. D. Nixon, who in turn made several calls. The Women's Political Council proposed a one-day boycott of the buses. The next morning, which was a Friday, Nixon called King, and he offered the Dexter Avenue Church as a meeting place for that night. Over forty black leaders showed up, and they agreed to boycott the buses on the following Monday and hold a mass meeting Monday night. Leaflets were mimeographed and distributed announcing these actions. Committees were organized, and alternative transportation was arranged. Recalling Thoreau's words about not cooperating with an evil system, King thought of the movement as massive noncooperation.

The word spread, and on Monday morning the Montgomery buses were practically empty except for a few white passengers. Mrs. Parks was convicted that morning of disobeying the city's segregation ordinance and fined ten dollars and court costs. Her attorney appealed. That afternoon Dr. King was elected president of what became the Montgomery Improvement Association (MIA). The Holt Street Baptist Church had five thousand people standing outside listening to loudspeakers for the evening meeting. King spoke for the hearts of many when he declared that they were "tired of being segregated and humiliated."[2] He affirmed that their only alternative was to protest for

freedom and justice. Christian love and nonviolent principles provided the basis for his advice. No one must be
intimidated to keep them from riding the buses. He said,
"Our method will be that of persuasion, not coercion. We
will only say to the people, 'Let your conscience be your
guide.'"[3] He quoted the statement by Booker T. Washington not to let anyone drag you down so low as to make
you hate him. King concluded his speech,

> If you will protest courageously,
> and yet with dignity and Christian love,
> when the history books are written in future generations,
> the historians will have to pause and say,
> "There lived a great people—a black people—
> who injected new meaning and dignity
> into the veins of civilization."
> This is our challenge and our overwhelming responsibility.[4]

Ralph Abernathy proposed three moderate demands,
which were unanimously approved at the mass meeting:

1) courteous treatment by bus operators;
2) passengers to be seated on a first-come, first-served
   basis with Negroes in the back and whites in the
   front; and
3) Negro bus drivers to be employed in predominantly
   Negro routes.

In his book *Stride Toward Freedom* King explained how
Christian love and nonviolent methods guided the movement and how he spoke in weekly meetings.

> I stressed that the use of violence in our struggle
> would be both impractical and immoral.
> To meet hate with retaliatory hate would do nothing
> but intensify the existence of evil in the universe.
> Hate begets hate; violence begets violence;
> toughness begets a greater toughness.
> We must meet the forces of hate with the power of love;

we must meet physical force with soul force.
Our aim must never be to defeat
or humiliate the white man,
but to win his friendship and understanding.[5]

Although to King nonviolence was a way of life, he was glad that the black people were willing to accept it as a method; he presented it simply as Christianity in action. In *Stride Toward Freedom* King elucidated six key points about the philosophy of nonviolence. First, it is not based on cowardice; although it may seem passive physically, it is spiritually active, requiring the courage to stand up against injustice. Second, nonviolence does not seek to defeat the opponent but rather to win his understanding to create "the beloved community." Third, the attack is directed at the evil, not at the people who are doing the evil; for King the conflict was not between whites and blacks but between justice and injustice. Fourth, in nonviolence there is a willingness to accept suffering without retaliating. Fifth, not only is physical violence avoided but also spiritual violence; love replaces hatred. Sixth, nonviolence has faith that justice will prevail because it is a universal law.

Meanwhile, to get people to work and back, black taxi companies had lowered their fares, car pools were arranged, and many people walked. However, the city prohibited the taxi companies from doing this business and threatened people with vagrancy and illegal-hitchhiking charges; rumors spread that drivers might lose their licenses or insurance. King was arrested in January for driving 30 in a 25 mile-per-hour zone, even though he was driving very carefully since he was aware of being followed. The Kings' house was bombed; Coretta and a friend escaped injury by moving quickly to the back of the house. Martin rushed home from his meeting, and a furious mob gathered outside. He calmed them down and advised them to put down their weapons and go home. He said, "We cannot solve this problem through retaliatory violence. We must meet violence with nonviolence.... We must love our white brothers no matter what they do to us."[6] When the mayor tried to speak, he was booed and threatened; but again King quieted the crowd. His presence and words had prevented a bloody riot. The Kings often received threatening phone calls; but even after the bomb blast, King would not allow a weapon in his house.

While King was away lecturing at Fisk University in Nashville, the Montgomery attorney began arresting MIA leaders for violating an old state law against boycotts. Against the advice of his father, Martin returned to Montgomery to be placed under arrest. He was released on bail. On March 22 Judge Carter found eighty-nine defendants guilty. King was sentenced to pay a fine of $500 or serve 386 days hard labor. Appeals were filed. On June 4, 1956 a federal court held that bus segregation was unconstitutional. However, the city attorneys appealed to the United States Supreme Court. In November the city tried to ban the car pools. While they were in a Montgomery court on this charge, the Supreme Court affirmed the decision declaring Alabama's state and local laws requiring segregation on buses unconstitutional.

Rev. King told a mass meeting that they must act with "calm dignity and wise restraint" and not let their emotions run wild. He said, "We must now move from protest to reconciliation."[7] Meetings were held to prepare the people for integration of the buses. Training sessions in nonviolent techniques enabled "actors" to play out different roles before a critical audience, which would discuss the results. Integrated bus suggestions were printed which recommended "complete nonviolence in word and action" and admonished them to be loving enough to absorb evil and understanding enough to convert an enemy into a friend. A few days before Christmas, after more than a year's boycott, the black ministers of Montgomery led the way in riding integrated buses. In January a few acts of terrorism by the Ku Klux Klan occurred, but again King urged nonviolence and the way of the cross. After a few weeks the transportation systems had returned to normal with integrated buses.

King and SCLC Campaigns

The Montgomery success gave King national prominence. Along with Ralph Abernathy, Fred Shuttlesworth, and C. K. Steele, he formed the Southern Christian Leadership Conference (SCLC) with headquarters in Atlanta. He urged President Eisenhower to call for a White House Conference on Civil Rights. When the Eisenhower administration failed to respond adequately, King organized a "Prayer Pilgrimage of Freedom" which drew 37,000 marchers to the Lincoln Memorial in Washington on May 17, 1957. King led the cry of blacks for the ballot so that they could participate more fully in the legislative process.

In 1958 *Stride Toward Freedom* came out calling for a militant and nonviolent mass movement. King suggested in this book that if they remain nonviolent, then public opinion will be magnetically attracted to them rather than to the instigators of violence. A nonviolent mass movement is power under discipline seeking justice. He summarized his nonviolent intentions this way:

We will take direct action against injustice
without waiting for other agencies to act.
We will not obey unjust laws or submit to unjust practices.
We will do this peacefully, openly, cheerfully
because our aim is to persuade.
We adopt the means of nonviolence
because our end is a community at peace with itself.
We will try to persuade with our words,
but if our words fail, we will try to persuade with our acts.
We will always be willing to talk and seek fair compromise,
but we are ready to suffer when necessary
and even risk our lives
to become witnesses to the truth as we see it.[8]

He pointed out that nonviolence first affects the hearts of those committed to it, gives them greater self-respect and courage, and then it stirs the conscience of the opponents until reconciliation is achieved. He warned against using power to oppress others.

In an effort to achieve freedom in America, Asia, and Africa
we must not try to leap from a position of disadvantage
to one of advantage, thus subverting justice.
We must seek democracy
and not the substitution of one tyranny for another.
Our aim must never be to defeat
or humiliate the white man.
We must not become victimized
with a philosophy of black supremacy.
God is not interested merely in the freedom
of black men, and brown men, and yellow men;
God is interested in the freedom of the whole human race.[9]

King suggested, "The constructive program ahead must include a campaign to get Negroes to register and vote."[10] He also warned that in a world of ballistic missiles the choice was no longer between violence and nonviolence but between nonviolence and nonexistence.

On Lincoln's birthday in 1958 twenty-one mass meetings were held simultaneously in key southern cities calling for "freedom now." In September, King was arbitrarily arrested while in the Montgomery courthouse. He decided to refuse to pay bail or the fine. However, the officials preferred to pay his fine for him so that the taxpayers would not have to feed King for fourteen days.

While autographing copies of his book in New York, a psychotic woman stabbed King in the chest with a sharp letter opener. He remained calm and waited for a surgeon to remove the knife-like weapon. Its point had been touching his aorta; he was told that if he had merely sneezed, he probably would have died.

In February 1959 Martin Luther King made a pilgrimage to India and returned even more confirmed in the principles of nonviolence. In December, King called for a broad and bold progress in the southern campaign for equality. In 1960 student activists organized numerous sit-ins at lunch counters in order to end discrimination. King and James Lawson spoke on nonviolence at a meeting in Raleigh, North Carolina, and the Student Nonviolent Coordinating Committee (SNCC) was formed. King and thirty-six others were arrested for sitting at the lunch counter in Rich's Department Store in Atlanta. The judge sentenced King to six months hard labor. This was on October 25, and the election was only a few days away. President Eisenhower considered making a public statement, but he and Vice President Nixon decided not to comment. However, John Kennedy and his brother Robert made some phone calls urging King's release. Some say that this gesture helped Kennedy win the election over Nixon by a narrow margin.

King was elected chairman of the committee on the Freedom Rides in 1961. To protect the freedom riders from the onslaught of violence, King requested Attorney General Robert Kennedy to send more federal marshals. King explained, "The law may not be able to make a man love me, but it can keep him from lynching me."[11] The Freedom Rides took the civil rights movement from the urban college campuses to the rural hamlets of the South.

King answered the call to help the movement in Albany, Georgia to desegregate public parks and other facilities. He and Ralph Abernathy were arrested in December 1961 for refusing to disperse. They were tried the following February and sentenced on July 10, 1962 to pay a fine or be imprisoned at hard labor for 45 days. They chose prison. Again an anonymous person paid the fines. King then announced a civil disobedience campaign. However, when two thousand people threw rocks and bottles at the police, he called for a "Day of Penitence" and a week of prayer vigils. King, Abernathy, and Dr. Anderson were arrested at the first vigil. They spent two weeks in jail before the trial and then were given suspended sentences. A new demonstration was planned after their release, but this time the city obtained a federal injunction against the demonstration. Since the federal courts had always been their ally, King reluctantly canceled the march. Many considered the Albany campaign a failure because it did not achieve desegregation; but King felt they learned tactical lessons and through increased voter registration began to affect elections more. Five percent of the black population had accepted nonviolence and had gone willingly to jail.

Fred Shuttlesworth of the Alabama Christian Movement for Human Rights had been working to desegregate Birmingham, but he was meeting much resistance. He requested the help of the SCLC, and in April 1963 after the elections involving Eugene "Bull" Connor, they acted. Their organization had improved since Albany, and workshops on nonviolence and direct-action techniques were conducted. They began with sit-ins involving a few arrests each day. Mass meetings with talks on nonviolence were held each evening. Many volunteers came forward, and the movement grew into a nonviolent army. Each volunteer signed the following Commitment Card:

I hereby pledge myself—my person and body—
   to the nonviolent movement.
Therefore, I will keep the following Ten Commandments:
1. Meditate daily on the teachings and life of Jesus.
2. Remember always that the nonviolent movement
   in Birmingham seeks justice and reconciliation, not victory.
3. Walk and Talk in the manner of love, for God is love.
4. Pray daily to be used by God
   in order that all men might be free.
5. Sacrifice personal wishes
   in order that all men might be free.
6. Observe with both friend and foe
   the ordinary rules of courtesy.
7. Seek to perform regular service for others
   and for the world.
8. Refrain from the violence of fist, tongue, or heart.
9. Strive to be in good spiritual and bodily health.
10. Follow the directions of the movement
   and of the captain on a demonstration.[12]

King chose to postpone his own arrest so that he could speak to meetings in the black community; he appealed to ministers for help in the struggle to improve social condi-

tions. On Saturday April 6, forty-two were arrested for
"parading without a permit." So far both sides were nonviolent, and they sang on their way to jail. The boycott of the
downtown merchants was effective. There were kneel-ins
at churches, sit-ins at the library, and a march to the county
building for voter registration; the jails began to fill. They
decided to disobey a state court injunction because they felt
Alabama was misusing the judicial process. Although most
of the leaders wanted King to stay free in order to raise
money, he asked Ralph Abernathy to go to jail with him.
On Good Friday they were arrested, and King was put in
solitary confinement. Coretta contacted President Kennedy
to request help in improving King's jail conditions, and
Harry Belafonte was able to raise $50,000 for bail bonds.

On scraps of paper Martin Luther King wrote his
famous letter from Birmingham jail in which he responded
to ministers' public charges that his actions were "unwise
and untimely." He explained that he came to Birmingham
because of the injustice there. They had gone through the
four basic steps of a nonviolent campaign: collection of
facts about injustice, negotiation, self-purification, and
direct action. Just as Socrates had been an intellectual
gadfly, he too must struggle against injustice. He stated the
hard truth, "We know through painful experience that
freedom is never voluntarily given by the oppressor; it
must be demanded by the oppressed."[13] He quoted Augustine, who said that "an unjust law is no law at all."[14] Segregation is unjust because it damages the personality and
creates false concepts of superiority and inferiority. To
break an unjust law "openly, lovingly, and with a willingness to accept the penalty"[15] is to express respect for real
justice. He pointed out that what Hitler did in Germany
was "legal," while aiding or comforting a Jew was "illegal."
Their action did not create the tension; it merely brought to
the surface the seething hidden tensions. Nonviolence
offers a creative outlet for repressed emotions which might
otherwise result in violence. He said that if he is an
extremist, then like Jesus he is an extremist for love.

After eight days King and Abernathy accepted bail. King then suggested that they enlist young people in the campaign. Andy Young sent some who were too young to the library to learn something. On May 2 over a thousand youths demonstrated and went to jail. King explained in his book *Why We Can't Wait* that all ages, sexes, races, and even the disabled can be accepted into a nonviolent army. When the jails were almost full, Bull Connor changed his tactics to violence, turning on the water hoses, sending in police with their clubs, and releasing the police dogs. Moral indignation swept across the nation. On May 4 the US Attorney General sent mediators to seek a truce. On May 10 an agreement was reached granting the major demands: desegregation of lunch counters, rest rooms, fitting rooms, and drinking fountains; upgrading and hiring of blacks on a nondiscriminatory basis; release of all jailed persons; and establishing communications between black and white leaders.

Segregationists reacted by bombing the house of Martin's brother A. D. King at midnight on Saturday in order to incite a riot. Followers of the movement sang "We Shall Overcome" to stop the violence. The next day President Kennedy sent in three thousand federal troops. On May 20 the Supreme Court decided that demonstrations against segregated institutions are legal. Justice had triumphed.

King went on a speaking tour from Los Angeles to New York. In Detroit on June 23, 1963 he led 125,000 people on a Freedom Walk. To this crowd he spoke of nonviolence as a strong method of disarming the opponent. He declared, "If a man hasn't discovered something that he will die for, he isn't fit to live!"[16]

At a conference with A. Philip Randolph and Roy Wilkins of the NAACP, John Lewis of SNCC, Dorothy Height of the National Council of Negro Women, James Farmer of CORE, and Whitney Young of the Urban League, they planned a march on Washington for "Jobs and Freedom" in order to put pressure on Congress to pass

President Kennedy's Civil Rights Bill. Some 250,000 people, about a third of them white, congregated at the Lincoln Memorial on August 28, 1963. Randolph introduced King as the "moral leader of the nation." King began with his prepared speech about how America had given the Negro a bad check, and they had come there to collect on the promises. The great crowd's response inspired him, and he put aside his text and began to speak of his dream of equality, brotherhood, and freedom—a dream where people are not judged by their skin color but by their character. His oratory symbolically tolled the bell of freedom so that it would ring out all across the land.

When the assassination of President Kennedy was announced, King privately told Coretta that the same thing would happen to him, because "this is a sick society."[17] The following June, Dr. King and Abernathy were arrested in St. Augustine, Florida. King explained how some people were trying to stop the movement by threatening them with physical death; but he responded, "If physical death is the price that I must pay to free my white brother and all my brothers and sisters from a permanent death of the spirit, then nothing can be more redemptive."[18] On July 2, 1964 King personally witnessed President Lyndon Johnson's signing of the Civil Rights law. King submitted an Economic Bill of Rights to the Democratic Party platform committee. He suggested that the disadvantaged, who have been denied so long, ought to receive something comparable to the G.I. Bill of Rights.

At age thirty-five Dr. Martin Luther King became the youngest person ever to receive a Nobel Prize. He accepted the prestigious award for peace on behalf of the Movement, saying it was "a profound recognition that nonviolence is the answer to the crucial political and racial questions of our time—the need for man to overcome oppression without resorting to violence."[19]

In 1965 the push for voter registration was accelerated, and Selma, Alabama was selected as the most challenging target. Mass meetings were held there throughout January

and February. On the first day of February, King and Abernathy led a march of 250 blacks and 15 whites to the courthouse, where they all were arrested. On March 5 King
spent two and a half hours with President Johnson urging
him to expedite the Voting Rights bill. Two days later he
announced a 54-mile march from Selma to Montgomery.
Although Governor Wallace prohibited the march, King
exhorted the people to stand up for what is right. SCLC
strategy was for the leaders to avoid arrest in the early
stages of a campaign. Thus King was not at the front of the
march when they were met by Alabama troopers with gas
masks, tear gas, clubs, horsemen with whips, and deputies
with electric cattle prods. The brutal attack was cheered by
whites on the sidelines.

King announced that he and Abernathy would lead
another march. A federal injunction was issued against it,
but King made a nationwide appeal for ministers and
others to join them. This time they crossed the bridge
before coming to the troopers. Fifteen hundred people
prayed on the road, and then to avoid a violent confrontation King asked them to turn back. That night a white
minister from Boston was murdered by four Klansmen in
Selma. Demonstrations were held across the country, and
four thousand religious leaders picketed the White House
to push for the Voting Rights bill. The evening of the
funeral President Johnson gave his "We shall overcome"
speech and made the Voting Rights bill his top priority. The
injunction against the march was lifted, and the President
federalized the Alabama National Guard and sent troops to
protect the marchers. On March 21 the march was successfully carried out; when they got to Montgomery, they were
a crowd of fifty thousand. Again King's oratory lifted the
people as he declared that they would not have to wait
long for freedom because "no lie can live forever," because
"you will reap what you sow," because "the arm of the
moral universe is long but it bends toward justice," and
because "mine eyes have seen the glory of the coming of
the Lord."[20] The Voting Rights bill was signed on August 6,

1965.

Student Nonviolent Coordinating Committee

James Lawson refused to fight in the Korean War and was sent to prison for his conscientious objection. Paroled under Methodist ministers, he went to India as a missionary and studied the nonviolent methods of Gandhi for three years. While enrolled at Oberlin College in Ohio, he traveled to Montgomery during the bus boycott and advised Martin Luther King, Jr. on applying nonviolence in a mass protest. In 1958 Lawson and FOR minister Glenn Smiley began offering workshops on nonviolence in Nashville. That year the NAACP won some desegregation victories using sit-ins in Kansas and Oklahoma.

On February 1, 1960 four black freshman from North Carolina Agricultural and Technical College sat in the Woolworth store in Greensboro without receiving service for an hour until the store closed. CORE was contacted, and Gordon Carey came from New York to organize more sit-ins by students. Fred Shuttlesworth was in North Carolina then and called SCLC's executive director, Ella Baker. She called people, and Ralph Abernathy helped students of Alabama State College to organize sit-ins in Montgomery. Columbia students picketed Woolworth's in New York city, and Harlem congressman Adam Clayton Powell called for a national boycott of Woolworth stores. In two weeks the sit-ins spread to fifteen southern cities. Julian Bond at Morehouse College led the effort in Atlanta.

The Nashville students were prepared, and on February 18 they mobilized two hundred people for sit-ins at several stores. On February 27 some white teens insulted and attacked the Negroes sitting at the lunch counter. The Nashville police arrived and arrested 81 black demonstrators but none of the whites; those arrested were replaced at the lunch counter by other protestors. The black community in Nashville raised nearly $50,000 for bail, but the judge turned his back on their black attorney, Z. Alexander Looby, and fined the demonstrators. On March 2 at the

Nashville bus terminal 63 students were arrested. Two weeks later four blacks were finally served food there; but while they ate, they were beaten. Black customers boycotted the offending Nashville stores. Young John Lewis was arrested four times. Lawson refused to withdraw from the movement and was expelled by Vanderbilt's Divinity School; eleven faculty later resigned in protest when he was not re-admitted. After four days of nonviolence classes at Orangeburg, South Carolina, on March 15 a thousand Negroes protested lunch-counter discrimination; police used fire hoses and tear gas, and 388 students were arrested. Atlanta was changed forever when 76 students were arrested. NAACP executive secretary Roy Wilkins and Martin Luther King both made statements that the students would end segregation.

In April 1960 Ella Baker of the SCLC organized a conference at Shaw University in Raleigh, North Carolina for students who wanted to challenge racial discrimination. Student leaders from 56 colleges in twelve southern states attended, and Lawson gave the keynote speech. They formed the Student Nonviolent Coordinating Committee (SNCC, pronounced "snick"), and the SCLC contributed $800 to get it started. After a bomb destroyed much of Looby's house in Nashville, 2,000 Negroes marched in protest to City Hall. In early May four theaters and six lunch counters in Nashville ended their Jim Crow policies. That spring lunch counters in seven Tennessee cities were desegregated. Although protestors remained nonviolent, sporadic acts of violence broke out against them in various places. In Jackson, Mississippi police used clubs, tear gas, and dogs against demonstrators, and in Biloxi whites with clubs and chains attacked Negroes at a public beach; ten were even wounded by gunshots.

In May 1960 SNCC met at Atlanta University, and James Lawson wrote the original draft for what became the following SNCC Statement of Purpose:

We affirm the philosophical or religious ideal of nonviolence as the foundation of our purpose,

the pre-supposition of our faith,
and the manner of our action.
Nonviolence as it grows from Judaic-Christian tradition
seeks a social order of justice permeated by love.
Integration of human endeavor represents
the crucial first step toward such a society.
 Through nonviolence,
courage displaces fear; love transforms hate.
Acceptance dissipates prejudice; hopes ends despair.
Peace dominates war; faith reconciles doubt.
Mutual regard cancels enmity.
Justice for all overthrows injustice.
The redemptive community supersedes
systems of gross social immorality.
 Love is the central motif of nonviolence.
Love is the force by which God binds
man to Himself and man to man.
Such love goes to the extreme;
it remains loving and forgiving even in the midst of hostility.
It matches the capacity of evil to inflict suffering
with an even more enduring capacity to absorb evil,
all the while persisting in love.
 By appealing to conscience
and standing on the moral nature of human existence,
nonviolence nurtures the atmosphere in which
reconciliation and justice become actual possibilities.[22]

SNCC elected Marion Barry chairman, and he testified before the platform committee at the Democratic Party's national convention at Los Angeles in July. By February 1961 more than 3,600 demonstrators had been in jail. That month SNCC began a no-bail tactic when Charles Sherrod, Charles Jones, Diane Nash, and Ruby Doris Smith were arrested at Rock Hill, South Carolina; they were sentenced to thirty days. In Atlanta eighty students stayed in jail. Also in February SNCC began testing the Boynton decision that declared discrimination at facilities of interstate travel illegal.

 Freedom riders left Washington on May 4, and at the Rock Hill bus station John Lewis and Albert Bigelow were beaten while entering a white waiting room. At Anniston, Alabama, a bomb was thrown onto the bus; passengers suffered smoke inhalation but escaped as the bus burned up. A second bus arrived an hour later, and eight men beat up the protesting riders with metal pipes; James Peck needed fifty stitches in his head. At Birmingham drivers refused to take them farther, and they flew to New Orleans. Diane Nash in Nashville organized ten students, who took a bus to Birmingham, but Police Chief Bull Connor arrested them and drove them 120 miles to the Tennessee border. They tried again, and after President Kennedy's phone calls, a bus took them from Birmingham to Montgomery on May 20. Kennedy's representative in the Justice Department, John Siegenthaler, flew to Montgomery. There a mob of three hundred with clubs and sticks knocked out Siegenthaler, and no ambulance would come to help him or the other wounded demonstrators. Attorney General Robert Kennedy learned what happened and sent his deputy Byron White with US marshals. Governor John Patterson declared martial law, and the freedom riders were joined by 1200 people at Abernathy's Baptist church, where the marshals used tear gas to disperse the surrounding mob. With the National Guard on the streets the twelve freedom riders made it to the bus and Jackson, Mississippi, where they were arrested for entering a white waiting room. They refused to pay fines and were beaten in jail. William Coffin led a group of white ministers, and they were arrested in Montgomery along with Abernathy and Shuttlesworth.

The freedom rides continued, and by the end of the summer in 1961 more than three hundred had been arrested. Treatment was the worst in Mississippi, where prisoners, such as Stokely Carmichael, had their bedding removed for singing. That summer President Kennedy's assistant Harris Wofford, Burke Marshall from the Civil Rights Division, and the Taconic and Field Foundations offered SNCC funds to work on voter registration in the South. Tim Jenkins took this idea to a SNCC meeting, but many wanted to continue the direct action effort. Ella Baker suggested a compromise, and they agreed to work on both.

Bob Moses led heroic efforts in McComb, Mississippi despite violent opposition. Although Mississippi was 43% Negro, only five percent of them were registered to vote. The federal government filed some lawsuits but did not reign in the abusive police power in Mississippi. Although the 5th Circuit Court of Appeals and Supreme Court Justice Hugo Black ordered the University of Mississippi to admit James Meredith, in the fall of 1962 Governor Ross Barnett tried to resist until September 30 when President Kennedy federalized the Mississippi national guard and sent 400 marshals, who were attacked by a mob of two thousand whites; two people were killed, and more than 300 were injured. Within ten days the US Army had 12,000 troops in Oxford, Mississippi. Meredith graduated the following year and was wounded on a "walk against fear" in June 1966. On March 23, 1963 the SNCC office used for voter registration in Greenwood was destroyed by a fire. Four days later leaders Moses, Jim Forman, and eight others were arrested for marching to the county courthouse. They were released after the US Justice Department postponed its suit against local officials. NAACP field secretary Medgar Evers was murdered in his driveway at Jackson on June 12. By the end of 1963 SNCC had 130 staff working in the South. Historian Howard Zinn participated in the Freedom Day demonstrations at Hattiesburg, Mississippi on January 22, 1964, and in his book *SNCC: The New Abolitionists* he wrote an account of their efforts to register voters led by Bob Moses.

Charles Sherrod and Cordell Reagon began the SNCC effort in Albany, Georgia in October 1961. On November first they rode a Trailways bus to Albany with Charles Jones and Jim Forman to test compliance with the Interstate Commerce Commission's recent barring of segregation in terminals. Police ordered them to leave a white waiting room, and the violation was reported to the US Justice Department. A coalition of groups called itself the Albany

Movement, and five students were arrested on November 22. When Albany State College expelled them and others were fired, students marched in protest. An interracial group of nine activists, which included Bob Zellner, Tom Hayden and his wife Sandra, were arrested with two others at the bus terminal by Albany Police Chief Laurie Pritchett on December 10. During their trial hundreds of students marched in protest, and a total of 737 were arrested, mostly for parading without a permit. A boycott of the city buses put the bus company out of business. Those disobeying segregation in the courtroom were dragged out. King and Abernathy returned to Albany for their trials in July 1962. They refused to pay a fine; but someone else did so secretly, and they left. That summer hundreds of youths were arrested for disobeying segregation at the library, restaurants, the park, the swimming pool, and the bowling alley. The Albany Movement registered five hundred Negroes to vote and began running candidates for office. When Charles Wingfield was expelled for putting up a petition on the wall of his school, more than a thousand students stayed out of school in protest. Wingfield was not re-admitted but began working for SNCC.

In April 1963 William Moore was carrying protest signs on a walk to Mississippi, but he was murdered on a highway in Alabama. SNCC and CORE organized an inter-racial group of ten to continue his walk. They left Chattanooga on the first of May and were accompanied by a group of reporters; they were frequently harassed by local racists. At the Alabama border Governor George Wallace had them arrested, and after 31 days in jail they were fined $200 each.

At the massive demonstration in Washington on August 28, 1963 SNCC chairman John Lewis was persuaded by other leaders to soften his criticism of the Kennedy administration's failure to protect civil rights in the South. Lawyers and historian Zinn pointed out that the US Code in Title 18 Section 242 makes it a crime to deprive any inhabitant of their rights, and Title 10 Section 333 authorizes the President to use armed forces to suppress domestic violence that opposes or obstructs the laws of the United States. Yet thousands of Negroes and some whites had been jailed and brutally treated in nonviolent efforts to secure their constitutional rights. Injunctions against officials could have been issued to deter violations and protect those rights. Judges could have jailed violators for civil contempt. Robert Moses brought a suit against Attorney General Robert Kennedy which had been denied and was being appealed. In his speech Lewis removed the complaint that the pending civil rights bill would not protect people from police brutality. He did criticize the federal government for indicting nine civil rights leaders for peacefully protesting in Albany, Georgia, and more than thirty FBI agents were on this case. His remark that this was a conspiracy to appease southern politicians was also self-censored.

Selma, Alabama had a history of being a slave market and a lynching town. In Dallas County 57% of the people were of African descent, but only one percent of eligible blacks were registered to vote compared to 64% of eligible whites. During voter registration efforts in early fall 1963 more than three hundred people were arrested as Sheriff Jim Clark and his deputies with clubs used electric cattle prods against demonstrators. At a church meeting Dick Gregory spoke for two hours, humorously pointing out the absurdities of segregation. On October 7, Freedom Day, 350 Negroes stood in line all day to try to register to vote; those trying to give them water or food were arrested while FBI officials watched and did nothing.

In June 1964 a group of 25 blacks traveled from Mississippi to Washington to ask the federal government for protection during Freedom Summer when seven hundred mostly white college students came to help the mostly black SNCC and other civil rights workers in Mississippi. On June 21 James Chaney, Michael Schwerner, and Andrew Goodman were murdered in Neshoba County. Harvard law school professor Mark Howe blamed the Attorney

General for not using the law to protect civil rights workers. About two thousand students attended more than thirty Freedom Schools that summer. The church in Glucks-tadt used for the school was burned down. The Mississippi Freedom Democratic Party (MFDP) led by Fannie Lou Hamer decided to register voters independently of the state, and 80,000 registered with the new party. During the Freedom Summer more than a thousand people were arrested in Mississippi. The MFDP tried to get its delegates seated at the Democratic national convention in Atlantic City, but they were only allowed two delegates.

Federal indifference to police brutality continued during demonstrations at Selma in the first three months of 1965. Only for the large march from Selma to Montgomery did President Johnson authorize the national guard to protect marchers. After the murders of Jimmie Lee Jackson, Rev. James Reeb, and Viola Liuzzo, in the spring of 1965 Stokely Carmichael (Kwame Ture) led the SNCC effort in Lowndes County, Alabama. In May the SNCC executive committee had a closed meeting about whether SNCC workers should carry guns, as some already were. Carmichael started the Lowndes County Freedom Organi-zation (LCFO) as a black political party with the black panther as its symbol. By the fall SNCC workers had moved beyond the South and were working Boston, Detroit, Chicago, Washington, San Francisco, and Philadel-phia, and Los Angeles. In January 1966 SNCC issued a strong statement opposing the Vietnam War. That month they started boycotting the buses in the District of Columbia and demanded home rule. In May 1966 Carmichael was elected chairman of SNCC, replacing John Lewis.

King Challenges Poverty and War

Meanwhile problems were surfacing outside the South. In one night of rioting in the Watts section of Los Angeles in August 1965 more people were killed than in ten years of nonviolent demonstrations across the country. On June 6,

1966 James Meredith was shot while leading a march in Mississippi. King visited him in the hospital and took his place on the march. Stokely Carmichael and the Black Power advocates wanted to exclude whites, but King said he would withdraw. They agreed to keep the march interracial and nonviolent.

In January 1966 King had moved his family into a Chicago slum to begin a protest for better housing and economic conditions. Mayor Daley closed up City Hall, but like his namesake Martin Luther, King nailed his specific demands to the closed door. Finally, to avoid a violent confrontation Mayor Daley met with King, Archbishop Cody, Chicago Real Estate Board representatives, the Chicago Housing Authority, business and industrial leaders, and black leaders of Chicago and the SCLC. An open housing agreement was announced on August 26. An SCLC poverty and unemployment program called Operation Breadbasket was put under the leadership of Jesse Jackson. At the annual SCLC convention in August 1966 at Jackson, Mississippi, King called for a "guaranteed annual income, and a convention resolution proposed $4,000 per year. In a debate on a 90-minute Meet the Press program on NBC television on August 21, King, Whitney Young, and Roy Wilkins argued for adhering to nonviolence while Stokely Carmichael, James Meredith, and Floyd McKissick advocated black power. King believed in black empowerment but considered it a tactical mistake to use the term "black power" because it tended to provoke the majority into crushing the minority.

In his last book, *Where Do We Go from Here: Chaos or Community?*, Rev. King responded to the concerns of those advocating black power; but he still recommended nonviolent methods and reconciliation with whites. He warned that power without love is reckless and abusive, but he admitted that love without power is sentimental and weak. The aim should be justice. He argued that the recent riots showed the futility of using violence in the struggle for racial justice. Murdering liars and haters does not end the lie and the hate. Only nonviolence can break the chain reaction of evil. He believed that both education and social action are needed. King perceived that the root cause of both racial hatred and war was fear. He hoped that the greatest application of the nonviolent methods used in the civil rights movement would be for world peace, asking, "Do we have the morality and courage required to live together as brothers and not be afraid?"[21] War, he said, had become obsolete; but he knew the danger when he saw the leaders of nations preparing for war while talking peace. He warned of the ultimate danger to the human race.

If we assume that life is worth living
and that man has a right to survive,
then we must find an alternative to war.
In a day when vehicles hurtle through outer space
and guided ballistic missiles carve highways of death
through the stratosphere,
no nation can claim victory in war.
A so-called limited war will leave
little more than a calamitous legacy of human suffering,
political turmoil and spiritual disillusionment.
A world war will leave only smoldering ashes
as mute testimony of a human race
whose folly led inexorably to ultimate death.
If modern man continues to flirt unhesitatingly with war,
he will transform his earthly habitat into an inferno
such as even the mind of Dante could not imagine.
   Therefore I suggest that
the philosophy and strategy of nonviolence
become immediately a subject for study
and for serious experimentation
in every field of human conflict,
by no means excluding the relations between nations.
It is, after all, nation-states which make war,
which have produced the weapons
that threaten the survival of mankind
and which are both genocidal and suicidal in character.[23]

He had faith that we can end war and violence as long

as we do not succumb to fear of the weapons we have created. He recommended that the United Nations consider using nonviolent direct action as an application of peaceable power. He prophesied that achieving disarmament and peace would depend on a spiritual re-evaluation. He warned that a nation, which spends year after year more money on military defense than on social programs, is moving toward spiritual death. Ultimately there must be a world-wide fellowship based on unconditional love for all people.

King's conscience told him that he must speak out against the Vietnam War, even though the SCLC leaders asked him not to speak as SCLC President but as a private citizen. Many civil rights leaders considered his denunciation of Johnson's Vietnam policy a mistake. However, his wife Coretta, his former professor Harold de Wolf, A. J. Muste, and UN Ambassador Arthur Goldberg supported him for his courageous stand. In January 1967 in Los Angeles he complained that the promises of the Great Society had been shot down on the battlefields of Vietnam. He suggested combining the fervor of the civil rights movement with the peace movement. He spoke at the Spring Mobilization campaign organized by A. J. Muste. While in Geneva, King called for an immediate negotiated settlement to the "immoral" war. At Riverside Church in New York on April 4, 1967 he proposed a five-point peace program for Vietnam: an end to all bombing, a unilateral cease-fire to prepare for negotiation, curtailment of military build-ups throughout Southeast Asia, realistic acceptance of the National Liberation Front (NLF), and the withdrawal of all foreign troops from Vietnam in accordance with the 1954 Geneva agreement. He criticized current American values and suggested radical changes that are still needed.

I am convinced that if we are to get
on the right side of the world revolution,
we as a nation must undergo a radical revolution of values.
We must rapidly begin the shift
from a "thing-oriented" society

to a "person-oriented" society.
When machines and computers,
profit motives and property rights
are considered more important than people,
the giant triplets of racism, materialism and militarism
are incapable of being conquered.[24]

King with Benjamin Spock and Harry Belafonte led a demonstration of more than 125,000 to the United Nations building in New York on April 15, and they sent a note to Ralph Bunche that they were supporting peace, equal rights, and the self-determination of peoples.

In 1968 Martin Luther King continued to criticize the war in Vietnam, and on January 14 he went to the Santa Rita jail to visit Joan Baez, who had been arrested with others at a draft board in California. He refused to segregate his moral concern for peace from that for justice, believing that there can be no justice without peace nor peace without justice. He recommended civil disobedience to stop the abominable and immoral Vietnam War. He was preparing a massive Poor People's Campaign for whites as well as blacks when he was called to Memphis to assist with a strike of the sanitation workers. Two thousand people at Clayborn Temple wanted to hear him speak. He declared his support for their cause, but then he began to reflect about the threats made against his life. He confessed that he would like a long life, but his main concern was to do God's will. He was glad that he had been to the mountain top and seen the Promised Land. The next day, April 4, 1968, Martin Luther King, Jr. was shot and killed. He had already requested a simple eulogy in a sermon he had given two months before when he had said,

I'd like someone to mention that day
that Martin Luther King, Jr. tried
to give his life serving others.
I'd like somebody to say that day
that Martin Luther King, Jr. tried to love somebody.
I want you to say that day,

that I tried to be right on the war question.
I want you to be able to say that day
that I did try to feed the hungry.
I want you to be able to say that day
that I did try in my life to clothe those who were naked.
I want you to say, on that day,
that I did try, in my life, to visit those who were in prison.
I want you to say that I tried to love and serve humanity.
Yes, if you want to say that I was a drum major,
say that I was a drum major for justice;
say that I was a drum major for peace.[25]

Chavez and the United Farm Workers

Cesar Estrada Chavez was born near Yuma, Arizona on March 31, 1927. His grandfather had migrated from Mexico in the 1880s, and his father, Librado Chavez, homesteaded land and ran a grocery store. During the Depression, Librado had to sell his store to pay his back taxes; a local banker had denied him a loan even though he qualified under federal guidelines. During the 1930s about a half million Mexicans were repatriated or deported from the United States. In 1939 the Chavez family along with thousands of poor whites from the Midwest and black sharecroppers from the South went to California looking for work. His father joined various unions, and the family often quit jobs in protest of bad treatment. Cesar completed the eighth grade before he left school to work when his father was temporarily incapacitated by a car accident in 1942. The back-aching experience of using a short-handled hoe stimulated Cesar to work years later for the banning of that tool. He experienced racial discrimination, and he had been punished at school for speaking Spanish. In 1944 he was arrested for refusing to sit in the Mexican section of a theater in Delano. That year he had joined the US Navy and was sent to the Mariana Islands and Guam, where he worked as a painter. Cesar married his sweetheart Helen Fabela in 1948, and on their honeymoon they visited all the California missions. He and his parents worked as sharecroppers growing strawberries for two years. Then Cesar with his growing family spent a year and a half working in the forests of northern California before settling in the Sal Si Puedes barrio of San Jose, where Cesar got a job in a lumber mill in 1952.

Ernesto Galarza had earned a Ph.D. from Columbia University and organized for the National Farm Labor Union (NFLU); he initiated the supermarket picket lines to boycott table grapes. Galarza also worked for the AFL-CIO's Agricultural Workers Organizing Committee (AWOC) and advised Cesar during his early years of organizing. Under the leadership of Saul Alinsky, the Community Service Organization (CSO) had registered 15,000 new voters in 1949 and helped Edward Roybal get elected to the city council in Los Angeles. When drunk police officers beat seven Chicanos nearly to death in 1951, CSO efforts made authorities hold the officers accountable for what navy men had gotten away with during the Zoot Suit riots of 1942. Cesar Chavez worked as a volunteer for the CSO registering people to vote, and he became a friend and assistant of Catholic priest Donald McDonnell, who also served farm workers. Cesar studied on his own and was especially influenced by Louis Fischer's *Life of Gandhi*. In 1952 Fred Ross hired Chavez to work full-time as a CSO organizer for $35 a week. During the McCarthy era the FBI conducted various investigations of liberal groups, but Chavez persuaded the FBI not to allow the Republican party to interfere with their voter registration efforts. From 1953 to 1955 the Immigration and Naturalization Service (INS) deported nearly two million Mexicans. Chavez was an effective and hard-working organizer, and his family moved to Oakland and then to various places in the San Joaquin Valley; his salary was increased to $58 a week.

In the summer of 1958 the United Packinghouse Workers union promised the CSO $20,000 for a new chapter in Oxnard, and Cesar Chavez was put in charge. At this time a big issue was the competition with the bracero program of guest workers from Mexico that had started during World War II to provide needed labor. During a lemon workers strike Chavez and the CSO used persistent applications for jobs, boycotts, and sit-down strikes in the fields; they won their campaign to have local workers hired first, and their wages went up from 65 to 90 cents an hour. In 1959 Cesar wanted to start a union, but he was appointed state director of CSO and was assigned to Los Angeles, where he worked for two years. That year McDonnell and another priest named Thomas McCullough along with Dolores Huerta persuaded the AFL-CIO to support the forming of a farm workers union, and they founded the Agricultural Workers Organizing Committee (AWOC). Huerta persuaded the Filipino Larry Itliong to join them. Chavez began to work with Huerta and Gil Padilla.

At the 1962 annual CSO convention in Calexico, Cesar proposed a union movement for farm workers; when this was rejected, he resigned and moved to Delano in April. With little savings for his family of eight children, Chavez often worked in the fields with his wife Helen from 6 a.m. to 2 p.m. and then organized on his own the rest of the day and evening. Traveling to their camps and fields and meeting workers in their houses, he passed out more than 80,000 questionnaires on the issues. Julio Hernandez had been blackballed for being in a union in 1951, but Cesar persuaded him to try again. Dolores Huerta was upset that AWOC organizers were too cozy with contractors, and she quit to work with Chavez, who set up an office in his brother Richard's garage.

In the fall of 1962 about 150 delegates of workers met at a theater and formed the National Farm Workers Association (NFWA) with a flag of a black eagle in a white circle on a red background and the motto "Viva la Causa!" Chavez was elected president with Huerta, Hernandez, and Padilla as vice presidents. Dues were set at $3.50 per month, and the goal was to get the $1.50 minimum wage for farm workers with unemployment insurance. Richard Chavez was a carpenter and had built a house, and his brother Cesar got him to mortgage it so that they could start a burial-insurance program and credit union. Helen Chavez set up a co-op for auto supplies and administered the credit union. Cesar was offered a $50,000 grant from a foundation but turned it down to retain independence. He was the only union official at that time whose salary came completely from the workers. Chavez was offered a job as director of the Peace Corps in Latin America with an annual salary of $21,000; yet he rejected that offer even though he only was getting $50 per week and sometimes he still had to work in the fields.

Chavez wanted to build up the organization before going on strike, and by 1964 the NFWA had a thousand dues-paying members and more than fifty locals. In December they began their newspaper, *El Malcriado*, which means "the unruly one." In March 1965 flower workers, who had been promised $9 per thousand plants but were paid less than $7, went on strike. During the summer Gilbert Padilla and Protestant minister Jim Drake organized protest marches and a rent-strike because of the miserable shacks in the labor camps in Tulare County. The bracero program had been ended in 1964, but in the summer of 1965 growers persuaded Governor Pat Brown to pressure President Lyndon Johnson into reviving the program; pay had to be at least $1.40 an hour. When growers paid the domestic workers only $1.25, the Filipinos of the AWOC in the Coachella Valley went on strike and got better wages. However, other growers in the Delano area also paid less and wanted to pay Mexican-Americans only $1.10 per hour. On September 8 Larry Itliong led the Filipino workers on a strike. Chavez had been learning from the nonviolent civil rights movement led by Dr. King. He called a meeting and warned against using violence even though violence would be used against them, and the vote for a strike was unanimous. Chavez and others found that when they did not react violently, they gained the sympathy of other workers. Cesar said,

People don't like to see
a nonviolent movement subjected to violence,

and there's a lot of support across the country for nonviolence.
That's the key point we have going for us.
We can turn the world if we can do it nonviolently.[26]

Law enforcement tended to be on the side of the
growers. Confrontations occurred on the picket lines, and
44 pickets, including Helen Chavez, were arrested and
transported to Bakersfield in October. Cesar Chavez publicized the violence used against them and found that such
unjust acts actually helped their cause. He coordinated
with AWOC leader Al Green. With Filipinos and Mexicans
on strike, 48 ranches were affected. Chavez immediately
sent letters to the growers to negotiate, but they were
returned unopened. SNCC organizers began arriving to
help, and Luis Valdez came from the San Francisco Mime
Troupe and started El Teatro de Campesino to perform
skits that would educate workers in the camps. In
December, Walter Reuther of the United Auto Workers
came to support their effort, and the UAW donated money
to the strike. Reuther, who led the sit-down strikes at
General Motors in 1937, said, "There is no power in the
world like the power of free men working together in a just
cause."[27] The NFWA was awarded a $267,887 grant from
the US Office of Economic Opportunity as part of its
poverty program, but Chavez asked Sargent Shriver to
postpone the grant until the strike was over. During hearings of the Subcommittee on Migratory Labor, Senator
Bobby Kennedy reminded Kern County sheriff Roy
Galyen, who had arrested picketers, of the US Constitution.
Kennedy even joined a picket line supporting the grape
strike.

In March 1966 Cesar Chavez organized a 250-mile
march to Sacramento in 25 days that ended on Easter
Sunday, but Gov. Brown chose to go to Palm Springs. The
Schenley Corporation was affected by the strike and
offered Chavez a contract, but the powerful Di Giorgios
made a deal with the Teamsters, who rushed an election on
union representation. Chavez advised boycotting that elec-

tion, and Dolores Huerta won the support of the Mexican-American Political Association (MAPA), which convinced Gov. Brown to investigate and invalidate the early election; a new election was scheduled for August 30. The NFWA merged with the AWOC to form the United Farm Workers Organizing Committee (UFWOC) within the AFL-CIO; Chavez became director and Itliong vice director. The UFWOC got 530 votes to 331 for the Teamsters, and only twelve workers voted not to have a union. Martin Luther King sent them a congratulatory telegram, saying, "The fight for equality must be fought on many fronts."[28] In another election at Arvin the UFW won by even more votes. Chavez began negotiating with Di Giorgio executives, but violence against strikers provoked Chavez into calling for a boycott against their TreeSweet juices and S&W canned foods. When Chavez went with newly converted strikers to pick up their things at a company labor camp, they were arrested and convicted of trespassing; but this outrage won over more workers.

In September 1966 the Perelli-Minetti winery made a deal with the Teamsters, and UFW declared a boycott against their labels and stores that sold their wines. In April 1967 Di Giorgio became the first employer that agreed to finance a health and welfare fund for farm workers with vacation and holiday pay. The UFW won another election against the Teamsters, and by July 1967 the biggest vintner Gallo and Christian Brothers, Almaden, and Paul Masson had all agreed to negotiate with the farm workers. Padilla and Drake went to Texas, where Rangers were breaking strikes. Chavez hired the lawyer Jerry Cohen, and he eventually won a suit against the Texas Rangers that was decided by the US Supreme Court in the 1970s. Cohen also proved that the injunctions against secondary boycotts did not apply because farm workers were excluded by the National Labor Relations Act. In August 1967 workers at the Giumara Vineyards voted to go on strike, and two-thirds of their 5,000 workers left their jobs during the harvest. Picketing was severely limited to three people at each entrance, and so Chavez announced a nation-wide boycott of Giumara grapes. Giumara used other names, and Huerta and Ross urged Chavez to broaden the boycott to all table grapes in January 1968.

Cesar Chavez was reading the writings of Gandhi and was adamant about holding to nonviolence. In October 1966 picketing Manuel Rivera was hit by a truck and disabled. An angry mob surrounded the truck, but Chavez pushed through the crowd and may have saved the driver's life. When Chavez found strikers with a few guns, he confiscated them. By February 1968 the black power movement and the Black Panthers had led Chicanos to form the militant Brown Berets. Chavez decided to go on a fast until the union members renewed their commitment to nonviolence. After thirteen days of fasting he had to appear in court and was supported by three thousand farm workers. After 25 days Cesar broke his fast with Bobby Kennedy, who announced his candidacy for President a week later. Chavez was too weak to speak standing, and his message was read aloud by Jim Drake. In their struggle of the poor against the rich he called upon their bodies and spirits in the cause of justice, noting that the true act of courage is sacrificing oneself for others in the nonviolent struggle. Their voter registration drive helped Kennedy win the California primary. However, that spring both Martin Luther King and Bobby Kennedy were assassinated. After Nixon's election, the Defense department greatly increased its purchase of grapes for soldiers in Vietnam.

To spread the boycott in 1969 Chavez sent Al and Elena Rojas to Pittsburgh, Jessica Govea to Toronto and Montreal, and Eliseo Medina to Chicago, where he used sit-down demonstrations in the grocery stores. Others got the distribution of grapes curtailed in Detroit, New York, Boston, and Philadelphia as well. In May 1969 Chavez and Rev. Ralph Abernathy led a march from Indio to the Mexican border. In April 1970 a committee of the National Conference of Catholic Bishops persuaded Coachella growers to negotiate. Finally, 26 grape growers went to the UFW head-quarters near Delano on July 29, 1970 and signed union contracts giving farm workers $1.80 an hour and contrib-uting ten cents an hour to the Robert Kennedy Health and Welfare Fund and two cents per hour for UFW service centers. Chavez acknowledged the sacrifices of the strikers, 95% of whom had lost their homes and cars, but 85% of table-grape growers in California were now under union contracts. Chavez recognized the power of individuals working together for a common good in peaceful ways that could bring about a cultural revolution.

By August 1970 about 170 firms still had not switched from the Teamsters to the UFW, and Cesar Chavez called for a general strike. On August 29 more than 20,000 people in Los Angeles marched in protest of the Vietnam War; police used tear gas, and three people were killed, including *Los Angeles Times* reporter Ruben Salazar. Violence by the Teamsters was increasing, and the UFW's attorney Cohen was hospitalized. Dolores Huerta negoti-ated a two-year contract with InterHarvest that raised base pay to $2.10 an hour and eliminated the use of DDT and other dangerous pesticides. Chavez spent most of December in jail for not obeying an injunction against boycotting Bud Antle lettuce, but in April 1971 the Cali-fornia Supreme Court ruled in his favor, deciding that the strike and boycott were legal and that the Teamsters had colluded with the growers. In the Salinas Valley the Team-sters had made secret agreements with the growers without consulting workers, and they fired any who refused to pay dues. The UFW moved its headquarters south from Delano to La Paz. Republicans in the Arizona legislature passed laws against boycotts and limiting strikes. In April 1972 Chavez fasted for 24 days to raise public awareness, and in the fall Arizona elected its first Mexican-American governor, Raul Castro.

Because many growers were signing contracts with the bullying Teamsters, in April 1973 Chavez called for a strike. After Gallo signed a contract with Teamsters on June 27,

Chavez announced a boycott of Gallo wines. Four days earlier Teamsters had attacked picket lines with weapons, injuring 25 people. In August two UFW members were killed, and Cesar asked union members to fast for three days. He cancelled the strike but continued the boycott. Under President Nixon and Governor Reagan law enforcement was hard on the strikers, and 3,500 were arrested in 1973; but most of the cases were dismissed by the courts. UFW membership fell from 40,000 to 6,500.

In 1974 Nixon resigned, and Democrat Jerry Brown was elected governor. In February 1975 the UFW organized a march from San Francisco to Merced, and that year the short-handled hoe was finally banned in California. Brown and his agriculture secretary, Rose Bird, pushed through the Agricultural Labor Relations Act in June. Yet growers still allowed Teamsters access while barring UFW organizers, who filed more than a thousand complaints. Eighty elections enabled the UFW to increase its membership. By the end of 1975 the UFW represented 27,000 workers to the Teamsters' 12,000, but then the legislature stopped funding the Agricultural Labor Relations Board (ALRB). The farm workers union tried to remedy this by putting Proposition 14 on the ballot, but the growers contributed two million dollars to defeat it at the polls in 1976. The next year the Teamsters stopped contesting the farm worker elections, and in 1978 UFW membership passed a hundred thousand. Chavez ended the grape and lettuce boycotts. Strikers had to withstand tear-gas attacks during the lettuce strike in the Imperial Valley in 1979. Two marches to Salinas resulted in the Meyer Tomato company agreeing to pay $5 an hour, union representatives' salaries, and for a better medical plan.

The United Farm Workers experienced some dissension in the 1980s. Chavez fired some Salinas organizers; after they went on a hunger strike, he filed a $25 million lawsuit against them for libel. However, in 1982 a judge ruled that the Salinas group had been fired illegally and awarded them back pay. Some on the UFW staff objected to using the challenging interpersonal game of Synanon founder Charles Dederich. In September 1983 a security guard shot dairy worker Rene Lopez, and the day after his death a judge granted the union's request to disarm the grower Sikkim's guards. By 1984 UFW membership dropped below 12,000. In June of that year Chavez announced a grape boycott to call attention to the use of dangerous pesticides. In 1988 Cesar fasted for 36 days to protest pesticides. In 1991 the UFW lost a suit to an Imperial Valley grower that would cost them $2.4 million. When they were threatened in Arizona by a $5.4 million suit by Bruce Church, Inc., Chavez went to Arizona near his birthplace and fasted before testifying in court. After breaking his fast, he felt tired and died in his sleep on April 23, 1993. His funeral at Delano was attended by 40,000 people. By his own standard of how well an institution helps the poor, the work of Cesar Chavez and the United Farm Workers should receive a favorable judgment by history.

Notes

1. Brown v. Board of Education, Supreme Court of the United States, 1954. 347 U.S. 483, 74 S.Ct. 686, 98 L.Ed. 873 in *Law and American History: Cases and Materials* by Stephen B. Presser and Jamil S. Zainaldin, p. 738.
2. *Stride Toward Freedom* by Martin Luther King Jr., p. 61.
3. *Ibid.*, p. 62.
4. *Ibid.*, p. 63.
5. *Ibid.*, p. 87.
6. *Ibid.*, p. 137.
7. *Ibid.*, p. 172.
8. *Ibid.*, p. 216.
9. *Ibid.*, p. 220-221.
10. *Ibid.*, p. 222.
11. *King* by David L. Lewis, p. 133.
12. *Ibid.*, p. 180-181.
13. *Why We Can't Wait* by Martin Luther King Jr., p. 80.
14. *Ibid.*, p. 82.
15. *Ibid.*, p. 83.

16. *King* by David L. Lewis, p. 211.
17. *Ibid.*, p. 236.
18. *Ibid.*, p. 242.
19. *My Life with Martin Luther King*, Jr.by Coretta Scott King, p. 12-13.
20. Speech on March 25, 1965 in *A Testament of Hope: The Essential Writings of Martin Luther King, Jr.*, p. 230.
21. *Where Do We Go from Here: Chaos or Community?* by Martin Luther King Jr., p. 182.
22. *The Eyes on the Prize Civil Rights Reader*, p. 119-120.
23. *Where Do We Go from Here: Chaos or Community?* by Martin Luther King Jr., p. 183-184.
24. *A Testament of Hope: The Essential Writings of Martin Luther King, Jr.*, p. 240.
25. *Ibid.*, 267.
26. Quoted in *Cesar Chavez: A Triumph of Spirit* by Richard Griswold del Castillo and Richard A. Garcia, p. 47.
27. Quoted in *The Fight in the Fields* by Susan Ferriss and Ricardo Sandoval, p. 114.
28. *Ibid.*, p. 133.

9
Lessons of the Vietnam War

All the peoples on the earth are equal from birth;
all the peoples have a right to live to be happy and free.
*Declaration of Independence
of the Democratic Republic of Vietnam*

The United States must be compelled
to get out of Vietnam immediately and without conditions.
Bertrand Russell

Let peace-minded persons and organizations
in every state of the United States
and in every country of the world
devise ways to call for an end to military intervention
in Vietnam as a first imperative step
to ending the threat of nuclear war
and bringing justice, freedom and peace to mankind.
A. J. Muste

This war turns the clock of history back
and perpetuates white colonialism.
The greatest irony and tragedy of it all
is that our own nation which initiated so much
of the revolutionary spirit in this modern world
is now cast in the mold of being an arch anti-revolutionary.
Martin Luther King, Jr.

I went to Vietnam a hard charging Marine 2nd Lieutenant,
sure that I had answered the plea of a victimized people
in their struggle against communist aggression.
That belief lasted about two weeks.
Instead of fighting communist aggressors
I found that 90% of the time our military actions
were directed against the people of South Vietnam.
These people had little sympathy
or for that matter knowledge of the Saigon Government.
We are engaged in a war in South Vietnam
to pound a people into submission to a government

that has little or no popular support
among the real people of South Vietnam.
By real people I mean all those Vietnamese people
who aren't war profiteers or who have not sold out
to their government or the United States
because it was the easy and/or profitable thing to do.
letter to Senator Fulbright

Obviously a major lesson of Vietnam
is that we must know ourselves better.
Daniel Ellsberg

Most people agree that the American military involvement in Vietnam was a tragedy, and as in classical drama we can learn many lessons from the suffering inflicted and undergone by the "hero." Our concern in this book is with peacemaking and the ways of establishing peace in the world. From this perspective the official policies of the United States Government were a colossal failure, since US influence in Vietnam resulted in the opposite of peace until the United States finally withdrew all of its influence. Even from the military point of view Indochina was the only war the USA. has ever really "lost," and it happened while America was generally considered to be the greatest military power in the history of the world and at the hands of an "enemy" who was considered "primitive" and "weak." Perhaps never before has history so clearly shown the stupidity, folly, and utter ineptness of using bombing and killing to try to solve human problems. Psychologically we may come to see that those problems were more in American attitudes than in the situations of the Vietnamese except insofar as they suffered from American "influence." In this chapter we will explore how those attitudes created a terrible situation and how we can change in order to prevent such misery and failures in the future.

French Colonial Vietnam

When World War II began, the area in Southeast Asia now known as Vietnam, Cambodia, and Laos was a colony called French Indochina. The French colonial government there declared allegiance to the Vichy regime, which the Nazis established in southern France after their invasion in 1940. During that war the Japanese, as allies of the Nazis, occupied Indochina and ruled through the French colonial administration until the Vichy regime in France fell. The Japanese then set up Vietnamese emperor Bao Dai to rule over the Vietnamese. Since 1940 a guerrilla resistance movement known as the Viet Minh, led by Communist Ho Chi Minh, had struggled against the Vichy French colonialists and the Japanese invaders. They were even aided by the United States and trained by their advisors.

In August 1945 when the Japanese surrendered to the Allies, a popular revolution swept Vietnam and placed the Viet Minh in power. Under Ho Chi Minh's chairmanship the Democratic Republic of Vietnam (DRV) was established on September 2, 1945, and the Declaration of Independence, which Ho had written, was announced. He quoted from the American Declaration of Independence and from the French Revolution's 1791 Declaration of Human and Civic Rights in order to appeal to the human rights principles of these two nations. As the Americans had done two centuries before, he listed the grievances the people had suffered under their colonial overlords, in this case the French. The document concludes:

Vietnam has the right to be free and independent
and, in fact, has become free and independent.
The people of Vietnam decide to mobilize
all their spiritual and material forces
and to sacrifice their lives and property
in order to safeguard their right
of liberty and independence.[1]

Although President Roosevelt had wanted to see Vietnam under a United Nations trusteeship to prepare it for independence, at the Potsdam conference President Truman and British prime minister Attlee agreed to divide French Indochina at the sixteenth parallel, leaving China in control in the north and giving the British operational control over southern Vietnam. The DRV accepted this and welcomed British troops into Saigon in September. However, some dissenting Vietnamese Trotskyites were arrested and killed. The British then attacked the independence forces of the Vietnamese in order to restore to power the French colonial government in the south. The United States tacitly accepted French sovereignty over Indochina, and President Truman neglected to respond to several letters of appeal from Ho Chi Minh. Yet General MacArthur complained,

> If there is anything that makes my blood boil,
> it is to see our Allies in Indochina and Java
> deploying Japanese troops to reconquer the little people
> we promised to liberate.
> It is the most ignoble kind of betrayal.

In February 1946 France and China agreed to let French troops replace the Chinese north of the sixteenth parallel. Ho Chi Minh negotiated with the French for a free Vietnamese state within the French Union. The agreement of March called for 15,000 French troops in the north along with 10,000 Vietnamese soldiers. Ho Chi Minh and some compatriots traveled to France for a conference; the rest of the delegation soon left in protest, but Ho stayed on to bargain for a *modus vivendi* which recognized some political freedoms of the Viet Minh in the south. Returning in October, Ho Chi Minh pleaded with the armies of the Vietnamese and French to stop fighting, ending his proclamation with the following words:

> If we use the right words, they will certainly listen to us.
> Violent actions are absolutely forbidden.
> This is what you have to do at present
> to create a peaceful atmosphere,
> paving the way democratically
> to reach the unification of our Vietnam.[2]

However, in November 1946 the French commander at Haiphong used a minor customs clash as a justification for launching an all-out French attack on the city. The Viet Minh were driven into the countryside, and the guerrilla war against the French had begun. Not only did the United States fail to support the rights of the Vietnamese people for self-determination, but the Truman administration gave military aid to France for its colonial war in Vietnam.

After the Chinese Communist revolution in 1949 the United States decided to increase its military aid to the French in Vietnam. In January 1950 China and the Soviet Union recognized the government of Ho Chi Minh. Dreadfully afraid of the Communists, the United States government wanted to help the French destroy the Viet Minh, but it could not publicly justify supporting a colonial war. Therefore Bao Dai, who had been in exile in Hong Kong for three years, was nominally recognized by France as the independent government of Vietnam. This enabled American military assistance to go to France while Bao Dai was the "publicized" recipient. On May 8, 1950 Secretary of State Dean Acheson made the following statement:

> The United States Government, convinced that
> neither national independence nor democratic evolution
> exist in any area dominated by Soviet imperialism,
> considers the situation to be such as to warrant
> its according economic aid and military equipment
> to the Associated States of Indochina and to France
> in order to assist them in restoring stability
> and permitting these states to pursue
> their peaceful and democratic development.[3]

To compare objectively this attitude to the facts of the situation, one cannot help but see the American paranoia and hypocrisy. First, America was helping France to squelch Vietnamese national independence and democratic evolution with imperialistic war and colonial oppression. Second, the only Soviet involvement was a simple diplomatic statement toward a purely ideological ally. Even aid from the Chinese Communists was minimal during this period. Yet from 1950 to 1954 the United States gave the Bao Dai government $126 million in economic, military, and technical assistance while supplying the French with $2.6 billion of military material, which accounted for four-fifths of the French military effort. With Eisenhower's election in 1952 the new secretary of state, John Foster Dulles, expressed the paranoia as the "Domino Theory." The Korean War was fought for these same reasons during this period. By 1952 the French were spending a third of their national budget on the Indochina War.

In spite of the military power of France aided by the United States, the Viet Minh were able to win an impressive victory at Dienbienphu in 1954. In this battle alone the Vietnamese estimated that they had 20,000 killed. In this Indochina War the French colonial forces lost about 95,000 killed. The French were ready now to give up control of Vietnam, and they agreed to an armistice at Geneva. However, the document was never signed by any of the parties because the United States refused to give even its oral consent. American officials wanted France to continue the struggle. Although President Eisenhower considered using tactical nuclear weapons or sending US troops, he had the good sense not to involve America in another land war in Asia. Dulles tried to consolidate interests in the area with the Southeast Asia Treaty Organization (SEATO), but only Thailand, Pakistan, and the Philippines agreed to assist each other against outside aggression.

American Vietnam War

The Geneva accords removed the French from northern Vietnam and recognized the Bao Dai government in the south for the two years the French had been given to depart from there. Then an election was supposed to unify the country. This temporary concession of southern territory by the Vietnamese to the French was a response to strong pressure from the Soviet and Chinese representatives Molotov and Zhou Enlai. The French left on schedule but were replaced in May 1955 by the United States and its military support for South Vietnam. Bao Dai was replaced by the pro-American dictator, Ngo Dinh Diem, who refused to hold elections because the Communists would have won. Diem re-established the landlords who had been removed by guerrillas for supporting the Japanese and the French. The peasants of the Viet Minh rebelled, and guerrilla fighting spread. Diem violated every article of the constitution and had thousands of people imprisoned in camps. By 1959 United States military "advisors" were being killed in Vietnam, and in 1960 the guerrillas formed the National Liberation Front (NLF). The Second Indochina War had begun.

Most of the NLF were southern Vietnamese. Very few northern troops entered South Vietnam until the American troops had arrived in force. The Americans were attempting to hold back a revolution more than prevent an invasion; it was primarily a civil war. On December 20, 1960 the National Liberation Front formulated the following Ten Points:

1. Overthrow the camouflaged colonial regime of the American imperialists and the dictatorial power of Ngo Dinh Diem, servant of the Americans, and institute a government of national democratic union.
2. Institute a largely liberal and democratic regime.
3. Establish an independent and sovereign economy, and improve the living conditions of the people.
4. Reduce land rent; implement agrarian reform with the aim of providing land to the tillers.
5. Develop a national and democratic culture and education.
6. Create a national army devoted to the defense of the Fatherland and the people.
7. Guarantee equality between the various minorities and between the sexes; protect the legitimate interests of foreign citizens established in Vietnam and

of Vietnamese citizens residing abroad.
8. Promote a foreign policy of peace and neutrality.
9. Re-establish normal relations between the two
zones, and prepare for the peaceful reunification of
the country.
10. Struggle against all aggressive war; actively
defend universal peace.

In the full manifesto each of these points included several specific means of implementation. The text of Point 2 is a good example:

2. To bring into being a broad and progressive democracy,
promulgate freedom of expression, of the press,
of belief, of assembly, of association,
of movement and other democratic freedoms.
To grant general amnesty to all political detainees,
dissolve all concentration camps dubbed "prosperity zones"
and "resettlement centers,"
abolish the fascist 10-59 law
and other anti-democratic laws.[4]

The Twelve Points of Discipline for the People's Liberation Army suggested that soldiers be fair and honest in business with civilians, never taking even a needle from the people. When staying in civilian houses, they should take care of them as if they were their own. They should be courteous with people and love them. With these ideals as standards, it is not surprising that the NLF made such successful inroads in South Vietnam.

By 1961 more than half of South Vietnamese territory was under Communist control. Over the next two years President Kennedy sent sixteen thousand American soldiers as advisors to the South Vietnamese army. In May 1963 the Buddhists rebelled against Diem's tyrannical government, and monks began setting themselves on fire in protest. The United States hinted that changes in the government were needed. On the first day of November a military coup deposed Diem, and he and his brother Nhu were assassinated. Over the next year and a half the government of South Vietnam changed hands among the generals several times. In February 1964 President Lyndon Johnson issued public warnings to North Vietnam and ordered the covert bombing of Laos near the border of North Vietnam.

In August 1964 the *USS Maddox* was attacked while patrolling in the Gulf of Tonkin, probably in retaliation for a South Vietnamese Navy attack on an island in the north two days before. The *Maddox* fired back; two days later another attack was reported, though there was never any evidence that this second attack actually occurred. The US ships were not damaged nor were any Americans hurt, while they had sunk three or four of the attacking torpedo boats. Nevertheless, Johnson ordered sixty-four bombing sorties over four North Vietnamese bases, and he requested approval from Congress to use armed force. This excessive response has been considered a violation of the rules of civilized warfare as interpreted in the Nuremberg trials. Senator Wayne Morse, who had been informed by a Pentagon officer that the *Maddox* had been involved in covert raids of North Vietnam, objected that the Gulf of Tonkin Resolution gave the President war-making powers without a declaration of war, and he lamented it as a historic mistake.

President Johnson was overwhelmingly elected over Goldwater's militaristic and reactionary programs, and on February 7, 1965 he ordered the bombing of North Vietnam. The next day the Students for a Democratic Society (SDS) issued a statement of outrage, saying that the US was supporting dictatorship, not freedom, and was intervening in a civil war, not a war of aggression. SDS called for a march on Washington in April and protested,

We are outraged that $2 million a day
is expended for a war on the poor in Vietnam,
while government financing is so desperately needed
to abolish poverty at home.
What kind of America is it whose response to poverty

and oppression in Vietnam is napalm and defoliation?
Whose response to poverty and oppression
in Mississippi is—silence?
It is a hideously immoral war.
America is committing pointless murder.[5]

A graduated bombing program was begun in March, and in April the United States began sending thousands of combat troops to South Vietnam. On April 17 the SDS march brought 20,000 people to the capitol. That month Hanoi offered its proposal for a settlement consisting of four points in accordance with the 1954 Geneva agreements:

1. Recognition of Vietnamese independence and territorial integrity by withdrawal of all US forces, bases, and weapons;
2. no foreign military bases or troops in Vietnam and no military alliances for the two zones;
3. settlement of South Vietnamese affairs according to the program of the NLF; and
4. peaceful reunification of Vietnam without any foreign interference.

This proposal was rejected in Washington out of hand, because they assumed the NLF program would exclude other groups.

In 1965 the Catholic Worker, the Committee for Nonviolent Action (CNVA), the Student Peace Union (SPU), and the War Resisters League (WRL) published the "Declaration of Conscience Against the War in Vietnam," which was signed by 6,000 people including David Dellinger, Dorothy Day, Ammon Hennacy, Bradford Lyttle, A. J. Muste, Robert Swann, James Bevel, John Lewis, Robert Moses, A. Philip Randolph, Bayard Rustin, Kenneth Boulding, W. H. Ferry, Erich Fromm, Paul Goodman, Linus Pauling, and Straughton Lynd and which read as follows:

Because the use of the military resources

of the United States in Vietnam and elsewhere
suppresses the aspirations of the people
for political independence and economic freedom;
Because inhuman torture and senseless killing
are being carried out by forces armed, uniformed, trained
and financed by the United States;
Because we believe that all peoples of the earth,
including both Americans and non-Americans,
have an inalienable right to life, liberty,
and the peaceful pursuit of happiness in their own way; and
Because we think that positive steps must be taken to put
an end to the threat of nuclear catastrophe and death
by chemical or biological warfare,
whether these result from accident or escalation—

We hereby declare our conscientious refusal
to cooperate with the United States government
in the prosecution of the war in Vietnam.
We encourage those who can conscientiously do so
to refuse to serve in the armed forces
and to ask for discharge if they are already in.
Those of us who are subject to the draft ourselves
declare our own intention to refuse to serve.
We urge others to refuse and refuse ourselves
to take part in the manufacture
or transportation of military equipment,
or to work in the fields of military research
and weapons development.
We shall encourage the development
of other nonviolent acts,
including acts which involve civil disobedience,
in order to stop the flow of American soldiers
and munitions to Vietnam.[6]

During Thanksgiving weekend there was another peace march in Washington, and the anti-war leaders urged the Communists to respond to American peace initiatives. Ho Chi Minh replied that the four points still held, and that the US must ease its criminal war of aggression against Vietnam. At Christmas the US temporarily halted the bombing, hoping for some capitulation from North

Vietnam. Hanoi replied that the United States was thousands of miles away and had no right to invade South Vietnam or to impose conditions on the DRV.

On December 21, 1965 the United Nations passed a resolution declaring that no state has the right to intervene in the affairs of another state and condemning armed intervention, because "every state has an inalienable right to choose its political, economic, social and cultural systems, without interference in any form by another state." A Citizens' White Paper by Schurmann, Scott, and Zelnik, studying nine critical periods from November 1963 to July 1966, concluded that efforts toward a political settlement were usually retarded or broken off by American military interventions, which often resulted in escalation. The *Pentagon Papers* later revealed that the expanded bombing of North Vietnam was against the judgment of the US Government's own intelligence advisors, who did not believe that it would stop Hanoi's support for the Vietcong insurgency in the South.

By 1967 nearly half a million American soldiers were fighting in South Vietnam, but at home the Spring Mobilization Committee called for a bombing halt, a US-initiated cease-fire, negotiations, and a phased withdrawal of American troops. About 200,000 people marched from the United Nations building to Central Park, and in San Francisco 50,000 gathered. Some 150 conscientious objectors burned their draft cards in a public protest. Young men were encouraged to turn in their draft cards on October 16. In Oakland, California after nonviolent demonstrators were arrested, thousands of people tried to close down an army induction center; the reaction of the police resulted in a riot. Violence also occurred in Madison, Wisconsin; so SANE, SDS, and other groups declined to sponsor the Washington rally that consequently on October 20 drew only about 100,000 people.

Six days later Jesuit priest Philip Berrigan, Rev. James Mengel, Tom Lewis, and David Eberhardt poured their blood on the selective service files in the Baltimore

Customs House and then waited to be arrested. On May 17, 1968 Phil and his brother Daniel Berrigan with Tom Lewis and six others used home-made napalm to burn 378 draft files of the Catonsville, Maryland draft board. In their statement to the press they explained that napalm had killed and burned so many people in Vietnam, and they noted that US nuclear and conventional weaponry exceeds that of the rest of the world. They were sentenced to three years in prison. In September 1968 fourteen people burned about 10,000 draft files in Milwaukee, and various other actions against draft files occurred around the country.

In November 1967 General Westmoreland announced that troop withdrawal could begin in 1969 if the bombing and military progress continued. However, on the Vietnamese holiday of Tet at the end of January 1968 the Vietcong (NLF) launched a massive attack on the major cities of South Vietnam. Within three weeks about 165,000 civilians had been killed, and there were two million new refugees. American forces bombed hamlets that the Vietcong occupied. A US major, looking at the devastated village of Ben Tre, said, "We had to destroy it in order to save it." The offensive, which included an invasion of the US embassy in Saigon, came as a great shock to Americans. The huge size of the action and its surprise to the Americans and South Vietnamese Army indicated that most of the people in the country were more loyal to the NLF than to the Government.

When Westmoreland and chief of staff General Wheeler asked for 200,000 more troops, President Johnson was visibly shaken and began to doubt seriously for the first time the military policies he was following. In March 1968 Senator Eugene McCarthy won a victory in the New Hampshire Presidential primary running against Johnson's Vietnam war policy. A few days later Robert Kennedy announced his candidacy. On March 31 President Johnson announced he would not seek re-election, and to begin de-escalation of the war he limited the bombing to a small strategic area. The war and the anti-war movement that had been aroused to protest it had ruined the Johnson presidency, which on domestic issues had been rather successful. In May formal negotiations began in Paris. If Robert Kennedy had not been assassinated on the night he won the California primary on June 5, he probably would have gained the Democratic nomination and if elected, could have ended the war. Instead, Vice President Hubert Humphrey, who followed Johnson's war policy, gained the nomination even though he had not won a single primary. Frustrated people protested this miscarriage of the popular will at the Democratic national convention in Chicago in August but were suppressed by the brutality of Mayor Richard Daley's police. Richard Nixon won a narrow victory over Humphrey, and under his presidency American military intervention in Indochina would drag on for five more years.

In February 1969 Nixon's national security advisor, Henry Kissinger, began arranging the secret bombing of Communist bases in Cambodia in violation of the US Constitution, which requires Congress to declare war before attacking another country. To hide these crimes, bombing pilots were ordered to bomb South Vietnam and then had their targets changed; but they still filed false reports that they had bombed South Vietnam when in reality they had bombed Cambodia. By March 1969 there were 541,000 US troops fighting in South Vietnam. From March 1969 to May 1970, the United States conducted 3,630 bombing raids on Cambodia, killing about 600,000 people there. Another 350,000 civilians were killed in Laos by US bombing.

The peace movement continued to grow and affected Nixon's policies. President Nixon wanted to strike a "savage blow" against North Vietnam in the fall of 1969 by mining Haiphong harbor and perhaps even using nuclear weapons, but the demonstrations were so large in October and November that he changed his mind for political reasons. The paid staff of 31 for the Vietnam Moratorium Committee (VMC) had been infiltrated by CIA informers.

Local rallies brought out about a quarter of a million people to protest the war on October 15. On November 9 a full-page ad appeared in the *New York Times* signed by 1365 active duty GIs, saying, "We are opposed to American involvement in the war in Vietnam. We resent the needless wasting of lives to save face for the politicians in Washington."[7] The story of the massacre of over seven hundred civilians at My Lai was exposed to public outcry. On November 15 three quarters of a million people gathered in Washington while one quarter of a million marched in San Francisco.

After Nixon announced the invasion of Cambodia on April 30, 1970, student strikes were called on American college campuses. On May 4 at Kent State University in Ohio four protesting students were shot to death by national guard troops, and many other students were wounded. Within a few days over four million students at about 350 college campuses were on strike. In June the Senate repealed the Gulf of Tonkin Resolution and barred future US military operations in Cambodia without Congressional approval. By 1970 the Vietnam Veterans Against the War (VVAW) had become active with creative actions such as a mock search-and-destroy operation in New Jersey and Pennsylvania. They also testified that atrocities such as the My Lai massacre were not isolated cases but part of a pattern of war crimes for which they held the commanders responsible. After testifying before the Senate Foreign Relations committee in April 1971, 700 veterans angrily stated their names and flung their medals and ribbons back at the Capital. On April 24 about 300,000 demonstrated peacefully at the same time as 125,000 rallied in San Francisco. In Washington 30,000 people remained in West Potomac Park on May Day in an attempt to shut down the government. On May 2 before dawn police warned people to leave because of the use of drugs and began making arrests using plastic handcuffs. About 12,000 stayed, and by the end of the day more than 7,000 had been arrested. The arrest total for three days was about 13,000, the largest mass arrest in US history.

In June 1967 Secretary of Defense Robert McNamara had secretly commissioned a detailed study of the war in Vietnam by 36 Pentagon bureaucrats. In eighteen months they wrote 1.5 million words of narrative history and collected a million words in documents that covered US involvement in Vietnam from World War II to May 1968 when peace talks began in Paris. An employee of the Pentagon named Daniel Ellsberg made a copy of all this and gave it to Neil Sheehan of the *New York Times*, which began publishing a summary on June 13, 1971. After three installments the US Justice department got a restraining order from a Federal court. *The Times* and the *Washington Post* took the case to the US Supreme Court, which on June 30 voted 6-3 to allow publication of the *Pentagon Papers*. Ellsberg was prosecuted under the Espionage Act; but after the judge discovered that Nixon had ordered the office of his psychiatrist raided, he was released.

Adapting to public pressure, President Nixon began withdrawing US troops, but he kept the war going by bombing Laos, Cambodia, and North Vietnam. The "Vietnamization" of the war was doomed to fail without US support. Running against the peace candidate George McGovern in 1972, Nixon promised peace. Using various illegal political tricks against his opponents that were later exposed in the Watergate scandal, Nixon gained an overwhelming electoral victory. After his 1972 Christmas bombing, several peace groups and ten religious peace groups formed the Coalition to Stop Funding the War (CSFW). A cease-fire agreement was signed in January 1973. However, it was only when the Watergate scandal began to weaken the Nixon presidency that Congress, on July 1, 1973, finally cut off all funds for any military activity in Indochina. Without American troops fighting their civil war, the government of South Vietnam could not last long. On August 9, 1974 Nixon resigned the Presidency in order to avoid being impeached. On April 21, 1975 President Thieu resigned and fled, followed a week later by his successor. On April 30 Vietnam became a unified country as US helicopters completed the evacuation of 1,373 Americans and 5,595 Vietnamese, abandoning their embassy in Saigon.

American Lessons from Vietnam

What were the results of American military involvement in Vietnam? Without American support the government of South Vietnam completely collapsed by 1975. More than three million Americans were sent to Vietnam. About 58,000 were killed, and about 300,000 were wounded. A conservative estimate of *civilian* casualties in South Vietnam was the Senate Subcommittee on Refugees estimates of 400,000 killed, 900,000 wounded, and 6.4 million turned into refugees. The total number of people who were killed during the American-Vietnam War has been estimated between one million and three million people. The United States dropped from the air 3.2 million tons of bombs on South Vietnam, 2.1 million tons on Laos (almost one ton per person), and 340,000 tons on North Vietnam. Both Johnson and Nixon each presided over more bombing than was used by all sides in World War II. An obvious result of American military involvement is that the people of Vietnam were terribly militarized for self-defense and forced to try to solve their problems with military means. This contagion spread with the war in Cambodia, where millions more were killed in the 1970s.

In South Vietnam alone the United States government directly spent $141 billion. In a country where the per capita income was $157 per year, the US poured in the equivalent of $7,000 per person for the twenty million inhabitants. If even one-tenth of this amount had been spent helping the people of Vietnam, surely they would have become our friends; but spending it destructively resulted not only in massive killing and maiming but also in a decadent type of economy involving large amounts of graft, favoritism, prostitution, and drugs. The world's most powerful and wealthy nation was unable to defeat an army of peasants using homemade and captured weapons. Ostensibly fighting to preserve freedom, the United States propped up a series of military dictators. The American forces traveled halfway around the world to attack Vietnamese people in North and South Vietnam supposedly to protect them from "external aggression." The only conceivable external aggression, other than that of the US, was the movement of people from North Vietnam to South Vietnam; yet the basis of the Geneva Accords was that Vietnam was to be one country. Then how can the movement of Vietnamese in their own country be considered external aggression? The United States claimed it must continue the fight for its honor and the respect of its allies; yet never before has America been so dishonored or lost the respect of its allies more than it did in Vietnam.

Using the weak justification of SEATO's collective defense arrangements, the United States violated the United Nations Charter, the Geneva Accords of 1954, the Nuremberg Code, the Hague Conventions, the Geneva Protocol of 1925, the 1928 Pact of Paris, the Geneva Conventions and Genocide Convention of 1949, and the Paris agreements of 1973. International law expert Richard A. Falk noted the following illegal war policies:

1. the Phoenix Program,
2. aerial and naval bombardment of undefended villages,
3. destruction of crops and forests.
4. "search-and-destroy" missions,
5. "harassment and interdiction" fire,
6. forcible removal of civilian population,
7. reliance on a variety of weapons prohibited by treaty.

After devastating the country of Vietnam, the rich United States has not even considered paying reparations. In fact the US was the only nation out of 141 that refused to endorse a United Nations resolution urging priority economic assistance to Vietnam.

Another result is the terrible injuries, both physical and psychological, which the Vietnam veterans have suffered.

The moral problems have caused severe psychological disturbances. Hundreds of thousands of Americans were trained to kill and did kill hundreds of thousands of Vietnamese. When they discovered it was for no good reason, the remorse, grief, guilt, anger, frustration, and resentment erupted. By 1980 the number of veterans, who had committed suicide, was already larger than the number of Americans killed in Vietnam. The veterans bear the heaviest psychological burden. Yet all Americans were responsible, especially the politicians and officers who gave the orders.

The only restraints on US military escalation were the fear of a conflict with China or the Soviet Union and the conscience of the American public as represented in the peace movement. During the Vietnam War about 170,000 young American men were granted Conscientious Objector (CO) status by their draft boards or from the military, and some 300,000 applied but were denied the deferment. The number of men who illegally avoided the draft has been estimated at 600,000, and about a third of these were formally charged. About 40,000 fled to Canada, while another 20,000 escaped to other countries or hid from authorities in the United States. The number of COs increased from 18,000 in 1964 to 61,000 in 1971, and the number of prosecutions went from 340 in 1965 to 5,000 for the year 1972. About 17,000 in the military applied to be Conscientious Objectors.

Noting that anti-war demonstrators did not kill a single person during the period the US Government killed hundreds of thousands in Indochina, Fred Halstead summarized the accomplishments of the anti-war movement as breaking the spell of anti-Communist hysteria, increasing healthy skepticism of political leaders, changing the stereotype of soldiers as obedient pawns, becoming reluctant to engage in military adventures abroad, and expanding social reform movements to issues of foreign policy. For the first time in American history the people successfully challenged the government's right to wage war.

Why, then, did America get bogged down in the quagmire of Vietnam for so long at such great cost? After World War II the United States became the greatest power in the history of the world. The abuse of greatness is the abuse of the power. America thought it could do no wrong. At the same time Americans had a tremendous fear of Communism. Historically, it took a decade and a half before the US even recognized the Soviet Union and more than two decades before it recognized nearly a billion people in China. With a world-wide military force the United States was arrogant enough to think that it could stop Communism by force of arms. Psychologically there was the irrational fear that if America did not intervene, somehow Communism would take over the world. The Soviet empire was likewise afraid of encroachment through Korea or eastern Europe and therefore took steps to place a protective ring around itself, while the United States has protective military bases all around the world.

Because of this combination of American power, fear of Communism, and self-righteous concepts about capitalist democracy, the US foolishly tried to set up a non-Communist government in a country that was trying to free itself from French colonialism by a combination of nationalistic independence and Marxist ideology. Politicians apparently believed that only by the influence of its military power could the United States try to hold back the tide of political revolution and national independence in Vietnam.

What are the lessons for the future that Americans and others can learn? Military methods ultimately do not solve political and social problems. Independence and self-determination are best attained without military interference. Military methods only militarize the opposition and escalate violence so that peaceful solutions are more unattainable. The security of the United States and its allies is not really threatened by what goes on in small underdeveloped countries. Nuclear weapons are of no use in these situations. Armed intervention will eventually backfire. The US has no legal right to be a policeman in another country. The veterans can teach others of the horrors and agonies of war. The American people must not allow the President to go astray while intoxicated with power. An effective peace movement can dramatically influence political policies. Finally, every person has the responsibility to refuse to support an illegal and immoral war.

Notes

1. *Vietnam: A History in Documents* ed. Gareth Porter, p. 30
2. Ho Chi Minh, *On Revolution*, p. 161.
3. *Viet-Nam Crisis: A Documentary History, Volume 1: 1940-1956*, p. 148.
4. *Vietnam: A History in Documents* ed. Gareth Porter, p. 206.
5. *Out Now! A Participant's Account of the American Movement Against the Vietnam War* by Fred Halstead, p. 35.
6. *Nonviolence in America: A Documentary History* ed. Straughton and Alice Lynd, p. 270-271.
7. *Out Now! A Participant's Account of the American Movement Against the Vietnam War* by Fred Halstead, p. 504.

10

Women for Peace

Perhaps the universal Sisterhood is necessary
before the Universal Brotherhood is possible.
Bertha von Suttner, June 1912

As women entered into politics
when clean milk and premature labor of children
became factors in political life,
so they might be concerned with international affairs
when these at least were dealing with
such human and poignant matters as food for starving peoples
who could be fed only through international activities....
There might be found an antidote to war in woman's affection
and all-embracing pity for helpless children.
Jane Addams, *Peace and Bread in Time of War*

Our function is to establish new values,
to create an overpowering sense of the sacredness of life,
so that war will be unthinkable;
so that when international disputes arise,
even of the most grave character—when lives have been lost,
when our rights have been clearly invaded—
we shall not turn to wholesale, deliberate destruction of life
as the means of settling those disputes,
of avenging those deaths, of asserting those rights.
Crystal Eastman, July 24, 1915

You can no more win a war than an earthquake!
Jeannette Rankin

If by strength is meant moral power,
then woman is immeasurably man's superior.
Has she not greater intuition,
is she not more self-sacrificing,
has she not greater powers of endurance,
has she not greater courage?
Without her man could not be.
If nonviolence is the law of our being,

the future is with woman.
Mohandas Gandhi, 1930

Love is the measure by which we will be judged.
Dorothy Day

This is the way to peace—overcome evil with good,
and falsehood with truth, and hatred with love.
Peace Pilgrim

Experiment with nonviolent struggle has barely begun.
But in a world in which traditional violent battle
can escalate into nuclear war,
it is an experiment that is absolutely necessary
to push to its furthest limits.
Barbara Deming

A liberation movement that is nonviolent
sets the oppressor free as well as the oppressed.
Barbara Deming

Feminism can help women respect their own power.
Nonviolence can help them use their power effectively
in a way which maintains that respect
and extends it to others.
Jane Meyerding

The true measure of justice of a system
is the amount of protection it guarantees to the weakest.
Where there is no justice there can be no peace.
Aung San Suu Kyi, "In Quest of Democracy"

The more we understand, appreciate, and humanize
people we are taught to see as enemies,
the harder it is for our government
to persuade us to fight them....
The struggle to end war will be the culmination
of a global movement that rejects violence
on the part of individuals, terrorist groups, and nation-states.
Medea Benjamin, 2005

Women make up more than half of the human race. Yet civilization has been suffering for five thousand years under the aggressive oppression of male dominance and authoritarian patriarchy. Some of the great philosophers of peace, such as 'Abdu'l-Bahá and Gandhi, have seen hope for a peaceful world in the future because of the softening of masculine force by the feminine qualities of love, service, intuition, and moral power. The women's movement is well on the way to healing a society so afflicted by militarism that it teeters on the brink of mass destruction. Whereas war used to be a masculine "sport" for warriors, in the twentieth century the percentage of civilian deaths in war steadily increased until now everyone is imperiled by the threat of nuclear holocaust. At the same time women have become increasingly involved in actively working for peace, responding instinctively to nurture the human race for the sake of its survival. Previous chapters have discussed how women contributed to the abolition of slavery, suffrage, and women's rights. As early as 1891 the National Council of Women (NCW) and the Women's Christian Temperance Union (WCTU) petitioned the US Government to avoid war with Chile, and in 1895 women's groups urged that a Venezuelan border dispute with England be settled by arbitration.

Suttner, Courtney, Royden, and Weil

Bertha Kinsky was born June 9, 1843 in Prague and married Baron von Suttner after serving as a governess in his house. She worked briefly for Alfred Bernhard Nobel, and he often supported her peace efforts with donations. She was influenced by Charles Darwin's theory of evolution and the progressive ideas of Herbert Spencer and the historian H. T. Buckle. She suggested that human progress was leading toward disarmament and peace in her *Inventory of a Soul*. In *The Machine Age* she argued that war is the opposite of survival of the fittest, because it kills the most fit while allowing the defective to survive; thus instead of evolving the species, it causes degeneration. She prophesied that someday more powerful weapons would be able to destroy entire armies at once and would thus eliminate the strategies that make war feasible, though her friend Nobel with his explosives business continued to believe that deterrence would prevent wars. She could understand a few sacrificing themselves for the majority; but she felt that to sacrifice all for none is extreme madness. In 1888 she heard a call from Hodgson Pratt of the London Peace Society to form a great league with branches in all European cities. She believed that everyone must contribute to humanity's well-being, and she saw the peace movement as a way to do so.

By far Bertha von Suttner's most famous and influential novel was the two-volume *Lay Down Your Arms*, which was published in 1889. Written from a woman's point of view as she loses two husbands in the wars of 1859 and 1870, she dramatically exposed the superficiality and folly of men going to war for honor to show their courage. Politicians and generals are particularly criticized for promoting armaments. In the last chapter the main character wrote in her diary,

Today there is hardly any one left
who has not dreamed this dream,
or who would not confess its beauty.
And there are watchers too;
watchers conspicuous enough, who are longing
to awake mankind out of the long sleep of savagery,
and energetically and with a single eye to their object
collecting themselves for the purpose
of planting the white flag.
Their battle-cry is, "War on War,"
their watchword, the only word which can have power
to deliver from ruin Europe armed against herself is,
"Lay down your arms."
In all places, in England and France, in Italy,
in the northern countries, in Germany
 in Switzerland, in America,
associations have been formed, whose object is,
through the compulsion of public opinion,

through the commanding pressure of the people's will,
to move the Governments to submit their differences
in future to an Arbitration Court, appointed by themselves,
and so once for all to enthrone justice
in place of brute force.[1]

Near the end of the book she predicted that the next
war would not be a gain for either side but ruin for all. This
novel was translated into dozens of languages and made
the international peace movement a major topic of discussion throughout Europe. Leo Tolstoy hoped that it would
have the same effect on the war problem that Harriet
Beecher Stowe had on slavery with *Uncle Tom's Cabin*,
though he called it "untalented" and believed that arbitration was not a complete solution. Nevertheless he did
correspond with "Peace Bertha" as she came to be called in
the satirical press.

Bertha von Suttner founded an Austrian peace society
in 1891 and the next year attended the international peace
congress at Bern, where she suggested a European confederation of states and last saw Nobel. It is widely believed
that he included the Peace Prize in his 1896 will because of
her, and she became the first woman to win this Nobel
Prize in 1906. She also urged Andrew Carnegie to do more
for peace than merely donating libraries. She promoted and
attended the Peace Conferences at The Hague in 1899 and
1907. Suttner traveled extensively, including a tour from
New York to California, and spoke to an estimated 400,000
people. She tried to calm the conflicts in the Balkans; but
she died on June 21, 1914, one week before the assassination at Sarajevo of Franz Ferdinand, the crown prince of the
Austro-Hungarian empire that touched off the Great War.
Suttner had also written a two-volume autobiography, and
in 1917 her political articles were published in two volumes
as *The Battle for the Prevention of World War*, which was
immediately banned in Austria and Germany.

In England in 1900 Kate Courtney (1847-1929) and
Emily Hobhouse founded a Women's Committee of the

South Africa Conciliation movement to urge settlement of the Boer War and the South African Women and Children's Distress Fund to help those made homeless by Britain's scorched-earth policy of burning farms. The British established large concentration camps in which 27,927 Boers died, mostly children and women. Also 14,000 African women died in black concentration camps. In 1911 Courtney complained that Italy's seizing Tripoli from the Turks would set back the Peace and Arbitration movement, and novelist Bertha von Suttner made the same point in her speeches in Bucharest and Budapest. Courtney objected to the imperialism of the French in Morocco, Austrians in Herzegovina and Bosnia, Russians in Persia, and the British in South Africa and Egypt; she noted that only poor Germany was still a "lion without a Christian." She complained that the secret Cabinet government could mobilize the nation without warning or consultation, that secret diplomacy was based on an "enemy psychosis," and that two rival imperialists were engaged in an uncontrolled and unstable arms race.

During the World War, Kate Courtney worked for an Emergency Committee to help "enemy aliens," in the Union for the Democratic Control of Foreign Policy (UDC), and with the emerging international women's peace movement. In 1915 she arranged for Jane Addams to meet with Robert Cecil at the Foreign Office. She tried to intervene on behalf of UDC chairman E. D. Morel after he was arrested and sentenced to six months under the Defence of the Realm Act for sending two pamphlets to pacifist Romain Rolland in neutral Switzerland. Courtney's *War Diary* expressed intelligent views about the terrible war and described what she was doing about it. After the war the first meeting of the Fight the Famine Committee was held at her house, and she prophesied that the humiliating terms being imposed on Germany were likely to push Germans into another war.

Maude Royden (1876-1956) studied at Oxford and as a

preacher tried to become the first woman ordained in the Church of England. In 1908 she became a speaker for the voting rights of women, and from 1912 to 1914 she edited the suffragists' weekly paper, *The Common Cause*. She embraced internationalism and peace and was appalled when the Great War broke out. She became an activist with the Fellowship of Reconciliation (FOR) and in 1915 published her first pacifist pamphlet, *The Great Adventure: The Way to Peace*, in which she advocated non-violent direct action (NVDA). She argued that the Christ offered humanity an alternative to violent reaction in the Sermon on the Mount. She suggested how England could have used nonviolent methods to resist German aggression, because many Germans were socialists and would have supported them.

We could have called for the peace-lovers in the world
to fling themselves—if need be—in front of the troop trains.
If millions of men will go out to offer their lives up in war,
surely there are those who would die for peace!
and if not men, we could have called out women![2]

Royden believed that the heroism of the cross is much greater than the heroism of the sword; the greater adventurer goes to the enemy with naked hands. The Christian ideal should not be sacrificed to national necessity because truth is better than victory. The Fellowship of Reconciliation organized a peace caravan, and they were nearly burned to death by a mob in Midland town; but police intervened and sent them away on a train. Royden realized that women could be as militaristic as men, but she believed that the women's movement could be a natural force for peace. Because they believed in moral force instead of physical force, they could work against militarism; the physically weaker sex would not agree that "Might is right."

When Royden attended the International Alliance for Women's Suffrage conference at Geneva in 1920, she was allowed to preach from Calvin's pulpit, inspiring people that only love can create and build, because without love the world perishes. In the 1920s she complained that the League of Nations was being betrayed as the "balance of power" once again was substituted for collective security. In 1931 Maude Royden appealed to both men and women to form a Peace Army that could intervene nonviolently between combatants. She was deeply disappointed that "only a thousand people" volunteered and that they were never organized, though she did initiate protest meetings at the London docks against shipping arms to Japan. She had compromised her pacifism to accept the collective security of the League; when World War II began in 1939, she repudiated her pacifism.

Simone Weil (1909-43) was a child during the First World War in France and "adopted" a soldier, who was killed. She felt she was cured of nationalistic patriotism when she saw the French humiliate the Germans after the war. She studied with the pacifist philosopher Alain for four years and noted that the slavery of soldiers is much worse than the slavery of workers. After the signing of the Kellogg-Briand Peace Pact, in 1929 she circulated a manifesto calling for immediate and complete disarmament. The next year she participated in a peace march to support Briand. When French President Lebrun came to unveil a local war memorial in October 1933, she opposed war by speaking to her socialist and pacifist friends from a window ledge.

The next month Simone Weil published her "Reflections on War" in *La Critique Sociale* magazine. She noted that war always strengthens the state over the people regardless of ideology. War affects not only foreign policy but domestic policy as well because a massacre is oppressive. She argued that a revolution dies when it becomes a war. Whether the enemy is fascist, democratic, or communist, the adversary becomes the bureaucracy and the military. The "protector" that makes its citizens slaves becomes just as much an enemy. The worst betrayal is to subordinate oneself to the war machine, which destroys human values. War is not only the supreme example of inhumanity but actually is a competition in inhumanity. The state machine fights in order to maintain its ability to make war. She prophesied that future wars would be an insane destruction of wealth built up by civilization over generations until civilization itself perished.

In 1936 Weil believed that the socialist government of Spain deserved her support in its fight for survival against the fascists, and that summer she pointed a rifle at planes but primarily served as a cook. She observed how pitiless killing became a way of life. She left the war after she was scalded by burning oil. Weil soon returned to her pacifist principles as she asked if war could ever bring the world more justice, liberty, or well being. In 1937 she wrote her powerful antimilitarist essay "Ne Recommencons pas la Guerre de Troie," which was translated as "The Power of Words." She asked why nations waged war against each other century after century. In the Trojan War she saw Helen as an empty symbol that could be replaced by any abstraction in capital letters such as nation, security, capitalism, communism, fascism, democracy, etc. She astutely observed,

> What a country calls its vital economic interests
> are not the things which enable its citizens to live,
> but the things which enable it to make war;
> petrol is much more likely than wheat
> to be a cause of international conflict.
> Thus when war is waged it is for the purpose
> of safeguarding or increasing one's capacity to make war.[3]

 A government cannot appear weak in its external relations without weakening its authority over its own people. She perceived that only complete and universal disarmament could resolve this dilemma, but she realized that was nearly inconceivable. The illusion of national security by retaining the capacity to make war is practically impossible, because the only way to achieve it is to deprive other countries of the same security.

In March 1938 Weil signed a statement by French anti-fascists urging their government to negotiate with Germany for the sake of world peace, and she agreed to speak that summer with Maria Montessori for peace. Yet the next month she wrote an article how they could resist invasion by decentralized armed resistance. She urged the democracies to gain the moral advantage over Hitler by renouncing their colonies in Africa and Asia, and she criticized French imperialism in Algeria and Indochina. If they adopted the methods of Hitler, she felt that a victory would not be much better than a defeat. Reflecting on the Roman empire, she warned, "Every people which turns itself into a nation by submitting to a centralized, bureaucratic, military State becomes and long remains a scourge to its neighbors and the world."[4] She believed that the League of Nations failed because it left in place the dogma of national sovereignty, and she proposed a federalist world order that would decentralize the nation states. She pessimistically predicted that if a just and magnanimous peace was not established after World War II, the continued mutual massacres would destroy all the states.

Simone Weil taught philosophy at various schools in France, but she refused to eat more than those people on relief. She worked in a factory to find out what that was like. Her essay *"The Iliad:* Poem of Force" explained the nature of violence as portrayed in one of the earliest and best examples of western literature. After the Nazis occupied Paris, she moved to Marseilles; though of a Jewish family, she had a mystical experience in a chapel. She went with her parents to the United States in 1942. She crossed back to England to work for the French resistance, but leaders would not let her parachute into France. Because of the Jewish victims in Europe, she ate little and died of tuberculosis on August 24, 1943.

Addams, Woman's Peace Party, and WILPF

Jane Addams was born on September 6, 1860 in Cedar-ville, Illinois. Her mother died before she was three, and she was raised by her father, who believed in Quaker prin-ciples and served eight terms in the Illinois Senate. Illness interrupted Jane's medical studies. Traveling to Europe, she was impressed by Toynbee Hall in the slum of London. In September 1889 she and her college friend, Ellen Gates Star, founded Hull House in Chicago to provide a social center for the poor working people in the neighborhood. This was the beginning of the social settlement movement in the United States. Hull House became a focal point for social reforms in child labor laws, protection of immigrants, labor unions, and working conditions as well as a meeting place for educational and cultural activities. Her excellent books *Twenty Years at Hull-House* and *The Second Twenty Years at Hull-House* described this experience.

In *Newer Ideals of Peace*, published in 1907, Jane Addams criticized the militarism in city government, the inadequate responses of legislation to the needs of an industrial society, the lack of immigrants and women in local government, the inadequate protection of children, and the social prob-lems in the labor movement. Based on her experience in working with immigrants from various countries, she developed a cosmopolitan attitude she called "cosmic patriotism." She became an ardent internationalist and hoped that people could move beyond their narrow nation-alist orientations toward a more universal human effort and affection.

Jane Addams was vice-president of the National Amer-ican Woman Suffrage Association from 1911 to 1914; but when the war broke out in Europe, she devoted all her energies to working for peace. In September 1914 Rosika Schwimmer, a Hungarian journalist and suffragist, came to America and spoke to President Wilson, Secretary of State Bryan, and then the general public about the United States intervening to negotiate a peace settlement. Emmeline Pethick-Lawrence, an English feminist, spoke at a suffrage rally in Carnegie Hall about organizing a woman's peace movement. Crystal Eastman formed a woman's peace committee and suggested that Pethick-Lawrence contact Jane Addams in Chicago. Carrie Chapman Catt also wrote Jane Addams a letter complaining that the present management of the peace movement in the United States was over-masculinized. Addams agreed that women were the most eager for action, and she and Catt called a national conference of women's organizations.

They gathered in Washington on January 9, 1915 and formed the Woman's Peace Party with a Preamble that stated, "As women we feel a peculiar moral passion of revolt against both the cruelty and waste of war,"[5] and with the following insightful platform:

1. The immediate calling of a convention of neutral nations in the interest of early peace.
2. Limitation of armaments and the nationalization of the manufacture.
3. Organized opposition to militarism in our own country.
4. Education of youth in the ideals of peace.
5. Democratic control of foreign policies.
6. The further humanizing of governments by the extension of the franchise of women.
7. "Concert of Nations" to supersede "Balance of Power."
8. Action toward the gradual organization of the world to substitute Law for War.
9. The substitution of an international police for rival armies and navies.
10. Removal of economic causes of war.
11. The appointment by our Government of a commission of men and women, with an adequate appropriation to promote international peace.[6]

Thus to stop the current war they suggested a conference of delegates from neutral nations or at least an unofficial conference of pacifists. To make sure that the settlement terms would not sow the seeds of new wars they recommended self-determination and autonomy for all disputed territories, no war indemnities unless international law had been violated, and democratic control of foreign policy and treaty arrangements. To secure world peace for the future they suggested replacing the "balance of power" with an international congress, an international police force, and courts to settle all disputes between nations; an immediate and permanent League of Neutral Nations could use binding arbitration, judicial, and legislative procedures and an international police force for protection. The progressive national disarmament should be protected by the peace program; until disarmament is complete, munitions manufacture should be nationalized. Private property at sea should be protected by international and national action to remove the economic causes of war.

The national program for the United States included approval of the Peace Commission Treaties that require a year's investigation before any declaration of war, protest against the increase of armaments, and a recommendation that the President and US Government set up a commission of men and women to work for the prevention of war. Three thousand people attended the mass meeting, and Jane Addams was elected chairman. National headquarters was established in Chicago, and within a year 25,000 women had joined.

Crystal Eastman felt that a Woman's Peace Party was good because women are mothers, or potential mothers, and "therefore have a more intimate sense of the value of human life."[7] Thus there can be more meaning and passion in their determination to end war than in an organization with both men and women. In an article for *Survey* Crystal Eastman explained how the Woman's Peace Congress at The Hague was organized by the Dutch suffragist Aletta Jacobs, whom she called, "one of a group of 'international' women who are challenging public opinion with the idea of world union for peace."[8] The Woman Suffrage Alliance meeting scheduled for Berlin had to be canceled because of the war. Instead, Dr. Jacobs called a meeting in February 1915 at Amsterdam to plan a larger congress of individuals to focus on methods of bringing about peace. Leaders from Belgium, Germany, and Britain met with their Dutch hostesses and issued a call for an international Congress of Women at The Hague on April 28; they invited Jane Addams to preside.

Representatives of over 150 organizations from twelve countries gathered that spring of 1915, and 1,136 women voted to adopt twenty resolutions. These were similar to the program of the Woman's Peace Party. The International Congress of Women advocated universal disarmament secured by international agreement. They believed that the private profits from armament factories were a strong hindrance to abolishing war. In addition they decided to urge the neutral countries to offer continuous mediation for a peace settlement between the belligerent nations, and they selected envoys to approach the different governments. Jane Addams, Aletta Jacobs, and the Italian Rosa Genoni went to Austro-Hungary, Belgium, Britain, France, Germany, Italy, and Switzerland. Emily Balch, Chrystal Macmillan, Cor Ramondt Hirschmann, and Rosika Schwimmer were sent to the Scandinavian countries and Russia. In Sweden alone 343 meetings were held on June 27, and The Hague resolutions were signed by 88,784 women. In August, Jane Addams met with President Wilson, who said that the resolutions were the best formulation he had seen so far.

After having witnessed the war, Jane Addams explained why the young soldiers and civilians were revolting against war. She found that every nation claimed that they were fighting in self-defense to preserve their traditions. Though the elderly men believed that war was right and should be fought to the finish, the young men in the trenches were not convinced that it was a legitimate way of settling disputes. She quoted a young man who said,

We are told that we are fighting for civilization
but I tell you that war destroys civilization.
The highest product of the universities,

the scholar, the philosopher, the poet,
when he is in the trenches,
when he spends his days and nights
in squalor and brutality and horror
is as low and brutal as the rudest peasant.[9]

He went on to explain that in the trenches there was neither courage nor cowardice, as chance determined who was blown up. Addams found war to be so unnatural that soldiers had to be drugged to make the bayonet charge. The English were given rum, the Germans ether, and the French used absinthe. She believed that if peace were made by negotiation, the civil authorities of the western democracies would have more influence; but if it was fought to victory, the military authorities would make the final settlement.

Of the factors that Jane Addams believed caused the war to continue, she placed first the influence of the press, observing,

The press everywhere tended to make
an entire nation responsible for the crimes of individuals,
a tendency which is certainly
fraught with awful consequences,
even though the crimes for which
the nation is held responsible
may have originated in the gross exaggeration
of some trivial incident.[10]

She also noticed that the domination by the press prevented the mobilization of the advocates for peace. She began to believe that "the next revolution against tyranny would have to be a revolution against the unscrupulous power of the press."[11] People of different countries were not able to get the information they needed to make sound judgments about the war, because the press selected the knowledge they wanted the people to have just as the church did in the past. The women at The Hague believed that the time had come to begin negotiations, or else the war would go on year after year until exhaustion. Some politicians called these women envoys foolish. However, one high official told Addams that hers were the first sensible words he had heard in his office for ten months; usually people just asked him for more ammunition and more money. To him the words "why not substitute negotiations for fighting" were the most sensible. Addams hoped that the breakdown of the philosophy of nationalism would bring about a new birth of internationalism, founded not just on arbitration treaties but upon governmental institutions designed to protect and enhance by cooperation a world becoming conscious of itself.

After visiting the capitals of the belligerent governments, Addams found they had no objection to a conference of neutral nations, even though they could not ask for mediation. To alleviate the fear of beginning a conference while one side had a military advantage, she argued "that the proposed conference would start mediation at a higher level than that of military advantage."[12] Three out of five neutral European nations were ready to join in such a conference, while the other two were still deliberating. By fall all the leading belligerent nations were willing to cooperate in a Neutral Conference, and the neutrals Norway, Sweden, Denmark, and Holland were eager to participate if the conference were to be called by the United States. Unfortunately the US declined for the reasons that Latin American countries could not be ignored nor was there room for many of them to participate; also the Central Powers had the technical military advantage at that time. Another neutral country would offer to call the conference if the United States would attend, but this made no difference. Even 10,000 telegrams to President Wilson from woman's organizations were of no avail.

In January 1916 the Woman's Peace Party became the United States section of the international organization which came to be named the Women's International League for Peace and Freedom (WILPF). Henry Ford donated a chartered ship to take women to Europe for a private Neutral Conference, which was held in Stockholm on January 26. They formulated further appeals to the neutral and belligerent nations to begin mediation.

Crystal Eastman started in November 1915 the "Truth About Preparedness Campaign" sponsored by the Woman's Peace Party and the American Union Against Militarism (AUAM). She revealed the economic exploitation behind the industrialists' propaganda for military increases through public debates and numerous articles. In the summer of 1916 AUAM's private investigation of the facts in Mexico revealed that the American troops were the aggressors in a skirmish, and a massive publicity campaign changed President Wilson's mind, preventing the United States from entering into a misguided war with Mexico. In 1917 Crystal Eastman and Roger Baldwin founded the American Civil Liberties Union (ACLU) to protect human rights. Alice Paul told Jeannette Rankin, "It would be a tragedy for the first woman ever in Congress to vote for war."[13] Rankin said, "I want to stand by my country, but I cannot vote for war."[14] Rankin voted against entering the war, and in 1941 she was in Congress again to vote against another World War. After America entered the war, Crystal Eastman and other radicals struggled for an early peace, opposed conscription, universal military training, and other repressive legislation; they sponsored classes led by pacifists such as Norman Angell and Emily Green Balch.

Disappointed by Wilson's entering into the war, Jane Addams turned her efforts to the struggle for food. She urged international cooperation and demanded that food blockades, still in place after the armistice, be immediately lifted. She felt that women could do much for international organization especially in regard to such a basic issue as food for survival.

In 1919 the International Congress of Women held in Zurich criticized the peace terms for sanctioning secret agreements, denying self-determination, giving spoils to the victors, creating discord in Europe, demanding disarmament only for the losing side, and condemning a hundred million people to poverty, disease, despair, hatred, and anarchy because of the economic proposals. They welcomed a League of Nations, which four years earlier had seemed so unrealistic to many; but they criticized the plan for varying from Wilson's fourteen points.

The Women's Peace Society (WPS) was founded in 1919 by William Lloyd Garrison's daughter Fanny Garrison Villard. As the League of Nations was forming, the Women's International League for Peace and Freedom (WILPF) established its headquarters in Geneva, where they kept a close watch on the League of Nations Assembly and Secretariat. WILPF helped to publicize its proceedings and offered frequent criticism. In lectures Jane Addams urged the United States to participate in the World Court.

In August 1921 Elinor Byrns was acting as chair of a conference that was held on the Canadian side of Niagara and formed the Woman's Peace Union (WPU) of the Western Hemisphere. They urged President Harding to work for "immediate, universal and complete disarmament" at the upcoming Washington Naval Conference. The WPU pledge was based on Garrison's 1838 "Declaration of Sentiments."

We women of the Western Hemisphere believe that
under no circumstances is it right to take human life
and pledge ourselves to work for world peace....
We affirm it is our intention never to aid in or sanction war,
offensive or defensive, international or civil, or in any way,
whether by making or handling munitions,
subscribing to war loans, using our labor
for the purpose of setting others free for war service,
helping by money or work any organization
which supports or condones war.[15]

In 1923 Elinor Byrns and Caroline Lexow Babcock of the WPU initiated a resolution for a constitutional amendment to outlaw war and remove the power of the US Congress to declare war, raise or support any military, or appropriate money for war. They promoted a "Declaration of Independence from the Tyranny of War" because war must be abolished before it abolishes the human race. They persuaded Republican Senator Lynn Joseph Frazier from North Dakota to present their resolution in every session of the Congress from 1926 to 1939. Elinor Byrnes published a pamphlet in 1927 entitled "Violence and Killing Always Wrong" in which she connected violence to ownership and the will to power. She condemned child abuse, capital punishment, and the use of force to break strikes. Jeannette Rankin worked for the WPU in 1929. The next year the WPU gained the support of the Women's Peace Society, the War Resisters League, the American Friends Service Committee (AFSC), the Pennsylvania Committee for Total Disarmament, the Fellowship of Reconciliation, and WILPF to testify at the hearing on the Senate Joint Resolution 45.

In 1923 the WILPF board in a resolution urged the US Congress to pass a bill forbidding the use of the military for collecting private debts or protecting private investments in foreign countries. WILPF believed that the United States could help developing countries without imposing "occupation or overlordship." They opposed increasing the US Navy. In 1924 WILPF suggested that governments agree to the compulsory jurisdiction of the Permanent Court of International Justice. Their Congress held in Washington that year also recommended better education to avoid mass suggestion, the abolition of capital punishment and the improvement of prisons, and a better balance of influence between men and women. The National Committee on the Causes and Cures of War (NCCCW) soon became the largest woman's peace group in the United States after it was founded by Carrie Chapman Catt in 1924; as the most broad-based, it was the most conservative. In 1928 the NCCCW organized 14,000 meetings to urge ratification of the Kellogg-Briand Pact to outlaw war. WILPF considered this treaty a valuable step toward substituting law for war and achieving the disarmament of all nations.

The 1929 WILPF Congress in Prague warned that modern warfare threatened civilian populations and that the only way to safety is disarmament. NCCCW and WILPF worked together in gathering 600,000 signatures in the US to contribute to the eight million that were presented to the 1932 Geneva Conference for the Reduction and Limitations of Armaments. After Japan invaded Manchuria, WILPF sent a letter to President Hoover urging the United States to cooperate with the League of Nations Council in challenging this treaty violation and to work with the signatories of the Nine Power Pact, to publish its diplomatic notes with Japan, and to prohibit arms shipments to Japan. In 1933 WILPF stimulated North Dakota Senator Gerald P. Nye, chairman of the Munitions Committee, to investigate the profits made by arms manufacturers in the World War and that industry's role in bribing public officials to vote for larger military budgets and fix prices. WILPF's 1934 Zurich Congress formulated aims that became its policy for the next quarter century. The primary goals read:

Total and universal disarmament,
the abolition of violent means of coercion
for the settlement of all conflicts,
the substitution in every case
of some form of peaceful settlement,
and the development of a world organization
for the political, social and economic
cooperation of peoples.[16]

In addition they committed themselves to studying and alleviating the causes of war by nonviolent social reform. Jane Addams donated to WILPF the money she got for winning the Nobel Peace Prize in 1931. She had been International President of WILPF for twenty years when she died in 1935.

When Chamberlain appeased Hitler in 1938 at Munich, WILPF issued this strong response:

It is a sham peace based on
the violation of law, justice and right.

It is a so-called 'peaceful change' dictated by four Powers
and forced upon a young and small State,
which was not represented
when its dismemberment was finally decided upon.[17]

The International Chairmen of WILPF sent out an
appeal to help Czechoslovakia financially and economically. In it they declared,

Pacifism is *not* the quietistic acceptance
of betrayal and lies for the sake of 'Peace.'
Pacifism is the struggle for truth, the struggle for right,
the struggle for clear political aims,
for firm political will and action.
Pacifism is *not* weak acceptance of 'faits accomplis'
achieved by brute force.
Pacifism is courageous initiative
for a constructive policy of just peace.[18]

In 1951 WILPF considered a plan for a nonviolent
national defense along Gandhian lines to deter aggression
without the disadvantages and dangers of armaments.
They discovered that nonviolent principles must be understood by the people before this can work on a national
scale, recognizing that violence breeds violence, upholding
truth before prestige, accepting the principle of equal
rights, freedom of conscience and of information, and
strengthening altruistic rather than materialistic values.

WILPF has supported the United Nations and criticized
the Korean War, nuclear arms and testing, civil rights violations, the Vietnam War, and the nuclear arms race. In March
1983 WILPF representatives visited the NATO governments to protest the deployment of more nuclear weapons
in Europe. WILPF holds to the Gandhian principle against
war and violence, because a good end cannot be attained
by a bad means. WILPF remains perhaps the largest and
most influential of all the international women's peace
organizations.

Dorothy Day and the Catholic Worker

Another great peacemaker and social reformer was Dorothy Day, who founded the Catholic Worker. Dorothy was born in Brooklyn on November 8, 1897. A scholarship helped her to attend the University of Illinois, where she joined a socialist group. In 1917 she went to Washington to picket the White House with the suffragists. She was arrested and bailed out. When the thirty-five of them appeared in court, they were convicted; but their sentencing was postponed. That afternoon they picketed and were arrested again, going through the same procedure. The third time they refused to pay bail. The leaders were sentenced to six months, the older women to fifteen days, and the rest, including Dorothy, to thirty days. They demanded to be treated as political prisoners and went on a hunger strike for ten days until their demands were met. Day was so obstreperous that she was handcuffed and thrown in a cell with leader Lucy Burns.

Dorothy Day moved back to New York, and she was soon mixing as a writer and activist with Eugene O'Neill, John Reed, Louise Bryant, and Max Eastman. She wrote for *The Masses* until it was suppressed by the US Government. For many years Dorothy worked as a free-lance writer. She published an autobiographical novel entitled *The Eleventh Virgin* and even sold its movie rights. She fell in love with an older writer, who did not want to marry, and she had an abortion. Later she formed a common law marriage with anarchist Forster Batterham and gave birth to the girl Tamar. She raised her daughter, and in 1928 she became a Catholic. Dorothy once said, "I believe because I want to believe; I hope because I want to hope; I love because I want to love."[19]

In December 1932 Dorothy went to Washington for the Hunger March of the Unemployed that was organized by her Communist friends. There she prayed to God for some way that she could help the poor. Returning to New York, she found waiting for her a homeless French priest named Peter Maurin, who had been told that she had similar beliefs as his. He was full of ideas and shared them with her in an uninterrupted flow. He disagreed with Communism because he considered the dictatorship of the proletariat and class warfare to be unsound means. He said, "A pure end requires pure means. Christian charity and voluntary poverty are the pure means for the realization of a Communist society."[20] He proposed publishing a newspaper to popularize his ideas for a communitarian revolution, round-table discussions to clarify thought, houses of hospitality as living centers to help the poor and provide hospices, and farming communes as "agronomic universities."

So Dorothy Day and Peter Maurin began the Catholic Worker movement in the depths of the Depression. They started publishing a newspaper called *The Catholic Worker* in May 1933. About twenty people moved into a house on the west side of New York; they fed the hungry, clothed the needy, and sheltered the homeless, not as an impersonal state agency but by personal sacrifice and care. Soon "houses of hospitality" were being started in Boston, Rochester, Milwaukee, and other cities. They lived in voluntary poverty, practicing Christ's teachings. By 1935 the circulation of the *Catholic Worker* newspaper went over 100,000. They moved into a large house on Mott Street and later also got a small farm outside of New York. Despite disagreement from Peter Maurin, Dorothy Day spent much of her efforts in the 1930s helping workers to organize unions. Dorothy traveled and spoke to groups. They picketed the German consulate to protest Nazi anti-Semitism and gave out literature criticizing Nazi policies. In May 1939 Dorothy and some friends formed the Committee of Catholics to Fight Anti-Semitism.

When the Second World War began, Dorothy Day still retained the Gospel teaching of human brotherhood and would not give up her pacifism. In June 1940 their "Peace Edition" of the *Catholic Worker* suggested they could use nonviolent means to resist an invader. Day wrote about the immorality of conscription, and she urged Catholics to be

Conscientious Objectors. After the bombing of Pearl Harbor, the *Catholic Worker* headline and subheadline read,

Our Country Passes from Undeclared to Declared War;
We Continue Our Christian Pacifist Stand.
In Addition to the Weapons of Starvation of Its Enemy,
Our Country Is Now Using the Weapons
of Army, Navy, and Air Force.[21]

Yet some Catholic Workers joined the army, and dissension within the community caused a precipitous drop in circulation of the newspaper. By January 1942 fifteen Catholic Worker houses of hospitality had closed because there were not enough people to take care of them. Day estimated that 80% of the Workers had "betrayed" their pacifist principles; but others formed the Association of Catholic Conscientious Objectors.

In 1955 Day organized a civil disobedience protest against New York City's compulsory air raid drill, and seven people were given suspended sentences. Another year Dorothy spent thirty days in jail for this simple protest. In 1957 she wrote,

We were setting our faces against the world,
against things as they are,
the terrible injustice of our capitalist industrial system
which lives by war and by preparing for war;
setting our faces against race hatred
and all nationalist strivings.
But especially we wanted to act against war
and the preparation for war: nerve gas, guided missiles,
the testing and stockpiling of nuclear bombs, conscription,
the collection of income tax
against the entire military state.
We made our gesture; we disobeyed a law.[22]

In 1959 they were sentenced to thirty days but were released after ten days. They did this every year until 1961, when after 2,000 people refused to take shelter, the city decided to drop the requirement.

Dorothy Day also worked for the civil rights of African Americans and traveled to the South to do so. In 1957 she went to support the pacifist and interracial community founded by Clarence Jordan called Koinonia near Americus, Georgia. As they were threatened by Ku Klux Klan violence, she volunteered to watch their produce-stand at night in a car; someone from a passing car fired a shotgun into the car, but she was not hit. Dorothy also went to Danville, Virginia to pray, march, boycott, and suffer imprisonment in the civil rights struggle.

On April 22, 1963 the Mothers for Peace, a group made up of Catholic Workers, members of PAX (which became Pax Christi in 1972), Women Strike for Peace, WILPF, the Fellowship of Reconciliation, and others, met with Pope John XXIII to plead for a condemnation of nuclear war and the development of nonviolent resistance. During the Vietnam War, Dorothy Day inspired the radical Catholic Left to protest. She continued to oppose conscription and taxes for war, and in October 1965 she spoke at the first draft card burning. A heckler shouted that they should burn themselves, not their draft cards. Three days later young Roger LaPorte, a student of religion and a Catholic Worker volunteer, poured gasoline on himself and struck a match in front of the United Nations building, dying 33 hours later. Dorothy believed that he knew it was wrong to take his own life; but in her column she explained his desire to end the Vietnam War. In the previous week six massive air strikes had killed the most since the war began. She called language satanic that described the Army's spending as adding extra "zip" to the economy. In 1948 Day had written, "Love must be tried and test and proved. It must be tried as though by fire. And fire burns."[23]

Day and many Catholic Workers had for many years refused to pay federal income tax because most of it went to pay for war. In 1972 the Internal Revenue Service (IRS) sent them a letter stating that they owed $296,359 in unpaid taxes, fines, and penalties for the past six years. In their newspaper Dorothy explained that they might lose their houses; but she remained firm in her belief, shared by the War Resisters International, that wars will cease when we refuse to pay for them. She wondered how much the IRS would think they owed if they had counted up all the way back from 1933! The Catholic Worker was too busy helping the poor to go through the legal hassles of becoming a non-profit corporation, which would also restrict their political activities. However, by verbal negotiation in June 1972 Government agents were persuaded that they acted out of religious conviction. Thus they were not prosecuted because officials realized that they would just continue to act as they had in the past. Ammon Hennacy was probably the best known of the Catholic Workers for refusing to pay income tax while publicizing his protest. He had been imprisoned for nearly two years by the US Government for refusing to be conscripted into the war in 1917. He worked as a laborer so that no tax would be withheld and lived simply.

Dorothy Day encouraged other radical Catholics to protest such as the Jesuit brothers Dan and Phil Berrigan. At the age of 75 she was arrested for picketing with Cesar Chavez and the United Farm Workers Union and spent twelve days in jail. She died November 29, 1980; the continuing Catholic Worker movement is her great legacy.

On January 1, 1953 a woman calling herself Peace Pilgrim began walking around the United States and Canada for world peace. By 1964 she had walked 25,000 miles, and she kept walking, praying, counseling and teaching until her death in an automobile accident on July 7, 1981. She owned only the clothes she wore, a comb, a folding toothbrush, a pen, and a few letters. She walked until she found shelter, and she fasted until she was given food. She discovered the golden rule as a child and believed she could make friends by being friendly. She had a deep belief in God and prayer and taught spiritual principles to all she met.

Peace Pilgrim described the steps of preparation for

peace as taking a right attitude toward life, bringing one's life into harmony with universal laws, finding one's special place in life by God's inner guidance, and simplifying life. She recommended purifying the body by a good diet, purifying thought by reducing negativity, purifying desire by seeking only God's will, and purifying motive by being of service. Peace Pilgrim advised relinquishing self-will, the feeling of separateness, attachments to things or people, and negative feelings. Then the lightness beyond time and space of peace could be attained in the oneness that binds all life together and permeates all. Spiritual maturity is when God or the higher self controls the body, the mind, and the emotions. Her credo was to use good to overcome evil, truth to overcome falsehood, and love to overcome hatred, and the key, she said, is practice. She believed that those who use violence are still spiritually immature. She noted the extreme contrast of the two choices we face— either a nuclear war of annihilation or the golden age of peace.

Women Strike for Peace

Dagmar Wilson was the mother of three and worked as an artist illustrating children's books. She became concerned about the policies of the Cold War and was influenced by the ideas of Linus Pauling, Bertrand Russell, and Albert Einstein. After hearing a speech by psychiatrist Jerome Frank, she joined the Committee for a Sane Nuclear Policy (SANE). During the Berlin wall crisis she read about the protest of Bertrand Russell and was moved to do something about his arrest. When she learned that SANE was planning no response, she called her friends. On September 21, 1961 they came up with the idea that for peace women could go on strike for one day. The next day the women began issuing their appeal to "End the Arms Race—Not the Human Race," proclaiming, "We strike against death, desolation, destruction and on behalf of life and liberty."[24] In October they explained that women devote their lives to raising children to be healthy and good citizens, but in the nuclear age all women, including mothers, have an urgent duty to work for peace so that their children will have a future. They were particularly concerned about reports that the levels of strontium 90 in milk had risen sharply since the atmospheric testing of hydrogen bombs. By the end of 1958 there had been at least 190 tests of hydrogen bombs including 125 by the United States. Now the US and USSR were arguing over who had broken the testing moratorium.

The women set November 1, 1961 as the strike day, and thousands of women in sixty cities refused to work on that day. Women Strike for Peace (WSP) gained much publicity, but the original initiators did not want to form a traditional "top-down bureaucratic peace organization."[25] Instead, each local group was free to plan and carry out their own activities on the first-of-the-month strike day. Some WILPF activists worked with both groups; other women preferred the freedom of Women Strike for Peace, which was "intentionally simple, pragmatic, non-ideological, moralistic, and emotional."[26] Instead of allowing the majority to rule by voting, they worked for consensus on decisions. Bella Abzug from New York became the chairperson of WSP's legislative committee. They used the slogan "Pure Milk Not Poison," and their numbers grew. In January 1962 Berkeley Women for Peace had a thousand women attend the California legislative session to oppose civil defense legislation. WSP urged women to boycott milk unless it was decontaminated, especially during periods of nuclear testing. This prompted the US Public Health Service to warn mothers on April 26, 1962 not to stop giving their children milk because of the protests. By then WSP had forty radiation committees pressuring dairies, milk processors, the US Department of Agriculture, and the US Congress to purify the milk.

In June 1962 the Midwest group met at Ann Arbor and formulated the following Women Strike for Peace policy statement:

We present a resolute stand of women in the United States

against the unprecedented threat to life
from nuclear holocaust.
  We are women of all races,
creeds, and political persuasions
who are dedicated to the achievement of
general and complete disarmament
under effective international control.
  We cherish the right and respect the responsibility
of the individual in a democratic society to act
to influence the course of government.
  We join with women throughout the world to challenge
the right of any nation or group of nations
to hold the power of life or death over the world.[27]

The House Un-American Activities Committee
(HUAC) subpoenaed fourteen WSP women from the New
York area for a hearing in December 1962. This absurd
endeavor was satirized by a cartoon in the *Washington Post*
showing a Congressman asking his colleague if these
people are subversive because they are women or because
they are for peace. A hundred women volunteered to
testify and were refused. Three of the subpoenaed women
refused to testify in secret, and two years later they were
indicted for contempt of Congress; but their convictions
were overturned by a higher court in August 1966. In his
book *Thirty Years of Treason* Eric Bentley gave WSP credit for
striking the crucial blow in the final demise of HUAC.

In 1963 Women Strike for Peace created a Clearing
House on the Economics of Disarmament to publish an
amateur bulletin, but they got expert advice from the dissident economist Seymour Melman, who skillfully showed
how bad militarism is for the economy. United Nations
Secretary-General U Thant recognized the influential role
of Women Strike for Peace by personally thanking Dagmar
Wilson, Lorraine Gordon, and Helen Frumin before going
to Moscow to witness the signing on August 5, 1963 of the
Treaty Banning Nuclear Weapons Tests in the Atmosphere,
in Outer Space, and Underwater. Popularly known as the
partial test ban treaty, this at least moved nuclear tests

underground.

By 1964 Women Strike for Peace had become as concerned about the Vietnam War as they were about disarmament. On March 16, 1965 Alice Hertz, an 82-year-old founder of Detroit WSP, sacrificed her own life by setting her body on fire in a Detroit shopping center in order to protest the escalation of the Vietnam War. WSP organized many protests and sent Christmas cards signed by thousands of women to President Johnson in 1965. The next year WSP opposed the renewal of the draft. In the summer of 1966 two women from WSP and two from WILPF were arrested for blocking a napalm shipment from Santa Clara, California. The following winter 2,500 women gathered outside the Pentagon with photos of napalmed Vietnamese children. They demanded to speak to generals and banged on the locked Pentagon doors with their shoes. In 1970 WSP proclaimed a "Declaration of Liberation from Military Domination." That year Bella Abzug was elected to the US House of Representatives from New York. She and WSP called for the impeachment of Richard Nixon as early as January 1972, because he thwarted the Congressional mandate and the will of the people to end the war.

Feminism and Nonviolence

The tremendous influence of feminism on the peace movement in the 1960s and 1970s is perhaps best typified by Barbara Deming. Writing for *The Nation* and *Liberation* magazines, she described her participation in various nonviolent protest movements. She visited Cuba and North Vietnam and reported the viewpoints of the other side. She explained the philosophy and methods of the Committee for Nonviolent Action (CNVA) and their recommendation of unilateral disarmament to all countries including the Soviet Union. In her account of the San Francisco to Moscow walk the mirror images of Russian and American fears and defense policies were revealed. At the same time the person-to-person effectiveness of nonviolent direct action was eloquently portrayed. By walking for peace in the South she combined the quest for civil rights and justice with peace and nonviolence. She was arrested for civil disobedience in Birmingham, Alabama and Albany, Georgia. During the Vietnam War she lectured and wrote about the atrocities the United States was perpetrating against the Vietnamese people. She particularly pointed out the Lazy Dog bombs that are ineffective against the "steel and concrete" targets but were designed to enter flesh. She told of how schools, hospitals, and homes were being bombed unmercifully.

Barbara Deming became a strong advocate of nonviolent revolution as the most effective way to transform a violent and oppressive society. Although she sympathized with revolutionaries who feel the need for violent methods of liberation, she argued that in nonviolent struggle there will be fewer casualties. She acknowledged that in standing up to violent power, some suffering is inevitable. Yet she believed that the nonviolent action of assertive noncooperation with the oppressors can be as strong and effective as violent struggle while maintaining the respect for everyone's human rights. She wrote,

> This is how we stand up for ourselves nonviolently:
> we refuse the authorities our labor,
> we refuse them our money (our taxes),
> we refuse them our bodies (to fight in their wars).
> We strike.[28]

She went on to recommend blocking, obstructing, and disrupting the operation of a system in which people are not free. At the same time the adversary is confronted, their rights are respected, and they are made to examine their conscience about what is just. A violent response to a nonviolent action further reveals the injustice and loses sympathy from allies and supporters. Deming believed that nonviolent methods have barely begun to be used with their full power.

Like Andrea Dworkin, Deming came to believe that nonviolence must be combined with radical feminism, for the patriarchal male dominance over submissive women pervades the entire society in deeply ingrained ways. Women and everyone in the peace movement must insist on the equality of the sexes and live the revolution in their personal lives. Feminism and pacifism have much in common. Caroline Wildflower described how feminism improved the peace movement. She explained how in the 1960s the male leaders were reluctant to give women shared leadership. Instead, women were assigned to secretarial work. When the Women's Movement started raising the consciousness about these injustices in society, changes began to happen in spite of the resistance of habit. Not only were the authorities and hierarchies of society being challenged, but the same structures within the peace groups were being scrutinized and criticized by empowered women. The results of this continuing evolution are that the group processes are becoming more egalitarian, jobs are rotated so that everyone is broadened, women are expressing an equal voice with more emotional power, men are becoming more sensitive to their own feminine qualities, and a more healthy overall balance is emerging.

In the 1980s the military buildup under President Reagan stimulated the peace movement to mobilize. Women, minorities, and the poor were being neglected while the Pentagon budget accelerated. The issues became especially obvious to women when increased expenditures on nuclear weapons, missiles, bombers, submarines, aircraft carriers, etc. were compared to decreases in education, health, job training, family aid, food, housing, energy, civil rights, environmental protection, etc. The five-year military budget for the US alone was projected at 1.6 trillion dollars. World military expenditures average $19,300 per soldier while public education spending averaged $380 per student. The governmental budgets of the western powers allotted four times as much money to military research as they did to health research. The world in 1982 spent 1800 times as much on military forces as it did on international peacekeeping. In April 1982 the Women's

Pentagon Action Unity Statement included the following:

Our cities are in ruins, bankrupt;
they suffer the devastation of war.
Hospitals are closed,
our schools deprived of books and teachers.
Our Black and Latino youth are without decent work.
They will be forced, drafted to become cannon fodder
for the very power that oppresses them.
Whatever help the poor receive is cut or withdrawn
to feed the Pentagon
which needs about $500,000,000 a day
for its murderous health....
We women are gathering
because life on the precipice is intolerable.[29]

Many women, such as Ann Davidon, spoke about breaking through the "macho mental barrier" and demilitarizing society by shifting resources to useful production. Sally Gearhart believed "the rising up of women in this century to be the human race's response to the threat of its own self-annihilation and the destruction of the planet."[30] She called upon the world's women to take the responsibility for sustaining life.

The women's peace movement is truly international. In October 1981 over a thousand women from 133 countries met in Prague, Czechoslovakia on the themes Equality, National Independence, and Peace. They all agreed that the nuclear arms race must be stopped and that women and men of good will can prevent nuclear war. The Women's International Democratic Federation (WIDF) reported on the activities of the women's peace movement in Europe and the Soviet Union. Hundreds of thousands of women were protesting the danger of war, not only in western Europe but in eastern Europe and the Soviet Union as well. The Soviet Women's Committee reported that during the last week of October 1982 Action for Disarmament was celebrated in the USSR by fifty million people with over 80,000 events in protest of the arms race. According to

WIDF, in the spring of 1982 women demonstrated for peace in Angola, Argentina, Australia, Belgium, Canada, Czechoslovakia, Finland, West Germany (800,000 citizens), East Germany (77,000 women), Great Britain (100,000), Greece, Italy, Japan (30,000 in Tokyo on Easter), Yemen, Mauritius, Mozambique (20,000 women), Nicaragua (100,000), Netherlands, New Zealand (20,000 women), Poland, Soviet Union, Sweden, and the USA. Women's peace camps were established at Greenham Common in England and at Seneca, New York.

Ruth Sivard published statistics comparing government expenditures on the military to social programs. She noted that in 1986 the total spending on military forces reached about $900 billion as what the world spent per soldier had increased to about $30,000 but what was provided per school-age child for education had only gone up to $455. The two superpowers, the USA and USSR, were spending 60% of the world's defense expenditures but had only 11% of the world's population. Yet military spending in underdeveloped nations had increased 800 percent since 1960 after adjusting for inflation.

In 1988 Women for a Meaningful Summit from the United States and Soviet Union included Coretta Scott King, California Assemblywoman Maxine Waters, and Cora Weiss of SANE/FREEZE International. Their peace platform urged that the agreement to reduce strategic nuclear weapons (START) be concluded without delay, and they declared that war is obsolete, that nuclear and conventional weapons do not provide security, and that the "real enemies are hunger, disease, racism, poverty, inequality, injustice, and violence." They suggested that by a partnership among all nations the systems of war could be "dismantled and replaced by systems of peace and justice" using nonviolent means. Comprehensive security would include the "political, economic, military, humanitarian, cultural, and environmental spheres." They affirmed that "no nation has the right to intervene in the internal affairs of other nations."[31] They demanded that the Universal

Declaration of Human Rights be fully implemented, and they called for strengthening international institutions so that the United Nations, the International Court of Justice, and other international bodies could resolve conflict peacefully.

In 1997 Jody Williams and the International Campaign to Ban Landmines (ICBL) won the Nobel Peace Prize for helping to get 121 nations to sign the Mine Ban Treaty in Ottawa. Before she died, Princess Diana had also worked on this issue. As of 2005 this treaty has been ratified by 143 nations, but the United States, Russia, China, India, both Koreas, Pakistan, Israel, Egypt, Iran, and Iraq are among the 42 nations that have refused. About a hundred million landmines exist in the earth, and despite these recent efforts about 15,000 to 20,000 casualties still occur each year. In her acceptance speech Williams explained how landmines, once they have been placed, do not discriminate between soldiers and civilians, and after the end of the war they remain deadly indefinitely unless they are removed. She estimated that seventy countries have been contaminated by tens of millions of mines. Cambodia still has about five million from the 1970s. The United States military reported that about thirty million mines were scattered throughout Afghanistan in the 1980s. Six million landmines were sown in the former Yugoslavia in the 1990s. Angola has nine million; Mozambique and Somalia have a million each. The number of landmines stockpiled throughout the world is estimated at 100-200 million. The Ottawa Mine Ban Treaty bans the use, production, trade and stockpiling of antipersonnel landmines.

Outstanding reporting on peace issues comes from Pacifica radio's Amy Goodman, who hosts Democracy Now! on weekdays broadcasting from New York City. Pacifist and conscientious objector Lew Hill founded Pacifica in April 1949 as a commercial-free community-supported radio network that is dedicated to peace and justice. The first station broadcasted as KPFA-FM in Berkeley. KPFK-FM began broadcasting from Los Angeles in 1957. The next year Nobel prize-winner Linus Pauling debated Edward Teller, the inventor of the H-bomb. WBAI in New York joined the Pacifica family in 1960. Pacifica radio has withstood numerous efforts to censor its content and an investigation by the House on Un-American Activities Committee (HUAC) in the early 1960s. In 1970 KPFT began broadcasting from Houston, and it survived two bombings of its transmitter towers by the Ku Klux Klan in its first year. WPFW started broadcasting from Washington DC in 1977 after winning a six-year battle for the last available radio frequency in the nation's capital.

Amy Goodman won several awards for her courageous reporting of the Santa Cruz massacre in Dili, East Timor on November 12, 1991 for WBAI's popular Morning Show. Jose Ramos-Horta, who won the Nobel Peace Prize in 1986, gave Goodman credit for publicizing this massacre of peaceful demonstrators that the Indonesia Government tried to deny even happened. She and Pacifica reporter Allan Nairn were beaten by the Indonesian army; but they were not killed probably because they said they were Americans. Goodman noted that the United States had supplied their weapons. Then they witnessed the soldiers open fire on the large crowd gathered for a funeral; 271 people were killed, and another 270 have "disappeared."

The Democracy Now! program that Amy Goodman hosts began in February 1996. In 1999 her program "Drilling and Killing: Chevron and Nigeria's Oil Dictatorship" resulted in her being banned from Chevron's public news conference. In October 2000 the Pacifica program director Stephen Yasko tried to interfere with the content of Democracy Now!, but Amy Goodman retained her independent journalism from "the embattled studios of WBAI." She continued to broadcast as "the exception to the rulers" her "resistance radio" that includes important news and interviews often ignored, neglected, or censored by the mainstream media. In August 2001 Pacifica took her program off the air, and Democracy Now! had to move out of the WBAI studio and broadcast from an alternate location for the one station that retained her program. After a struggle for power, a new Pacifica board was elected in December, and her program was fully restored in January 2002 along with its employees who had been banned and fired.

Amy and her brother Andrew Goodman wrote *The Exception to the Rulers: Exposing Oily Politicians, War Profiteers, and the Media that Love Them,* and it was published in 2004. Some of the outstanding people given a voice on her program include Mumia Abu-Jamal, Phyllis Bennis, Dan Berrigan, Noam Chomsky, Ramsey Clark, Ani DiFranco, Phil Donohue, Ariel Dorfman, Robert Fisk, Michael Franti, Col. Sam Gardiner, Danny Glover, Jason Halperin, Jennifer Harbury, Chris Hedges, Seymour Hersh, Yolanda Huet-Vaughan, Dennis Kucinich, Rita Lasar, Michael Meacher, Michael Moore, Ralph Nader, Allan Nairn, John Perkins, Michael Ratner, Ken Saro-Wiwa, Jeremy Scahill, Danny Schechter, Norman Solomon, Lynne Stewart, Maxine Waters, Howard Zinn, and Andreas Zumach. As of 2006 Democracy Now! is syndicated on weekdays on more than four hundred radio stations, satellite television, and on the Internet at democracynow.org.

Aung San Suu Kyi in Burma

Aung San Suu Kyi was born in Rangoon on June 19, 1945. Her father Aung San, who led the independence revolution and was a national hero, was assassinated on July 19, 1947. Her mother Khin Kyi was ambassador to India 1960-67, and Suu Kyi was influenced by the nonviolent philosophy of Gandhi. She earned a degree in philosophy, politics, and economics at Oxford University in 1967, and she worked for the United Nations Secretariat in New York from 1969 to 1971. While working as a research officer in the Foreign Ministry of Bhutan in 1972, Suu Kyi married Michael Aris, a scholar of Tibetan culture. She was working on her doctoral dissertation at Oxford on Burmese literature in March 1988 when she learned that her mother had a stroke. Suu Kyi immediately went back to Rangoon to take care of her and was later joined by her British husband and their two sons. On July 23 General Ne Win, who had ruled Burma as a one-party state since 1962, announced his retirement and proposed a referendum on whether to have a one-party or multi-party system. The central committee of the Burma Socialist Programme Party (BSPP) elected new leaders who decided not to have the referendum.

Student demonstrations led to some arrests, curfews, and declaration of martial law on August 3 as 10,000 people gathered. Five days later on 8-8-88 at 8:08 a.m. the pro-democracy movement was founded, and a general strike began with tens of thousands demonstrating in Rangoon. On August 15 Aung San Suu Kyi proposed a People's Consultative Committee to act as an intermediary between the students and the government. Eleven days later she spoke to a rally of a half million people outside the Shwedagon Pagoda, calling for free and fair elections as soon as possible. On September 12 she, Tin U, and Aung Gyi suggested an interim government. Six days later army officers took over the government under the State Law and Order Restoration Council (SLORC). On September 24 Aung San Suu Kyi, Tin U, and Aung Gyi formed the National League for Democracy (NLD) with Suu Kyi as General Secretary as mass arrests and summary executions of pro-democracy activists occurred throughout Burma. The BSPP became the National Unity Party (NUP) and by threatening punishment and dismissal brought an end to the general strike on October 3. Aung San Suu Kyi sent two letters to Amnesty International, complaining that on October 15 more than six hundred men had been arrested in Rangoon while sitting at tea shops or eating stalls.

Aung San Suu Kyi traveled throughout Burma for seven months and spoke to large crowds in more than a hundred places. Aung San's widow and Suu Kyi's mother, Khin Kyi, died on December 27, and hundreds of thousands attended the funeral in Rangoon. Later in January

1989 Aung San Suu Kyi's tour was disrupted by the military, and 34 NLD workers were arrested. In February she criticized the human rights violations and the resumption of Japanese aid. In April, Captain Myint Oo threatened to kill Aung San Suu Kyi in Danubyu. Six soldiers jumped out of a jeep and pointed their guns at her. She calmly waved away her supporters and kept walking down the road. When *The Working People's Daily* launched fierce attacks on the NLD and Aung San Suu Kyi in June, she began criticizing Ne Win openly at mass rallies in Rangoon. She announced that she would lead a march on Martyrs' Day, July 19; but eleven trucks with troops were stationed outside her house, and thousands of soldiers patrolled the streets of Rangoon to prevent the NLD from marching. The next day SLORC put Aung San Suu Kyi and Tin U under house arrest while scores of NLD workers were jailed across Burma. Aung San Suu Kyi asked to be held in prison with the other activists. She fasted on water for twelve days until she was assured that they would not be tortured.

In December 1989 a hundred political parties announced their intention to participate in the May 1990 elections. Aung San Suu Kyi's candidacy was challenged in January for her alleged connections with insurgent groups, and the Elections Commission barred her. In the election on May 27, 1990 the people of Burma elected the National League for Democracy (NLD) to 392 of the 485 seats contested. However, SLORC refused to transfer power, and Aung San Suu Kyi remained under house arrest for six years until July 1995. She did not even leave the country to accept the 1991 Nobel Peace Prize because she would not have been allowed back into Myanmar, the name given to Burma by the military authorities in 1989. She had the prize money put in a trust for the health and education of the Burmese people.

Aung San Suu Kyi has written about the need for democracy, nonviolence, and national unity. She countered criticisms that democracy is not Burmese. In "Quest of Democracy" she described the ten Buddhist duties of kings, which are liberality, morality, generosity (self-sacrifice), integrity, kindness (courage), austerity (self-discipline), non-anger, nonviolence, patience, and not opposing the will of the people. She argued that these Buddhist values and principles of accountability were more likely to produce democracy, respect for public opinion, and just laws than a ruling class that does not honor the will of the people.

In "Freedom from Fear" Aung San Suu Kyi suggested that fear corrupts more than power.

It is not power that corrupts but fear.
Fear of losing power corrupts those who wield it
and fear of the scourge of power
corrupts those who are subject to it.[32]

She wrote that the Burmese are aware of four kinds of corruption. These are desire (from bribes or for one's friends), doing wrong from ill will toward enemies, committing errors from ignorance, and fear, which she believed was the root cause of the other three. She noted that public dissatisfaction with economic hardship was the primary motive of the democracy movement in Burma since 1988. She suggested that one must have determination to persevere in the struggle and make sacrifices, that saints are sinners who keep on trying, and that the free are the oppressed who continue to work for a free society. She agreed with her father, who though he founded Burma's national army, believed that army officers should stay out of politics.

On August 14, 1994 the United Nations representative Jehan Raheem, US Congressman Bill Richardson, and *New York Times* reporter Philip Shenon were allowed to interview Aung San Suu Kyi, and the following month she met with two SLORC generals. She was depicted in John Boorman's film *Beyond Rangoon* in 1995. Aung San Suu Kyi was released from detention on July 11, 1995. The next day she asked international businesses not to invest in Burma until democracy was restored. She also started a tourist boycott. In October the NLD reappointed her General Secretary despite a SLORC ban, and she asked any organization working with the regime in Burma also to consult with the NLD. In 1996 the Ministry of Information conducted a propaganda campaign against Aung San Suu Kyi by having the state media portray her as an untrustworthy female, a prostitute of her body and the nation, and that her husband Michael Aris was manipulating her like a puppet at the behest of the US Central Intelligence Agency (CIA). SLORC accused Aung San Suu Kyi of receiving $82,000 from the United States for her personal use while the US was providing $2.5 million through the National Endowment for Democracy (NED) and the International Rescue Committee. A cult was developing that suggested she is an archetypal "Lady" and a powerful spirit (Nat) of Democracy, and she was portrayed by the media as an un-Buddhist animist.

On Human Rights Day, December 10, 1997 Aung San Suu Kyi asked why the government found it necessary to put their people in jail if they do not have the support of the Burmese people. In May 1998 Aung San Suu Kyi and the NLD formed the Committee Representing People's Parliament (CRPP) based on those elected in May 1990. However, an effort was made to divide the NLD as 25 members criticized her for this. The NLD demanded that the elected government be seated by August 1998. In July and August 1998 the army blocked her car at a bridge twice to keep her from leaving Rangoon even though she spent several days in the car. Burma suffers from severe ethnic conflicts, but Aung San Suu Kyi believes that democratic institutions could provide the proper means of conflict resolution. One does not need recourse to violence in order to rebel against tyranny and oppression as long as human rights are protected by the rule of law. Her husband had been diagnosed with prostate cancer in 1997; but he was not even allowed a visa so that he could visit her, and he died in March 1999.

Police stopped her car from leaving Rangoon on

August 24, 2000, and a week later 200 riot police forced the convoy to return to the capital. The next day police raided her headquarters, seized documents, and arrested several members of the party. On September 23, 2000 Aung San Suu Kyi and other party leaders were detained in their homes. The next month the State Peace and Development Council (SPDC) was persuaded by the Malaysian prime minister Datuk Seri Dr. Mahathir Mohamad to open a dialog with Aung San Suu Kyi. In January 2001 NLD chairman Tin U and 84 other members were released from custody, and Suu Kyi hoped that her talks with the SPDC would be productive. That month the military stopped the outrageous propaganda campaign against her in the state-run media. In April more than thirty US Senators warned President George W. Bush not to lift the sanctions against the Myanmar regime. Secret negotiations by the United Nations led to her release in May 2002. Eight other members of the NLD were also let go, but according to Amnesty International more than 1,500 others were still in Burmese jails.

In 2003 Aung San Suu Kyi still would not leave Myanmar to accept awards because she would not be allowed to return. In March she was interviewed by the BBC, and she said that she did not look upon the generals as the enemy but that she wanted to work together for a settlement that would be beneficial to everyone, including the military. She was so popular that it was difficult for the regime to arrest her in Rangoon. However, in May 2003 they got three hundred members of the Union Solidarity and Development Association (USDA) to attack her caravan in the country near Mandalay. Three weeks later some of her supporters were killed when the army fired at her vehicle. She remained with her supporters but then was taken away by her driver. Later they were arrested and sent to Insein Prison. The government claimed that she was under protective custody. After undergoing surgery in September, she was moved back to house arrest. Large banks helped the Myanmar regime get around the tough sanctions imposed by the United States that went into effect in August 2003. International protests of her detention were held in June 2004, and the rock band U2 dedicated two songs to her. In November 2005 the NLD confirmed that her house arrest had been extended for another year, and in response the United States raised the issue in the UN Security Council.

Medea Benjamin and Code Pink

Medea Benjamin worked for ten years as an economist and nutritionist in Latin America and Africa for the United Nations Food and Agriculture Organization, the World Health Organization, and the Swedish International Development Agency. After being a senior analyst for Food First, in San Francisco she co-founded Global Exchange in 1988. Ten years later the *Washington Post* credited this organization with putting labor rights on the human rights agenda. Global Exchange helped to organize large protests against the World Trade Organization (WTO) meeting at Seattle in December 1999. Benjamin was criticized by some activists for her statement that it was correct for Seattle police to arrest "anarchists" who destroyed property. Benjamin was instrumental in coordinating the anti-sweatshop campaigns that have sprung up on college campuses, and she has led the effort to get corporations, such as Nike and the Gap, to establish ethical codes of conduct. In 1999 her work helped expose the indentured servitude of garment workers in Saipan that led to a billion-dollar lawsuit against seventeen retailers. She has also promoted worker rights in China, the liberation of Indonesia from the tyranny of General Suharto, and self-determination for East Timor. Benjamin supported the peace process between the Zapatistas and the Mexican government and has struggled to get the embargoes against Cuba and Iraq lifted. In 2000 Medea Benjamin was the Green Party candidate for the US Senate in California. She has written and edited books to help link citizens of the first and third worlds, and she wrote a biography of Brazil's first poor and black woman senator, Benedita da Silva.

Code Pink: Women for Peace was founded by Medea Benjamin, Jodie Evans, Starhawk, Diane Wilson, and about a hundred other women on November 17, 2002 in order to protest the impending invasion of Iraq by the George W. Bush administration. They marched through the streets of Washington and began a vigil in front of the White House that lasted four months. Their vigil was supported by Greenpeace, WILPF, WAND, Public Citizen, NOW, Women for Women International, Neighbors for Peace and Justice, and others. In September 2002 when Donald Rumsfeld was testifying at a House Armed Services Committee hearing, Benjamin and Diane Wilson chanted, "Inspections, not war" and were removed. A month later Wilson scaled the fence at the White House and was arrested by the Secret Service; she was banned from Washington for one year. Wilson and two other protestors were arrested in Austin when the Texas legislature was passing a resolution supporting the war. In February 2003 Benjamin and eleven other women visited Baghdad to assess the likely impact of war, and they concluded that the UN inspections to remove weapons were working. On International Women's Day, March 8, more than 10,000 people marched in Washington, and about two dozen women were arrested for protesting the imminent war. By the end of 2003 there were more than a hundred Code Pink chapters which act autonomously. Code Pink Central sends out weekly Code Pink Alerts to more than 30,000 people. Code Pink activists have presented themselves in pink slips (women's lingerie) to warn politicians and other public figures such as Fox News' Bill O'Reilly and FCC director Michael Powell that the people may fire them from their jobs.

In 2004 Medea Benjamin was dragged off the floor of the Democratic national convention in handcuffs for having displayed a banner which read, "End the Occupation! Bring the Troops Home Now!" At the Republican convention she was also removed, and her sign read, "Pro-Life: Stop the Killing in Iraq." Benjamin was also ejected from Bush's second inaugural ceremony. After the destruction of Falluja in November 2004, Code Pink helped Global Exchange and Families for Peace to raise $600,000 in humanitarian relief for the refugees from Falluja. In 2005 Benjamin traveled to Iraq with military families who had lost loved ones in the war, and she organized the Occupation Watch Center to coordinate humanitarian aid to Iraqis. To protest the closing of the Salinas library in California because of lack of funding, Code Pink organized a 24-hour read-in in April 2005. That month women unfurled banners and spoke out at the Congressional hearing for UN ambassador nominee John Bolton.

In the book *Stop the Next War Now: Effective Responses to Violence and Terrorism*, which she edited with Jodie Evans, Benjamin recommends the following ten actions for peace:

1. Educate yourself on the issues.
2. Demand truthful media.
3. Communicate!
4. Hold your leaders accountable.
5. Help the United States kick our oil addiction.
6. Build the peace movement.
7. Support members of the military who are speaking out.
8. Protect our civil liberties and oppose the backlash against immigrants.
9. Support the creation of a Department of Peace.
10. Teach peace.[33]

If men through their aggression, power urges, and rigid stubbornness have caused war after war, then women through their love, nurturing, and flexibility can help us to learn how to prevent wars in order to save our civilization. Western civilization in the twentieth century became pathologically destructive, endangering all life. Much therapy and healing is needed to cure the disease of masculine militarism. Feminist nonviolence is clearly the remedy recommended by the greatest of the peacemakers. Our society as a whole and each person individually must learn to revere the loving, sensitive, caring, empathetic qualities of our being. Women are excellent teachers of peace in this process that will evolve into a balanced, healthy, integrated, and just society. Feminism has enabled women to take their rightful place in the anti-nuclear movement, thus strengthening the power and health of the peace movement. The empowerment of women is exemplified in the anti-nuclear movement by three of its most important voices: Helen Caldicott, Petra Kelly, and Randall Forsberg, as can be seen in the next chapter.

Notes

1. *Lay Down Your Arms* by Bertha von Suttner, tr. T. Holmes, p. 424.
2. *The Great Adventure* by Maude Royden quoted in *Women Against the Iron Fist* by Sybil Oldfield, p. 53.
3. "The Power of Words" by Simone Weil quoted in *Women Against the Iron Fist* by Sybil Oldfield, p. 77.
4. "Europe's Colonialism in Africa and Asia" by Simone Weil quoted in *Women Against the Iron Fist* by Sybil Oldfield, p. 84.
5. Quoted in *Women Strike for Peace* by Amy Swerdlow, p. 27.
6. Quoted in *American Women's Activism in World War I* by Barbara J. Steinson, p. 35.
7. Crystal Eastman to Jane Addams, 28 June 1917, quoted in *Women Strike for Peace* by Amy Swerdlow, p. 31.
8. *On Women & Revolution* by Crystal Eastman, p. 238.
9. *Women at The Hague* by Jane Addams, p. 71.
10. *Ibid.*, p. 84.
11. *Ibid.*, p. 91.
12. *Ibid.*, p. 164.
13. Quoted in *Women Strike for Peace* by Amy Swerdlow, p. 32.
14. *Ibid.*
15. Niagara Falls Conference Minutes, 19 Aug. 1921, WPU: NYPL, quoted in *The Women's Peace Union and the Outlawry of War: 1921-1942* by Harriet Hyman Alonso, p. 19.

16. *Women's International League for Peace and Freedom: 1915-1965* by Gertrude Bussey and Margaret Tims, p. 122.
17. *Ibid.*, p. 162.
18. *Ibid.*, p. 163.
19. *By Little and By Little: The Selected Writings of Dorothy Day,* p. 48.
20. Quoted in *Dorothy Day* by William D. Miller, p. 241.
21. *By Little and By Little: The Selected Writings of Dorothy Day,* p. 261.
22. *Ibid.*, p. 280.
23. *Ibid.*, p. 228.
24. *Women Strike for Peace* by Amy Swerdlow, p. 18.
25. *Ibid.*, p. 49.
26. *Ibid.*, p. 51.
27. *Ibid.*, p. 88.
28. "Nonviolence and Radical Social Change" by Barbara Deming in *Revolution & Equilibrium*, p. 223.
29. *Reweaving the Web of Life: Feminism and Nonviolence*, p. 415.
30. *Ibid.*, p. 266.
31. "Women for a Meaningful Summit" in *Women on War*, p. 66.
32. *Freedom from Fear and Other Writings* by Aung San Suu Kyi, p. 180.
33. *Stop the Next War Now*, p. 223-225.

11

Anti-Nuclear Protests

The people in the long run are going to do more
to promote peace than our government.
Indeed, I think that people want peace so much
that one of these days government better
get out of the way and let them have it.
Dwight Eisenhower, 1959

In the name of God, let us abolish nuclear weapons.
New Abolitionist Covenant

We are the curators of life on earth,
standing at a crossroads in time.
We must awake from our false sense of security
and commit ourselves to using democracy constructively
to save the human species.
Helen Caldicott

We reject violence completely,
because the structural violence caused by this decision
to place these missiles or to continue the arms race
on both sides is violence.
Petra Kelly

To end the danger of nuclear war the nations must
not merely freeze nuclear weapons but abolish them.
Randall Forsberg

We must protest if we are to survive.
Protest is the only realistic form of civil defense.
E. P. Thompson

Protesting Nuclear Testing

In April 1954 India's Prime Minister Jawaharlal Nehru
led the non-aligned nations in criticizing the US H-bomb
tests in the Pacific. He also encouraged Norman Cousins to
persuade Albert Schweitzer to alert the world to the

dangers of nuclear weapons and their testing. In the summer of 1957 Nevil Shute's novel *On the Beach* about the survivors of a nuclear war was published, and Republican Senator Wayne Morse of Oregon introduced a resolution to halt nuclear tests because of their radiation hazards but also as the first step toward disarmament and peace.

On July 15, 1955 the Mainau Declaration signed by 52 Nobel Laureates warned humanity, "All nations must come to the decision to renounce force as a final resort of policy. If they are not prepared to do this, they will cease to exist."[1] On May15, 1957 Dr. Linus Pauling referred to Schweitzer's appeal when he spoke at Washington University in St. Louis, arguing that no human being should be sacrificed to a project that could kill hundreds of millions. Two other professors, Barry Commoner and Edward Condon, helped Pauling write a petition that garnered signatures from 2,000 scientists by June, when it was released to the press and sent to the White House. Pauling had won a Nobel Prize for Chemistry; but he gave up his administrative position at Cal Tech in 1958 to write the book *No More War!* that warned against the harmful effects of radioactive fallout from nuclear weapons testing. In the Preface, he wrote

We shall enter upon the continuing period of peace,
a period when there will be no more war,
when disputes between nations will be settled
by the application of man's power of reason,
by international law.
It is the development of great nuclear weapons
that requires that war be given up, for all time.
The forces that can destroy the world must not be used.[2]

Pauling described what hydrogen bombs would do to major cities and predicted that the fallout from testing could result in a million seriously defective children and about two million embryonic and neonatal deaths. He proposed a World Peace Research Organization and sent 1500 copies of the book to influential people, including every member of Congress. In July 1957 Bertrand Russell had initiated the Pugwash conference that brought together scientists from both sides of the Cold War. This was so successful that it became the first of a series of conferences. On January 15, 1958 Pauling handed United Nations Secretary-General Dag Hammarskjold a petition signed by 9,235 scientists, including 37 Nobel Laureates, urging an international agreement to stop testing.

Inspired by Dr. King and the Montgomery bus boycott of 1956 and the Catholic Workers and War Resisters who had refused to take shelter during civil defense drills in New York, some activists formed the Committee for Non-Violent Action (CNVA). On August 12, 1957 they held vigils at the office of the Atomic Energy Commission in Las Vegas, Nevada. When they tried to enter the gates of the atomic test site at Camp Mercury, they were arrested for trespassing. After they received suspended sentences, they returned to a prayer vigil at the test site and saw the extraordinary light of the first test in a series. The next spring Albert Bigelow and four Quakers sailed the *Golden Rule* into the Pacific test zone near the Eniwetok atoll, where H-bomb tests were planned. They defied a court injunction twice, were arrested, and went to jail. Hearing of their trial, Earle Reynolds sailed his *Phoenix* into the test zone and spent two days in jail. In the summer of 1959 CNVA activists organized civil disobedience in Omaha at the Strategic Air Command (SAC) base. Others held a vigil to protest the germ warfare at Fort Detrick in Maryland, and the Polaris submarine was picketed in Connecticut. For ten months starting in December 1960 a walk for peace traversed from San Francisco to the east coast through Europe and on to Moscow.

Also in 1957 the National Committee for a Sane Nuclear Policy (SANE) was founded; the name was suggested by psychologist Erich Fromm, and the main organizers were long-time executive secretary of the American Friends Service Committee (AFSC) Clarence Pickett and the United World Federalist (UWF) Norman Cousins, editor of *Saturday Review*. Unitarian minister Homer Jack became coordinator. After Sputnik was launched on October 4, their full-page advertisement in the *New York Times* warned people, "We are facing a danger unlike any danger that has ever existed."[3] The ad was then run in many local papers, and 25,000 reprints were distributed. SANE ran a series of effective ads including one which said "Dr. Spock is worried," featuring the famous pediatrician Benjamin Spock, whose book *Baby and Child Care* was extraordinarily influential. Within a year SANE had 25,000 members in 130 chapters. On May 19, 1958 Madison Square Garden in New York was filled with 20,000 supporters. In July President Eisenhower offered to stop nuclear testing on October 31 for one year provided that the Soviet Union also refrained from testing during this moratorium, though the US did conduct a series of tests in October. In 1959 negotiations for a test ban bogged down at Geneva, because the Soviets feared that on-site inspections by the United States would be used for spying.

The Student Peace Union was started at the University of Chicago by CNVA activist Kenneth Calkins, and they adopted the logo of the British Campaign for Nuclear Disarmament (CND) based on the semaphore signs for N and D in a circle that became the universally recognized peace symbol.

After tensions in Germany over the building of the Berlin wall in August 1961, the Soviets resumed nuclear testing on September 1. Two weeks later the United States began testing underground, but in April 1962 the United States resumed testing in the atmosphere. The effort to stop nuclear testing was greatly enhanced by the actions of Women Strike for Peace (WSP), starting in the fall of 1961. In 1963 SANE urged its members to write to the Senate and White House, and 18,000 letters were sent asking for an end to nuclear testing. Norman Cousins consulted with Secretary of State Dean Rusk and flew to Moscow to talk with Soviet premier Khrushchev about a test ban treaty. After Cousins returned and advised President Kennedy that the Russians would respond favorably to a diplomatic initiative, Kennedy included the proposal in his speech at the American University in June, 1963. By the end of July the partial test ban treaty had been signed by the two superpowers. However, the French continued to test nuclear weapons in the South Pacific. Between 1972 and 1974 Greenpeace's *Rainbow Warrior* made a series of voyages to the Moruroa and Fangataufa atolls in order to disrupt the tests. After French gendarmes beat Greenpeace crew member David McTaggart on the *Vega*, the outrage to the publicity was so vociferous that the French decided to move their tests underground also. Greenpeace has continued with many creative actions to protest nuclear weapons. In July 1985 when France was about to resume nuclear testing, its secret agents bombed the *Rainbow Warrior* in Auckland Harbour, killing a crew member. *Rainbow Warrior II* returned to Moruroa and was seized by the French. Greenpeace's Nuclear Free Seas campaign started in 1987 and got results four years later when Britain, Russia, and the United States all withdrew their nuclear weapons from on board surface ships. In 1995 the French seized the *Rainbow Warrior II* and arrested the crew prior to more testing, but international outrage persuaded them to stop testing there after January 1996. That year several Greenpeace executive directors were arrested in Tianamen Square for protesting China's nuclear testing. Since 2000 Greenpeace has been protesting the testing of the US ballistic missile defense (BMD) tests at Vandenberg Air Force Base and the Kwajalein atoll.

Nonviolent protests began at the underground nuclear test site at Mercury, Nevada in 1981. Numbers of those getting arrested were small until 1986, when 775 protested and 154 were arrested. From then until 1994 there were 536 American Peace Test demonstrations at the Nevada test site with a total of 37,488 participants with 15,740 arrests. After 1994 the American Peace Test disbanded, but the faith-based Nevada Desert Experience (NDE) continued to protest every year.

Protesting Nuclear Power

Demonstrations against nuclear power plants in western Europe began in France and West Germany in 1971. Protests increased, and in February 1975 a major breakthrough for the anti-nuclear movement occurred in Wyhl of southwestern Germany. When construction of the power plant was about to begin, several hundred local activists (farmers, housewives, merchants, and students) held a press conference at the construction site and sat down in front of the bulldozers. Police cleared the area by using water cannons and by arresting people. Nevertheless, some local people stayed there overnight, and they returned the next week with 28,000 supporters from all over Germany and from Alsace in France. People occupied the land for over a year and operated a school to educate people on nuclear issues. They agreed to leave when a panel of judges was established, and in 1977 the panel ruled against the plant.

During the summer of 1976 the construction site for a nuclear power plant at Seabrook, New Hampshire was occupied by 180 people, and the following April more than 2,000 members of the Clamshell Alliance marched onto the site where construction had begun. On the first of May 1,414 people were arrested at the Seabrook site. The Clams were well organized into affinity groups of 10-20 people who were trained in non-violence and practiced consensus decision-making. They attempted to avoid a hierarchical and authoritarian leadership structure by letting every person in each group and each group within the whole participate in the process. Of those arrested, more than half refused to pay bail and stayed in custody for two weeks.

The example of the Clamshell Alliance stimulated a more active resistance in California to the almost completed Diablo Canyon nuclear reactors. The Movement for a New Society (MNS) from Philadelphia had influenced the Clamshell, and David Hartsough, who had also worked for civil rights in the South, brought their nonviolence tactics, affinity group structure, and consensus processes to

California, persuading the American Friends Service Committee (AFSC) board to support the Diablo Canyon action in order to develop the nonviolent movement. In June 1977 the Abalone Alliance was formed. The Mothers For Peace had filed as interveners in 1973 and were glad to see the effort mobilizing. Nonviolence was strictly adhered to when 47 people were arrested for trespassing on August 7, 1977. One year later 5,000 people rallied, and 487 occupiers and blockaders were arrested for their civil disobedience.

By the time fuel-loading was due to begin in September 1981 a nonviolence handbook had been published to educate new activists on the processes; numerous affinity groups were prepared from all over California; and the direct action was extended for two weeks with more than 1900 arrests. Shortly after the action, numerous errors were discovered in the plans and buildings of the plant, and two years later the plant was still not close to becoming operational. Although a minor earthquake fault was found near the plant, it eventually did go on-line.

For many people, including myself, the experience at Diablo Canyon in the encampment, the nonviolence training, the affinity group friendship, feminist awareness, the consensus processes, the arrest, and the time together in jail were deeply moving and inspiring. The Nonviolence Code, which was agreed to by every affinity group, was as follows:

1. Our attitude will be one of openness, friendliness, and respect towards all people we encounter.
2. We will use no violence, verbal or physical, toward any person.
3. We will not damage any property.
4. We will not bring or use any drugs or alcohol other than for medical purposes.
5. We will not run.
6. We will carry no weapons.

These Nonviolence Guidelines were adopted by various direct actions in California sponsored by the Livermore Action Group, the Vandenberg Action Coalition, and others.

At Diablo Canyon in 1981 strong solidarity was achieved on refusing to pay any money for bail or fines and also on refusing to accept probation. Most people were released after four days for time served, but over five hundred people became defendants represented by Richard Frischman using the necessity argument—that people had to act out of a moral necessity in order to prevent a greater harm or danger. This defense of necessity has been used by many anti-nuclear activists in order to challenge these evils through the judicial process.

During my week in jail I got to know the white-haired "Berkeley Bob" Schneider, who had won the Silver Star in World War II and later became known as Eldred. He told me that this Diablo action was so fantastic that he wanted to help organize the same thing at the Livermore Laboratory in northern California, where research for nuclear weapons is conducted. I agreed that the danger of nuclear weapons is even greater than that of nuclear power. In February 1982 the Livermore Action Group had their first action, and on June 21 of that year 1,400 blockaders, including Daniel Ellsberg, disrupted business as usual at the lab and were arrested. That same month 1,691 blockaded the United Nations offices of the nuclear weapons powers, and nearly a million people marched in the streets of New York for an end to the nuclear arms race.

Protesting Nuclear Weapons

In June 1978 the United Nations held its First Special Session on Disarmament, and a coalition called the Mobilization for Survival (MfS) sponsored a rally of 20,000 protesters. That year hundreds of people had been arrested over a period of eight months at Rocky Flats, Colorado, where the plutonium triggers for nuclear bombs are manufactured. Daniel Ellsberg called Rocky Flats the Auschwitz of our time. The next year 15,000 people participated in the demonstrations at Rocky Flats. In April 1979 at Groton, Connecticut, more than 3000 people demonstrated, and over 200 people blockaded the launching of the first Trident submarine, the *Ohio*.

On September 9, 1980 Daniel Berrigan, Philip Berrigan, Dean Hammer, Elmer Maas, Carl Kabat, Anne Montgomery, Molly Rush, and John Schuchardt of the "Plowshares Eight" entered a General Electric plant in King of Prussia, Pennsylvania and hammered on Mark 12A nuclear warheads (a first-strike weapon for the MX missile). During their trial they were not allowed to present evidence on international law or the defense of necessity but were convicted of burglary, conspiracy, and criminal mischief and were sentenced to five to ten years in prison. They were defended by Ramsey Clark and others, and their appeals took ten years. Their trial is depicted in the movie *In the King of Prussia* with Martin Sheen playing the judge and the defendants playing themselves. Their disarmament action was followed by many other plowshare actions at General Dynamics Electric Boatyard at Groton, Connecticut, protesting the Trident submarines, and at other facilities where nuclear weapons are developed or at missile silos, ELF (Extremely Low Frequency) towers used for communication during a nuclear war, or at military bases. Starting in 1984 some judges began to allow juries to hear expert evidence based on justification by necessity and to uphold international law. As of 1986 seventeen of these disarmament actions had taken place with some sentences as long as 12 years, and by the year 2001 there had been 68 plowshares actions involving 150 individuals, many of whom committed more than one action. The average sentences have been between one and two years. In October 2002 three Dominican sisters hammered on a Minuteman missile silo near Greeley, Colorado; after a trial they were sentenced to 41, 33, and 30 months, a $3,080 fine, and three years probation. Plowshares actions have also taken place in Australia, Germany, Holland, Sweden,

England, and Ireland.

The conversion of two Catholic bishops, Matthiesen in Amarillo, Texas and Hunthausen of Seattle, was stimulated by personal contact with individuals arrested for civil disobedience. Matthiesen urged workers to quit Pantex, where nuclear weapons are assembled, and Hunthausen refused to pay part of his federal income tax to protest military spending. Jim and Shelley Douglass, who influenced Bishop Hunthausen in Washington, organized a group called Ground Zero, which began protesting Trident submarines in 1975 and, starting in 1983, the white train carrying nuclear weapons. Their dual focus in their nonviolent civil disobedience campaign is Christ's kingdom of God and international law.

The Los Angeles Catholic Workers, who operate a free soup kitchen on skid row to feed about 800 people a day, have been active in civil disobedience for several years protesting nuclear weapons businesses in southern California and also other wars since then. Following in Dorothy Day's tradition, Jeff Dietrich, Catherine Morris, and others have been arrested many times.

The planned flight testing of the MX missile at Vandenberg Air Force Base on the central coast of California brought protesters from all over the state in January and March of 1983. About 200 were arrested and banned from the base in the first action. Many of these people returned in March and were joined by hundreds more who stayed in jail a week in solidarity for equal sentences; in this second action 777 were arrested. Congress had delayed some of the MX missile funds, which were to be voted on again in May. That month Jim Wallis of the Sojourners led 242 Christians into the halls of the US Congress to pray; they were arrested for an illegal demonstration. On June 17 the first MX missile flight test was delayed for several days at Vandenberg as forty protesters were arrested on the base. The Vandenberg Action Coalition is just one of the many activist groups that have sprung up around the world. Since the missile flights are targeted at the Marshall Islands, these protests are connected to the efforts of Pacific Islanders for a nuclear-free Pacific.

The first flight test of the MX missile seems to have been scheduled to coincide with the first annual International Day of Nuclear Disarmament on June 20, 1983 organized by the Livermore Action Group (LAG) of Berkeley. On that day legal rallies and nonviolent civil disobedience occurred in over fifty locations across the United States. At Livermore alone 1,066 people were arrested. Most of them refused to be arraigned because they would not accept probation; after a week the judge relented on the probation. The objectives of this action were to further the causes of global nuclear disarmament, demilitarization and nonintervention, equitable distribution of wealth and resources within and among nations, and a sustainable relationship between the human race and the planet. The aim was to "protest, halt, and disrupt the design, production, transport, and deployment of nuclear weapons worldwide for at least one working day."

In August 1981 some women in England organized a march from Cardiff to the US Air Force base at Greenham Common 125 miles away in order to protest the planned deployment of 96 cruise missiles there. Because it flies low so as not to be picked up by radar, the cruise missile is considered a first-strike weapon rather than a deterrent. The marchers arrived at Greenham Common on September 5. The media had ignored the march; so four women chained themselves to the main gate. Many decided to stay and set up a peace camp on base property; they were soon joined by others. On January 20, 1982 the nearby town of Newbury threatened to evict them; but they decided to remain and wanted to encourage the Labour party, which was currently considering unilateral disarmament. That year it became a peace camp for women only. The evictions began in May 1982; but those arrested were soon replaced by others as they had a decentralized social structure. Following the example of the US Women's Pentagon

Action, they issued a call to surround the base. On December 12, 1982 more than 30,000 women did exactly that, and the next day about 2,000 women were arrested for blockading the base. On New Year's Day 1982 forty-four women climbed over the fence and danced on a partially built missile silo.

The women named the seven gates of the Greenham Common base after the colors of the rainbow. Inspired by the encirclement, many towns and cities formed Greenham groups and supported the peace camp by raising money, spreading publicity, and arranging child care and transportation. Local affinity groups were able to initiate their own actions and be independent while still being part of the movement. After the cruise missiles were deployed in November 1983, a group of women decided to file a lawsuit in New York against President Reagan; the court denied them a hearing, but the effort created an extensive network in the United States. Another independent action that was opposed by many in the camp was when London Greenham groups brought blankets to the fences. In December 1983 about 40,000 women came to Greenham Common with mirrors to reflect back the reality of the base to those inside.

During a ten-day action in September 1984 about 10,000 women camped at the base. That month British prime minister Margaret Thatcher announced that she would get rid of the camp, and after that evictions occurred almost every day. Military by-laws were imposed in April 1985, making trespass a criminal offense with a possible fine of 100 pounds or 28 days in prison. The US Air Force even "zapped" women with microwaves of ultrasound that silently interfered with brainwave patterns, causing headaches, drowsiness, loss of memory, and even worse symptoms. On December 12, 1985, the sixth anniversary of the NATO decision to deploy cruise missiles, actions were carried out in home areas as well as at the base. Cruisewatch monitored the 44 deployments that occurred at the base between 1984 and 1988 so that missiles could not be deployed outside the base in secret. The women believed that these convoys were enough to cause the Soviet Union to go on nuclear alert because an exercise could not be distinguished from a real threat. In 1987 women at the camp debated who could call themselves "Greenham women," some believing that only those at the camp should do so. All these and many other decisions were made by using consensus process.

In her articles Gwyn Kirk described the feminist and nonviolent practices of the Greenham women, whom she believed practice nonviolence as a way of life. She described the six principles as assertiveness (challenging the police, politicians, judges, and the military), enjoyment (celebrating and affirming life with power, creativity and imagination), openness (making the business of war public and having clear communication), support and preparation (providing for the needs of the blockaders), flexibility of tactics (responding to new situations and being creatively unpredictable to keep up the pressure), and resistance (maintaining the protest despite harassment, prosecution, and persecution). The values she observed that the experience at Greenham Common used and taught are personal responsibility (not being victims and initiating actions), diversity (the variety of people and overcoming racism), a decentralized network (friendly groups providing emotional support), nonhierarchical decision-making (feminist and consensus processes), communication, coordination, and continuity (by personal contacts), and flexibility.

Many women at Greenham Common found that their experience was transformative, and the peace camp there lasted until the year 2000. Inspired by their example, many other peace camps sprang up in such places as Cosimo in Sicily, Seneca in New York, Puget Sound, Savannah River, St. Paul, and in Holland and Australia. At the Seneca Women's Peace Camp the attributes of responsibility, self-discipline, cooperation, and struggle were emphasized, and the consensus process was closely followed.

In West Germany the anti-nuclear and ecology movements grew into a full-fledged political party—the Greens. They managed to combine direct action protests with electoral politics, and in March 1983 the Green Party won 27 seats in the national Parliament. As their most articulate spokesperson in English, Petra Kelly pointed out that one of their main concerns was the US deployment of Pershing II and cruise missiles in western Europe that was scheduled to begin in December 1983. Kelly argued that nonviolent action and parliamentary democracy are complementary, writing,

Nonviolent opposition in no way diminishes
or undermines representative democracy;
in fact, it strengthens and stabilizes it.
The will of the electorate is not expressed
simply by putting one's mark
on a political blank cheque every four years.[4]

Petra Kelly believed that the Greens must demonstrate how to resolve conflicts by not treating adversaries as enemies but as people who need to be liberated from their slavery to violence. Practically every violent action results in violence in return. Thus violent revolutions usually only change the personnel at the top, but the system of violence remains. Like Gandhi, she recommended not cooperating with the violent elements in the social system.

The anti-nuclear movement is active throughout western Europe, while in eastern Europe during the Cold War it primarily operated through official organizations. In the Netherlands the No Cruise Missiles Committee organized massive rallies with 400,000 people in Amsterdam in November 1981 and 550,000 in The Hague in October 1983. An anti-missile petition was signed in 1985 by 3.75 million Dutch citizens. In England more than a dozen peace camps were established, Greenham Common being the most well-known. European Nuclear Disarmament (END) under the leadership of E. P. Thompson grew quickly in a few years. The nonviolent direct action portion of the anti-nuclear movement emphasizes the egalitarian methods of shifting roles and leadership positions so that many people can develop leadership skills. Most protesters shy away from the word "leader," preferring the role names of facilitator or spokesperson. Feminist awareness and consensus process attempt to be sensitive to every person's feelings, and the effort is always to keep a sense of group unity by resolving dissension. Yet every person and each group is considered autonomous. One group or even one person in a group can block consensus if there is an ethical objection to an action. Actually it is a moral responsibility to protest an immoral action which may affect the group. This is in reality the basis of civil disobedience toward a society which is allowing immoral actions. As with Gandhi, people in the nonviolent movement feel that the means is as important as the end. Therefore a great emphasis is placed on the purity of the process. When affinity groups of five to twenty people all agree on something, and when a spokes-council of representatives from those groups all achieve a unanimous decision involving hundreds of people, the moral and spiritual power of the resulting action can be awesome. Through this process of alternating spokes-council and affinity group meetings, goals are determined, strategies and tactics develop and change, and virtually every decision important to the group is made in such a way that every individual can influence the result.

The Great Peace March of 1986 showed how many peace groups made a transition from the top-down organization that typifies political campaigns of "leaders" to a more democratic movement that is shaped by all the active participants. Initiated by the former campaign manager, David Mixner, the publicity failed to produce the 5,000 marchers and funding support the staff of one hundred expected. The march began from Los Angeles on March first with about 1200 marching. The lack of organization resulted in numerous problems, and on March 14 Mixner announced that the March was broke, had failed, and people might as well go home. At Barstow in the Mojave

Desert about 400 people decided that they would continue and appealed for assistance. Renamed the Great Peace March for Global Nuclear Disarmament, on March 28 they continued walking as a reformed democratic organization on the move—Peace City. They found support along the way, and by the time they reached Washington DC on November 15 they were about 800 strong. Those who persisted found that they had the most challenging and memorable experiences of their lives.

Other protests of nuclear weapons continued to occur throughout the 1980s. For example, Pax Christi sponsored a protest of the Trident II submarine base at King's Bay, Georgia on May 6, 1989. After a short rally 54 people were given traffic citations for blocking the road into the main gate. Then twenty of us were arrested on the federal property of the base for stepping over a designated line on the sidewalk outside the fence of the base and were later charged with a federal petty offense. When the Berlin wall came down seven months later, I was still in prison for having a trial in that action; but it was clear that the direct actions protesting nuclear weapons were rapidly diminishing as the Soviet Union collapsed and was transformed by the end of the Cold War.

Nuclear Weapons Freeze Campaign

At the same time as the nonviolent direct action movement was growing, a nation-wide campaign in the United States for serious nuclear arms control developed a ground-swell of support through the bilateral nuclear weapons freeze proposal. The Freeze was conceived in the summer of 1979 when the American Friends Service Committee (AFSC) proposed a "Nuclear Moratorium," and arms-control scholar Randall Forsberg, who had done research for the Stockholm International Peace Research Institute (SIPRI), wrote the essay "Confining the Military to Defense as a Route to Disarmament" in which she suggested that both the USA and USSR stop producing nuclear weapons as a first step. This idea struck a chord with leaders in the peace movement when she spoke at the Mobilization for Survival annual convention in September. Encouraged by them, she wrote up her proposal in a four-page "Call to Halt the Arms Race." The following paragraph from that document was to become the basis of Freeze resolutions all around the country:

> To improve national and international security,
> the United States and the Soviet Union
> should stop the nuclear arms race.
> Specifically, they should adopt a mutual freeze
> on the testing, production and deployment
> of nuclear weapons and of missiles and new aircraft
> designed primarily to deliver nuclear weapons.
> This is an essential, verifiable first step
> toward lessening the risk of nuclear war
> and reducing the nuclear arsenals.[5]

The AFSC distributed 5,000 copies, and endorsements soon came in from Clergy and Laity Concerned (CALC), FOR, WILPF, Pax Christi USA, and the Coalition for a New Foreign and Military Policy.

Republican Senator Mark Hatfield introduced in the US Senate an amendment to the SALT II treaty calling for a Freeze, and in January 1980 a conference of about 30 peace groups endorsed Forsberg's Freeze proposal. The Freeze resolution was placed on the ballot in 62 cities and towns in Massachusetts, and in November it passed in all but three; the Freeze even passed in 30 where Reagan also won. More than 300 peace activists met at Georgetown University in March 1981 and set up committees to work for a nuclear weapons freeze. Forsberg's Institute for Defense and Disarmament Studies (IDDS) became a clearinghouse for information until the national Nuclear Weapons Freeze Campaign (NWFC) established an office in St. Louis in December 1981. That year Freeze resolutions were endorsed by the legislatures of Massachusetts, Oregon, New York, Connecticut, Maine, Minnesota, Vermont, Wisconsin, Kansas, Iowa, and Maryland. In November

300,000 West Germans demonstrated against nuclear weapons in Bonn, and the Women's Pentagon Action involved about 1,300 women in civil disobedience. In February 1982 Jonathan Schell published a detailed analysis of the consequences of a nuclear war in *The New Yorker* magazine, and his book *The Fate of the Earth* came out in April and became a best-seller.

Senators Ted Kennedy and Hatfield introduced a Freeze resolution in March 1982 and immediately attracted 25 co-sponsors in the Senate and 125 in the House of Representatives. Although 60-85% of the American people favored a Freeze, pressure against it from two thousand corporate lobbyists led to its narrow defeat in the House on August 5 by a vote of 204 to 202. However, in the 1982 elections Nuclear Freeze Initiatives were passed by the people in California, Massachusetts, Michigan, Montana, New Jersey, North Dakota, Oregon, Rhode Island, Chicago, Denver, Philadelphia, Washington DC, and Dade County. For the first time in history as many as 18 million people voted on the issue of nuclear weapons; 60% of them voted for the Freeze even though President Reagan opposed it. In seventy Congressional races where the Freeze was a key issue, pro-Freeze candidates won in 64% of them. On May 4, 1983 the US House of Representatives passed a non-binding Freeze resolution 278-149.

A bilateral nuclear weapons freeze that is verifiable was a fair proposal at that time because the Soviet Union had just recently caught up to parity with the United States in military power. Yet the Reagan Administration was attempting to forge ahead to military superiority again by developing and deploying new first-strike weapons such as the Trident II, MX, Pershing II, and cruise missiles, which actually had been approved by President Carter in December 1979, shortly *before* the Russians invaded Afghanistan. A complete Freeze would also be a comprehensive test ban and would be easier to verify than SALT I or II, according to Herbert Scoville, former deputy director of the Central Intelligence Agency (CIA). Common sense told people that the arms race had to be stopped before it could be reversed.

The Freeze campaign became a national, mainstream issue, and much of the effort behind it came from professional organizations such as the Physicians for Social Responsibility (PSR), which was led for four years by Dr. Helen Caldicott. In her care for children's health as a pediatrician and as a native of Australia in the south Pacific, where many nuclear tests occurred, Caldicott became aware of the medical dangers from radioactivity and had worked to end French nuclear testing there. Her lectures, films, and books on nuclear madness stirred thousands of anti-nuclear activists. In 1979 she organized a symposium of experts on the subject of "The Medical Consequences of Nuclear War" which addressed large audiences in major cities across the United States. A short film showing the highlights of the symposium called "The Last Epidemic" was shown by peace groups and Freeze advocates to thousands of small groups. Another short film of one of Caldicott's moving lectures on the nuclear arms issue, "If You Love this Planet," won an Academy Award in 1983.

Caldicott is not afraid to use strong and deep emotions of concern for the survival of our human civilization in order to stir her listeners to action. She considers this issue of human survival to be the ultimate issue of all time. In 1980 she started the Women's Party for Survival with the symbol for it being a baby. Later her driving force turned this into the many groups that sprang up around the country called Women's Action for Nuclear Disarmament (WAND). Her work also stimulated the forming of the International Physicians for the Prevention of Nuclear War (IPPNW), and in the fall of 1982 they presented a television program that was shown uncensored in both the Soviet Union and the United States. Three Soviet physicians and three American physicians all agreed that the only cure for nuclear war was prevention and the elimination of nuclear weapons.

An indication of how widespread and diverse the peace

movement had become can be seen by the various professional organizations that sprang up so rapidly. They included Educators for Social Responsibility, Lawyers Committee for Nuclear Policy, High Technology Professionals for Peace, Lawyers Alliance for Nuclear Arms Control, Union of Concerned Scientists, Business Executives for National Security, Architects for Social Responsibility, Social Workers for Peace and Nuclear Disarmament, Union of Concerned Psychoanalysts and Psychotherapists, Artists for Survival, Nurses for Social Responsibility, and many others. Religious and church groups became more active than ever. The US Catholic bishops, the World Council of Churches, the United Presbyterian Church, the Episcopal House of Bishops, the United Methodist Council of Bishops, the National Council of Churches of Christ in the US that includes thirty Protestant denominations, and many other churches, including the Lutherans in East Germany, made strong criticisms of the nuclear arms race.

Even though polls showed that three-quarters of the American people favored freezing the testing, production, and deployment of nuclear weapons, half-hearted support by Democratic Presidential candidates and Republican victories in 1984 and 1988 delayed the cessation of the nuclear arms race. Even after the end of the Cold War and major reductions in military spending by Russia and the other former Soviet republics, American politicians still refused to reduce US nuclear arsenals and weapon technology that would have provided a valuable "peace dividend." Yet even stopping the accelerated arms race by leveling it off helped to bring about the economic prosperity of the late 1990s. In 1986 the Nuclear Weapons Freeze Campaign (NWFC) merged with SANE to become SANE/Freeze, and in 1993 the name was changed to Peace Action. As of 2005 Peace Action was still actively working on many peace issues, including abolishing nuclear weapons.

In July 1996 the World Court ruled that the threat or use of nuclear weapons would violate international law. In

May 1995 the Abolition 2000 statement was initiated, and 400 organizations signed on. In 1997 a treaty was drafted for the abolition of nuclear weapons, and it was introduced into the UN General Assembly. In 1998 Jimmy Carter, Mikhail Gorbachev, Helmut Schmidt, and Pierre Trudeau were some of the 120 leaders from 48 countries who issued an appeal to abolish nuclear weapons. By the year 2000 the Abolition 2000 campaign had more than two thousand groups, and the petition had been signed by 13.4 million people.

In 2002 Dr. Caldicott published *The New Nuclear Danger*, warning about the revived military industrial complex under George W. Bush, and that year she founded the Nuclear Policy Research Institute. She described how the Clinton administration had greatly increased arms sales to other countries, and she noted that despite the end of the Cold War it was the first administration since Eisenhower that did not negotiate a major arms control treaty. Under George W. Bush the Department of Energy embarked on the nuclear Stockpile Stewardship and Management (SS&M) program that would cost more than $5 billion per year. Since the Cold War was long over and the US had no enemies for which these new weapons were needed, she wondered what could be the motivations of the tremendous project. The explanations she found were the enriching of weapons makers, rival competition between the air force, army, navy, and marines, donations to politicians by weapons manufacturers, and giving the United States a huge arsenal to enforce its corporate globalization.

Caldicott was concerned because the new Bush administration withdrew from the Anti-Ballistic Missile (ABM) Treaty so that it could go forward with its Ballistic Missile Defense (BMD) or National Missile Defense (NMD) system that had been promoted for years by the new Defense Secretary, Donald Rumsfeld. She noted that both President Putin of Russia and the Chinese arms control ambassador warned the United States that this acceleration of the arms race would stop the process of nuclear disarmament. Policy statements have made clear that in its drive for world domination the Bush administration is intent on gaining military supremacy in space. Representative Dennis Kucinich has proposed a bill to prohibit the weaponization of outer space. Caldicott also warned about the radioactive depleted uranium (DU) that was used in Iraq in 1991, Bosnia in 1994 and 1995, Kosovo in 1999, and Afghanistan in 2001 and 2002. She discovered that already at least five Italian soldiers who fought in Bosnia had died of leukemia. Caldicott reviewed the records of the warmongering advisors influencing Bush's foreign policy—Dick Cheney, Donald Rumsfeld, Colin Powell, Condoleezza Rice, Paul Wolfowitz, Richard Perle, and others. At the beginning of her book she contrasted these horrifying dangers with the vision of a wise president leading the world toward disarmament and peaceful recovery.

Randall Forsberg was appointed by President Clinton to the Advisory Committee of the US Arms Control and Disarmament Agency, and she continues to work diligently for nuclear disarmament. She noted that the US invasion of Iraq in 2003 flagrantly violated US and international laws. At the same time the United States was justifying its invasion with the erroneous contention that Iraq still had remnants of chemical weapons, the US was blocking and undermining treaties that would verify the reduction of nuclear, chemical, and biological weapons. Forsberg has pointed out that in 2001 Russia proposed reducing its arsenal of ten thousand nuclear weapons to 1,500 with verification of their dismantling; but President George W. Bush refused this offer and in May 2002 signed the Strategic Offensive Reduction Treaty (SORT) that merely put thousands of weapons on reserve instead of dismantling them. The limits do not take effect for ten years, at which time the treaty expires. Bush made the US the only country to block the implementation of the Comprehensive Test Ban Treaty. The Bush administration has also blocked verification of the ban on biological weapons with the excuse that they would expose the secrets of the biotech companies.

The US has refused to ban weapons in space, and is the only country developing such weapons. President Bush also announced that the US was withdrawing from the Anti-Ballistic Missile (ABM) Treaty, which had been in effect since 1968. In 2004 the Bush administration began deployment of Ballistic Missile Defense (BMD) even though the system has failed most of its tests. According to Forsberg, the Bush team reversed the policy aimed at getting North Korea to end its testing and export of missiles with a range of more than two hundred miles, and China will not negotiate on fissile material unless the US is willing to discuss its program for weapons in space. Information from the nuclear-posture review has leaked out indicating that the Bush administration is threatening to use nuclear weapons against several countries including Cuba, Syria, and Iran. Forsberg believes that these Bush policies are more likely to foster the spread of weapons of mass destruction than the reverse.

Notes

1. *No More War!* by Linus Pauling p. 223.
2. *Ibid.*, p. vii.
3. *The American Peace Movement* by Charles Chatfield, p. 105.
4. "Women and Ecology" in *Women on War*, p. 312.
5. "Call to Halt the Nuclear Arms Race - Proposal for a Mutual U.S. Soviet Nuclear Weapons Freeze," *Bulletin of Peace Proposals*, Vol. 12, No. 4 (1981).

12

Resisting Wars in Central America

The bishops of Latin America, in our meeting in Puebla,
publicly recognized "the legitimate right
to self-determination by our peoples,
which permits them to organize as they wish,
set their own historical direction,
and participate in a new international order."
Oscar Romero, letter to President Carter, January 17, 1980

Each week I go about the country
listening to the cries of the people,
their pain from so much crime,
and the ignominy of so much violence.
Each week I ask the Lord to give me the right words
to console, to denounce, to call for repentance.
Oscar Romero, March 24, 1980

If the United States significantly escalates
its intervention on Central America,
I pledge to join with others
in acts of legal protest and civil disobedience
as conscience leads me.
Pledge of Resistance, 1984

We are not worth more; they are not worth less.
S. Brian Willson

Let us then combat war with peace.
Let us combat totalitarianism with the power of democracy.
United in ideals and principles,
joined by dialogue and democracy,
we can and will bring hostilities to an end.
We must give peace a chance.
Oscar Arias to the US Congress, September 22, 1987

Peace is a process which never ends.
It is the result of innumerable decisions
made by many persons in many lands.

It is an attitude, a way of life,
a way of solving problems and of resolving conflicts.
It cannot be forced on the smallest nation,
nor can it be imposed by the largest.
It can neither ignore our differences
nor overlook our common interests.
It requires us to work and live together.
Oscar Arias, *The Art of Peace* 115

I have no doubt at all that one day ...
the School of the Americas which has caused so much
suffering and death to our sisters and brothers abroad
and has been a theft from the poor here at home,... will close.
We will speak from prison, your honor.
We will speak from our cells.
The truth cannot be silenced, it can't be chained.
Roy Bourgeois

Central American History

In 1821 Central America abolished slavery and
followed the example of Mexico's Agustin Iturbide and
declared its independence from Spain, and the next year
they became a part of his Mexican empire. When Iturbide
was overthrown in 1823, the United Provinces of Central
America declared their independence. That year United
States president James Monroe proclaimed the paternalistic
policy toward Latin America that became known as the
Monroe Doctrine in order to warn Europeans not to intervene anymore in the western hemisphere. During the California gold rush in 1850 US businessmen began financing a
railroad across the isthmus of Panama; it was completed
after five years and was protected by US troops. Also in
1855 adventurer William Walker declared himself president
of Nicaragua so that the United States could secure rights
to a canal; he reestablished slavery in Nicaragua and was
recognized by the US. Two years later shipping magnate
Cornelius Vanderbilt helped the US invade Nicaragua to
overthrow Walker with assistance from Costa Ricans at
Rivas.

The United States intervened in Nicaragua four times

between 1894 and 1899. After another intervention in 1910, the US Marines occupied Nicaragua for the next quarter century. A rebellion led by the mystical Augusto Sandino, a theosophist, in 1927 was not quelled until 1934, when he was treacherously murdered by order of Anastasio Somoza Garcia after he had dinner with him. Somoza established the National Guard, and his family ruled Nicaragua until 1979.

El Salvador became an independent nation in 1838, and in 1886 the communal lands were privatized as an oligarchy of mostly coffee growers called "the fourteen families" dominated the country for the next 45 years. As the Depression devastated the coffee market, the Communist Party of El Salvador (CPS) won many municipal elections in 1931; but Minister of War General Maximiliano Hernandez Martinez refused to accept the results. The Congress elected the reformer Arturo Araujo; but amid Communist agitation Farabundo Marti led a CPS revolt with Indian peasants; this was quickly defeated by the army, and in 1932 Marti and CPS leaders were publicly executed as about 30,000 peasants were massacred in the infamous *la matanza*. General Martinez took dictatorial power that delayed industrialization. Labor unions were illegal until Martinez was persuaded to resign by the United States in 1944 during a sit-down strike, though military rule continued. The *Partido Revolutionario de Unificacion Democratica* (PRUD) was founded in 1948 by Oscar Osorio, who became President in 1950, when El Salvador got a new constitution and began industrializing. The elections of 1956 were fixed by the government party (PRUD) of Lt. Col. Jose Maria Lemus.

In 1961 in response to the Cuban revolution the anticommunist *Organizacion Democratica Nacionalista* (ORDEN) was founded in El Salvador by General Jose Alberto Medrano. Vatican II of Pope John XXIII influenced Latin America when the bishops met at Medellin, Columbia in 1968 and were inspired to dedicate themselves to alleviating injustice and oppression. *A Theology of Liberation* by

Gustavo Gutierrez inspired many priests to become active in social and political reforms. In 1969 after Salvadorans in Honduras were mistreated, the "Soccer War" broke out and lasted four days; about 25,000 impoverished peasants were pushed back into El Salvador, and the border was closed. Throughout the 1970s in El Salvador, Nicaragua, and Guatemala civil wars developed in reaction to government repression and right-wing death squads under General Medrano and others. San Salvador mayor Jose Napoleon Duarte was apparently elected President in 1972, but Col. Arturo Molina of the PRUD, renamed as the *Partido de Conciliacion Nacional* (PCN), was chosen by the Assembly instead. After an attempted revolt by reformist officers failed, Duarte was arrested, tortured, and exiled.

The United Fruit Company had been in Guatemala for a half century when Jacobo Arbenz was elected President in 1950 to succeed peacefully Juan Jose Arévalo, who had been democratically elected in 1944. Arbenz implemented agrarian reform, but the United Fruit Company complained that they were only compensated for their 234,000 acres according to the fraudulent value they had reported on their tax forms. In 1954 mercenaries trained by the US Central Intelligence Agency (CIA) at military bases in Honduras and Nicaragua, supported by four US fighter planes, overthrew Arbenz and put Col. Carlos Castillo Armas of the National Liberation Movement (MLN) in power. Thousands of people were killed as land was returned to previous owners, taxes on interest and dividends to foreign investors were abolished, and all unions were disbanded. After President Armas was assassinated in 1957, riots resulted in the military taking control; a conservative was elected the next year. United States Special Forces began intervening in Guatemala in 1966, and in the next seven years right-wing death squads killed about 30,000 people. In 1974 a right-wing candidate seems to have stolen the election from General Rios Montt.

When President Jimmy Carter attached human rights requirements to US aid in 1977, Guatemala, El Salvador,

Brazil, and Argentina refused to accept it; the next year the US banned arms sales to Guatemala. In 1982 General Rios Montt took power, and the World Council of Churches reported that the government had killed more than 9,000 people in five months. Under President Ronald Reagan in 1983 the US resumed shipping military supplies to Guatemala. Many changes of government occurred in the next few years, and the Church continued to complain of human rights abuses.

The United Fruit Company was also dominant in Honduras, which was invaded by US troops in 1923. The United States let the United Fruit Company take control and rule by a dictator from 1932 to 1948. An army coup in 1963 was led by Col. Oswaldo Lopez in 1963, who ruled until he was overthrown in 1975 when a scandal exposed that United Brands had paid an official $1.25 million and then saved $7.5 million in taxes. After Nicaragua's Somoza fell in 1979, President Carter strengthened relations with Honduras.

El Salvador's Civil War

In February 1977 another fraudulent election made General Carlos Humberto Romero president of El Salvador as more than two hundred peaceful protesters were killed; the Catholic Church boycotted his inauguration. In June the White Warriors' Union accused Catholics in El Salvador of promoting Communism and threatened to kill all the Jesuits in the country, distributing leaflets inciting, "Be a Patriot! Kill a Priest!" Since several priests had already been assassinated by death squads, the US warned President Romero; the US Congress began holding hearings on religious persecution in El Salvador. Over the next few months the Romero government was condemned for human rights violations by reports from Amnesty International, the International Commission of Jurists, the Organization of American States (OAS), and the US State Department. The Legal Aid office of Archbishop Oscar Romero found that 727 people had been killed by death squads in 1978 and

1979. On October 15, 1979 General Humberto Romero's government was overthrown by a coup of young officers. They formed a ruling junta, and a few weeks later the Carter administration announced that it would send "nonlethal" military aid to El Salvador.

In January 1980 a struggle for power resulted in the civilians resigning as the right-wing General Jose Guill-ermo Garcia gained the upper hand, though Christian Democrats joined his junta. In February the banks of El Salvador were nationalized, and land reform was decreed; but death-squad killings escalated. On the 17th Archbishop Oscar Romero wrote a letter to President Carter warning him,

> Your government's contribution, instead of favoring
> the cause of justice and peace in El Salvador,
> will surely increase injustice here
> and sharpen the repression that has been unleashed
> against the people's organizations
> fighting to defend their most fundamental rights.[1]

The archbishop explained that neither the junta nor the Christian Democrats were governing the country, because the armed forces had the political power and used it unscrupulously to repress the people and defend the oligarchy. Therefore Romero asked Carter to prohibit all military aid to El Salvador and not let the US intervene in any way so that the people's organizations could resolve the crisis, and he cited the statement by the bishops of Latin America recognizing the right of self-determination of their peoples.

After Attorney General Mario Zamora sued Roberto D'Aubuisson for libel for having accused him of collabo-rating with guerrillas, Zamora was assassinated. D'Aubuisson was generally recognized as a leader of ORDEN death squads in the 1970s under General Medrano. After the October 1979 coup Major D'Aubuisson had been forced out of the army; but he began accusing "Communist traitors" on television so that troops would kill them. After Zamora's death, many Christian Democrats withdrew from the government in protest and formed a new party called the Popular Social Christian Movement; but on March 9 the Christian Democrat Jose Napoleon Duarte joined the ruling junta.

In his last sermon the day before he was assassinated while saying mass on March 24, 1980, Archbishop Oscar Romero made this dramatic plea,

> I would like to make a special appeal
> to the men of the army,
> and specifically to the ranks of the National Guard,
> the police and the military.
> Brothers, you come from our own people.
> You are killing your own brother peasants
> when any human order to kill must be subordinate
> to the law of God which says, "Thou shalt not kill."
> No soldier is obliged to obey an order
> contrary to the law of God.
> No one has to obey an immoral law.
> It is high time you recovered your consciences
> and obeyed your consciences rather than a sinful order.
> The church, the defender of the rights of God,
> of the law of God, of human dignity, of the person,
> cannot remain silent before such an abomination.
> We want the government to face the fact
> that reforms are valueless
> if they are to be carried out at the cost of so much blood.
> In the name of God, in the name of this suffering people
> whose cries rise to heaven more loudly each day,
> I implore you, I beg you, I order you in the name of God,
> stop the repression.[2]

About 30,000 people attended Romero's funeral; gunshots and explosions caused panic, resulting in the death of thirty and injuries to hundreds. Three days after Romero's death USAID granted $13 million to El Salvador, and on April first the US House Appropriations Committee approved $5.7 million in military aid. That month the *Frente Democratico Revolucionario* (FDR) formed in El

Salvador as the political party allied with the rebels.

On May 7, 1980 the progressive Col. Adolfo Majano discovered a plot by the extreme right led by D'Aubuisson, who was arrested with 23 others. One week later six hundred Salvadoran peasants fleeing into Honduras were massacred at the Rio Sumpul by troops from both El Salvador and Honduras. After right-wing supporters chanted "Communist" outside the home of US ambassador Robert White, D'Aubuisson was released. On June 26 soldiers stormed the National University and killed fifty as the government closed the university. In October the Salvadoran army killed 3,000 peasants in Morazan, and more US military advisors secretly arrived in El Salvador. Five rebel groups joined together to form the *Frente Farabundo Marti para la Liberacion Nacional* (FMLN).

After Ronald Reagan was elected President of the United States, he assured Salvadoran business leaders that he would resume military aid. Six FDR leaders in San Salvador were kidnapped, tortured, and murdered. On December 4 the bodies of Maryknoll sisters Ita Ford and Maura Clarke, Ursuline sister Dorothy Kazel, and missionary Jean Donovan were found near the airport after they had been raped and murdered by soldiers of the National Guard. The next day President Carter suspended aid to El Salvador. After the third junta disbanded as Duarte became provisional President of El Salvador, Carter restored economic aid. On January 5, 1981 three agrarian reform advisors, two from the United States, were shot to death in San Salvador. Concerned that President-elect Reagan would intervene, the FMLN tried to launch a final offensive before he took office; but the popular organizations had been so devastated by the death squads that a general strike failed. On January 14 Carter's National Security Council approved $5.9 million in lethal aid to El Salvador.

The capable and outspoken US ambassador to El Salvador, Robert White, was fired by the new Secretary of State Alexander Haig within a week after Reagan's inauguration. In February the Reagan administration issued a

White Paper claiming that Salvadoran guerrillas were receiving arms and training from Cuba and Nicaragua; they proposed $25 million in additional military aid to El Salvador with 26 more advisors. By June the US press had refuted virtually every point of the White Paper. On March 9 Reagan signed a Presidential finding authorizing CIA covert operations to support the government of El Salvador with $19.5 million, ostensibly to interdict arms supplies coming from Nicaragua and Honduras.

In January 1982 the US began training Salvadoran troops at Fort Bragg and Fort Benning. To keep aid going to El Salvador the Reagan administration had to certify that it was making progress on human rights. This finding was immediately refuted in the press by numerous human rights organizations. The Salvadoran Communal Union (UCS) complained that at least ninety officials of peasant organizations had been killed in 1981. Amnesty International reported human rights violations on a "massive scale." The American Civil Liberties Union (ACLU) and Americas Watch argued there were hundreds of politically motivated murders, torture, and mutilation by paramilitary forces. The *Washington Post* and the *New York Times* reported extensively on the El Mozote massacre. Relatives of the four murdered churchwomen complained that the Salvadoran government had covered up the case and had not tried anyone for their murders. Dozens of those in the US Congress were so appalled that they sponsored a resolution to declare the certification null and void. A *Newsweek* poll found that 89% of those familiar with US policy said that the United States should not send troops to El Salvador.

Roberto D'Aubuisson had founded the Nationalist Republican Alliance (ARENA) that drew policies from the 1980 platform of the US Republican Party. The US ambassador Deane Hinton warned that a victory by the right-wing ARENA party in the upcoming election could be a disaster; so the CIA spent two million dollars to help the Christian Democrats. In the March 1982 election about 85%

of El Salvador's eligible voters cast ballots. The Christian Democrats won 24 of the sixty seats in the Assembly; but the rest were taken by five rightist parties with ARENA getting 19 seats and the PCN fourteen. Ambassador Hinton persuaded the parties not to challenge the election results nor block agrarian reform and warned them that if they elected D'Aubuisson president, US aid may stop. Despite opposition by ARENA, the Christian Democrat Alvaro Magaña was elected President, though D'Aubuisson became the leader of the Constituent Assembly, which in May suspended the agrarian reform.

In July 1982 the Reagan administration had to certify El Salvador's human rights record again and argued that the 1,573 political murders in the first half of the year were less than the year before, though the number was more than the previous six months. In October leaders of the FDR and FMLN offered to negotiate without preconditions by sending a letter that was delivered to President Magaña by Archbishop Rivera y Damas. That month Ambassador Hinton warned the US-Salvadoran Chamber of Commerce that the "Mafia" that was murdering innocent civilians and Americans must be stopped. After guerrilla commandos destroyed most of the Salvadoran air force at the Ilopango air base in late January 1983, President Reagan used his emergency powers to send $55 million in military aid to El Salvador without congressional approval.

In January 1983 President Reagan issued his third certification of human rights progress in El Salvador, and on April 27 he spoke to a joint session of Congress urging them to support his anti-Communist effort in Central America, arguing, "The national security of all the Americas is at stake in Central America."[3] In late May assistant secretary of state for Inter-American affairs Thomas Ender and Ambassador Hinton were both replaced for trying to get the Salvadorans to stop human rights violations. In June a hundred US military advisers began training Salvadoran troops in Honduras. In July, Reagan certified El Salvador's human rights record again even though no one had been brought to trial for the deaths of the church-women or the agrarian workers, and in November the President vetoed a bill that would have continued the certification requirements. On October 25, 1983 US Marines and Army Rangers invaded the Caribbean island of Grenada, where a military coup led by the Marxist deputy prime minister Bernard Coard had taken power on October 13; that government and resisting Cuban workers were removed as Reagan argued that US medical students had to be protected.

For the fiscal year of 1984 the US Congress gave the Reagan administration a third less military aid for El Salvador than they requested, but the $64.8 million was still more than twice that of the previous year. On December 11 Vice President George Bush visited President Magaña but in a toast warned him, "Your cause is being undermined by the murderous violence of reactionary minorities,"[4] and he denounced the "cowardly death squads."

On March 25, 1984 Salvadorans voted for president, and a runoff was scheduled for May between Christian Democrat Duarte and D'Aubuisson of ARENA. During the congressional recess in April, President Reagan invoked his emergency powers to send $32 million in military aid to El Salvador. Meanwhile the CIA spent $2.1 million covertly to back Duarte, using the German Konrad Adenauer Foundation, a Venezuelan Institute, and the US Agency for International Development (USAID). D'Aubuisson's friend Jesse Helms learned of it and complained on the Senate floor, and death threats were made against US ambassador Thomas Pickering. Duarte won the election and promised to end the death squads, implement reform, and negotiate peace with the guerrillas. This was enough to persuade the US House of Representatives to vote 212-208 to resume military aid. After a Salvadoran jury convicted five former National Guardsmen of killing the four church women, Congress was more willing to pass aid for El Salvador. The Reagan administration managed to compile $196.6 million for the war in El Salvador in 1984, and $123.25 million was authorized for 1985.

In March 1988 the ARENA party won control of El Salvador's National Assembly. Peace-loving senators Mark Hatfield and Tom Harkin tried to hold back half of El Salvador's military aid for six months so that they would negotiate an end to the war; but their amendment was stopped in committee after dying Duarte sent a message from Walter Reed Hospital. ARENA candidate Alfredo Christiani was elected president in March 1989. In November the guerrillas launched a major offensive but could not get the support they wanted in the capital San Salvador. The military reacted to this by sending out death-squads against journalists, clerics, relief workers, and intellectuals, murdering six Jesuit priests and two women at the Central American University on November 16. The US Congress responded to these developments by cutting the military aid for 1990 in half. In the 1980s the US had given El Salvador nearly $4 billion in overt aid. In April 1990 representatives of the FMLN and the El Salvador government met at Geneva under the auspices of the United Nations. The next month the US House adopted the Moakly-Murtha amendment that cut military aid in half again unless the FMLN refused to negotiate or got weapons from abroad or murdered civilians. In July an important accord on human rights was reached by the FMLN and the El Salvador government.

After a US helicopter was shot down in January 1991, the Bush administration restored the extra military aid. In October the FMLN agreed to disarm when they were promised major reforms in the government and economic improvements such as land reform. Finally at the very end of UN Secretary-General Perez de Cuellar's term on the last day of 1991, a peace agreement was made. The United Nations Observer Mission in El Salvador (ONUSAL) successfully monitored the peace accord and supervised elections in 1994. The UN also mediated an end to 36 years of civil war in Guatemala in 1996. Altogether the low-intensity wars of the 1980s had killed more than two hundred thousand people in Nicaragua, El Salvador, and Guate-mala, resulting in more than two million refugees.

Nicaragua's Sandinistas and Contras

Anastasio Somoza was elected President of Nicaragua in 1967, succeeding his late brother Luis Somoza. Four years later Congress dissolved itself and transferred its constitutional authority to Somoza. After the 1972 earthquake Somoza declared martial law that lasted until 1977. That year the *Frente Sandinista de Liberacion Nacional* (FSLN), which had been founded after the Cuban revolution in 1961 by Carlos Fonseca, Tomas Borge, and Silvio Moraga, began a major offensive. The Somoza government was criticized by *La Prenza* editor Pedro Joaquin Chamorro, but he was assassinated on January 10, 1978. FSLN insurrections spread in Nicaraguan provinces and closed in on Managua. In November the United States blocked $65 million in loans from the International Monetary Fund (IMF) because Somoza refused mediation; but in May 1979 they released the money. On June 20 captured ABC reporter Bill Stewart was shot in the head by a National Guard soldier while his crew filmed from a van. The US called for a meeting of the Organization of American States (OAS), and Secretary of State Cyrus Vance urged a peacekeeping force. The FSLN got most of its weapons from Venezuela and Panama, as Cuba restrained itself to keep the US from opposing the revolution. On July 17, 1979 President Somoza fled to Miami.

Two days later an unusual combination of Marxist guerrillas and conservative businessmen took power in Managua, declaring the Government of National Reconstruction and promising a mixed economy, political pluralism, and a non-aligned foreign policy. Although the National Directorate was led by the moderate brothers Daniel and Humberto Ortega, the private sector opposed the Sandinistas' emphasis on social welfare with free education and health care, taxes on the wealthy, and agrarian reform. The US contributed about $20 million in relief aid to feed and house those displaced by the civil war. In February 1980 the US Congress appropriated $75 million in humanitarian aid for Nicaragua along with $5 million in military aid for its neighbors. In September, President Carter certified that Nicaragua was not harboring terrorists nor supporting them in other countries. Carter's moderate policy was designed to avoid the past mistakes with Cuba that had pushed Castro toward the Communists.

In April 1981 the Reagan administration canceled the $118 million in US aid to Nicaragua that Carter had obtained, and the President approved CIA director Bill Casey's plan to back anti-Sandinista insurgents based in Honduras. On November 16 Reagan approved $19.95 million to support these *contra* rebels. Without US assistance the Nicaraguans turned to others for help. The Soviet Union provided 20,000 tons of wheat; Libya loaned them $100 million; and Cuba sent $64 million in technical aid. In February 1982 Mexican president Jose Lopez Portillo gave a speech in Nicaragua and offered to mediate to help release the "three knots of tension" involving the United States and Nicaragua, the US and Cuba, and the El Salvador civil war. Many in the US Congress welcomed his assistance, and to mollify the public the Reagan administration reluctantly promised to cooperate. After anti-Sandinista Contras destroyed two major bridges on the border between Nicaragua and Honduras in March, the Sandinistas declared a state of emergency on March 15.

In December 1982 US Representative Tom Harkin proposed an amendment that would prohibit US assistance to any group "carrying out military activities in or against Nicaragua."[5] Edward Boland then offered a substitute with language acceptable to the Republicans, prohibiting funds "for the purpose of overthrowing the government of Nicaragua,"[6] which passed the House 411-0. Yet the number of Contras the US was supporting increased from less than 2,000 in August 1982 to 7,000 by the following May. Thirty-seven members of the House wrote to President Reagan complaining that the Boland amendment was being violated, and on July 28, 1983 the House voted 228-195 to end covert operations against Nicaragua.

Throughout the second half of 1983 the US military conducted extensive exercises in the western Caribbean to intimidate Nicaragua, Salvadoran rebels, and Cuba. In September the Contras sabotaged Nicaragua's only coastal oil terminal, and the next month they attacked oil storage facilities. The House voted again 227-194 in the annual intelligence authorization to ban spending on covert operations against Nicaragua, and in November they passed a resolution in support of negotiations by the Contadora process mediated by Mexico, Venezuela, Colombia, and Panama; but the conference committee added $24 million dollars for the Contras for the next fiscal year. Without telling the oversight committees, the National Security Council (NSC) increased the authorized strength of the Contras to 18,000.

Early in 1984 the CIA used a ship off Nicaragua's coast to help Latin American commandos lay mines in three Nicaraguan harbors; but the Senate Intelligence committee was not fully informed until March 27 after Dutch, Panamanian, and Soviet ships were damaged, and Nicaraguan fishermen were killed. Then a Liberian tanker and a Japanese ship were damaged, and speedboats with machine guns and explosives attacked the Corinto harbor. By overwhelming votes both houses of Congress voted to condemn the mining, 84-12 in the Senate. On May 24 the House voted 241-177 to prohibit aid to the Contras.

Since the Reagan administration could not get money from Congress for the Contras, they looked for other ways. On June 25 at a meeting with President Reagan, Vice President Bush, CIA Director Casey, National Security Advisor McFarlane, Chairman of the Joint Chiefs of Staff Vessey, Secretary of State Schultz, and Secretary of Defense Weinberger, they discussed getting military support for the Contras from other countries. Prince Bandar of Saudi Arabia had already offered a million dollars a month. Casey had got $10 million in arms that Israel had captured from the Palestinian Liberation Organization (PLO), though he had denied this when he testified before the House Intelligence Committee. Schultz and the White House chief of staff Jim Baker warned that such solicitations could be an "impeachable offense," and Reagan demanded secrecy, warning "If such a story gets out, we'll all be hanging by our thumbs in front of the White House."[7] Within days of Congress voting to end all funding for the Contras, more than $20 million was sent by Saudis into Contra bank accounts.

The Contadora nations were mediating peace talks at Manzanillo, and in September 1984 Nicaragua surprised many by agreeing to the proposed treaty that would ban foreign military bases, training, and exercises; it meant that US advisers would have to leave Honduras and El Salvador, and the Cuban advisers would have to leave Nicaragua. Reagan's diplomats found ways to delay the treaty, irritating Mexico. In October the Associated Press reported that a CIA murder manual called *Psychological Operations in Guerrilla Warfare* had been sent to Contras, urging them to hire criminals to provoke violence at large urban demonstrations to cause deaths and make martyrs. They also advised them to "neutralize" (assassinate) judges, police, security officials, and Sandinista leaders. On November 2 Nicaragua held elections, and the Sandinistas won about two-thirds of the votes. Two days later Reagan won re-election with 59% of the popular vote.

After Reagan's large electoral victory in 1984, his administration imposed an economic embargo against Nicaragua on May 1, 1985. The next month Congress approved $27 million for the Contras but only in overt and nonlethal aid. However, a year later Congress authorized $100 million, including $70 million in military aid, for the Nicaraguan Contras to be administered by the CIA. Meanwhile during the restricted period from 1985 to 1986 Lt. Col. Oliver North, working for the National Security Council (NSC), had secretly raised $34 million dollars from other countries and $2.7 million from wealthy citizens as covert aid for the Contras, using an offshore enterprise managed by former general Richard Secord. By March 1985 the secret arms were flowing into Honduras. North thanked Guatemala for its help by promising military aid, and Salvadoran president Duarte let them use the Ilopango air base for logistics. Panama's General Noriega had been working for the CIA for two decades and allowed them to use Panama for training camps and his drug-smuggling planes for transporting the arms (and drugs to pay for them). China sent surface-to-air missiles through Guatemala, and Taiwan donated two million dollars. In 1986 the US secretly sold arms to Iran for a profit of $16.1 million, of which $3.8 million was spent for the Contras' war.

As early as 1985 the Central American Crisis Monitoring Team of the Institute for Policy Studies had published the pamphlet *In Contempt of Congress*, quoting official statements of Reagan officials with the counterevidence showing that they were lies, deceptions, and distortions. Former New York assistant attorney general Reed Brody documented with 145 sworn affidavits 28 cases of human rights violations by the Contras. Columnist Charles Krauthammer dubbed American support for anti-communist revolutions the Reagan Doctrine. Neither the United States nor El Salvador ever brought their allegations against Nicaragua to the Organization of American States or the United Nations. Yet Article 51 of the UN Charter requires any nation claiming the right of self-defense to lodge a formal complaint in the Security Council. The Reagan administration was apparently unwilling to have its actions scrutinized by international law. On June 25, 1986 the House passed Reagan's $100 million in aid for the Contras, and the next day the World Court announced that it had found the United States guilty of fifteen violations against international law for arming the Contras, attacking Nicaragua, mining their harbors, embargoing their trade, and violating their airspace. The US Government had withdrawn from the World Court and ignored its judgment.

On October 5, 1986 the Sandinista army shot down a

plane carrying 10,000 pounds of ammunition and supplies for the Contras. The surviving crew member was the American Eugene Hasenfus, and evidence indicated it was a CIA operation. CIA Central America Task Force chief Alan Fiers lied to the House Intelligence Committee about it and was later convicted for that. His boss, CIA deputy director of operations Clair George, had instructed him to lie, and in 1992 George was also found guilty of making false statements to Congress. In November the press revealed that the Reagan administration had sold arms to Iran in order to get US hostages in Lebanon released. The Justice Department found a memo by North planning to use $12 million from the arms sale to purchase supplies for the Nicaraguan resistance forces. Attorney General Edwin Meese warned President Reagan that he could be impeached if he tried to cover it up; over the objection of CIA director Casey, both held a news conference to admit the "Iran-Contra" scandal. They announced that National Security Advisor John Poindexter and his assistant Oliver North were both dismissed. After a congressional investigation involving extensive public hearings that were televised, on November 18, 1987 the Iran-Contra committees reported that they found "secrecy, deception, and disdain for the law."[8]

Democratic House Speaker Jim Wright and President Reagan announced a proposal for a cease-fire on August 5, 1987, but two days later the presidents of all five Central American nations signed the Arias peace accord in Guatemala. Wright liked this peace plan, but Reagan considered it "fatally flawed," because it would allow Soviet aid to the Sandinistas to continue. In January 1988 the Sandinistas ended their state of emergency, allowed exiles to return, released some political prisoners, and agreed to negotiate directly with the Contra rebels. In February the US House of Representatives rejected the entire Contra aid package. In March the Sandinistas met with the Contras at Sapoas on the Costa Rica border and signed a sixty-day cease-fire. Soviet president Mikhail Gorbachev suspended their military aid to Nicaragua at the end of 1988 and urged the Sandinistas to hold a fair election.

In February 1989 the five Central American presidents met in El Salvador and planned the voluntary demobilization, repatriation, and relocation of the Nicaraguan Contras and their families. In a meeting at Tela, Honduras in August the Central American leaders agreed not to allow insurgent forces in their territories, and an international commission to verify this was created, making it difficult for the Contras to operate out of Honduras and Costa Rica. During the 1980s the US had given the Contras $350 million to fight the Sandinistas. During the administration of George Bush the effort was shifted to influencing the next election in Nicaragua through the National Endowment for Democracy (NED), which contributed $11.6 million to the opposition. The CIA found $6 million to help the opposing coalition and even gave $600,000 to former Contra leaders for the election campaign. This paid off when Violeta Chamorro defeated Daniel Ortega 55% to 41% on February 25, 1990. During the campaign Ortega complained that his country was facing an election with a gun pointed at its head, because the Bush administration threatened that a Sandinista victory would mean more war. Nonetheless the Sandinistas accepted the election results and became the opposition party. The Contra war, financed and supplied by the US, had caused $15 billion damage in Nicaragua and killed about 30,000 people, not counting those who died from hunger and disease.

Resisting Reagan's Proxy Wars

In the summer of 1980 the US Border Patrol discovered that about half of 27 illegal Salvadoran immigrants had died of thirst and exposure; the survivors were taken in by churches in Tucson. The following May Quaker philosopher and goat rancher Jim Corbett tried to get a Salvadoran hitchhiker he had met released but learned that he had already been deported. Jim and his wife Pat borrowed $4,500 to bail out four Salvadoran women and a baby, and they learned about the violence in El Salvador that people were fleeing. Corbett went to Los Angeles and argued with the US Immigration and Naturalization Service (INS) that Salvadoran refugees should not be deported. He wrote five hundred letters to Quaker meetings, asking for donations to pay bail for refugees. By June, Corbett and the Manzo Area Council had raised $150,000; but the INS raised the bails from $250 to $1,000 and then to $3,000. Normally refugees, who would likely be persecuted if they were returned to their countries, are allowed to stay in the United States; but under the Reagan administration policy even Salvadorans with marks of torture on their bodies were deported. Statistics later showed that from 1983 to 1986 only 2.6% of Salvadorans and only 0.9% of Guatemalans requesting asylum were approved.

When the INS demanded $9,000 bail for three Salvadoran refugees that Corbett had turned in on June 26, 1981, he protested they were forcing him to go outside the law. Corbett's father was a lawyer and had taught him about the Nuremberg trials. So Corbett organized a refugee support group and began a smuggling operation in the tradition of the Quaker underground railroad for fleeing slaves before the Civil War or of those who had helped Jews escape from the Nazis. By July another $175,000 was donated to free the remaining 115 Salvadorans from the detention center, and in August, Corbett was making one or two trips a day smuggling undocumented refugees. Corbett asked Presbyterian pastor John Fife for help in placing all these Central Americans. Fife suggested to his congregation that they provide a sanctuary in their church, and in January 1982 by secret ballot they approved 59-2. By the time of their public declaration on March 24 five churches in the San Francisco bay area and three others were declaring sanctuary also. The INS publicly scoffed at the idea, but secretly they sent a paid informant to infiltrate the movement.

In August 1982 national coordination was taken over by the Chicago Religious Task Force on Central America (CRTF). They distributed 30,000 manuals on how to provide sanctuary, and the movement spread across the country; 150 churches and synagogues had become sanctuaries by the middle of 1984. In January 1985 Corbett, Fife, and fourteen others in Arizona were indicted, publicizing the movement. The number increased to 250, and even the city of Los Angeles and the state of New Mexico declared themselves sanctuaries. The Sanctuary movement reached its height in 1987 when four hundred faith-based communities were taking in political refugees from Central America.

Charles Clements, a former Air Force pilot who had been put in a psychiatric hospital for refusing to fly more bombing missions in Vietnam, became a physician and spent a year treating the *campesinos* and witnessing the horrendous war in El Salvador, starting in March 1982. He saw jets and helicopter gunships, supplied by the US, strafe defenseless peasants. Others he treated had been tortured or suffered from attacks using napalm, gasoline bombs, and white phosphorus rockets.

On March 23, 1984 two hundred people went to see Vermont Senator Robert Stafford at his office in Winooski to express their opposition to funding the Contra war and to ask him to hold a public meeting. When he refused, many stayed; three days later 44 protesters were arrested for trespassing. In the trial refugees told of their experience in the war zones of Central America, and experts testified. The judge charged the jurors that a significant State interest would have to be proved to override the defendants right to petition their government for redress of grievances, and he allowed the defense of necessity—that in an emergency a minor law may be violated in order to prevent a greater harm. The jury found all 26 defendants not guilty.

In April 1983 the ex-Maryknoll nun Gail Phares of the Carolina Interfaith Task Force on Central America (CITCA) organized a group of 33 people to travel to El Porvenir by Nicaragua's Honduran border that was under attack by the Contras. They observed that the Contras stopped shooting because of their presence. Jeff Boyer suggested that US citizens could hold vigils in the war zones. By July, Action for Peace in Nicaragua had 153 volunteers from forty states. The second delegation prayed to be forgiven for the killings their government was funding, and the Nicaraguans began to respond, "You are forgiven."[9] More delegations traveled to Nicaragua, observed the villages that were assaulted by the Contras, and reported back to their churches and friends in the United States. Soon all the major religious peace groups and churches were supporting Witness for Peace by publicizing the issue, raising money, and sending delegations. Over the next few years about two hundred long-term delegates and four thousand short-term delegates traveled to Nicaragua as part of Witness for Peace in order to diminish the violence there.

The Reagan administration used various dirty tricks to try to destroy the Central American peace movement. In June 1983 the US State Department officially discouraged travel to Nicaragua and closed all six Nicaraguan consulates in the United States. The Federal Bureau of Investigation (FBI) and Customs began harassing citizens traveling to Nicaragua. The FBI also tried to intimidate activists by investigating them in their homes. When President Reagan declared a state of national emergency in May 1985, US landing rights for Nicaragua's airline were revoked. The Internal Revenue Service (IRS) audited many activists, and organizers found that their phones often made funny noises because of surveillance. An activist once made a call and heard a recording of a previous call. The government also tampered with and interfered with people's mail. As early as 1981 the FBI had begun to spy on the Committee in Solidarity with the People of El Salvador (CISPES), and later Freedom of Information Act (FOIA) requests revealed that it had become a major surveillance operation by 1985, spinning off into 178 separate investigations involving all 59 FBI field offices probing 1,330 organizations. These operations were supposed to have been closed down in 1985, but many believe information was still gathered. In 1987 the important testimony of FBI agent Frank Varelli was sabotaged by altering his previous lie detector results and reports to make it look like he was lying to a congressional committee.

A propaganda campaign by the government tried to associate peace activists with Communism or terrorism, and critical journalists and professors were intimidated. In August 1985 a Contra kidnapping of a Witness for Peace delegation was falsely leaked as if it were planned by Nicaraguan president Daniel Ortega to help his cause. This disinformation caused reporters to doubt whether the story was newsworthy. In the 1980s more than 140 break-ins into the offices, churches, and homes of peace activists were documented. Often money and valuable equipment was left while documents, records, and photos were ransacked. In 1987 an American Friends Service Committee (AFSC) coordinator in Pasadena had boxes of documents stolen from her car; but expensive clothes and jewelry were left behind. In all these 140 cases only one time was any suspect ever identified or arrested. In Los Angeles death threats by death-squads were often made against Salvadoran and Guatemalan activists. In 1984 the Federal Emergency Management Agency (FEMA) designed the Rex 84 contingency plan to suspend the US Constitution, declare martial law, and detain thousands of people as threats to national security after the President declared a state of domestic national emergency. During the 1987 Iran-Contra hearings this plan was not allowed to be discussed in open session.

During a gathering of peace and justice activists at the Kirkridge Retreat Center in Pennsylvania in November 1983 Jim Wallis and Jim Rice of *Sojourners* magazine drafted a "Promise of Resistance" that was revised and signed by 33 activists, vowing that if the US invaded Nicaragua, they would go there unarmed as a loving barrier. They sent copies of the statement to members of Congress, President Reagan, the Defense Department, and the CIA. In the August 1984 issue of *Sojourners* the idea was altered to occupy congressional offices and was called a "Pledge of

Resistance."

In Berkeley theology student Ken Butigan was working for Witness for Peace and was inspired by the original "Promise." He began circulating a document called "A Commitment to Stop the Killing in Central America." David Hartsough of the AFSC in San Francisco liked the idea and got Butigan $50 a week and an office to work on it. He revised slightly the *Sojourners* pledge and persuaded the Committee in Solidarity with the People of El Salvador (CISPES) to gather signatures. On October 9, 1984 outside the Federal Building in San Francisco seven hundred people signed the pledge in the first hour as two hundred people spoke why they were willing to risk going to jail. A week later Butigan attended a *Sojourners* meeting in Washington and urged a decentralized campaign. The language was changed so that any major military escalation in Central America would lead to protests and civil disobedience. Butigan then compiled a Pledge of Resistance handbook called *Basta! No Mandate for War*, drawing upon the affinity group structure and consensus processes of the anti-nuclear movement and the handbooks used by the Livermore Action Group (LAG). By December 42,352 had signed, half of them pledging civil disobedience.

In May 1985 the US Congress voted against aid to the Contras, but the Reagan administration imposed a trade embargo on Nicaragua. Activists were divided whether to act. The national organization chose to wait; but in Boston 2,600 protested, and 559 were arrested for occupying the Federal Building. In San Francisco 3,000 demonstrated, and six hundred were arrested. Nationwide more than 2,000 had been arrested for nonviolent civil disobedience. A month later Congress passed $27 million for the Contras. This time the national organization acted with demonstrations in more than two hundred cities as more than 1,200 protesters were arrested. By September 70,000 had signed the Pledge of Resistance.

In 1986 during four votes over Contra aid, demonstrations took place in a thousand places, and another two thousand people were arrested. When National Guard troops were sent to Honduras the next year, demonstrators protested at a hundred congressional offices. A hundred thousand people marched for peace and justice in Central America in Washington at the April Mobilization, and 567 were arrested for protesting at CIA headquarters. At the Pentagon in 1988 five hundred protesters committed civil disobedience, but only 240 of them were arrested. In the fall of 1989 there were seven hundred protests around the country because of increases in military aid to El Salvador. 2,440 protesters risked arrest, and 1,452 of them were taken into custody. On March 24, 1990 during a Washington snowstorm 580 people were arrested for demonstrating in front of the White House, the largest number for any single pledge action.

In 1966 S. Brian Willson went to Air Force officer training school; but while being trained for combat at Fort Benning, he refused to stab a dummy one hundred times, yelling, "Kill!" Nonetheless he was deployed in March 1969 to Vietnam, where he was asked to make reports on bombed villages. Later he was haunted by the faces of the dead women and children he had seen. After criticizing the bombings and civilian deaths, he was transferred to Louisiana. He completed law school and became the director of the Vietnam Veterans Outreach Center in his native Massachusetts. In January 1986 he traveled to Nicaragua to see if the Contras were "freedom fighters" as President Reagan claimed. When he saw the corpses of their civilian victims, he wept. He became sick of what he called the demonic American Way Of Life (AWOL), and he stopped paying federal income tax. On the steps of the Capitol in Washington, Brian and three other veterans fasted from September 1, 1986 to October 17. Senator Warren Rudman compared the fasting veterans to the terrorists holding hostages in Beirut. FBI agent John C. Ryan refused to investigate a group that was "totally nonviolent," and he was fired after more than twenty years of service.

Willson organized Veterans Peace Action Teams and returned to Nicaragua. His team of nine veterans walked 73 miles on a dangerous road, where in October 1986 eleven persons had been killed and twelve lost legs because of land mines. Willson learned that during the Vietnam War demonstrators had blocked trains carrying troops from the Concord Naval Weapons Station (CNWS) at Port Chicago east of Berkeley. Concerned that 230 Salvadoran villages had been bombed or strafed from the air in 1986, he organized a protest campaign on the tracks. He wrote a letter to the CNWS, and on June 10 demonstrators began blocking trains and trucks carrying munitions from CNWS across the public road to Port Chicago for shipment. Willson, Duncan Murphy, and Rev. David Duncombe decided to begin another forty-day water fast on September 1 and also planned to stay on the tracks to block every train unless they were arrested. On August 21 Willson sent a letter to the CNWS commander with copies to the Sheriff, the Police Department, the Highway Patrol, and to several politicians, stating their intention not to move for an approaching train.

On September 1 Brian took another note to CNWS and made a speech in which he said, "You can't move these munitions without moving my body or destroying my body."[10] The speed limit for the train crossing the road there was five miles per hour; but the video of the event revealed that the train was traveling 17 miles per hour and did not slow down until after Willson had been run over. Duncombe was kneeling and was able to move at the last moment; Murphy was kneeling and leaped up and grabbed ahold of the train; but Willson was sitting and was not able to get out of the way. One leg was severed, and the other was so badly mangled that it had to be amputated; a large hole in his skull was opened, and part of his brain was damaged. His wife Holly Rauen, whom he had married nine days before, managed to stop the bleeding, and Brian eventually recovered. Later it was learned that the Navy had ordered the train not to stop, because they were afraid the protesters would try to board the train. The train engineers actually sued Willson for psychological stress they suffered; but he counter-sued and won the case. No jurisdiction was willing to bring criminal charges against the Navy for this atrocity.

After this horrendous incident the Nuremberg Actions protest continued as more people joined. For the next five years the vigil at the tracks was constant, and almost every train was blocked, resulting in 1,700 arrests. For a while the sheriffs tried to remove people by using pain holds; but after David Hartsough and David Wylie suffered broken arms, this tactic was abandoned. For more information on this Nuremberg Actions campaign see "My Efforts for World Peace" in the appendix.

Costa Rica and Arias

Costa Rica has a long history of liberalism and education. General Tomas Guardia did take over the country in 1870 and ruled it as president for twelve years, but in 1877 he promulgated a liberal "Law of Individual Rights" that protected freedom of religion, speech, and the press. Public education was greatly expanded when he made primary education free and obligatory for both sexes. In 1889 President Bernard Soto allowed an honest election and was persuaded by demonstrators to let the opposition party take office after they won.

Rafael Angel Calderon came to power as a representative of the upper class in 1940, but he formed an alliance with Catholics and Communists to form the United Social Christian Party. In his four years he brought about major social and economic reforms, letting cultivators claim unused land, making taxes progressive, establishing a minimum wage, providing unemployment compensation, and codifying workers' rights. However, World War II caused economic hardship and inflation. In 1948 a disputed election erupted into civil war and brought Jose Figueres (known as Costa Rica's national hero "Don Pepe") to power. He ruled as the president of the Founding Junta of the Second Republic for eighteen months, disbanding the army and nationalizing the banks and insurance companies. The 1949 constitution promoted even more public education and made it compulsory to age 14. He was opposed by Nicaragua's Somoza, who became his bitter enemy. Figueres founded the National Liberation Party and was twice elected President, governing Costa Rica 1953-1957 and 1970-1974.

The welfare state of Costa Rica reached a crisis in 1980 when its debt became the largest per person in the world. Sandinistas had used Costa Rica as a base for attacking the Somoza regime, and in 1979 about 50,000 Nicaraguans took refuge in Costa Rica. Also tens of thousands of Salvadorans fled the civil war in their country by settling in Costa Rica. In the early 1980s Contras led by disgruntled Sandinista Eden Pastora operated from there. The Reagan administration's proxy war against the Sandinistas also secretly sent $9.6 million in military aid to Costa Rica, giving their Civil and Rural Guard 4,000 M-16 rifles, 200 M-79 grenade launchers, and 120 M-60 machine guns. Reagan propaganda was gladly accepted by Costa Rica's three daily newspapers, and US military advisors arrived in 1985. Roads in northern Costa Rica were paved, and helicopters and four small planes were purchased for the Civil Guard. *Soldier of Fortune* magazine recruited mercenaries to join the Contras.

Former Sandinista "Commander Zero" Eden Pastora led the Democratic Revolutionary Alliance (ARDE) in Costa Rica; but he refused to be dominated by the Somacista Contras in the northern Nicaraguan Democratic Force (FDN) operating from Honduras, and he resisted CIA pressure to unite with them. On May 30, 1984 Pastora held a press conference at La Penca at which a powerful bomb killed three journalists and five Contras, wounding 26 others including journalist Tony Avirgan. Costa Rican security officers and US officials immediately blamed the Sandinistas for trying to assassinate Pastora, who eventually withdrew completely from the Contra effort in May 1986.

However, an investigation by Avirgan and Martha Honey indicated that this was a cover-up for a CIA operation that was connected to John Hull, who owned a ranch in Costa Rica. They got information from a Carlos, who explained that Hull's ranch was used for trafficking in arms, cocaine, and marijuana. Avirgan and Honey published their findings and were sued for libel by John Hull; but they won the case in a Costa Rica court.

The most remarkable thing about Costa Rica is that it survived amid these Central American wars with little or no army, relying since 1947 on the Rio Mutual Defense Treaty. On February 2, 1986 Oscar Arias was the first peace candidate to be elected president of Costa Rica, and on the day of his inauguration he quietly ordered US ambassador Lewis Tambs to shut down the Santa Elena airstrip that had been used to supply the Contras in Costa Rica. Arias fired its administrator, Col. Jose Montero, and ordered Security Minister Hernan Garron to have a Civil Guard patrol the airstrip to prevent its being used. However, in June his orders were secretly countermanded as Garron and Vice Minister Rogelio Castro removed the guards and only ordered occasional patrols. In July the government of Nicaragua sued Honduras and Costa Rica in the World Court. Unlike the US and Honduras, the government of Costa Rica accepted the jurisdiction of the World Court. Tambs persuaded Arias not to publicize his stationing of the guards on the Santa Elena base on September 8, the day they impounded 77 drums of aviation fuel and put them on the runway to prevent use of the airstrip. Speaking to the United Nations General Assembly on September 24 President Arias expressed his concern about Nicaragua's "totalitarian regime of Marxist ideology," but the next day Minister Garron announced that the covert air strip used by the Contras had been closed.

In October 1986 CIA director Casey flew to San Jose, but Arias refused to meet with him in secret. When Arias went to Washington to meet with President Reagan in December, he made sure many people were present when he met with Casey. Arias urged peaceful solutions, especially in Nicaragua and was promised that $40 million in frozen USAID would be released for Costa Rica. At San Jose in February 1987 he presented his peace proposal to the presidents of Guatemala, El Salvador, and Honduras, calling for cease-fires, suspending outside military aid to guerrillas, amnesty for political prisoners, free elections, and negotiations between governments and unarmed opposition forces. The next month the US Senate voted 97-1 to support the Arias plan. In July, Arias announced that the Santa Elena property would become part of the Santa Rosa National Park to protect the largest dry tropical forest in Central America. In August 1987 at Esquipulas in Guatemala all five Central American presidents signed the peace accord that called for verification by the United Nations and the Organization of American States. They agreed to implement by November cease-fires, democratization, stopping aid to the Contras and other insurgents, and removal of the Contra bases from Honduras and Costa Rica. They planned to meet in January to certify this implementation. President Reagan denounced this Central American Peace Plan as "fatally flawed." The USAID funds for Costa Rica had been stopped since the peace process began in February 1987, but by threatening a scandal Democrats led by Senator John Kerry got the aid resumed. The government of Nicaragua withdrew its suit against Costa Rica and lifted its press restrictions.

On September 22 Arias addressed the US Congress, informing them that he would not let the US dehumanize the Costa Rican economy because of foreign creditors' demands and saying, "The new economic organization must be based on equity and security. No economy based on greed and intimidation can ever be established in Costa Rica in the name of efficiency."[11] Arias announced that schoolchildren would compete to design a new uniform to replace the camouflage fatigues donated by the US. He commended the United States on the bicentennial of its Constitution, and he quoted John Kennedy's words during his visit to Costa Rica in 1963,

> Today the principles of nonintervention
> and the peaceful resolution of disputes
> have been so firmly imbedded in our tradition
> that the heroic democracy in which we meet today
> can pursue its national goals
> without an armed force to guard its frontiers.[12]

Arias concluded his speech by suggesting that they could overcome war and totalitarianism with peace and the power of democracy. In October 1987 he was awarded the Nobel Peace Prize.

When the five Central American presidents met again at San Jose on January 15, 1988, they found that most of the agreements had been implemented except that Honduras had not closed down the Contra camps in its territory. Nicaragua's Daniel Ortega announced not only the end of its six-year-old state of emergency but also cease-fire talks with the Contras, freeing the remaining 3,200 political prisoners, and the scheduling of municipal elections. In an article in the *New York Times* Ortega wrote that Nicaragua was ready to negotiate limiting armed forces, removing foreign military advisors, and banning foreign military bases. Arias also announced in January that all Contra leaders living in Costa Rica must renounce the armed struggle or leave. On March 23 OAS Secretary General Jolo Baena Soares presided at Sapoa on the Costa Rican border for the signing of the cease-fire agreement between Nicaragua and the Contras. In 1988 Arias complained that the United States was secretly funding private-sector organizations in order to subvert Costa Rica's government institutions. The Central Bank had to pay a market interest on loans that was currently 21 percent. Economic Support Funds (ESF) paid for by US and Costa Rican taxpayers were being used to finance private companies that threatened government agencies. Arias solved this problem by withdrawing from the Agency for International Development (USAID) programs. Without even having an army or navy Costa Rica had survived the war years relatively unscathed and had led the region to a peaceful solution despite the hostile interference from the United States in its fear of Communism.

In the spring of 1984 Christic Institute attorney Daniel Sheehan became concerned about plans by the Reagan administration to lock up 400,000 Central American immigrants as part of a "State of Domestic National Emergency" if US troops invaded Central America. Tony Avirgan and Martha Honey asked Daniel Sheehan to bring a lawsuit under the Racketeering Influence and Corrupt Organization Act (RICO), and he publicized the elaborate story of how a secret team of ex-military and CIA operatives illegally arranged for the Contras to receive weapons, smuggled cocaine, and plotted to murder Pastora at the La Penca news conference. Sheehan carefully avoided including any current government employees so that the resources of the US Justice Department would not be used against him. The suit charged 29 people with criminal misconduct including John Hull, Tom Posey, Robert Owen, Theodore Shackley, Thomas Clines, Richard Secord, Edwin Wilson, Albert Hakim, Rafael Quintero, Adolfo Calero, and John Singlaub.

In June 1988, Judge James Lawrence King dismissed the suit before it even went to trial for lack of evidence on the alleged bomber Amac Galil; yet King had not allowed them to present that evidence. Then Judge King ordered Daniel Sheehan and plaintiffs Tony Avirgan and Martha Honey to pay a million dollars for frivolous litigation. When they appealed to the 11th Circuit Court, a liberal judge on that court, Robert S. Vance, was murdered by a pipe bomb in the mail. Another bomb was found in the 11th Circuit clerk's office and was defused, but a third bomb killed a civil rights attorney. 11th Circuit Judge J. L. Edmundson was being protected by US Marshals, because Vance's murder was unsolved, and a shot shattered a window in his limousine. The 11th Circuit Court denied the appeal, and the US Supreme Court refused to hear the case.

In 1996 reporter Gary Webb retold the whole story in

his three-part series "Dark Alliance" in the *San Jose Mercury News*, emphasizing how this criminal conspiracy that was intent on supplying wars had also greatly contributed to the crack epidemic of the 1980s by importing so much cocaine. During the 1987 Iran-Contra hearings in Congress a man had been arrested for unfurling a banner saying "Ask about cocaine;" for this effort to raise public awareness he was imprisoned for more than a year. Yet most of the criminals in the Iran-Contra conspiracy that subverted American foreign policy never spent any time in prison, because they were pardoned by President Bush or, as in the case of North and Poindexter, had their cases overturned because Congress had given them immunity.

Bush's Panama Invasion

US troops intervened in Panama three times between 1865 and 1873. The US Congress in 1902 authorized buying a strip of land in Panama from Colombia for a canal, and the next year US gunboats helped "secessionists" break away from Colombia. The United States then signed a treaty with these Panamanians and used troops while they built the canal that opened in 1914. President Theodore Roosevelt in 1904 proclaimed his corollary to the Monroe Doctrine—that the United States would be an "international police force" in Central America. US troops intervened in Panama in 1918 during elections, in 1921 because of a border conflict with Costa Rica, and in 1925 because of a rent strike in Panama City. From 1930 to 1945 the government of Panama prohibited labor organizing. During World War II the US built many more military bases in Panama. In 1953 the US established the Panamanian National Guard that was based on Anastasio Somoza's Nicaraguan National Guard. A controversy over whether Panamanian flags could be flown in the Canal Zone erupted into riots in 1964, and 21 people were killed. In 1968 the elected president was deposed when Col. Omar Torrijos took power as the commander-in-chief of the defense forces. A new constitution in 1972 gave Torrijos extraordinary power, which he used to bring about some social reforms.

In 1977 US President Jimmy Carter completed negotiation of a new Panama Canal treaty that would give Panama control of the canal on the last day of 1999. In 1981 Torrijos died in a mysterious plane crash, which was called an accident; but because Ronald Reagan had vociferously opposed the new canal treaty, some suspected the CIA. In 1983 General Manuel Noriega became commander of the Panamanian Defense Forces (PDF). Noriega had been working for the CIA for more than twenty years and claimed that he was paid $10 million for this. He had been trained at the School of the Americas and was head of military intelligence. The next year Nicolas Ardito-Barletta won a narrow victory in an election considered fraudulent; US Secretary of State George Schultz attended his inauguration. In 1985 the former health vice minister, Dr. Hugo Spadafora was assassinated after visiting Costa Rica; the military was accused, and Ardito-Barletta resigned. Noriega appointed the industrialist Eric Arturo Delvalle president. In 1986 many newspapers in the United States accused Noriega of drug trafficking. That year by seizing the ship and exposing the plot he foiled Oliver North's scheme to pretend to capture Communist arms on a ship in the canal bound for the Sandinistas.

Col. Roberto Diaz Herrera had been second-in-command of the PDF but was dismissed. At a press conference in June 1987 he accused Noriega of working with the CIA to murder Torrijos, claiming Reagan and Bush knew of this. He accused Noriega of ordering the assassination of Spadafora because he was trying to expose corruption in the Panama government. Diaz Herrera also claimed that Noriega had made millions in bribes by allowing drugs to pass through Panama and for providing false end-user certificates for shipped US arms. Panama's government announced that it was stopping all payments on its debts, and rumors it was printing money led to bank withdrawals. The US Senate suggested that Noriega resign and called for elections. A rally was held on June 30 protesting US interference in Panamanian affairs; a hundred demonstrators marched to the US embassy and did much damage to the building. The United States suspended its aid to Panama and demanded reparations. The Panama government apologized and paid the $106,000; but the US aid was not resumed.

On January 8, 1988 Jose Blandon, Panama's consul general in New York City, resigned and blamed Noriega for turning the Panamanian government into a "criminal empire" by selling passports, visas, airport landing rights, and allowing drug smugglers to use Panama's airports and banking system for payment of more than $300 million. In Miami and Tampa, Florida, US indictments against General Noriega were unsealed on February 4, charging him with smuggling huge amounts of marijuana into the United States in 1983 and 1984 and of selling ether and acetone for processing cocaine. In February President Delvalle met with the US assistant secretary of state Elliott Abrams in Miami. Returning to Panama, he told Noriega to step down; but the General refused. Delvalle played a tape for the Panamanian people on February 25 saying he was "separating" Noriega for his trial; but that night Delvalle was removed by the Panamanian Assembly, and he went into hiding, still recognized as President by the US.

In May 1988 the Reagan administration was in the middle of complicated negotiations with Panama. At that time George Bush was facing a challenge by Democrat Michael Dukakis, and with political advice from James Baker he slighted the current Reagan approach by announcing that *he* would never bargain with drug dealers. In May 1989 Guillermo Endara was apparently elected president of Panama with about three-quarters of the votes, but Noriega declared the election fraudulent and nullified. The OAS and the Panamanian Assembly also declined to recognize Endara because the United States had contributed $10 million to his campaign. On October 4 some officers asked Noriega to resign, but he refused again.

Early in the morning on December 20, 1989 President
George Bush sent a force of 26,000 from the US Army, Navy,
and Air Force to attack Panama. The reasons given that
American lives and the Canal needed to be protected have
been dismissed, because no evidence has been shown that
they were in any danger. The main reason was to remove
Noriega so that he could be tried in the United States.
Under international law this is hardly a valid reason for
attacking an entire country. The United States claimed that
they killed only 324 or 516 Panamanians; but others estimated the number of civilians killed at between one thousand and five thousand. The Panamanian Defense Forces
were targeted, and their capability was destroyed.
Although they had also served as police, the US troops did
not take over law enforcement, resulting in looting and
chaos. Endara and his two vice presidents were sworn in at
the US Southern Command and moments later formally
requested US help in removing Noriega. Many of Endara's
political opponents and union leaders were arrested. The
United States was in flagrant violation of Article 19 of the
OAS Charter which reads,

No state may use or encourage
the use of coercive measures
of an economic or political character
in order to force the sovereign will of another state
and obtain from it advantages of any kind.[13]

The US invasion of Panama was condemned both by
the United Nations General Assembly and by the Organization of American States. Two weeks after the invasion,
Noriega surrendered; he was later convicted of the drug
crimes and was sentenced to forty years in prison.

The patriotic propaganda of the US news media offered
a stark contrast to the Oscar-winning documentary film,
The Panama Deception directed by Barbara Trent. After
demonizing Noriega, the US media focused on the "Operation Just Cause" as a heroic victory, dwelling only on the
few US deaths while ignoring how many Panamanians

were killed. The film shows a greater context for the invasion and portrays the suffering of the Panamanian people as certain poor neighborhoods were devastated. The film also brought out the many political ramifications as the US punished Panama first economically and then military to make sure that it would control the Canal that was scheduled for a partial shift in control in January 1990 and complete control by Panama in 2000. By destroying the PDF and making sure there was a compliant regime, the US made sure that its business interests would prevail.

School of the Americas Protests

Roy Bourgeois had been a Navy officer in Vietnam, where he was wounded; but after spending time with Vietnamese orphans, he went to the seminary of the Maryknoll Missionary Order and was ordained a Catholic priest in 1972. He worked as a missionary in Bolivia for five years, and he reported to Washington that the government of Bolivia was torturing people. He became especially concerned about El Salvador because two of the nuns murdered in December 1980 were his friends. He went to El Salvador and after returning began to speak out. He learned that the United States was training 525 Salvadoran officers at its School of the Americas (SOA), which had been transferred from Panama to Fort Benning, Georgia. In August 1983, dressed as military officers, Bourgeois and two others entered the base and from a pine tree played a tape of Archbishop Romero's sermon so that the Salvadorans could hear it. The three were arrested and sentenced to eighteen months in prison.

After six Jesuit priests and two women were murdered in 1989 at San Salvador, Bourgeois learned that they had been killed by men who had been trained at the School of the Americas, which he began calling the School of the Assassins. Roy and nine others fasted on water at the gate to Fort Benning for 35 days. On the first anniversary of the Jesuit murders, Bourgeois and the two Liteky brothers went on the base to pour blood and leave photos of the victims. Research showed that officers were being trained at SOA before and after they committed atrocities in El Salvador. In the spring of 1994 Bourgeois and others fasted for forty days on the steps of the Capitol in Washington to persuade Congress to defund the School of the Americas. Two years later a White House Intelligence Oversight board admitted that for ten years training manuals had instructed officers to use murder, torture, and false imprisonment; they were also taught to kidnap, blackmail, and spy on nonviolent opponents. That spring twelve protesters were arrested for trespassing and were sentenced from two to six months. Bringing signatures of a million people to close the school, 601 protesters were arrested for entering the base on November 16, 1997; only 31 repeat offenders were indicted, but 22, including Bourgeois, spent six months in prison.

A documentary of Roy Bourgeois was televised by Public Broadcasting (PBS) in 1998. The next year the US House of Representatives voted 230-197 to delete the funds of SOA; but the House-Senate conference committee restored the funding. In January 2001 the School of the Americas was closed for one month and then reopened under the name Western Hemisphere Institute for Security Cooperation (WHISC). Nearly a hundred people were arrested for protesting the school that year, and 26 were sentenced to six months in prison. Annual demonstrations in November 2002 and 2003 drew about 10,000 protesters to Fort Benning each time; 95 people were arrested in 2002, and 44 in 2003. In 2004 an estimated 16,000 attended the demonstration; at least twenty people were arrested, plus eleven people were arrested for the same cause at the federal building in Sacramento, California. As of 2005 the total time served in prison by 171 demonstrators protesting SOA is 85 years.

Notes

1. "Letter to President Carter, February 17, 1980" in *Revolution in Central America*, p. 355.

2. Archbishop Oscar Romero: "The Last Sermon" in *The Central American Crisis Reader*, p. 377.
3. Quoted in *Crossroads* by Cynthia J. Arnson, p. 128.
4. *Ibid.*, p. 143.
5. Quoted in *Our Own Backyard* by William M. LeoGrande, p. 303.
6. *Ibid.*, p. 304.
7. Quoted in *Crossroads* by Cynthia J. Arnson, p. 174.
8. *Ibid.*, p. 220.
9. Quoted in *Resisting Reagan* by Christian Smith, p. 74.
10. "The Tracks," by Brian Willson, in *Nonviolence in America* ed Staughton and Alice Lynd, p. 465.
11. "Let's Give Peace a Chance" in *The Costa Rica Reader*, p. 371.
12. *Ibid.*, p. 374.
13. Quoted in *The Panamanian Problem* by Guillermo de St. Malo A and Godfrey Harris, p. 286.

13
Gorbachev and Ending the Cold War

Never before has so terrible a threat hung over mankind as now.
The only reasonable way out of the existing situation
is the reaching of an agreement by the opposing forces
on the immediate termination of the arms race,
the nuclear arms race on earth
and the prevention of arms in space.
We need an agreement on an honest and equitable basis
without attempts at "outplaying" the other side
and dictating terms to it.
We need an agreement which would help all
to advance toward the cherished goal:
the complete elimination and prohibition
of nuclear weapons for all time,
toward the complete removal of the threat of nuclear war.
This is our firm conviction.
Mikhail Gorbachev, March 11, 1985

We want freedom to reign supreme
in the coming century everywhere in the world.
We want peaceful competition between different social systems
to develop unimpeded,
to encourage mutually advantageous cooperation
rather than confrontation and an arms race.
We want people of every country
to enjoy prosperity, welfare and happiness.
The road to this lies through proceeding
to a nuclear-free, nonviolent world.
We have embarked on this road,
and call on other countries and nations to follow suit.
Mikhail Gorbachev, *Perestroika*

Freedom and democracy, after all,
mean joint participation and shared responsibility....
Your government, my people, has returned to you.
Vaclav Havel, January 1, 1990

We need a new system of values,

a system of the organic unity between mankind and nature
and the ethic of global responsibility
Mikhail Gorbachev

Nonviolently Resisting Tyranny

Modern history has many examples of people resisting imperial domination by using more or less nonviolent methods. Between 1567 and 1579 Dutch Protestants revolted against the Catholic Spanish imperialism of Philip II and established a republic governed by States-General. American colonists nonviolently refused to cooperate with the British Stamp Act of 1765 until it was repealed. Another tax imposed without representation was resisted by the "Boston tea party" in 1773 when merchants dressed as Mohawks threw imported tea into the harbor. John Adams later wrote that the real American revolution was nonviolent and had occurred between 1760 and 1775, when the colonists had essentially become independent. This was followed by a war between the newly independent republic and British imperialism. Hungarians resisted domination by Austria; but the violent revolt led by Kossuth was a failure, while the reformer Ferenc Deak got Austrian emperor Franz Josef to recognize rights of Hungarians in the Compromise of 1867 that made the empire Austro-Hungarian.

The best revolutions are nonviolent. On January 9, 1905 thousands of Russians marched peacefully to the Winter Palace of Czar Nicholas II; but guards mowed down demonstrators with machine guns. Russian sailors on the cruiser *Potemkin* mutinied in July at Odessa, and in October a general strike was called. On October 17 Nicholas granted a constitution with a parliament (Duma) and civil liberties, but later he withdrew his concessions and repressed dissent.

The 1917 revolution began with marches celebrating International Women's Day on March 8 (February 23 in the old Julian calendar). After two days of strikes and riots, the Russian troops fighting in the Great War mutinied, and on

March 15 Czar Nicholas II abdicated. In July, Minister of War Kerensky headed a provisional government. Housewives, who had to wait in long bread lines, began demonstrating, and on November 6 (old October 24) V. I. Lenin ordered the signal that sent soldiers, sailors, and factory workers rushing into government offices and the Winter Palace. Kerensky accepted Bolshevik support to prevent General Kornilov from being dictator, and Bolsheviks led by Leon Trotsky gained a majority of the Petrograd Soviet; but the next day Kerensky fled, and Lenin took control as the Council of People's Commissars with Leon Trotsky as commissar for foreign affairs and Stalin as commissar for national minorities. The first reform the Soviets made was to abolish capital punishment. Peasants began seizing fields of the landlords. Lenin kept his promise by withdrawing the Russian army from the war; but they were soon attacked by their former western allies. This is not the place to tell the sad story of how this revolution degenerated into a totalitarian empire, especially after Stalin took power.

After Germany lost the Great War, on March 10, 1920 the right-wing Wolfgang Kapp and top army officers seized the government in Berlin; but the Weimar Republic used nonviolent methods to survive this coup *(Putsch)*. The Ebert government fled Berlin but told people not to cooperate with the new regime. When officers occupied newspaper offices, the Berlin printers went on strike, followed by other workers. A general strike was declared by the Ebert cabinet and the executives of the Social Democratic Party (SDP). The Kappist regime had no money and could not make the bureaucrats cooperate. The Ebert government refused to compromise with the Kappists. An airplane dropped leaflets announcing, "The Collapse of the Military Dictatorship." Even threats to shoot people and the shooting of some failed to stop the strike. On March 17 the Berlin Security Police demanded that Kapp resign, and later that day he did resign and fled to Sweden. General Luttwitz remained as Commander-in-Chief, but he resigned that night. The next day the Baltic Brigades marched out of Berlin, shooting some civilians who jeered at them. The Ebert government resumed its functions but still faced some chaos in the country.

The Versailles Treaty had forced Germany to give up the coal-mining Ruhr region to French and Belgian control. By 1923 Germans resented severe French repression and increased their non-cooperation and acts of sabotage. The French realized that they were losing more than they were gaining. They agreed to withdraw French troops, and the Germans ended the passive resistance campaign.

During World War II as Nazi Germany took over countries in Europe, nonviolent resistance gradually developed, especially in Norway and Denmark. The Nordic countries had declared neutrality; but the German invasion in the spring of 1940 defeated the Norwegian defense forces as the cabinet fled to London. Pressure groups tried to influence political decisions under the German occupation. In September all Norwegian political parties were dissolved, and the Parliament was disbanded as German commissioners took control. Radios were confiscated, but a few remained or were built to hear the British Broadcasting Company (BBC) news.

Norwegian teachers were threatened with dismissal if they did not follow the policies of the new government; but instead of signing on to that, teachers signed a counter-declaration saying they would teach according to their own consciences. They refused to teach Nazi propaganda in the schools or cooperate with the Nazi youth organization. In February 1942 the Germans set up the Norwegian Vidkun Quisling as Minister-President but controlled all his decisions. He proclaimed a law creating the Norwegian Teachers' Union. Teachers and parents sent in letters of protest. In March more than a thousand teachers were arrested and sent to concentration camps. In April Quisling allowed the teachers to teach even though they still refused to indoctrinate. Church leaders also criticized the violence of the German occupation and refused to reveal the secrets of the confessional. A pastoral letter was printed and distributed, though the Germans confiscated half of the 50,000 printed. On Easter in 1942 the clergy renounced their state-paid salaries but continued to perform their spiritual duties.

Denmark had also declared neutrality and offered little armed resistance as the Germans invaded their country on April 9, 1940. The Danish government remained in place; although they had to make some concessions to the Germans, they rejected a common currency and customs with Germany and refused to let the Danish Nazis take power. The resistance developed gradually but increased in violence when the Germans were losing the war. The Danes, especially the students, began to wear red, white, and blue caps, and more Danes began giving the German occupiers the "cold shoulder." The BBC broadcasted to Danes in Danish. Sabotage attacks dramatically increased in 1942 to more than a hundred, and in 1943 there were more than a thousand. In August 1943 spontaneous strikes and demonstrations spread. Germans gave the Danish government an ultimatum, which Erik Scavenius refused. The Germans took over the government, but that month the British recognized the Danes' Freedom Council that was trying to coordinate the resistance and would not allow army officers to participate until 1944. In October 1943 Berlin ordered all the 7,000 Jews in Denmark arrested; but the Danes managed to help all but 500 to escape to Sweden. During the occupation 538 illegal newspapers circulated, reaching ten million people in 1944. They effectively counteracted German propaganda.

Rebelling Against Soviet Domination

The Soviet Union used their share of the military victory in World War II to expand their Communist empire into eastern Europe. This turned into a conflict with the western capitalist nations that became known as the Cold War. The United States already had atomic weapons; when the Soviet Union developed them in 1949 and the hydrogen bomb in 1953, these rival nations became known as "super-powers." Yet despite the lack of free elections and civil liberties in Communist nations dominated by the Soviet Union, nonviolent resistance began to develop in certain places.

After Stalin died in March 1953, 250,000 political prisoners at Vorkuta in the Soviet Union were informed that they should not expect amnesty. So they went on strike and were encouraged when the hated head of the secret police, Beria, fell; but strike leaders were removed, and some were shot. After three months lack of food and fuel forced the strikers to go back to work, but they had gained some concessions.

East German workers proclaimed a more liberal course on June 11, 1953 and refused to accept an increase in hours without an increase in pay. Workers marched in Berlin and called for a general strike. About 300,000 workers were on strike in 272 towns by June 17. The demonstrations the day before had been peaceful; but on this day posters and newspaper kiosks were smashed and burned, and scuffling began with the police. Some prisons were stormed, and more than just political prisoners escaped. Crowds even beat to death a few officials and informers. At 1 p.m. the strike committee met and decided to tell workers to go back into the firms but stay on strike. Two hours later a state of emergency was declared, and Soviet tanks rolled in with machine guns to quell the uprising, killing 569 and wounding 1,744. The Red Army took up strategic positions along the border with West Berlin, at post offices, railway stations, and docks. They were ordered to act with restraint, and in the entire country only 21 more people were killed. Later *Neues Deutschland* portrayed the episode as "Fascism Shows its Ugly Face." Not wanting to start another world war, US President Eisenhower limited his response to sending food aid to the East Germans.

In Poland Cardinal Wyszynski was arrested in 1953 and held in prison. In 1955 the Soviet empire formed the Warsaw Pact to counter the western North Atlantic Treaty

Organization (NATO) that had been formed in 1949. When Nikita Khrushchev became the leader of the Soviet Union in 1956, he criticized Stalin and exposed his cruel policies. In June striking workers in Poland gained some concessions although seventy workers were killed in clashes with the Polish army and police.

Stalin had imposed the leader Rakosi on Hungary, and he was forced to resign in July 1956 as a gesture to the Hungarian people. Khrushchev visited Warsaw on October 19, and two days later the Central Committee elected Gomulka first secretary of the Polish Communist Party. The next day demonstrations occurred in Budapest to support the Poles. After a poor harvest and fuel shortages, Hungarian students and workers began demonstrating in the streets for their Sixteen Points, demanding personal freedom, more food, and removal of secret police and Russian domination. Imre Nagy was named prime minister, and Janos Kadar became foreign minister. The Red Army withdrew, and Nagy announced he was allowing political parties. In Poland, Gomulka released Cardinal Wyszynski from prison. When Nagy broadcast on October 31 that Hungary was going to withdraw from the Warsaw Pact, Kadar left and formed a government in eastern Hungary supported by Soviet tanks. Four days later Soviet tanks entered Budapest and brutally killed even the wounded, dragging around their bodies with tanks to scare away others. An estimated 30,000 people were killed, and approximately 200,000 fled to the west without their belongings. Nagy was tried and executed, as Kadar took control. These dramatic events coincided with the Suez crisis.

On January 5, 1968 Alexander Dubcek became first secretary of the Czech Communist Party. His liberal policy ended censorship; but in Warsaw on January 30 a play portraying Poland suffering under Russian imperialism in the 19th century was shut down, and student leader Adam Michnik was arrested. On March 8 Polish students began protesting these and shouting that Poland is waiting for a

Dubcek. Three days later the police and workers militia were brought in to quell the students in a battle that lasted eight hours. On March 14 students in Krakow began a sympathy strike, and student protests spread throughout Poland. Gomulka blamed Zionists, and Moczar began anti-Semitic purges, causing two-thirds of the 30,000 Polish Jews, who had survived the holocaust, to leave the country. After Kolakowski and five other Jewish professors were dismissed from the University of Warsaw, students demanded that Kolakowski be reinstated; 1,300 students were expelled. That spring major student demonstrations erupted in Paris.

On August 20, 1968 the Soviet Union with its Warsaw allies invaded Czechoslovakia with half a million troops and abducted Dubcek, Prime Minister Cernik, National Assembly President Smrkovsky, and National Front Chairman Kriegel. The popular Czech President Ludvik Svoboda was put under house arrest, but he refused to sign a document for the conservative regime. Czech officials issued emergency orders for all troops to stay in their barracks. The Czech news agency refused to broadcast an announcement that party and government officials had requested Soviet help. The Extraordinary Fourteenth Party Congress, the National Assembly, and remaining government ministers announced that the invasion had begun without their knowledge or consent. The National Assembly also demanded the release of their constitutional representatives and the immediate withdrawal of the Warsaw Pact forces. They called for one-hour general strikes and asked rail workers to slow the trains bringing equipment to jam radio broadcasts.

The Czech police refused to collaborate with the invaders. Radio broadcasts warned that violence was futile and advised nonviolent resistance; students were asked to calm explosive situations. The Soviet empire had militarily occupied Czechoslovakia, but they still faced a political challenge. Svoboda was flown to Moscow but refused to negotiate without Dubcek, Cernik, and Smrkovsky. They agreed on a compromise that retained them in their positions but that gave the party a more leading role and left Russian troops in the country. Many Czechs resented the loss of reforms and would not accept it for a week. Apparently the leaders did not think the people would continue their resistance. The next April, Dubcek was replaced as party leader by Gustav Husak. The lessons of Prague 1968 would not be forgotten.

On December 14, 1970 workers from the Lenin Shipyards in Gdansk went on strike; but the Polish students, who felt they had been betrayed by the workers in 1968, refused to join them. The next day was called Bloody Tuesday as fighting broke out all over Gdansk, and the following day there were terrible tank and helicopter battles. The strike spread to Gdynia and Szczecin, and the battles shifted there on December 17. Three days later Gomulka resigned and was replaced by Edvard Gierek, and the Christmas season ended the battles. The official report counted 45 dead and 1,165 wounded; but other estimates were much higher. On January 22, 1971 workers went on strike because of a speed-up and demanded to meet with Gierek, who talked with them for nine hours and said he was a worker too. The workers decided to give him a chance, and he developed a revised five-year plan that expanded the consumer sector.

On June 24, 1976 an official announcement that food prices would be raised up to 60% caused sit-down strikes throughout Poland. The price increases were canceled, and the strikes ended; but many labor leaders had been arrested. In September, Kuron, Michnik, and other intellectuals formed the Workers' Defense Committee (KOR) to give workers legal advice and inform the public. An underground press spread ideas. Michnik wrote how the bond between force and deception kept people from establishing honest relations with each other as they used deceit for self-preservation in the totalitarian system. The KOR broke through this isolation, and they were wise enough to reject violence and revenge. Now people could gather and look each other in the eye. Michnik gave many writers credit for sacrificing material comforts to do their writing even though it could only be published unofficially on a small scale as *samizdat* (self-published). On October 16, 1978 Archbishop Karol Wojtyla of Krakow was elected Pope John Paul II. His visit to Poland in June 1979 was an inspiration to many. In September KOR's journal published a Charter of Workers' Rights. In December, Lech Walesa and Andrezej Gwiazda organized a memorial service for the 1970 martyrs, and many people were arrested. Walesa warned that if a memorial was not built, in one year 35 million Poles would each bring a brick to build it themselves.

In July 1980 the government nearly doubled meat prices, causing strikes around Poland. Warsaw strikers immediately gained pay increases of ten percent or more, and the strikes spread. On August 14 the dismissed electrician Lech Walesa climbed into the Lenin Shipyard at Gdansk and began a sit-down strike over the illegal dismissal of a worker as 16,000 workers demanded an independent union. The sit-ins spread, and an Interfactory Strike Committee was formed. On August 20 Kuron and Michnik were arrested along with twelve other KOR activists. Strike leaders demanded communication lines be restored before continuing talks with the government, and they posted their 21 demands. By the end of August the government had agreed to allow free trade unions, free information and media, and civil rights. The new unions adopted the name Solidarity and soon had more than ten million members. Suddenly a closed society was allowed to exchange information openly, and the effect was euphoric. However, the economy was a mess with a huge foreign debt, and the media was still mostly controlled. A polluted environment and malnutrition caused diseases the health care system could not handle. The Polish Communist Party lost hundreds of thousands of members.

In September 1981 Walesa was elected president of Solidarity but wanted it to stay a trade union and not become a political movement; yet many wanted political reforms. In November, Solidarity insisted on discussing major reforms with the Communist Party, and student strikes spread. In December, Walesa warned that they could not remain passive any longer. The loyal Communist, General Wojciech Jaruzelski, had been made prime minister in February 1981, and on December 13 he declared a state of war and ordered thousands arrested as tanks patrolled the streets. Strikes were crushed one after another. The Solidarity Union was officially dissolved in October 1982, and the next month Walesa was released but kept under surveillance. In December the state of war was suspended. Walesa was awarded the Nobel Peace Prize but declined to leave Poland lest he not be allowed to return. Martial law was formally lifted in July 1983, but more restrictive laws had been instituted. The economy continued in stagnation. Thirty-three university presidents were removed by authorities in 1985; but the next year they released 20,000 out of 114,000, freeing 225 political prisoners including Michnik. In June 1987 Pope John Paul II made his third pilgrimage to Poland and proclaimed that Solidarity had "eternal significance."

Gorbachev's Reforms and Arms Race Reversal

Mikhail Gorbachev was born on March 2, 1931 during a famine on the Stavropol steppe. He was active in the Young Communist League, then in the Komsomol, and joined the Communist Party in 1952. He studied law at Moscow State University, graduating at the same time as his wife Raisa in 1955. The next year Gorbachev became first secretary of the Komsomol in Stavropol, and he continued to rise in the government. In 1964 his mentor Kulakov became head of the agriculture department on the Central Committee, and three years later Gorbachev earned his degree from the Stavropol Agricultural Institute. In 1970 he was elected first secretary of the Stavropol Krai party and was promoted to the Central Committee. Raisa had studied the self-accounting system used in Krasnodar that gave people cash incentives for larger harvests, and her husband gained attention for the success of the new Ipatovsky harvesting methods. When Kulakov died in 1978, Gorbachev became Secretary of Agriculture and moved to Moscow; two years later he became a voting member of the elite Politburo.

In 1982 his patron, KGB Chief Yuri Andropov, became General Secretary. While Andropov was dying, Gorbachev was his main link to the Party elite. When Soviet jets shot down the straying Korean Air Lines Flight 007, Gorbachev headed the crisis-management team. In 1984 Konstantin Chernenko became General Secretary; but he was ailing too, and as his second, Gorbachev presided over meetings. In December 1984 Gorbachev went to England and met with Prime Minister Margaret Thatcher. He hoped that with her help he could persuade President Reagan to agree to free western Europe of US missiles and not go forward on his Strategic Defense Initiative (SDI or Star Wars). Gorbachev complained about the folly of the nuclear arms race and challenged Britain's acquiescence to US missiles in Europe. He asked for her suggestions on how he might decentralize the Soviet economy and wanted to learn how Britain had adjusted to the transformation of its empire to a commonwealth. Afterward Thatcher announced, "I like Mr. Gorbachev. We can do business together."[1]

On March 10, 1985 Chernenko died, and Mikhail Gorbachev became the leader of the Soviet Union. The very next day he called for an end to the arms race and for the complete abolition of nuclear weapons. He proposed freezing nuclear arsenals and stopping further deployment of missiles as steps leading to a substantial reduction of the stockpiles, and he warned against developing new weapons in space or on Earth.

Gorbachev wanted to improve the inefficient Soviet economy and brought Boris Yeltsin from Sverdlovsk to head the Moscow party. He moved aside the aging foreign minister Andrei Gromyko by giving him a ceremonial position as Soviet president, appointing Eduard Shevardnadze from Georgia. A more hidden adviser was the bold intellectual Alexander Yakovlev. In April, Gorbachev began to discuss restructuring *(perestroika)* the economy by using flexible cost accounting and retooling. Because the enormous consumption of vodka had been weakening the economy and culture, Gorbachev decreed fines and punishments for being drunk in public, introduced treatment programs, and restricted the sale of alcohol, raising the drinking age from 18 to 21. He courted the intellectuals by encouraging writers, such as Vitaly Korotich, whom he made editor of *Ogonyok (Little Flame)*. Gorbachev and Yakovlev wanted the press and literature to help people to understand they could express their own power.

Gorbachev began cutting back the military by making officers retire, and he was the first Soviet leader to take personal control over the nuclear weapons. In April he announced that he was suspending the deployment of Soviet SS-20 missiles in Europe. He announced a unilateral moratorium on nuclear testing in July, began making proposals for cutting the large numbers of strategic weapons in half, and for the first time opened Soviet military installations to verification of disarmament treaties. He wanted to keep the commitment of the Non-Proliferation Treaty by halting and reversing the nuclear arms race. In September 1985 Gorbachev met with President Ronald Reagan at Geneva. He quoted Reagan's famous statement, "A nuclear war could never be won and must never be fought"[2] and then asked why both nations were building new weapons when they were never even going to use the ones they already had.

In January 1986 Gorbachev proposed the complete elimination of all nuclear weapons by the year 2000. The next month the political prisoner Anatoly Shcharansky was freed and allowed to leave the Soviet Union in a spy exchange. During a satellite broadcast in August 1986 Gorbachev accused Reagan of escalating the arms race in order to exhaust the Soviet economy, imposing hardships on people. He announced that the Soviet Union would extend its unilateral moratorium on nuclear testing for another six months. Also in 1986 Gorbachev proposed withdrawing 7,000 troops from Afghanistan, and he planned to start converting defense industries to produce consumer goods.

On April 26, 1986 the worst nuclear power disaster in history so far occurred when the plant at Chernobyl exploded and caused much radioactive poisoning. Gorbachev was troubled by international criticism but took control of the bureaucratic ineptness. He learned that several other plants were also in danger, and he made experts sign papers that they would be responsible for fixing them. As a result he had the plant in Armenia shut down, and five others were ordered to stop operating. Gorbachev urged historians to report on the extensive horrors of the Stalin era so that they could understand their own past and learn.

Gorbachev and Reagan met again in October 1986 at Reykjavik, Iceland. Gorbachev proposed eliminating all strategic nuclear weapons by 1996 and insisted that the Strategic Defense Initiative (SDI) be delayed for ten years. Never before had superpower leaders even discussed reducing their nuclear arsenals. In private he even seems to have persuaded the US President, but Reagan's advisers did not agree because of the Star Wars program. At the press conference Gorbachev said that SDI did not scare them and that their response would be asymmetrical and would not cost as much. He warned that if they attacked the constraints of the Anti-Ballistic Missile (ABM) Treaty, they would be worthless politicians.

In December 1986 Gorbachev called Andrei Sakharov to tell him he could return to Moscow. Gorbachev would not immediately agree to free all the prisoners, but in the next three months about three hundred political prisoners were released. He initiated his democratization campaign at the beginning of 1987. He realized that it would be a good and bad process of dialectic, but he declared that is real life; we must learn from the mistakes and go forward. Publication of Pasternak's *Doctor Zhivago* was allowed, and Gorbachev had the moving anti-Stalin film *Repentance* shown on television. Russian broadcasts by the BBC and Voice of America were no longer jammed.

In March 1987 Margaret Thatcher visited Gorbachev in Moscow. He asked her what world opinion would think if the Soviets removed their medium-range missiles from Europe and reduced their strategic weapons by half while she continued building up her forces. He condemned the Brezhnev doctrine and called the iron curtain archaic, suggesting that his policy toward eastern Europe would be more liberal. The next month Gorbachev traveled to Prague and began implying that these countries could be independent, indicating his sympathy for the Dubcek reforms. In July, Gorbachev proposed the elimination of all intermediate-range nuclear missiles in the world.

Gorbachev got his reform program enacted into law by the Supreme Soviet in June 1987 to begin decentralizing the economy by some experimentation with free markets, letting the nation's 50,000 businesses reorganize themselves under their own management and allowing them to make a profit or go out of business. However, the top Party administrators persuaded him to let them have seven years to make the transition, enabling them to get around many of the new laws. Gorbachev went into seclusion for 52 days during the summer of 1987, and in the fall he published his book *Perestroika*. He called for "new thinking" and tried to find a synthesis of what worked in other countries—production in the United States, labor-management relations in Japan, and the social solutions of Sweden. A totalitarian bureaucracy was falling apart as the democratic politics brought criticisms and reforms. The outspoken Yeltsin became a rival and advocated taking on the bureaucracy directly.

Gorbachev visited Washington in December 1987, and the two superpower leaders agreed on the Intermediate Nuclear Forces (INF) treaty that would eliminate two categories of nuclear weapons. Reagan lectured the Soviet leader on human rights and challenged him to open up his society to allow free ideas and travel. Gorbachev restrained his temper, but privately he told his advisers to commit the Soviet Union to human rights reform. As in Iceland, greater strategic reductions were blocked at the last moment because of a disagreement on SDI and the interpretation of the Anti-Ballistic Missile (ABM) treaty. In February 1988 Gorbachev announced that all Soviet troops would be withdrawn from Afghanistan, and this was completed one year later. In April this process began, and the USSR and the US both pledged not to interfere in the internal affairs of Afghanistan and Pakistan.

In March 1988 conservative Communists led by Yegor Ligachev tried to overthrow Gorbachev, who was able to fragment them and isolate Ligachev in order to lessen his power. Generally the Soviet economy was still in a mess although some reforms using private enterprise and cooperatives created more wealth; but these tended to be in services such as restaurants rather than in industry. *Glasnost* had opened the floodgates on much pent-up criticism. Gorbachev gradually developed *perestroika* from restructuring of the economy into a larger moral reform and psychological empowerment. At the Party Conference in June, Gorbachev proposed increasing local power and forming a new parliament called the Congress of People's Deputies. In October, Gorbachev was elected to replace Gromyko as president of the Supreme Soviet.

Gorbachev made an important speech to the United Nations in December 1988. He described his vision for a new era that would leave the Cold War behind. As a Christmas gift he announced that the Soviet Union was going to reduce its military forces by a half million men by the end of 1990; six tank divisions would be withdrawn from Czechoslovakia, Hungary, and East Germany and be disbanded by 1991. He called for a "new world order" and renounced the use of force. The next day he promised that the Soviet Union would reform its laws to conform to the international human rights convention that had been signed at Helsinki in 1975. The Soviet Union had lost more than 50,000 men in the costly Afghanistan war, and for the first time since Soviet troops had left Austria in 1955, they would withdraw from a nation they had conquered. Unlike American presidents in their attitude toward Vietnam, Gorbachev would later admit that the Afghanistan war was morally wrong and a crime against humanity. Polls of Europeans showed that he was twice as popular as Reagan.

Liberation of Eastern Europe 1989-91

The leadership of Janos Kadar allowed some reforms in Hungary and free travel, and as a result living standards in Hungary were rising. In 1987 some young Communist academics wrote *Turn and Reform*, calling for the government to dialog with the people on reforms, and the following year Kadar and others were replaced by reformers. The Hungarians had learned from their failed uprising of 1956, and the Democratic Forum was committed to nonviolence. In March 1989 at Budapest 75,000 people were allowed to demonstrate without being disrupted by the police.

That month the Soviet Union Army stopped drafting university students. The antireligious edicts of the 1960s were rescinded. In April the Polish government legalized the Solidarity Union and agreed to elections. By staying nonviolent Solidarity could now engage in a dialog with the Communist leaders in a Round Table discussion. After the Soviet Army suppressed a demonstration at Tbilisi, killing at least twenty people and wounding hundreds, the leader of the Communist Party in Georgia was replaced. Seventy-four Communist members of the Soviet Union Central Committee were also removed on the same day Soviet troops began leaving Hungary. In May the Hungarian government gave up Party control of the Interior Ministry for a multi-party system and began removing the electrified fence on its Austrian border; by September the border was opened, and thousands of East Germans started going west.

Gorbachev visited China for five days in May to

normalize relations, sparking the students' democracy demonstrations. While he was there, Lithuania and Estonia passed legislation declaring their sovereignty, followed by Latvia in July. The Soviet Union voted to elect 2,250 members of the People's Deputies; though about a third were selected by Party organizations, many new voices were elected directly by the people. On May 25 at the first session of the Congress of People's Deputies, Gorbachev was elected president of the Soviet Union.

On June 4, 1989 Solidarity won every open election in Poland except for one. Meanwhile ethnic riots in Uzbekistan killed scores of people. On the first of July, Gorbachev went on television to warn people about ethnic conflict. Five days later in Strasbourg he pledged that the USSR would not block reforms in eastern Europe, and the next day he announced at Bucharest that the Warsaw Pact nations were free to choose their own paths to socialism. At home Gorbachev's liberalization was doing more for the intelligentsia than for the workers; in July about two million suffering coal miners went on strike all across Siberia, though on television he announced his support of the striking miners. In August, Gorbachev called Rakowski, the leader of Poland's Communist Party, and urged him to let Solidarity help lead the government. Two days later for the first time a Communist party was voted out of power as Tadeusz Mazowiecki was elected prime minister of Poland.

By early October people were leaving East Germany at the rate of two hundred per hour. 2,500 East Germans had taken refuge at the West Germany embassy in Prague, and Erich Honecker agreed to let them pass through East Germany to the West; but on October 4 when he directed their train through Dresden, thousands tried to board the train and were brutally beaten by police as 1,300 were arrested. Dresden's Party leader Modrow was soon leading the large demonstrations there. Three days later the visiting "Gorby" was cheered in East Berlin when he announced that political decisions for the German Democratic Republic were decided in Berlin, not in Moscow. The unpopular Honecker had ordered German police to club demonstrators, but a few days later he resigned.

The Hungarian Communist Party changed its name to the Socialist Party, and the Parliament planned multi-party elections. Hungarians rallied on the 23rd anniversary of the 1956 uprising, and on October 24 hundreds of thousands of Hungarians nonviolently overthrew their Communist government and proclaimed a republic. At Warsaw three days later the Warsaw Pact nations announced their decision allowing each nation the right to choose its own course and prohibiting any intervention by one member in the affairs of another. In early November, Honecker's successor Egon Krenz opened the border to the West, and East Germans began rushing through the opening in the Berlin Wall. In Bulgaria hard-line Communist leaders were removed.

In Czechoslovakia in 1977 playwright Vaclav Havel and other intellectuals had formed Charter 77 as an informal community to monitor respect for human rights. They were committed to nonviolent and legal methods and tried to engage the authorities in dialog. Yet in 1979 Havel was imprisoned for four years for having stood with people who laid flowers by a statue in Wenceslas Square. After he was released, Havel inspired many with his long essay, "The Power of the Powerless." Authorities arrested dissidents on October 28, but Gorbachev urged them to allow change. On November 17, 1989 a rally of 15,000 in Prague formed the Civic Forum; but student demonstrators were beaten by police; more than a hundred were arrested, and 561 were injured. Over the weekend the first student strike committee was organized as Havel and other Civic Forum leaders directed a nonviolent revolution. On November 22 leaders of Civic Forum's sister organization, Public Against Violence, spoke to a hundred thousand people in Slovakia's capital at Bratislava. The next day 300,000 people gathered during very cold weather in Wenceslas Square in Prague as Czech television employees voted to give full coverage to the demonstrations. A general strike was called for

November 27 and was observed by 80% of the workers. The next day Havel met with Ladislav Adamec, who agreed to a new federal government. The day after that the Federal Assembly ended political domination by the Communist Party. When Alexander Dubcek spoke to a gathering of 250,000 people, the Communist leaders resigned.

Even in Russia the 72nd anniversary of the Soviet Union on November 7 turned into a protest of Communism by 5,000 students. The Supreme Soviet of Georgia declared its sovereignty. Gorbachev loved change and said Europe must advance even faster toward "a commonwealth of sovereign democratic states."[3] He visited the Pope in Rome and announced a new law respecting freedom of religion. Old Russian churches became popular again, and in Central Asia mosques began to reopen. The Supreme Soviet passed a law banning censorship of the media and another law that gave the Baltic republics some economic autonomy.

At Malta in early December 1989 Gorbachev met US President George Bush and pledged he would not use force to prop up Communist regimes in eastern Europe. Bush agreed to cancel most prohibitions against US trade with the liberalizing Soviet Union. The Bush administration had been concerned that the charismatic Gorbachev had taken advantage of Reagan, and they had spent a year reviewing their policy. In East Germany the Central Committee, Egon Krenz, and the ruling Politburo all resigned on December 3, and a week later President Gustav Husak of Czechoslovakia resigned as non-communists took over the government in Prague. Romania was the only country that used violence to overthrow its Communist rulers. Riots began breaking out, and on December 25 the dictatorial Nicolae Ceauscescu and his wife were convicted by a military tribunal of murdering 60,000 people during their rule; they were executed by a firing squad. Four days later playwright Vaclav Havel was inaugurated as president of Czechoslovakia as Dubcek became chairman of the Czechoslovak parliament. The accelerated pace of these revolutions was indicated by some who said that they took ten years in Poland, ten months in Hungary, ten weeks in East Germany, ten days in Czechoslovakia, and ten hours in Romania. In January 1990 Soviet troops were sent to quell riots in Azerbaijan near the Iranian border. When Gorbachev visited Vilnius, 250,000 Lithuanians rallied for independence on January 11. On the same day Armenia declared its right to veto Soviet laws. After conflicts between Armenia and Azerbaijan killed thirty people, the Soviet army occupied Baku, taking sixty lives before order was restored. In February, Gorbachev negotiated a deal with West German chancellor Helmut Kohl whereby a reunified Germany could remain in NATO if its united forces were smaller than those of West Germany alone had been. Gorbachev promised to withdraw Soviet troops within three or four years, and he hoped that the United States would withdraw its forces too. In exchange Germany would give the Soviet Union economic assistance and greater cooperation in all areas. The nuclear arms race had also cost the United States, which was suffering a recession and had become the world's largest debtor.

Glasnost had allowed national and ethnic conflicts to be expressed. Gorbachev hoped to keep the union together in a constitutional federation, but secession fever was spreading. He advised the Communist Party to allow multi-party elections, and many opponents won places on local councils (soviets). On February 27 Gorbachev got the Supreme Soviet to increase his presidential powers on the same day the Congress of People's Deputies nullified Article 6 of the Constitution that had given the Communist Party dominant control. On March 11 Lithuania declared its independence and elected Landsbergis president, though Gorbachev called Lithuania's action illegal and invalid. Four days later Gorbachev was re-elected president of the Soviet Union with 59% of the Deputies' votes; the next election in 1995 would be by popular vote. Gorbachev excluded the use of military forces outside of the Soviet Union with the only exception being after a sudden attack from outside. He appointed Yakovlev head of his Presidential Council with authority over the KGB and other security; this ended the investigation whether Gorbachev had taken bribes while he was in Stavropol. Lithuanians were not intimidated by the Soviet Army and refused conscription, holding to their right by international law to secede. In April, Gorbachev shut down oil and gas lines to Lithuania.

In 1990 Gorbachev was being severely criticized by the conservative Communists for destroying the old system and by the liberal progressives like Yeltsin for not freeing the economy and expression even more. Gorbachev still would not allow undesirables to speak on television or radio stations or publish in newspapers he controlled. He had tried to reform much of the corruption but had maintained his luxurious perks. At Party meetings furious debates took place, and Gorbachev often became angry with those he called "adventurers." He was trying to ride the tiger of revolution he had unleashed, and getting the conservatives and progressives to work together became increasingly difficult. Gorbachev still believed in socialism and was not willing to take one side or the other. Under Communism the state socialism had become very corrupt with bribes of bureaucrats and a legal system that seldom provided justice because of organized crime. Ironically freeing the economy tended to increase this corruption as the black market was legalized. Shifting toward a more capitalistic system gave great advantages to those already in positions of power. The gross domestic product of the Soviet Union was now declining ten percent a year, and crime was increasing.

Radicals had won many elections, and at the May Day parade protesters chanted that Gorbachev should resign; he issued a presidential decree banning demonstrations in central Moscow, and he pushed through a law making it a crime to damage the honor and dignity of the newly created Soviet President. At the end of May the price of bread was to be tripled, and panicking buyers emptied the markets. Gorbachev opposed Yeltsin, who won a close vote to become the president of Russia's parliament. In June they proclaimed that Russia's laws were sovereign over those of the Soviet Union. In July, Yeltsin resigned from the Communist Party, and Gorbachev decreed the end of Party control over the media and approved Yeltsin's 500-day plan for a market economy. The Ukraine and Byelorussia declared their sovereignty, followed in August by Armenia, Turkmenistan, and Tajikistan. In September the Soviet Union agreed to friendship treaties recognizing the reunification of Germany, ending the authority by the "four powers" (US, Britain, France, and USSR) in Germany. That month the Supreme Soviet gave Gorbachev special powers for the transition to a market economy.

In October 1990 mass demonstrations in the Ukraine led to the resignation of Prime Minister Vitaly Masol. That month the United States and the Soviet Union agreed to a treaty on conventional forces in Europe and for reducing greatly their nuclear arsenals. Gorbachev was awarded the Nobel Peace Prize. He devalued the ruble and announced that foreigners could now own Soviet enterprises. Nationalists defeated the Communists in the republic of Georgia. Kazakhstan and Kyrgyzstan declared their sovereignty. In November, Gorbachev promised the military that he would preserve the country's unity and warned that disintegration could mean a bloodbath. Four days later the Supreme Soviet approved a Federation Council that would include the leaders of the fifteen republics. The next week the name of the country was changed to the Union of Sovereign Socialist Republics. Gorbachev barred the republics from controlling nuclear weapons in their territories and authorized soldiers to use force if they were harassed. In December the Russian parliament legalized private ownership of land, and Lech Walesa was elected president of Poland. Fearing a coming dictatorship, Foreign Minister Shevardnadze resigned. Three days later KGB head

Kryuchkov warned that violence may be necessary to restore order as he accused the CIA of fomenting dissent in the USSR

In January 1991 Soviet troops began seizing media outlets in Lithuania and used force to quell demonstrations opposing this. Gorbachev said he had not ordered it but approved nonetheless, causing many intellectuals to withdraw their support from Gorbachev. In response the European Parliament voted to withhold one billion dollars' worth of food aid. In February, Yeltsin called for Gorbachev's resignation, and strikes by coal miners spread. The next month troops were brought into Moscow but were unable to stop a large Yeltsin demonstration. The Warsaw Pact was officially dissolved. The Russian Supreme Soviet gave Yeltsin greater powers. Strikes began in Minsk, and Georgia declared independence. In June, Yeltsin was elected president of Russia with 57% of the votes. In July the USSR Supreme Soviet approved the idea of a union treaty but suggested changes, and Gorbachev was unable to get much economic assistance from the capitalist Group of Seven meeting at London.

On August 17, 1991 Kryuchkov, Pavlov, and Yazov demanded that Gorbachev relinquish power to them. When Gorbachev refused to order a crack-down the next day, Vice President Yanayev claimed presidential powers. The day after that an emergency committee assumed power, but Yeltsin declared the coup illegal. On August 21 the coup failed, and Gorbachev returned to Moscow. No longer believing that the Communist Party could be reformed, three days later he suspended the Communist Party and resigned as general secretary. Now Gorbachev could see no other way but democracy. In the next week the Ukraine, Belarus (Byelorussia), Moldova, Azerbaijan, Uzbekistan, and Kyrgyzstan all proclaimed their independence. On September 6 Georgia broke free of the USSR, whose council that day recognized the independence of Estonia, Latvia, and Lithuania, supporting their membership in the United Nations. Residents of Leningrad voted to change the name of their city back to St. Petersburg, and Tajikistan and Armenia declared their independence.

In October the Russian Congress gave Yeltsin power to implement economic reforms by decree, and the next month he banned the Communist Party. Yeltsin and leaders of the other republics in the USSR State Council agreed on a new confederation. In December the Ukraine voted to be independent and elected Leonid Kravchuk president. A week later Yeltsin, Kravchuk, and the Belarussian chief of state Shushkevish met and decided to replace the Soviet Union with a Commonwealth of Independent States (CIS). Two days later Belarus and the Ukraine ratified the CIS agreement, followed the next day by the Russian parliament. Central Asian leaders met in Ashkhabad the day after that and requested membership in the CIS. By December 22 the leaders of eleven republics (all except Georgia) signed the Commonwealth Declaration, and three days later Gorbachev resigned on television as the Russian flag replaced the Soviet flag over the Kremlin.

Gorbachev and the Earth Charter

On April 20, 1993 at the Global Forum in Kyoto, Gorbachev announced the birth of Green Cross International nine months after it had been conceived at the Rio summit in order to help sustain and manage life on planet Earth. He noted that the environmental movement usually focuses on local threats, but he warned that global problems such as the greenhouse effect required urgent action. He called for the united efforts of natural and social scientists to work for human survival. He suggested that state self-determination needs to be harmonized with the principles of international relations. He noted that the end of the Cold War had not ended the conflicts between nations and that the growth of freedom did not automatically bring a growth in morality. He recommended an "ecology of spirit" and a moral strengthening of humanism. Human pride and passion must be curbed by a philosophy of limits, for plundering Nature is stealing from ourselves.

The civilization of the future must be planetary with high diversity. He urged research and international cooperation.

The Earth Charter initiative was begun by Earth Council chairman Maurice Strong and Gorbachev in 1994 in order to implement the action plan of the 1992 Earth Summit at Rio de Janeiro. The first international workshop was held at The Hague in May 1995 with representatives from thirty countries and seventy organizations. A commission of 23 people issued a Draft Earth Charter at the Rio+5 Forum in March 1997. The consultation process continued for two more years, and in April 1999 the Earth Charter Benchmark Draft II was issued. The mission of the Earth Charter was officially launched in June 2000 at The Hague "to establish a sound ethical foundation for the emerging global society and to help build a sustainable world based on respect for nature, universal human rights, economic justice, and a culture of peace."[4] In 2002 the Earth Charter was recognized by the United Nations, and many countries and organizations have adopted it as an educational tool. The main principles of the Earth Charter are the following:

I. RESPECT AND CARE FOR THE COMMUNITY OF LIFE
1. Respect Earth and life in all its diversity.
2. Care for the community of life with understanding, compassion, and love.
3. Build democratic societies that are just, participatory, sustainable, and peaceful.
4. Secure Earth's bounty and beauty for present and future generations.

II. ECOLOGICAL INTEGRITY
5. Protect and restore the integrity of Earth's ecological systems, with special concern for biological diversity and the natural processes that sustain life.
6. Prevent harm as the best method of environmental protection and, when knowledge is limited, apply a precautionary approach.
7. Adopt patterns of production, consumption, and reproduction that safeguard Earth's regenerative

capacities, human rights, and community well-being.
8. Advance the study of ecological sustainability and promote the open exchange and wide application of the knowledge acquired.

III. SOCIAL AND ECONOMIC JUSTICE
9. Eradicate poverty as an ethical, social, and environmental imperative.
10. Ensure that economic activities and institutions at all levels promote human development in an equitable and sustainable manner.
11. Affirm gender equality and equity as prerequisites to sustainable development and ensure universal access to education, health care, and economic opportunity.
12. Uphold the right of all, without discrimination, to a natural and social environment supportive of human dignity, bodily health, and spiritual well-being, with special attention to the rights of indigenous peoples and minorities.
IV. DEMOCRACY, NONVIOLENCE, AND PEACE
13. Strengthen democratic institutions at all levels, and provide transparency and accountability in governance, inclusive participation in decision making, and access to justice.
14. Integrate into formal education and life-long learning the knowledge, values, and skills needed for a sustainable way of life.
15. Treat all living beings with respect and consideration.
16. Promote a culture of tolerance, nonviolence, and peace.[5]

Gorbachev attended the third global summit of Nobel Peace Laureates in October 2002, and in their final statement they lamented that the United Nations World Summit on Sustainable Development in Johannesburg the previous month had not addressed such fundamental problems as poverty, environmental degradation, and the increasingly acute energy crisis. The participants declared that unilateral action against Iraq was unacceptable, and they supported the "Water for Peace" initiative of Green Cross International to resolve the global water crisis.

Notes

1. Quoted in *The Man Who Changed the World* by Gail Sheehy, p. 164.
2. *Ibid.*, p. 194.
3. *Ibid.*, p. 219.
4. The Earth Charter brochure of the Earth Charter Commission published in 2002.
5. *Ibid.*

14

Mandela and Freeing South Africa

To overthrow oppression has been sanctioned by humanity
and is the highest aspiration of every free man.
Nelson Mandela, September 1953

Our goal is a united Africa
in which the standards of life and liberty
are constantly expanding;
in which the ancient legacy of illiteracy and disease
is swept aside;
in which the dignity of man
is rescued from beneath the heels of colonialism
which have trampled it....
Our vision has always been
that of a non-racial democratic South Africa
which upholds the rights of all who live in our country.
Albert Luthuli, Nobel Peace Prize Address

We have set out on a quest for true humanity,
and somewhere on the distant horizon
we can see the glittering prize.
Let us march forth with courage and determination,
drawing strength from our common plight and our brotherhood.
In time we shall be in a position to bestow upon South Africa
the greatest gift possible—a more human face.
Steve Biko, 1973

I am trying to eradicate the thinking
that is prevalent in white society
which makes them operate from fear as a basis.
In other words they do not necessarily
look at things that are done by blacks logically.
They look at them in terms of to what extent
they are threatened in their position as whites,
and this is the basis for police brutality.
Steve Biko, May 1976

I cherish my freedom dearly,

but I care even more for your freedom.
Too many have died since I went to prison.
Too many have suffered for the love of freedom....
But I cannot sell my birthright,
nor am I prepared to sell the birthright
of the people to be free.
Nelson Mandela, 1985

When we make the so-called preferential option for the poor;
when we become the voice of the voiceless ones;
when we stand in solidarity with the hungry and the homeless,
the uprooted ones, the down-trodden,
those that are marginalised,
we must not be surprised that the world will hate us,
and yet, another part of the world will love us.
Desmond Tutu, sermon in September 1987

We, who were outlaws not so long ago,
have today been given the rare privilege
to be the host to the nations of the world on our own soil.
We thank all of our distinguished international guests
for having come to take possession
with the people of our country of what is, after all,
a common victory for justice, for peace, for human dignity.
We have, at last, achieved our political emancipation.
We pledge ourselves to liberate all our people
from the continuing bondage of poverty,
deprivation, suffering, gender, and other discrimination.
Nelson Mandela, May 10, 1994

To be free is not merely to cast off one's chains,
but to live in a way that
respects and enhances the freedom of others.
Nelson Mandela, 1994

The very right to be human is denied every day
to hundreds of millions of people as a result of poverty,
the unavailability of basic necessities
such as food, jobs, water and shelter,
education, health care and a healthy environment.
Nelson Mandela at the UN, September 21, 1998

Even after the agreements are signed,
peacemaking is never finished.
Peace is not a goal to be reached
but a way of life to be lived.
Violence erupts in moments of hatred and rejection,
but peace is created in long years of love and acceptance.
Trust must be built over generations.
Desmond Tutu, *God Has a Dream* 120

In 1910 the two Boer republics of Transvaal and the Orange Free State and the two British colonies of the Cape and Natal formed the Union of South Africa. Four lawyers founded the Natal African National Congress in 1912. Africans were pushed into slums by the 1913 Land Act, the 1923 Urban Areas Act, the 1926 Color Bar Act, and the 1927 Native Administration Act. The Congress began protesting the pass laws in 1919 when 700 demonstrators in Johannesburg went to prison. Two years later soldiers massacred 163 blacks for refusing to vacate white land in the eastern Cape. In 1922 thousands of striking miners marched in Johannesburg; Prime Minister J. C. Smuts called in the army and air force, and 153 strikers were killed with more than five hundred wounded. During the 1930s General Barry Hertzog led the National Party, and after gaining two-thirds of the Parliament he removed the last 11,000 black voters from the rolls in the Cape. A bill allowed Cape Town blacks to elect seven white representatives in Parliament and twelve blacks to the advisory Native Representation Council. The African National Congress (ANC) elected the physician Albert Xuma president in 1940.

Luthuli, Mandela, and the ANC 1943-61

Albert Luthuli was born in 1898 in Rhodesia; ten years later his father died, and his family returned to South Africa. Albert was educated by American Congregational missionaries, and from 1921 to 1935 he taught teachers at Adams College. To reconcile Christianity with his Zulu heritage he sponsored a cultural society for the study of Zulu folklore. He became the Zulu chief of 5,000 people at

Umvoti in 1936 but continued to preach every Sunday.

Nelson Mandela was born July 18, 1918 in Umtata, capital of the Transkei in South Africa. His father was a chief of the Thembu people in the Xhosa nation and had four wives; after losing his fortune and his title, he died when Nelson was nine years old. Nelson studied English as well as Xhosa. In 1937 he went to the Wesleyan College at Healdtown before studying law at Fort Hare, the only university open to blacks in South Africa. The food was so terrible that Mandela resigned during a protest. He returned to the Transkei; but when the regent arranged a marriage for him and his friend Justice, both young men decided to run away instead and went to Johannesburg. Mandela completed his B.A. degree in 1942.

Moved by the democratic principles of the Atlantic Charter signed by Roosevelt and Churchill, the African National Congress (ANC) formulated African Claims demanding full citizenship for Africans. Anton Lembede spoke and wrote to get people to think of themselves as Africans, instead of as Xhosas or Zulus, and to overcome their feelings of inferiority by looking to heroes such as W. E. B. Du Bois, Marcus Garvey, and Haile Selassie. At the ANC conference in December 1943 they proposed forming a Youth League and did so on Easter Sunday in 1944. Lembede was elected its president, Oliver Tambo secretary, and Walter Sisulu treasurer; the executive committee included A. P. Mda and Nelson Mandela. The Youth League rejected communism as a foreign ideology. In his autobiography, *Long Walk to Freedom*, Mandela admitted that he went so far as to break up Communist Party meetings by tearing up signs and capturing the microphone. Lembede, Sisulu, and Mandela wanted to exclude whites from the League, but others such as Tambo disagreed. Communist J. B. Marks led a successful strike of 70,000 miners and in 1945 was elected president of the League.

Luthuli joined the African National Congress (ANC) in 1945. That year he was elected to the Native Representative Council, and they demanded the government abolish all discriminatory laws. At its annual convention in December 1945 the ANC drew up a bill of rights for full citizenship. Prime Minister J. C. Smuts appointed the Fagan Commission, which reported in 1948 that complete segregation in South Africa was not only undesirable but also impossible. When the Smuts government passed the Asiatic Land Tenure Act in 1946, the Transvaal Indian Congress (TIC) and the Natal Indian Congress (NIC) launched a two-year campaign of nonviolent resistance in which two thousand people went to jail. The leaders, Drs. Dadoo and Naicker, were sentenced to six months hard labor. While Dr. Xuma was speaking at the United Nations, the Youth Leaguers organized an ANC boycott of the Native Representative Council. Xuma opposed this and Lembede's call to boycott the visit of British royalty in 1947, but the charismatic Lembede died of a stomach ailment. That year Mandela was elected to the executive committee of the Transvaal ANC. In 1948 Luthuli spent nine months lecturing to churches, schools, and fraternal organizations in the United States, warning that communism, Islam, materialism, and secularism were threatening the soul of Africa. He recommended combining Christianity with African culture.

In the 1948 elections Dr. Malan's National Party won a large plurality over the United party of General Smuts and began to implement its apartheid policy that denied Africans permanent residence in the towns. Malan pardoned those who had supported Nazi Germany, and his government took the vote away from the Coloreds (Africans of mixed race). Mixed marriages were prohibited in 1949, and the Immorality Act made sexual relations between white and nonwhite a crime. The Population Registration Act defined all South Africans by race, and the Group Areas Act restricted where they could live under the apartheid system. The Youth League demanded that Dr. Xuma, the ANC president, support a program of action, or they would elect someone else. He refused, and Dr. Moroka was elected president and Sisulu secretary-general. Mandela could not get permission from his law firm to attend the

1949 conference, but Oliver Tambo was elected to the national executive committee. The Communist Party and the Indian Congress proposed a general strike for May 1, 1950 and the ANC convention approved the Freedom Day. The South Africa government then passed the Suppression of Communism Act, which made any protest of state policy illegal. On May 1, Malan sent in 2,000 police to disperse protestors, and their guns killed eighteen people.

The ANC planned a national day of protest for June 26, 1950 and was supported by the South African Indian Congress (SAIC) and the African People's Party (APO). Nelson Mandela was won over to multi-racial nationalism and coordinated the various actions from the office by phone. Because he had a driver's license, Mandela was chosen to deliver a letter to Prime Minister Malan demanding repeal of six unjust laws by the end of February, 1952. Luthuli had been elected president of the Natal branch of the African National Congress in May 1951, and a year later they announced a defiance campaign with the SAIC and the communist-influenced white Congress of Democrats. The Indians had past experience under Mahatma Gandhi's leadership and were influenced by his son Manilal Gandhi. Mandela accepted nonviolence as a tactic as long as it was effective. A banned person could not meet with any designated organizations and was allowed to speak to only one person at a time without risking imprisonment. After J. B. Marks was banned, Mandela was elected president of the Youth League.

The first stage of the Defiance Campaign included entering prohibited areas without permits, using "Whites Only" facilities, and staying in town after curfew. On June 26, 1952 some 250 ANC leaders risked arrest by infringing color-bar regulations, and in the next five months more than eight thousand people went to prison without a single incident of violence on their side. The volunteers refused to pay bail or a fine. The police raided the offices and homes of ANC and Indian leaders on July 30, and two weeks later they arrested Dr. Moroka, Mandela, Sisulu, Marks, Dadoo,

Yusuf Cachalia, Ahmed Kathrada, and thirteen other leaders for "promoting communism." By then they were bailing out. Although the campaign had no full-time organizers, during this period ANC membership increased from 20,000 to 100,000. Mandela and Tambo formed a law partnership in August, and they had much work defending Africans from prosecution by apartheid laws. In October and November the police killed several Africans, and blacks killed a few white civilians. Luthuli was ordered by the secretary of Native Affairs, Dr. Eiselen, to resign from the ANC or from his chieftainship. He refused, and the Native Commissioner dismissed Chief Luthuli in November 1952; he was banned from all South African towns for a year. The next month Luthuli was elected president of the ANC with Mandela as the deputy from the Transvaal. Luthuli disagreed with communists such as Walter Sisulu, but he accepted them as allies in the struggle for social justice. During the Cold War he agreed with the neutral foreign policy of India's prime minister Nehru. In December after a trial Justice Rumpff sentenced the twenty leaders to nine months but suspended them for two years.

The South African government banned the ANC in the reserves (bantustans); 52 leaders were banned for six months, and Mandela was forbidden to leave Johannesburg. Mandela suggested a strategy that was called the M-Plan so that they could communicate from small cells by street up to ANC branches. Government authorities threatened to evict Mandela and Tambo from their law office because of the Urban Areas Act. In 1953 the ANC called off the resistance campaign so as not to help the National Party in the elections. The Public Safety Act authorized the minister of Native Affairs to suspend civil liberties, and the Criminal Laws Amendment Act set punishments of three years' imprisonment for any protests against laws and five years for inciting others to do so. Soon after Luthuli's first ban expired, he was banned again for two years. Mandela began to question whether violence would be needed to overturn the power of the white minority; but he was reprimanded by the ANC executive committee and agreed to defend the policy of nonviolence in public. He urged Walter Sisulu to ask the People's Republic of China for weapons, but the Chinese rejected the request. In April 1954 the Law Society of the Transvaal tried to disbar Mandela because of his political activities, but expert lawyers working for free won his case in court. Efforts by the ANC and the TIC were unable to stop the government from using 4,000 police and soldiers to remove more than 60,000 people from Johannesburg's popular communities of Sophiatown, Martindale, and Newclare in February 1955 even though ten thousand people had gathered to hear Chief Luthuli speak.

The Parliament had passed the Bantu Education Act in 1953, and the Native Affairs minister Hendrik Verwoerd said that the Bantu needed no education in European society above a certain level of labor. In protest of the government take-over, Bishop Ambrose Reeves closed his schools in Johannesburg that had ten thousand students. The transfer to the Native Affairs department was scheduled for April 1955, and the ANC planned a boycott. Schools were improvised, and the government made offering unauthorized education a crime.

Professor Zachariah Matthews suggested drawing up a Freedom Charter for all Africans. A coalition of groups formed the Congress of the People (COP) and chose Luthuli as chairman with Sisulu (ANC), Yusuf Cachalia (SAIC), Stanley Lollan (South African Colored People's Organization), and Lionel Bernstein (Congress of Democrats) as secretaries. The South African Congress of Trade Unions (SACTU) was formed in March 1955 and collected workers' demands for the Charter. After widespread and extensive discussions, three thousand delegates, including three hundred Indians, two hundred coloreds, and one hundred whites, met at Kliptown near Johannesburg in June and agreed on the Freedom Charter before the police disbanded them after two days of meetings. The preamble reads as follows:

We, the People of South Africa,
declare for all our country and the world to know:
that South Africa belongs to all who live in it,
black and white,
and that no government can justly claim authority
unless it is based on the will of all the people;
that our people have been robbed of their birthright
to land, liberty and peace by a form of government
founded on injustice and inequality;
that our country will never be prosperous or free
until all our people live in brotherhood,
enjoying equal rights and opportunities;
that only a democratic state,
based on the will of all the people,
can secure to all their birthright
without distinction of colour, race, sex or belief;
And therefore, we, the people of South Africa,
black and white together—equals, countrymen and brothers
adopt this Freedom Charter;
And we pledge ourselves to strive together,
sparing neither strength nor courage,
until the democratic changes here set out have been won.[1]

Because communists in the Congress of Democrats had also participated, the government of South Africa prepared treason charges. Although the Freedom Charter called for national mineral wealth to be restored to the people and industries be controlled to benefit the people, it also stated, "All people shall have equal rights to trade where they choose, to manufacture and to enter all trades, crafts, and professions."[2] On September 27, 1955 more than a thousand police officers raided the homes and offices of five hundred people. In March 1956 Mandela was banned for five years. After pass laws were extended to women, the Federation of South African Women (FEDSAW) was formed, and 20,000 women protested at Pretoria in August. In December the police arrested 156 leaders, including Mandela and Luthuli. The Congress responded by organizing a bus boycott in which 45,000 people walked to work for three months, and to avoid a general strike the government required employers to subsidize the bus fares.

In 1957 the ANC Women's League became active, and about two thousand women were arrested at the Central Pass Office in Johannesburg. They stayed in prison for two weeks before bailing out, and Mandela and Tambo defended most of them in court. Luthuli said, "When the women begin to take an active part in the struggle, no power on earth can stop us from achieving freedom in our lifetime."[3] At the end of 1957 the government dropped the treason charges against Luthuli and sixty others because they failed to prove a Communist conspiracy or the use of violence; a year later charges were dropped on 64 more, leaving thirty on trial. Luthuli spoke to audiences of all races emphasizing the dignity of the individual and the importance of defending it. When Chief Luthuli was assaulted at an Afrikaans university, Henderik Claasens was sentenced to three months and a fine. The treason trial went on for three more years. The evidence on Mandela amounted to 400 pages; Capetown university professor Murray testified on Marxism for 23 days, and Chief Luthuli was a defense witness for three weeks. Luthuli distinguished the nonviolent from pacifists who refuse to defend themselves; he believed that nonviolent men and nations have a right to defend themselves when attacked.

After Mandela's wife Evelyn became too dissatisfied because of Nelson's dedication to the freedom movement, they decided to divorce. Mandela was attracted to young Winnie and married her in June 1958. That year another general election occurred in which three million whites could vote while thirteen million Africans were excluded. The ANC, other Congresses, and SACTU called for a three-day strike during the April elections. They campaigned against the National Party; but the strike was a failure, and the Nationals increased their popular vote by more than ten percent.

Luthuli believed in a multi-racial society, but Africanists wanted Africa for Africans only. At the 1958 ANC conference Luthuli's leadership survived a challenge by the

Africanists who believed that white communists and Indians were dominating the ANC; so they formed the Pan-African Congress (PAC) under the leadership of Robert Sobukwe in April 1959. That month Luthuli proposed a boycott of farms and factories owned by National party supporters. The potato boycott was most effective, and some manufacturing concerns made concessions. Luthuli published "Boycott Us" to encourage those in other countries to boycott South African goods even though it meant sacrifices for the Africans. He hoped that nonviolent methods would reconcile the races and prevent the country's destruction. Luthuli was banned again in May 1959, this time for five years. In 1959 the Parliament of South Africa created eight isolated bantustans for different ethnic groups, and they excluded non-whites from universities. Now 70% of the population was confined to 13% of the land. People in Sekhukhuneland refused to pay taxes; their main chief and other counselors were arrested or banished, and the new chief was perceived as a government puppet and was assassinated. In February 1960 British prime minister Harold Macmillan spoke to the South African Parliament and urged them to change their racial policies because "winds of change" were liberating Africans. Seventeen former colonies in Africa were scheduled to become independent states in 1960. Demonstrations against requiring passes for women were provoking clashes with the police.

At their conference in December 1959 the ANC agreed to begin a nation-wide anti-pass campaign on March 31, 1960, but the Pan-African Congress launched their campaign to resist the Pass Laws on March 21. Their leaders turned themselves in at the Orlando police station, and Sobukwe was sentenced to three years in prison. On the first day 75 police fired on thousands of unarmed demonstrators at Sharpeville in the Transvaal, killing 69 Africans and wounding 178. News reports of the Sharpeville massacre spread around the world, and for the first time the United Nations Security Council condemned

South Africa. Luthuli was testifying for the defense at the treason trial in Pretoria. He immediately called for Africans to stay home from work on March 28 to mourn the victims, and he publicly burned his Reference Book on March 26. Arrests for Pass Law violations were suspended the next day. Mandela and many Africans destroyed their Reference Books on March 28, but most renewed them a week later. The Pan-Africanists called for continued resistance, and some churches and schools were burned. On March 30 the Government declared a state of emergency and arrested 234 people; Luthuli, who had a weak heart, was assaulted by a prison guard and was taken to a hospital. Oliver Tambo escaped and found political asylum in Bechuanaland. On April 5 the South African Parliament banned both the Pan-African Congress and the ANC. More than two thousand people were detained without being given trials. In April the thirty defendants in the treason trial dismissed their lawyers as Mandela and Duma Nokwe began defending themselves and the others. During the emergency they were held in the Pretoria jail.

South Africa lifted the state of emergency on August 31, 1960, but more than 5,000 people were still being detained. Luthuli was sentenced that day for burning his Reference Book; but already having been imprisoned for five months, he was released on condition that he not commit a similar offense for three years. The Government implemented its Bantu administration and replaced traditional chiefs with those loyal to the Government. At the All-African Convention at Pietermaritzburg on March 25, 1961 Mandela was allowed to speak to an audience for the first time in five years, and Luthuli recommended defiance of apartheid and "active sacrificial service." The chief urged the Commonwealth prime ministers meeting at London to expel South Africa from the Commonwealth, and at Capetown the South African Colored People's Congress nominated Luthuli for president of the newly forming republic of South Africa. On March 29, 1961 the long treason trial finally ended as Justice Rumpff announced acquittals for all the accused. Mandela sent a letter to Prime Minister Verwoerd demanding a national constitutional convention or they would stage a three-day strike from May 29 to the day South Africa was to be proclaimed a republic. Mandela advocated the stay-at-home tactic because the enemy could not easily strike back.

Mandela's Sabotage and Imprisonment

Nelson Mandela went underground and disguised himself as a chauffeur or gardener to avoid detection. He began suggesting a turn toward violent methods. Although the Communist Party was considering forming a military wing, at a meeting in June their secretary Moses Kotane believed the nonviolent methods could work if they were imaginative and determined enough, warning Mandela that violence could provoke the enemy into massacring innocent people. Chief Luthuli insisted that the ANC remain nonviolent, but he said that Mandela and others were free to form an independent military movement. The Communist Party decided to support an armed effort, but the Indian leaders wanted to stay with nonviolence. J. N. Singh said, "Nonviolence has not failed us; we have failed nonviolence."[4] Mandela joined with communist Joe Slovo and Walter Sisulu to form the Spear of the Nation (Umkhonto we Sizwe or MK). Their strategy was to begin with sabotage that would damage the state but not be violent to individual persons, and they recruited demolitions experts. On December 16 when South Africans were celebrating Dingane's Day, MK attacked electric power plants and government offices in Johannesburg, Port Elizabeth, and Durban with home-made bombs; one of their men was accidentally killed. At the same time the MK Manifesto was distributed in leaflets explaining their national liberation movement. Ironically, Albert Luthuli had just returned from Oslo, where he had received the Nobel Peace Prize on December 10, 1961.

Mandela managed to escape the police for seventeen months. In February 1962 he attended the Pan African

Freedom Movement for East, Central, and Southern Africa (PAFMECSA) conference in Addis Ababa. From Ethiopia he traveled to Egypt, Tunisia, Morocco, Sierra Leone, Liberia, Ghana, Mali, Senegal, Guinea, and Uganda, raising money and support for the armed struggle. In London he stayed with Oliver Tambo, who had set up ANC offices there and in Ghana, Egypt, and Tanganyika. Mandela went back to Addis Ababa for eight weeks of military training. In June 1962 South Africa enacted the Sabotage Act with penalties ranging from five years to death. Returning to South Africa in July, Mandela met secretly at Liliesleaf Farm with Sisulu, Kotane, Govan Mbeki, Dan Tloome, J. B. Marks, and Duma Nokwe. He visited Luthuli at Groutville, and disguised as Cecil Williams' chauffeur they headed for Johannesburg; but on August 5th police cars stopped them and arrested Mandela. In prison he found that Walter Sisulu had also been arrested.

Mandela chose to defend himself and asked Joe Slovo to be his legal advisor. While he was awaiting trial in prison, the MK sabotage campaign was led by Raymond Mhlaba and Joe Modise. The banned African National Congress (ANC) held its conference in Bechuanaland in October, the month of Mandela's trial. He was not charged with any violence, and in his trial he accused the government of being the criminals; he was sentenced to three years for inciting a strike plus two years for leaving South Africa without a passport. He joined Sobukwe in the Pretoria prison. Sisulu was sentenced to six years; but he appealed and was released on bail. The movement advised him to go underground, and Sisulu did so. Meanwhile the United Nations General Assembly had voted for sanctions against South Africa for the first time.

In May 1963 the government of South Africa enacted what was called the Ninety-Day Detention Law, authorizing the detaining of any person without a warrant for ninety days, which could be extended indefinitely. When Sobukwe's sentence ended, he was redetained and sent to Robben Island, where he was isolated in a cottage for six more years. Mandela was also transferred to the island. In July the police captured most of the MK commanders at Liliesleaf in Rivonia. Mandela was also charged with sabotage along with Sisulu, Govan Mbeki, Kathrada, Andrew Mlangeni, Bob Hepple, Mhlaba, Elias Motsoaledi, Dennis Goldberg, Rusty Bernstein, and Jimmy Kantor. Arthur Goldreich and Harold Wolpe escaped from prison along with two Indians.

The Rivonia trial began in December, and the state called 173 witnesses. They were tried for sabotage and conspiracy because these were much easier to prove than treason under South African law. The charges included sabotage, guerrilla warfare, conspiracy to aid invasion by foreign military, and soliciting and receiving funds from foreign countries for these purposes. As they each pleaded not guilty, they accused the government of being criminal. In his long statement Mandela admitted that he had planned sabotage, but he denied that they had moved on to the second step of guerrilla warfare. He emphasized that they were still committed to not harming human life. He concluded with the following words:

> During my lifetime I have dedicated myself
> to this struggle of the African people.
> I have fought against white domination,
> and I have fought against black domination.
> I have cherished the ideal of a democratic and free society
> in which all persons live together
> in harmony and with equal opportunities.
> It is an ideal which I hope to live for and to achieve.
> But if needs be, it is an ideal for which I am prepared to die.[5]

Most of the defendants expected that the gallows was likely. However, Justice de Wet had been appointed by the party of Smuts; all the defendants decided not to appeal even if they got the death penalty. He found Kantor and Bernstein not guilty but sentenced all the others to life imprisonment.

On Robben Island all the warders and none of the prisoners were white. Mandela and the other Africans and Indians from the ANC decided to continue their fight against apartheid in the prison. To avoid pressure to work faster, they worked at half speed. Blacks were given short trousers and were treated like boys. Mandela asked for long ones; but when given them he refused to wear them unless all the blacks were given long trousers. Rules preventing communication were strict. Each prisoner was only allowed two visits and two letters per year; they had to be immediate family members, and anything but family matters was censored. The prisoners used bribery and blackmail just to get a daily newspaper. They worked in the limestone quarry for thirteen years, but after 1966 they were allowed to talk while they worked. They struggled to improve their conditions and to be able to study for degrees. Mandela wrote that the only organization that really responded to their complaints was the International Red Cross. The ANC prisoners supported a hunger strike by other prisoners without even knowing what the issue was; but fasting was usually ineffective because they could not alert people on the outside. Winnie Mandela had difficulties trying to visit her husband Nelson, and she lost two jobs as a social worker. In May 1969 she was charged under the 1967 Terrorism Act and was detained for seventeen months. Section 6 of the Terrorism Act allowed the police to detain and interrogate anyone suspected of terrorism or of withholding information related to terrorism.

The political prisoners formed their own university. Walter Sisulu taught the history of the ANC, Ahmed Kathrada the history of the Indian struggle, and Mandela political economy. Mandela also used his legal skills to help some inmates with their appeals. Once Mandela was taunted into threatening a warder and was going to be charged; but he responded by indicting the racist prison system as a whole, and the prosecutor withdrew the case. Mandela worked at night writing his memoirs, and Mac Maharaj smuggled out a complete copy upon his release in 1976. They buried the originals in three parts in the garden;

but one of them was discovered, and Mandela, Sisulu, and Kathrada lost their study privileges for four years. Also in 1976 the minister of prisons, Jimmy Kruger, came and offered Mandela a shorter sentence if he would recognize the Transkei government of his nephew K. D. Matanzima; but Mandela disagreed with the collaboration of his nephew and declined. After the Soweto uprising, young people from the South African Students' Organization (SASO) and the Black People's Convention (BPC) began arriving at Robben Island. They had radical attitudes and considered the older prisoners too moderate. Mandela welcomed them, and SASO leader "Terror" Lekota and others decided to join the ANC. They were in the second year of a go-slow work strike and began demanding an end to all manual labor.

On May 16, 1977 Winnie Mandela was banished to the Brandfort township. In June 1978 the ANC guerrilla fighter Solomon Mahlangu was sentenced to death, and he was executed on April 6, 1979. The Robben Island prison began broadcasting their censored version of the news in 1978. Some newspapers with numerous holes were allowed, and movies were occasionally shown. In 1979 discrimination in the meals was ended, and the Africans, Indians, and Colored all got the same food. Because almost all the prisoners were now political, the siphoning off of the better food by kitchen workers decreased. India selected Mandela for its Nehru Human Rights award. In 1980 the ANC began a "Free Mandela" campaign, and the MK stepped up its sabotage activities. In reaction P. W. Botha and General Magnus Malan militarized the country with their "total onslaught" policy. When Matanzima deposed the Transkei king Sabata, Mandela advised supporting Sabata and because of popular sentiment refused to meet with his nephew.

Biko and Black Consciousness

Stephen Bantu Biko was born on December 18, 1946 at King William's Town in the Cape Province. After his older

brother was arrested, Steve was expelled from Lovedale
High School in 1963. He graduated from St. Francis College
boarding school in 1966 and began studying medicine at
Natal University. Biko was elected to the Students' Representative Council (SRC) and worked with the multi-racial
National Union of South African Students (NUSAS), but he
complained it was dominated by white liberals. In 1968 he
was elected the first president of the all-black South African
Students' Organization (SASO); they included the Indians
and Colored (mixed race) who were categorized as non-
white in the apartheid system. Their purposes were to help
the non-white students make known their grievances,
establish their identity, protect their interests, heighten
their confidence, and solve their problems.

For the SASO newsletter Biko wrote a regular column
called "I Write What I Like" which was often signed by
Frank Talk. In 1971 he wrote an article about how fear is
used in South African politics. Once the Europeans had
cruelly imposed themselves on the Africans, fear was used
to perpetuate their domination. Attempts by blacks to
protest were intimidated by security visits, banning orders,
house arrests, and worse. Europeans were not respected for
such injustices, but they were feared. Whites claimed an
exclusive monopoly on comfort and security. Yet because of
their greed for power and wealth, they continued to feel
insecure. Biko criticized blacks who agreed to prop up such
a system. In a paper on Black Consciousness, he urged
them "to operate as a group in order to rid themselves of
the shackles that bind them to perpetual servitude."[6] He
argued that blacks cannot reform a system that implies
acceptance of its injustice; instead blacks must completely
transform the system. In South Africa the whites were the
haves, and the blacks were the *have-nots*. The one major
force that Black Consciousness had to challenge was white
racism. Biko also wrote on black theology within the
context of the black man's suffering.

After completing three years of study, Biko was
dismissed from the university in 1972. He was a leader in

the Black Consciousness movement, and in July they formed the Black Peoples' Convention (BPC). Biko began working for Black Community Programs (BCP) in Durban and contributed to the *Black Review*. In February 1973 several SASO and BPC officials were banned; Biko was restricted to King William's Town for five years. He founded the Eastern Cape branch of BCP and worked as branch executive until he was banned from doing that also at the end of 1975. That year he founded the Zimele Trust Fund to support political prisoners and their families and the Ginsberg Educational Trust to help black students. In 1975 Biko was one of many black militants detained for 137 days without being charged.

When Mozambique was near its independence from Portugal in 1974, rallies were organized in South Africa. On the evening before the rallies of September 25, Minister of Justice Jimmy Kruger announced that SASO and BPC were banned until October 20. Nearly five thousand people gathered outside Curries Fountain Stadium in Durban. The police released dogs, and many fleeing people were arrested and injured. Police raided the SASO offices in October and arrested SASO and BPC activists. Nine people including Lekota were eventually indicted and were held in jail for nearly sixteen months as the trial went on for 136 days with 61 state witnesses and 21 for the defense. They were charged under the Terrorism Act, which states that a person is guilty of terrorism if he (or she) "with intent to endanger the maintenance of law and order in the Republic or elsewhere, commits any act or attempts to commit any act."[7] This Act also placed the burden on the accused to prove that one did not have such intent. Although no physical act of terrorism was alleged, the nine were prosecuted for the ideas of "black consciousness" which the government feared could cause terrorism.

Biko had not been charged because he was already restricted to King William's Town; but as the foremost proponent of Black Consciousness he testified for the defense for four and a half days during the first week of

May 1976. He explained that black people were oppressed by "institutionalized machinery" that caused them to develop in a state of alienation. He said they tried to get blacks to grapple with their problems by "conscientization." They asked foreign investors to help build up the humanity of blacks, and they encouraged foreign companies to criticize South Africa's racist policies. For Africa he suggested, "As black people live in Europe on terms laid down by Europeans, whites shall be subjected to the same conditions."[8] He said they believed that voting should be on the basis of one person, one vote, and they advocated the economic sharing of black communalism. He also explained that they were committed to using peaceful means. Finally in December 1976 Justice Boshoff found all the defendants not guilty of eleven counts because SASO and BPC were not revolutionary organizations; but he convicted them of conspiracy to commit acts that would further racial hostility and for holding rallies in support of the Mozambique liberation movement (FRELIMO). He sentenced six of the defendants to six years and the other three to five years. Since 1950 more than 40,000 Africans had been incarcerated under the repressive apartheid system.

The government of South Africa was spending more than six times as much for each white student than it did for each black student. In 1974 the government began to deliver textbooks in the Afrikaner language, and students organized to protest in 1975. On June 16, 1976 about 15,000 schoolchildren in Soweto rallied against the government's attempt to impose the Afrikaner language on half their classes. The demonstration was peaceful until the police began shooting and killed a student. Then the children fought with sticks and stones, and riots spread in the townships of South Africa. Students boycotted the schools. On August 4, about ten thousand adults joined 12,000 students in the first major political strike in South Africa since 1961. Many black schoolchildren were shot by police, and 700 people had been killed by October 1977; 2,430 students were being detained. Students organized against proposed rent increases in Soweto, and the Government's control was replaced by the more democratic Committee of Ten. Biko recommended smaller demonstrations but more of them so that the police would not kill so many people. He believed that boycotts were helpful and pointed to the sports policies adopted by most countries toward South Africa's apartheid.

After being arrested in August 1976, Biko was detained for 101 days. A few days after his release he sent a memo to and met with US Senator Dick Clark on American policy toward Azania, which is what he called South Africa. The memo urged President Jimmy Carter to reverse US policies and implied that he could use trade boycotts, an arms embargo, and withdrawal of investments even though Biko was prohibited for calling for such things. Biko suggested that the United States could demand the release of political prisoners and stop tolerating bantustan leaders such as Gatcha Buthelezi, Matanzima, and Lucas Mangope. Biko rejected the division into Zulus, Xhosas, and Pedis but wanted to unite the Africans of Azania against their common enemy. Biko was arrested and released again in March and July 1977; he was never accused of any violence, and he was never convicted of a crime.

Biko's last arrest was on August 18, 1977 when his car was stopped at a roadblock outside of King William's Town. He was kept naked and manacled in the Port Elizabeth jail for the next twenty days. When a magistrate visited him on September 1, he complained that he had not been allowed to wash. On September 6 the police interrogated Biko from 10:30 a.m. until 6 p.m. All night he was left handcuffed with a leg chained to the wall. The next morning at 7 a.m. he was released from the handcuffs and manacle but was given several blows to the head, apparently causing the brain damage that led to his death six days later. After being examined by doctors and spending time in the prison hospital, on September 11 he was put into a land rover naked and manacled and driven 740 miles to Pretoria, where he was left on the floor of a cell and died after several hours. Pathologists reported that the cause of death was the three brain lesions from blows to the head. Biko's funeral was attended by 15,000 people despite police efforts that kept thousands more away. Bishop Desmond Tutu spoke about how injustice and oppression can dehumanize both victims and perpetrators.

Biko was the 46th detainee to die while being interrogated by South African police since the detention law of 1963, but no one was ever charged for these homicides. Donald Woods, editor of the *Daily Dispatch*, became a close friend of Biko and wrote a personal biography. He praised Biko for his wisdom, humor, compassion, understanding, brilliancy of intellect, unselfishness, modesty, and courage. He noted how Biko would sit in the back during meetings and after others had spoken would offer incisive suggestions that others would accept. Woods tried to persuade South African authorities that Biko was a man of peace who was standing up for his principles and could be a moderating influence in bringing about the reconciliation needed. Instead of heeding this advice, the government began investigating Woods and banned him on October 19, 1977. He wrote his book about Biko secretly and then escaped from South African with his family.

Steve Biko saw the Black Consciousness movement as a way to emancipate the entire continent of Africa by making whites realize they are not superior but human and blacks that they are not inferior but also human. When a reporter noted that most blacks are really brown, Biko replied that whites are actually pink. Biko was committed to using only nonviolent methods. The Black Peoples' Convention (BPC) operated within the law. Thus it was not a communist organization and had no military wing.

Mandela's ANC Negotiation with South Africa

In April 1982 Nelson Mandela, Walter Sisulu, Raymond Mhlaba, and Andrew Mlangeni were transferred from Robben Island to Pollsmoor prison in a suburb of Cape

Town. In August the ANC activist Ruth First was murdered by a letter bomb. In December the ANC's MK used bombs to damage the unfinished Koeberg nuclear power plant and other military targets of the apartheid regime. That month the South African army killed 42 people while attacking the ANC outpost in Maseru, Lesotho. In May 1983 MK used its first car bomb against a military intelligence officer in Pretoria. In November, P. W. Botha's referendum to form chambers in Parliament for Indians and Colored was passed by white voters; but they could be vetoed by the white portion of the Parliament, and eighty percent of Indian and Colored voters boycotted the election to these two houses in 1984. The colored priest Allan Boesak had called a meeting that led to the forming of the United Democratic Front (UDF) with delegates from three hundred civic associations, churches, unions, student groups, and sports bodies. They opposed the racially separate chambers that excluded black Africans.

Mandela told visiting dignitaries that he wanted a nonracial South Africa without segregation by homelands and with one-person-one-vote for a nonracial Parliament. He called the concessions that repealed some apartheid laws such as the Mixed Marriages Act and the Immorality Act a "pinprick," warning that the ANC could make governing difficult even if it could not win a military victory. Yet Mandela indicated that he wanted the whites to continue to live in South Africa after they shared power with the Africans. When Americans asked Mandela why he did not stay with the nonviolence of Martin Luther King, he reminded them that the United States had constitutional guarantees to protect equal rights; but South Africa was a police state based on inequality that used force against nonviolent protests. He noted that even Jesus used some force to expel the moneychangers from the temple.

Violence increased in 1984. In October a force of 7,000 police and soldiers raided nearly 20,000 homes and arrested 350 people. The UDF organized a massive stay-away-from-work-and-school day on November 5 in the

Transvaal, and 6,000 of the 800,000 strikers lost their jobs. By the end of the year 160 people had been killed, and more than a thousand were detained. On January 31, 1985 President Botha announced in Parliament that he would release Mandela if he "unconditionally rejected violence as a political instrument." Mandela rejected the offer and sent a message that was read by his daughter Zindzi to a cheering UDF rally at the Soweto stadium, asking Botha to renounce violence, dismantle apartheid, unban the ANC, free political prisoners, and guarantee free political activity. While Mandela was having a prostate operation, he was casually visited by Kobie Coetsee, the minister of justice. Next Mandela was transferred to a large three-room cell by himself. He sent a letter to Coetsee suggesting talks.

Meanwhile demonstrations continued to be suppressed violently; 879 people were killed in 1985, and 1,298 in 1986. Some blacks had taken to "necklacing" those they considered traitors by burning a car tire around their necks. At a black funeral Bishop Desmond Tutu saved a suspected informer from being murdered by a mob. Tutu had been given the Nobel Peace Prize for 1984, and in August 1985 he defied the ban to lead a funeral procession in Daveyton, pleading with the officers for pity and the dignity of a burial. Pope John Paul II criticized apartheid, and the US House of Representatives voted 380-48 for economic sanctions against South Africa. The Congress of South African Trade Unions (COSATU) was founded in December 1985.

At the beginning of 1986 Oliver Tambo promised that South Africa would continue to be ungovernable until apartheid was destroyed and power was transferred. Seven eminent persons from the British Commonwealth conference visited Mandela, who advised them to see Tambo in Lusaka because he was the head of the movement. Mandela proposed that if the government withdrew its soldiers and police from the townships, the ANC might suspend the armed struggle to prepare for talks. More than a hundred thousand blacks had been arrested for pass violations the previous year; but in April the pass laws were repealed, and those people were released. However, Botha ordered air raids on ANC bases in Botswana, Zambia, and Zimbabwe, and on June 12 he declared a state of emergency. Mandela contacted the head of the prisons and asked to see Coetsee again. Mandela wrote to Tambo that he was negotiating only to set up a meeting between the ANC executive committee and the South African government. Mandela had meetings for months with government officials, discussing such issues as giving up the armed struggle and socialism. He explained that the ANC was only defending itself from violence and that they would prefer to use peaceful methods if the state renounced violence. He believed that the Freedom Charter called for "African-style capitalism" and that he had not changed his mind. He did not want to drive the whites into the sea but promised to respect the rights of the minority.

Mandela complained about dampness in his cell, and in 1988 he was taken to a hospital to be treated for tuberculosis. In December he was moved to a comfortable warder's house and was allowed a cook. In January 1989 P. W. Botha suffered a stroke; the next month he resigned as head of the National party but continued as state president. By the beginning of 1989 more than 30,000 political activists had been jailed in the last two and a half years. In February they went on a nationwide hunger strike, and most of those detained were released. The UDF allied with the COSATU to form the Mass Democratic Movement (MDM) and began planning civil disobedience to challenge apartheid. F. W. de Klerk became president of South Africa in August 1989, and in September he allowed Tutu and Boesak to lead a big march in Cape Town. In October he released all the ANC leaders except Mandela, and they were not banned from speaking.

Early in 1990 the ANC secretary general Alfred Nzo admitted that they could no longer depend on Soviet support for a war against Pretoria. On February 2 de Klerk announced in Parliament the lifting of the bans against the ANC, the PAC, the Communist Party, and 31 other organizations. Nelson Mandela was released at Cape Town on February 11 to jubilant crowds. At a press conference he expressed his loyalty to the African National Congress (ANC). Reflecting on his 27 years in prison, he said that his anger toward whites diminished while his hatred of the apartheid system increased. He noticed that poverty and conditions had worsened in many ways. At a Soweto stadium he asked students to return to school, pleaded for less crime, and said there could be no freedom without civility and peace. Rivalry between Buthelezi's Inkatha Freedom Party (IFP) and the ANC caused violence between Zulus, killing 230 people in March. Mandela asked them to end the war. On March 26 the police killed twelve demonstrators, and Mandela suspended the talks with de Klerk. Mandela met with African leaders at Lusaka and toured Africa. He visited Robben Island to persuade 25 MK prisoners to accept the government's pardon.

Preliminary talks with the government began in May 1990, and Joe Slovo of the Communist Party and MK commander Joe Modise were allowed to participate. The state of emergency was lifted except in Natal. Mandela traveled abroad to promote continuation of the sanctions against apartheid South Africa. He met with British prime minister Margaret Thatcher, and in New York city he was cheered by a million people. He addressed a joint session of the United States Congress, talked with President George H. W. Bush, spoke before Canada's Parliament, and met with Prime Minister Mulroney. The death toll in South Africa from political violence reached a high of 3,460 in 1990, and in July about forty ANC members were arrested. Slovo suggested that the ANC suspend the armed struggle for the negotiations, and Mandela supported that. On August 6 the ANC and the government agreed on the Pretoria Minute. Mandela learned of collusion between the Inkatha Party and the security forces that had caused many murders. In December the ANC held a conference in Johannesburg with more than fifteen hundred delegates.

Mandela met with Buthelezi to reduce the violence, but

neither the Inkatha party nor the ANC members kept the accord. The ANC asked de Klerk to dismiss two ministers, ban the carrying of weapons in public, dismantle secret counterinsurgency units, and investigate misconduct by security forces; when he refused, the ANC suspended the talks in May 1991. In July at their first annual conference inside South Africa in thirty years Mandela was elected ANC president. Winnie Mandela had become an aggressive activist, and she was convicted of kidnapping and accessory to assault. Nelson believed she was innocent, but they separated the next year. In December 1991 the government, the ANC, and other parties in South Africa began the Convention for a Democratic South Africa (CODESA). Observers from the United Nations, the British Commonwealth, the European Community, and the Organization of African Unity also attended. On the first day Mandela and the ANC agreed to let de Klerk speak last; but his negative criticism provoked a reply from Mandela in which he stated that they would not turn in their weapons until they were part of the government that was collecting them. He complained that the government had been financing covertly the Inkatha violence.

While attending the world economic forum at Davos in February 1992 Mandela renounced economic nationalization, though the ANC still wanted to do some state planning. De Klerk put his reform process before the white voters on March 17, and 69% approved of the negotiations. On April 10 the popular Chris Hani, who was general secretary of the Communist party, was shot dead near Johannesburg; but an Afrikaner woman identified the assassin's car, and he was captured. To calm the rioting that killed seventy people in the Cape and Natal, Mandela made a crucial speech praising the white woman's action. Two weeks later Tambo died of a stroke.

The second CODESA began in May 1992, but the white minority was trying to hang on to a veto power. The ANC planned "rolling mass actions." On June 17 an Inkatha raid killed 46 people at Biopatong. In July the United Nations

Security Council heard arguments from Pik Botha and Mandela. The UN passed a resolution calling for those responsible for the Biopatong massacre to be held accountable, and they sent Cyrus Vance as an envoy to encourage the resumption of talks. The ANC called a general strike, and on August 3 and 4 more than four million people stayed home. When 70,000 marched to Bisho's stadium on September 7, troops killed 29 people and wounded more than two hundred. Later that month Mandela and de Klerk signed a Record of Understanding as a basis for the negotiations, agreeing on a single elected assembly to serve as a transitional legislature to adopt a new constitution. Chief Buthelezi rejected it and withdrew from the negotiations. De Klerk insisted on a two-thirds majority for deciding crucial issues; but Mandela held out for majority rule, and on November 18 they agreed on an interim constitution.

The ANC executive committee decided to support the government's demand for proportional representation in the cabinet, and both agreed on a five-year government of national unity in February 1993. The next month de Klerk announced that South Africa had secretly manufactured six atomic bombs; but they had joined the Nuclear Non-Proliferation Treaty in 1991, and now the weapons and their technology were dismantled. The ANC was opposed to nuclear weapons, and Mandela repudiated all weapons of mass destruction. The ANC favored making Africa a nuclear-free zone. Thus South Africa became the first nation to renounce nuclear weapons after having obtained them.

In June a forum with 26 parties, which included Inkatha, the Pan African Congress, and the Conservative party, set the first one-person-one-vote election in South Africa for April 27, 1994. President Clinton awarded Mandela and de Klerk the Philadelphia Liberty Medal and promised generous aid after the election. Mandela and de Klerk were jointly awarded the Nobel Peace Prize for 1993. Mandela donated the money from his prize to children's charities; later he would give a third of his salary to similar charities. In March 1994 Inkatha members tried to sabotage the election and killed 53 people. Ten days before the election Mandela and de Klerk debated each other on television. Mandela later admitted that he asked twenty businessmen for at least one million rands each for his campaign, and only one did not comply. The voting was by party, and the ANC got 63%, the National Party 20%, and Inkatha 11%. The assembly elected the president, and on May 10 Mandela was inaugurated as president with de Klerk and Thabo Mbeki as his deputies.

Mandela's Presidency of South Africa

During the Government of National Unity (GNU), President Mandela had a cabinet that represented all the major parties, and he handled most issues in a non-partisan manner. He appointed Winnie Mandela minister of Arts; but her diamond deals and large expenses led to scandal, and Nelson Mandela dismissed her from the government. He appeared in court in March 1996 to ask her for a divorce. During the ANC conference at the end of 1994, Mandela asked for fiscal discipline to avoid waste and inefficiency. Sometimes he let his deputies Thabo Mbeki or de Klerk preside at cabinet meetings, but Mandela could take over whenever he wanted. Buthelezi had been appointed minister of Home Affairs, but his relationship with Mandela was still stormy. Mandela wanted to abolish capital punishment, and the new court declared it unconstitutional. The court over-ruled two of Mandela's proclamations affecting elections in the Western Cape, and he quickly accepted their judgment. Joe Slovo was minister of Housing, but he died. Lack of experience and education made it difficult to find many black managers. Mandela treated black and white civil servants with special attention and often won their support.

In May 1996 de Klerk announced that he and his National party were withdrawing from the government. He wanted the Inkatha party to leave also, but Buthelezi stayed. Mandela acted more as head of state, and he let

Thabo Mbeki preside over most cabinet meetings and take over more of the governmental administration. In December 1997 Mandela gave up his presidency of the ANC, and Mbeki was elected without opposition. Mandela spoke for four hours about the problems of the government in a wide-ranging and controversial assessment. By then the ANC's moderate economic policy was even endorsed by the trade unionists and communists. Mandela was still attracted to women and began to travel and live with Graça Machel, widow of Mozambique's former president. They got along very well and married on the day before his 80th birthday. Two thousand people were invited to the celebration, and some conservatives criticized the extravagance and his pardoning of nine thousand prisoners.

The ANC's Reconstruction and Development Program (RDP) was designed to meet basic needs, improve human resources, strengthen the economy, democratize society, and reorganize the public sector. They had ambitious goals and problems, but some of the accomplishments were remarkable. By the year 2000 nearly five million people had access to clean water for the first time from 236 water projects completed since 1994. Five million people were also accommodated by the 1,129,612 houses that were given government subsidies as the government spent R40 billion on housing over six years. Rural homes with electricity increased from 12% to 42%. By the end of 1998 about five hundred new health clinics were serving an additional five million people. President Mandela immediately doubled the annual HIV/Aids budget from R21 million to R42 million, and by 1997 it was up to R80 million. They increased the number of condoms distributed from five million in 1994 to 140 million in 1997. More than ten thousand secondary school teachers had been trained by 1998.

The economy had its challenges. The price of gold was down; labor became more expensive; and capitalists avoided Africa to invest in Southeast Asia. In May 1998 speculators gambled with the currency, and the rand lost a quarter of its value against the US dollar in two months.

Archbishop Tutu criticized the salary increases for the members of Parliament who were making thirty times the average income, but he believed that Mandela's leadership saved the country from destruction. Mandela reminded them that corruption was a problem that South Africa and the ANC had to face. Allan Boesak was charged with embezzlement, and in 1999 he was convicted and sentenced to six years. Although the number of murders leveled off after 1994, other serious crimes continued to rise. A quarter of the previously all-white police force quit; 874 policeman were murdered; and three hundred committed suicide. Mandela accused the right-wing newspapers of giving crime extra publicity in order to discourage foreign investors.

The more conservative policy of Growth, Employment, and Redistribution (GEAR) was announced in 1996 and emphasized deficit reduction, limited government, tariff reduction, privatization, and linking productivity to wages. GEAR was aimed at helping the economy grow quickly in order to provide jobs for those seeking work.

Mandela became a diplomatic peacemaker and had come to rely on brains more than blood for thinking. The apartheid regime had developed its own arms industry to counteract the sanctions, and by 1989 the Armaments Corporation of South Africa (Armscor) employed 130,000 people and gave work to a thousand subcontractors. In the 1990s South Africa's defense spending decreased by more than fifty percent. In 1993 de Klerk had the moral restraint not to sell arms to Rwanda and Burundi for R45 million because of their civil wars. In 1994 the sanctions against South Africa's arms sales ended, and Denel tried to promote arms manufacturing and sales. They were selling $40 million in weapons to Zaire that were probably headed for Rwanda, and in September 1994 the new government discovered they were sending guns to Yemen and appointed a commission under Justice Cameron to investigate. Three Armscor executives were charged with fraud and resigned.

After receiving Cameron's report the government formed the National Commercial Arms Control Committee (NCACC). Some wanted to create jobs by increasing exports, and Denel planned to expand exports by 300% over five years. The government discerned which nations could buy arms based on their human rights, adherence to international law, and internal considerations. In 1995 the NCACC rejected a R2.1 billion arms deal with Turkey, but chairman Kadar Asmal lifted the ban two years later. Arms became South Africa's second largest exporting industry in 1997, a year when the exports were more than double the average of the previous five years. In July 1997 Mandela visited Indonesia and urged President Suharto to grant democratic rights to East Timor, but he also agreed to supply him with weapons. Mandela rationalized the sale of arms to other countries for their national defense, and in 1998 South Africa sold weapons (in decreasing order of magnitude) to Algeria, United States, Thailand, Switzerland, Rwanda, Peru, Denmark, Colombia, Brazil, and Australia.

The South Africa National Defense Force (SANDF) combined the previous army with the ANC's liberation movement and the homelands' forces. At first the Foreign Affairs department still had mostly Afrikaners, but in 1998 Mandela appointed Jackie Selebi director-general. The cautious Alfred Nzo was foreign minister, but Thabo Mbeki took a more influential role. In November 1995 at the Commonwealth Summit in New Zealand, President Mandela was using "quiet diplomacy" in regard to Nigeria until General Sani Abacha had Ken Saro-Wiwa executed. Mandela accused Abacha of judicial murder and called for sanctions; but he could not convince British prime minister John Major, and his appeal to the UN Security Council also failed. Nigeria had valuable oil but was eventually suspended from the Commonwealth until Abacha died in 1998. In the region Mandela worked with the eleven other nations of the Southern African Development Community (SADC). In 1998 Mandela and Mbeki were traveling when acting president Buthelezi approved a force of 600 South African peacekeepers to intervene in Lesotho. Mandela approved the policy, and his relations with Buthelezi improved.

Taiwan had contributed $10 million to the ANC in 1993 for their election campaign, and later they donated one billion rands for South Africa's RDP; but in November 1996 Mandela recognized the People's Republic of China (PRC). Early in 1997 the United States objected to South Africa selling Syria tanks for $650 million, and senators threatened to cut off aid to South Africa; but Mandela resented the interference and also met with Libya's Qaddafi and Cuba's Fidel Castro. When Qaddafi showed him how American bombers had destroyed his presidential palace, Mandela criticized nations that try to be police for the world. Mandela argued that those suspected of bombing the Lockerbie flight should be tried in a neutral country because the same country should not be prosecutor and judge. In March 1999 Mandela was able to persuade Qadaffi to turn over the two suspects in exchange for the lifting of UN sanctions against Libya.

Mandela supported the effort to ban landmines. In February 1997 South Africa imposed a complete ban on anti-personnel mines, and in May they promoted the Ottawa process by hosting an OAU conference on banning landmines. Jackie Selebi became chairman of the negotiations for the Landmine Treaty that began at Oslo in September. By December 1997 the Ottawa Convention had been signed by 120 nations, though the US, China, and Russia refused. Mandela spoke to the United Nations General Assembly on September 21, 1998. He expressed his concern for the dire poverty in the world and the many challenges to fulfilling the promises of the Universal Declaration of Human Rights. He noted that South Africa was working with Brazil, Egypt, Ireland, Mexico, New Zealand, Slovenia, and Sweden to eliminate all nuclear weapons from the world.

Mandela did not run for re-election in 1999. In his last

424 Mandela's Presidency of South Africa

annual speech to Parliament he reflected on how equality, the right to vote, and freedom of speech had come to be taken for granted in a nation where most people did not have those rights before 1994. In a farewell speech on March 29 Mandela was naturally proud of how they had achieved democracy and revolution by a "profoundly legal path." In June 1999 the ANC received 66% of the votes, and Thabo Mbeki was elected president. In the 2004 elections the National Party received less than two percent of the vote and dissolved itself the next year.

Truth and Reconciliation Commission

The interim Constitution for South Africa ended with a section called "National Unity and Reconciliation," which began as follows:

This Constitution provides a historic bridge
between the past of a deeply divided society
characterised by strife, conflict, untold suffering and injustice,
and a future founded on the recognition of human rights,
democracy and peaceful co-existence
and development opportunities for all South Africans,
irrespective of colour, race, class, belief or sex.
  The pursuit of national unity,
the well being of all South African citizens and peace
require reconciliation between the people of South Africa
and the reconstruction of society.
  The adoption of this Constitution
lays the secure foundation for the people of South Africa
to transcend the divisions and strife of the past,
which generated gross violations of human rights,
the transgression of humanitarian principles in violent conflicts
and a legacy of hatred, fear, guilt and revenge.
  These can now be addressed on the basis
that there is a need for understanding but not for vengeance,
a need for reparation but not for retaliation,
a need for *ubuntu* (humanity) but not for victimisation
  In order to advance such reconciliation and reconstruction,
amnesty shall be granted in respect of acts, omissions
and offences associated with political objectives

and committed in the course of the conflicts of the past.[9]

The ANC had already appointed commissions in 1991 and 1993 to investigate abuses of human rights in ANC detention camps, and the executive committee publicly apologized for its collective responsibility. Those in the ANC believed that most of the violations were by the apartheid regime, and law professor Kadar Asmal suggested a truth commission. Alex Boraine of Justice in Transition studied prior truth commissions and lobbied with thirty South African organizations. De Klerk wanted amnesty for those in the apartheid regime, but the ANC would not let them grant amnesty to themselves. Jose Zalaquett had served on the Chilean National Commission for Truth and Reconciliation, and he recommended that amnesty should be based on acknowledgements of truth so that people will know for what one is being pardoned. He also suggested that democratic approval of the amnesty process enables the nation to forgive, and the purposes of amnesty should included reparations and prevention.

After three hundred hours of debate, the new Parliament of South Africa passed the National Unity and Reconciliation Act. Individuals could apply for amnesty for their politically motivated acts, but the pardon depended on their full disclosure. Unlike many of the previous truth commissions, in South Africa detailed accounts from perpetrators and institutions would make public much information so that it would be difficult in the future for people to deny what had happened. Those not applying for amnesty or not qualifying could still be prosecuted. Confessions before the commission could not be used as evidence in court cases, but they might help prosecuting attorneys do their own investigations.

The Truth and Reconciliation Commission (TRC) would give amnesty to perpetrators who confessed what they did and could show that their motives were political for actions between 1960 and December 6, 1993. The TRC soon got this deadline extended to May 10, 1994. The commissioners were to direct the work of the three committees on human rights violations, on reparations and rehabilitation, and on amnesty, plus the investigation unit. The President was to select the commissioners, but Mandela invited the public to make suggestions and set up a panel that reduced three hundred names to 25 nominations. From these on December 15, 1995 Mandela chose fifteen and appointed Anglican archbishop Desmond Tutu as chairman with the Methodist leader Boraine as his deputy. Later two more commissioners were added to make the commission more representative. Mandela stated that he did not approve all fifteen but selected them for the sake of national unity. The commission had ten men and seven women; they were seven blacks, six whites, two colored, and two Indians. The National Party was successful in making the Amnesty Committee independent.

The hearings on human rights violations were held in civic centers, town halls, and churches throughout South Africa. A candle was lit to remember the victims, and hearings often began with prayer and the singing of hymns. The South African Broadcasting Corporation (SABC) covered TRC hearings on radio daily and on television in a weekly report. When ANC leaders said they would not apply for amnesty because their fight against the apartheid regime was a "just war," Tutu threatened to resign from the TRC. However, the ANC decided to encourage its members to apply for amnesty, and Tutu remained as chairman. Early in the process 37 ANC leaders (including Thabo Mbeki) were given a general amnesty based on their assuming collective responsibility for any human rights violations committed by ANC members in the anti-apartheid struggle. This was criticized for going against the requirement of full disclosure, and the TRC challenged the Amnesty Committee in court before the National party could do so. In March 1999 the Amnesty Committee cancelled its amnesty of the 37 ANC leaders as an application outside their scope. They also denied amnesty to the murderers of Chris Hani and Steve Biko.

In August 1995 Eugene de Kock, a hit-squad commander for the South African Police (SAP) was convicted on 89 charges and was sentenced to life imprisonment, plus 212 years. Several of the SAP officers and former cabinet officials he implicated, such as General Johan van der Merwe, applied for amnesty. The Defense minister General Magnus Malan had a controversial trial for ordering the murder of thirteen people in KwaMakutha in 1987, but he was acquitted. Based on these cases, those in the police were more in danger than those in the army. The SANDF delayed investigations by resisting requests from the TRC research department for information from the military archives. Merwe's testimony led to Adriaan Vlok, the former minister of law and order, and he implicated former president P. W. Botha, who was head of the notorious State Security Council (SSC) but defied a subpoena to testify before the Commission. After the National Party left the government of national unity, they stopped cooperating with the TRC and often tried to block its work in court. Other legal challenges against the amnesty process were brought by the Azanian People's Organization (AZAPO) and by the relatives of Steve Biko and other murdered activists.

Before the report was published, the TRC notified those who were going to be receiving derogatory findings. De Klerk used this warning to get the findings on him blacked out of the report. The ANC objected to its liberation struggle being criminalized by the TRC. The Truth and Reconciliation Commission published its five-volume report in October 1998. Mandela approved of the TRC and declined to grant a general amnesty. Buthelezi and the IFP had boycotted the TRC altogether, and controversy surrounded the question of whether prosecutions of them would cause more harm than good. Eventually they settled out of court, and the TRC amended many passages on Inkatha from the report that originally had blamed them for 30% of all the violations. The TRC was criticized by many for providing more amnesty than reparations. The reparations cases were divided into two classes—the victims of gross human rights violations and those who suffered generally from the apartheid system. As of November 2001 the Reparations and Rehabilitation Committee processed 17,016 applications, and the total amount paid for reparations was R50 million; but the final TRC report of March 2003 indicated that reparations were still being delayed. Out of nearly 22,000 applications only ten percent testified orally in public. About 850 human rights violators received amnesty.

For many the process of reconciliation came to be symbolized by chairman Desmond Tutu. He was born on October 7, 1931 to Xhosa and Tswana parents. His father was a schoolmaster; because they were unable to afford a medical school, Desmond became a teacher as well. After three years of teaching, he rebelled against the inferior Bantu education system and decided to study religion. Tutu was ordained an Anglican priest in 1961. He earned a bachelor's and a master's degree from King's College in London and then taught theology in South Africa. Returning to England, he was an assistant director of the World Council of Churches from 1972 to 1975. After speaking at the funeral of Steve Biko, as the new bishop of Lesotho, Tutu took a more active political role in the struggle to overthrow the apartheid regime. He was appointed general secretary of the South African Council of Churches in 1978, but the next year the Government revoked his passport because of his criticism. Tutu emerged as one of the leaders of the United Democratic Front (UDF). His four main political objectives were equal civil rights for all, abolishing the passport laws, better public education, and an end to the deporting of Africans to the "home-lands." In 1984 he was given the Nobel Peace Prize as a representative of the black South Africans' nonviolent struggle for brotherhood and democracy. In 1986 Tutu was elected archbishop of Capetown. He promoted the international economic sanctions against South Africa's apartheid regime; he castigated President Reagan for calling them a "historic act of folly," but in October the US Congress enacted mandatory sanctions against South Africa. During the 1989 elections Tutu led a protest march that police using whips chased off a whites-only beach.

When Tutu became chairman of the Truth and Reconciliation Commission, he hoped that by opening the wounds to cleanse them the commission could stop the festering so that past evils would no longer haunt them. He noted that reconciliation depends on forgiveness, which must be based on acknowledging what was done wrong. Instead of the retribution of punishment, Tutu recommended restorative justice that corrects imbalances and heals broken relationships. He had compassion even for those who had imposed the apartheid system because no one was diminished more by it than the violators of human rights. He was happy to see people repenting because it restored not only their own decency but also helped to revive the integrity of the whole nation. Whites who had hated him during the struggle against apartheid were won over by his kindness. He forgave white perpetrators and had so much empathy for white victims that many blacks began to resent him. He knew that the therapeutic process of reconciliation would take a long time. Tutu applied the traditional Xhosa concept of *ubuntu* (humanity) in his Christian theology. He saw African communitarian values as "delicate networks of interdependence." Tutu described those who have *ubuntu*.

They are generous, hospitable, friendly,
caring, and compassionate.
They share what they have.
It also means my humanity is caught up,
is inextricably bound up, in theirs.
We belong to a bundle of life.
We say, "A person is a person through other people."[10]

Tutu advocated terminating South Africa's weapons industry, and he criticized President Thabo Mbeki for stifling political debate. He condemned Israel's treatment of Palestinians as a form of apartheid, and he favored the West Papuans' movement for independence from Indonesia. He denounced the dictatorial Robert Mugabe of Zimbabwe and the timidity of South Africa's quiet diplomacy. Tutu has stood up for the rights of homosexuals in the Anglican Church because he believes their contributions are valuable. He protested the US invasion of Iraq and the abuse of prisoners at Guantanamo Bay, and he has called for restorative justice in Iraq. Tutu spoke out against Pope Benedict XVI's policy against condoms that affects the spread of HIV/AIDS in Africa.

Notes

1. Quoted in *Long Walk to Freedom* by Nelson Mandela, p. 151-152.
2. *Ibid.*, p. 152.
3. *Ibid.*, p. 191.
4. *Ibid.*, p. 238.
5. *Ibid.*, p. 322.
6. *I Write What I Like* by Steve Biko, p. 49.
7. Quoted in Millard Arnold's introduction to *Black Consciousness in South Africa* by Steve Biko, p. xxvii.
8. *Black Consciousness in South Africa* by Steve Biko, p. 40.
9. Quoted in *Commissioning the Past*, p. 222.
10. *No Future without Forgiveness* by Desmond Tutu, p. 34.

15

Chomsky and Zinn on US Imperialism

It is the responsibility of intellectuals
to speak truth and to expose lies.
Noam Chomsky

The first step towards political sanity
must be intensive self-examination,
exposure not only of what we do
and what we represent in the world today,
but also of the attitudes that color and distort
our perception of our international behavior.
Noam Chomsky, "The Logic of Withdrawal"

Commitment to work on the problems
of racism, oppression, imperialism, and so on,
is in the United States an absolute necessity.
Noam Chomsky, *Language and Politics*

Things happen in the world because of the efforts
of dedicated and courageous people
whose names no one has heard,
and who disappear from history.
Noam Chomsky, 1993

War is inherently unjust,
and the great challenge of our time is
how to deal with evil, tyranny, and oppression
without killing huge numbers of people.
Howard Zinn, 2002

We have enough examples—
in the history of our own country and that of others—
that show it is possible for organized citizens
to resist and overcome what seem like hopeless odds.
The power of determined people armed with a moral cause is,
I believe, "the ultimate power."
Howard Zinn, 2003

Revenge knows few limits
when the privileged and powerful
are subjected to the kind of terror
they regularly mete out to their victims.
Noam Chomsky, *Hegemony or Survival* 182

Chomsky's Analysis of US Foreign Policy

Noam Chomsky was born in Philadelphia on December 7, 1928 and began studying language with his father, who was a Hebrew scholar. He has been interested in politics since childhood and said he was influenced by the radical Jewish community in New York. At the University of Pennsylvania he studied linguistics, mathematics, and philosophy, and he was given a Ph.D. there after having done research as a Harvard Fellow from 1951 to 1955. He and his wife lived for a few months in 1953 on a kibbutz in Israel. Chomsky was influenced by George Orwell and the anarchists in Spain that were attacked by fascists in the Spanish Civil War. He especially admired Bertrand Russell and compared his life and reputation to another great pacifist, Albert Einstein. Both responded to the "grave dangers facing humanity."

Einstein responded by living
a very comfortable life in Princeton
and dedicating himself to research that he loved,
taking a few moments for an occasional oracular statement.
Russell responded by leading demonstrations
and getting himself dragged off by the cops,
writing extensively on the problems of the day,
organizing war crimes trials, etc.
The result? Russell was and is reviled and condemned.
Einstein is admired as a saint.
Should that surprise us? Not at all.[1]

Chomsky taught at the Massachusetts Institute of Technology (MIT) from 1955 until he retired to do more speaking. His writings have been cited more times than those of any other living person. He is one of the most influential thinkers in the field of linguistics for his theory of generative and transformational grammar with deep structure. His understanding of the uniqueness of human language led him to criticize the reductionist behaviorism of B. F. Skinner that tried to explain human behavior as a simple process of conditioning by the environment. Chomsky argued that language is more than a set of mechanical habits because it is creative and rational. He considered it offensive to human dignity to treat people as if they were like laboratory rats or pigeons.

Chomsky became perhaps the most articulate critic of the American war in Vietnam and dedicated his book of essays, *American Power and the New Mandarins*, "to the brave young men who refuse to serve in a criminal war."[2] During an anti-draft protest at the Pentagon in October 1967 Chomsky himself was arrested during a teach-in with Dave Dellinger and Dagmar Wilson. He also refused to pay half his federal income tax. He observed that anti-Communism was a useful device to get the American people to support an imperial intervention, which was really to make sure that American power dominated Southeast Asia. He suggested that it did not take great intelligence to see the need for de-escalation by the greatest power in the world that had become the most aggressive. This book included a long essay on "The Revolutionary Pacifism of A. J. Muste" about the great pacifist's response to the US going to war against Japan in 1941. Chomsky agreed with Muste that the tragedy might have been averted

> by a serious attempt at peaceful reconciliation
> with no attempt to fasten sole war-guilt on any nation,
> assurance to all peoples of equitable access
> to markets and essential materials,
> armament reduction, massive economic rehabilitation,
> and moves towards international federation.[3]

Chomsky admitted, though, that such a proposal then would have seemed as senseless as during the time he wrote. Yet he found Muste's revolutionary pacifism realistic and ethical. In his essay on "The Logic of Withdrawal" Chomsky agreed with Howard Zinn that since 1954 the problems of Vietnam should have been solved at the local level by the Vietnamese instead of raising them to an international conflict. He argued that if enough people spoke for withdrawal, it would become politically feasible. In the essay "On Resistance" Chomsky described his arrest at the Pentagon and offered these reflections on the value of nonviolent protest:

The argument that resistance to the war
should remain strictly nonviolent seems to me overwhelming.
As a tactic, violence is absurd.
No one can compete with the government in this arena,
and the resort to violence, which will surely fail,
will simply frighten and alienate some who can be reached,
and will further encourage the ideologists
and administrators of forceful repression.
What is more, one hopes that participants
in nonviolent resistance will themselves
become human beings of a more admirable sort.
No one can fail to be impressed
by the personal qualities of those
who have grown to maturity in the civil rights movement.
Whatever else it may have accomplished,
the civil rights movement has made
an inestimable contribution to American society
in transforming the lives and characters
of those who took part in it.
Perhaps a program of principled, nonviolent resistance
can do the same for many others,
in the particular circumstances that we face today.
It is not impossible that this may save the country
from a terrible future.[4]

Chomsky went on to say that resistance need not replace dissent, which is still needed. Those who refuse to pay taxes and resist the draft and the war can also speak to church groups and town meetings or participate in electoral politics by supporting peace candidates. He concluded that the United States had become the greatest threat to peace, national self-determination, and international cooperation, while the American people still enjoyed internal freedom.

In 1969 Chomsky became aware that the Pentagon and NASA were financing two laboratories at MIT. He believed it was impossible for the university to sever ties with the military-industrial complex at that time, and therefore he worked to make people aware of what was going on so that they would know how to act.

In 1970 Chomsky complained that Laos was being bombed even more than Vietnam. He argued that Cambodia's "decade of genocide" by the Khmer Rouge was partly a reaction to and an effect of US bombing. The United States military killed nearly three million people in the Vietnam War and perhaps another million in Laos and Cambodia. Surprisingly, though it was hardly reported, postwar Vietnam had little retribution after so much violence. Yet the US not only refused to pay reparations for its massive devastation, but it also tried to punish the Vietnamese even further. When India wanted to send a hundred buffalo to Vietnam in 1977, the US threatened to stop its Food for Peace program in India. President Carter said he would not help Vietnam because the "destruction was mutual."

Chomsky wrote to the *New York Times*, noting that the term "bloodbath" was never applied to the war but only to the possibility of ending the war. In 1973 the book *Counter-revolutionary Violence: Bloodbaths in Fact and Propaganda*, which he wrote with Edward S. Herman, was denied distribution by the Warner Communications corporation after 20,000 copies had been printed.

In 1976 Chomsky was interviewed in French by Mitsou Ronat for the book *Language and Responsibility*. He said that anyone can see through the deceptions of the system of shared ideology and propaganda if one analyzes how they are designed to protect special interests. In 1972 Henry Kissinger appeared on television to say that peace was at hand; but he was rejecting the negotiating principles on crucial points. Thus Chomsky predicted more escalation, which took place during the Christmas bombing. He noted how revisionist historians were changing the previously prevalent view that Russia and China were responsible for the Cold War. Such revisionist views were hardly noticed until there were enough students aroused by the civil rights movement and anti-war protests in the 1960s. He noted that state censorship is unnecessary in the American system because the ideological controls are complex and decentralized.

He cited cases exposed by the Church Committee in which the FBI in its Counter-Intelligence Program (Cointelpro) infiltrated and murdered Fred Hampton and Mark Clark in Chicago. The FBI did little to stop the Rangers criminal gang until the Black Panthers got them interested in politics; then they tried to make the groups fight each other. The FBI hired the leader of the Secret Army Organization to shoot a student at San Diego State, wounding a woman. In Seattle the FBI infiltrated left-wing groups; their agent tried to instigate the bombing of a bridge, and another even initiated a robbery in which a man was killed. In 1960 the FBI tried to disrupt the Puerto Rican independence movement. The next year under Attorney General Robert Kennedy they targeted the Socialist Workers Party, because they ran candidates in elections and supported racial integration and Castro. Chomsky believed that Cointelpro made Watergate look like a tea party. Some people were shocked that the CIA tried to assassinate foreign leaders, but the Phoenix program in Vietnam exterminated forty thousand people. Chomsky asked why those people were considered less significant.

During the Carter presidency, which tried to bring more human rights into US foreign policy, Chomsky and Herman published their two-volume *Political Economy of Human Rights*. In the first volume, *The Washington Connection and Third World Fascism*, they demonstrated that since World War II the United States has been imposing oppressive and terrorist regimes from the CIA-sponsored coups in Iran in 1953 and in Guatemala in 1954 to Indonesia in 1965 and Chile in 1973. In the 1960s eleven constitutionally elected governments in Latin America were displaced by military dictators. The US was overthrowing democratic reformers and radicals in order to "stabilize" countries for business with right-wing military regimes. For a quarter of a century until 1975 in the name of freedom the US tried

to subjugate Vietnam by force and subversion,
in the process violating the UN Charter,
the Geneva Accords of 1954, the Nuremberg Code,
the Hague Convention, the Geneva Protocol of 1925,
and finally the Paris agreements of 1973.[5]

Saturation bombing resulted in mass murder; but the wars in Laos and Cambodia were kept secret, because the mass media refused to report them. Freedom in this case was for US business to make profits; but the rights of students, peasants, labor unions, and political critics were massively suppressed.

In 1965 the United States backed a coup in Indonesia that resulted in a massacre of perhaps 700,000 people while 750,000 were arrested. These figures are unknown to most Americans, but the crimes of the Khmer Rouge were repeatedly reported. After centuries of colonialism in Indonesia, Portuguese fascism was overthrown in 1974. People in East Timor wanted to be independent and the following year found themselves in a civil war with Indonesia that in the next four years slaughtered about 200,000 people in East Timor from a population of 700,000. In 1976 US Secretary of State Henry Kissinger took credit for blocking United Nations action on behalf of Timor. The Carter administration increased the shipment of weapons to Indonesia even though 100,000 people had already been massacred.

Some people think these are exceptions, but a pattern emerges. Solzhenitsyn and Sakharov may be praised for their criticism of Soviet oppression; but what is their moral level when they complained that the US did not fight hard enough to win in Vietnam? Chomsky saw better ethics in the resisters and deserters who tried to defend the rights of others, namely the victims of American aggression. The bias of the media is found in the emphasis on two or three dissidents in the Soviet Union while 20,000 cases of severe torture in Latin America are completely ignored. The military-industrial-intelligence com-plex invested and made huge profits by promoting weapons, fear, and insecurity. A murder network of death squads operated in Argentina, Brazil, Chile, Paraguay, and Uruguay to hunt down dissidents. Neither President Carter nor the mainstream press would refer to the Shah of Iran as a dictator even though between 1974 and 1977 of at least 25,000 political prisoners some 300 were executed.

Because the right-wing military leaders of these third-world countries do not usually have a large following, as did Mussolini and Hitler, Chomsky called them "subfascists." He noted that the Carter administration continued sending arms to the Philippines, South Korea, Thailand, Indonesia, Morocco, and Iran even though they seriously violated human rights. When as many as 250,000 people were systematically murdered by the minority tribal government of Burundi, the Carnegie Endowment's study could not find a single mention of it by the US Government nor a condemnation. In Paraguay the Aché Indians were treated atrociously by the government and fundamentalist missionaries; yet US economic and military aid continued to go there despite Carter's human rights policy. Chomsky noted that Paraguayan fascism was ignored by US media even though it was widely reported in Europe. Since the military coup of 1964 Brazil gained much support from international lending organizations and multinational corporations despite their bad treatment of Indians, the poor, and the Amazon environment.

Chomsky and Herman discussed the horrendous problems of East Timor at length. In twenty years starting in 1949 the United States gave Thailand more than two billion dollars in aid and arms to meet Communist threats even though in the police state they established there was little opposition. During the Vietnam War 50,000 US forces used Thailand as a base for bombing raids, causing the prostitution industry to boom. Thailand managed to elect a democratic government in 1973, but aid was reduced despite their economic difficulties. Yet after the US assisted a military coup in 1976, the aid was increased; that year the US sold them $89.6 million in military equipment, more than Thailand had purchased in the previous quarter century. In 1977 the Marcos regime in the Philippines arrested more than 60,000 people under martial law, but visiting Vice President Mondale was placated by an announcement that a few political prisoners would be released. Lending drove the Philippines debt from $2.2 billion in 1972, when martial law was declared, to $6 billion in 1977; apparently capitalists approved of this subfascism.

In the Dominican Republic the constitutional government of Juan Bosch was overthrown by the military in 1963. Two years later 23,000 US forces invaded the island to prevent Bosch from replacing the fascist regime of Donald Reid Cabral. President Johnson claimed Communism was a threat, but Bosch was a democratic reformer. Ten years later Bosch complained, "This country is not pro-American; it is United States property."[6] Chomsky and Herman explained how Nazis had escaped to Latin America, and, helped by US military and intelligence agencies, military elites were ruling in Argentina, Bolivia, Brazil, Chile, Ecuador, Paraguay, Peru, and Uruguay.

In their second volume on human rights, Chomsky and Herman examined the results of the Indochina War and the reconstruction of the failed US foreign policy. The United States was only partially defeated by Vietnam, which had suffered so much more. The US refused to pay reparations or give aid to help rebuild the country they destroyed, unlike the policy toward Germany and Japan after World War II, and they even blocked trade. The US was the only country out of 141 to oppose a United Nations resolution urging priority economic assistance to Vietnam. In Laos people died from malnutrition, disease, and unexploded bombs. The United States had dropped more than 500,000 tons of bombs on Cambodia; so it is not too surprising that the country was militarized and degenerated into a horrible civil war. The devastation that was caused by the US military intervention was explained as proof that Communism is evil. Kissinger directed the CIA to start subverting Angola from South Africa and Zaire.

After Israel invaded Lebanon in 1982, Chomsky wrote *The Fateful Triangle* about the United States, Israel, and the Palestinians. He began by noting the hypocrisy of complaining about Israel's establishing settlements in the occupied territories when the US is essentially paying for them with huge amounts of aid and discounted military sales. Chomsky complained about Israel's policy of rejecting the Palestinians' rights that is condoned by the US. Since the mid-1970s the international consensus has been that there should be a Palestinian state in the West Bank and Gaza strip; but Israel has continually rejected this solution, and over the protest of everyone, including the US, Israel annexed Arab East Jerusalem. In January 1976 the United States vetoed a UN Security Council resolution calling for a peace settlement according to the international consensus for a Palestinian state with 1967 borders. In November 1977 Egypt's Anwar Sadat made his daring trip to Jerusalem, hoping to convene a Geneva conference to settle the conflict; but the US opposed this, because it would include European powers. The Camp David peace treaty of 1979 did little to solve the Palestinian conflict and even allowed more settlements; but Egypt was separated from Arab allies and became a major recipient of US aid, gaining $2 billion per year for more than twenty years.

In April 1982 the US alone vetoed a UN Security Council resolution calling on Israel to reinstate the ousted mayors of Nablus, Ramallah, and El Bireh. Israel has not recognized rights of one-sixth of their population that is not

Jewish. In June 1982 the US was alone in vetoing a UN Security Council resolution that called for a simultaneous withdrawal from Beirut by Israeli and Palestinian forces. In the previous four years Israel had received 48% of all US military aid. The Israeli lobby consists not only of Jews but also Christian fundamentalists, some liberals and labor leaders, and conservatives who support a strong military policy. Public opinion is swayed as the Anti-Defamation League (ADL) accuses any critics of being "anti-Semitic" or "self-hating" Jews. Since Israel captured the West Bank, Gaza, and the Golan Heights in the 1967 war, the US has considered Israel an important strategic asset in the Middle East, where oil is so important.

When Israeli forces invaded West Beirut on September 15, 1982, the United States did not object, though the atrocious massacres of Palestinians at the Sabra and Shatila refugee camps aroused angry condemnation. Israeli soldiers would not allow *Newsweek* reporter James Pringle into the Sabra camp during the massacre. An ABC news investigation learned that at least 45 Israeli officers knew of the slaughter while it was occurring; but the Begin government refused to allow an independent inquiry. US envoy Philip Habib had assured the Lebanese and Palestinians that they would be safe after the Palestinian Liberation Organization (PLO) fighters left. The Habib cease-fire of 1981 had also guaranteed Israeli security, which was their rationale for the invasion. Chomsky considered it a reflection of American racism that Israel's security was the issue instead of the Palestinians' security. He predicted that terrorism in the occupied territories and Israel was the likely forecast, and he hoped that more of the peace movement would start facing the issue.

Israel's attack on Lebanon was designed to disperse the refugees and destroy Palestinians' nationalist organization. Israel dissolved the elected councils of Nablus and Dura on the West Bank and dismissed the mayors of Jenin and Gaza, where city employees were arrested. Lebanese police estimated that the Israeli invasion killed 19,085 and wounded more than 30,000; 84% of those killed were civilians. Chomsky considered these underestimates. President Reagan proposed a peace plan calling for a freeze on settlements; but Israeli prime minister Menachem Begin angrily rejected this even though it excluded the PLO by denying the right of inhabitants to choose their own political representative. Begin announced new settlements in Judea and Samaria. Another consequence of the Lebanon invasion was that Israel took over complete control of the scarce water resources of the West Bank even though this violated the Camp David accords.

In 1985 Chomsky published *Turning the Tide* on the current US intervention in Central America. He noted the bias in the US media. Edward Herman had done a study of the *New York Times* reporting on the elections in El Salvador and Nicaragua. The coercion by armed forces was discussed in 37.5% of the Nicaragua articles but only in 3.6% of the El Salvador reports even though such human rights abuses were much more common in El Salvador than in Nicaragua. (The wars in Central America are discussed in a previous chapter of this book.)

Chomsky's book *Deterring Democracy* (1992) reflected on the end of the Cold War, which had caused an economic recession. He predicted,

The United States remains the only power with the will
and the capacity to exercise force on a global scale—
even more freely than before,
with the fading of the Soviet deterrent.
But the US no longer enjoys
the preponderance of economic power
that had enabled it to maintain an aggressive
and interventionist military posture since World War II.
Military power not backed by a comparable economic base
has its limits as a means if coercion and domination.
It may well inspire adventurism,
a tendency to lead with one's strength,
possibly with catastrophic consequences.[7]

Chomsky observed that in the past the United States and its clients were often politically weak (lacking popular support), but it made up for this with military and economic strength, instead of following international law. He feared that with less economic power the temptation to use force was increased, and as in the Gulf War, the US police force would have to be paid for by other countries, making Americans mercenaries.

Chomsky accused the United States of using the Cold War to justify international subversion, aggression, and state terrorism while the huge military-industrial complex, which President Eisenhower warned against, became a government welfare program for high technology in the "private sector." Sacrifice and discipline for this imperial cause meant, especially under Reagan, reducing the social programs that meet human needs. In 1990 Defense Secretary Dick Cheney announced that a large Navy would continue to be necessary to further American interests in Latin America and Asia. In response to the initiatives of Gorbachev, the United States did agree to a treaty on intermediate-range missiles in Europe (INF Treaty) in 1987; but at the United Nations the US stood alone against 154 nations that voted against weapons in outer space, alone against 135 nations voting against developing new weapons of mass destruction (WMD), and only with France against 143 nations voting for a comprehensive test ban. The United States was the only country to boycott the 1987 UN disarmament conference.

Chomsky sharply criticized President Bush's 1989 invasion of Panama which violated the UN Charter, the OAS Charter, and the Panama Canal treaty. Wondering how the United States would learn, he quoted A. J. Muste, who said, "The problem after a war is with the victor. He thinks he has just proved that war and violence pay. Who will now teach him a lesson?"[8] Chomsky exposed the hypocrisy in the pretexts Bush gave for the invasion. The wife of an officer had been beaten, but numerous cases much worse could be found in Latin America. Panama's 1989 election was fraudulent, but the election of 1984 had been also. Noriega was corrupt, but he had been for years. Noriega was involved in drug smuggling, but he had been doing that with the CIA. As for bank money-laundering, Bush himself had cancelled the federal program aimed at stopping that in the early 1980s when he was the Drug Czar. The press complained that they could not cover the Panamanian casualties because of the US military; but Chomsky suggested they could have checked the hospitals.

One real reason for the US turning against Noriega is that he was supporting the Contadora peace process the US opposed, and another was because he allowed trading with Nicaragua and Cuba. Of course the main reason was to maintain control of the Panama Canal that was to be turned over mostly to Panamanian authority in 1990. The invasion put back in power the white Europeans, who had been displaced when the reforming General Torrijos took control in 1968. Chomsky learned that the "US military sent hundreds of psywar specialists into Panama to 'spread pro-American propaganda messages throughout the country.'"[9] He reported that the forgotten 1983 invasion of Grenada had left the island much worse off as the health care system was dismantled by Herbert Blaize, who had died just before the Panama invasion. F-117A stealth fighters were used for the first time in Panama, dropping 2,000-pound bombs with time-delay mechanisms. Chomsky found that casualty figures reported in the US media were ludicrously low; human rights groups had found that at least 2,000 Panamanians had been killed.

Chomsky on Propaganda and Profits

Noam Chomsky and Edward S. Herman published *Manufacturing Consent* on the political economy of the mass media in 1988. The expression "manufacturing consent" was used by Walter Lippman to describe propaganda, the manipulation of public opinion for political purposes. They observed that the biased choices made by the media in deciding what to report and how were based on selecting people with internalized preconceptions that are adapted to ownership, big organizations, markets, and political power. Overt censorship is not used as too crude; rather reporters and commentators censor themselves to suit the requirements of the media. Those individuals who do not conform are dismissed or marginalized so that their views have little influence. Chomsky and Herman studied the pattern of US propaganda and found that evidence of US violence and aggression is systematically suppressed while the faults of enemies are greatly emphasized by media coverage. Uncomfortable facts can be found by a diligent researcher in the back pages of newspapers or in minor or alternative media.

In the commercial market mass media entertain as much as inform in order to maximize profits. Chomsky and Herman analyzed the pressures that shape the values, beliefs, and behavior patterns that are inculcated in American society by the mass media. They described five main factors that filter the news. First is the immense size of the dominant media corporations, the increasing concentration of ownership, their great wealth, and the ultimate importance of making large profits (bottom-line motivation). Since *Manufacturing Consent* was written, media ownership has been concentrated even more by mergers and acquisitions under the relaxing of Federal Communications Commission (FCC) regulations. Many in the past would publish well written books, expecting about three or four percent profit; but lately the big publishers usually will not publish a book unless they expect it will make 15% profit; this often means that it is either by or about an already marketable celebrity.

The second major factor is how advertising affects what makes it into the mass media. Advertisers have become the licensers because they will not sustain content in television, radio, and magazines that does not boost their sales. This means that the media are designed primarily for those with money who buy things. Very few corporations will sponsor any programs or material that is critical of corporate activities or the military-industrial complex.

Third, reporters increasingly are gathering their information from government sources, business entities, or from
"experts" funded by these agents of power. The mass
media assumes that these are "objective" sources of news,
and they rarely challenge those powerful interests; but
other sources of news are harder to find and are scrutinized
carefully through the biased lens of the establishment, if
they are considered at all. The government and the corporate sector have immense financial, human, and technical
resources to generate huge amounts of information for the
media, thus subsidizing and facilitating the work of the
communications media. A comparison between the
resources of the Pentagon and those of the largest peace
organizations shows how overwhelming is this imbalance.
Most scientists and researchers in the universities and in
business have been bought by the government or the
corporations. An analysis of the experts presented on
Public Broadcasting's *MacNeil-Lehrer News Hour* in 1985
showed that 70% of the nonjournalists presented were
either government officials, former government officials, or
from conservative think-tanks.

The fourth factor looked at the criticism of the media,
referred to as "flak." Advertisers are especially concerned
about this and endeavor to make sure that audiences are
not made uncomfortable. Those who criticize powerful
constituencies are seldom heard in the mass media. Such
"unpopular" voices, no matter how brilliant nor well
informed they may be, are rarely allowed on talk shows.
Yet right-wing commentators, who are so well represented
in the major media, often rail on about the "liberal bias" of
the media. How often does a peace activist even get a
chance to speak? In *Manufacturing Consent,* the fifth filter
used in the media was described as "anti-Communism,"
which during the Cold War was a way of describing the
dominant concern; but in the 1996 book, *The Common Good,*
Chomsky explained that the fear used to control people
was broadened out during and after the Reagan years to

include "international terrorism," "drug traffickers," "immigrants, black criminals, welfare mothers,"[10] and others.

A clear dichotomy contrasts how the enemies of the United States are reported in comparison to its allies. Victims of an enemy get extraordinary coverage in the media; but those suffering from the policies of the United States are given as little attention as possible. For example, the murder of the Polish priest, Jerzy Popieluszko, received extensive media coverage; but murders by client states in Latin America are virtually ignored unless the victim happens to be a US citizen. Chomsky and Herman detailed how biased was the coverage of the Indochina wars and the retrospectives such that the idea that these were major war crimes is "inexpressible." That American bombing killed more than a half million Cambodians is not even mentioned; but the atrocities that followed these attacks are emphasized. When the US was convicted by the World Court for mining Nicaraguan harbors, this was a minor story; but when the Reagan administration went against the will of Congress, this became the Iran-Contra scandal.

In 1999 Chomsky published *Profit Over People* on neoliberalism and the global order. He described the "Washington consensus" that has promoted a free-market ideology to apply to other countries in order to increase the profits of the wealthy, while the United States, Britain and other economic powers have used government controls to protect their own economies. In 1945 the US proposed an "Economic Charter of the Americas" to keep Latin American countries from adopting economic nationalism that would raise the living standards of the masses. Thus the US has managed to exploit the cheap labor and natural resources of Latin America for its own profit. In 1948 the CIA intervened in the Italian elections to protect the world capitalist system. Since the end of the Cold War, economic experiments with private capital in Russia have driven a quarter of the population below subsistence. Chomsky noted how the British empire exploited India using the

"Permanent Settlement" two centuries ago, resulting in India's financing 40% of Britain's trade deficit as its textile industry was destroyed by British protectionism. England exported opium from India to China while banning its importation.

Especially since the Reagan presidency, the United States has been enriching the wealthy at the expense of the poor and middle class so that now it has the highest child poverty rate of any industrial country. Thanks to the heartless policies of Margaret Thatcher, one-third of British babies were being born in poverty. Chomsky found that neoliberal doctrines hurt education and health, promote more inequality, and reduce the incomes of workers while helping the very rich get richer. In Latin America the wealthy are exempt from social obligations such as taxes. Chomsky analyzed that the United States and Japan have prospered because they used the British means of market interference. During the Cold War the US used its Food for Peace program as a way to subsidize US agribusiness and shipping while undercutting foreign agriculture. The huge military spending subsidized the private aircraft industry and spread into computers, electronics, automation, biotechnology, communications, and many other private sectors. The Reagan administration provided more protection to US industry for import relief than at any time since the 1930s. These continuing policies amount to "socialism for the rich," according to Chomsky.

He pointed out that Adam Smith, the founding capitalist theorist, warned that the division of labor should not turn workers into objects and that regulation to help workers is always just. Chomsky noted that public opinion in the United States is shifting as now more than 80% think the government is run to benefit special interests, not the people, and they believe that the economic system is inherently unfair; 95% agree that corporations should sacrifice some profits to make things better for workers and communities. The manipulation of people's buying habits and opinions results from a trillion-dollar-a-year marketing industry, one-sixth of the entire economy. Chomsky noted that even the *Wall Street Journal* recognized that President Clinton was on the side of corporate America on issue after issue.

Chomsky explained the United States has used the World Trade Organization (WTO) to pressure seventy countries to open up their markets to US corporations and investors. Against much popular opposition, Brazil decided to privatize its successful Vale Company that controls uranium, iron, and other minerals; its income in 1996 was over $5 billion. The 1997 privatization reduced the Vale labor force by 4,618, but profit growth in the next five years was 36% for its lucky new owners. The UN Food and Agriculture Organization (FAO) has warned developing countries to reverse the policies imposed on them by the "Washington consensus" that are having disastrous effects on people while increasing corporate profits. Chomsky summarized the American values of the WTO as a tool for US intervention in the internal affairs of other nations, taking over crucial sectors of foreign economies by US corporations, benefiting business and the wealthy while shifting costs to the general population, and as a powerful new weapon against democracy. Clinton's re-election campaign was greatly aided by the telecommunications sector, which was rewarded by the 1996 Telecommunications Act.

Most egregious is the Helms-Burton Act, which makes the US impose sanctions on any nation that trades with Cuba. This economic strangulation is a clear violation of ethics and the WTO. Only Israel and Uzbekistan voted with the US against a UN resolution condemning this, and the Organization of American States (OAS) rejected the Helms-Burton Act unanimously. By the late 1990s the United States had used its veto at the United Nations more than seventy times since 1967. The Clinton administration said that the WTO could not force the US to change its laws. Lacking medicine and food, Cuba has managed to train skilled doctors and since 1963 has sent 51,820 doctors, dentists, and nurses to help poor nations, especially in Africa. In 1985 Cuba had more than twice as many specialists helping third-world countries than the US had in the Peace Corps and AID. The so-called Cuban Democracy Act of 1992 caused the number of companies granted US licenses to sell medicines to Cuba to be reduced by 96%. Chomsky wrote that the greatest human rights violator, Colombia, receives more US military aid than any other Latin American country while it terrorizes people in the name of the "drug war."

While speaking in South Africa in 1997, Chomsky noted that during his talk a thousand children would die of preventable diseases. UNICEF has estimated that these tragedies could be alleviated by about ten percent of US military spending. In discussing the Zapatista uprising in response to the North American Free Trade Agreement (NAFTA), Chomsky noted that they were struggling "for work, land, housing, food, health care, education, independence, freedom, democracy, justice, and peace."[11] He reminded readers that a few days after NAFTA was passed, the US Congress financed 100,000 more police with more high security prisons and militaristic "boot camps" for youthful offenders, extended the death penalty, and made sentences more harsh. Chomsky warned that secrecy was trying to bypass public awareness and criticism by giving the President "Fast Track" authority and on the Multilateral Agreement on Investment (MAI) treaty, which would allow a foreign corporation or investor to sue the United States for damages if it restrained their investment. Chomsky complained that the full text of the MAI is not even available to the public. During the stock market boom of the 1990s Chomsky noted that in 1997 half the stocks were owned by the top one percent and 90% by the wealthiest ten percent.

Zinn on US History and Wars

Howard Zinn was born into a poor family of immigrant Jews in New York City on August 24, 1922. He loved to read and learned about social injustice in the novels of Charles Dickens. After being a bombardier in World War II, Howard Zinn worked as a laborer. The G.I. Bill helped him earn his B.A. at New York University, and Zinn got his M.A. and Ph.D. at Columbia University. He observed the anti-Communist hysteria, wrote a thesis on the Colorado coal strike of 1913-14, and published his doctoral dissertation on Fiorello LaGuardia in Congress. In 1956 he was appointed chairman of the history department at Spelman College, where he taught African Americans and participated in the civil rights movement for several years. He advised the Student Nonviolent Coordinating Committee (SNCC) and wrote *SNCC: The New Abolitionists* about their efforts. He found that by the end of 1961 more than 50,000 people had demonstrated for civil rights, and at least 3,600 had been to jail. Zinn estimated that about 150 dedicated SNCC workers in Georgia, Alabama, and Mississippi did much to bring about a civil rights revolution.

In 1965 Zinn began speaking out against the Vietnam War. He described atrocities and gave powerful reasons for ending the Vietnam War in his 1967 book *Vietnam: The Logic of Withdrawal*. At that time the US was spending twenty billion dollars annually on the Vietnam War, and he calculated that this was enough to give every Vietnamese family $5,000, which was nearly ten times their annual income. Each month the US was spending more on the war than it spent annually on the federal poverty program for the Great Society. He discovered that in 1966 the Pentagon paid an average of $34 for condolence to relatives for each Vietnamese killed accidentally but $87 for each rubber tree accidentally destroyed. They were killing four civilians for every enemy soldier killed. Zinn noted that the United States replaced the French as the aggressors in Vietnam, and he observed that the main thrust of the war was bombing and shelling civilians. The number of Vietcong revolutionaries they were fighting in South Vietnam far outnumbered the North Vietnamese soldiers opposing them. To those concerned about the loss of prestige if the

United States pulled out of Vietnam, Zinn answered that compared to being bogged down in a war that they were afraid to lose, a clean and swift withdrawal would be right and would improve the declining prestige. He concluded his book on Vietnam by summarizing his arguments in an imaginary speech by President Johnson announcing that the United States was no longer at war in Vietnam.

During the Tet offensive on January 30, 1968 Zinn traveled with Daniel Berrigan to Hanoi because the North Vietnamese wanted to release the first captured American pilots to someone in the peace movement. Zinn learned that the leaders in Hanoi were willing to negotiate; but when he returned to the United States, no one in the government would even debrief him on what he had learned during his week in Hanoi.

In 1968 Zinn published *Disobedience and Democracy* to refute what he considered nine fallacies on law and order put forth by US Supreme Court justice Abe Fortas in his booklet *Concerning Dissent and Civil Disobedience.* Zinn argued that human laws are fallible. When the laws and the government fail the moral test of protecting human needs, then conscientious citizens have the right to take actions to reform the social or political injustice. He pointed out that during the two greatest crises in American history—the revolution against the British empire and the Civil War that freed the slaves—people had to go beyond the limits of British law and the Constitution. Zinn acknowledged that protesting by civil disobedience is not enough by itself because it does not construct a new society. Also not all forms of civil disobedience are moral or effective. Yet he concluded,

The only way to escape the twin evils
of stagnation and chaotic violence at home,
and to avoid devastating wars abroad,
is for citizens to accept, utilize,
control the disorder of civil disobedience,
enriching it with countless possibilities
and tactics not yet imagined,

to make life more human for us and others on this earth.[12]

Despite his political protests, Zinn got tenure at Boston University, probably because he had published more and had excellent student evaluations. In 1972 he criticized BU President John Silber for inviting US Marines to recruit on campus and for arresting protestors. Zinn was denied raises and teaching assistants even though he had 400 students. He was arrested five times for protesting during the Vietnam War, and he was often called as an expert witness in the trials of demonstrators. When he found that several jurors regretted voting guilty, he wrote about the right of "jury nullification"—that jurors have the right to vote their conscience regardless of the specific instructions of the judge.

Zinn became friends with Daniel Ellsberg and Noam Chomsky when they were in the same affinity group during the demonstrations against the war in 1971. When Beacon Press published a four-volume edition of the *Pentagon Papers*, a political history of the Vietnam War, they asked Zinn and Chomsky to edit an accompanying collection of critical essays. In 1973 Zinn testified for several hours on the history of the Vietnam War during the trial of Ellsberg and Tony Russo , who were accused of revealing military secrets for exposing the *Pentagon Papers*. Zinn argued that this information did not harm the defense of the nation and the people although it might have embarrassed special interests, politicians, and corporations going after tin, rubber, and oil. Apparently the jury would not have convicted them even if the case had not been dismissed because of Nixon's sending men to burglarize the files of Ellsberg's psychiatrist and others to beat him up at an anti-war rally.

Zinn wrote the volume *Postwar America* for the History of American Society series. He could not help emphasizing his own views and dedicated the book to Dave Dellinger for his revolutionary courage. The reviewer James T. Patterson reported that Zinn showed the nasty side of

American life and concluded "by calling for a humane new socialism, the demise of the nation-state, the abolition of prisons, and the end of authoritarianism in personal and familial relationships."[13]

In 1974 Zinn edited *Justice in Everyday Life* that gave accounts by various people on efforts to improve society. The next year he satirized the report on the CIA by a commission under Nelson Rockefeller by calling it "Attica Massacre Chief Clears Assassination Plotters."[14] Zinn wrote a play about the anarchist Emma Goldman, and it was directed by his son in Greenwich Village. In 1976 Zinn's biweekly column in the *Boston Globe* was canceled after he wrote about whom he thought should *not* be honored on Memorial Day.

No politician who voted funds for war,
no business contractor for the military,
no general who ordered young men into battle,
no FBI man who spied on anti-war activities,
should be invited to public ceremonies on this sacred day.[15]

Zinn learned how the writing of history was being revised by people with social concerns. This provided him with the research that enabled him to write his popular *People's History of the United States* in the late 1970s. This book is an excellent supplement to traditional American histories, because it brings out the history of those often neglected before, such as native Americans, African-Americans, women, immigrants, labor movements, socialists, anarchists, etc.

Zinn signed the Pledge of Resistance, and in 1986 he was arrested with 550 people at the federal building in Boston. After being charged with failing to quit the premises, the charges were dropped. He retired from teaching in 1988 in order to do more speaking and writing.

In 1990 Howard Zinn published his *Declarations of Independence* as he cross-examined American ideology. He criticized the very rich class that dominates the media and public policy and the so-called "experts" that serve them. He described how modern politicians use Machiavellian deception which they call "plausible denial." Dissenters like Leo Szilard, Albert Einstein, and Daniel Ellsberg have tried to change the vicious policies that result from the abuse of such power. In discussing violence and human nature he noted that zoologist Konrad Lorenz wrote in his book *On Aggression* that the animal instincts are not as dangerous as our "emotional allegiance to cultural values."[16] Zinn observed that men do not rush into battle with a ferocious desire to kill. Rather, they joined the armed forces for the security of a career, or they were conscripted by law with the threat of imprisonment if they refused. His own experience in war told him that people do not delight in destruction. He noted that at the My Lai massacre several soldiers refused to follow orders to kill, and Warrant Officer Hugh Thompson actually saved some Vietnamese lives by ordering his helicopter crew to fire on American GIs if they shot any more civilians.

Zinn recounted how Mark Twain wrote satires of war hysteria and opposed the Spanish-American War of 1898. Helen Keller in 1916 told American men not to fight but strike and become heroes in construction instead of obedient slaves in a destructive army. Zinn was moved by the anti-war novel *Johnny Got His Gun* by Dalton Trumbo, who had been blacklisted in Hollywood. The lies that Americans were told to get them into the First World War were analyzed by Walter Millis in *The Road to War*. Sinking the *Lusitania* was publicized as an attack on a harmless passenger ship, but later it was learned that it was loaded with munitions to be used against Germans.

Zinn discovered that two weeks before the Atlantic Charter was proclaimed, acting Secretary of State Sumner Welles assured the French they would be allowed to keep their colonies. Zinn pointed out that the United States imposed a total embargo on selling scrap iron and oil to Japan in the summer of 1941. He discovered that John J.

McCloy deleted a footnote that questioned whether the internment of the Japanese on the West Coast was really necessary. Zinn lamented that a million Jews were murdered in Europe in 1942 while the US State Department was checking to see if the story was true. He believed that the war against Hitler probably brought on the massive extermination of the Jews. He questioned a "war against racism" in which the US armed forces were still segregated. Black soldiers were given dangerous jobs like loading munitions, and many were killed at Port Chicago on July 17, 1944 when two transport ships blew up. Survivors who refused to load munitions in unsafe conditions were put in jail.

Zinn challenged the saturation bombing of cities such as Cologne, Essen, Frankfurt, Hamburg, Dresden, and Tokyo. He himself had been ordered to drop napalm on the French resort at Royan in April 1945, because it was occupied by Germans. Five allied planes were lost in the mission, and he went back years later to discover the effects on the town. He wrote a paper to show that the atomic bombing of Hiroshima and Nagasaki was unnecessary. Zinn noted that 350,000 Americans had evaded the draft during that "good war," and 6,000 conscientious objectors went to prison.

Zinn taught a political science course on "Law and Justice in America" in which they explored when disobedience is appropriate. He noted that after Shays' Rebellion, Thomas Jefferson hoped that the government would pardon them because he believed the spirit of resistance to government was worth keeping alive. Zinn described the extreme economic injustices that had gotten worse during the Reagan years, and he felt that *A Theory of Justice* by John Rawls had a philosophical argument for a more just distribution of wealth but not a practical plan that would persuade the corporations. Zinn reported how free speech was hampered by "national security," and he agreed with Chomsky that the media are strongly controlled by the wealthy interests. Dissenters often have to commit civil disobedience to get any attention in the media at all. Zinn noted that Daniel Schorr was fired from CBS for publicizing a suppressed report on the CIA in 1976. The CIA in fact had employees working for many major news outlets such as *Newsweek*, *Time*, the *New York Times*, UPI, and CBS News. In 1982 Ray Bonner was removed from covering Central America for the *New York Times* after he wrote an article critical of US policy in El Salvador. In 1988 it was learned that the FBI was asking librarians to report suspicious behavior. In his final chapter on ultimate power Zinn called for justice without violence.

In 1998 Howard Zinn wrote that the US bombing of Iraq to keep Saddam Hussein from getting weapons of mass destruction was unlikely to fulfill that purpose. In December the US bombed Iraq using 250 cruise missiles that cost $1 million each. He questioned American priorities that killed people abroad while the homeless froze in the US. Zinn did find some cause for hope that demonstrators in Seattle challenged globalization, protectionism, export trade, intellectual property, and other difficult issues that hurt the poor and the environment.

Yugoslavia War

Zinn wrote that the atrocities of Milosevic did not justify US-led NATO committing more atrocities during the Yugoslavia War in 1999. He was horrified that cluster bombs were being used, because he recalled seeing wounded children in Hanoi hospitals in 1968 with tiny pellets in their bodies. He believed that "our" terrorism was just as bad as "their" terrorism. Milosevic should be prosecuted for war crimes, but so should Clinton, Albright, Cohen, and Gen. Wesley Clark. He suggested that they should stop bombing and start talking.

After the US bombing of Yugoslavia for ten weeks in the spring of 1999, Chomsky wrote *The New Military Humanism: Lessons from Kosovo*. Since the Clinton administration claimed that this was a humanitarian intervention, Chomsky examined other cases that were somewhat comparable. The number of refugees created by the bombing was nearly as many as the three-quarters of a million Palestinians, who were displaced in 1948 by Israel's founding war. The Universal Declaration of Human Rights (UDHR), adopted by the United Nations on December 10, 1948, and UN Resolution 194 passed the next day both required respect for the right of refugees; but President Clinton renounced adherence to this UDHR Article 13 (2).

The Serbian government of Slobodan Milosevic took away the autonomy of Kosovo in 1989 and also took control of the Hungarian minority in Vojvodina. The Kosovar intellectual Ibrahim Rugova led a nonviolent movement for the rights of the Albanian Kosovars, and in 1990 they declared Kosovo an independent state. In May 1992 Rugova was elected president with 99.5% of the vote as the Democratic League of Kosovo (LDK) won three-quarters of the seats in the Parliament; but the Serb government considered this Kosovo government illegal. In 1995 the Albanian Kosovars were excluded from the Dayton negotiations as the US partitioned Bosnia-Herzegovina between Croatia and Serbia. As a result the Albanians turned to guerrilla warfare, forming the Kosovo Liberation Army (KLA), and in April 1996 they began killing Serb policemen and civilians. The Clinton administration called the KLA terrorists. The fighting escalated in February 1998 as the KLA took on the Serbian Army and started killing Serbian mail carriers. After Serbian forces massacred nearly a hundred people at the headquarters of the Jashari clan, Albanians rose up to fight the Serbs as the KLA distributed arms. By summer the KLA controlled 40% of Kosovo. In seven months nearly 2,000 Albanians had been killed as about 350,000 fled their homes. In October a cease-fire led to the deployment of 2,000 monitors from the Organization for Security and Cooperation in Europe (OSCE).

Although US intelligence reported that the Kosovo rebels were trying to draw NATO into its independence struggle by provoking Serbian atrocities, NATO took the bait after 45 civilians were massacred at Racak on January

15, 1999. UN refugee workers and Catholic Relief Services warned that the threat of bombing would endanger tens of thousands of refugees hiding in the woods, as NATO bombing would cause these workers to leave. On March 19 the OSCE monitors of the Kosovo Verification Mission were withdrawn to prepare for the bombing, and the Serbs began attacking KLA strongholds. The Serb National Assembly rejected NATO's Rambouillet ultimatum on March 23 but objected to the withdrawal of the monitors as part of the "blackmail" threats made against their country. The next day the Serbs greatly escalated their attacks, and NATO began bombing that night. The US led the NATO forces as the infrastructure of Yugoslavia was targeted. President Bill Clinton and Prime Minister Tony Blair explained that a "new internationalism" was aimed at stopping brutal repression of ethnic groups, but they acted without United Nations authorization.

The war actually increased the ethnic conflict and created about 350,000 more refugees from Kosovo in the next two weeks. NATO commander Wesley Clark stated that neither Clinton nor Blair notified him there would be a flood of refugees. In the first three weeks casualties of Serb civilians were higher than the previous three months, which were supposed to have been a humanitarian catastrophe. By May 1999 the KLA was functioning as the ground forces for NATO, though NATO spokesperson Jamie Shea said NATO had no direct contact with the KLA. By the middle of May more than 300 villages had been burned. American B-52s dropped cluster bombs, which Chomsky noted had been banned except the US had refused to sign the conventions. The unexploded bombs would continue to kill for years. The infrastructure of Vojvodina was attacked because it was an agriculture center, turning the Hungarian democrats there against NATO. In Belgrade and other parts of Yugoslavia the bombing targeted oil refineries, storage areas, ammunition depots, bridges, television and radio transmitters, metal processing plants, and even the president's villa.

In late May 1999 more than 5,000 KLA troops launched an offensive. On June 3 Serbia agreed to a treaty; after they withdrew their forces from Kosovo a week later, the bombing stopped. The UN High Commissioner for Refugees (UNHCR) reported 671,500 refugees left Yugoslavia; but their relief services had been cut back since 1998 because the US was so far behind in paying its UN dues. Yugoslavia had denounced the NATO bombing as illegal aggression against a sovereign state; Russia had opposed it; and China was deeply offended because their embassy in Belgrade was bombed, killing three and wounding many. China was concerned that the United States was starting a new Cold War against socialist countries. Russia, China, and India agreed with Serbia that the bombing violated the UN Charter. After the treaty the peace-keeping mission was under the United Nations as KFOR with mostly NATO forces but also Russians.

Surprisingly, the Russian dissident Alexander Solzhenitsyn said, "The aggressors have kicked aside the UN, opening a new era where might is right."[17] He said that if NATO really wanted to defend the Kosovars, they would have defended the persecuted Kurds too. Chomsky noted that there had been many massacres worse than the one at Racak in East Timor, where in 1999 a few thousand were killed as Indonesians put thousands in concentration camps. In Colombia recently there had been about 2,000 killed annually with 300,000 new refugees, as many as in Kosovo; but in Colombia the atrocities were ongoing. Turkey, a NATO member, had been repressing the Kurds for many years. In the mid-1990s more than a million Kurds had to flee the Turkish army as 3,200 were killed by death squads. Human Rights Watch in 1995 called this a scorched-earth campaign that violated international law. By 1999 Turkey had 300,000 forces in the southeastern region fighting the ethnic war. After Saddam Hussein gassed the Kurds in northern Iraq in March 1988, the United States increased its military aid to Iraq. Thousands of people, many of them children, were killed by unexploded ordinance in Laos; yet the US did nothing to help remove those bombs. In England a suit was brought against Tony Blair and others for using cluster bombs in Kosovo; but American officials could not be charged, because the US had not signed the Ottawa Convention.

The United States has neglected much more severe crises in Africa. In October 1993 thirty-four US soldiers were killed in Somalia; according to Chomsky between 7,000 and 10,000 Somalis were killed before US forces withdrew in March 1994. After that embarrassment, Clinton issued Presidential Directive 25, announcing that future peace-keeping efforts would be limited by the following conditions: the national interest must be at stake; allies must be engaged; there must be a clear mandate and exit strategy; the force must be under US command; and there must be a peace to keep.

Because of the sanctions against Iraq half a million Iraqi children had died, mostly from lack of water purification by 1996 US when Madeleine Albright, soon to become US Secretary of State, said on the 60 Minutes television program that the price was worth it. UN humanitarian coordinator Denis Halliday called this policy genocidal and resigned in protest. The US would not let Iran help Muslims in Bosnia, because Iran had been convicted of a crime by the World Court. The only other nation to have been convicted by the World Court is the United States, which alone vetoed a UN Security Council resolution calling upon all states to obey international law. Chomsky cited these recent examples but also noted that US history has many more instances going back to the extermination of ten million native Americans and the exploitation of African slavery as Europeans conquered North America. He concluded that the new "humanitarian" intervention was just the old intervention. Chomsky also expressed concern that the NATO bombing undermined the already precarious international law.

Chomsky further commented on the implications of the Kosovo war in his 2000 book *A New Generation Draws the*

Line. Representatives of 133 nations with 80% of the world population met in April 2000 in Havana at the South Summit of G-77, and they rejected the "humanitarian intervention" of NATO along with other forms of coercion as part of "globalization." Nelson Mandela accused Britain and the United States of ignoring other nations while playing the world's policemen; he considered their intervention more serious than what was happening in Africa. Political scientist John Mearsheimer observed that the Gulf War and Kosovo War had made India more determined than ever to keep nuclear weapons to deter the United States. When Israel retreated from Lebanon in June 2000, the United Nations General Assembly voted 110-2 to provide nearly $150 million for UNIFIL monitors; Israel and the US alone opposed. Israel was asked to pay $1.28 million to compensate for its attack on a UN compound that killed more than a hundred civilians during its 1996 invasion of Lebanon.

Chomsky discussed recent events in East Timor, where the people voted overwhelmingly for independence on August 30, 1999. The Indonesian military (TNI) reacted to this with numerous atrocities that drove about 800,000 people from their homes, a quarter of a million to West Timor. Amnesty International reported that at the end of the year more than a hundred thousand were still virtually imprisoned there in makeshift camps ruled by militia groups. A month later the UN International Commission of Inquiry on East Timor called for a human rights tribunal under the United Nations for accountability. The US had been supporting the Indonesian military for a long time. A massacre at Dili in 1991 could not be denied, because Pacifica Radio reporters Amy Goodman and Allan Nairn witnessed it as they were severely beaten. Chomsky calculated that since 1975 the US had sold more than one billion dollars worth of weapons to Indonesia, and in the year 1998 the sales had increased five times over the previous year. Britain's Hawk jets were used to terrorize civilians.

George W. Bush's War on Terrorism

On September 11, 2001 Americans were shocked by the terrorist attacks on the World Trade Center and the Pentagon. Despite the many millions of people US bombing had killed in the previous six decades, most Americans had never felt the consequences of mass slaughter as something that could affect them. On September 19, President George W. Bush gave a speech in which he declared war on terrorists, those who harbor terrorists, and even on those who refuse to cooperate with his war on terrorists.

Noam Chomsky gave several interviews in September and early October in order to give people some context to understand the meaning of this traumatic event. He particularly emphasized those aspects of the story that the mass media tended to leave out. Although the analogy of Pearl Harbor had been used, that was actually an attack on two military targets in a US colony. For an attack on the United States itself one has to go back to the War of 1812, though New York's World Trade Center had already been the target of a terrorist bombing in 1993. Chomsky pointed out that much of the world considers the US the leading terrorist state, and he noted that the US was convicted by the World Court in 1986 for the "unlawful use of force"[18] against Nicaragua. This is only one of many examples of international terrorism by the United States. When the Irish Republican Army (IRA) exploded bombs in London, the English did not bomb West Belfast, nor after the Oklahoma City bombing was there a call to bomb militia groups. Chomsky lamented that there was little discussion of solving this crisis by adhering to the rule of law. Instead, there was a drumbeat to attack the Taliban in Afghanistan. Yet killing innocent victims there would likely help the network of Osama bin Laden gain new recruits.

Chomsky asked the fundamental question why this terrible deed was committed. Zbigniew Brzezinski claimed that in 1979 the US supported Islamic terrorists in order to draw the Russians into an "Afghan trap." After the

Russians invaded Afghanistan, the US by way of Pakistan supported a mercenary army of about 100,000 Islamic radicals called Mujahidin. The wealthy Osama bin Laden joined these terrorist camps in the 1980s and was then an ally of the United States. Chomsky suggested that Egypt's Anwar Sadat was assassinated by allied Islamist radicals in 1981, and a suicide bomber drove the US Marines out of Beirut in 1983. Two years later the Reagan administration instigated a terrorist bombing that killed eighty and wounded 250 in Beirut. Israel's 1993 and 1996 invasions of Lebanon killed about 20,000 civilians. Chomsky estimated that in the 1990s Turkey's counterinsurgency campaign against the Kurds killed tens of thousands, drove over two million from their homes, and destroyed 3,500 villages. In retaliation for the bombing of two US embassies in Kenya and Tanzania in August 1998, the US retaliated by destroying the Al-Shifa pharmaceutical plant in Sudan that provided half the medicines for that poor country; it is hard to measure how much misery resulted from that atrocity.

Chomsky brought up the fact that millions in Afghanistan were starving and that a war against their country would be a humanitarian disaster; but few even wanted to discuss this. In forming an alliance against terrorists the United States was willing to let Russia, China, Indonesia, Pakistan, India, Israel, Egypt, Turkey, and Algeria terrorize those rebelling against them. The Taliban had tried to eradicate the huge Afghan heroin production; but the US quickly made alliances with the Northern Alliance and Tajikistan, who were very involved in this lucrative drug-trafficking.

Chomsky warned the US not to fall into Bin Laden's "diabolical trap" by massacring innocent civilians. We must understand the motivations behind the terrorist atrocities and not escalate the cycle of violence. The Taliban offered to turn over Bin Laden if the US would give them evidence of his complicity in the crime. Arundhati Roy in India suggested that the US could extradite Union Carbide chairman Warren Anderson to be prosecuted for the

Bhopal gas leak that killed 16,000 people in 1984. The Haitian government has been asking the US to extradite Emmanuel Constant for the slaughter of 5,000 people in Haiti. Chomsky reminded people that the new US ambassador to the United Nations, John Negroponte, had overseen the terrorist war against Nicaragua when he was ambassador to Honduras in the 1980s.

Retired historian Howard Zinn reflected on Bush's policies in his book *Terrorism and War* in early 2002. He cited a 1997 Defense Science Board report that found increased terrorism directed against the United States was correlated with US intervention in other countries, and he lamented that Bush's desire to increase US domination was likely to make the situation worse. He observed that the bombing of Afghanistan had increased the harm; professor Marc Herold calculated that already 3,700 people had been killed by the bombing as more than 350,000 Afghans were driven from their homes. The *Guardian* reported that a hundred of these were dying of exposure and starvation each day. Zinn doubted that terrorism would be ended by perpetrating more terrorism. He explained that Osama bin Laden turned the al-Qaida network against the US after its foreign policy changed in 1990. Bin Laden particularly resented US military bases in his native land of Saudi Arabia and US support for Israel's crimes against the Palestinians.

Zinn traced the US interest in the oil back to Franklin Roosevelt's agreement with King Ibn Saud of Saudi Arabia during World War II. Zinn recommended that the United States remove its troops from Saudi Arabia, stop the sanctions that cause such suffering in Iraq, and persuade Israel to improve its treatment of the Palestinians. By reducing its military budget, the US could help solve many health problems. Even though he had enthusiastically volunteered for World War II, Zinn after much study came to the conclusion that no war is just, that better alternatives can always be found to the killing of large numbers of people. He observed that the US bombing of Afghanistan did not destroy the al-Qaida leadership nor its network of terrorists. He predicted that if the US extended its war on terrorism from Afghanistan to Iraq that relations with the Muslim world would become much worse. Zinn noted that many of the relatives of the 9-11 victims did not want the US retaliating in revenge. He complained that the Bush administration was giving tax breaks of $70 billion to corporations like IBM, GM, and Ford. Economist Seymour Melman reminded people that spending on war causes economic injustice.

Zinn complained that the USA Patriot Act authorized arbitrary arrests, indefinite detention, and even military tribunals. Constitutional lawyer Nancy Chang warned that it criminalized legitimate political dissent. The patriotic hysteria in the media dismissed any criticism of war as "anti-American." The Afghanistan War was already given $17.5 billion, and Bush's National Missile Defense (NMD) could cost $200 billion. During the panic even liberals were afraid to criticize President Bush after he made outrageously bellicose speeches; the attitude in the country was like a lynch mob. Bush claimed that the US is a peaceful nation, but historian Zinn has shown that since World War II the US has been the most warlike nation. He compared President Bush's order to keep the records of the Reagan administration secret from the American people analogous to Stalin's effort to cover up his sordid past.

Zinn cried out against a foreign policy that uses massive bombing to try to solve problems. Journalists complained that the war in Afghanistan restricted them more than ever before, as they were prevented from showing wounded US soldiers or Afghan civilians. Zinn complained that capitalist corporations promote war in order to make profits on the weapons they make. He reviewed the history of anti-war activity in the United States and noted that since the Vietnam War was stopped, politicians have tried to break out of the "Vietnam syndrome" so that there will be no restraint on their war-making. Yet Zinn remained an optimist, because he trusted in the people and their ability to change the policies of their government. He believed that those who oppose war will be vindicated eventually.

Chomsky on US Hegemony

In 2003 Chomsky published *Hegemony or Survival: America's Quest for Global Dominance.* He noted that only the United States and Israel abstained from resolutions by the United Nations Committee on Disarmament and International Security for measures to prevent the militarization of space and to confirm the 1925 Geneva Protocol against chemical and biological warfare. The Bush administration brought the comprehensive UN weapons inspections in Iraq to a sudden end by launching an invasion without approval of the UN Security Council in March 2003. Many intelligence specialists warned that this would increase international terrorism and the spread of weapons of mass destruction (WMD). So many millions protested this imminent invasion that the press began calling world public opinion the second superpower. The historian Arthur Schlesinger called the invasion of Iraq "anticipatory self-defense" but found it similar to the Japanese attack on Pearl Harbor. International law expert Richard Falk concluded that the invasion of Iraq was a Crime against Peace; Germany's Nazi leaders had been convicted of this at Nuremberg. Chomsky was concerned that the American quest for hegemony was making human survival precarious.

Chomsky reported that between November 2000 and April 2003 Israel's security forces in 175 attacks killed 235 people; of these they suspected 156 had committed crimes. In his war on terrorists George W. Bush began using these liquidation tactics. In late October 2002 the CIA used a Predator drone and its Hellfire missile to kill six suspected al-Qaida operatives while they were driving a car in Yemen; one of those murdered was a US citizen. After 9-11 the Bush administration began declaring people, even US citizens, enemy combatants or suspected terrorists so that they could be imprisoned without a charge or access to a lawyer. The portion of Cuba the US still occupied at Guantanamo Bay was used in order to attempt to escape the jurisdiction of US courts. Chomsky warned that the primacy of law over force that had been an important part of American foreign policy since World War II was being reversed by Bush's new strategy.

The US had rejected UN Resolution 687 that called for an end to sanctions against Iraq after the Security Council determined they had complied by eliminating weapons of mass destruction (WMDs) and their delivery systems. President George H. W. Bush had refused to lift the sanctions as long as Saddam Hussein was in power, and the US would not agree to eliminating WMDs from the Middle East because of Israel. Chomsky noted that President Clinton also followed this policy. Iraq complained that UN inspectors (UNSCOM) were spying for Washington. UNSCOM was withdrawn in December 1998 so that Clinton and British prime minister Tony Blair could bomb Iraq in defiance of the UN. To me it is ironic that at this time Clinton was being impeached for an irrelevant issue while the US Congress was overwhelmingly supporting this bombing, which should be an impeachable offense.

Chomsky noted that George W. Bush was determined to invade Iraq regardless of whether Saddam Hussein had disarmed his country or not, and at the Azores summit in March 2003 Bush said that he would invade even if Saddam Hussein left Iraq. The US attack on an already disarmed Iraq made North Korea and others realize that perhaps only possession of WMDs could deter American attacks. The sympathy for the United States because of the 9-11 attack had been radically reversed. A *Time* magazine poll found that more than 80% of Europeans believed that the US had become the greatest threat to world peace. Turkey refused to allow its territory to be used for the invasion of Iraq because 95% of its people opposed the US policy.

Chomsky reviewed the 1962 Cuban missile crisis when

forty years later it was announced that only the Soviet submarine officer Vasili Arkhipov had prevented the launching of nuclear-armed torpedoes that could have started a war, which President Eisenhower had warned could destroy the northern hemisphere. Yet even after the agreement that ended the crisis, President Kennedy approved covert sabotage against Cuban targets, and according to the Cuban government a CIA team of six men killed 400 Cuban factory workers on November 8, 1962. It is ironic that a plot to kill Castro was initiated on the day Kennedy was assassinated. Bush's anti-terrorism policies have been challenged by his reluctance to extradite Luis Posada Carriles, who was responsible for the 1997 bombings in Cuba and is the prime suspect for the bombing of a Cubana Airlines flight in October 1976 that killed 73 people. Posada had also supported the Contras in the 1980s, and he was convicted in Panama of conspiring to assassinate Fidel Castro in 2000. Yet in 1998 the FBI arrested five Cubans who had infiltrated anti-Castro terrorist groups in the United States, and they were sentenced to long prison terms.

Once again Chomsky reviewed the imperial strategy of the United States and its disregard for international law. The World Court had ordered the US to pay indemnities for its mining Nicaraguan harbors in the 1980s, but this was contemptuously ignored. Reparations were estimated at $17 billion, the amount Iraq was obligated to pay Kuwait for its 1990 invasion that killed about the same number of people as Bush I's invasion of Panama a few months earlier. Chomsky noted that Latin Americans know that the United States is a major sponsor of terrorism, and he asked why the Cubans and Nicaraguans would not feel justified in attacking the United States by Bush's logic after 9-11.

Over the years the United States has supported such dictators as the Shah of Iran, George Papadopoulos in Greece, Saddam Hussein in his war against Iran, Ferdinand Marcos in the Philippines, Baby Doc Duvalier in Haiti, Nicolae Ceausescu in Romania, Suharto in Indonesia,

Mobutu Sese Seko in Zaire, South Korean leaders prior to 1987, and Manuel Noriega in Panama. George W. Bush has closed his eyes to the human rights violations of many dominant leaders who have agreed to be allies in his war on terrorists, including Islam Karimov in Uzbekistan, Saparmurat Niyazov in Turkmenistan, and Teodoro Obiang in Equatorial Guinea. The US has extended its network of military bases to Bulgaria and Romania, and the invasion and occupation of Afghanistan has enabled the US to build new bases there and in Central Asia. The US has more than seven hundred military bases in at least forty countries, plus others that are kept secret. The United States has insisted on maintaining its base on Okinawa ever since the San Francisco Peace Treaty (SFPT) in 1951 despite protests from the Okinawans. Neither China, Korea, nor the Philippines ever received any reparations from imperial Japan's conquests, but the US made Japan pay for the costs of its post-war occupation.

Chomsky cited US intelligence and other sources for the estimate that Israel has several hundred nuclear weapons and that it is developing chemical and biological weapons. The air and armored forces of the Israel Defense Forces (IDF) are considered more advanced than any NATO nation's except the US. In the Middle East the US-Israel-Turkey alliance has been called an "axis of evil." Twelve percent of Israel's offensive aircraft are based in Turkey. Early in 2002 the Arab League accepted a Saudi Plan that offered Israel full recognition and integration into the region if they would withdraw to the 1967 borders. Chomsky noted that American public opinion supports such a proposal and also equalizing the aid the US gives to Israel with comparable aid to the Palestinians under a negotiated settlement. The US has continued its support of Israel even while they have been illegally building new settlements in the West Bank in the 1990s and recently. Part of Bush II's "road map" requires Israel to cut public sector jobs and wages while lowering taxes; this proposal caused 700,000 workers to go on strike. George W. Bush has called the war criminal Ariel Sharon "a man of peace," and the wall Israel is building in the West Bank will leave nearly 100,000 Palestinians and much rich agricultural land on the Israeli side. Another quarter million Palestinians will be isolated.

Chomsky commented that useful truisms are no longer followed. The first is that actions should be evaluated as to their likely consequences. The second is that the standards we apply to others should also apply to ourselves. He recalled that the first war on terrorism was declared in 1981 by the Reagan administration. Unwanted facts were ignored, and terrorist attacks carried out by the US and its allies were even praised. After the attacks of September 11, according to a Gallup poll most people preferred that the US government extradite the terrorists to stand trial rather than attack militarily the country where they were based. In Europe support for military action ranged from 8% in Greece to 29% in France. In Latin America the range was from only 2% in Mexico to a high of 16% in Panama. Support was much lower if civilian targets were to be included. This is assuming that those who were responsible for the attack were known; but they were not known as the US government admitted eight months later. Even the thousand Afghan leaders who opposed the Taliban asked the US to stop the air raids in October 2002. The US bombing was also opposed by the Afghan women's organization RAWA and the relief agencies. The Taliban had offered to hand over suspected criminals, but the US refused to provide any evidence of who the criminals were. Yet when Haiti renewed its request that the US extradite Emmanuel Constant, whose paramilitary forces had murdered thousands in the early 1990s with support from Bush I and Clinton, the US Government did not even respond because of concerns that Constant might reveal contacts between his state terrorists and Washington.

Many have pointed out that destroying al-Qaida will have little effect if the political repression and economic injustices that provoke terrorists continue to persist. The US approach of firing missiles and dropping bombs tends to spread violence like a virus. A United Nations report found that during the period of threats to invade Iraq recruitment for al-Qaida increased in more than thirty countries, and since the US occupation Iraq has become a magnet for terrorists who want to attack Americans. Ami Ayalon, who ran Israel's General Security Service (Shabak) in the late 1990s, learned that those who fight terror without facing its underlying grievances desire an unending war, which Bush II apparently has accepted. Chomsky observed that the reasons why the terrorists seem to hate Americans are easily found in the policies of the United States. Anger is increasing in Pakistan because Musharraf's military regime has delayed democracy as it cooperates with the US war on terrorists. The US support for the repressive regimes in Saudi Arabia and Egypt also fuels Arab anti-Americanism.

Chomsky warned that an even greater threat to human survival than the war on terrorism is found in the weapons of mass destruction and the US attempt to achieve world domination by gaining a monopoly on the militarization of space. The developing program of missile defense is provoking a new arms race. China is greatly expanding its arsenal of nuclear-armed missiles and will probably add multiple warheads (MIRV). This causes India to react, and that provokes Pakistan. American intelligence predicts that Russia and China are likely to sell countermeasures to North Korea, Iran, Syria, and other countries. China has been urgently pleading since 1998 to keep space for only peaceful uses, and since then the US militarization of space programs has blocked the UN Conference on Disarmament from making progress. Chomsky noted that even Sam Nunn dismissed the 2002 Bush-Putin SORT treaty as meaningless. Missile defense is getting more funds than the US State Department and four times as much as what is spent on safeguarding dangerous weapons in the former Soviet Union. In May 2003 the US Congress approved Bush's program for a new generation of nuclear weapons. Analysts have found that "missile defense" is not really for defense but combines with offensive forces to achieve the goal of military supremacy and global domination. To monopolize the militarization of space, the US would have to be able to protect satellites that are easy targets. This means that they would have to achieve "full spectrum dominance." According to the Strategic Master Plan of the Air Force Space Command, the military ownership of space would

provide war-fighting commanders the ability to rapidly
deny, delay, deceive, disrupt, destroy,
exploit and neutralize targets
in hours/minutes rather than weeks/days
even when US and allied forces
have a limited forward presence.[19]

Hypersonic drones (airplanes directed by remote control) are already being used to monitor and destroy targets. In the Clinton era the Space Command put out publicity indicating their goal of "dominating the space dimension of military operations to protect US interests and investments."[20] The economic globalization process that is widening the gap between the rich and the poor is expected to require this full-spectrum dominance to prevent rogue elements from gaining WMDs and to fight terrorism that resists the US hegemony.

Noam Chomsky raised the existential question whether hegemony will continue to be considered more important than survival, as it has for the past half century. The United States recently refused to reaffirm or strengthen the 1967 Outer Space Treaty that reserved space for peaceful purposes, and it is the only nation out of 66 member states that is opposing formal negotiations on outer space. Since 2001 the United States has declined to fund and refused to cooperate with international verification of the ban on chemical weapons. The Bush II administration has also withdrawn from negotiations for verification of the 1972 Biological and Toxic Weapons Convention, claiming the pharmaceutical and biotechnology companies must protect their trade secrets. The US apparently has three clandestine defense projects related to bioweapons, and it is suspected that Russia and the US are working on genetically engineering vaccine-resistant anthrax. Thus a bioweapons arms race is also likely, and the 2002 Hart-Rudman report warned that the chances are increasing that terrorists could use chemical or bioweapons.

The Bush administration has ignored and announced that it no longer supports the essential Article 6 of the important Nuclear Non-Proliferation Treaty (NPT) that calls for complete nuclear disarmament. Bush has revoked the Anti-Ballistic Missile (ABM) Treaty and opposed the Comprehensive Test Ban Treaty. Chomsky noted that Bush undermined the first UN conference to try to control the black market in small arms and that he designated John Bolton to back US opposition to international advocacy by non-governmental organizations (NGOs).

Despite the overwhelming evidence that Chomsky garnered to show how precarious human survival is, he concluded his book with the hope that recent developments in human rights culture and solidarity movements in Central America and elsewhere could join with the global justice movements that are becoming a superpower. These he believed could evolve into a global movement that could yet save our civilization.

Notes

1. Quoted in *Noam Chomsky* by Robert F. Barsky, p. 33.
2. Chomsky, Noam, *American Power and the New Mandarins.*
3. *Ibid.*, p. 165.
4. *Ibid.*, p. 374-375.
5. Chomsky, Noam, and Edward S. Herman, *The Washington Connection and Third World Fascism*, p. 3.
6. Alan Riding, "Balaguer and His Firm Ally, the U.S." *New York Times* (6 June 1975) quoted in *The Washington Connection and Third World Fascism*, p. 243.
7. Chomsky, Noam, *Deterring Democracy*, p. 2-3.
8. *Ibid.*, p. 148.

9. *Ibid.*, p. 161.
10. Chomsky, Noam, *The Common Good*, p. 42.
11. Chomsky, Noam, "The Zapatists Uprising" in *Profit Over People*, p. 122.
12. *Disobedience and Democracy* by Howard Zinn, p. 123.
13. Quoted in *Howard Zinn: A Radical American Vision* by Davis D. Joyce, p. 144.
14. "The CIA, Rockefeller, and the Boys in the Club" in *The Zinn Reader*, p. 326.
15. "Whom Will We Honor Memorial Day?" in *The Zinn Reader*, p. 329.
16. Quoted in *Declarations of Independence* by Howard Zinn, p. 39.
17. Chomsky, Noam, *The New Military Humanism*, p. 9.
18. Chomsky, Noam, *9-11*, p. 23.
19. Quoted in *Hegemony or Survival* by Noam Chomsky, p. 228.
20. *Ibid.*, p. 229.

16

Protesting the Bush-Iraq Wars

The bombing constitutes the most grievous
violation of international law.
It is intended to destroy the civilian life and economy of Iraq.
It is not necessary, meaningful or permissible
as a means of driving Iraq from Kuwait.
Ramsey Clark, letter to Bush, February 12, 1991

From several trips I have made to Iraq,
it is obvious where one should go to find
overwhelming evidence of a weapon of mass destruction.
Inspectors have only to enter the wards of any hospital
to see that the sanctions themselves are a lethal weapon,
destroying the lives of Iraq's most vulnerable people.
In children's wards, tiny victims writhe in pain
on blood-stained mats, bereft of anesthetics and antibiotics.
Thousands of children, poisoned by contaminated water,
die from dysentery, cholera, and diarrhea.
Others succumb to respiratory infections
that become fatal full-body infections.
Five thousand children under age five perish each month.
Almost a million children who are severely malnourished
will bear lifelong consequences of
stunted growth, brain deficiencies, disabilities.
At the hands of UN/US policy makers,
childhood in Iraq has, for thousands, become a living hell.
Kathy Kelly, February 1998

If people in the US had seen their images, day after day,
the economic sanctions would never have lasted long enough
to claim the lives of over a half million children.
Kathy Kelly, *Other Lands Have Dreams* 103

George Bush will invade Iraq
unless restrained by the United Nations....
A UN or US policy of selecting enemies of the US for attack
is criminal and can only heighten hatred,
division, terrorism and lead to war....

Do not let this happen.
Ramsey Clark, letter to Kofi Annan, September 30, 2002

We feel sure that preventing a "next" war requires
effectively countering the present war propaganda.
Kathy Kelly, *Other Lands Have Dreams* 78

Yearn for peace.
Try very hard not to pay for war.
And, most of all, think of the children.
Kathy Kelly, *Other Lands Have Dreams* 150

Let us, collectively, free our minds, soften our hearts,
comfort the wounded, put down our weapons,
and reassert ourselves as human beings by putting an end to war.
Camilo Mejia, 2005

Clark on the 1991 Iraq War

Ramsey Clark has written an insightful account of the causes and effects of the 1991 war with Iraq in *The Fire This Time: U. S. War Crimes in the Gulf*. Clark was Assistant Attorney General and then Attorney General during the Kennedy and Johnson administrations. Clark recounted the pertinent history of Iraq, Kuwait, and the United States. After the First World War in 1921 Sir Percy Cox of the British Colonial Office drew new borders between Iraq and Saudi Arabia, establishing Kuwait as a small kingdom that took away most of Iraq's coastline. The rich oil deposits in the region were exploited and controlled by seven oil companies from England, France, and the United States until Iran's Mossadegh government nationalized their oil in 1951, taking it from the Anglo-Iranian Oil Company (now British Petroleum). Western nations imposed sanctions on Iran until 1953, when the CIA helped overthrow Mossadegh. Then General Norman Schwarzkopf Sr. helped Shah Reza Pahlevi set up the oppressive SAVAK state police. The Hashemite monarchy in Iraq was overthrown in 1958 by a nationalist revolution led by Abdel Karim Kassem, and two years later the Organization of Petroleum

Exporting Countries (OPEC) was founded to counter the western oil monopolies. In 1963 a CIA-backed coup killed Kassem and thousands of his supporters.

Five years later the secular Ba'ath Party gained power in Iraq, and they nationalized Iraq's oil in 1972. In May of that year President Nixon, Henry Kissinger, and the Shah of Iran began instigating the Kurds in northern Iraq to rebel by giving them weapons. When Iraq agreed to share the disputed Shatt-al-Arab waterway with Iran in 1975, the Shah stopped supporting the Kurds. The Shah was overthrown by the Iranian revolution in February 1979. Saddam Hussein replaced al-Bakr as president of Iraq in June, and the next month he executed 21 government officials. After the Americans in the Tehran embassy were taken hostage by the Iranian radicals in November, US National Security Advisor Zbigniew Brzezinski began urging Iraq to attack Iran to take back the waterway. A year later Iraq's Saddam Hussein, guided by US intelligence, went to war against Iran, a war that would last eight years and kill about a million people. Weaker Iraq was supported in this war effort at first by the Soviet empire, Arab states including Kuwait and Saudi Arabia, and then by the western powers Britain, France, West Germany, and the United States, which provided satellite and AWACS intelligence. Egypt, which was receiving $2 billion per year in US aid, sent Iraq troops, tanks, and heavy artillery. Another US aid recipient, Turkey, helped Iraq by fighting its Kurdish rebels. Saudi Arabia provided money, and Kuwait alone loaned Iraq $30 billion.

The US sold arms worth $20 billion to Gulf states, and the Reagan administration illegally allowed Saudi Arabia to transfer weapons to Iraq. In 1972 the US had declared Iraq a nation that supports terrorism, but the Reagan regime took Iraq off that list. How the White House illegally armed Iraq is explained in detail by investigative reporter Alan Friedman in *Spider's Web*. In December 1983 President Reagan sent special envoy Donald Rumsfeld to Baghdad to restore diplomatic relations with Saddam

Hussein's government and to offer US loan guarantees to Iraq. The next spring the Export-Import Bank sent Iraq $500 million. The US also became Iraq's major trading partner by increasing its purchases of Iraqi oil. Vice President Bush, the State Department, and the CIA urged the Export-Import Bank to finance US exports to Iraq. The Atlanta branch of the Italian Banca Nazionale del Lavoro arranged for $5.5 billion in fraudulent loans that were guaranteed by the Commodity Credit Corporation. In 1986 a CIA team was sent to Baghdad as military advisors. Meanwhile Oliver North had been secretly shipping arms to Iran until this illegal trade was exposed in late 1986. The next year the US helped Iraq by protecting Kuwaiti oil tankers. In the late 1980s CIA fronts in Saudi Arabia and Chile sent 73 weapons transactions to Baghdad that included weapons-grade anthrax and equipment to repair rockets.

The Iraq-Iran War ended with a cease-fire on August 7, 1988, and the next day Kuwait drastically increased its oil production, breaking OPEC agreements and driving the price from $21 a barrel down to $11. The *New York Times* calculated that this would cost Iraq $14 billion a year. While Iraq had been preoccupied fighting Iran, Kuwait had moved the border to the north and, using slant-drilling technology supplied by the US, was pumping oil from Iraq's Rumaila oil field. Iraq needed peace to rebuild and pay its $80 billion war debt, but it was being economically squeezed; Iraq's inflation was at 40% as the *dinar* sank. During an Arab summit meeting at Amman in February 1990 Saddam Hussein asked the US to withdraw from the Gulf and alerted others that the US wanted to dominate the Gulf region and fix oil prices. The next month Kuwait and the United Arab Emirates (UAE) refused to follow OPEC production limits. Israel had bombed Iraq's nuclear power complex in 1981, and in April 1990 Saddam Hussein proposed that the Middle East become a nuclear, chemical, and biological weapons-free zone. In May, Saddam Hussein complained of economic warfare, and on July 17 he publicly accused Kuwait and the US of conspiring to destroy Iraq's economy. He warned them, and the next day Iraqi troops moved to the Kuwaiti border.

Since the 1979 Iranian revolution and the Soviet invasion of Afghanistan, the United States had been developing the Rapid Deployment Joint Task Force (RDJTF) to back up the Carter Doctrine's pledge to protect Middle Eastern oil as vital to US national security. By 1985 the US Central Command (CENTCOM) had gotten Saudi Arabia to agree to provide access. Only after the Iraq-Iran War ended did the US complain that Saddam Hussein had used chemical weapons on the Kurds six months before. Yet the US had helped supply such weapons that also had been used against Iran. The US Senate voted to cancel technology and food sales to Iraq. In 1989 CENTCOM's war plan 1002 was revised to make Iraq the enemy instead of the Soviet Union. The end of the Cold War meant that the US was no longer deterred from being aggressive in this region. Early in 1990 the CENTCOM commander General Norman Schwarzkopf Jr. told Congress that Middle Eastern oil is the West's lifeblood, and he recommended a permanent military presence in the region. He also conducted four war games directed at Iraq; some of these were based on an Iraqi invasion of Kuwait. On July 25 the US announced more Gulf war exercises; but US ambassador April Glaspie told Saddam Hussein that State Department policy was that the US had no position on Arab-Arab conflicts.

On August 2, 1990 Iraq invaded Kuwait. President Bush immediately prohibited US trade with Iraq and froze $30 billion in Iraqi assets, making Iraq unable to pay its UN dues. The US insisted that Iraq's vote be taken away even though the US owed the UN $1.6 billion in unpaid dues at the time. The same day a US battle group of seven warships was dispatched, and the next day the United Nations Security Council condemned Iraq. Saddam Hussein told Jordan's King Hussein that he would withdraw if the Arab League did not condemn Iraq. King Hussein tried to persuade Egypt's Hosni Mubarak; but Egypt was pressured by the US and introduced the condemnation resolution. So instead of withdrawing, Saddam Hussein claimed that Kuwait was part of Iraq. On August 6 the UN Security Council imposed international sanctions on Iraq, and the next day the US persuaded King Fahd to let the US military use territory in Saudi Arabia. The US claimed that Iraqi troops were near the Saudi border, but satellite photos later refuted this. On August 8 President Bush ordered 40,000 troops to defend Saudi Arabia. Four days later Saddam Hussein offered to withdraw from Kuwait if Israel would pull out of the occupied territories. Then he made another offer without linking it to Israel, but the US rejected these. Saddam Hussein even offered to debate President Bush and Prime Minister Thatcher on television. In September embargoed Iraq began rationing food supplies. Chomsky considered Iraq's invasion of Kuwait roughly comparable to Israel's invasion of Lebanon in 1978 or 1982 and the US invasion of Panama in 1989.

In the United States the media began demonizing Saddam Hussein, and Secretary of State James Baker even argued that the war was necessary to provide jobs for the sagging economy. When a poll showed that Americans would support an invasion to prevent Iraq from getting nuclear weapons, that argument was used even though the International Atomic Energy Agency (IAEA) estimated that Iraq was at least three years away from having even one atomic bomb. A girl, who turned out to be the daughter of the Kuwaiti ambassador, testified before a Congressional committee that Iraqi soldiers had taken babies from incubators, but this was later exposed as a hoax devised by the public relations firm Hill & Knowlton. By October, Bush had massed 400,000 US troops in the region, and this increased to 573,000 before the war began. President Bush refused to negotiate except to give Iraq an ultimatum to withdraw by January 15, 1991, the UN deadline. The United States used bribery and threats to get the United Nations Security Council to give it authorization for the war. Ethiopia, Zaire, and Colombia got new aid. China got a loan from the World Bank and better diplomatic relations.

After its vote, the Soviet Union was loaned $4 billion by Saudi Arabia, Kuwait, and the UAE. Egypt altogether had $14 billion of debt canceled. Cuba and Yemen were punished for not voting in favor. The UN allowed the US and its allies to act without any limitation, and the US never even reported what it did. Essentially the UN had relinquished its authority to the US.

On January 16 Bush ordered General Schwarzkopf to begin the attack. Iraq was immediately hit with thousands of missiles and bombs that destroyed 85% of its power and vital services within two days. This attack on the civilian infrastructure that destroyed Iraq's energy, sewage, and water systems has been considered a form of biological warfare because of the diseases caused. This was probably the most one-sided war in history, and it is more accurate to call it a massacre or genocide. Iraq had between 125,000 and 150,000 soldiers killed, while the US lost only 148 killed in combat, 37 of them by "friendly fire." In six weeks the US flew 109,000 sorties over Kuwait and Iraq. Although the purpose was supposed to be to drive the Iraqi soldiers out of Kuwait, 88,500 tons of explosives were dropped on Iraq; only 6,520 tons were the precision-guided "smart bombs," which were so well publicized.

On February 13 a US bomb killed 1,500 civilians in a Baghdad bomb shelter, and two days later President Bush urged the Iraqi people to overthrow Saddam Hussein. On February 21 Soviet diplomats announced that Iraq had agreed to withdraw unconditionally from Kuwait. The US gave them two days to do so before starting the ground attack. On February 26 as Iraqi troops tried to retreat or surrender along the Basra road, thousands were slaughtered during the "turkey shoot" on the "highway of death." Two days later Iraq and the US agreed on a cease-fire; but two days after that, thousands of Iraqi soldiers were killed in another battle that did not kill a single American.

Ramsey Clark estimated that the bombing killed at least 25,000 Iraqi civilians directly and another 25,000 indirectly. American bombing hit 28 hospitals, 52 community clinics, and 676 schools, completely destroying 38 schools. Civilian vehicles on highways were strafed. The Pentagon admitted that civilian targets were attacked to demoralize the people and make the sanctions more effective. Modern Iraq was reduced to a pre-industrial condition as sewage and sanitation systems were destroyed; power was scarce, and most communications systems could not operate. The Iraqi people were held hostage as the US and its allies hoped that Saddam Hussein would be overthrown, causing tens of thousands to die of starvation and disease. After President Bush had repeatedly urged the southern Shi'is and northern Kurds to rise up against Saddam Hussein, he let them be slaughtered by the ruthless dictator, further weakening the country.

The embargo imposed to get Iraq to leave Kuwait was not lifted, and continuing sanctions prevented recovery. Oil-exporting Iraq had been importing 70% of its food. With its assets frozen it had little revenue to purchase food. In June 1992 the US even bombed grain and wheat fields near Mosul in northern Iraq. The United States dominated the UN committee that severely restricted Iraq's importation of food and medicine. These conditions caused several thousand Iraqis, many of them children, to die each month and would continue for at least a dozen years. The sanctions were not lifted because Iraq was expected to pay at least $70 billion in reparations despite its previous debt and ruined country. The cost of rebuilding Iraq was estimated at $200 billion. The United Nations offered to let Iraq sell $1.6 billion worth of oil each six months; but 30% of this was to go for reparations and 5% for weapons destruction and border decisions, leaving Iraq with $1.04 billion over six months for food and medicine even though that would only cover food alone for four months. Iraq considered the offer so unfair that they declined. The UN committee gave most of the disputed Ramaila oil field to Kuwait.

The US Congress estimated that the first Gulf War cost the US $61.1 billion; but the superpower had become a mercenary and was reimbursed for $54 billion of this in cash and services. Kuwait contributed $16 billion, Saudi Arabia $16 billion, Japan $10 billion, Germany more than $6 billion, and the United Arab Emirates (UAE) $4 billion. Japan and Germany did not participate militarily in the coalition because of their treaties made at the end of World War II. The United Kingdom spent $4.1 billion.

The intensive bombing also caused an environmental disaster. In August 1990 the Bush administration had signed a waiver to exempt the military operations from the National Environmental Protection Act. In December 1990 the United Nations passed a resolution to prohibit attacks on nuclear facilities; but Gen. Schwarzkopf announced that these were primary targets, and on January 23 General Colin Powell confirmed that Iraq's two nuclear reactors had been destroyed. A week later Schwarzkopf said that eighteen chemical, ten biological, and three nuclear plants had been attacked. The US and British aircraft launched some 50,000 rockets and missiles containing depleted uranium (DU), and the US forces fired a total of 944,000 rounds of the DU armor-piercing shells. The uranium-238 causes cancer and birth defects and will remain in those areas indefinitely. Iraq did spill and burn oil, but Saudi scientists estimated that 30% of the oil spilled was caused by the bombing. The oil spilled into the Gulf was estimated to be twenty times that of the *Exxon Valdez* spill, by far the worst in history. University of Toronto Peace Institute researchers have estimated that 30% of all environmental degradation in the world is caused by military activities. Clark also summarized the human rights abuses of foreign nationals that were reported by Middle East Watch in Kuwait after the Iraqis departed. Women in Kuwait had no civil rights.

Ramsey Clark noted that the media self-censorship and manipulation by the Pentagon that he had found in the Grenada and Panama invasions became even worse in this tightly controlled war. Clark had legally defended the 340 civilian victims of the US bombing in April 1986 of Qaddafi's private residence in Libya; but the press had refused to cover the story, and the judge threw out the case, fining Clark's law office $20,000 to deter others from filing such suits. Clark also wrote how the US media had neglected to report that the Thai military slaughtered hundreds of students in 1976, that Indonesia murdered thousands in East Timor, and that Turks were killing thousands of Kurds. The Pentagon pools that took some reporters to battle scenes were so closely controlled that many reporters preferred not to go. Walter Cronkite said military briefings in Saudi Arabia were "ridiculously inadequate," and he called the US military arrogant. *The Nation*, the *Village Voice*, and *Harper's Magazine* tried to test the constitutionality of the press rules, but the courts were too slow to help. News stories and film footage were censored by the military.

So Ramsey Clark and award-winning documentary film-maker Jon Alpert went to Iraq themselves, and in the first week of February during the war Alpert took six hours of video in Baghdad and Basra. Of the major news networks only the *MacNeil-Lehrer News Hour* would show a short segment of it. On February 12, 1991 Clark wrote a long letter to President Bush describing what he witnessed in Iraq and asking him to stop the war crimes. Some journalists were fired for reporting something besides the US side of the war. An incident in which Americans dressed as Iraqis went in Soviet-built helicopters to place homing devices for the bombing was covered up. One of these helicopters was shot down by Americans, and Clark noted that this CIA operation violated the Geneva Convention. Most of all, Clark complained that the media did not report the effects by the US bombing on the Grenadians, the Libyans, the Panamanians, and the Iraqis.

On January 16, 1991, the day the attack began, Congressman Henry Gonzalez submitted a resolution for the impeachment of President Bush on five charges. Clark expressed concern that the United States was seeking military supremacy and committing crimes with impunity. When the *USS Stark* was torpedoed during the Iraq-Iran

War, Iraq paid $36 million in damages; but when the US shot down a commercial Iranian airliner in 1987, killing 270 people, the US paid nothing.

A peace coalition had been organized to try to stop US military intervention in the Middle East, and Clark's op-ed piece "Peril from an Imperial Presidency" was printed in the *Los Angeles Times* on August 24, 1990. That fall rallies in New York and San Francisco drew 20,000 people. Two days after the war started, a hundred thousand people gathered across from the White House, and an even larger crowd demonstrated in San Francisco; yet a few pro-war supporters were given equal coverage by the media. The Commission of Inquiry for the International War Crimes Tribunal held its first hearings in New York City on May 11, 1991. These war crimes tribunals were held in thirty US cities and more than twenty countries but were ignored by the American media; one *New York Times* reporter said he would be fired if he wrote about it. Yet these tribunals were given substantial coverage in other countries.

Clark and others carefully documented the violations of international law, citing the US Constitution, the UN Charter, the Nuremberg Principles, and the Geneva Conventions. Protocol I of the 1977 Additional Geneva Convention states in Article 48,

> In order to ensure respect for and protection of
> the civilian population and civilian objects,
> the Parties to the conflict shall at all times distinguish
> between the civilian population and combatants
> and between civilian objects and military objectives
> and accordingly shall direct their operations
> only against military objectives.[1]

Article 54 states,

> 1. Starvation of civilians as a method of warfare is prohibited.
> 2. It is prohibited to attack, destroy, remove
>   or render useless objects indispensable
>   to the survival of the civilian population,

such as foodstuffs, agricultural areas for the production
of foodstuffs, crops, livestock,
drinking water installations
and supplies and irrigation works,
for the specific purpose of denying them
for their sustenance value
to the civilian population or to the adverse Party,
whatever the motive, whether in order to starve out civilians,
to cause them to move away, or for any other motive.[2]

Article 55 states that care should be taken to protect the natural environment against damage. Clark charged that the one-sided casualty figures proved that the force used was not proportional to a legitimate military objective, thus violating the Hague Convention.

The nineteen charges against Bush and others included provoking the war; destroying Iraq economically and militarily; bombing civilian targets; bombing indiscriminately; slaughtering unresisting soldiers; using prohibited weapons; attacking dangerous installations; invading Panama and killing Panamanians; corrupting the UN; usurping authority of the US Congress; waging war on the environment; urging Shi'is and Kurds to rebel and then occupying parts of Iraq; depriving Iraqi people of medicine, potable water, food, and other necessities; continuing to assault Iraq after the cease-fire; violating human rights; destroying Iraq's economy by threatening famine and epidemic; controlling and manipulating media coverage; and controlling Gulf oil resources. One year after the war ended, the 22 judges from 18 nations found the absent defendants guilty of all the charges. Clark noted that this was the first time a victorious government had been charged with war crimes on its own soil.

The Commission also made more than fifty proposals to remedy the situation, such as ending the sanctions, sending emergency food and supplies, removing unexploded bombs, assessing legitimate reparations, ceasing military threats, and withdrawing foreign troops. Long-term proposals include prohibiting weapons of mass destruction, disarmament, prohibiting military in foreign countries, creating effective institutions to resolve disputes and prevent war, reforming the United Nations, promoting health, agriculture, clean water, fair labor, education, birth control, housing, environmental protection and proper use of resources, preventing economic exploitation, and restricting the use of embargoes and sanctions. The United States needs to be liberated from militarism, unconstitutional government, plutocratic control, concentration of wealth, punitive social control, and the consequences of foreign intervention. The media also needs to be freed from the corporate monopolies. Peace and justice organizations need to grow and spread their influence so that people can monitor and reform governmental institutions.

Sanctions Against Iraq

In response to Iraq's invasion of Kuwait, on August 6, 1990 UN Security Council Resolution 661 passed 13-0 with Yemen and Cuba abstaining; it called for all states to boycott Iraq and Kuwait. Three days later President Bush strengthened US sanctions against Iraq. On August 13 Secretary of State Jim Baker announced that the US would "interdict" Iraqi oil shipments, and the White House announced that foodstuffs would be included in the ban. UNSCR 665 called upon all states to halt all shipping to and from Iraq. Bulgaria wanted to ship baby food to Iraq, but in September the US and western nations blocked this. On November 29 UNSCR 678 passed 12-2 and authorized member states to "restore international peace and security in the area." China abstained. In response to Yemen's vote against, two days later the US canceled all its $24 million in annual aid to Yemen. The United Nations Children's Fund (UNICEF) reported that 32,464 Iraqi children had died because of the sanctions by the end of 1990.

On January 16, 1991 the US began the bombing that destroyed Iraq's power stations, electrical grids, sewage and sanitation systems, food production and storage facilities, water purification and desalination plants, and other infrastructure. After two days the incubators in Iraq no longer functioned. By February the Iraqi civilians' daily intake of calories had fallen from 3,340 to 1,000. In March the World Health Organization (WHO) calculated that Iraq's water supply had dropped to 5% of the pre-war level. On April 3 UNSCR 687 called upon all states to continue the sanctions against Iraq until it dismantled and destroyed its chemical, biological, and nuclear weapons programs and its ballistic missiles. The Security Council was to review compliance with its resolutions every sixty days. The US without UN authorization imposed "no-fly zones" over northern and southern Iraq. Prime Minister John Major announced in May that England would veto any attempt to weaken the sanctions as long as Saddam Hussein was still in power. UNSCR 692 established a war damage fund to collect revenues from future Iraqi oil exports. A Harvard medical team predicted that 170,000 Iraqi children would die by the end of 1991 because of the war and sanctions. Basra had two doctors to cope with 80,000 people suffering from a cholera epidemic. A UN official announced that $6.85 billion would be needed in the next year to avert massive starvation in Iraq, but only $216 million was raised. UNSCR 705 required Iraq to pay 30% of future oil revenues for reparations, and UNSCR 706 limited future oil revenues used for humanitarian needs to $1.6 billion. By the end of 1991 the UNICEF cumulative death toll of children under 12 reached 118,406.

In April 1992 a shipment from Pakistan that included clothes, pencils, and schoolbooks was stopped, and the US blocked water purification chemicals. Pencils were banned because of the graphite, and the prohibited chlorine was desperately needed not only to purify water but also to control mosquitoes and flies. The UNICEF death toll was 241,869 children by the end of the year. Ramsey Clark wrote again to the new UN secretary general Boutros-Ghali requesting that the sanctions be lifted. He cited how the sanctions were violating the Geneva Conventions, the FAO/WHO World Declaration on Nutrition, UN General

Assembly Resolution 44/215, the Constitution of the World Health Organization, and the Universal Declaration of Human Rights. For five years Clark sent letters every two months to each member of the UN Security Council pleading for an end to the genocidal sanctions. On June 27, 1993 President Clinton ordered 23 cruise missiles to attack Baghdad in retaliation for an assassination attempt against former president Bush which was alleged to have been plotted by Iraq; eight civilians were killed including the respected painter Leyla Attar. In July the British blocked a shipment of cotton for medical swabs and gauze, and Japan's attempt to send hospital and ambulance communications equipment was stopped in August. In October IAEA director general Hans Blix reported that Iraq's nuclear weapons program was neutralized by the war and no longer existed. The Security Council maintained the sanctions despite Iraq's compliance and acceptance of monitoring programs. The death toll for children reached 369,892 at the end of 1993.

In 1994 the Iraqi minister of health announced that the infant mortality rate that was 40 per 1000 in 1989 had risen to 126, and the average number of monthly deaths, which was 2,545 before the sanctions, had passed eleven thousand. In August 1994 Jordan's King Hussein and Turkey's President Suleyman called for easing of the sanctions against Iraq. At the end of the year UNICEF reported that 503,573 children had died because of the sanctions.

In April 1995 UNSCR 986 established the Oil for Food Program allowing Iraq to sell up to $2 billion in oil every six months; 30% of revenues were to be deducted for compensation payments and 2.2% to administer the program, but the first shipment of food did not reach Iraq until March 1997. In May 1995 the UN Special Commission (UNSCOM) alleged that 17 tons of bioweapons material, which had been obtained from western countries in the 1980s, was still missing, and so the embargo was continued. Iraq claimed they had destroyed these in October 1990 but agreed to destroy the suspected facilities in July. The Food & Agriculture Organization (FAO) Mission visited Iraq for five weeks and reported that $2.7 billion would be needed in the next year to meet the food shortages. Already that summer the World Food Program (WFP) had no more food to provide in south and central Iraq, and they ran out in the north in August. Sewage disposal in Basra had deteriorated even more since 1993. Typhoid cases had risen to 24,436 in 1994. They concluded that the UN Security Council must agree to let Iraq sell oil so that food and farm equipment could be imported. Sanitation and access to potable water needed essential equipment, and medical supplies and drugs were urgently required. The UN World Food Program's regional manager, Mona Hamman, reported that four million Iraqis were at severe nutritional risk, as only 34% of nutritional needs were being met. At the end of 1995 the UNICEF death toll reached 642,357.

In July 1996 two thousand Iranian troops invaded northern Iraq, but the UN Security Council took no action. Yet the Oil for Food Program was suspended because of the security concerns in northern Iraq. In early September the US used 44 cruise missiles to bomb targets south of Baghdad and extended the No-fly zone in southern Iraq. France's President Jacques Chirac urged implementation of the UNSCR 986 food program in October, as WFP food stores ran out in Iraq. France withdrew completely from the No-fly zone aerial patrols. After more than six years' hiatus, Iraqi oil exports resumed in December. The UNICEF death toll of children was now 782,638.

In April 1997 the US blocked forty contracts for medical equipment supplies intended for Iraq and seven food contracts for rice, beans, and cooking oil. UNICEF published a report that 750,000 Iraqi children under the age of five were suffering from malnutrition. In May more than 50,000 Turkish troops invaded Kurdish separatists in northern Iraq, and again the UN Security Council failed to act. Clinton and Russia's President Boris Yeltsin considered tougher sanctions to pressure Iraq. In August the UNICEF total for the Iraqi children who had died because of the economic sanctions reached 878,856. After visiting Iraq's hospitals again, Ramsey Clark sent another detailed report to the members of the Security Council in November. The sanctions had increased the child mortality rate eight times for those under five and more than four-fold for those over five. Diseases from malnutrition had increased exponentially with kwashiorkor reaching 21,000 cases a year and marasmus 192,000 cases the previous year. In 1996 about 1,354,000 suffered from illnesses related to malnutrition. He estimated that the sanctions had cost a total of one and a half million lives. He considered this genocide, and he also charged that these sanctions and the US punitive bombing were crimes against peace and humanity. The Security Council ban against Iraqi leaders traveling outside their country violated their human rights and prevented them from telling others their side of the story.

In January 1998 Egyptian organizations presented to the United Nations the Cairo Declaration with eighteen million signatures calling for an end to the economic blockade of Iraq in order to save the children. Eighty-four people, including Ramsey Clark, Bishop Thomas Gumbleton, and Kathy Kelly, traveled to Iraq in May as the Iraq Sanctions Challenge, taking $4 million worth of medicine without having secured a license from the United States Government. In August UNSCOM team leader Scott Ritter resigned "in protest over the inaction of the Security Council in Iraq and interference by the Britain and the US in UNSCOM's work." UNSCR 1194 ended the periodic reviews of the sanctions, requiring a new resolution to end them that could be vetoed by the US. On September 30 Denis Halliday, UN Humanitarian Aid Coordinator, resigned in protest of the sanctions and inadequate food program, calling the situation "illegal and immoral." He was replaced by Hans von Sponeck. The US appropriated $97 million for military equipment and training for those attempting to overthrow Saddam Hussein, who in reaction stopped cooperating with UNSCOM inspections. President

Clinton ordered preparations for a massive air attack. Iraq sent letters to Washington offering to resume cooperation, and UNSCOM inspectors returned to Iraq in November. UNSCOM reported lack of cooperation and withdrew on December 16. The next day US and UK forces began four days of bombing. Later it was learned that the US had placed spying devices inside equipment used by UN inspectors. Ritter revealed that inspectors had attempted to coordinate a coup by the Special Republican Guard against Saddam Hussein.

In January 1999 Noam Chomsky published an article denouncing the US bombing as contemptuous of the UN Security Council and a call for a lawless world ruled by the powerful. Chomsky, Zinn, Edward Said, and others praised the sanction-busting efforts by Voices in the Wilderness. In response to France's call for lifting sanctions, the US agreed to remove the $5.2 billion cap on the Oil for Food Program; but this was considered propaganda because the low price of crude oil prevented Iraq from earning much more. In February journalist Robert Fisk reported that the US and UK had staged more than 70 air strikes in five weeks. The Washington Fellowship of Reconciliation (FOR) and Physicians for Social Responsibility (PSR) delegation took medicine to Baghdad and met in April with Hans von Sponeck, who complained that the UNSCR 986 food program was not meeting the needs of Iraqis. UN Secretary General Kofi Annan cited a WHO report in May that refuted the claims made by the US and Britain that Saddam Hussein was to blame for not distributing supplies. In the first eight months of 1999 the US and UK fired 1,100 missiles at 359 targets, and Robert Fisk reported that more than a hundred civilians had been killed. Scientists found that the use of depleted uranium (DU) had caused radiation five thousand times the permissible level and had increased cancers seven-fold and deformities fourfold in southern Iraq. In September the *New Internationalist* magazine published an issue charging that US planes had caused an infestation of screw worm flies resulting in 70,000 cases of the disease in

Iraq; they compared it to a similar epidemic that struck Libya in 1989 when US relations were strained. In October 1999 Kofi Annan accused the US of disrupting the Oil for Food Program.

In February 2000 UN Humanitarian Aid Coordinator Hans von Sponeck again criticized the Oil for Food program as inadequate to the needs of the Iraqi people, and two days later he resigned. Iraqi officials indicated their unwillingness to cooperate with the UN Monitoring, Verification, and Inspection Commission (UNMOVIC), which was directed by Hans Blix and replaced UNSCOM. In September the UN Compensation Commission approved a $15.9 billion claim by Kuwait against Iraq for lost oil production. Iraq objected; but the percentage of oil sales paid for compensation was reduced from 30% to 25%, and Iraq continued to export oil.

Kelly on the Sanctions and War

Kathy Kelly grew up in Chicago and graduated from Loyola University in 1974. Three years later she moved uptown to work with the Francis of Assisi Catholic Worker House. After the Maryknoll priest Roy Bourgeois was sentenced to six months for flinging blood on a political poster, she was inspired to act and was arrested with Karl Meyer for protesting draft registration. Karl became her mentor and husband for twelve years. Kelly began resisting war taxes by keeping her income below the taxable level. She has continued to do so for 25 years and has said that not paying federal income tax is a spiritual discipline. She taught at Saint Ignatius College Prep for six years. In the summer of 1985 Jesuits gave her a development grant to visit Nicaragua, and she fasted with Foreign Minister Miguel D'Escoto, who urged people to protest Contra terror nonviolently. The next year she quit her job in order to devote herself to opposing military aid to the Contras. Kelly has been arrested about fifty times for protesting draft registration, wars in Central America, nuclear missile silos, Project ELF (Extreme Low Frequency used for military communications), and the sanctions against Iraq as well as for protests in Israel, Croatia, Haiti, and Italy. In 1988 she was sentenced to one year for planting corn on nuclear missile silos in Missouri and served nine months. She learned from the elderly activists Maurice McCracken and Ernest Bromley that courage is the ability to control your fear, and from their examples she found that courage can be contagious.

Kathy Kelly joined a Gulf Peace Team that occupied the border between Iraq and Kuwait during the first two weeks of the air war in January 1991. Then concerned Iraqi officials evacuated them to Baghdad, and after the explosions of bombs near their hotel they were moved to Amman in Jordan. Six months later Kelly returned to the United States. She visited Bosnia in December 1992 and August 1993. She was part of a Christian Peacemaker team in Haiti that discouraged militias from threatening their neighbors in 1994. She learned how the United Nations economic sanctions imposed against Iraq by the United States were causing great suffering and death. Kelly helped found Voices in the Wilderness (VitW), and in January 1996 they sent a letter to Attorney General Janet Reno declaring that they would break the sanctions to take medical supplies to Iraq. The US Treasury Department warned them they could face twelve years in prison and a fine of one million dollars. In March 1996 Kelly led the first of many VitW delegations (seventy as of 2005) to bring relief to the families and children of Iraq; Kelly herself has been there 26 times.

Instead of the sanctions that were wrecking Iraqi society, Kelly suggested that strengthening their educational institutions and social services would improve communication and their society. She observed that the sanctions made it more difficult for the Iraqi people to challenge the tyranny of Saddam Hussein. The bombing of Desert Storm had destroyed Iraq's electrical grid, refrigeration, sanitation facilities, and much medical equipment, and the sanctions prevented Iraqis from importing or repairing their damaged incubators. Their VitW delegations tried to treat the Iraqi people with warm respect, and they were amazed at the hospitality they received despite the pain of the sanctions inflicted by the US and UK. Instead of Bush's question, "Why do they hate us so much?" Kelly wondered, "Why do they love us so much?"[3]

In January 1997 during the confirmation hearings for Madeleine Albright five members of VitW held up pictures of Iraqi children and were detained. A year later when Kelly returned to the United States, customs agents gave her passport to the State Department as evidence she had been to Iraq. In 1998 their delegation took $110,000 worth of medicines to Iraq. Kelly described how five thousand children were dying each month mostly from contaminated water that caused dysentery, cholera, and diarrhea. Nearly a million children were suffering from malnutrition that would stunt their growth and cause disabilities. Camera crews visited hospitals, but the reports that were seen in Europe rarely appeared on American television. Secretary of State Madeleine Albright had said on the *60 Minutes* television program in 1996 that she thought the death of five hundred thousand Iraqi children was "worth it." In June 1999 six people on a Commence with Compassion fast were arrested for protesting at her commencement address at Northwestern University. In November 1999 Albright spoke to the Chicago Council on Foreign Relations; after she refused to answer whether the sanctions were worth the children's' deaths, fifteen activists were removed; Kathy Kelly and four others were arrested. In February 2000 the second UN Humanitarian Coordinator for Iraq, Hans von Sponeck, resigned to protest the sanctions. Four days later during a VitW and FOR demonstration at the US Mission to the United Nations 86 people were arrested.

In April 2002 Kelly went with a team to the Jenin Camp in Palestine during the Israeli Defense Force's Operation Defensive Shield. Because the United States has given Israel over $100 billion of mostly military aid during their 37 years of occupying Palestine, she felt responsible for the devastation but could only say that she refused to pay taxes.

In June 2002 Bert Sacks announced that he would not pay the $10,000 fine for having taken medicine and food to Iraq, but instead he raised another $10,000 to buy more medicine for Iraq. Voices in the Wilderness wanted the United Nations Charter to be upheld, and they opposed the impending US invasion of Iraq. In October 2002 their demonstrations in Iraq were erroneously described by *New York Times* reporter John Burns as "in support of Saddam Hussein." They believed the reports of the chief UN weapons inspector Hans Blix and former inspector Scott Ritter that the task of disarming Iraq was nearly complete. Kelly learned that she was going to be fined $20,000, but she refused to pay. She was in Baghdad trying to comfort Iraqi families when the invasion began on March 20, 2003. During the shock-and-awe attacks they learned that more than a thousand cruise missiles had been used in one night. They were angry at the devastation and killing, but they hoped that activists around the world would be demonstrating against the war.

Kathy Kelly has described many heart-rending experiences in Iraq. The musicians Majid al-Ghazali and Hisham al-Sharaf had their Baghdad School of Folk Music and Ballet ransacked by looters. Kelly was driven to Amman by her friend Sattar, a civil engineer who had helped three physicians perform emergency medical care for several days with little rest. He observed that the US tanks were only protecting the Oil Ministry. He saw another American tank break into a facility that stored two years' worth of grain and rice; the US officer told the looters to take what they wanted and burn the rest. Sattar had the courage to tell US soldiers that they could not manage the situation themselves or protect the civilians. Sattar commented that nothing had changed except that Saddam was gone, and he told the Americans that it was their country now. Kelly agreed with Tom Paine, who said that his country is the world and his religion is to do good. She wanted "to convince people that our over-consumption and wasteful lifestyles aren't worth the price paid by people we conquer."[4]

In the summer of 2003 Kelly found that Iraq was very insecure as armed robbers attacked pedestrians on the streets in the daytime. The occupying soldiers and the people in Baghdad were living in fear and dread. Saddam City was renamed Sadr City, and families tried to survive in appalling conditions. Kelly saw first-hand how relying on threats and force to solve problems provokes other leaders and societies to do the same. Some of her friends, who were students from Palestine, were detained by US troops as terrorists. Fadi Elayyan and Jihad Tahboub were released after two months; but they had to sign a paper saying the US had no responsibility for their treatment. They had been held for seven days without being given food or water. They suffered in the cold outside for a month, and those who complained were beaten. They observed children being abused by criminals, but the US guards only laughed.

Early in 2005 *The Lancet*, a British medical journal, estimated that about a hundred thousand Iraqi civilians had already been killed in the latest war. The Tigris and Euphrates rivers were polluted, and the continuing lack of electricity made it difficult to preserve food and medicine or treat water and sewage. The US occupation brought chaos and corruption with a security situation that was worse than before. Kelly has recommended that the US find the courage to admit a horrible mistake. The US could rectify the situation by closing their military bases, scheduling troop withdrawal, and cleaning up the depleted uranium, cluster bombs, landmines, and other unexploded bombs in Iraq. Restitution should be paid to Iraqis for fourteen years of economic and military warfare. The US and its allies should fund the reconstruction of Iraq; it should be directed by Iraqis, who should be employed and paid a living wage for the rebuilding. Finally, Kelly advised that the US should renounce its effort to create a puppet government in Iraq for its own national interests.

In October 2003 Kelly spoke to Judge Crocker at her sentencing for protesting the Navy's ELF system that is designed to facilitate the fighting of a nuclear war. She compared the war she witnessed in Iraq to the immensely worse effects that Trident nuclear missiles could cause. She and her team had knelt and prayed at the Iraq-Kuwait border that US soldiers would not cross the line to invade Iraq because of missiles they might have. She crossed the line at the Wisconsin ELF facility to call attention to the real weapons of mass destruction in the US arsenal that can destroy any country in the world. She was sentenced to a month but has not yet served that sentence.

In November 2003 Kathy Kelly was arrested with 27 activists at Fort Benning in Georgia during the School of the Americas protests when 14,000 people demonstrated. She was so badly abused during the booking that she stopped cooperating and was hog-tied and got a black eye. For that peaceful protest she served three more months in 2004. She has criticized the futility of the US prison-industrial complex which fails mainly because it intends to punish people instead of help them. She noted that the US prison population had quadrupled in the last 25 years. She regrets that so much money and resources are wasted on the military and prison systems when they could be used for health, education, and welfare systems. More than half of prison inmates were convicted of nonviolent crimes, and 78% of those were drug-related. Half of the prisoners who are serving mandatory minimum sentences are first-time offenders. She prophetically wrote, "Our society desperately needs the social imagining that could envision alternatives."[5] She summarized how the US has been constantly at war in the nuclear age since World War II in Korea, Vietnam, Nicaragua, El Salvador, Grenada, Panama, Iraq, Kosovo, Colombia, Afghanistan, and Iraq again. Kelly has written that we need to practice the old adage to live simply so that others may simply live.

Bush II's War on Iraq

In February 2001 US and UK planes attacked air defense targets in Baghdad. In August after Iraq claimed they shot down a US spy plane, the US conducted retaliatory strikes. Iraq in November said it would not allow inspectors back into the country unless the sanctions were lifted and the no-fly zones were abolished. In his 2002 state of the union address US President George W. Bush called Iraq, Iran, and North Korea the "axis of evil" and said he would not let them threaten the US with the "world's most destructive weapons." He illegally diverted $700 million that was appropriated for the Afghanistan War and used it to prepare for the invasion of Iraq. Bush spoke at West Point in June and threatened that the US may need to take preemptive action. On September 12 Bush called upon the United Nations to act against Iraq because he considered it a "grave and gathering danger." Four days later Iraq agreed to unconditional weapons inspections. The next day Bush announced his National Security Strategy (NSS), which asserted that the United States would maintain its military supremacy and act alone if necessary against states harboring terrorists or weapons of mass destruction. Also in September the US and UK stepped up their air attacks that bombed Iraq's western air defense installations, probably hoping to provoke a reaction by Saddam Hussein that could be used to justify invading Iraq.

In October 2002 the US Congress passed a resolution authorizing the use of force against Iraq. On November 8 UNSCR 1441 required Iraq to accept UN inspectors with unconditional rights and to make full declaration of its nuclear, chemical, biological, and ballistic weapons and related materials. Other members of the UN Security Council blocked the US attempt to include an explicit authorization to use force; most members believed that another resolution would be necessary for that. Iraq denied having any weapons of mass destruction and agreed to the UN inspections, which resumed on November 27. On December 7 Iraq submitted a 11,800-page report on its previous programs related to weapons of mass destruction, but US officials edited out 8,000 pages before turning the redacted copies over to the ten non-permanent members of the UN Security Council. Hans von Sponeck called the US tampering "outrageous." On December 19 US Secretary of State Colin Powell declared Iraq in "material breach" of UN resolutions, and two days later President Bush approved the deployment of 200,000 troops.

Publication of a secret memo in January 2003 exposed US attempts to spy on the private communications of the delegations of UN Security Council members. During his state of the union address President Bush accused Saddam Hussein of deception, but Bush's assertion that Iraq had obtained uranium from Africa was false. Powell presented the US case against Iraq at the UN Security Council on February 5, 2003. US claims that Iraq had weapons of mass destruction and connections to al-Qaida terrorists were doubted by many and believed by others, but neither of these charges have been proven despite extensive efforts to find evidence. Nine days later the chief UN inspector Hans Blix presented a report that found progress in Iraq's cooperation. On February 22 Blix ordered Iraq to destroy Al Samoud 2 missiles that were a little beyond the 150-kilometer range allowed. Two days later the US, UK, and Spain submitted a resolution to the UN Security Council to authorize the use of military force against Iraq. On March 7 after Iraq destroyed seventy of the questionable missiles, Blix commended their improved cooperation as a "substantial measure of disarmament" and asked for more time to complete the UN inspections. Because the US, Britain, and Spain could only persuade Bulgaria to favor their resolution, they did not present it for a vote in the UN Security Council.

On March 17, 2003 as UN inspectors were evacuating Iraq, President Bush publicly gave Saddam Hussein and his sons 48 hours to leave Iraq or face war. Two days later the US launched an air attack on Baghdad in an attempt to kill Saddam Hussein. This was soon followed by "shock and awe" bombing and an armed invasion from Kuwait by the US, the British, and a few other allies. In the north invading US forces were joined by Kurdish allies and captured Kirkuk and Mosul. The British occupied Basra, and the US captured Baghdad on April 9. Looting was widespread and included the museums with ancient artifacts while the US troops guarded only the Oil Ministry. The official name of the war was originally Operation Iraqi Liberation (OIL), but this had been quickly changed to Operation Iraqi Freedom (OIF). When US soldiers took over a school to use it as a military base in Falluja, many unarmed Iraqis asked them to leave on April 29; but US forces shot dead twenty people and wounded about 75 of the civilian demonstrators. On May 1 Bush declared victory and the end of the combat phase. Thousands of Iraqis protested the US occupation.

After General Jay Garner resisted US plans to sell off Iraq's oil and national assets, President George W. Bush put Paul Bremer in charge of the occupation of Iraq on May 12. Ten days later the UN Security Council recognized the US and UK as occupying powers and gave the Coalition Provisional Authority (CPA) a mandate to administer Iraq; the sanctions against Iraq were terminated. The next day Bremer dissolved the Ba'ath government, and US forces began disbanding the Iraqi military. This policy removed Iraq's security forces and many of its administrative personnel, greatly exacerbating an already huge unemployment problem and causing chaos in much of Iraq. All the reconstruction contracts in Iraq were awarded by the US Agency for International Development (USAID), the US Army Corps of Engineers, and the US State Department to private US companies. Halliburton, which was formerly run by Vice President Cheney, and its subsidiary Brown and Root received contracts worth more than $1.7 billion, and Bechtel also gained contracts totaling more than one billion dollars.

On June 28, 2003 the US military began canceling local elections and self-rule in Iraq's provinces and started appointing mayors and administrators. In July the US Defense secretary Donald Rumsfeld testified that the occupation would require 140,000 US troops and was costing the US $3.9 billion per month. That month US and UK officials appointed a governing council of 25 Iraqis, but Bremer remained in control. Leaders of the former regime had their pictures printed on packs of cards, and they were hunted down. American forces killed Saddam Hussein's sons Uday and Qusay during a raid on Mosul in July. A growing insurgency was developing. Twenty UN employees were killed by a suicide bombing at Baghdad in August, and another bombing killed 19 Italians at Nasiriya in November. US forces captured Saddam Hussein in December. In 2003 the US Army had 370,000 troops deployed in 120 countries.

In 2004 attacks by insurgents and the coalition killed hundreds each month. In March the Shi'a majority wanted early elections, but the UN officials advised delay. After the dead bodies of four American civilians were abused in April, the US military retaliated with a major assault on Falluja that killed six hundred civilians. Bremer declared Muqtada al-Sadr an outlaw and shut down his weekly newspaper. US forces killed seven more journalists, bringing the number of media workers killed to 28. Also in April charges were brought against US soldiers for abusing Iraqis held at the Abu Ghraib prison. In June the CPA conducted a poll of Iraqis and found that 92% viewed the US as occupiers, 3% saw them as peacekeepers, and 2% thought they were liberators.

On June 28, 2004 the US transferred governmental authority to the Iraqi council, and Bremer departed. A week later interim prime minister Iyad Allawi, a former employee of the CIA, declared a state of emergency and martial law. In August after three weeks of fighting in Najaf, the Shi'a leader Ali al-Sistani returned from London, where he had medical treatment for his heart, and he mediated a truce that allowed the withdrawal of al-Sadr's forces from the Imam Ali mosque. In September the number of US

military killed in Iraq passed one thousand. UN Secretary
General Kofi Annan declared that the US invasion of Iraq
violated the UN Charter and was illegal. *The Lancet* estimated that 100,000 Iraqis had been killed since March 2003,
and most of them were civilians. President Bush asked for
$87 billion for the military occupations of Iraq and Afghan-
istan, and Congress approved this funding in November in
addition to the $403 billion for the annual defense budget.
After its November elections the US launched a heavy
assault with 10,000 soldiers on the resistance in Falluja. The
UN and aid agencies reported that the number of children
suffering from malnutrition in Iraq had doubled since the
invasion.

In January 2005 Lynn Woolsey and 25 members of
Congress introduced the first resolution calling for the
immediate withdrawal of US troops from Iraq. An estimated 8.5 million Iraqis voted on January 30. The Shi'a
coalition called the United Iraq Alliance got 48% and
Kurdish parties 26%, but Sunnis only got 2% because of
their boycott. A report by the Special Inspector General for
Iraq Reconstruction could not account for $8.8 billion in
reconstruction funds that came from the former UN Oil for
Food Program, oil revenues, and other seized Iraqi assets.
By spring the US was holding more than 12,000 Iraqis in
four major prisons. In May 2005 the US Congress passed
another supplemental appropriation of $82 billion for the
war, but the same month the number of members voting
for withdrawal from Iraq had increased to 128. By 2005 the
US-led coalition had established more than a hundred military bases in Iraq, each with more than five hundred
troops. Pentagon plans included maintaining four major
bases away from population centers indefinitely. In June
2005 UN Secretary General Kofi Annan criticized the US
military for violating the Fourth Geneva Convention by
continuing to hold 6,000 Iraqi prisoners one year after the
occupation had been formally ended. On June 16, 2005 US
Representative Maxine Waters announced the forming of
an Out of Iraq Congressional Caucus with 41 members.

News leaked out that the CIA has been secretly abducting people and flying them to countries in the Middle East and Europe where abusive interrogation methods were used without public scrutiny. In December 2005 both houses of Congress passed John McCain's amendment to ban the use of torture, specifically prohibiting "cruel, inhuman, or degrading treatment or punishment of persons under custody or control of the United States Government."

After holding back the story for more than a year at the request of President Bush, in December 2005 the *New York Times* made public the secret spying by the National Security Agency (NSA) on thousands of people and citizens inside the United States without using the lawful method of reporting these wiretaps to the secret court established by the Foreign Intelligence Surveillance Act (FISA). Yet that court has secretly approved all but four of 18,748 such requests since 1978. Bush's argument that they did not have time to gain approval is invalid, because the government was allowed to begin each wiretap at will and must only report it within 72 hours. This blatant disregard for Congress, the courts, and the privacy of the American people drew immediate charges that these are felonies and impeachable offenses. Representative John Conyers moved to organize hearings with committees similar to those used during the Watergate investigations and charged President Bush and Vice President Cheney with defrauding the United States, making false statements to Congress, violating the War Powers Resolution, misusing Government funds, violating federal laws and treaties against torture,, using federal laws to retaliate against witnesses, and violating federal laws in leaking and misusing intelligence.

Millions Protest the War Against Iraq

In response to the bellicose reaction of President George W. Bush to the attacks of September 11, 2001, the International Action Center organized a march in Washington on

September 29, forming Act Now to Stop War and End Racism (ANSWER). In 2002 a group calling itself Not In Our Name formed around a statement of conscience that began "Let it not be said that people in the United States did nothing when their government declared a war without limit and instituted stark new measures of repression." In April about a hundred thousand people in Washington protested the war in Afghanistan and at home. In September those pledging resistance to a US invasion of Iraq were organized into a nation-wide network of activists called the Iraq Pledge of Resistance. On September 30 Ramsey Clark sent a strong letter to UN Secretary General Kofi Annan, asking the United Nations to oppose George W. Bush's intended invasion of Iraq. In October 2002 many peace groups came together to form United for Peace and Justice (UFPJ), which was soon joined by hundreds of local groups.

Active civil disobedience attempting to prevent the US invasion of Iraq began in October when the Dominican nuns Ardeth Platte, Carol Gilbert, and Jackie Hudson, wearing suits with the words "Disarmament Specialists and Citizens Inspections Teams," broke into an N-8 missile silo in northern Colorado to try to help with the effort to dismantle all weapons of mass destruction; after a trial they were sentenced to 41, 33, and 30 months. In November 2002 Military Families Speak Out (MFSO) was organized, and fifteen parents of soldiers and marines began a lawsuit against President Bush and Defense Secretary Rumsfeld. That month protests included 6 people being arrested in Louisville, 5 in Atlanta, 12 in Dallas, 16 in New York, and 30 in San Francisco. In December eight people were arrested at Senator Allard's office in Englewood, Colorado, 123 in New York City, 9 in San Francisco, 7 in Austin, 19 in Chicago, 14 in Hartford, 9 in Sacramento, 36 in Washington, 13 in Ithaca, and 7 in Richmond.

Arrests in January 2003 included 19 in Los Angeles, 8 in Oswego, 9 in Chicopee, 8 in Milwaukee, 16 in Syracuse, 38 in New York City, 11 in Tucson, 16 in Washington, 5 in

Bangor, 19 in Valley Forge, 12 in Vieques, 22 in Chicago, 20 in Denver, and 13 in Grand Rapids. In February arrests to stop the war included 8 in Raleigh, 355 in New York City, 13 in Tucson, 8 in Washington, 6 in Ann Arbor, 34 in Colorado Springs, 5 in Eugene, 6 in Phoenix, 59 in San Francisco, 8 in Seattle, 6 in Los Angeles, 10 in Somerville, and 11 in Boston.

Protests continued in March and increased as the invasion of Iraq became more imminent. Arrests on March 5 included 18 in Los Angeles, 20 in San Francisco, 12 in Santa Rosa, and 13 in Rochester. Code Pink had 26 people arrested in front of the White House on International Women's Day (March 8), and 23 from the Iraq Pledge of Resistance were detained the next day at the Capitol. On March 12 New York City passed a resolution opposing a preemptive or unilateral war against Iraq; about 150 other cities had already expressed such an opinion, including Philadelphia, Chicago, and Los Angeles. On March 14 there were 22 arrested in Sacramento and 80 in San Francisco. The next day 175 more were arrested in San Francisco, plus 19 in Aurora, Colorado at Buckley AFB. Arrests on March 17 included 55 in Washington, 44 in New York City, 40 in San Francisco, 26 in Toledo, and 10 in Salt Lake City. The next day 27 were detained in Detroit and 38 in Los Angeles. On March 19 Boston had 77 arrests, Madison 23, Portland in Maine 20, New Haven 16, Olympia 11, Seattle 11, Los Angeles 42, and Washington 29.

As the war began, many thousands demonstrated in the streets across the country, and those arrested for protesting on March 20 included 1500 in San Francisco, 900 in Chicago, 135 in Portland, Oregon, 122 in Pittsburgh, 120 in Berkeley, 104 in Philadelphia, 50 in Santa Rosa, 47 in Austin, 40 in Nevada City, 36 in New York City, 26 in Asheville, 22 in New Orleans, 22 in Chico, 21 in Flagstaff, 21 in Albany, 19 in Ann Arbor, 17 in Albuquerque, 15 in Bangor, 15 in Lewiston, and 14 in Indianapolis. The next day 800 more were arrested in San Francisco, 69 in Chicago, 40 in Baltimore, 37 in Sacramento, 27 in Los Angeles, 26 in

Washington, and 14 in Lansing. On March 22 in Hollywood 78 people were taken into custody; 91 more were arrested in New York City, 55 in Chicopee, 35 in Ithaca, 40 more in San Francisco, 14 in Seattle, and 16 in Johnston, Iowa.

Protests continued in various places. On Monday March 24 fifty people were arrested in Austin and 24 in St. Paul. The next day 67 were arrested in Minneapolis, 68 in Washington, 18 in Madison, and 10 in Olympia. On March 27 in New York City 214 more people, including some spectators, were arrested during a die-in. The next day another 83 were arrested in San Francisco. March 29 saw 23 arrested in Northampton and 22 in Seattle. In the next three days 32 people were arrested in Madison, and on April 2 a rally at Alliant Tech in Edina, Minnesota resulted in 28 arrests. On April 7 one hundred more people were arrested in New York City. That day in Oakland police shot rubber bullets and beanbags at demonstrators, many in the back as they were trying to flee; only 31 of the demonstrators were arrested. On April 14 in Richmond, California forty people were arrested for blockading Chevron-Texaco. On April 22 in Sunnyvale 52 people were detained for blocking entrances to Lockheed Martin. On May 4 in Kent, Ohio 14 were arrested, and that week in New York City 83 people were arrested during Operation Homeland Resistance. According to the *Nuclear Resistor* for the year beginning from the fall of 2002 more than 9,500 arrests were related to anti-war protests. On March 20, 2004 in San Francisco 80 people were arrested. During the Republican national convention in New York City more than 1,800 people were arrested on August 31 and the following days.

Many more people were involved in peace vigils and marches, often on a weekly basis. These reached a peak on February 15 when more than six hundred cities around the world had major peace marches or demonstrations. Never before had so many people mobilized to prevent a war or even to protest one in progress. More than twelve million people demonstrated their desire for peace on the same weekend. About 2,000,000 people marched in Rome,

1,750,000 in London, 1,300,000 in Barcelona, 700,000 in Madrid, 500,000 in Berlin, 375,000 in New York City, 250,000 in Paris and in Sydney, 200,000 in Damascus and in the Athens area, 100,000 in Montreal, in Melbourne, in Dublin, in Oviedo, and in Cadiz, 80,000 in Lisbon and in Toronto, 75,000 in Los Angeles, 70,000 in Amsterdam and in Seattle, 60,000 in Oslo, in Buenos Aires, and in Seville, and 50,000 in Brussels, in Montevideo, and in Stuttgart. A detailed study of 287 demonstrations for peace on February 15 in all fifty states of the US based on the conservative estimates printed in the media calculated that they were attended by between 862,282 and 1,033,839 people. Numerous voices in the media began calling the peace movement the second superpower. On March 20, 2004 two million people in Rome demonstrated against the military occupation of Iraq.

In June 2003 the first conference of United for Peace and Justice was held in Chicago and was attended by representatives from 325 organizations. By the end of 2004 UFPJ had more than 900 groups, and MFSO included nearly two thousand military families. In January 2005 nine parents of killed veterans, including Cindy Sheehan, founded Gold Star Families for Peace. In 2005 Pentagon figures indicated that more than five thousand US military personnel were away without leave (AWOL). Marine Stephen Funk was the first conscientious objector to be imprisoned for refusing to fight in the Iraq War, and he completed his six months in a North Carolina military prison in March 2004. Camilo Mejia also publicly refused to commit war crimes in Iraq after a two-week leave. During his trial in May 2004 international law expert Francis Boyle testified that the US invasion and occupation of Iraq not only violated international law but also the US Army Field Manual 27-10 which incorporates the Geneva Conventions. Law professor Marjorie Cohn was also an expert witness that the Iraq War violated the United Nations Charter, which only authorizes force for self defense. Mejia came to believe that his cowardice was going along with the war at first. Then he courageously fulfilled his duty according to the Nuremberg Principles by refusing to obey illegal orders, but he was convicted by the court martial and served nine months in prison. He learned that being in prison was not as bad as participating in an illegal war. Cohn also testified in the trial of Pablo Paredes, who had also denounced the war as illegal and refused to ship out; he was given hard labor and was confined to his base but was not imprisoned.

Many in the US military who have been refused Conscientious Objector (CO) status have fled to Canada. Conscientious Objector Chris Harrison co-founded Peace-Out to help people get out of the military. On March 1, 2005 in Vermont 52 towns approved resolutions opposing the use of Vermont national guard troops in Iraq. Iraq Veterans Against the War (IVAW) demonstrated in Fayetteville, North Carolina near Fort Bragg on the second anniversary of the Iraq invasion along with others in 765 cities and towns in all fifty states. As military recruiting goals fell seriously short in 2005, the Coalition Against Militarism in Our Schools (CAMS), other peace groups, and students organized counter-recruitment campaigns. On March 19 in New York City 24 people were arrested for demonstrating at recruiting centers, and on April 5 at UC Santa Cruz 300 students persuaded the Army, Navy, and Marine recruiters to leave the campus.

Former US Attorney General Ramsey Clark has drawn up Articles of Impeachment of President George W. Bush, Vice President Richard B. Cheney, and Secretary of Defense Donald H. Rumsfeld for waging wars of aggression in defiance of the US Constitution, the UN Charter and the rule of law; for carrying out a massive assault on and occupation of Iraq, a country that was not threatening the United States, resulting in the death and maiming of tens of thousands of Iraqis, and hundreds of US GIs; for lying to the people of the US, to Congress, and to the UN, giving false and deceptive rationales for war; for attacking civilians; for ordering assassinations, kidnappings, secret and other illegal detentions of individuals, torture and physical and psychological coercion of prisoners; for aggression against Afghanistan, Iraq and others and usurping powers of the United Nations and the peoples of its nations by bribery, coercion and other corrupt acts; for rejecting treaties, committing treaty violations, and frustrating compliance with treaties in order to destroy any means by which international law and institutions can prevent, affect, or adjudicate the exercise of US military and economic power against the international community; for ordering indefinite detention of citizens without access to counsel, without charge, and without opportunity to appear before a civil judicial officer to challenge the detention; for ordering indefinite detention of non-citizens in the United States and elsewhere without charge at the discretionary designation of the Attorney General or the Secretary of Defense; for authorizing the Attorney General to override judicial orders of release of detainees under INS jurisdiction; for authorizing secret military tribunals and summary execution of persons who are not citizens; for refusing to provide public disclosure of the identities and locations of persons who have been arrested, detained and imprisoned by the US Government in the United States; for using secret arrests and denying the right to public trials; for authorizing the monitoring of confidential attorney-client privileged communications by the government; for authorizing the seizure of assets of persons in the United States; for using racial and religious profiling and authorization of domestic spying by federal law enforcement on persons based on their engagement in noncriminal religious and political activity; for refusing to provide information and records necessary and appropriate for the constitutional right of legislative oversight of executive functions; for rejecting treaties protective of peace and human rights and for abrogating and withdrawing from international treaties and obligations without consent of the legislative branch, including termination of the ABM treaty between the United States and Russia and rescission of the authorizing signature from the Treaty of Rome which served as the basis for the International Criminal Court (ICC).

In addition to these serious charges the Bush administration has violated numerous laws. The website http://
zzpat.tripod.com/cvb/ has cited more than 150 news articles with evidence of impeachable offenses during the first
term of the George W. Bush presidency. In June hearings
were held by Democrats on the Judiciary Committee led by
Representative John Conyers to investigate deceptions the
Bush administration used to justify the Iraq invasion.

In May 2005 legal summons were delivered to US and
UK embassies in Istanbul, Tokyo, Lisbon, Brussels, and
other capitals for President G. W. Bush and Prime Minister
Tony Blair to face charges before the World Tribunal on Iraq
(WTI) in Istanbul for war crimes. Preliminary tribunals
were already held in Paris, Tokyo, New York, Barcelona,
Brussels, Seoul, London, Mumbai, and other cities, though
Bush and Blair did not appear. The culminating session of
the WTI was held in Istanbul June 24-27, 2005. This was a
major news story in Turkey, the Middle East, Europe, and
on the world wide web, but the tribunals findings were
ignored by US media. Arundhati Roy was the chairperson
of the 15-member Jury of Conscience, and the panel of
advocates was organized by Richard Falk and Turgut
Tarhanli, dean of the Bilgi Law School in Istanbul. The
advocates included Denis Halliday, Hans von Sponeck,
Tim Goodrich, Samir Amin, Johan Galtung, and Walden
Bello. The unanimous verdict condemned George W. Bush,
Tony Blair, Donald Rumsfeld, Dick Cheney, Colin Powell
and Paul Wolfowitz for planning and waging a war of
aggression in violation of the United Nations Charter and
international law. The governments of the United States
and United Kingdom were found guilty of 16 charges, and
the Security Council of the United Nations was convicted
on six counts for not protecting its member states against
aggression. Other governments, private corporations, and
the major media were also found to be complicit in contributing to the illegal war. The Tribunal recommended
boycotting US corporations doing business in Iraq such as

Halliburton, Coca-Cola, Bechtel and Boeing.

On August 6, 2005 Cindy Sheehan and members of Gold Star Families for Peace requested to meet with President George W. Bush and began a continuous vigil outside his ranch in Crawford, Texas while he was there on vacation. Cindy Sheehan and 383 other people were arrested for protesting at the White House on September 26, 2005.

In Cuba 25 Christians from the United States walked seventy miles from Santiago to visit the fasting detainees at the US Naval Base at Guantanamo Bay, but on December 11, 2005 they were not allowed to do so.

Notes

1. Quoted in *The Fire This Time* by Ramsey Clark, p. 174.
2. *Ibid.*, p. 175-176.
3. *Other Lands Have Dreams* by Kathy Kelly, p. 27.
4. *Ibid.*, p. 75.
5. *Ibid.*, p. 106.

17

Nonviolent Revolution for Global Justice

Global Emergency

Humanity is currently facing its greatest crisis in human history. I call it an evolutionary crisis, because the survival of the human species is threatened with extinction. The large arsenals of weapons of mass destruction, especially the thermonuclear weapons, could be used in an all-out war that might bring about a nuclear winter and the demise of the human race. I have faith that we will learn how to solve our problems without degenerating into such massive self-destruction; but we must recognize that given current destructive tendencies such a catastrophic event is a distinct possibility if we do not solve our problems in more peaceful ways. I think it is very important for people to understand that these dangers exist so that we will act to prevent them. In addition to a sudden disaster from nuclear war, the environmental problem of gradual pollution is making the Earth less habitable. This danger is less risky, because we may have more time to reverse the negative trends. Nonetheless, to prevent the increase of human misery and to protect the Earth habitat, we must address ecological concerns as well. The supply of fresh water is a major concern. If we are not able to resolve conflicts over the distribution and use of water, many wars could result, making the problem worse. Likewise, conflicts over diminishing fossil fuels could cause wars and possibly trigger mutual destruction.

Despite the outstanding efforts of Mikhail Gorbachev that helped to bring about an end to the Cold War and the nuclear arms race between the two superpowers, the United States has obstinately refused to disarm as it promised and is obligated to do by international law because of the Nuclear Non-Proliferation (NPT) Treaty, Article 6, which reads,

Each of the Parties to the Treaty undertakes
to pursue negotiations in good faith on effective measures
relating to cessation of the nuclear arms race at an early date
and to nuclear disarmament,
and on a treaty on general and complete disarmament
under strict and effective international control.

The recent (NPT) conference at the United Nations in May 2005 failed to make progress mainly because of US intransigence on disarmament. Under Presidents George H. W. Bush, Bill Clinton, and especially under George W. Bush, the United States has proclaimed itself the only superpower and is making strong efforts to attain world domination by continuing to increase its military power, arrogating to itself and its expanding NATO allies the authority to be the police wherever their selfish interests are in contention while neglecting or giving low priority to humanitarian crises in poor countries, especially in Africa. The previous chapters show this trend by the recent wars in Panama, Iraq, Yugoslavia, Afghanistan, and Iraq again.

No US president has shown more contempt for international law and treaties than George W. Bush. Since taking office in 2001 he has withdrawn from the 1972 Anti-Ballistic Missile Treaty, rejected the 1972 Biological and Toxic Weapons Convention ratified by 144 nations including the United States, alone opposed the UN Agreement to Curb the International Flow of Illicit Small Arms, withheld dues from the United Nations, rejected the International Criminal Court (ICC) Treaty, disavowed Clinton's promise to join the Land Mine Treaty, blocked negotiations on the Kyoto Protocol of 1997 for controlling global warming, declined to participate in the Organization for Economic Co-operation and Development (OECD) efforts to crack down on off-shore and other tax and money-laundering havens, refused to join 123 nations pledged to ban the use and production of anti-personnel bombs and mines, withdrawn from the International Conference on Racism, opposed the G-8's International Plan for Cleaner Energy, enforced an illegal boycott of Cuba, rejected the Comprehensive Test Ban Treaty, refused to rejoin UNESCO (UN Educational, Scientific and Cultural Organization) or contribute to its budget, rejected abolition of the death penalty in the UN's International Covenant on Civil and Political Rights, declined to sign the Framework Convention on Tobacco Control, violated the UN Charter and numerous treaties by invading Iraq, and failed to ratify the 1979 UN Convention on the Elimination of All Forms of Discrimination against Women, the 1989 UN Convention on the Rights of the Child, and the 1966 UN International Covenant on Economic, Social and Cultural Rights. The Bush II administration has used brutal force to overthrow the governments of Afghanistan, Iraq, and Haiti.

In 2002 the warmongering policies of George W. Bush went beyond even his 2001 proclamation of an endless war on terrorism everywhere in the world, when he declared the nations Iraq, Iran, and North Korea an "axis of evil." In reviewing the option for the first use of nuclear weapons, the Bush administration added the nations of Syria, Libya, China, and Russia and began implying that the US would even be justified in making "pre-emptive" strikes or even launching preventive wars of aggression in its national interest. Bush II also announced an expensive program to develop new nuclear weapons and a massive program to monopolize weaponry in outer space in order to gain complete military supremacy for world domination. These extremely dangerous and outrageous policies have been supported in the mass media and by many prominent politicians. Yet the belligerent attitudes of George W. Bush and his drive toward global domination and war with Iraq have stimulated great concern and massive demonstrations around the world.

The crisis was worsened by the 2004 US elections in which the Democrats nominated a candidate who supported the illegal war in Iraq in order to try to defeat Bush. The election cheating and fraud, especially in Ohio, were not adequately investigated and reported by the major media. One can only conclude that the United States, like Germany, Italy, and Japan in the 1930s, has become a criminal nation. In June 2005 widely respected Amnesty International published a report calling the US policy of detaining people and abusing their rights a gulag.

According to WHO's 2005 world health report, eleven million children under the age of five are dying annually from preventable causes. More than half the people in the world struggle to survive on less than two dollars a day, and over one billion try to live on less than one dollar a day. More than 800 million people go to bed hungry. This extreme poverty throughout the world could be ended if the wealthy nations that are worth $30 trillion contributed just $150 billion a year. Yet the US alone is now spending more than $500 billion annually on the military. The AIDS epidemic is killing millions in Africa and is spreading in Asia. Minor wars rage in dozens of countries, and most people have little faith in their governmental leaders. Humans' use of fossil fuels is causing global warming, which is already beginning to affect weather patterns, melting of polar ice, and rising sea levels. This book is mostly concerned with the issues of war and peace and social justice; but we also need to work on solving all these problems.

Since the neo-imperialist policies of the United States are currently posing the greatest threat to world peace and stability, I believe that US citizens have a special responsibility and a great opportunity to help all of humanity by changing the policies of our government. The US and Russia have far more weapons of mass destruction than any other nation. Yet President Bush is hypocritically demanding that other countries, which are attempting to gain such weapons, cease doing so or face a pre-emptive war from the United States. This is not a wise nor safe way to keep other nations from developing nuclear weapons. In fact, such warlike behavior tends to stimulate other countries, such as North Korea, Iran, China, Russia, India, and Pakistan, to develop their nuclear arsenals so that they can deter the US from attacking them. How long will it take for people to learn that war is not the way to peace and justice? Those of us who understand this cannot afford to wait for foolish leaders to learn this lesson the hard way. The wise who care about the future of humanity must act to change these dangerous policies. This chapter explains ways to do that so that we can establish a world of peace and justice.

Nonviolent Strategies

Naturally we must begin from where we are, which is a very difficult situation. We need to realize that this global emergency requires dedicated sacrifice by thousands and millions of people who are committed to make the changes needed. William James called it the "moral equivalent of war." In 1910 he wrote,

> So long as antimilitarists propose no substitute
> for war's disciplinary function, no *moral equivalent* of war,
> analogous, as one might say,
> to the mechanical equivalent of heat,
> so long they fail to realize the full inwardness of the situation.
> And as a rule they do fail.
> The duties, penalties, and sanctions
> pictured in the utopias they paint
> are all too weak and tame to touch the military-minded.[1]

James went on to cite Tolstoy as the only one who suggested turning away from worldly values enough. In other words, we need to be more energetic in our efforts for peace than those who go to war. This is certainly an awesome challenge; but what could be more noble and heroic than saving human civilization from its impending trend toward self-destruction?

I believe that Jesus gave the greatest call when he told people to seek first the sovereignty of God and not worry about food, clothing, and shelter, because one cannot serve both God and money. He advised those who would be his disciples to sell all they had and give the money to the poor. I believe that if enough people will actually do this, we will be able to transform our society to one that takes care of all without intentionally harming any. Renouncing violence means we must give up the special privileges that those with extra power have taken from others. We must accept equality with all people and work for the good of everyone. Most difficult, perhaps, is that we must learn to love our enemies and do good even to those who harm us. This does not mean that we should support their crimes; but instead of retaliating or punishing, we must seek reconciliation and justice for all. We need to learn how to trust the Spirit of goodness in all with the faith that even if we are killed or die after much struggle, that others will carry on our work until the good triumphs. We must purify ourselves by adhering to the way of love and its discipline of nonviolence. Such methods are not only the best; I believe they will also prove to be the most effective in the long run, because they reduce the amount of violence and injustice in the world.

Yet to transform the serious situation we face we must do more than simply live peacefully ourselves in loving relationship with those near us. To change governmental policies that threaten the well-being of all, we must work actively to transform our society by communicating and educating in every way possible and by demonstrating the ways of peace in our nonviolent actions that courageously challenge the war-makers and the war preparations. During the Roman empire Jesus demonstrated and taught the way of the cross, which was the punishment for non-Roman revolutionaries. Our current civilization is even more militarized than that empire was, and thus our efforts for peace and disarmament are punished by those in power also, usually by imprisonment. Yet I believe that these are the sacrifices our generation must make in order to redeem our civilization from the powerful who use violence. The rapid acceleration of modern technology and the destructive power of current weapons indicate that the fate of the Earth will be decided in the near future. Because of this danger, we cannot afford to wait for a gradual evolution nor sit back while the greedy plunder the Earth and endanger humanity. We must appeal to others to help and act together boldly with courage, if our civilization is to be saved.

Early in his presidency Dwight Eisenhower gave a speech in which he outlined what the policy of the United States should be, ironically a contrast to what it actually became during his administration, the huge military-industrial establishment he warned about in his 1961 farewell address. Yet in April 1953 Eisenhower prophetically said,

The way chosen by the United States
was plainly marked by a few clear precepts,
which govern its conduct in world affairs.
First: no people on earth can be held,
as a people, to be an enemy,
for all humanity shares the common hunger
for peace and fellowship and justice.
Second: no nation's security and well-being
can be lastingly achieved in isolation
but only in effective cooperation with fellow-nations.
Third: any nation's right to a form of government
and an economic system of its own choosing is inalienable.
Fourth: any nation's attempt to dictate to other nations
their form of government is indefensible.
And fifth: a nation's hope of lasting peace
cannot be firmly based upon any race in armaments
but rather upon just relations
and honest understanding with all other nations.
   In the light of these principles
the citizens of the United States
defined the way they proposed to follow,
through the aftermath of war, toward true peace.
This way was faithful to the spirit
that inspired the United Nations:
to prohibit strife, to relieve tensions, to banish fears.
This way was to control and to reduce armaments.
This way was to allow all nations
to devote their energies and resources
to the great and good tasks of healing the war's wounds,
of clothing and feeding and housing the needy,
of perfecting a just political life,

of enjoying the fruits of their own free toil.
   Every gun that is made, every warship launched,
every rocket fired signifies, in the final sense,
a theft from those who hunger and are not fed,
those who are cold and are not clothed.
This world in arms is not spending money alone.
It is spending the sweat of its laborers,
the genius of its scientists, the hopes of its children.
The cost of one modern heavy bomber is this:
a modern brick school in more than 30 cities.
It is two electric power plants,
each serving a town of 60,000 population.
It is two fine, fully equipped hospitals.
It is some 50 miles of concrete highway.
We pay for a single fighter
with a half million bushels of wheat.
We pay for a single destroyer with new homes
that could have housed more than 8,000 people.
This, I repeat, is the best way of life to be found
on the road the world has been taking.
This is not a way of life at all, in any true sense.
Under the cloud of threatening war,
it is humanity hanging from a cross of iron.[2]

Of course, the costs of bombers, fighter planes, and
other modern weapons in our time are much larger than
then, and so the stealing from the poor is that much greater.
The millions of starving children are the ones crucified by
our neglect. Those deformed by the birth defects that are
caused by radiation or who die slowly from its cancers are
the ones who suffer from using nuclear weapons such as
depleted uranium or worse.

I believe that this emergency is an urgent call for us to
act nonviolently to save humanity. War also destroys the
humanity in those doing the killing. We must be guided by
the divine principles of love, goodness, and justice; we
must act for the good of everyone in the world; and we
must make the sacrifices necessary wherever we may find
ourselves. To sacrifice is to make something sacred. When
we risk our lives and freedom to help save others, we are

magnifying our souls and extending our love. On the back
of the *Nonviolent Action Handbook* I published the following:

A Call to Conscience

For the good of all the people in the world,
for the preservation of our mother Earth,
for the future of all the children,
let us work together in harmony
to remove all the nuclear weapons,
to stop all the wars,
to learn to live together in peace,
to establish justice throughout the world
by using nonviolent judicial processes.
In this time of mortal crisis for humanity,
let us commit our lives to loving nonviolent action
to transform our own consciousness and our society,
by refusing to be complicit with war crimes,
by going willingly to jail to protest violent wrongs,
to suffer without inflicting any harm in return,
to persist until these goals are attained,
to communicate the truth as clearly as we can,
to share in community with the poor,
to live in friendship with all the people in the world,
to respect and care for our mother Earth,
to trust Spirit to sustain us in this life and beyond,
and to maintain our own center of peace.

This book you are now reading shows how nonviolent
actions have helped to bring about the end of slavery, votes
for women, civil rights for minorities, an end to the
Vietnam War, a limiting and resolution to the conflicts in
Central America, and to a reduction in nuclear weapons.
Recent efforts to intervene nonviolently in festering wars
have been organized by the International Solidarity Move-
ment (ISM), Peace Brigades International (PBI), Christian
Peacemaker Teams (CPT), the Nonviolent Peace Force
(NPF), Voices in the Wilderness (VitW), and Witness for
Peace. They are looking for volunteers and financial
support. Now we need to unify our efforts in order to

complete the task by bringing about the complete disarmament of all weapons of mass destruction, great reductions in national armed forces, and the use of international courts of justice to resolve all disputes between nations.

We can no longer afford to tolerate the ambitious and the greedy promoting wars that harm so many. The people who understand that nonviolent methods solve problems better than relying on massive national armaments for security need to act in ways that demonstrate these principles in order to persuade others that human beings can in fact solve conflicts without violence. We need to exert economic pressures with boycotts, strikes, and noncooperation with crimes against international law so that others will have to face the consequences of those crimes and so will eventually be moved to change wrong policies that harm people. We must act in solidarity with all the good people in the world who want peace and justice for all.

What does this mean in practical terms? As Gandhi often pointed out, not cooperating with evil is as much a duty as cooperating with good. Thus if our government is using our taxes to prepare for and finance wars, then in order not to be complicit with those crimes we must withhold our tax money. In the United States more than half of federal income tax is spent on war-related activity. Does this mean that one will be put in prison for refusing to pay one's taxes? Actually, so far people are not being imprisoned for simply refusing to pay federal income tax, although those who cheat on the income tax may be prosecuted and imprisoned. When someone honestly and openly refuses to pay, the Internal Revenue Service (IRS) may attempt to confiscate the tax they think is owed by attaching wages or property. However, there are restrictions, because they are not allowed to leave people completely destitute. Therefore only those with significant assets or a large income are in much danger of such confiscations. Many people, like myself, simply do not make enough money to owe any income tax; or the tax is so small that it is not worth the trouble for the IRS to try to collect it.

Kathy Kelly of Voices in the Wilderness for twenty-five years has found that not paying federal income tax is a spiritual discipline. The North American colonies began their revolution by refusing to pay the taxes to the British empire that were imposed to pay for its imperialist wars.

I recommend that people take the advice of Jesus, who was crucified for telling people not to pay tax to Rome. (See *Luke* 23:2) One can give income over the taxable level, which is usually around what is called the poverty line, to nonprofit or charitable institutions that are tax deductible. The people and these non-governmental organizations (NGOs) are the emerging superpower that will bring about the peaceful revolution that will transform the world to peace and justice. Such contributions help improve society while at the same time preventing the government from having resources for war-making. I envision a large movement of people, who dedicate themselves to the good of all humanity and so live in community with others by sharing their wealth that is beyond the taxable level. The examples were set by Buddha and his followers, Jains, Jesus and his disciples, monasteries, Sufis, Franciscans, Gandhi's ashrams, and others. I foresee that such groups could form charitable organizations in which all the employees would be earning less than the taxable level; but by living in community they would have everything that they need. In contrast to corporate charities such as the United Way, which pays huge salaries to its executives and spends much of the money donated raising more money with junk mailings, advertising, and so on, these spiritually disciplined charities would be able to guarantee to donors that a much larger percentage of the money they contribute will actually go to help people in need or for the educational purposes of the institution.

This peace and justice movement will make it clear that having great wealth that is not used to help others is in fact being in complicity with imperialist domination, which is designed to protect the interests of the wealthy. People, especially in the United States, must choose whether they serve the almighty dollar or whether they want to dedicate their lives to the love and sharing that Jesus the Christ demonstrated and taught. We must expose the hypocrisy of those who claim to be Christians and yet support right-wing politicians who promote imperialist wars and oppress the poor while favoring the rich who contribute to their campaigns. This great struggle between those who use violence and those who do not is part of the conflict that Jesus predicted would precede the second coming of the Christ. I believe that the cosmic Christ is in every soul, because the soul is part of God. In my opinion the second coming of Christ is when it comes to the awareness of each person. That is why Jesus warned people not to follow those who said the Christ is over here or over there; but the second coming of the Christ will be as obvious as lightning from east to west, because when a person realizes that the Christ is within, one can never be separated from that reality. The Buddha and others also taught the ways of peace and nonviolence. We need to respect the religious beliefs of all as well as the rights of those who do not believe in God.

People can be creative in resisting the militarism of our society. Military bases and weapons manufacturers and researchers are near almost every community in the United States, which has more than 700 overseas bases as well. Demonstrations and protests can be organized, especially in times of war. I believe that extra efforts need to be made in communicating and educating people in the schools, churches, civic groups, by media, art, music, and so on. Nonviolent protests that result in arrests are also very effective; but they are not the only ways to persuade people to change. Einstein said that we need a chain reaction of awareness. Nonviolent action is most effective person to person. Those who do not wish to take time from work to protest or risk arrest can contribute money to peace education and support others who are making sacrifices. As the peace and justice movement grows and expands, strikes and boycotts become even more effective. The United

States Government already owes nearly eight trillion dollars and is currently running an annual deficit of about a half trillion. When enough people sell their US Treasury bonds, the US war machine will be bankrupt. Meanwhile efforts can also be made to influence the politicians and to elect those people who will lead society toward the reforms needed.

Democratic Revolution

In this phase of the nonviolent revolution the sacrifices of committed individuals and groups and the massive educational campaigns catalyze society to elect reformers to high offices in the government. Thus it is very important that people work on the political campaigns of those candidates who will make the changes. In the United States the current political process has become so corrupted by money that this is a challenge. People need to learn not to be overly influenced by paid political advertisements. Again we need committed individuals who will work hard to spread the word so that the pervasive apathy and cynicism can be overcome; then more people will vote. Fortunately the Internet and other modern communication technologies can help us get around the domination of the mass media by the huge corporations. People need to work to improve the mass media, but they can also find alternative media such as Pacifica radio that will tell them the truth and let them hear the voices that are calling for peace and justice more than those who have been bought by wealthy interests.

In the last twenty-five years the Republican Party has been taken over by the rich in order to implement policies to their selfish advantage even though they result in imperialist wars and greater suffering and hardship for the poor and middle class. Yet most of the politicians in the Democratic Party have also become subservient to the corporate interests of those who contribute to their campaigns. These two powerful parties that have become so similar have colluded to exclude other parties from getting a fair hearing in the media or in the formal debates that precede elections. Outstanding candidates from the Green Party have been excluded from these debates, and the winner-take-all system has marginalized this progressive party. Even when Ralph Nader was interviewed by the media in 2000, half the time was spent discussing how he was acting as a spoiler against the Democrats. In 2004 Nader ran as an independent and was generally ignored, as was Green candidate David Cobb.

Progressive candidates can run in Democratic primaries in order to transform that party. A "green Democrat" has a better chance of winning a Democratic primary than a general election as a Green Party candidate. Then the green Democrat also has a better chance of winning the final election. After many such green Democrats are elected, this struggle may result in the Democratic Party splitting, and then there would be three major parties. Visionary candidates can also run through the Green Party to educate people and may be able win in three-way races. Instant Runoff Voting (IRV) is a major election reform that is urgently needed. I also have suggested amending the US Constitution so that the Senate could be elected by proportional representation to make it more democratic.

If we can get more of the poor and middle class voting, I believe that the narrow interests of the Republican Party will result in its being greatly weakened. I believe that people will eventually realize that the party of Bush really only helps the selfishness of the richest people and that its policies are not in the long-term interests of the United States or of the world. How long it takes before this revolution in consciousness takes place depends upon how bad things have to get before people learn but also on how well we can educate people that there are better ways. I believe that if we can learn from our wisdom, we will not have to suffer as much before we make the improvements. Let us work hard so that it does not take a limited nuclear war before people learn! We need political leadership that envisions a much better world and will bring about disarmament and justice for all.

Disarmament and World Justice

Since the United States has the most powerful military forces ever assembled and spends nearly as much or more on the military than the rest of the world combined, this country can lead the way toward disarmament. Despite the efforts of the Bush administration to create a new set of enemies to replace the Communist menace of the Cold War, the US is not really threatened by invasion from any foreign power. The scattered terrorist enemies that have arisen to fight the US are a direct result of the international crimes of the US in what is called "blow-back." This is essentially karma, the consequences of US foreign policy and its attempts to dominate the world. I believe that if the United States elects an enlightened president, that she or he could lead the world to peace and disarmament. I recommend that this process of disarmament be verified by an international organization such as the United Nations; but because the UN is dominated by the five nuclear powers that are the permanent members of the Security Council, I believe that either the UN needs to be reformed to be more democratic, or the people of the world need to form a democratic federal world government.

The new US president could call for a world constitutional convention so that representatives from every country could gather and draw up a constitution for a limited federal government that could oversee the process of disarmament and have three balanced branches of government to settle international disputes and protect human rights. Nations would remain sovereign over their own territories and would be free to choose their economic and social policies as long as they did not violate other nations or human rights. This world constitution would need to be ratified by all the major nations of the world before it would take effect. People could elect representatives to the world legislature. I have suggested that the executive branch could be headed by a council of nine presidents representing North America, South America, Africa, Europe, the Middle East, North Asia, India, China, and East Asia. Elections could be held regularly, and the nine presidents would be elected by the people of their region. Each president would appoint one judge to the World Court for one nine-year term, one new judge being appointed each year. The judges would have to be confirmed by the legislators.

The disarmament process could begin with a thorough inventory of all weapons of mass destruction, and then these could be eliminated with inspections verifying that they have been dismantled. Conventional weapons could also be eliminated over several years. Peacekeeping would be as nonviolent as possible, and volunteers could come from all nations but not too many from any one nation. If any group or nation tried to resist an arrest for a violation of world law, then the executive council could authorize whatever force might be needed to bring the violators to trial before the World Court. Thus national armed forces would no longer be needed. Each nation could have their own local police, but all international disputes would be under the jurisdiction of the world's federal authorities. In the early stages of the disarmament all military forces in foreign countries could be removed, and all weapons sales could be banned. I believe that diplomacy and judicial decisions can resolve the conflicts between nations and peoples when the unjust use of force or its threat is removed. The world legislature could pass laws banning the weapons of war. As long as nuclear power plants exist, all nuclear materials could be monitored by world inspectors. All military bases would be closed and could be converted to university campuses, hospitals, and other productive uses. This is only a brief sketch of what would need to be a very carefully designed process.

Sustainable Civilization

At the same time as we are working for peace and disarmament, we need to be making efforts to bring the world into a more harmonious balance by correcting the social and economic injustices, by providing the charitable resources to alleviate the suffering, and by preserving the ecological integrity of the environment to protect human health. Recent inequities perpetrated by predatory capitalism through the World Trade Organization (WTO), the World Bank, the International Monetary Fund (IMF), and the powerful nations of the North have aroused cries of protest from the poorer peoples of the South. The expanding movement for global justice needs to be supported by conscientious people everywhere so that trade can be not only free but also fair and responsible to the needs of the people and their environment. Letting the rich continue to exploit the poor in order to become even richer and more powerful while the poor become weaker and more miserable is not an economically sustainable situation. Therefore the exploited need to organize and work to improve their situations while those who care about them need to help educate and persuade the powerful to be more just and charitable in their economic policies. The processes that govern trade should not be controlled by the powerful few in secret but should be open and democratic for the benefit of all.

The rich and powerful nations, such as the United States, which uses a quarter of the world's resources and produces proportionally as much pollution, need to be responsible by accepting and adhering to global treaties that are designed to prevent global warming, depletion of the ozone layer, reduction of fisheries, and pollution of air, water, and land. More enlightened governmental policies will subsidize and encourage sustainable energies while taxing all forms of pollution in order to make corporations accountable for the consequences of their actions. These progressive policies will make our civilization much less dependent on petroleum, coal, and nuclear energy.

I believe that we have the intelligence and technical skill to make this Earth a paradise for all if we will stop wasting so much of our human and material resources on destructive military activities and the ruthless pursuit of excessive profits. The challenge humanity faces in the next generation or two will probably decide the fate of the Earth for centuries to come. Will we use our wisdom and move back from the brink of disaster? Will we join together with others and work for the good of all so that our children and grandchildren may enjoy a bright and happy future?

To summarize, here are some of the things that we can do to make this world a better place. We can pray and meditate for peace in order to exude that peace to others. We can examine our lives and our conscience to see how we can correct our faults, improve ourselves, and do more to help others. We can study the issues of peace and justice so that we will make intelligent decisions and so that we can communicate well and educate others. We can work on projects with others that will benefit society. We can be frugal or spend our money in ways that are most beneficial for the world. We can have the courage to confront those who are harming others in order to persuade them to change their behavior. We can work with groups to organize people so that we can magnify our power and bring about major improvements in society and government.

By acting nonviolently we can heal the wounds caused by violence and transform our society; through the democratic process of world law we can keep the peace. May God guide us all, and may we all work together in harmony for a world that is best for everyone.

Notes

1. "The Moral Equivalent of War" by William James in *The Pacifist Conscience* ed. Peter Mayer, p. 185-186.
2. "Chance for Peace" address delivered before the American Society of Newspaper Editors, April 16, 1953.

Appendix
My Efforts for World Peace

Since world public opinion now favors democratic means,
I believe the time has come for the people of the world
to unite in establishing institutions of global democracy.
The evolution of education and the ability to communicate
almost instantly with technology anywhere on the Earth
enables us to organize ourselves in this global village.
So many problems which the nations have failed to solve
cry out for responsible decisions from global institutions
that can represent the interests of all the people on Earth
as well as those who will come after us in the future.
First, humanity demands that human rights be protected
in every country of the world regardless of social system.
Second, military disarmament will probably not be secure
until there is a world authority that people and nations
can respect and rely on to act in the best interests of all
without allowing favoritism to any ethnic group or nation.
Third, economic relationships need to be based on justice
rather than military power and exploitation by the wealthy.
Fourth, big decreases in military spending will enable
every society to provide better education and health care
for all their people in the best way they see fit locally.
Fifth, the environmental crises require world cooperation
so that comprehensive solutions can be implemented globally.
Also the prevention of wars will help humanity and nature.
Sixth, at the same time world institutions can protect
and allow various social groups to express themselves freely
so that the rich cultural diversity of peoples can flourish.
Seventh, when such global peace and harmony is nurtured,
when everyone works together in a fair and just economy
so that all are relatively well educated and healthy,
and the creatures of the Earth are respected and sustained,
giving future generations a safe home environment,
then personal and social enlightenment will bloom everywhere
and bear much fruit in the arts, humanities and sciences
that a great spiritual renaissance as never seen before
will turn this planet into a paradise with knowledge
and a marvelous school for souls to learn more about

the nature of creation in relative comfort and ease.
Sanderson Beck, "A Plea for Love" (1992)

My Path to the World Peace Movement

I was born in Los Angeles on March 5, 1947 and had a happy and peaceful childhood growing up in the Pacific Palisades. My parents were Republicans, and I had a conservative upbringing. When I was a freshman at the University of California at Berkeley, I participated in the earliest phase of the Free Speech Movement that was led by Mario Savio in 1964. The Dean of Women had made a rule that literature could no longer be passed out on the edge of campus. Nonviolent student protests eventually resulted in opening up the entire campus to this First Amendment right. At first I wanted to study psychology and political science, but I did not like the way the course in each I took was taught. I decided to major in Dramatic Art, because I wanted to study life, motivation, and emotions as well as theories, and it was more experiential than most academic subjects. I believed very strongly in freedom, and during the summer of 1967 I did an independent study, reading just about everything written by Jean-Paul Sartre. After I graduated in December of that year, I continued right on in graduate school.

As a graduate student I no longer had a deferment from the draft. I knew I could not go into the military, because I would not give up my freedom to such an organization. Although I had little religious background, I decided to apply for Conscientious Objector status. When I was 16, I had started reading the *Bible*; but I got bogged down in *Chronicles*. Now I began with the *New Testament* and was impressed with Jesus in the *Gospels*. I read the *Portable World Bible* and other existential philosophers such as Ortega y Gasset and Friedrich Nietzsche. I was drawn to Eastern philosophy and was so overwhelmed by Lao-zi's *Dao De Jing* that I used that as the basis for my conscientious objection to war. Although I had been raised to compete and strive in sports, to be an Eagle Scout, and get good grades, I responded very deeply to this peaceful philosophy of not striving. During the summer of 1968 I was doing research to write a screenplay on Phaedra and discovered the Minoan civilization. While radicals were rebelling against the police in the streets, I was being pulled up to spiritual ideas. I did not like the riots and decided to leave Berkeley. I came back on a weekend in October and on a peace march met friends from my high school who gave me a ride to Santa Barbara, where I enrolled in the Religious Studies program at UCSB.

There I was lucky to find a roommate, Venustiano Olguin, who had worked closely with Cesar Chavez and came to UCSB to study nonviolence and Gandhi. I was to give a presentation to the seminar of Mircea Eliade on the same day I was called before my draft board in Westwood. I asked for an extension; it was denied, and I appealed. In the spring I met Bishop James Pike, who broke bread with us after a one-day fast for peace. Finally in December 1969 I told the draft board that I could not hurt another human being, because we are all one. I said I had never been in a fight in my life. I was granted Conscientious Objector status. As I was having mystical experiences and no longer had financial support for my studies from my parents, I decided to give up all my possessions and dedicate my life to God through the Christ, which I believe is a divine energy in us all. At that time I met John-Roger, who had founded the Movement of Spiritual Inner Awareness (MSIA) and called himself the Mystical Traveler Consciousness. His ability to soul travel and help people spiritually amazed me. I had taken some psychedelic drugs, but in June 1970 I decided to give those up for good and have not taken any illegal drugs since.

I completed my Masters degree in Religious Studies in June 1971, and the next year I was ordained a minister by John-Roger through the office of the Christ. In Los Angeles I was very active in MSIA, co-authored and directed a musical comedy, and served on the ministerial board for two years. I founded a spiritual university called the

University of the Golden Age (UGA), co-edited and published *Across the Golden Bridge* about 62 people's experiences in MSIA, taught philosophy in community colleges, wrote and had published *Living In God's Holy Thoughts,* and went to UCLA for a Ph.D. in the Philosophy of Education. In 1976 I began teaching at the World University in Ojai. After I wrote a 500-page dissertation on Confucius and Socrates, my faculty committee at UCLA sabotaged my thesis because of my spiritual philosophy and wholistic approach, deciding I had to do it over their way. I decided to complete my Ph.D. in Philosophy at World University, and I moved to Ojai in 1979.

When President Carter reacted to the Soviet invasion of Afghanistan with more militarization, I became very concerned and wrote him a letter. I began teaching courses at World University in world peace and Gandhi's nonviolence as well as in philosophy, religion, and psychology. After translating the *Gospels* from Greek and putting together a book on the soul, I began researching and writing *The Way to Peace,* which became the 282-page book that has been replaced by this much longer revision under a new title. I was horrified by the policies of Ronald Reagan and began to consider the need for civil disobedience. I was only earning $400 a month but lived simply, though I collected a library of used books. In the summer of 1981 I was called before the MSIA ministerial board, because I had offered $25 donation instead of the expected $125 for their ministerial training seminar. I raised the issue of civil disobedience because John-Roger had said that ministers should obey all the laws. The board did not think that was important, and they revoked my ministerial credential for being too poor.

In September 1981 I read in the *Los Angeles Times* about the nonviolent action to stop the nuclear power plant at Diablo Canyon. I took the nonviolence training at the camp, joined an affinity group, and the next day was arrested for the first time. The men were put in an old gymnasium for more than a week, and I found the experience very instructive and inspiring. In 1982 I worked on the campaign to freeze nuclear weapons and had a letter complaining about the Cold War mentality of Defense Secretary Caspar Weinberger printed in the *Los Angeles Times*. I attended a World Federalist conference, PSR's forum on the medical consequences of nuclear war and other peace activities. I started a networking organization called the World Peace Movement, formulating and printing in a brochure the following Principles, Purposes, and Methods:

Principles

1. The Earth is one world, and its human beings must learn to live in peace with each other or perish.
2. The human race is one and interdependent; the good of each depends on the good of all and our love for each other.
3. The way of love and peace is nonviolent and does not hurt anyone.
4. The uniting power of love, peace, and friendship is stronger than the divisive strife of hatred, war, and enmity.
5. The conversion of a hostile and militaristic world into a peaceful global society is primarily an educational process of changing consciousness from fear, suspicion, and mistrust to love, confidence, and trust in the human capacity to solve problems, cooperate, and establish justice.
6. Every human being has the equal right to life, liberty, security, and justice.
7. Respect for individual freedom and dignity requires the protection of all human rights by means of a universal system of justice.
8. Justice in human affairs evolves through democratic means and due process of law.
9. The use of force is justified only when a legal authority, designated by consent of the people, is required to restrain and bring to justice a violator of the law.
10. A law enforcement official has legal authority only within the territory of the people who designate that official. No nation has the sovereign right to use any force

outside its national borders.

11. War, the use of force outside one's territory,
    the threat to use such force,
    and the sale or transfer of military weapons
    outside one's territory
    should be prohibited by international law.
12. International wars and internal oppression
    of human rights are allowed to occur
    because there is no enforceable world law.
13. Enforceable world law and justice
    may be established by instituting
    a democratically elected federal world government
    to protect human rights and solve international disputes
    through a compulsory system of jurisprudence.
14. In a federal world government each nation
    would maintain sovereignty over its own internal affairs,
    except that the federal world government
    would have legal authority to protect human rights
    and settle international disputes.
15. Education, communication, democratic process,
    and nonviolent protest of wrongs are the purest
    and most effective means of social reform.
    Peace and justice are attained
    only by peaceful and just means.
16. Biological, chemical, and nuclear weapons
    are so horrendously deadly to people
    and damaging to the environment
    for such long periods of time
    that only deluded minds seriously contemplate their use.
17. Belief in deterrence of war
    by massive armaments and nuclear weapons
    is based on fear, suspicion, mistrust, and insecurity;
    this weapons policy perpetuates
    more fear, suspicion, mistrust, and insecurity in the world.
18. Those people who have moral courage and faith
    in the justice of their economic and political philosophies
    and in nonviolent social change and democratic processes
    will support enforceable world law
    instead of massive national armaments.
19. Huge expenditures on massive armaments of destruction
    are a colossal waste of human and material resources,
    causing poverty, inflation, and a lower quality of life.

Such resources could otherwise be used for
improvement of the environment,
food production and distribution,
education, health, and other beneficial purposes.

Purposes

1. To awaken the inner peace
   that dwells in the hearts of all beings.
2. To create the consciousness of world peace
   and to foster friendship and harmony among all people.
3. To promote and protect the human rights of all people,
   regardless of race, color, sex, language, religion,
   political or other opinion, national or social origin, property,
   birth or other status, as delineated in the
   United Nations' Universal Declaration of Human Rights.
4. To assure international justice and universal human rights
   by developing ways to preserve them,
   such as a federal world government,
   democratically elected by all the people of the Earth,
   with a world court of justice having compulsory jurisdiction
   to decide all cases of international disputes
   and violations of world law and human rights,
   and with a world peacekeeping force
   of individuals from all countries
   who would be dedicated to the whole of humanity
   and who would enforce world law
   and the decisions of the world court of justice
   by the most peaceful means possible.
5. To achieve disarmament and the total elimination of all
   biological, chemical, and nuclear weapons in the world.
6. To purify and maintain a clean
   and ecologically balanced environment
   for our health and prosperity and for future generations.
7. To alleviate poverty and hunger, and to improve the health,
   education, and living conditions of all people on earth.
8. To encourage all schools
   from the primary grades to the university
   to offer peace education from a global perspective.

Methods

1. To live peacefully and lovingly as examples to all.
2. To educate ourselves and others by every means

to increase awareness of the oneness of life,
the interdependence of all beings,
the ecological unity of the environment,
the way of love and nonviolence,
and the urgent need for transnational attitudes,
programs, and institutions for the sake of mutual survival.
3. To communicate by every means the truth
and the facts which reveal and nourish world peace.
4. To pray and meditate
and expand the consciousness of peace.
5. To respect and nurture human rights
with tolerance and understanding.
6. To refrain from contributing
to the preparations and activities of war
and from hostile and aggressive attitudes.
7. To protest nonviolently against oppression, militarism,
nuclear weapons, pollution, and violations of human rights.
8. To work for the total elimination of
biological, chemical, and nuclear weapons in every country.
9. To promote and practice world citizenship,
and to work to organize a world constitutional convention
to plan the democratic institution
of a federal world government.
10. To use all human wisdom, sciences, and technologies
in developing and purifying the environment,
eradicating hunger and sickness in all countries,
and making global education available to all people.
11. To communicate closely with all peace organizations
and dedicated peace workers
to facilitate the forming of a united worldwide network
to bring about the establishment of world peace.

Protesting the MX and Cruise Missiles

In January 1983 I participated with the Vandenberg Action Coalition in an occupation of Vandenberg Air Force Base to protest the upcoming testing of the MX missile, a destabilizing first-strike weapon capable of destroying ten Soviet missiles. Defense expert Herbert Scoville had stated that the MX missile would not deter a Soviet attack but would give them an incentive to launch their missiles on warning. About two hundred of us were given letters banning and barring us from the base, and we were released. The next month I was arrested in Orange County in an action organized by the Los Angeles Catholic Worker. I cited out of jail so that I could moderate a panel discussion at the Mind-Body-Spirit Festival on Nuclear Disarmament with Daniel Ellsberg, Danaan Parry, Richard Moss, and Yogi Bhajan. In March about eight hundred of us were arrested at Vandenberg, and most stayed in custody in solidarity with those of us who had been banned before. Most of the men were put in the gym at the Lompoc prison camp, and the experience was similar to Diablo Canyon with many educational and entertaining activities.

I had written a letter to Col. Farney warning him and the base that they were violating international law, and I quoted the Nuremberg Principles. In May at a long meeting taken up mostly with people reflecting on the previous action, I was able to get the Vandenberg Action Coalition to approve a letter I wrote to President Reagan, declaring that unless the US Congress stopped all funding for the MX missile, there would be a nonviolent occupation of Vandenberg AFB. I signed the letter, and copies were sent to every member of Congress and to major newspapers and media networks. I insisted on my right to be tried by a federal judge and represented myself in the trial at Los Angeles. Ironically, Judge A. Wallace Tashima would not let my expert witness, Dr. Jimmy Hara, testify on the effects of nuclear weapons, because he would not allow the defense of necessity nor international law. However, his attitude seemed to soften during the one-day trial, and he did not sentence me to any more time in prison. The lawyer Leon Vickman was challenging the legality of nuclear weapons in the Provisional District World Court and asked to add my case to his suit; I agreed. My action was also defended by the legal opinions of Dr. T. P. Amerasinghe from Sri Lanka and A. B. Patel of India.

Meanwhile we organized a local group to protest the testing of cruise missiles at the Point Mugu Naval Base; a cruise missile had even crashed in the national forest near

Ojai. In the San Francisco Bay area the Livermore Action Group declared June 20, 1983 International Day of Nuclear Disarmament; so we planned our action for that day. The US Government used this opportunity to begin testing the MX missile in mid-June, and so only about forty people were arrested at Vandenberg then. After much preparation eleven of us blocked traffic going into the Pt. Mugu base on June 20. We stayed outside the federal property line so that we would be given a jury trial. Later it was discovered that they had painted the line in the wrong place, and so those charges were dropped so that we could be tried without a jury by a federal magistrate. We were found guilty, but sentencing was delayed. On August 6 several people began a water fast for life to stop the nuclear arms race. In solidarity I fasted on juices and ended my fast when they did after forty days. On the 28th day of the fast I was arrested in the office of Congressman Lagomarsino, who refused to see me; but I was not prosecuted.

In October 1983 there was a world-wide effort to stop the deployment of the cruise missiles in Europe, and that was the weekend that the Reagan administration chose to invade Grenada. I joined the action at El Segundo organized by the Los Angeles Catholic Worker and the Alliance for Survival. In the Los Angeles jail I was badly treated for refusing to submit to a chest x-ray. The elderly Glafko Sikelianos (son of a famous Greek poet) and I pleaded not guilty and represented ourselves in a jury trial. Although the judge and most of the jury were African Americans, they did not really seem to understand the ideas and methods of Martin Luther King. Refusing probation, Glafko and I were sentenced to 120 days for trespassing. After a month in jail the lawyer Doug Booth got us a sentence modification hearing, and later our sentences were suspended. We both went back and had to serve two-thirds of our 21-day sentences in the Ventura County jail for the Pt. Mugu action. I was moved by the support we got at the sentencing hearings, and the time in jail was easily spent reading. I had appealed my Vandenberg case to the federal circuit court of appeals; but I was not allowed to present oral arguments, because I was in jail on these other cases.

Networking for Peace

I wrote a short book called *IRENE: Realizing World Peace* and had 2,000 copies printed in March 1985. The vision of how we can bring about a peaceful world is expressed in rhymed couplets.

When angels do descend to Earth, they call,
"Let there be peace on Earth, good will to all."
Relating so, they know the way that's best:
In living love the sacred heart is blessed.
Can human beings find that clear purity
In using love for our security?
Can we with our intelligent good will
Bring healing to a troubled world that's ill?
When what is best the people truly know,
They feel and think, and then they make it so.
Each person does what she believes is right
For her to do by her own inner light.
People don't act on what they know is wrong;
They love something to which they want to belong.
But if we don't love what is truly good,
Then we don't know the way we really could.
Our love depends on whether we're aware,
Because we give ourselves to where we care.
Thus when we act by this limitation,
The consequences bring education.
Humans evolve and learn through interaction,
Always seeking inner satisfaction.
For all to take responsibility,
Becoming wise with full ability,
Would bring to our society new birth,
A living paradise set up on Earth.
Ignorant abuses must be prevented
By institutions global now invented,
For clearly people are not angels yet,
So every need and problem must be met.
To learn and grow without hurting others

We all must love our sisters and brothers.
With all on Earth as one big family
Our differences we can settle happily,
For common needs and wants are similar;
Our hopes and dreams are so familiar.
To survive as a civilization
Changes must come in one generation.
Our greed, intolerance, oppression, and fear
Will not just magically disappear,
But we can awaken greater love, sharing,
Communication, justice, and caring
By working all together for the whole
Of the world and the good of each soul.
We'll find a way to govern the nations,
Preventing war's cruel abominations
With effective global law and government
Protecting human rights, environment,
Democracy, and due process of law,
With peace and dignity the prophets saw.

To find out where a peaceful world leads
Let's start with just the basic human needs.
Everyone surely wants to breathe fresh air
And drink the water that is clean and clear.
All people want to have enough to eat,
With adequate shelter, clothing, and heat.
If we want a peaceful world of wealth,
It must be based on every person's health,
For who would want to live with pollution
When in our hands there is a solution?
World, national, and local government
Can monitor the whole environment
To keep the water and the food chain pure
To prevent diseases as well as cure.
All natural resources we can share
If we discover systems that are fair.
Every local culture can grow their foods
To be supplemented by trading goods.
Less land will be taken for raising meat
So that crops can be grown for all to eat.

Now no one wants to be killed in a war

Or be facing nuclear weapons in horror.
We won't allow the military to kill
Civilians innocent of any bad will,
And those who work in defense industries
Will surely rather earn their salaries
For doing useful and constructive tasks
That answer calmly when the conscience asks,
"Am I contributing to peace and life,
Or does the work I do fuel greater strife?"
The sale of weapons we must not permit
To any country; we would challenge it.
No military aid or troops must go
Outside a nation's borders, and although
We must enforce the laws that keep us free
It must be by the right authority.
No nation has the sovereign right to be
A police force in some other country.
International laws can only be
Correctly served by world legality.
Certainly people want to feel secure
Aware that laws and police will assure
Us all that criminals are apprehended
When human rights violations are intended,
And people want their law courts to be fair,
Protecting the accused's rights everywhere.
People want their freedom of expression
Of art and speech, writing, and religion.
Within these broad and universal rights
Let social groups each live by their own lights.

If all the world's peoples want these things,
And since we have the technical means, that brings
Us to the social and political
Questions of how to make our ideals real.
How can we organize society
To fill all needs and safeguard liberty?
When people have become aware of what
Is best for all and have found the ways that
Will work to make our dream be manifest,
Then we will see that it was all a test
For us to grow in love for all mankind
And understand the universal mind.

If we're to live peacefully together,
Then we must learn to trust in each other
And have faith that human institutions
Can work for us to find real solutions.
If we will work for social improvement,
We can magnify our enlightenment.
And thus the values that we've seen above—
Peace, health, prosperity, human rights, and love—
Require major political revision;
Now look into the future for this vision:

The basic needs of all are being filled;
There is no war, and none are being killed,
Because the people of the world agreed
That desperate problems created the need
To form a democratic federal
World government that would represent all.
Every person may vote in elections.
World laws and courts provide the protections
For human rights, ecology, and peace.
The living standard is on the increase
Among the poor and middle class persons,
Disarmament prospering conversions.
Once a sufficient number of people learned
That change and social justice can be earned
By using methods that are nonviolent,
We no longer were fearful and silent
In facing up to violent repression,
But started acting to remove oppression.
Our moral power from an inner source
Was not intimidated by threat of force.
Nuclear weapons soon became useless,
Because immoral threats were powerless.
No nation could maintain or justify
Its genocidal weapons with a lie.
The treaties on nuclear disarmament
Agreed upon by every government
Proved that peaceful judicial processes
Can replace large military forces,
When backed by strong and active moral will
That's pure and free of any threat to kill.
Humanity's concern for its safety

And for the long-standing misery
Of poor people and the environment
Inspired a democratic government
To form based on a world constitution
To keep the peace and find a solution.
Peacekeeping forces loyal to the world
Constitution enforce the law of world
Authority, replacing the nations'
Military forces' occupations.
Threat of invasion has become so slight
That now the nations have no need to fight.
Disputes receive the world court's decision,
Which is accepted by world opinion.
Our technical and human resources,
Lost before on military forces,
Are now directed to food production
Throughout the world with good distribution,
Environmental cleanup and health care,
Renewing energy for all to share,
Providing everyone education,
Inspiring arts, and communication.
Nuclear power plants have been removed
As natural technologies improved.
While every person's basic needs are met,
There still are ways for those who wish to get
More money, if we work a little more,
Take jobs less popular or needing more
Training, creating value we can sell
To other people, if we do it well.
Most people now pursue education,
Spiritual growth and celebration;
We play in sports and learn new crafts and arts,
But most of all we share with open hearts.
There still are difficulties day to day,
But now they're handled in a humane way.
The few convicted criminals receive
True rehabilitation to relieve
The circumstances that did cause their plight,
Instead of punishment which isn't right.
The difference between the past and now
Is that the good in people has learned how
To use its power to prevent nations

From using armies and corporations
To exploit people, violate their rights,
And dominate their lives with strife and fights.
But now society is much more fair,
For everyone is learning how to share
And help the struggling with some special care
So that everyone can be more aware.

Then I diagnosed the many causes of wars such as population pressures, eating of meat, tribal hunting, territoriality, male dominance, military organization, warrior elites, honor, religious conflicts, weapons technology, the nuclear arms race, superpower rivalry, a military economy, psychological factors, masculine aggression, ambition for power, belief in deterrence, competition, apathy and despair, and various other current problems. Then I gave a prognosis, describing the tendencies since the reaction to the dramatic events of 1979, when the conflicts with Muslims over Middle-Eastern oil accelerated as did the superpower arms race. The elections of Margaret Thatcher and Ronald Reagan made the 1980s dangerous from the hostile policies of these western powers. I examined the current political trends with the wars in the Middle East and Central America and the nuclear arms race. The current economic trends were also short-sighted.

In the last section of the book called "Healing" I described how I believed we could bring about world peace. I suggested that a popular peace movement could change the policies of their governments to reverse the arms race and end the wars, and Green politics could begin healing the Earth and society. I prophesied that Europe would remove all their nuclear weapons and become a nuclear-free zone. I predicted that West and East Germans would unify into one nation, followed later by the reunification of the Koreas as Asia was also demilitarized. A Pan-African movement would also throw off military support. The Scandinavian countries would lead the way by showing how a balance of some socialism and a free market can work well. Corporate profits would be taxed to help to improve the environment, and as society became more efficient and less materialistic, the work week could be reduced gradually from forty hours to 24 hours or less.

Eventually as disarmament proceeded, the people of the world would join together to form a democratic government to resolve international disputes and protect human rights everywhere. A World Assembly would be elected by the people to make world law, and nine presidents from North America, Latin America, Europe, Africa, North Asia, West Asia, India, China, and East Asia would be elected to the World Executive Council to make sure that world law was enforced by an International Peacekeeping Service. Each president would appoint one justice to the World Court of Justice. So far only a small part of this has actually happened; but I believe that something like the rest will occur if we are to survive. I mailed a copy of *IRENE* to about 1300 peace organizations, more than two hundred of them outside of North America.

When I heard about the Great Peace March, I went down to Los Angeles to talk to them about their plans. I was aghast at how naïve they were about the processes needed to keep a moving city of 5,000 functioning well. Apparently the staff expected to give the orders and that everyone would just obey. One person even said to me, "What is there for them to decide? They can't not march." They wanted each marcher to raise $1,000. I decided that if I was going to have to raise more money (after sending out *IRENE*) that it would be for my book *The Way to Peace*, which I published in 1986.

By the end of the year I had decided to go on my own peace tour in 1987, and I sent out a mailing to more than three thousand peace groups in the 140 cities on my itinerary from April to November and to about 300 Unitarian ministers. My strategy was to influence the policies of the candidates running for President so that we could elect someone who would go along with the enlightened proposals of Gorbachev. I drew up a "Peace by 2000" petition that asked politicians to work for a plan of complete nuclear disarmament by that year. I hoped that each peace group would make copies of the petition and circulate them. I also included an article of about 5,000 words called "Will We Make Peace in 1989?" that described the current issues and how I believed we could solve them. The mailing also contained the brochure on the World Peace Movement Principles, Purposes, and Methods, a local news article about my peace efforts, and my schedule so that they would know when I would be in their city. I received about thirty responses to this mailing offering to arrange some event for my visit.

Except when I spent a few days in a big city, I traveled nearly every day except on Sundays. I kept a peace journal that I wrote in about once a week, summarizing the contacts that I made, what I learned about their activities, and what we worked on together. At the beginning I spent extra time in San Francisco preparing for a large mobilization rally in April. Then I proceeded up the coast to Seattle. In Great Falls, Montana 22 peace groups had gathered to hear me speak. I managed to contact the most active peace workers in each city and gave out the materials, sold a few books, and cooperated as best I could with whatever they were doing. After crossing South Dakota I went down to Little Rock for the Unitarians General Assembly. Then I went to Oklahoma and turned north. In Dubuque I was able to speak to Michael Dukakis, who claimed he was converted to disarmament, and in Des Moines I talked briefly to Joe Biden, who actually said I would be in trouble if he were elected. From Minnesota I went east across the Midwest to New England. In New York I picked up copies of my new book *LIFE AS A WHOLE: Principles of Education Based on a Spiritual Philosophy of Love*, but I did not sell many copies of that on the rest of my tour.

I met every person in the Plowshares 8 except Carl Kabat, who was in prison. I attended the Atlantic Life Community retreat in Pennsylvania and went to a trial in Virginia, where some from Jonah House were convicted. In Washington Senator Jesse Helms invited me into the Senators elevator which gave me the chance to warn him that a vote for aid to the Contras is a crime according to the Nuremberg Principles. I also found that there were fine peace activists in the deep South, though not as many. Miami was the only city where I was warned that peace bumper stickers could be dangerous for your car. I stayed with people wherever I went and never had difficulty finding hospitality. I stayed in several Catholic Worker houses. I found that most of the active peace workers were generous and kind although they were often financially poor. Those in smaller cities tended to be more friendly, and some of the more sophisticated were not too helpful. At St. Mary's University in San Antonio I was their featured speaker during their conference on conflict resolution. On my last stop in Las Vegas I was arrested at the test site; but everyone was released without any consequences. When I returned home to Ojai, I had just enough money to pay off the debt for publishing *LIFE AS A WHOLE.* I had met with about six hundred peace groups and stayed in 130 cities.

Nuremberg Actions at Concord

When I visited the Walnut Creek Peace Center on my tour, Chuck Goodmacher told me that they were planning Nuremberg Actions to block the trains at Concord that were taking weapons to Central America. I felt drawn to this area and favored the approach of using international law. I was in New York City on September 1 when I heard that Brian Willson had been run over by a munitions train at Concord. So after I completed my peace tour, I decided to go up to Concord and join Nuremberg Actions. The first night I was there, I saw a truck coming out of the base and stood in front of it. They moved me out of the way and said they thought we had an agreement about that. I attended the meetings, worked as a volunteer at the peace center, and began blocking trains. I was hoping to organize a peace community there. When Scot Rutherford purchased a house in a poor section of Pittsburg near Concord, I moved in there.

I was planning on going south to see my family for Christmas and bring back my library that I had reduced to 1500 books. So on December 23 I was not planning on getting arrested; but Greg Getty refused to put his arms behind his back, and because the deputies were inflicting pain on him instead of picking him up, I decided to join him. As I walked into the closed road, I was immediately put in handcuffs and arrested. We were soon released, and Greg, Spalding, and April went south with me to help me move my books and things. Brian's wife Holly Rauen and I organized an event at Bill O'Donnell's Catholic church in Berkeley so that people could hear Katya Komisaruk speak about how she destroyed the Navstar computer at Vandenberg in her plowshares action before turning herself in. Brian Willson also spoke, and there was good music. I did not like to spend long hours at the vigils in the cold wind by the highway and preferred to study and write; but I was intent on blocking every train I could. I also managed to teach a class on Literature and Psychology at John F. Kennedy University one night a week. I was getting arrested at the tracks about once a week, but for a while they would just take names and let us go. Shawna even used the name Emma Goldman, and they did not know the difference. In February we had a fast, and I sent a letter urging every member of Congress to vote against aid to the Contras. After that, Saul Steinberg of Coleman Publishing no longer sent me any more copies of my book *The Way to Peace* even though I owned the books. I had seen a photo of him standing next to Ronald Reagan.

When I was indicted for the arrest before Christmas, I did not want to waive time. I defended myself in the first trial of Nuremberg Actions, and Lowell Richards represented Bill Minkwitz. Lowell and I decided not to challenge any jurors. An outstanding videographer named Mark Coplan was allowed to tape the trial. Judge Cunningham seemed reasonable on many things, but he would not allow us to present international law or the defense of necessity.

He did allow me to explain my motivation, and in the closing argument he let me read and interpret the Nuremberg Principles. Because my arrest was questionable on this day, the jury acquitted me. One juror refused to convict Bill, and so his was a hung jury. In March 1988 the sheriffs began holding people in jail for up to 48 hours (not counting weekends) and then releasing people without charging them, using some statute designed for holding prostitutes, drunks, and drug addicts. That meant that an arrest on Thursday or Friday resulted on four days in jail. Then they would release us without charging us. I refused to bail out even for my last class, and my teaching opportunity faded to giving one small workshop on nonviolence.

In June we learned that the US Customs was stopping trucks carrying medicine and toys for children from crossing the Texas border, because they were going to Nicaragua. So a group of us went to the Customs building in San Francisco and were arrested sitting outside the door they locked to keep us out. We were given a trial fairly quickly, and some of us were convicted for being in front of the door. I refused to cooperate with probation, and it was terminated "with prejudice." Thirty people from Nuremberg Actions were indicted and tried together in Concord, but once again the jury was hung. I helped Mark with the videotaping by holding the shotgun microphone. Expert witnesses included Karen Parker on international law, ex-CIA agent David MacMichael, a judge from El Salvador, and the Vietnam veteran and physician Charlie Clements.

I offered to write and edit a Nonviolence Handbook; but Holly said they already had one from the Pledge of Resistance, though no one seemed to be using it. Greg would cook soup at the house, and I let him use my car to take it to the vigil. Richard Wilhelm told me he was eating only raw oats; he was not complaining, but I was concerned that people living at the tracks were not even getting enough to eat. I finally convinced a meeting to authorize $75 a week for food. Efforts to draw more people into the campaign were not very successful. There was a large demonstration on a weekend; but the fence gate was locked, and no one was even arrested. We did have one action occupying the area by the nuclear bunkers, and Diane Poole poured her blood. I was discouraged when I was not invited to be on KPFA radio, because a newly hired coordinator wanted "people with jobs." When Joe Cohen completed his walk across the country from Georgia, he stayed at peace house. I had met him several times on my tour, and he offered to let me rent his house on 125 acres of pine forest in Georgia for only $100 per month. So in September 1988 I decided to leave, and after house-sitting for my vacationing parents, I moved to Buena Vista, Georgia. I had been arrested in Concord more than forty times in the ten months I was there.

Protesting the Trident Missiles

On May 6, 1989 I participated in a Pax Christi protest at the Trident Submarine base at Kings Bay, Georgia. Twenty of us were arrested for stepping over an imaginary line on the sidewalk outside the fence near the main gate that they had arbitrarily drawn, because my friend Joe Cohen and others had tried to climb the fence in a previous protest. Also 54 others were arrested for blocking the road into the base; but they were not even charged. Before I stepped over the line, I said,

> This base is in violation of international law;
> it is in violation of the United Nations Charter,
> the Pact of Paris, the Nuremberg Principles,
> and the Geneva Conventions.
> It is an obscenity against humanity
> and an abomination in the sight of God!
> Today I am taking one more small step
> for peace in the world.

At the time the Navy was playing loudly over and over a tape of the commander warning people they would be arrested so that it was difficult for people to hear. Because we were obviously peace protesters, they would not even let us walk to the building where people normally requested permission to enter the base.

We were released and later ordered to appear for arraignment on June 12, and several protesters came back from New Orleans and Michigan for the arraignment. Because of these distances most agreed to pay a fine or spend five days in jail. Only Miriam Hope and I pleaded not guilty and requested a trial by a federal judge. Once again our right to a trial by a jury was denied, and on July 11 we were tried by Judge Alaimo. Miriam wanted more time to prepare and was supposed to have at least 30 days; but Judge Alaimo decided that 29 days was enough. These facts were later missing in the court record. After the prosecution presented their case, I made an offer of proof for the defense of necessity and international law. Judge Alaimo kept interrupting me and asked if I wanted to testify. Only when I was testifying did he inform me that he had ruled against my defense. Judge Alaimo asked me several questions as if he were prosecuting me. During Miriam's testimony Judge Alaimo agreed to assume that the Trident submarine is the worst weapon ever invented. In my closing argument I said among many other things that Gorbachev was moving the Soviet Union toward disarmament, while the United States was developing these offensive first-strike weapons.

Judge Alaimo found us both guilty but postponed sentencing so that an investigative report could be made. I said I did not want to travel back and forth again and would refuse probation or a fine; so he allowed me to start serving my time. I was taken to the new but already overcrowded Glynn County jail. During the ten weeks I waited for my sentencing hearing I read many books and did some writing. Even though she was not in jail, Miriam was sentenced before I was and was allowed to pay her fine to a charity and had to do 500 hours of community service. Knowing I would probably get the maximum sentence of six months, I spoke to Judge Alaimo for about an hour at my hearing without using any notes. I had had a long time to think about it and gave an impassioned speech about my concern for our country and the danger of a nuclear war, how absurd militarization was, the value of nonviolent methods, and I explained the many efforts I had made to bring about peace. I also complained that many inmates in the jail were waiting several weeks just to be arraigned. I was given the maximum sentence and never did pay the fine. I said I wanted to appeal and was assigned a public defender for that.

Because of the overcrowding I advised the officer running the jail to stop accepting federal prisoners, and soon I was transferred to Taladega, Alabama. There we were crowded three men into single cells. When the televangelist Jim Bakker was brought to Taladega only two men were put in each cell in his building so that the media would not learn how overcrowded the prison was. I even had to go to the hole for one day, because every cell in our building had three men. After about a month I was transferred by plane to El Reno in Oklahoma and from there to California. This was apparently done so that California would prosecute me for the Nuremberg Actions at Concord even though moving me for that purpose was a clear violation of federal prison policy. California does not extradite for misdemeanors, and they did not try to pick me up.

I was taken to the camp at Lompoc. I considered myself a political prisoner and refused to work for the Government. So I was taken across the street to a maximum security prison and put in the hole for a month. Because they would not let me use the law library or a typewriter to work on my appeal, I agreed to work and went back to the camp. My lawyer had refused to argue my right to a jury trial or international law, because he was afraid of being fined for a "frivolous" appeal. So I used his research on my solid First Amendment argument and wrote the appeal myself. I was allowed to work on this at the camp until the deadline of December 18. Even though I applied for an extension, I had to take a job during the last two weeks; but I managed to finish my appeal and mail it before I was released on January 5, 1990. By then the Berlin Wall had come down, and the new decade brought a new era. I was given $25 to get a new start in life and was flown back to Georgia. My appeal was later denied, and I was not even given the opportunity to make an oral argument.

2003 Peace Campaign

The questionable election of George W. Bush and his warlike policies, especially after September 11, 2001, caused another major crisis for the world. So I decided that I could travel around the United States again in order to make my books available personally and speak to people about world peace. I scheduled an itinerary of 180 college campuses to visit in seven months. In November 2002 this crisis inspired me to run for President of the United States myself as a Democrat in an effort to raise public awareness on more enlightened solutions for peace and justice issues. I hoped that I would gain enough support to be included in the televised debates before the Democratic primaries.

I sent the following letter on January 6, 2003 to the United Nations with supportive signatures by 79 people from Citizens for Peaceful Resolutions in Ventura, California:

Dear Secretary-General Kofi Annan,

For twelve years the military forces of the United States and the United Kingdom have been violating international law in Iraq. Those of us in the world peace movement are especially concerned about the imminent war threatened against Iraq by the United States and the United Kingdom. We believe that the numerous attacks on Iraqi air defenses and other targets in the so-called "no-fly zones" are illegal by international law according to the United Nations Charter, Article 2, Sections 3 and 4, which read,

3. All Members shall settle their international disputes by peaceful means in such a manner that international peace and security, and justice, are not endangered.
4. All Members shall refrain in their international relations from the threat or use of force against the territorial integrity or

political independence of any state, or in any other manner inconsistent with the Purposes of the United Nations.

These attacks and the preparations for the aggressive war are also crimes against peace according to the Nuremberg Principles, which are defined as,

> Planning, preparation, initiation or waging of a war of aggression or a war in violation of international treaties, agreements or assurances.

Although the economic sanctions that were imposed on Iraq by the United Nations Security Council in 1990 may have been justified in order to get Iraq to withdraw from Kuwait, since that goal has been achieved, we believe that they are no longer justified. Hundreds of thousands of Iraqi children have died as a result of these immoral and illegal sanctions. We believe they are crimes against humanity according to the Nuremberg Principles, which are defined as

> Murder, extermination, enslavement, deportation and other inhuman acts done against any civilian population, or persecutions on political, racial or religious grounds, when such acts are done or such persecutions are carried on in execution of or in connection with any crime against peace or any war crime.

They also clearly violate the Geneva Convention Relative to the Protection of Civilian Persons in Time of War, Articles 27, 30, and 31, which read:

> Article 27. Protected persons are entitled, in all circumstances, to respect for their persons, their honor, their family rights, their religious convictions and practices, and their manners and customs. They shall at all times be humanely treated, and shall be protected specifically against all acts of violence or threats thereof and against insults and public curiosity. Women shall be especially protected against any attack on their honor, in particular against rape, enforced prostitution, or any form of indecent assault. Without prejudice to the provisions relating to their state of health, age and sex, all protected persons shall be treated with the same consideration by the Party to the conflict in whose power they are, without any adverse distinction based, in particular, on race, religion or political opinion.

Article 30. The High Contracting Parties specifically agree that each of them is prohibited from taking any measure of such character as to cause physical suffering or extermination of protected persons in their lands. This prohibition applies not only to murder, torture, corporal punishment, mutilation and medical or scientific experiments not necessitated by the medical treatment of a protected person, but also to any other measures of brutality whether applied by civilian or military agents.

Article 31. No protected person may be punished for an offense he or she has not personally committed. Collective penalties and likewise all measures of intimidation or of terrorism are prohibited. Pillage is prohibited. Reprisals against protected persons and their property are prohibited.

The stated purpose of these sanctions and the threatened war against Iraq is to make sure that they do not have any weapons of mass destruction, and we support thorough inspections in Iraq by agents of the United Nations to make sure that Iraq does not have any such weapons. Thus far several weeks of inspections have not revealed any evidence that they do. If any programs for developing weapons of mass destruction are found, they should simply be dismantled. A war over this would be unnecessary, immoral, and illegal.

Yet the United States and the United Kingdom are in clear violation of the Treaty on the Non-Proliferation of Nuclear Weapons, Article 6, which reads,

Each of the Parties to the Treaty undertakes to pursue negotiations in good faith on effective measures relating to cessation of the nuclear arms race at an early date and to nuclear disarmament, and on a treaty on general and complete disarmament under strict and effective international control.

Therefore we call upon the United Nations General Assembly, as the representatives of the political voices of humanity, to pass a resolution condemning these violations of international law by the United States and the United Kingdom.

We further request that the United Nations Security Council keep their inspectors in Iraq to prevent an aggressive war by the United States and the United Kingdom against the people of Iraq until the United States removes its threatening forces from the region.

We also ask the International Court of Justice to bring charges against the United States and the United Kingdom so that they will cease and desist from committing these crimes against international law.

In the Light of God,
Sanderson Beck
for the world peace movement

The practical *Nonviolent Action Handbook* was published in January 2003 to assist peace activists, and the long, one-volume edition of *Guides to Peace and Justice* came out in February. During the weekly marches for peace in Santa Barbara I urged people to do more and recommended a general strike if Bush gave Saddam Hussein an ultimatum. I said I would begin a juice fast and did so on March 17. As the war began two days later, we formed an affinity group in Ventura to protest at Republican Congressman Elton Gallegly's office on April 1. During the next two evenings I marched with protestors in the streets of Santa Barbara, but only a few people had been arrested for blocking traffic on the 101 freeway in the afternoon. I urged people to protest at Raytheon or Vandenberg Air Force Base as a more direct confrontation with the war activities.

I was arrested on Saturday March 22 for crossing the line at Vandenberg AFB, where they were using computers and the space command system to direct the shock-and-awe attacks on Iraq. I made a short speech while Captain Quigley was reading a warning into a loudspeaker. I had to shout and complained that US hypocrisy was demanding a weak country disarm while the US had more weapons of mass destruction than anyone. I appealed to Christians to follow what Jesus taught by loving our enemies. I said that I was running for president on a true disarmament platform, and I prophesied that there would be a new nonviolent revolution "to throw the fascists out." After I was taken into custody, I appealed to the soldiers in riot gear to become conscientious objections by refusing to obey illegal orders according to the Nuremberg Principles. Two women had been arrested before me; after being questioned by the FBI, we were released with court dates in June.

The next day I helped facilitate nonviolence workshops in Santa Barbara at the Nuclear Age Peace Foundation and in Ventura. Some in Santa Barbara were considering protesting at Raytheon, the county's largest employer and one of the biggest weapons manufacturers. On Monday I felt called to return to Vandenberg AFB, and I arranged to announce my intentions on KPFK's Morning Show with Sonali Kolhatkar and then on KCSB radio. In the afternoon I crossed the line at Vandenberg AFB and again asked to speak to the base commander to tell him to stop committing war crimes. I told Sergeant Malcolm Walton that if they released me I would keep coming back until I could go before a judge with my charge. He arranged for me to be arraigned in Los Angeles on Wednesday and let me go. I stayed at the Los Angeles Catholic Worker, and on Wednesday morning joined their weekly protest at the federal building. Because Martin Sheen was there, numerous media were present. Before being arrested with two other women, I was allowed to make a very brief statement in which I called for massive civil disobedience to stop the illegal war. After an hour I was released and walked next door to my arraignment for the Vandenberg arrests. Magistrate Patrick Walsh showed his prejudice by saying he would not allow any argument related to international law even though he knew nothing yet about my case; he quickly denied my motion for a new judge. He permitted me to defend myself and allowed me to have the advice of a public defender, Davina Chen. In solidarity with the 2300 people in San Francisco I remained in custody for a month until the hearing on April 24.

On that day Judge Walsh would not hear my arguments in response to the prosecution's motion to disallow any defense using international law, necessity, crime prevention, and the first amendment. He urged me to go home, saying "The war is over," and I did not have to pay bail. That weekend I attended the Book Festival at UCLA and saw a woman handing out ANSWER flyers about an anti-war conference; she was doing it furtively because she had been warned she could not do that. I risked arrest for handing out my presidential campaign brochures in the outdoor areas outside of the limited "free speech zone" they set up near one entrance. I talked with the UCLA official in charge about their policy, and he told me that I could do so. I was then interviewed on the KPFK news and explained how this "little victory" had changed their repressive policy about free speech.

The day before my trial the prosecuting attorney told me that they would stipulate to the fact that Vandenberg AFB was involved in the Iraq War so that none of their officers would have to testify. At the trial on May 1 during my testimony and closing argument I tried to explain that I was merely trying to stop the ongoing crimes of murder, crimes against peace, and violation of the UN Charter and other treaties, but Judge Walsh kept trying to limit my time and went past the lunch break well into the afternoon. I defended myself on the Vandenberg charges, and Davina provided an excellent technical defense on the charge at the federal building; but Judge Walsh ignored all but the most narrow-minded issues and found me guilty on all three counts. On May 13 he sentenced me to probation and community service even though I told him that I would not accept probation. In the *Nonviolent Action Handbook* I had recommended refusing probation, and I would not accept it even though I was alone in this case. I went back to court on August 3 to be sentenced for refusing the probation and was given another three months in prison. I considered myself a political prisoner and would not accept a job because I needed to work on my appeal. I found this time in prison to be a spiritual experience.

I attended a conference in Santa Barbara sponsored by the Nuclear Age Peace Foundation in May 2004 called Charting a New Course for US Nuclear Policy that included David Krieger, Helen Caldicott, Randall Forsberg, Jonathan Schell, Daniel Ellsberg, Richard Falk, Alice Slater, Brent Blackwelder, Michele Boyd, John Burroughs, Jackie Cabasso, Michael Flynn, George Lakoff, Adil Najam, Thomas G. Plate, Tom Reifer, and Douglas Roche. I wrote and distributed the following proposal:

As Randy Forsberg suggested,
I think we should formulate specific goals,
but I think we also need to discuss strategies
for effectively achieving those goals.
Complete nuclear disarmament,
providing clean water for everyone in the world,
health care and education for all,
and phasing out nuclear power
would mean a radical revolution in the United States.
I think we need to realize that
the current US Government is a criminal regime
and that even to pay its taxes is to be complicit in its crimes.
I believe that we can bring about these goals in our lifetimes
if we are willing to make the necessary sacrifices.
Because the problems are complex and immense,
I think we should proceed in stages.
To begin the discussion I am making the following proposal:

OBJECTIVES:
1. Reduce nuclear weapons
   so that no nation has more than 100.
2. All national military forces must be withdrawn
   from nations outside their borders and be greatly reduced.
3. IAEA or UN inspections must ensure
   that #1 has been achieved,
   and then they should make sure that
   all remaining nuclear weapons are also eliminated.
   All nuclear materials must be monitored
   until nuclear power plants are phased out.
4. All disputes between nations shall be settled
   by a judicial process in an international court of justice.
5. Violators of international peace shall be arrested
   and brought to the International Criminal Court (ICC)
   in as nonviolent a way as possible.

6. We should make sure that everyone in the world
has access to clean water, health care, and education.

STRATEGIES:
1. Boycott the US Government
by refusing to pay its income tax
or cooperate with its crimes
until the first three objectives are achieved.
2. Dedicate our lives to working for these goals full-time
and by donating income
above the taxable level to nonprofits.
For some this may mean nonviolent civil disobedience
and refusing to work in prison
for an oppressive government.
For others it may mean communicating with people
and organizing nonviolent demonstrations.

After getting out of prison I have completed the first six volumes of the *Ethics of Civilization* and revised and extended *Guides to Peace and Justice* into this two-volume *History of Peace*. In 2005 I wrote and published two short books. *The Art of Gentle Living* is a self-help book with a spiritual philosophy and psychology with ideas how we each can live joyfully, lovingly, peacefully, and frugally so that we can be happy and get along better with others in an increasingly crowded world. Topics include spiritual awareness, conscious self-mastery and cooperation with the natural self, understanding feelings, using clear thinking, practicing compassionate communication, and demonstrating ethical economics and politics. *Best For All: How We Can Save the World* is a visionary book that suggests practical solutions to the most challenging crises humanity faces today in the current global emergency by focusing on alleviating poverty, disarming the weapons of war, creating global democracy, radically reforming the United States government, using restorative justice to improve the judicial system, developing ecological management for a sustainable economy, freeing communication from commercial pollution, inspiring spiritual awakening of truly humane values, and implementing these reforms by

using nonviolent strategies for social and political change.
The appendix includes proposed drafts for a Global Disarmament Treaty, a Federal Earth Democracy Constitution,
and a revised US Constitution.

Bibliography

General

Barash, David P. and Charles P. Webel, *Peace and Conflict Studies*. Thousand Oaks, 2002.

Encyclopaedia Britannica, 30 volumes. Chicago, 1975.

Encyclopedia of Philosophy, 8 volumes ed. Paul Edwards. New York, 1967.

Encyclopedia of World History, An ed. William L. Langer. Boston, 1980.

Instead of Violence ed. Arthur and Lila Weinberg. Boston, 1963.

Pacifist Conscience, The ed. Peter Mayer. New York, 1966.

Peace and War ed. Charles R. Beitz and Theodore Herman. San Francisco, 1973.

Peace/Mir: An Anthology of Historic Alternatives to War ed. Charles Hatfield and Ruzanna Ilukhina. Syracuse, 1994.

Peace Reader, A ed. Joseph J. Fahey and Richard Armstrong. New York, 1992.

1. Gandhi's Nonviolent Revolution

Ashe, Geoffrey, *Gandhi: A Study in Revolution*. London, 1968.

Bondurant, Joan, *Conquest of Violence*. Berkeley, 1965.

Chadha, Yogesh, *Gandhi: A Life*. New York, 1997.

Chaudhuri, Nirad D., *Thy Hand, Great Anarch! India 1921-1952*. Reading, 1987.

Easwaran, Eknath, *Gandhi the Man*. Berkeley, 1972.

Erikson, Erik H., *Gandhi's Truth*. New York, 1969.

Fischer, Louis, *The Life of Mahatma Gandhi*. New York, 1950.

Gandhi: His Relevance for Our Times ed. G. Ramachandran and T. K. Mahadevan. Bombay, 1964.

Gandhi, M. K., *An Autobiography or the Story of My Experiments with Truth* tr. Mahadev Desai. Ahmedabad, 1940.

Gandhi, M. K., *For Pacifists*. Ahmedabad, 1949.

Gandhi, M. K., *In Search of the Supreme*, 3 volumes ed. V. B. Kher. Ahmedabad, 1961 1962.

Gandhi, M. K., *Non-violence I Peace & War*, 2 volumes. Ahmedabad, 1942, 1949.

Gandhi, M. K., *Non-violent Resistance (Satyagraha)*. New York, 1951.

Gandhi, M. K., *Satyagraha in South Africa* tr. Valji Govindji Desai. Ahmedabad, 1950.

Gandhi, Mahatma, *Hind Swaraj or Indian Home Rule*. Madras, 1943.

Gandhi, Mahatma, Speeches and Writings of. Madras, fourth edition, no date.

Gandhi Reader, The ed. Homer A. Jack. Bloomington, 1956.

Gandhi, The Moral and Political Writings of Mahatma, Vol. 3: Non-Violent Resistance and Social Transformation. Oxford, 1987.

Gupta, R. K., *A Dictionary of Moral Concepts in Gandhi*. New Delhi, 2000.

Hunt, James D., *Gandhi and the Nonconformists: Encounters in South Africa*. New Delhi, 1986.

Iyer, Raghavan, *The Moral and Political Thought of Mahatma Gandhi*. London, 1983.

Keer, Dhananjay, *Mahatma Gandhi: Political Saint and Unarmed Prophet*. Bombay, 1973.

Mallac, Guy de, *Seven Steps to Global Change: Gandhi's Message for Today*. Santa Fe, 1987.

Meaning of the Mahatma for the Millennium, The ed. Kuruvilla Pandikattu. Delhi, 2000.

Mehta, Ved, *Mahatma Gandhi and His Apostles*. Middlesex, 1976.

Pyarelal, *Mahatma Gandhi: The Discovery of Satyagraha—On the Threshold*. Bombay, 1980.

Pyarelal, *Mahatma Gandhi: The Early Phase*. Ahmedabad, 1965.

Pyarelal, *Mahatma Gandhi: The Last Phase*, 2 volumes. Ahmedabad, 1958, 1965, 1966.

Rolland, Romain, *Mahatma Gandhi*. London, 1924.

Sharp, Gene, *Gandhi as a Political Strategist*. Boston, 1979.

Sheean, Vincent, *Lead, Kindly Light*. New York, 1949.

Shirer, William Laurence, *Gandhi: A Memoir*. New York,

1979.

Struggle for Freedom: History and Culture of the Indian People, Vol. 11 ed. R. C. Majumdar. Bombay, 1969.

Tendulkar, D. G., *Mahatma: Life of Mohandas Karamchand Gandhi,* Vol. 6-8. Delhi, 1984, 1985.

Torgerson, Don Arthur, *Gandhi.* Chicago, 1968.

Verma, M. M., *Gandhi's Technique of Mass Mobilization.* New Delhi, 1990.

2. Wilson and the League of Nations

Angell, Norman, *The Great Illusion: A Study of the Relation of Military Power to National Advantage.* New York, 1913.

Armstrong, Hamilton Fish, *Peace and Counterpeace: From Wilson to Hitler.* New York, 1971.

Bailey, Thomas A., *Woodrow Wilson and the Great Betrayal.* New York, 1947.

Bailey, Thomas A., *Woodrow Wilson and the Lost Peace.* New York, 1947.

Baker, Ray Stannard, *Woodrow Wilson and World Settlement,* Volumes 1-2. Garden City, 1922.

Baker, Ray Stannard, *Woodrow Wilson: Life and Letters,* 8 volumes. New York, 1946.

Bendiner, Elmer, *A Time for Angels: The Tragicomic History of the League of Nations.* New York, 1975.

Bledsoe, Robert L. and Boleslaw A. Boczek, *The International Law Dictionary.* Santa Barbara, 1987.

Blum, John Morton, *Woodrow Wilson and the Politics of Morality.* Boston, 1956.

Brierly, J. L., *The Law of Nations: An Introduction to the International Law of Peace.* New York, 1963.

Claude, Inis L., *Swords into Plowshares: The Problems and Progress of International Organization.* New York, 1971.

Davis, Calvin DeArmond, *The United States and the Second Hague Peace Conference: American Diplomacy and International Organization 1899-1914.* Durham, 1976.

Dillon, E. J., *The Inside Story of the Peace Conference.* New York, 1920.

Ferrell, Robert H., *Peace in Their Time: The Origins of the*

Kellog-Briand Pact. New York, 1952.

Forster, Kent, *The Failures of Peace: The Search for a Negotiated Peace During the First World War*. Washington, 1941.

Freud, Sigmund and William C. Bullitt, *Thomas Woodrow Wilson: A Psychological Study*. Boston, 1966.

George, Alexander L. and Juliette L. George, *Woodrow Wilson and Colonel House: A Personality Study*. New York, 1964.

George, David Lloyd, *Memoirs of the Peace Conference*, 2 volumes. New Haven, 1939.

Gill, George, *The League of Nations from 1929 to 1946*. Garden City Park, 1996.

Glahn, Gerhard von, *Law Among Nations: An Introduction to Public International Law*. New York, 1986.

Hinsley, F. H., *Power and the Pursuit of Peace: Theory and Practice in the History of Relations Between States*. Cambridge, 1963.

Holls, Frederick W., *The Peace Conference at the Hague*. New York, 1900.

Lansing, Robert, *The Big Four and Others of the Peace Conference*. Boston, 1921.

Lansing, Robert, *The Peace Negotiations: A Personal Narrative*. Boston, 1921.

Law of War, The: A Documentary History, Volume 1 ed. Leon Friedman. New York, 1972.

League of Nations: Ten Years of World Co-operation (Secretariat of the League of Nations). London, 1930.

Levin, N. Gordon, Jr., *Woodrow Wilson and World Politics*. London, 1968.

Link, Arthur S., *Wilson: Campaigns for Progressivism and Peace 1916-1917*. Princeton, 1965.

Mayer, Arno J., *Politics and Diplomacy of Peacemaking: Containment and Counterrevolution at Versailles, 1918-1919*. New York, 1947.

Mee, Charles L., *The End of Order: Versailles 1919*. New York, 1980.

Northedge, F. S., *The League of Nations: its life and times 1920-1946*. New York, 1986.

Pringle, Henry F., *The Life and Times of William Howard Taft*, 2 volumes. New York, 1939.

Rovine, Arthur W., *The First Fifty Years: The Secretary-General in World Politics 1920-1970*. Leyden, 1970.

Scott, James Brown, *The Hague Peace Conferences of 1899 and 1907*, 2 volumes. New York, 1972.

Smith, Gene, *When the Cheering Stopped: the last years of Woodrow Wilson*. New York, 1964.

Smith, Page, *America Enters the World: A People's History of the Progressive Era and World War I*. New York, 1985.

Stone, Ralph, *The Irreconcilables: The Fight Against the League of Nations*. New York, 1970.

Towards an Enduring Peace: A Symposium of Peace Proposals and Programs 1914-1916 ed. Randolph S. Bourne. New York, 1971.

Viereck, George Sylvester, *The Strangest Friendship in History: Woodrow Wilson and Colonel House*. New York, 1932.

Walters, F. P., *A History of the League of Nations*, 2 volumes. London, 1952.

Walworth, Arthur, *Woodrow Wilson*. Baltimore, 1965.

White, William Allen, *Woodrow Wilson: The Man, His Times and His Task*. Boston, 1924.

Wilson, Woodrow, The Messages and Papers of, 2 volumes. New York, 1924.

Woodrow Wilson and the Paris Peace Conference ed. N. Gordon Levin, Jr. Lexington, 1972.

Ziegler, David W., War, *Peace, and International Politics*. Boston, 1977.

Zimmern, Alfred, *The League of Nations and the Rule of Law 1918-1935*. London, 1936.

3. United Nations and Human Rights

Brackman, Arnold C., *The Other Nuremberg: The Untold Story of the Tokyo War Crimes Trials*. New York, 1987.

Burns, James MacGregor, *Roosevelt: The Lion and the Fox 1882-1940*. New York, 1956.

Burns, James MacGregor, *Roosevelt: The Soldier of Freedom*

1940-1945. New York, 1970.

Conot, Robert E., *Justice at Nuremberg*. New York, 1983.

Dallek, Robert, *Franklin D. Roosevelt and American Foreign Policy 1932-1945.* Oxford, 1979.

Eichelberger, Clark M., *Organizing for Peace: A Personal History of the Founding of the United Nations.* New York, 1977.

Franklin D. Roosevelt's Own Story Told in His Own Words ed. Donald Day. Boston, 1951.

Lash, Joseph P., *Eleanor: The Years Alone.* New York, 1972.

Roosevelt, Eleanor, *The Autobiography of.* New York, 1961.

Roosevelt, Eleanor, *On My Own: The Years Since the White House.* New York, 1958.

Roosevelt, Eleanor, *This I Remember.* New York, 1949.

Roosevelt, Franklin Delano, *The Selected Addresses of, 1932-1945 (Nothing to Fear)* ed. B. D. Zevin. Cambridge, 1946.

Russell, Ruth B., *A History of the United Nations Charter: The Role of the United States 1940-1945.* Washington, 1958.

Tavares de Sa, Hernane, *The Play within the Play: The Inside Story of the UN.* New York, 1966.

Tusa, Ann and John, *The Nuremberg Trial.* New York, 1983.

United Nations and Human Rights: 18th Report of the Commission to Study the Organization of Peace. Dobbs Ferry, 1968.

4. United Nations Peacekeeping

Blue Helmets: A Review of United Nations Peace-keeping. New York, 1996.

Boyd, Andrew, *Fifteen Men on a Powder Keg: A History of the U.N. Security Council.* New York, 1971.

Claude, Inis L., *Swords into Plowshares: The Problems and Progress of International Organization.* New York, 1971.

Evolution of Peacekeeping, The ed. William J. Durch. New York, 1993.

Ferenc, Benjamin B., *An International Criminal Court, A Step Toward World Peace: A Documentary History and Analysis, Volume 2: The Beginning of Wisdom.* London, 1980.

Glahn, Gerhard von, *Law Among Nations: An Introduction to*

Public International Law. New York, 1986.

James, Alan, *The Politics of Peace-Keeping.* New York, 1969.

Law of War, The: A Documentary History, 2 volumes ed. Leon Friedman. New York, 1972.

Lie, Trygve, *In the Cause of Peace: Seven Years with the United Nations.* New York, 1954.

McNamara, Robert S. and James G. Blight, *Wilson's Ghost: Reducing the Risk of Conflict, Killing, and Catastrophe in the 21st Century.* New York, 2001.

Peacekeeping: Appraisals and Proposals ed. Henry Wiseman. New York, 1983.

Raimundo, Bernard A., *Peaceful Coexistence: International Law in the Building of Communism.* Baltimore, 1967.

Rovine, Arthur W., *The First Fifty Years: The Secretary-General in World Politics 1920-1970.* Leyden, 1970.

Thant, U, *Toward World Peace: Speeches and Public Statements 1957-1963.* New York, 1964.

UN Security Council from the Cold War to the 21st Century, The ed. David M. Malone. Boulder, 2004.

Wainhouse, David W., *Arms Control Agreements: Designs for Verification and Organization.* 1968.

Wainhouse, David W., *International Peacekeeping at the Crossroads: National Support-Experience and Prospects.* Baltimore, 1973..

Wainhouse, David W., *International Peace Observation: A History and Forecast.* Baltimore, 1966.

5. Einstein and Schweitzer
on Peace in the Atomic Age

Albert Einstein: Philosopher-Scientist ed. Paul Arthur Schilpp. La Salle, 1970.

Barnett, Lincoln, *The Universe and Dr. Einstein.* London, 1949.

Clark, Ronald W., *Einstein: The Life and Times.* New York, 1971.

Einstein, Albert, *Ideas and Opinions.* London, 1964.

Einstein, Albert, *On Peace* ed. Otto Nathan and Heinz Norden. New York, 1960.

Einstein, Albert, *Out of My Later Years*. Secaucus, 1956.

Einstein, Albert, *The World As I See It*. London, 1935.

Joy, Charles R. and Melvin Arnold, *The Africa of Albert Schweitzer*. New York, 1948.

Pais, Abraham, *'Subtle is the Lord ...' The Science and the Life of Albert Einstein*. Oxford, 1982.

Schweitzer, Albert, *An Anthology* ed. Charles R. Joy. Boston, 1956.

Schweitzer, Albert, *Indian Thought and Its Development*. London, 1936.

Schweitzer, Albert, *Out of My Life and Thought: An Autobiography* tr. C. T. Campion. New York, 1949.

Schweitzer, Albert, *Peace or Atomic War?* New York, 1958.

Schweitzer, Albert, *The Philosophy of Civilization* tr. C. T. Campion. New York, 1950.

Schweitzer, Albert, *The Primeval Forest*. New York, 1931.

Schweitzer, Albert, *The Quest for the Historical Jesus* tr. W. Montgomery. New York, 1968.

Schweitzer, Albert, *Reverence for Life* tr. Reginald H. Fuller. New York, 1969.

6. Pacifism of Bertrand Russell and A. J. Muste

Bertrand Russell's Philosophy ed. George Nakhnikian. London, 1974.

Chatfield, Charles, *For Peace and Justice: Pacifism in America 1914-1941*. Knoxville, 1971.

Clark, Ronald W., *The Life of Bertrand Russell*. New York, 1975.

Cooney, Robert and Helen Michalowski, *The Power of the People: Active Nonviolence in the United States*. Culver City, 1977.

Ethics of War: Bertrand Russell and Ralph Barton Perry on World War I ed. Charles Chatfield. New York, 1972.

Feinberg, Barry and Ronald Kasrils, *Bertrand Russell's America, Volume 2: 1945-1970*. Boston, 1983.

Hentoff, Nat, *Peace Agitator: The Story of A. J. Muste*. New York, 1963.

Intellect and Social Conscience: Essays on Bertrand Russell's

Early Work ed. Margaret Moran and Carl Spadoni. Hamilton, 1984.

Monk, Ray, *Bertrand Russell: The Ghost of Madness 1921-1970*. New York, 2000.

Muste, A. J., *Non-Violence in an Aggressive World*. New York, 1940.

Muste, The Essays of A. J. ed. Nat Hentoff. New York, 1967.

Russell, *The Autobiography of Bertrand*, 3 volumes. 1967, 1968, and 1969.

Russell, The Basic Writings of Bertrand ed. Robert E. Egner and Lester E. Denonn. New York, 1961.

Russell, Bertrand, *Common Sense and Nuclear War*. New York, 1959.

Russell, Bertrand, *The Conquest of Happiness*. Garden City, 1930.

Russell, Bertrand, *Education and the Good Life*. New York, 1926.

Russell, Bertrand, *Fact and Fiction*. New York, 1961.

Russell, Bertrand, *Has Man a Future?* New York, 1961.

Russell, Bertrand, *A History of Western Philosophy*. New York, 1945.

Russell, Bertrand, *Human Society in Ethics and Politics*. New York, 1955.

Russell, Bertrand, *The Impact of Science on Society*. New York, 1952.

Russell, Bertrand, *An Inquiry into Meaning and Truth*. New York, 1940.

Russell, Bertrand, *Justice in War Time*. New York, 1916.

Russell, Bertrand, *Marriage and Morals*. New York, 1929.

Russell, Bertrand, *Mysticism and Logic*. Garden City, 1917.

Russell, Bertrand, *New Hopes for a Changing World*, 1951.

Russell, Bertrand, *An Outline of Philosophy*. Cleveland, 1927.

Russell, Bertrand, *Political Ideals*. New York, 1917.

Russell, Bertrand, *Power: A New Social Analysis*. New York, 1938.

Russell, Bertrand, *The Problems of Philosophy*. London, 1912.

Russell, Bertrand and Dora Russell, *Prospects of Industrial Civilization*. New York, 1923.

Russell, Bertrand, *Religion and Science*. New York, 1935.
Russell, Bertrand, *Roads to Freedom*. New York, 1966.
Russell, Bertrand, *Sceptical Essays*. London, 1928.
Russell, Bertrand, *The Scientific Outlook*. London, 1931.
Russell, Bertrand, Speaks His Mind. Cleveland, 1960.
Russell, Bertrand, *Unarmed Victory*. 1963.
Russell, Bertrand, *Unpopular Essays*. New York, 1950.
Russell, Bertrand, *War Crimes in Vietnam*. London, 1967.
Russell, Bertrand, *Which Way to Peace?* London, 1936.
Russell, Bertrand, *Why Men Fight: A Method of Abolishing the International Duel*. New York, 1930.
Russell, Bertrand, *Wisdom of the West*. London, 1959.
Vellacott, Jo, *Bertrand Russell and the Pacifists in the First World War*. New York, 1980.

7. Clark-Sohn Plan for World Law and Disarmament

Clark, Grenville, *A Plan for Peace*. New York, 1950.
Clark, Grenville and Louis B. Sohn, *World Peace Through World Law*. Cambridge, 1960.
Davis, Garry, *World Government, Ready or Not!* Sorrento, no date.
Disarmament: Negotiations and Treaties 1946-1971 Keesing's Research Report. New York, 1972.
Documentary History of Arms Control and Disarmament, A ed. Trevor N. Depuy and Gay M. Hammerman. New York, 1973.
Dunne, Gerald T., *Grenville Clark: Public Citizen*. New York, 1986.
Falk, Richard, *A Study of Future Worlds*. New York, 1975.
Ferencz, Benjamin B., and Ken Keyes, Jr., *Planethood: The Key to Your Survival and Prosperity*. Coos Bay, 1988.
Kiang, John, *One World: The Approach to Permanent Peace on Earth and the General Happiness of Mankind*. Notre Dame, 1984.
Legal and Political Problems of World Order ed. Saul H. Mendlowitz. New York, 1962.
Myrdal, Alva and others, *Dynamics of European Nuclear*

Disarmament. Nottingham, 1981.

Preventing World War III: Some Proposals ed. Quincy Wright, William M. Evan and Morton Deutsch. New York, 1962.

Reves, Emery, *The Anatomy of Peace.* New York, 1945.

Schlesinger, Arthur M. Jr., *A Thousand Days: John F. Kennedy in the White House.* Boston, 1965.

Sorensen, Theodore C., *Kennedy.* New York, 1965.

Strategy of World Order, The, 4 volumes ed. Richard Falk and Saul Mendlowitz. New York, 1966.

Toward Nuclear Disarmament and Global Security: A Search for Alternatives ed. Burns H. Weston. Boulder, 1984.

Wainhouse, David W., *Arms Control Agreements: Designs for Verification and Organization.* Baltimore, 1968.

Wilson, Andrew, *The Disarmament Handbook of Military Technology and Organization.* Middlesex, 1983.

8. King and the Civil Rights Movement

Anderson, Jervis, *Bayard Rustin: Troubles I've Seen.* New York, 1997.

Branch, Taylor, *Parting the Waters: America in the King Years 1954-63.* New York, 1988.

Burns, Stewart, *To the Mountain Top: Martin Luther King's Sacred Mission to Save America 1955-1968.* New York, 2004.

Carmichael, Stokely and Charles V. Hamilton, *Black Power.* New York, 1967.

Castillo, Richard Griswold del and Richard A. Garcia, *César Chavez: A Triumph of the Spirit.* Norman, 1995.

Churchill, Ward and Jim Vander Wall, *The Cointelpro Papers.* Boston, 1990.

Civil Rights 1960-66 ed. Lester A. Sobel. New York, 1967.

Civil Rights Reader, The ed. Leon Friedman. New York, 1967.

Eyes on the Prize Civil Rights Reader, The ed. Clayborne Carson *et al.* New York, 1991.

Ferriss, Susan and Ricardo Sandoval, *The Fight in the Fields: Cesar Chavez and the Farmworkers Movement.* New York, 1997.

Franklin, John Hope and Alfred A. Moss, Jr., *From Slavery to Freedom: A History of African Americans.* New York, 1994.

Garrow, David J., *The FBI and Martin Luther King, Jr. From Solo to Memphis*. New York, 1981.

Hampton, Henry and Steve Fayer, *Voice of Freedom: An Oral History of the Civil Rights Movement from the 1950s through the 1980s*. New York, 1990.

Kasher, Steven, *The Civil Rights Movement: A Photographic History, 1954-68*. New York, 1996.

King, Coretta Scott, *My Life with Martin Luther King, Jr.* New York, 1969.

King, Martin Luther Jr., *A Testament of Hope: The Essential Writings of* ed. James Melvin Washington. San Francisco, 1986.

King, Martin Luther Jr., *Strength to Love*. New York, 1963.

King, Martin Luther Jr.,*Stride Toward Freedom: The Montgomery Story*. New York, 1958.

King, Martin Luther Jr., *Where Do We Go from Here: Chaos or Community?* Boston, 1967.

King, Martin Luther Jr., *Why We Can't Wait*. New York, 1964.

Let Freedom Ring: A Documentary History of the Modern Civil Rights Movement ed. Peter B. Levy. New York, 1992.

Lewis, David L., *King: A Critical Biography*. New York, 1970.

Reporting Civil Rights, Part One: American Journalism 1941-1963. New York, 2003.

Reporting Civil Rights, Part Two: American Journalism 1964-1973. New York, 2003.

Riches, William T. Martin, *The Civil Rights Movement*. New York, 1997.

Rodriguez, Consuelo, *Cesar Chavez*. New York, 1991.

Ross, Fred, *Conquering Goliath: Cesar Chavez at the Beginning*. Keene, 1989.

Stoper, Emily, *The Student Nonviolent Coordinating Committee*. Brooklyn, 1989.

Williams, Juan, *Eyes on the Prize: America's Civil Rights Years, 1954-1965*. New York, 1987.

Zinn, Howard, *SNCC: The New Abolitionists*. Boston, 1965.

9. Lessons of the Vietnam War

Ashmore, Harry S. and William C. Baggs *Mission to Hanoi*. New York, 1968.

Berman, Larry, *No Peace, No Honor: Nixon, Kissinger, and Betrayal in Vietnam*. New York, 2001.

Caputo, Philip, *A Rumor of War*. New York, 1977.

Chomsky, Noam and Edward S. Herman, *The Political Economy of Human Rights. Volume 1: The Washington Connection and Third World Fascism. Volume 2: After the Cataclysm: Postwar Indochina & the Reconstruction of Imperial Ideology*. Boston, 1979.

Cooper, Chester L., *The Lost Crusade*. New York, 1970.

Crimes of War ed. Richard A. Falk, Gabriel Kolko, and Robert Jay Lifton. New York, 1971.

Duncason, Dennis J., *Government and Revolution in Vietnam*. London, 1968.

Ellsberg, Daniel, *Papers on the War*. New York, 1972.

Fitzgerald, Frances, *Fire in the Lake: The Vietnamese and the Americans in Vietnam*. Boston, 1972.

Halberstam, David, *The Best and the Brightest*. New York, 1972.

Halstead, Fred, *Out Now: A Participant's Account of the American Movement Against the Vietnam War*. New York, 1978.

Ho Chi Minh, *On Revolution: Selected Writings 1920-66*. New York, 1967.

Karnow, Stanley, *Vietnam: A History*. New York, 1983.

Lacouture, Jean, *Ho Chi Minh: A Political Biography* tr. Peter Wiles. New York, 1968.

Languth, A. J., *Our Vietnam: The War 1954-1975*. New York, 2000.

Pentagon Papers, The ed. Neil Sheehan, Hedrick Smith, Fox Butterfield, and E. W. Kenworthy. New York, 1971.

Raskin, Marcus G. and Bernard B. Fall, *The Vietnam Reader*. New York, 1965.

Salisbury, Harrison E., *Behind the Lines—Hanoi*. New York, 1967.

Santoli, Al, *Everything We Had*. New York, 1981.

Shawcross, William, *Sideshow: Kissinger, Nixon and the Destruction of Cambodia*. New York, 1979.

Sheehan, Neil, *A Bright Shining Lie: John Paul Vann and America in Vietnam*. New York, 1988.

Taylor, Telford, *Nuremberg and Vietnam: an American Tragedy*. Chicago, 1970.

Vietnam: A History in Documents ed. Gareth Porter. New York, 1979.

Viet-Nam Crisis: A Documentary History, Volume 1: 1940-1956 ed. Allan W. Cameron. Ithaca, 1971.

Vietnam Hearings, The. New York, 1966.

We Won't Go: Personal Accounts of War Objectors collected by Alice Lynd. Boston, 1968.

Woodstone, Norma Sue, *Up Against the War.* New York, 1970.

Zinn, Howard, *Vietnam: The Logic of Withdrawal.* Boston, 1967.

10. Women for Peace

Addams, Jane, *Forty Years at Hull-House.* New York, 1935.

Addams, Jane, *Newer Ideals of Peace.* 1907.

Addams, Jane *et al, The Overthrow of the War System.* Boston, 1915.

Addams, Jane, *Peace and Bread in Time of War.* Boston, 1945.

Addams, Jane, Emily G. Balch, and Alice Hamilton, *Women at The Hague: The International Congress of Women and its Results.* New York, 1915.

Alonso, Harriet Hyman, *The Women's Peace Union and the Outlawry of War, 1921-1942.* Knoxville, 1989.

Aung San Suu Kyi, *Freedom from Fear and Other Writings.* London, 1995.

Aung San Suu Kyi, *The Voice of Hope: Conversations with Alan Clements.* New York, 1997.

Brittain, Vera, *The Rebel Passion: A Short History of Some Pioneer Peacemakers.* Nyack, 1964.

Burma: The Challenge of Change in a Divided Society ed. Peter Carey. London, 1997.

Bussey, Gertrude and Margaret Tims, *Women's International*

League for Peace and Freedom 1915-1965. London, 1965.

Clements, Alan, *Burma: The Next Killing Fields?* Berkeley, 1992.

Cooney, Robert and Helen Michalowski, *The Power of the People: Active Nonviolence in the United States.* Culver City, 1977.

Day, Dorothy, *Loaves and Fishes.* New York, 1963.

Day, Dorothy, *The Long Loneliness: An Autobiography.* Garden City, 1952.

Day, Dorothy, *By Little and Little: The Selected Writings of.* New York, 1983.

Dear Sisters: Dispatches from the Women's Liberation Movement ed. Rosalyn Baxandall and Linda Gordon. New York, 2000.

Degen, Marie Louise, *The History of the Woman's Peace Party.* Baltimore, 1939.

Deming, Barbara, *Revolution & Equilibrium.* New York, 1971.

Deming, Barbara, *We Are All Part of One Another: A Reader* ed. Jane Meyerding. Philadelphia, 1984.

Eastman, Crystal, *On Women and Revolution.* Oxford, 1978.

Feminism: The Essential Historical Writings ed. Miram Schneir. New York, 1972.

Fink, Christina, *Living Silence: Burma Under Military Rule.* Bangkok, 2001.

Foster, Carrie A., *The Women and the Warriors: The U.S. Section of the Women's International League for Peace and Freedom 1915-1946.* Syracuse, 1995.

Goodman, Amy, *The Exception to the Rulers.* New York, 2004.

Gravers, Mikael, *Nationalism as Political Paranoia in Burma.* Surrey, 1999.

Hamann, Brigitte, *Bertha von Suttner: A Life for Peace* tr. Ann Dubsky. Syracuse, 1996.

Hennacy, Ammon, *The Autobiography of a Catholic Anarchist.* New York, 1954.

Hymowitz, Carol and Michael Weissman, *A History of Women in America.* New York, 1978.

Lintner, Bertil, *Outrage: Burma's Struggle for Democracy.*

London, 1990.

Miller, William D., *Dorothy Day: A Biography*. San Francisco, 1982.

Nevin, Thomas R., *Simone Weil: Portrait of a Self-Exiled Jew*. Chapel Hill, 1991.

Nonviolence in America: A Documentary History ed. Staughton Lynd and Alice Lynd. Maryknoll, 1995.

Oldfield, Sybil, *Women Against the Iron Fist: Alternatives to Militarism 1900-1989*. Oxford, 1989.

Peace Pilgrim: Her Life and Work in Her Own Words. Santa Fe, 1982.

Peacemaking: A Guide to Conflict Resolution for Individuals, Groups, and Nations ed. Barbara Stanford. New York, 1976.

Reweaving the Web of Life: Feminism and Nonviolence ed. Pam McAlister. Philadelphia, 1982.

Rocking the Ship of State: Toward a Feminist Peace Politics ed. Adrienne Harris and Ynestra King. Boulder, 1989.

Root of Bitterness: Documents of the Social History of American Women ed. Nancy F. Cott. Boston, 1986.

Skidmore, Monique, *Karaoke Freedom: Burma and the Politics of Fear*. Philadelphia, 2004.

Smith, Martin, *Burma: Insurgency and the Politics of Ethnicity*. Dhaka, 1999.

Steinberg, David I., *Burma: The State of Myanmar*. Washington, 2001.

Steinson, Barbara J., *American Women's Activism in World War I*. New York, 1982.

Stop the Next War Now: Effective Responses to Violence and Terrorism ed. Medea Benjamin and Jodie Evans. Maui, 2005.

Suttner, Bertha von, *Lay Down Your Arms* tr. T. Holmes. New York, 1914.

Swerdlow, Amy, *Women Strike for Peace: Traditional Motherhood and Radical Politics in the 1960s*. Chicago, 1993.

Tucker, Shelby, *Burma: The Curse of Independence*. London, 2001.

Victor, Barbara, *The Lady Aung San Suu Kyi: Nobel Laureate and Burma's Prisoner*. New York, 2002.

Voices from the Catholic Worker ed. Rosalie Riegle Troester. Philadelphia, 1993.

Woloch, Nancy, *Women and the American Experience*. New York, 1984.

Women on War: Essential Voices for the Nuclear Age ed. Daniela Gioseffi. New York, 1988.

11. Anti-Nuclear Protests

Aldridge, Robert C., *First Strike! The Pentagon's Strategy for Nuclear War*. Boston, 1983.

Arms Race and Nuclear War, The ed. William M. Evan and Stephen Hilgartner. Englewood Cliffs, 1987.

Barash, David P., and Judith Eve Lipton, *Stop Nuclear War! A Handbook*. New York, 1982.

Berrigan, Philip, Fighting the Lamb's War: The Autobiography of. Monroe, 1996.

Bowman, Robert, *Star Wars: Defense or Death Star?* No city, 1985.

Breakthrough: Emerging New Thinking: Soviet and Western Scholars Issue a Challenge to Build a World Beyond War. New York, 1988.

Breakthrough to Peace: Twelve Views on the Threat of Thermonuclear Extermination. Norfolk, 1962.

Breyman, Steve, *Why Movements Matter: The West German Peace Movement and U.S. Arms Control Policy.* Albany, 2001.

Cabasso, Jackie, and Susan Moon, *Risking Peace: Why We Sat in the Road.* Berkeley, 1985.

Calder, Nigel, *Nuclear Nightmares: An Investigation into Possible Wars.* New York, 1981.

Caldicott, Helen, *A Desperate Passion: An Autobiography.* New York, 1996.

Caldicott, Helen, *If You Love This Planet: A Plan to Heal the Earth.* New York, 1992.

Caldicott, Helen, *Missile Envy: The Arms Race and Nuclear War.* Toronto, 1986.

Caldicott, Helen, *The New Nuclear Danger: George W. Bush's Military-Industrial Complex.* New York, 2002.

Caldicott, Helen, *Nuclear Madness: What You Can Do!*

Toronto, 1982.

Chatfield, Charles, *The American Peace Movement: Ideals and Activism.* New York, 1992.

Common Security: A Blueprint for Survival by the Independent Commission on Disarmament and Security Issues. New York, 1982.

Defence Without the Bomb, The Report of the Alternative Defence Commission. London, 1983.

Dellums, Ronald V., *Defense Sense: The Search for a Rational Military Policy.* Cambridge, 1983.

Epstein, Barbara, *Political Protest and Cultural Revolution: Nonviolent Direct Action in the 1970s and 1980s.* Berkeley, 1991.

Final Epidemic, The: Physicians and Scientists on Nuclear War ed. Ruth Adams and Susan Cullen. Chicago, 1981.

Forsberg, Randall *et al, Nonproliferation Primer: Preventing the Spread of Nuclear, Chemical, and Biological Weapons.* Cambridge, 1995.

Frank, Jerome D., *Sanity & Survival: Psychological Aspects of War and Peace.* New York, 1967.

Goodwin, Peter, *Nuclear War: The Facts on Our Survival.* New York, 1981.

Hersh, Seymour, *Chemical & Biological Warfare: America's Hidden Arsenal.* Garden City, 1968.

Kaku, Michio, and Daniel Axelrod, *To Win a Nuclear War: The Pentagon's Secret War Plans.* Boston, 1987.

Kaplan, Fred, *Wizards of Armageddon,* New York, 1983.

Katz, Milton S., *Ban the Bomb: A History of SANE, the Committee for a Sane Nuclear Policy, 1957-1985.* New York, 1986.

Kennan, George F., *The Nuclear Delusion: Soviet-American Relations in the Atomic Age.* New York, 1982.

Kennedy, Edward M., and Mark O. Hatfield, *Freeze!* Toronto, 1982.

Keyes, Ken, Jr., *The Hundredth Monkey.* St. Mary, 1982.

Kleidman, Robert, *Organizing for Peace: Neutrality, the Test Ban, and the Freeze.* Syracuse, 1993.

Lifton, Robert Jay, and Eric Markusen, *The Genocidal*

Mentality: Nazi Holocaust and Nuclear Threat. New York, 1990.

Lifton, Robert Jay, and Richard Falk, *Indefensible Weapons: The Political and Psychological Case Against Nuclearism.* New York, 1982.

Loeb, Paul Rogat, *Hope in Hard Times: America's Peace Movement and the Reagan Era.* Lexington, 1987.

Lovins, Amory, and Hunter L. Lovins, *Energy/War: Breaking the Nuclear Link.* San Francisco, 1980.

Macy, Joanna Rogers, *Despair and Personal Power in the Nuclear Age.* Philadelphia, 1983.

McGuinness, Elizabeth Anne, *People Waging Peace: Stories of Americans striving for peace and justice in the world today.* San Pedro, 1988.

Melman, Seymour, *Pentagon Capitalism: The Political Economy of War.* New York, 1970.

No Place to Hide: fallout shelters—fact and fiction ed. Seymour Melman. New York, 1962.

Nonviolent Social Movements: A Geographical Perspective ed. Stephen Zunes *et al.* Malden, 1999.

Nuclear War: What's in It for you? Ground Zero. New York, 1982.

Nuclear Weapons, Report of the Secretary-General of the United Nations. Brookline, 1980.

O'Heffernan, Patrick, Amory B. Lovins, and L. Hunter Lovins, *The First Nuclear World War: A Strategy for Preventing Nuclear Wars and the Spread of Nuclear Weapons.* New York, 1983.

Pauling, Linus, *No More War!* New York, 1958.

Peacemakers: Christian Voices from the New Abolitionist Movement ed. Jim Wallis. San Francisco, 1983.

Polner, Murray and Jim O'Grady, *Disarmed and Dangerous: The Radical Lives and Times of Daniel and Philip Berrigan.* New York, 1997.

Preventing World War III ed. Quincy Wright. New York, 1962.

Protest and Survive ed. E. P. Thompson and Dan Smith. New York, 1981.

Rocking the Ship of State: Toward a Feminist Peace Politics ed. Adrienne Harris and Ynestra King. Boulder, 1989.

Scheer, Robert, *With Enough Shovels: Reagan, Bush and Nuclear War*. New York, 1983.

Schell, Jonathan, *The Abolition*. New York, 1984.

Schell, Jonathan, *Fate of the Earth*. New York, 1982.

Schindler, Craig, and Gary Lapid, *The Great Turning: personal peace, global victory.* Santa Fe, 1989.

Sharp, Gene, *The Politics of Nonviolent Action*. Boston, 1973.

Swords into Plowshares: Nonviolent Direct Action for Disarmament ed. Arthur L. Laffin and Anne Montgomery. San Francisco, 1987.

Waging Peace: A Handbook for the Struggle to Abolish Nuclear Weapons ed. Jim Wallis. San Francisco, 1982.

Waging Peace: Vision and Hope for the 21st Century ed. David Krieger and Frank Kelly. Chicago, 1992.

Wittner, Lawrence S., *One World or None: A History of the World Nuclear Disarmament Movement Through 1953*. Stanford, 1993.

Wittner, Lawrence S., *Resisting the Bomb: A History of the World Nuclear Disarmament Movement 1954-1970*. Stanford, 1997.

Wittner, Lawrence S., *Toward Nuclear Abolition: A History of the World Nuclear Disarmament Movement 1971 to the Present*. Stanford, 1997.

Women on War: Essential Voices for the Nuclear Age ed. Daniela Gioseffi. New York, 1988.

12. Resisting Wars in Central America

Arias, Esther and Mortimer, *Cry of My People: Out of Captivity in Latin America*. New York, 1980.

Annis, Sheldon et al, *Poverty, Natural Resources, and Public Policy in Central America*. New Brunswick. 1992.

Arnson, Cynthia J., *Crossroads: Congress, the President, and Central America 1976-1993*. University Park, 1993.

Barry, Tom, *Central America Inside Out*. New York, 1991.

Barry, Tom, *Roots of Rebellion: Land & Hunger in Central America*. Boston, 1987.

Bonner, Raymond, *Weakness and Deceit: U.S. Policy and El Salvador.* New York, 1984.

Central American Crisis Reader, The ed. Robert S. Leiken and Barry Rubin. New York, 1987.

Child, Jack, *The Central American Peace Process, 1983-1991.* Boulder, 1992.

Clements, Charles, *Witness to War: An American Doctor in El Salvador.* Toronto, 1984.

Cockburn, Leslie, *Out of Control: The Story of the Reagan Administration's Secret War in Nicaragua, the Illegal Arms Pipeline, and the Contra Drug Connection.* New York, 1987.

Collins, Joseph, *Nicaragua: What Difference Could a Revolution Make?* New York, 1986.

Comparative Peace Processes in Latin America ed. Cynthia J. Arnson. Washington, 1999.

Costa Rica Reader, The ed. Marc Edelman and Joanne Kenen. New York, 1989.

Gutman, Roy, *Panama Diplomacy: The Making of American Policy in Nicaragua 1981-1987.* New York, 1988.

Harris, Godfrey, and Guillermo de St. Malo A., *The Panamanian Problem: How the Reagan and Bush Administrations Dealt with the Noriega Regime.* Los Angeles, 1993.

Honey, Martha, *Hostile Acts: U.S. Policy in Costa Rica in the 1980s.* Gainesville, 1994.

In Contempt of Congress: The Reagan Record of Deceit & Illegality on Central America ed. Institute for Policy Studies. Washington, 1985.

LeoGrande, William M., *Our Own Backyard: The United States in Central America, 1977-1992.* Chapel Hill, 1998.

Lernoux, Penny, *Cry of the People: The Struggle for Human Rights in Latin America—The Catholic Church in Conflict with U.S. Policy.* Middlesex, 1982.

Nuccio, Richard A., *What's Wrong, Who's Right in Central America?* New York, 1989.

Revolution in Central America ed. Stanford Central America Action Network. Boulder, 1983.

Rolbein, Seth, *Nobel Costa Rica.* New York, 1989.

Smith, Christian, *Resisting Reagan: The U.S. Central America*

Peace Movement. Chicago, 1996.

Woodward, Bob, *Veil: The Secret Wars of the CIA 1981-1987.* New York, 1987.

13. Gorbachev and Ending the Cold War

Citizen Summitry ed. Don Carlson and Craig Comstock. Los Angeles, 1986.

Civilian Resistance as a National Defense: Non-violent Action against Aggression ed. Adam Roberts. Harrisburg, 1967.

Cold War and After, The: Prospects for Peace ed. Sean M. Lynn-Jones. Cambridge, 1992.

Collapse of Communism, The ed. Bernard Gwertzman and Michael T. Kaufman. New York, 1990.

Doder, Dusko, and Louise Branson, *Gorbachev: Heretic in the Kremlin.* New York, 1990.

Frankland, Mark, *The Patriots Revolution: How Eastern Europe Toppled Communism and Won its Freedom.* Chicago, 1992.

Gorbachev, Mikhail, *Address at the UN.* New York, December 7, 1988.

Gorbachev, Mikhail, *The August Coup: The Truth and the Lessons.* London, 1991.

Gorbachev, Mikhail, *October and Perestroika: the Revolution Continues.* Moscow, 1987.

Gorbachev, Mikhail, *Perestroika: New Thinking for Our Country and the World.* New York, 1987.

Gorbachev, Mikhail S., *A Time for Peace.* New York, 1985.

Gorbachev, Mikhail S., *Toward a Better World.* New York, 1987.

Havel, Vaclav, *Disturbing the Peace* tr. Paul Wilson. New York, 1990.

Kaiser, Robert G., *Why Gorbachev Happened: His Triumph and His Failure.* New York, 1991.

Matlock, Jack F. Jr., *Autopsy on an Empire: The American Ambassador's Account of the Collapse of the Soviet Union.* New York, 1995.

Medvedev, Roy, and Guiletto Chiesa, *Time of Change: An Insider's View of Russia's Transformation* tr. Michael Moore.

New York, 1989.

Mikhail S. Gorbachev: An Intimate Biography ed. Donald Morrison. New York, 1988.

Parker, Tony, *Russian Voices*. New York, 1991.

Sharp, Gene, *Making Europe Unconquerable: The Potential of Civilian-based Deterrence and Defense*. Cambridge, 1985.

Sharp, Gene, *The Politics of Nonviolent Action*. Boston, 1973.

Sheehy, Gail, *The Man Who Changed the World: The Lives of Mikhail S. Gorbachev*. New York, 1990.

Talbot, Strobe, *Deadly Gambits: The Reagan Administration and the Stalemate in Nuclear Arms Control*. New York, 1985.

Walesa, Lech, *A Way of Hope: An Autobiography*. New York, 1987.

Weschler, Lawrence, *Solidarity: Poland in the Season of its Passion*. New York, 1982.

Without Force or Lies: Voices from the Revolution of Central Europe in 1989-90 ed. William M. Brinton and Alan Rinzler.

Zamoyski, Adam, *The Polish Way: A Thousand-year History of the Poles and their Culture*. New York, 1987.

14. Mandela and Freeing South Africa

Barber, James, *Mandela's World: The International Dimension of South Africa's Political Revolution 1990-99*. Oxford, 2004.

Bell, Terry, *Unfinished Business: South Africa, Apartheid and Truth*. London, 2003.

Berstein, Hilda, *No. 46—Steve Biko*. London, 1978.

Biko, Steve, *Black Consciousness in South Africa*. New York, 1978.

Biko, Steve, *I Write What Like*. New York, 1978.

Callan, Edward, *Albert John Luthuli and the South African Race Conflict*. Kalamazoo, 1962.

Commissioning the Past: Understanding South Africa's Truth and Reconciliation Commission ed. Deborah Posel and Graeme Simpson. Johannesburg, 2002.

Daye, Russell, *Political Forgiveness: Lessons from South Africa*. Maryknoll, 2004.

Du Boulay, Shirley, *Tutu: Voice of the Voiceless*. London, 1988.

Dugard, John, *Human Rights and the South African Legal Order*. Princeton, 1978.

Gibson, James L., *Overcoming Apartheid: Can Truth Reconcile a Divided Nation?* New York, 2004.

Holland, Heidi, *The Struggle: A History of the African National Congress*. New York, 1990.

Illustrated History of South Africa. Pleasantville, 1988.

Lodge, Tom, *Politics in South Africa from Mandela to Mbeki*. Bloomington, 2002.

Mandela: An Illustrated Autobiography. Boston, 1996.

Mandela, Nelson, *In His Own Words*. New York, 2003.

Mandela, Nelson, *Long Walk to Freedom: The Autobiography of*. Boston, 1994.

Meer, Fatima, *Higher Than Hope: The Authorized Biography of Nelson Mandela*. New York, 1988.

Moriarty, Thomas A., *Finding the Words: A Rhetorical History of South Africa's Transition from Apartheid to Democracy*. Westport, 2003.

Sampson, Anthony, *Mandela: The Authorized   Biography*. New York, 1999.

Shea, Dorothy, *The South African Truth Commission: The Politics of Reconciliation*. Washington, 2000.

Tutu, Desmond, *God Has a Dream*. New York, 2004.

Waldmeir, Patti, *Anatomy of a Miracle: The End of Apartheid and the Birth of the New South Africa*. New York, 1997.

Woods, Donald, *Biko*. New York, 1978.

15. Chomsky and Zinn on US Imperialism

Barsky, Robert F., *Noam Chomsky: A Life of Dissent*. Cambridge, 1997.

Blum, William, *Rogue State: A Guide to the World's Only Superpower*. Monroe, 2000.

Chomsky, Noam, *American Power and the New Mandarins*. New York, 1969.

Chomsky, Noam, *The Chomsky Reader* ed. James Peck. New York, 1987.

Chomsky, Noam, *The Common Good*. Monroe, 1998.

Chomsky, Noam, *Deterring Democracy*. New York, 1992.

Chomsky, Noam, *The Fateful Triangle: The United States, Israel and the Palestinians*. Boston, 1983.

Chomsky, Noam, *Hegemony or Survival: America's Quest for Global Dominance*. New York, 2003.

Chomsky, Noam, *Language and Responsibility* tr. John Viertel. New York, 1977.

Chomsky, Noam, *A New Generation Draws the Line: Kosovo, East Timor and the Standards of the West*. London, 2000.

Chomsky, Noam, *The New Military Humanism: Lessons from Kosovo*. Monroe, 1999.

Chomsky, Noam, *9-11*. New York, 2001.

Chomsky, Noam, *Pirates & Emperors: International Terrorism in the Real World*. Montreal, 1987.

Chomsky, Noam, and Edward S. Herman, *The Political Economy of Human Rights, Volume 1: The Washington Connection and Third World Fascism. Volume 2: After the Cataclysm: Postwar Indochina and the Reconstruction of Imperial Ideology*. Boston, 1979.

Chomsky, Noam, *Profit Over People: Neoliberalism and Global Order*. New York, 1999.

Chomsky, Noam, *The Prosperous Few and the Restless Many*. Berkeley, 1994.

Chomsky, Noam, *Rogue States: The Rule of Force in World Affairs*. Cambridge, 2000.

Chomsky, Noam, *Terrorizing the Neighborhood: American Foreign Policy in the Post-Cold War Era*. Stirling, 1991.

Chomsky, Noam, *Turning the Tide: U.S. Intervention in Central America and the Struggle for Peace*. Boston, 1985.

Cold War and the University, The: Toward an Intellectual History of the Postwar Years ed. André Schiffrin. New York, 1997.

Getting Haiti Right This Time: The U.S. and the Coup. Monroe, 2004.

Globalization ed. Katrin Sjursen. New York, 2000.

Joyce, Davis D., *Howard Zinn: A Radical American Vision*. Amherst, 2003.

Justice in Everyday Life: The Way It Really Works ed. Howard Zinn. New York, 1974.

Kosovo and the Challenge of Humanitarian Intervention ed. Albrecht Schnabel and Ramesh Thakur. Tokyo, 2000.

Lyons, John, *Noam Chomsky.* New York, 1970.

NATO in the Balkans: Voices of Opposition. New York, 1998.

Stockwell, John, *The Praetorian Guard: The U.S. Role in the New World Order.* Boston, 1991.

Zinn, Howard, *Artists in Times of War.* New York, 2003.

Zinn, Howard, *Declarations of Independence: Cross-examining American Ideology.* New York, 1990.

Zinn, Howard, *Disobedience and Democracy: Nine Fallacies on Law and Order.* New York, 1968.

Zinn, Howard, *Failure to Quit: Reflections of an Optimistic Historian.* Cambridge, 1993.

Zinn, Howard, *The Future of History.* Monroe, 1999.

Zinn, Howard, *On History.* New York, 2001.

Zinn, Howard, *On War.* New York, 2001.

Zinn, Howard, *Passionate Declarations: Essays on War and Justice.* New York, 2003.

Zinn, Howard, *A People's History of the United States.* New York, 1980.

Zinn, Howard, *The Politics of History.* Boston, 1970.

Zinn, Howard, *SNCC: The New Abolitionists.* Boston, 1965.

Zinn, Howard, *Terrorism and War.* New York, 2002.

Zinn, Howard, *Vietnam: The Logic of Withdrawal.* Boston, 1967.

Zinn, Howard, *The Zinn Reader: Writings on Disobedience and Democracy.* New York, 1997.

16. Protesting the Bush-Iraq Wars

Atkinson, Rick, *Crusade: The Untold Story of the Persian Gulf War.* Boston, 1993.

Blix, Hans, *Disarming Iraq.* New York, 2004.

Children are Dying: The Impact of Sanctions on Iraq, The Reports by UN Food and Agriculture Organization, Ramsey Clark. New York, 1998.

Clark, Ramsey, *Challenge to Genocide: Let Iraq Live.* New York, 1998.

Clark, Ramsey, *The Fire This Time: U.S. War Crimes in the*

Gulf. New York, 1992.

Clark, Ramsey, *War Crimes: A Report on United States War Crimes Against Iraq.* Washington, 1992.

Collateral Damage: The New World Order at Home and Abroad ed. Cynthia Peters. Boston, 1992.

Everest, Larry, *Oil, Power and Empire: Iraq and the U.S. Global Agenda.* Monroe, 2004.

Friedman, Alan, *Spider's Web: The Secret History of How the White House Illegally Armed Iraq.* New York, 1993.

Iraq: The Human Cost of History ed. Tareq Y. Ismael and William W. Haddad. London, 2004.

Iraq: Opposing Viewpoints ed. William Dudley. San Diego, 2004.

Iraq War and its Consequences: Thoughts of Nobel Peace Laureates and Eminent Scholars, The ed. Irwin Abrams and Wang Gungwu. Singapore, 2003.

Kelly, Kathy, *Other Lands Have Dreams: From Baghdad to Pekin Prison.* Petrolia, 2005.

U.S. News & World Report, *Triumph Without Victory: The Unreported History of the Gulf War.* New York, 1992.

17. Nonviolent Revolution for Global Justice

Andreas, Joel, *Addicted to War: Why the U.S. Can't Kick Militarism.* Oakland, 2003.

Art of Peace, The ed. Jeffrey Hopkins. Ithaca, 2000.

Boulding, Elise, *Cultures of Peace: The Hidden Side of History.* Syracuse, 2000.

Brock, Peter, and Nigel Young, *Pacifism in the Twentieth Century.* Syracuse, 1999.

Cobban, Helena, *The Moral Architecture of World Peace: Nobel Laureates Discuss Our Global Future.* Charlottesville, 2000.

Dean, John W., *Worse than Watergate: The Secret Presidency of George W. Bush.* New York, 2004.

Disarmament: The World at a Critical Turning Point. New York, 1999.

Ending War: The Force of Reason ed. Maxwell Bruce and Tom Milne. New York, 1999.

Galtung, Johan, Carl G. Jacobsen and Kai Frithjof Brand-

Jacobsen, *Searching for Peace: The Road to Transcend.* London, 2002.

Johnson, Chalmers, *Blowback: The Costs and Consequences of American Empire.* New York, 2000.

Johnson, Chalmers, *The Sorrows of Empire: Militarism, Secrecy, and the End of the Republic.* New York, 2004.

Khatchadourian, Haig, *War, Terrorism, Genocide, and the Quest for Peace – Contemporary Problems in Political Ethics.* Lewiston, 2003.

Nader, Ralph, *Crashing the Party: Taking on the Corporate Government in an Age of Surrender.* New York, 2002.

Natural History of Peace, A ed Thomas Gregor. Nashville, 1996.

Nonviolent Intervention Across Borders: A Recurrent Vision. Honolulu, 2000.

Power of Nonviolence, The: Writings by Advocates of Peace. Boston, 2002.

Turbulent Peace: The Challenges of Managing International Conflict ed. Chester A. Crocker. Washington, 2001.

Chronological Index of Events

Dates	Events	Pages
1867	Deak gained rights for Hungarians.	364
1868	St. Petersburg conference banned cruel weapons.	29
1889	Bertha von Suttner wrote *Lay Down Your Arms.*	257-8
1889	Jane Addams founded Hull House in Chicago.	264
1899, 1907	Hague conventions limited war.	29-32
1905, 1917	Russian revolution had nonviolent phases.	364-5
1907	Gandhi used noncooperation in South Africa.	4-5
1909	Gandhi wrote *Hind Swaraj.*	7
1909	NAACP was founded.	194
1912	African National Congress was founded.	393
1913	H. G. Wells wrote *The World Set Free.*	174
1915	Addams founded the Woman's Peace Party.	265-70
1915	Maude Royden advocated nonviolent action.	260
1915-35	Jane Addams led WILPF.	271-3
1916	Russell led the No Conscription Fellowship.	153
1918.1.8	US President Wilson proposed 14 Points.	40-1
1918	Russell was imprisoned for his writing.	154
1919.4	Gandhi called and canceled a general strike.	9-10
1919	Versailles Treaty established League of Nations.	42-9
1921	Gandhi led mass noncooperation in India.	11-2
1921	Permanent Court of International Justice began.	53-4
1921.12	Yugoslavia withdrew from Albania.	55
1922.3	British sentenced Gandhi to six years.	12
1922	Austria became independent.	55-6
1925.6	Geneva Protocol banned poisonous weapons.	56
1925.10	Locarno Treaty set German borders.	56
1925.10	League made peace with Greece and Bulgaria.	56-7
1927	France withdrew its garrison from the Saar.	57
1928	Einstein advised refusing military service.	128-9
1928.8.27	Kellogg-Briand Pact outlawed war.	57-8
1929	Simone Weil advocated complete disarmament.	261
1930.3	Gandhi led the salt campaign in India.	14-5
1931.9.18	Japan invaded Manchuria.	58
1931	Maude Royden proposed a Peace Army.	261
1932.1	30,000 peasants were massacred in El Salvador.	326
1932.2	59 nations attended disarmament conference.	59-60
1932.9	Gandhi's fast gained rights for untouchables.	15-6
1933	Day and Maurin founded the Catholic Worker.	276

1933	Japan and Germany withdrew from League.	59, 61
1934	Somoza had Sandino murdered in Nicaragua.	326
1935-36	Ethiopia's Selassie asked the League for help.	62-4
1935	The Saar voted to rejoin Germany.	62
1935.10.3	Italy's army invaded Ethiopia.	63
1936.3.7	Hitler sent German troops into the Rhineland.	63
1936.7	Franco attacked the government of Spain.	64
1936	A. J. Muste used sit-down strikes.	168
1937	Japan attacked China, who appealed to League.	65-6
1938.3	Germany occupied Austria and Sudetanland.	66
1939.4.7	Italy invaded Albania.	67
1939.5	Spain withdrew from the League of Nations.	65
1939.8.2	Einstein wrote Roosevelt about atomic energy.	137-8
1939.9.1	Germany invaded Poland.	67
1939.11.30	USSR invaded Finland.	67
1940	*Nonviolence in an Aggressive World* by Muste .	168-9
1940-45	Danes resisted German occupation.	367
1941.8	Roosevelt and Churchill signed Atlantic Charter.	76-7
1942	Rustin and Farmer founded CORE.	195
1942-44	Gandhi was under arrest for protesting war.	17-8
1942-45	Norwegian teachers refused to teach Nazi ideas.	366
1943	Wendell Wilkie published *One World*.	177
1944	ANC formed a Youth League.	394
1944	Myrdal published *An American Dilemma*.	195
1945	Chief Luthuli joined the ANC.	394
1945.8	World War II ended with atomic bombings.	176, 456
1945.10.24	United Nations was formed.	81-3
1945	Emery Reves wrote *The Anatomy of Peace*.	177
1946.5	Soviet troops withdrew from Iran.	99
1946.12.11	UN affirmed Nuremberg Principles.	86-7
1947.8.15	India and Pakistan gained independence.	19, 101-2
1948.1.30	Gandhi was assassinated by a Hindu.	19
1948.5.14	Israel became a nation.	101
1948	CIA intervened in Italian elections.	447
1948.12.10	UN got Universal Declaration of Human Rights.	89-98
1949.4.4	NATO alliance was formed.	368-9
1949.4	Pacifica radio was founded.	288
1949.7.27	UN gained a cease-fire in Kashmir.	102
1949.8.12	Geneva Conventions were signed.	88-9
1949.12.27	Indonesia became independent.	100
1950.6.25	UN reacted to North Korea's invasion.	103-5
1950	Grenville Clark published *A Plan for Peace*.	179-80

1952	Luthuli was elected ANC president.	397
1953	Peace Pilgrim began walking around the US.	279-80
1953.6	300,000 East Germans went on strike.	368
1953.7.27	US agreed to an armistice in Korea.	105
1953.8.19	CIA helped overthrow Mossadegh in Iran.	477
1954.5.7	French were defeated at Dienbienphu.	238
1954.5.17	US Supreme Court overturned racial segregation.	196
1954.6	CIA helped overthrow Arbenz in Guatemala.	327, 437
1954.12.23	Russell spoke over BBC on "Man's Peril."	159
1955.5.14	Warsaw Pact alliance was formed.	368-9
1955.6	Freedom Charter proclaimed in South Africa.	398-9
1955	Day and others refused a civil defense drill.	171, 277
1955-56	King led the Montgomery bus boycott.	198-201
1956.11.2	UN gained a cease-fire at the Suez Canal.	105-6
1956.11	Soviet tanks crushed Hungarian uprising.	106, 369
1957	Russell organized Pugwash Conferences.	160, 302-3
1957	SANE founded to abolish nuclear weapons.	303-4
1957.9	Arkansas schools were integrated.	196
1958	Linus Pauling wrote *No More War!*	302-3
1958.4	Schweitzer broadcast on atomic weapons.	146-8
1958.6	UN observers went to Lebanon.	106-7
1958	King published *Stride Toward Freedom.*	199-200
1958	*World Peace Through World Law* was published.	181
1959.4	Sobukwe founded Pan-African Congress.	401
1959.9.19	Khrushchev suggested complete disarmament.	187
1960.3.21	Police killed 69 Africans at Sharpeville.	401
1960-61	Mandela defended in treason trial.	402
1960	Sit-ins led to founding of SNCC.	210-7
1960-64	UN intervened in the Congo.	107-8
1961	King led Freedom Rides.	204
1961.9.25	Kennedy proposed complete disarmament.	187-8
1961	20,000 sat down at a US Polaris base.	161
1961	Women Strike for Peace began protesting.	280-1
1961	ANC formed MK for sabotage.	403
1961	Luthuli won Nobel Peace Prize.	403
1962	Chavez organized National Farm Workers.	224-5
1962.9	Meredith went to University of Mississippi.	214
1962.10	UN, Russell mediated Cuban missile crisis.	109, 161-3
1962.11	Dutch withdrew from West New Guinea.	108-9
1963.2.9	CIA helped overthrow Kassem in Iraq.	478
1963.4	King wrote a letter from Birmingham jail.	205-7
1963.6.12	Medgar Evers was murdered in Jackson.	214

1963.8.5	Partial test ban treaty was signed.	282, 305
1963.8.28	250,000 heard King's "I Have a Dream" speech.	208
1963-64	UN observers went to Yemen.	110
1963-90	Mandela was in prison in South Africa.	404-7, 412-6
1964.3	UN peacekeepers went to Cyprus.	110
1964	SNCC organized Freedom Summer.	216-7
1964.7	US Civil Rights Act became law.	208
1964.8.7	US Congress passed Gulf of Tonkin Resolution.	241
1964.9	Savio led Free Speech Movement at Berkeley.	533
1965	SDS and others protested the Vietnam War.	241-2
1965.4	US intervened in the Dominican Republic.	110-1
1965.8	US Voting Rights Act became law.	209-10
1965.10	US backed a coup in Indonesia.	437
1966.1	SNCC opposed the Vietnam War.	217
1966	Russell opened Vietnam War Crimes Tribunal.	165-6
1966	United Farm Workers began grape boycott.	227
1966, 1971	UN observed cease-fire in Kashmir.	111
1967	King called for an end to the Vietnam War.	220-1
1967	Many thousands protested the Vietnam War.	244
1967.6	Israel occupied West Bank and territories.	111-2
1967	Chomsky and Zinn wrote against Vietnam War.	434
1967	Outer Space Treaty was signed.	473
1968	Latin American bishops decided to help the poor.	326
1968	Dubcek led Czech liberalization.	369-71
1968.4.4	King was killed while working for the poor.	221
1968.5.17	Catonsville 9 led by Berrigans burned draft files.	245
1969.11.15	Million people marched against the Vietnam War.	247
1969-70	US bombing killed 600,000 Cambodians.	247
1970.5.4	4 protesting students were killed at Kent State.	247
1971.4	Vietnam veterans protested in Washington.	247
1971.6	Ellsberg leaked the *Pentagon Papers*.	248, 453
1972	Duarte was elected but exiled from El Salvador.	327
1972	Biological Weapons Convention was signed.	473-4
1972-74	Greenpeace disrupted French nuclear tests.	305
1973.7	US Congress stopped funding the Vietnam War.	248
1973.9.11	CIA helped overthrow Allende in Chile.	437
1973.10.6	Egypt and Syria attacked Israel.	112-3
1975.2	People stopped a nuclear power plant at Wyhl.	306
1975.4.30	Last Americans evacuated Vietnam.	249
1975-77	200,000 were killed in East Timor.	437
1976.6.1	Syria invaded Lebanon.	113
1976-77	Soweto uprising was repressed.	410-1

1977.5.1	1,414 were arrested at Seabrook.	306
1977.9.12	Biko was killed in custody in Pretoria.	411-2
1978.6	UN held first session on disarmament.	308
1978, 1982	Israel invaded Lebanon.	113-4
1979.3.26	Carter made peace between Israel & Egypt.	113, 440
1979.7.19	Sandinistas overthrew Somoza in Nicaragua.	336
1979.12.27	Soviet army invaded Afghanistan.	114-5
1979-2005	Dr. Caldicott of PSR warned of nuclear war.	319-22
1980.3.24	Romero was assassinated in El Salvador.	330
1980	Solidarity Union grew to ten million in Poland.	372
1980	Nuclear weapons freeze proposal was supported.	317
1980.9.9	Berrigans led Plowshares 8 action.	309
1980-88	Iraq attacked Iran and fought a war.	115-6
1981.9	1,900 were arrested at Diablo Canyon.	307
1981.11	1,300 arrested in Women's Pentagon Action.	318
1982.1	Sanctuary movement helped Salvadorans.	343
1982.2	Schell published *The Fate of the Earth*.	318
1982	Millions of women demonstrated for peace.	286-7
1982.6.14	1,691 were arrested at the United Nations.	308
1982.6.21	1,400 were arrested at Livermore Lab.	308
1982.9	Israel massacred Palestinians at Sabra & Shatila.	441
1982.12.13	2,000 Greenham Common women arrested.	312
1983.3	777 were arrested at Vandenberg Air Force Base.	310
1983.3	Green Party won 27 seats in the Bundestag.	314
1983.4	Witness for Peace began visiting Nicaragua.	344-5
1983.6.20	1,066 were arrested at Livermore Lab.	311
1983.10.25	US Marines invaded Grenada.	334, 444
1984	Desmond Tutu won Nobel Peace Prize.	414, 428
1984	Winooski 44 were acquitted by a jury.	344
1984	Pledge of Resistance began.	347
1985.3.11	Gorbachev proposed ending nuclear arms race.	374
1985-89	Gorbachev implemented *perestroika* & *glasnost*.	375-8
1986	Great Peace March crossed the United States.	315-6
1986.6.27	World Court convicted US of attacking Nicaragua.	447
1986.10	Iran-Contra scandal was exposed.	341
1986-94	15,740 were arrested at Nevada test site.	305
1987	Greenpeace began Nuclear Free Seas campaign.	305
1987.9.1	Brian Willson was run over by a munitions train.	349
1987	US boycotted UN Disarmament Conference.	443
1988	Medea Benjamin co-founded Global Exchange.	296
1988.9	Burmese formed National League for Democracy.	291
1988-89	Soviet army withdrew from Afghanistan.	115, 379

1988-91	UN verified peace in Angola.	118-9
1989.11.1	Independent Namibia held elections.	118
1989	Poland, Hungary, Czechoslovakia became free.	379-82
1989	1,452 in Pledge of Resistance were arrested.	348
1989.12.20	US invaded Panama to capture Noriega.	359, 443-4
1989-95	Aung San Suu Kyi was under house arrest.	292-3
1990.2	East and West Germany were reunited.	383
1990	UN demobilized the Contras.	117
1990.8.2	Iraq invaded Kuwait.	469, 124
1990-91	USSR dissolved into independent republics.	383-7
1990-92	El Salvador and the FMLN made peace.	117-8
1990	UN authorized US to force Iraq out of Kuwait.	124
1990-2003	UN sanctions caused a million deaths in Iraq.	488-94
1991	US military killed 175,000 Iraqis.	482-3
1991	Warsaw Pact was dissolved.	386
1991	Aung San Suu Kyi won the Nobel Peace Prize.	292
1991.11.12	Goodman reported massacre in East Timor.	289, 462
1991-93	UN intervened in Cambodia.	124
1991-96	UN intervened in Yugoslavia.	127-8
1992	Earth Summit met at Rio de Janeiro.	388
1992-95	UN monitored cease-fire in Somalia.	120
1993	Gorbachev founded Green Cross International.	387
1993	Mandela and De Klerk won Nobel Peace Prize.	418
1993-96	UN intervened in Haiti.	125-6
1994-99	Mandela was president of South Africa.	419-24
1996.3	VitW delegations began visiting Iraq.	495
1996	UN verified peace in Guatemala.	118
1996	Amy Goodman began Pacifica's Democracy Now.	289
1996-98	TRC helped heal South Africa.	424-9
1997.3	UN began Oil for Food program in Iraq.	490
1997.11.16	601 were arrested at the School of the Americas.	361
1997.12	Mine Ban Treaty was signed in Ottawa.	288
1998.12	US and UK bombed Iraq.	468
1999	NATO bombed Serbs in Kosovo.	128, 459-60
1999.12	Protests disturbed WTO meeting in Seattle.	296
2000.6	Earth Charter mission was launched.	388-9
2000-02	Aung San Suu Kyi was under house arrest.	295
2001.9.11	Al-Qaida destroyed the World Trade Center.	463
2001.10.7	US attacked Taliban in Afghanistan.	471
2001.10.26	US Patriot Act became law.	466
2002.5.20	East Timor became an independent nation.	128-9
2002.10	US Congress authorized Iraq invasion.	500

2002.10	CIA killed 6 al-Qaida in Yemen.	467
2002.11	Code Pink: Women for Peace was founded.	297
2002	Earth Charter was recognized by the UN.	388-9
2003.2.15	Millions marched to protest imminent Iraq War.	508-9
2003.3.19	US, UK, and others invaded Iraq.	501-2
2003.3	Thousands arrested for protesting Iraq War.	507-8
2003.5	US Congress approved new nuclear weapons.	472
2003	Chomsky wrote *Hegemony or Survival*.	467-74
2003-06	Aung San Suu Kyi was under house arrest.	295-6
2004.2.28	US forces abducted Aristide from Haiti.	126
2004.4	Abu Ghraib prison abuse was exposed.	503
2005.1	UN mediated a peace agreement in the Sudan.	123
2005	Thousands of US military went AWOL.	509
2005.6	Democrats held hearings on Bush's lies.	512
2005.6	US Congress formed Out of Iraq caucus.	504
2005.6	World Tribunal on Iraq convicted Bush and Blair.	512
2005.8.6	Cindy Sheehan began vigil in Crawford, Texas.	513
2005.9.26	Sheehan and 382 arrested at White House.	513
2005.12	Bush admitted unwarranted spying on citizens.	505

Alphabetical Index of Names

Abacha, Sani 422
Abalone Alliance 307
ABC 441
'Abdu'l-Bahá 256
Abdulla 19
Abernathy, Ralph 199, 202, 204, 206-10, 213, 215, 228
ABM Treaty 321, 323, 376, 378, 474, 511, 515
Abrams, Elliott 358
Abu Ghraib prison 503
Abu-Jamal, Mumia 290
Abzug, Bella 281, 283
Aché Indians 438
Acheson, Dean 237
ACLU 270, 332
Across the Golden Bridge 535
Adamec, Ladislav 382
Adams, John 364
Addams, Jane 194, 254, 259, 264-71, 273
ADL 441
Adoula 108
Afghanistan War 466, 500
AFL-CIO 223-4, 227
African National Congress 393-8, 400-1, 403-4, 406-7, 413-9, 421, 423-6
African Union 122
AFSC 171, 272, 303, 307, 316-7, 346-7
Against the Crime of Silence by Russell 166
Agenda for Peace by Boutros-Ghali 129
Aidid 120
Alabama Christian Movement for Human Rights 205
Alaimo 554
Alain 261
Albany Movement 214-5
Albright, Madeleine 457, 461, 496

Alexander II, Czar 29
Algiers Treaty 115
Alinsky, Saul 223
Allard 506
Allawi, Iyad 503
Alliance for Survival 541
Alpert, Jon 485
ALRB 230
Amalgamated Textile Workers 167
Amerasinghe, T. P. 540
American Dilemma by Myrdal 195
American Peace Society 30
American Peace Test 305
American Power by Chomsky 433
Americas Watch 332
Amin, Hafizullah 114
Amin, Samir 512
Amnesty International 291, 328, 332, 462, 517
Amritsar Congress 11
Anatomy of Peace by Reves 177
ANC 393-8, 400-1, 403-4, 406-7, 413-9, 421, 423-6
Anderson, Warren 464
Andrews, Charles F. 8, 10
Andropov, Yuri 374
Angell, Norman 33, 270
Annan, Kofi 477, 493-4, 504, 506, 556
ANSWER 506, 561
Antarctic Treaty 187
Anti-Ballistic Missile Treaty 321, 323, 376, 378, 474, 511, 515
anti-Communists 164
Arab League 107, 470, 480
Arab Mahgreb Union 119
Arafat, Yasser 113
Araujo, Arturo 326
Arbenz, Jacobo 327
Architects for Social Responsibility 320
ARDE 351

Ardito-Barletta, Nicolas 357
ARENA 332-5
Arévalo, Juan Jose 327
Arias, Oscar 324-5, 341, 352, 354
Aris, Michael 290, 294
Aristide, Jean-Bertrand 125
Arkhipov, Vasili 469
Armas, Carlos Castillo 327
Arnold, Edwin 2
Artists for Survival 320
Asiatic Registration Act 4
Asmal, Kadar 422, 425
Asquith, Henry 35
Atlantic Charter 76, 455
Atlantic Life Community 549
Attlee, Clement 63, 235
Attar, Leyla 490
AUAM 270
Augustine 206
Aung Gyi 291
Aung San 290
Aung San Suu Kyi 290-5
Autobiography by Gandhi 1, 13
Autobiography by Russell 151
Avenol, Joseph 53, 61, 63-5, 67
Avirgan, Tony 351, 355
AWOC 223-5, 227
Ayalon, Ami 472
Azaña, Manuel 64
AZAPO 427

Ba'ath Party 478, 502
Babcock, Caroline Lexow 271
Bach, Johann Sebastian 141
Baez, Joan 221
Baker, Ella 210-1, 214
Baker, James 339, 358, 481, 488
Bakker, Jim 555
al-Bakr 478
Balch, Emily 267, 270
Baldwin, Roger 270
Baldwin, Stanley 63
Bandar of Saudi Arabia 338
Bao Dai 235, 237-9
Barnett, Ross 214
Barre, Siad 120

Barry, Marion 212
Baruch Plan 157, 177-8
Batterham, Forster 275
Battle for the Prevention of World War by Suttner 258
BBC 159, 295, 366-7, 377
BCP 409
Bechtel 502, 513
Begin, Menachem 114, 441-2
Belafonte, Harry 206, 221
Bello, Walden 512
Benedict XVI 430
Benes 67
Benjamin, Medea 296-7
Bennis, Phyllis 290
Bentley, Eric 282
Beria 368
Berkeley Women for Peace 281
Bernadotte 101
Bernstein, Lionel 398
Bernstein, Rusty 405
Berrigan, Daniel 245, 279, 290, 309, 452
Berrigan, Philip 244, 279, 309
Bertrand Russell Peace Foundation 164, 166
Besant, Annie 9
Bethe 177
Bevel, James 242
Beyond Rangoon 293
Bhagavad-Gita 2
Bhave, Vinoba 17
Bible 533
Biden, Joe 549
Bigelow, Albert 212, 303
Biko, Steve 391, 407-12, 426
Biological and Toxic Weapons Convention 473, 515
Bird, Rose 230
Black Act 4-5
Black Consciousness 408-9, 412
Black Panthers 228, 436
Black People's Convention 407
Black Power 218
Black Review 409
Black, Hugo 214

Blackwelder, Brent 562
Blair, Tony 459, 461, 468, 512
Blaize, Herbert 444
Blandon, Jose 358
Blix, Hans 490, 497, 501
Bloch, Ivan 30
Blum, Leon 64
BMD 305, 321, 323
Boeing 513
Boer War 3, 259
Boesak, Allan 413, 415, 421
Bohr 177
Boland, Edward 337
Bolsheviks 365
Bolton, John 298, 474
Bond, Julian 210
Bonner, Ray 457
Boorman, John 293
Booth, Doug 541
Borah 72
Boraine, Alex 425
Borge, Tomas 336
Bormann 85
Bosch, Juan 110, 439
Boshoff 410
Boston Globe 454
Botha, P. W. 407, 413, 415, 427
Botha, Pik 418
Boulding, Kenneth 242
Bourgeois, Roy 325, 360-1, 494
Boutros-Ghali 120-1, 125, 129, 489
Boyd, Michele 562
Boyer, Jeff 344
Boyle, Francis 126, 509
BPC 407, 409-10, 412
Brandegee 72
Bremer, Paul 502-3
Brezhnev 113
Brezhnev doctrine 377
Briand, Aristide 56-7, 261
Brody, Reed 340
Bromley, Ernest 495
Brookwood Labor College 168
Broomfield, Robert 12
Brown and Root 502

Brown Berets 228
Brown v. Board of Education 196
Brown, Jerry 230
Brown, Pat 225-6
Bruening, Heinrich 60
Bryan, William Jennings 35, 264
Bryant, Louise 275
Brzezinski, Zbigniew 463, 478
BSPP 291
Buckle, H. T. 256
Buddha 1, 152, 524
Buddhists 172, 240, 292-3
Bulletin of Atomic Scientists 177
Bunche, Ralph 101, 107, 110, 221
Burns, John 497
Burns, Lucy 275
Burroughs, John 562
Bush, George H. W. 334-5, 338, 342, 356-8, 382, 416, 443, 468, 471, 476, 479-82, 485, 487-8, 490, 515
Bush, George W. 295, 297-8, 321-322, 463, 465-7, 469-70, 472, 474, 476, 496, 500-2, 504-6, 510, 512-3, 515-6, 527-8, 556, 559
Business Executives for National Security 320
Buthelezi, Gatcha 411, 416, 418-419, 423, 427
Butigan, Ken 347
Byrnes, Elinor 272
Byrnes, James F. 175
Byrns, Elinor 271

Cabasso, Jackie 562
Cabral, Donald Reid 439
Cachalia, Yusuf 397-8
Caetano 118
Cairo Declaration 492
CALC 317
Calderon, Rafael Angel 350
Caldicott, Helen 299, 301, 319, 321-2, 562
Calero, Adolfo 355
Calkins, Kenneth 304

Callaghan, General 114
Calvin 260
Calvinist 166
Cameron 421
CAMS 510
Carey, Gordon 210
CARICOM 126
Carlos 352
Carmichael, Stokely 213, 217-8
Carnegie, Andrew 258
Carriles, Luis Posada 469
Carter, Jimmy 113, 125, 318, 324, 327, 329, 331, 337, 357, 411, 435-8, 480, 535
Casey, Bill 337-8, 341, 352
Castro, Fidel 163, 337, 423, 436, 469
Castro, Raul 229
Castro, Rogelio 352
Catholic Relief Services 459
Catholic Worker 171, 242, 275-9, 303, 310, 494, 540-1, 550, 560
Catholics 172, 276, 328, 350
Catt, Carrie Chapman 265, 272
CBS News 457
Ceausescu, Nicolae 382, 469
Cecil, Robert 46, 66, 259
Cédras, Raoul 125
CENTCOM 480
Cernik 370
Chamberlain, Austen 56
Chamberlain, Neville 66, 273
Chamorro, Pedro Joaquin 336
Chamorro, Violeta 342
Chamoun, Camille 106
Chaney, James 216
Chang, Nancy 466
Chaplin, Charlie 15
Charter 77 381
Chavez, Cesar 194, 222-31, 279, 534
Chavez, Helen 225-6
Chavez, Richard 224
Chen, Davina 560
Cheney, Richard B. 322, 443, 502, 505, 510, 512

Chernenko 374
Chernobyl 376
Chirac, Jacques 491
Chissano 119
Chomsky, Noam 290, 431-50, 453, 456-7, 459-64, 467-8, 470-4, 481, 493
Christ 6, 133, 260, 276, 310, 525, 534
Christian Democrats 329-30, 332, 334
Christian Peacemaker Teams 495, 522
Christiani, Alfredo 335
Christians 6, 19, 168, 172, 180, 200, 310, 429, 441, 525, 559
Christic Institute 355
Church Committee 436
Churchill, Winston 4, 76-8, 80, 394
CIA 246, 294, 318, 327, 332, 334, 337-9, 341-2, 346, 348, 351-2, 355, 357, 386, 436-7, 440, 444, 447, 454, 457, 467, 469, 477-9, 485, 503, 505, 552
CIO 168
CIS 387
CISPES 345, 347
CITCA 344
Citizens for Peaceful Resolutions 556
City of Corpses by Yoko Ota 176
Civic Forum 381
Civil Rights Bill 208
Civil War (Spanish) 65, 432
Civil War (US) 29, 343, 452
Civilization and Ethics by Albert Schweitzer 131, 144
Claasens, Henderik 400
Clamshell Alliance 306
Clark, Dick 411
Clark, Grenville 174, 178-81, 183-184, 187, 190
Clark, Jim 216
Clark, Mark 436
Clark, Ramsey 290, 309, 476-7,

482, 484-7, 489, 492, 506, 510
Clark, Wesley 457, 459
Clarke, Maura 331
Clark-Sohn Plan 181-2, 184, 186-187, 190-1
Clemenceau 28, 45, 49
Clements, Charles 344, 552
Clines, Thomas 355
Clinton, Bill 321-2, 418, 449, 457-459, 461, 468, 471, 473, 490-1, 493, 515
CND 160-1, 172, 304
CNVA 171-2, 242, 283, 303-4
CNWS 349
Coalition for a New Foreign and Military Policy 317
Coalition Provisional Authority 502-3
Coard, Bernard 334
Cobb, David 527
Cobb, Frank 38
Coca-Cola 513
Code for the Government of Armies 29
Code Pink 297-8, 507
CODESA 417
Cody, Archbishop 218
Coetsee, Kobie 414
Coffin, William 213
Cohen, Jerry 227
Cohen, Joe 553
Cohen, William 457
Cohn 510
Cohn, Marjorie 509
Cointelpro 436
Cold War 84, 100, 105, 117, 129, 190, 280, 303, 314, 316, 320-1, 367, 378, 387, 397, 436, 442, 446-7, 460, 480, 514, 528, 536
Commission of Inquiry 486-7
Committee of 100 161, 172
Common Sense and Nuclear Warfare by Russell 150, 160
Commoner, Barry 302
Communists 100, 102, 158, 163-164, 168, 171-2, 177, 180, 237,

239, 243, 252, 276, 328, 337, 346, 350, 355, 373, 378-9, 382-6, 394, 396, 403, 415-6, 439, 528
Comprehensive Test Ban Treaty 322, 474, 515
Concerning Dissent by Fortas 452
Condon, Edward 302
Confucius 535
Congress of Racial Equality 171, 195, 207, 210, 215
Congress of Vienna 29
Connally Resolution 78
Connor, Eugene "Bull" 205, 207, 213
Conscientious Objectors 251, 277, 510, 533-4
Constant, Emmanuel 465, 471
Contadora 338-9, 444
Contras 116-7, 337-42, 344-7, 351-5, 469, 494, 550-1
Conyers, John 505, 512
Coolidge, Calvin 57
COP 398
Coplan, Mark 551
Corbett, Jim 342-4
CORE 171, 195, 207, 210, 215
COSATU 414-5
Counterrevolutionary Violence by Chomsky 435
Courtney, Kate 258-9
Cousins, Norman 146, 174, 176-7, 301, 303-4
Covenant on Civil and Political Rights 516
Covenant on Economic, Social and Cultural Rights 516
Cox, James 71
Cox, Percy 477
CPA 502-3
CPLA 168
CPS 326
Crisis magazine 194
Crocker 499
Cronkite, Walter 485
CRPP 294

CRTF 343
CSCE 127
CSFW 248
CSO 223-4
Cuban Democracy Act 450
Czernin 41

D'Aubuisson, Roberto 329, 331-4
D'Escoto, Miguel 494
Dadoo 395-6
Daily Dispatch 412
Daladier, Edouard 66
Daley, Richard 218, 246
Danes' Freedom Council 367
Dante 219
Dao De Jing by Lao-zi 533
Darwin 256
Das, D. R. 11
Davidon, Ann 286
Dawes 56
Day, Dorothy 171, 242, 255, 275-279, 310
De Klerk 415-9, 421, 425
De Kock, Eugene 427
De Wet 405
Deak, Ferenc 364
Decay and the Restoration of Civilization by Schweitzer 143
Declaration of Independence 235
Declaration of London 32
Declarations of Independence by Zinn 454
Dederich, Charles 231
Defense Science Board 465
Delbos 65
Delhi Pact 15
Dellinger, David 242, 433, 453
Delvalle, Eric Arturo 357-8
Deming, Barbara 255, 283-4
Democracy Now! 288-90
Democrats 212, 217, 230, 297, 320, 341, 353, 358, 516, 526
Depression 222
Deterring Democracy by Chomsky 442
Dewey, John 156, 194

Dhlakama, Afonso 119
Di Giorgios 226
Diana, Princess 288
Diem, Ngo Dinh 239-40
Dietrich, Jeff 310
DiFranco, Ani 290
Disobedience and Democracy by Zinn 452
Doctor Zhivago by Pasternak 376
Doenitz 85
Doke, Joseph 5
Dollfuss, Engelbert 61
Donohue, Phil 290
Donovan, Jean 331
Dorfman, Ariel 290
Douglass, Jim and Shelley 310
Drake, Jim 225, 227
Drake-Brockman, General 11
Drummond, James Eric 53, 61
DRV 235-6, 244
DU 322
Du Bois, W. E. B. 194, 394
Duarte, Jose Napoleon 327, 330-331, 334-5, 340
Dubcek, Alexander 369-70, 377, 382
Dudley, Katherine 153
Dukakis, Michael 358, 549
Dukhobors 6
Dulles, John Foster 105, 238
Dunant, Henri 29
Duncombe, David 349
Dutch Protestants 364
Duvalier, Baby Doc 469
Dworkin, Andrea 284
Dyer, General Reginald 10

Earth 542, 547
Earth Charter 388
Eastman, Crystal 254, 265-6, 270
Eastman, Max 275
Eberhardt, David 244
Ebert 365
ECOMIL 122
ECOMOG 121
ECOWAS 121-2

Eddington, Arthur 132
Eden, Anthony 64, 77, 105
Edmundson, J. L. 355
Educators for Social Responsibility 320
Edward VIII 11
Einstein, Albert 20, 130-40, 145, 157, 159, 171, 175, 177, 280, 432, 455, 525
Eiselen 397
Eisenhower, Dwight 104-6, 146, 159, 181, 196, 202, 204, 238, 301, 304, 321, 368, 443, 469, 520
Eitan 114
Elayyan, Fadi 498
Eldred 308
ELF 309, 494, 499
Eliade, Mircea 534
Elizabeth of Belgium 137
Ellsberg, Daniel 234, 248, 308, 453, 455, 540, 562
Emerson, Ralph Waldo 80
END 314
Endara, Guillermo 358-9
Ender, Thomas 333
Episcopal House of Bishops 320
ESF 354
Eshkol, Levi 111
Etzioni, Amitai 191
European Nuclear Disarmament 314
Evans, Jodie 297-8
Everett, Ernest 153
Evers, Medgar 214
Exception to the Rulers by Goodman 290

Fabela, Helen 222
Fahd 481
Faisal 107, 112
Falk, Richard A. 191, 250, 467, 512, 562
Families for Peace 298
FAO 186, 449, 489, 491
Farmer, James 171, 195, 207

Farney 540
FAS 177
Fascists 25, 62, 75, 136
Fate of the Earth by Schell 318
Fateful Triangle by Chomsky 440
Faubus, Orval 196
Fawzi 111
FBI 216, 223, 345, 348, 436, 454, 457, 560
FCC 445
FDN 351
FDR 330, 333
Federation of American Scientists 177
FEDSAW 399
Fellowship of Reconciliation 128, 171, 176, 195, 210, 260, 272, 278, 317, 493, 496
FEMA 346
FEPC 194-5
Ferry, W. H. 242
Fiers, Alan 341
Fife, John 343-4
Figueres, Jose 350
Fire This Time by Clark 477
First, Ruth 413
FISA 505
Fisher, Louis 223
Fisk, Robert 290, 493
Flynn, Michael 562
FMLN 117, 331, 333, 335
Foch 43, 49
FOIA 345
Fonseca, Carlos 336
Food First 296
Food for Peace 435, 448
FOR 128, 171, 176, 195, 210, 260, 272, 278, 317, 493, 496
Ford, Henry 269
Ford, Ita 331
Forman, James 214
Forsberg, Randall 299, 301, 316-317, 322-3, 562
Fortas, Abe 452
Fourteen Points 40-1, 43, 49
Francis Joseph 364

Franciscans 524
Franco, Francisco 64
Frank 85
Frank, Jerome 280
Franti, Michael 290
Franz Ferdinand 258
Frazier, Lynn Joseph 272
Free Speech Movement 533
Freedom Charter 398-9, 415
Freeze 316-20
FRELIMO 410
French Chamber of Deputies 63
French Revolution 235
Freud, Sigmund 136
Frick 85
Friedman, Alan 478
Frischman, Richard 308
Fritzsche 85
Fromm, Erich 242, 303
Frumin, Helen 282
FSLN 336
Fulbright, Senator 234
Funk 85
Funk, Stephen 509
Future of Mankind by Russell 150
Future of War by Bloch 30

G.I. Bill 451
Gaines, Lloyd Lionel 194
Galarza, Ernesto 223
Galil, Amac 355
Gallegly, Elton 559
Galtung, Johan 512
Galyen, Roy 226
Gandhi, Mohandas 1-26, 46, 139,
    169, 172, 195, 197, 210, 228,
    255-6, 290, 314-5, 396, 523-4,
    534-5
Gandhi, Kasturbai 7
Gandhi, Manilal 396
Gandhian 274
Garcia, Jose Guillermo 329
Gardiner, Col. Sam 290
Garner, Jay 502
Garrison, William Lloyd 271
Garron, Hernan 352

Garvey, Marcus 394
GEAR 421
Gearhart, Sally 286
Geneva Conventions 88, 250,
    486, 489, 504, 509, 553, 557
Geneva Protocol 56, 63, 250, 467
Genoni, Rosa 267
George, Clair 341
Getty, Greg 551-2
al-Ghazali, Majid 497
Gierek, Edvard 371
Gilbert, Carol 506
Gilbert, Prentiss 58
Gladstone 34
Glaspie, April 480
Global Exchange 296, 298
Glover, Danny 290
God 4, 18-9, 22, 24, 64, 131, 133,
    141-2, 145, 168, 197, 203, 205,
    221, 275, 279-80, 301, 310,
    330, 518, 525, 531, 534, 553,
    559
God Has a Dream by Tutu 393
Goering 85
Gokhale 3
Gold Star Families for Peace 509,
    513
Goldberg, Arthur 220
Goldberg, Dennis 405
Golden Rule 303
Goldman, Emma 454
Goldreich, Arthur 405
Goldwater 241
Gomulka 369-71
Gonzalez, Henry 485
Goodmacher, Chuck 550
Goodman, Amy 288-90, 462
Goodman, Andrew 216
Goodman, Paul 242
Goodrich, Tim 512
Gorbachev, Mikhail 115, 341, 363-
    364, 373-89, 443, 514, 548,
    554
Gordon, Lorraine 282
Gospels 533, 535
Govea, Jessica 228

Graça Machel 420
Great Illusion by Angell 33
Great Peace March 315-6, 548
Green Cross International 387, 389
Green Party 296, 314, 527
Greenham Common 311-4
Greenpeace 297, 305
Gregory, Dick 216
Grey, Edward 34-5
Gromyko, Andrei 79, 104, 374, 378
Groves, General 175-6
Guardia, Tomas 350
Guardian 465
Gulf of Tonkin Resolution 241, 247
Gulf Peace Team 495
Gulf War 443, 462, 483
Gumbleton, Thomas 492
Gutierrez, Gustavo 327
Gwiazda, Andrezej 372

Habib, Philip 441
Hague Conferences 29-33, 85, 250, 258, 437, 487
Haig, Alexander 331
Hakim, Albert 355
Haliday, Denis 492
Halliburton 502, 513
Halliday, Denis 461, 512
Halperin, Jason 290
Halstead, Fred 251
Hamer, Fannie Lou 217
Hamman, Mona 491
Hammarskjold, Dag 99, 105, 107, 303
Hammer, Dean 309
Hampton, Fred 436
Hani, Chris 417, 426
Hara, Jimmy 540
Hara, Tamiki 177
Harbury, Jennifer 290
Hard Way to Peace by Etzioni 191
Harding, Warren 50, 52, 271
Harijans 9, 15-7

Harkin, Tom 335, 337
Harper's 485
Harrison, Chris 510
Hart-Rudman report 474
Hartsough, David 306, 347, 350
Has Man a Future? by Russell 160
Hasenfus, Eugene 341
Hassan 119-20
Hatfield, Mark 317, 335
Havel, Vaclav 363, 381-2
Hayden, Tom 215
Hays, Will 72
Hedges, Chris 290
Hegemony or Survival by Chomsky 432, 467
Height, Dorothy 207
Helen 262
Helms, Jesse 334, 549
Helms-Burton Act 449
Hennacy, Ammon 242, 279
Hepple, Bob 405
Herman, Edward S. 435-6, 438-9, 442, 444-5, 447
Hernandez, Julio 224
Herold, Marc 465
Herrera, Roberto Diaz 357
Herriot 136
Hersey, John 177
Hersh, Seymour 290
Hertling, Count von 41
Hertz, Alice 283
Hertzog, Barry 393
Hess 85
High Technology Professionals for Peace 320
Hill & Knowlton 481
Hill, Lew 288
Hind Swaraj by Gandhi 1, 7, 21
Hindenburg, Paul von 60
Hindus 4, 9-10, 12, 19-20, 23
Hinton, Deane 332
Hiroshima 176, 456
Hiroshima by Hersey 177
Hirschmann, Cor Ramondt 267
Hitler, Adolf 16-7, 60, 63, 66-7, 75, 136, 157, 206, 263, 273,

438, 456
Ho Chi Minh 172, 235-7, 243
Hoare, Samuel 63
Hobhouse, Emily 258
Hodgkin, Henry 176
Holt, Hamilton 35
Honecker, Erich 380-1
Honey, Martha 352, 355
Hoover, Herbert 49, 52, 60, 73, 273
Hope, Miriam 554
House of Lords 157
House, Edward M. 34, 46-7
Houser, George 195
Houston, Charles 194
Howe, Mark 216
Howells, William Dean 194
Howland, William B. 35
HUAC 139, 282, 289
Hudson, Jackie 506
Huerta, Dolores 224, 227-9
Huet-Vaughan, Yolanda 290
Hull House 264
Hull, Cordell 77
Hull, John 352, 355
Human Rights Watch 460
Humphrey, Hubert 246
Hunter Report 10
Hunthausen 310
Husak, Gustav 371, 382
Hussein (Jordan king) 107, 480, 490
Hussein, Qusay 503
Hussein, Saddam 115, 457, 460, 468-9, 478-83, 489, 492, 495, 497, 500-1, 503, 559
Hussein, Uday 503
Hutus 121

IAEA 125, 481, 490, 562
Ibn Saud 465
ICBL 288
ICC 512, 515, 562
IDDS 317
IDF 470, 496
IFOR 128, 176

IFP 427
IMF 336, 530
In Contempt of Congress 340
In the King of Prussia 309
Indian Congress 3, 11, 13, 15-7, 396
Indian Opinion 4, 7-8
Indian Relief Act 8
Indochina War 238, 439, 447
INF Treaty 377, 443
Inkatha Freedom Party 416-9
INS 223, 343, 511
Instant Runoff Voting 527
Institute for Policy Studies 340
Institute for World Order 191
INTERFET 128
International Action Center 505
International Conference of Parliamentarians 166
International Conference on Racism 515
International Criminal Court 512, 515, 562
International Plan for Cleaner Energy 515
International Red Cross 406
International Solidarity Movement 522
International Women's Day 364, 507
Inventory of a Soul by Suttner 256
Ipatovsky 374
IPPNW 319
IRA 463
Iran-Contra 341, 346, 356, 447
Iraq Pledge of Resistance 506-7
Iraq Veterans Against the War 510
Iraq War 509, 561
Iraq-Iran War 479-80, 485
IRS 278, 345, 523
Irwin, Viceroy 14-5
Islamist 464
Israeli Defense Force 470, 496
Itliong, Larry 224-5

Iturbide, Agustin 325
IVAW 510

Jack, Homer 303
Jackson, Jesse 218
Jackson, Jimmie Lee 217
Jackson, Robert H. 84
Jacobs, Aletta 266-7
Jains 524
James, William 518
Jaruzelski 373
Jefferson, Thomas 81, 456
Jesuits 328
Jesus 6, 133, 141, 197, 205-6,
  413, 518-9, 524-5, 533
Jews 16, 19, 85, 101, 343, 367,
  370, 441, 456
Jinnah 18
Jodl 85
John Paul II 372-3, 382, 414
John XXIII 278, 326
Johnny Got His Gun by Trumbo
  455
John-Roger 534-5
Johnson, Lyndon 208-9, 217, 220,
  225, 241, 245, 283, 439, 477
Johnson, Mordecai 197
Jones, Charles 212, 214
Jordan, Clarence 278
Justice in Everyday Life 454
Justice in War Time by Russell
  155

Kabat, Carl 309, 549
Kadar, Janos 369, 379
Kahn, Herman 191
Kallenbach, Hermann 7
Kaltenbrunner 85
Kant, Immanuel 30, 145
Kantor, Jimmy 405
Kapp, Wolfgang 365
Kappists 365
Karachi Agreement 102
Karimov, Islam 470
Karmal, Babrak 114
Kassem, Abdel Karim 477-8

Kathrada, Ahmed 397, 405-7
Kazel, Dorothy 331
KCSB 560
Keitel 85
Keller, Helen 455
Kellogg, Frank 57
Kellogg-Briand Pact 57-8, 85, 261,
  272, 553
Kelly, Kathy 476-7, 492, 494-9,
  524
Kelly, Petra 299, 301, 314
Kennedy, Edward 318
Kennedy, John 108-9, 161-2, 187-
  188, 204, 206-8, 213-5, 240,
  304, 353, 469, 477
Kennedy, Robert 204, 213, 216,
  226, 228, 245, 436
Kent State 247
Kerensky 365
Kerry, John 353
KFOR 128, 460
KGB 374, 384-5
Khan, Mir Alam 5
Khmer Rouge 435, 437
Khomeini 115
Khrushchev 109, 159, 162, 164,
  187, 304, 369
King, A. D. 207
King, Coretta Scott 197, 200, 206,
  208, 220, 287
King, James Lawrence 355
King Jr., Martin Luther 171, 193,
  197-211, 215, 218, 220-1, 225,
  227, 233, 303, 413, 541
Kingdom of God is Within You by
  Tolstoy 6
Kirk, Gwyn 313
Kissinger, Henry 113, 246, 435,
  437, 440, 478
KLA 458-9
Knox, Geoffrey 62
Kohl, Helmut 383
Koinonia 278
Kolakowski 370
Kolhatkar, Sonali 560
Komisaruk, Katya 551

Komsomol 373
Koo, Wellington 66
KOR 371-2
Korean War 105, 117, 210, 238, 274
Kornilov 365
Korotich, Vitaly 375
Kosovo Verification Mission 459
Kosovo War 462
Kossuth 364
Kotane, Moses 403-4
KPFA 289, 553
KPFK 289, 560-1
KPFT 289
Krauthammer, Charles 340
Kravchuk, Leonid 387
Krenz, Egon 381-2
Kriegel 370
Krieger, David 562
Kruger, Jimmy 409
Kryuchkov 386
Ku Klux Klan 201, 209, 278, 289
Kucinich, Dennis 290, 322
Kulakov 374
Kurds 57, 460, 464, 487, 491
Kuron 371-2
Kyoto Protocol 515

La Prenza 336
Ladd, William 30
Laden, Osama bin 463-5
LAG 311
Lagomarsino 541
LaGuardia, Fiorello 451
Lakoff, George 562
Lancet 498, 504
Landsbergis 383
Language and Politics by Chomsky 431
Lao-zi 145, 533
LaPorte, Roger 278
Lasar, Rita 290
Laval, Pierre 63
Law of the Sea Treaty 181
Lawson, James 203, 210-1
Lawyers Alliance for Nuclear Arms

Control 320
Lawyers Committee for Nuclear Policy 320
Lay Down Your Arms by Suttner 257
LCFO 217
LDK 458
League Assembly 59, 64, 67
League Council 58-9, 63, 65
League mandate 100
League of Nations 29, 33, 35, 42, 45-7, 49-56, 59, 61-5, 67, 71-5, 118, 134-6, 143, 156, 178, 261, 263, 271, 273
Lebrun 261
Lembede, Anton 394-5
Lemus, Jose Maria 326
Lenin 365
Lester, Sean 67
Lewis, John 207, 211-2, 215-7, 242
Lewis, Tom 244
Liberation 283
Lie, Trygve 102-5
Lieber, Francis 29
Life of Gandhi by Fisher 223
Ligachev, Yegor 378
Lincoln 29
Lippman, Walter 444
Liteky 360
Litvinov, Maxim 59, 77
Liuzzo, Viola 217
Livermore Action Group 308, 311, 347, 541
Lloyd George 44, 49-50, 55
Locarno Treaty 56, 63, 85
Lodge, Henry Cabot 31, 35, 50, 72
Lollan, Stanley 398
London Naval Treaty 59
Long Walk to Freedom by Mandela 394
Looby, Z. Alexander 210
Lopez, Oswaldo 328
Lopez, Rene 231
Lorenz, Konrad 455

Los Angeles Times 229, 486, 535
Lowndes County Freedom Organization 217
Luke 23:2 524
Lumumba, Patrice 107
Luthuli, Albert 391, 393-400, 402-403
Luttwitz 365
Lynd, Staughton 242
Lyttle, Bradford 242
Lytton Commission 59
Lytton, Victor 59

Maas, Elmer 309
MacArthur, Douglas 103-4, 236
MacDonald, Ramsay 15, 56, 60
Machiavellian 455
Machine Age by Suttner 256
Macmillan, Chrystal 267
Macmillan, Harold 401
MacNeil-Lehrer News Hour 446, 485
Malcriado 225
Magaña 333-4
Maharaj, Mac 406
Mahathir Mohamad 295
Mahdi, Ali 120
Mahlangu, Solomon 407
MAI Treaty 450
Majano, Adolfo 331
Major, John 422, 489
Makarios 110
Malan, Magnus 395-6, 407, 427
Malik, Charles H. 89
Malik, Jacob 104
Malval, Robert 125
Mandela, Nelson 391-7, 399-407, 412-24, 426-7, 462
Mandela, Winnie 400, 406-7, 417, 419
Mandela, Zindzi 414
Mangope, Lucas 411
Manhattan Project 175
Manufacturing Consent by Chomsky 444-6
Mao Zedong 102

MAPA 227
Marcos, Ferdinand 439, 469
Marks, J. B. 394, 396, 404
Marshall, Burke 213
Marshall, Thurgood 194, 196
Marti, Farabundo 326
Martinez, Maximiliano Hernandez 326
Marx, Karl 197
Marxism 252, 400
Masol, Vitaly 385
Mass Democratic Movement 415
Massey, Raymond 177
Matanzima, K. D. 407, 411
Matsuoka, Yosuke 59
Matthews, Zachariah 398
Matthiesen 310
Maurin, Peter 275-6
Mazowiecki, Tadeusz 380
Mbeki, Govan 404-5
Mbeki, Thabo 419-20, 422, 424, 426, 429
McCain, John 505
McCarthy, Eugene 245
McCarthyism 158, 171, 223
McCloy, John J. 176, 187, 190, 456
McCloy-Zorin Agreement 188
McCracken, Maurice 495
McCullough, Thomas 224
McDonnell, Donald 223
McGovern, George 248
McKissick, Floyd 218
McMichael, David 552
McNamara, Robert 248
McTaggart, David 305
Mda, A. P. 394
Meacher, Michael 290
Mearsheimer, John 462
Medina, Eliseo 228
Medrano, Jose Alberto 326, 329
Meese, Edwin 341
Meet the Press 218
Mejia, Camilo 477, 509
Melman, Seymour 282, 466
Mendlovitz, Saul 191

Mengel, James 244
Meredith, James 214, 218
Merwe, Johan van der 427
Meyer, Karl 494
Meyerding, Jane 255
MFDP 217
MFSO 506, 509
Mhlaba, Raymond 404-5, 412
Michnik, Adam 369, 371-2
Middle East Watch 484
MIF 126
Miller, Webb 14
Millis, Walter 455
Milobs 100
Milosevic 457-8
Mine Ban Treaty 288
Minkwitz, Bill 551
MINUCI 123
MINUGUA 118
MINURCA 122
MINURSO 120
MINUSTAH 126
MIPONUH 126
MISAB 122
Mississippi Freedom Democratic
    Party 217
MIT 432, 435
Mixner, David 315
MK 403, 405, 407, 413, 416
Mlangeni, Andrew 405, 412
MNS 306
Moakly-Murtha 335
Mobilization for Survival 308, 317
Mobilization to End the War in
    Vietnam 173
Mobutu Sese Seko 470
Moczar 370
Modise, Joe 404, 416
Modrow 380
Mohawks 364
Molina, Arturo 327
Molotov 67, 77, 238
Mondale, Walter 439
Monroe Doctrine 38, 47, 50, 72,
    163, 325, 356
Monroe, James 325

Montero, Jose 352
Montessori, Maria 15, 263
Montgomery Improvement Asso-
    ciation 198, 201
Montgomery, Anne 309
Montt, Rios 327
MONUA 119
MONUC 123
Moore, Michael 290
Moore, William 215
Moraga, Silvio 336
Morel, E. D. 259
Morgan v. Virginia 195
Morley, John 4
Moroka 395-6
Morris, Catherine 310
Morse, Wayne 241, 302
Moscicki 75
Moscow Declaration 77
Moses, Robert 214, 216, 242
Moss, Richard 540
Mossadegh 477
Mothers for Peace 278, 307
Motsoaledi, Elias 405
Mountbatten 18
MSIA 534-5
Mubarak, Hosni 480
Mugabe, Robert 430
Mujahidin 464
Mulroney 416
Murphy, Duncan 349
Murray 400
Musharraf 472
Muslim League 18
Muslims 4, 10-2, 19, 23, 90, 102,
    106, 461, 547
Mussolini, Benito 16, 60-3, 65, 67,
    75, 156-7, 438
Muste, A. J. 151, 162, 166-72,
    195, 197, 220, 233, 242, 433,
    443
My Lai massacre 247, 455
Myrdal, Gunnar 195

NAACP 194, 196, 198, 207, 210-1,
    214

Nader, Ralph 290, 527
NAFTA 450
Nagasaki 176, 456
Nagy, Imre 369
Naicker 395
Naidu, Sarojini 14
Nairn, Allan 289-90, 462
Najam, Adil 562
Napoleonic wars 29
Narayan, Jayaprakash 172
NASA 435
Nash, Diane 212-3
Nasser, Gamal Abdel 105, 109
Natal Indian Congress 3, 395
Nation, The 283, 485
National Conference of Catholic
  Bishops 228
National Council of Churches of
  Christ 320
National Farm Labor Union 223
National Labor Relations Act 227
National Party 393, 395, 397, 400,
  419, 424, 426-7
NATO 128, 147, 274, 312, 369,
  383, 457-8, 460-1, 470, 515
Navajivan 11
Nazis 80, 136, 175, 178, 235,
  263, 343, 367, 439
NCACC 422
NCCCW 272-3
NCW 256
NDE 305
NED 294, 342
Negrin, Juan 65
Negroponte, John 465
Nehru, Jawaharlal 163, 301, 397
Nehru, Motilal 11
Neighbors for Peace and Justice
  297
Neurath 85
New Hopes for a Changing World
  by Russell 158
New Internationalist 493
New Military Humanism by Chom-
  sky 457
New Nuclear Danger by Caldicott

321
New York Times 178, 247-8, 293,
  304, 332, 354, 435, 442, 457,
  479, 486, 497, 505
Newer Ideals of Peace by Addams
  264
Newsweek 332, 441, 457
NFLU 223
NFWA 224-7
NGOs 474, 524
Nicholai, Georg Friedrich 133
Nicholas II, Czar 29, 364
Nietzsche, Friedrich 533
Nine Power Treaty 66
Nixon, E. D. 198
Nixon, Richard 113, 204, 228,
  230, 246-8, 283, 478
Niyazov, Saparmurat 470
NLD 291-2, 294-6
NLF 164, 220, 239-40, 242, 245
NMD 321, 466
No Conscription Fellowship 153
No More War! by Pauling 302
Nobel Peace Prize 32, 145, 208,
  258, 273, 288, 292, 354, 373,
  391, 403, 414, 418, 428
Nobel, Alfred 256, 258
Nokwe, Duma 402, 404
Non-Proliferation Treaty 375
Nonviolence Guidelines 308
*Non-violence in an Aggressive
  World* by Muste 168
Nonviolent Action Handbook by
  Beck 522, 559, 561
Nonviolent Peace Force 522
Noriega, Manuel 340, 357-9, 444,
  470
North, Oliver 339, 341, 356-7,
  479
Northern Alliance 464
Norwegian Teachers' Union 366
Not In Our Name 506
NOW 297
NPT 418, 474, 514-5, 558
NSA 505
NSC 338-9

Nuclear Age Peace Foundation 560-1
Nuclear Free Seas 305
Nuclear Non-Proliferation Treaty 418, 474, 514-5, 558
Nuclear Policy Research Institute 321
Nuclear Resistor 508
Nunn, Sam 472
Nuremberg Actions 350, 550-1, 555
Nuremberg Principles 85-7, 250, 437, 486, 510, 540, 550, 552-3, 557, 560
Nuremberg trials 84-6, 241, 343
Nurses for Social Responsibility 320
NUSAS 408
NVDA 260
NWFC 317, 320
Nye, Gerald P. 273
Nzo, Alfred 415, 422

O'Donnell, Bill 551
O'Neill, Eugene 275
O'Reilly, Bill 297
OAS 111, 117, 328, 336, 340, 353-4, 358-9, 443, 449
OAU 119-20, 122, 423
Obiang, Teodoro 470
OECD 515
Oil for Food Program 490, 493-4, 504
Olguin, Venustiano 534
On Aggression by Lorenz 455
On the Beach by Shute 302
One World by Wilkie 177
One World or None 177
ONUB 123
ONUC 108
ONUCA 117
ONUMOZ 119
ONUSAL 117, 335
OPEC 478-9
Operation Breadbasket 218
Oppenheimer 177

ORDEN 326, 329
Orlando 45
Ortega y Gasset 533
Ortega, Daniel 336, 342, 346, 354
Ortega, Humberto 336
Orwell, George 432
OSCE 458-9
Osorio, Oscar 326
Ota, Yoko 177
Other Lands Have Dreams by Kelly 476-7
Ottawa Convention 461
Out of Iraq Caucus 504
Outer Space Treaty 473
Owen, Lord 127
Owen, Robert 355

Pacifica radio 288-9, 526
Padilla, Gilbert 224-5, 227
Paine, Tom 497
Palestinian Liberation Organization 113, 339, 441-2
Palestinians 101, 113, 440-1, 458, 465
Pan-African Congress 401, 418
Panama Canal treaty 357, 443
Panama Deception 359
Pan-American Conference 31
Papadopoulos, George 469
Papen, Franz von 60, 85
Paredes, Pablo 510
Parker, Karen 552
Parks, Rosa 198
Parliament of South Africa 425
Parliamentary Association for World Government 159
Parry, Danaan 540
Pasternak 376
Pastora, Eden 351, 355
Patel, A. B. 540
Patel, Vallabhbhai 11
Patterson, James T. 453
Patterson, John 213
Paul, Alice 270
Pauling, Linus 146, 160, 242, 280, 289, 302-3

PAX 278
Pax Christi 278, 316-7, 553
PBS 361
PCIJ 53-4, 62, 272
PCN 327, 333
PDF 357, 359-60
Peace Action 320
Peace Brigades International 522
Peace Corps 225
Peace or Atomic War? by Albert
    Schweitzer 131
Peace Pilgrim 255, 279-80
Peace-Out 510
Peck, James 213
Peng-Chun Chang 89
Pentagon Papers 244, 248, 453
*People's History of the United
    States* by Zinn 454
Perestroika by Gorbachev 363,
    377
Pérez de Cuellar 114-5, 119, 335
Perkins, John 290
Perle, Richard 322
Permanent Court of Arbitration 32
Pethick-Lawrence, Emmeline 264
Phares, Gail 344
Philip II of Spain 364
Philosophy of Civilization by
    Schweitzer 142
Pickering, Thomas 334
Pickett, Clarence 303
Pike, James 534
Plan for Peace by Clark 179
Plate, Thomas G. 562
Platte, Ardeth 506
Plea for Vegetarianism by Salt 2
Pledge of Resistance 324, 347,
    454, 552
Plessy v. Ferguson 196
PLO 113, 339, 441-2
Plowshares 8 309, 549
Poindexter, John 341, 356
POLISARIO 119
Polish Communist Party 372, 380
*Political Economy of Human
    Rights* by Chomsky 436

Political Ideals by Russell 156
Poole, Diane 553
Poor People's Campaign 221
Popieluszko, Jerzy 447
Portable World Bible 533
Portillo, Jose Lopez 337
Posey, Tom 355
Postwar America by Zinn 453
Potemkin 364
Powell, Adam Clayton 210
Powell, Colin 322, 484, 501, 512
Powell, Michael 297
Pratt, Hodgson 257
Pringle, James 441
Pritchett, Laurie 215
Profit Over People by Chomsky
    447
PRUD 326
PSR 319, 493, 536
*Psychological Operations in Guer-
    rilla Warfare* 339
Pu Yi 59
Public Citizen 297
Pugwash Conferences 160, 303
Putin 321, 472

Qaddafi 423, 484
al-Qaida 465-7, 471, 501
Quakers 30, 155, 303, 343
Quest of the Historical Jesus by
    Schweitzer 141
Quigley 559
Quintero, Rafael 355
Quisling, Vidkun 366
Qur'an 19, 90

Rabinowitch, Eugene 175, 177
Raeder 85
Raheem, Jehan 293
Rainbow Warrior 305
Rakosi 369
Rakowski 380
Ramos-Horta, Jose 289
Randolph, A. Philip 194, 196, 207,
    242
Rangers 436

Rankin, Jeannette 254, 270, 272
Ratner, Michael 290
Rauen, Holly 349, 551-2
Rauschenbusch, Walter 197
RAWA 471
Rawls, John 456
RDP 420, 423
Reagan Doctrine 340
Reagan, Ronald 230, 285, 312, 317-8, 328, 331-4, 337-41, 343, 345-6, 348, 351-2, 355, 357-8, 374-5, 377, 379, 382, 429, 442-3, 446-8, 456, 464, 466, 471, 478, 535, 540-1, 547, 551
Reagon, Cordell 214
Red Cross 51, 88
Red Cross convention 29
Reeb, James 217
Reed, John 275
Reeves, Ambrose 398
Reifer, Tom 562
Reno, Janet 495
Repentance 377
Republicans 223, 229, 297, 320, 337, 508, 526, 533
Reuther, Walter 226
Reves, Emery 177
Reynolds, Earle 303
Reza Shah Pahlevi 438, 469, 477-478
Ribbentrop 67, 85
Rice, Condoleezza 322
Rice, Jim 346
Richards, Lowell 551
Richardson, Bill 293
RICO 355
Rio Mutual Defense Treaty 352
Ritter, Scott 492, 497
Rivera y Damas 333
Rivera, Manuel 228
Road to War by Millis 455
Roads to Freedom by Russell 156
Robert Kennedy Health and Welfare Fund 229
Roche, Douglas 562

Rockefeller, Nelson 454
Rojas, Al and Elena 228
Rolland, Romain 133, 259
Romero, Carlos Humberto 328
Romero, Oscar 324, 328, 330, 360
Ronat, Mitsou 435
Roosevelt, Eleanor 71, 73, 89
Roosevelt, Franklin 52, 60, 62, 66, 70-8, 80, 84, 137, 175, 177, 194, 235, 394, 465
Roosevelt, Theodore 31-4, 71, 356
Rosenberg 85
Ross, Fred 223, 228
Rowlatt Act 10
Roy, Arundhati 464
Roybal, Edward 223
Royden, Maude 259-61
Rudman, Warren 348
Rugova, Ibrahim 458
Rumpff 397, 402
Rumsfeld, Donald 321-2, 478, 503, 506, 510, 512
Rush, Molly 309
Rusk, Dean 304
Ruskin, John 4
Russell, Bertrand 140, 145, 150-165, 233, 280, 302, 432
Russell-Einstein Manifesto 159
Russo, Tony 453
Rustin, Bayard 171, 195, 242
Rutherford, Scot 550
Ryan, John C. 348

Sabata 407
SABC 426
SAC 303
Sachs, Alexander 137
Sacks, Bert 497
SACTU 398, 400
Sadat, Anwar 113, 440, 464
SADC 422
al-Sadr, Muqtada 503
SAIC 396, 398
Said, Edward 493

Sakharov, Andrei 191, 376, 437
Salazar, Ruben 229
SALT I 318
SALT II 317-8
Salt, Henry 2
San Francisco Mime Troupe 226
San Jose Mercury News 356
Sanctuary movement 344
SANDF 422, 427
Sandinistas 336-7, 339, 341-2, 351, 357
Sandino, Augusto 326
SANE 244, 280, 287, 303-4, 320
Saro-Wiwa, Ken 290, 422
Sartre, Jean-Paul 533
SASO 407-10
Sattar 497
Saturday Review 303
Satyagraha in South Africa by Gandhi 6
Sauckel 85
SAVAK 477
Savio, Mario 533
Scahill, Jeremy 290
Scavenius, Erik 367
Schacht 85
Schechter, Danny 290
Schell, Jonathan 318, 562
Schirach 85
Schlesinger, Arthur 467
Schneider, Berkeley Bob 308
School of the Americas 325, 499
Schorr, Daniel 457
Schuchardt, John 309
Schultz, George 338, 357
Schuschnigg, Kurt von 66
Schwarzkopf Jr., Norman 480, 482, 484
Schwarzkopf Sr., Norman 477
Schweitzer, Albert 1, 131, 141-7, 301-2
Schwerner, Michael 216
Schwimmer, Rosika 264, 267
SCLC 202, 205, 209-11, 218, 220
Scott, Michael 162, 172
Scoville, Herbert 318, 539

SDI 374, 376, 378
SDP 365
SDS 241, 244
SEATO 238, 250
Secord, Richard 340, 355
Secret Army Organization 436
Selassie, Haile 62-3, 120, 394
Selebi, Jackie 422-3
Seneca Women's Peace Camp 313
Serbian Army 458
Seyss-Inquart 85
SFPT 470
Shackley, Theodore 355
Shape of Things to Come by Wells 177
al-Sharaf, Hisham 497
Sharon, Ariel 471
Shaw, Bernard 15
Shays' Rebellion 456
Shcharansky, Anatoly 375
Shea, Jamie 459
Sheehan, Cindy 509, 513
Sheehan, Daniel 355
Sheehan, Neil 248
Sheen, Martin 309, 560
Sherrod, Charles 212, 214
Sheth, Dada Abdulla 3
Shevardnadze, Eduard 374, 385
Shi'a 483, 487, 503
Shiozawa, Admiral Koichi 59
Shridharani, Krishnalal 195
Shriver, Sargent 226
Shushkevish 387
Shute, Nevil 302
Shuttlesworth, Fred 202, 205, 213
Siegenthaler, John 213
Siegmund-Schultze, Friedrich 176
Sikelianos, Glafko 541
Sikhs 19
Silber, John 453
Silva, Benedita da 297
Singh, J. N. 403
Singlaub, John 355
SIPRI 316
al-Sistani, Ali 503
Sisulu, Walter 394-8, 403-4, 406-

407, 412
Sivard, Ruth 287
60 Minutes 496
Skinner, B. F. 433
Slater, Alice 562
SLORC 291-2, 294
Slovo, Joe 403-4, 416, 419
Smiley, Alfred K. 30
Smiley, Glenn 210
Smith, Adam 448
Smith, Al 73
Smith, Ruby Doris 212
Smrkovsky 370
Smuts, Jan Christiaan 5, 8, 46, 393, 395, 405
SNCC 204, 207, 211, 213-7, 451
SNCC by Zinn 214, 451
SOA 357, 360-1
Soares, Jolo Baena 354
Sobukwe, Robert 401, 404
Soccer War 327
Social Democratic Party 365
Social Workers for Peace 320
Socialist Workers Party 436
Socrates 206, 535
Sohn, Louis B. 174, 178, 181, 183-7, 190
Sojourners 346-7
Soldier of Fortune 351
Solidarity Union 372, 379-80
Solomon, Norman 290
Solzhenitsyn 437, 460
Somoza, Anastasio 328, 336, 351, 356
Somoza, Luis 336
Somoza Garcia, Anastasio 326
Soong 77
SORT 322, 472
Soto, Bernard 350
Spaak, Paul-Henri 108
Spadafora, Hugo 357
Spanish Civil War 65, 432
Spanish-American War 455
SPDC 295
Speer 85
Spencer, Herbert 256

Spider's Web by Friedman 478
Spingarn, Arthur B. 194
Spock, Benjamin 221, 304
Sponeck, Hans von 492, 494, 496, 501, 512
SPU 242
Sputnik 304
Stafford, Robert 344
Stalin 78, 80, 157, 365, 368-9, 376, 466
Stamp Act 364
Star Wars 376
Star, Ellen Gates 264
Starhawk 297
START 287
Steele, C. K. 202
Steinberg, Saul 551
Stewart, Bill 336
Stewart, Lynne 290
Stimson, Henry 58, 176, 178
Stop the Next War Now 298
Stowe, Harriet Beecher 258
Streicher 85
Stride Toward Freedom by King 193, 199, 202
Strong, Maurice 388
Student Peace Union 304
Study of Future Worlds by Falk 191
Sufis 524
Suharto 296, 422, 469
Sukarno 109, 163
Suleyman 490
Summer Flower by Tamiki Hara 177
Sunnis 504
Suttner, Bertha von 254, 256-9
Svoboda, Ludvik 370
Swann, Robert 242
Swedish International Development Agency 296
Sykes-Picot Treaty 48, 55
Synanon 231
Syngman Rhee 104
Szilard, Leo 137, 174-7, 455

Taft, William Howard 32, 35, 50
Tagore, Rabindranath 9, 14
Tahboub, Jihad 498
Taliban 463-4, 471
Tambo, Oliver 394, 396-7, 400, 402, 404, 414, 417
Tambs, Lewis 352
Tarhanli, Turgut 512
Tashima, A. Wallace 540
Taylor, Charles 122
Teamsters 227, 229
Teatro de Campesino 226
Telecommunications Act 449
Teller, Edward 289
Terrorism and War by Zinn 465
Thant, U 99, 108-9, 111, 116, 163, 282
Thatcher, Margaret 312, 374, 377, 416, 448, 481, 547
Theology of Liberation by Gutierrez 326
Theory of Justice by Rawls 456
Thieu 248
Thomas Aquinas 89
Thompson, E. P. 301, 314
Thompson, Hugh 455
Thoreau, Henry David 6, 197-8
Time 457, 468
Tin U 291-2, 295
Tloome, Dan 404
Tobacco Control 516
Tolstoy, Leo 6-7, 155, 258, 518
Torrijos, Omar 356, 444
Toynbee 139
Transvaal Indian Congress 395
TRC 425, 427-9
Treaty of London 48
Trent, Barbara 359
Trojan War 262
Trotsky, Leon 365
Trotskyism 168, 236
Trueblood, Benjamin 30
Trujillo 110
Truman, Harry 84, 103, 175-7, 195-6, 235-7
Trumbo, Dalton 455

Truth and Reconciliation Commission 425, 427-9
Tshombé, Moishe 107
Ture, Kwame 217
Turn and Reform 379
Turning the Tide by Chomsky 442
Tutsis 121
Tutu, Desmond 392-3, 412, 414-415, 421, 426, 428-30
Twain, Mark 455

U2 296
UAW 226
UCS 332
UDC 259
UDF 413, 415, 428
UDHR 287, 458
UFPJ 506, 509
UFW 229-31, 279
UFWOC 227
UN Commission on Human Rights 89
UN Compensation Commission 494
UN Convention on Discrimination against Women 516
UN Convention on the Rights of the Child 516
UN Economic and Social Council 89
UN General Assembly 79-80, 83, 87, 89, 100-1, 104, 106, 108, 112, 127, 183, 352, 404, 423, 489
UN Human Rights Commission 90
UN Security Council 83, 99-107, 110, 112, 114, 116, 118, 121-2, 124-5, 127-8, 183, 190, 296, 340, 401, 422, 440-1, 461, 467-8, 480, 488-93, 500-2, 512, 528, 557-8
UNAMIR 121
UNAMSIL 123
UNASOG 120
UNAVEM 119
UNAVEM II 119

UNAVEM III 119
UNCIP 102
Uncle Tom's Cabin by Stowe 258
UNCOK 103
UNCRO 127
UNDOF 113
UNEF 106, 108, 111
UNEF II 113
Unemployed Leagues 168
UNESCO 186, 516
UNFAO 296
UNFICYP 110
UNGOMAP 115
UNHCR 460
UNICEF 450, 488-91
UNIFIL 114, 462
UNIIMOG 116
UNIKOM 124-5
Union of Concerned Psychoana-
    lysts 320
Union of Concerned Scientists 320
UNIPOM 111
Unitarians 303, 548-9
United Farm Workers 229-31, 279
United for Peace and Justice 506,
    509
United Fruit Company 327-8
United Iraq Alliance 504
United Methodist Council of Bish-
    ops 320
United Nations 17, 67, 70-1, 74,
    77-84, 86-7, 89, 91, 94, 96-7,
    99-128, 130, 138, 146, 162-3,
    171, 178-9, 181-2, 186-90,
    220-1, 235, 244, 250, 274, 278,
    282, 288, 290, 293, 295, 303,
    308, 335, 340, 353, 359, 378,
    386, 388-9, 395, 417, 437, 439,
    443, 449, 458-60, 462, 465,
    467, 472, 476, 483, 488, 492,
    495-6, 500, 506, 511-2, 515,
    528, 538, 556, 558
United Nations Charter 81-4, 91,
    103, 111, 125, 127, 163, 181,
    185, 189, 250, 340, 437, 443,
    460, 486, 497, 504, 509-10,

512, 516, 553, 556, 561
United Packinghouse Workers 223
United Presbyterian Church 320
United Social Christian Party 350
United States Constitution 226,
    246, 346, 486, 510, 527
United Way 524
United World Federalists 177
Universal Declaration of Human
    Rights 71, 89-97, 423, 490, 538
UNMEE 121
UNMIBH 128
UNMIH 125
UNMIK 128
UNMIL 122
UNMIS 123
UNMISET 128
UNMOGIP 102, 111
UNMOP 128
UNMOT 126
UNMOVIC 494
UNOCI 123
UNOGIL 107
UNOMIG 126
UNOMIL 122
UNOMSIL 123
UNOMUR 121
UNOSOM 120
UNOSOM II 120
UNPREDEP 128
UNPROFOR 127-8
UNRRA 78
UNSCOB 100
UNSCOM 468, 490, 492-4
UNSF 109
UNSMIH 126
UNTAC 124
UNTAES 127
UNTAET 128
UNTAG 118
UNTCOK 103
UNTEA 109
UNTMIH 126
Unto This Last by Ruskin 4
UNTSO 101
UNYOM 110

UPI 457
Urban League 207
Urey 177
URNG 118
US Arms Control and Disarmament Agency 187
US Congress 40, 195, 246, 248, 271, 283, 337-8, 347, 353, 356, 361, 416, 429, 468, 472, 480, 483, 487, 500, 504-5, 510
US House of Representatives 334, 338, 340-1, 414
US Senate 32-3, 58, 62, 78-9, 353, 357, 480, 527
US Supreme Court 195-6, 201, 207, 214, 227, 248, 452
USA Patriot Act 466
USAID 330, 334, 353-4, 450, 502
USDA 295
UWF 177, 303
Uwilingiyimana, Agathe 121

Valdez, Luis 226
Vale Company 449
Van Gogh 142
Vance, Cyrus 127, 336, 418
Vance, Robert S. 355
Vandenberg Action Coalition 308, 310, 539-40
Vanderbilt 325
Varelli, Frank 345
Vatican II 326
Vayo, Julio Alvarez del 64
Vega 305
Versailles Treaty 45, 49-50, 52, 56, 59, 61, 63, 85, 366
Verwoerd, Hendrik 398, 403
Vessey 338
Veterans Peace Action Teams 349
Vickman, Leon 540
Victor Emmanuel 75
Viet Minh 235-9
Vietnam Moratorium Committee 246
Vietnam War 148, 165, 172, 217, 220-1, 228, 233-4, 239, 243, 245, 247-9, 251-2, 274, 278, 283-4, 349, 433, 435-6, 438-9, 451, 453, 466
Village Voice 485
Villard, Fanny Garrison 271
Villard, Oswald Garrison 194
VitW 493, 495-7, 522, 524
Vlok, Adriaan 427
Voice of America 377
Voices in the Wilderness 493, 495-7, 522, 524
Voting Rights Bill 209
VVAW 247

Waldheim, Kurt 115-6
Walesa, Lech 372, 385
Walker, William 325
Wall Street Journal 449
Wallace, George 209, 215
Wallis, Jim 310, 346
Walsh, Patrick 560
Walton, Malcolm 560
WAND 297, 319
War Crimes Tribunal 165-6
War Diary by Courtney 259
War of 1812 463
War Powers Resolution 505
War Resisters League 171, 176, 242, 272, 279, 303
War Without Violence by Shridharani 195
Warren, Earl 196
Warsaw Pact 163, 368-70, 380-1, 386
Washington Naval Conference 271
Washington Post 248, 282, 296, 332
Washington, Booker T. 199
Washington, George 35-6
Watergate 248, 436
Waters, Maxine 287, 290, 504
WBAI 289
WCTU 256
Webb, Gary 355
Weil, Simone 261-3

Weinberger, Caspar 338, 536
Weiss, Cora 287
Welles, Sumner 455
Wells, H. G. 174, 177
Wells, Ida B. 194
Westmoreland, General 245
Wheeler, General 245
Where Do We Go from Here? by King 218
Which Way to Peace? by Russell 157
WHISC 361
White, Robert 331
White, Walter 194
Whitehead, Alfred North 151
WHO 186, 296, 489-90, 493, 517
Why Men Fight by Russell 154
Why We Can't Wait by King 207
WIDF 286-7
Wildflower, Caroline 285
Wilhelm, Richard 552
Wilkie, Wendell 177
Wilkins, Roy 207, 211, 218
Williams, Cecil 404
Williams, Jody 288
Willson, S. Brian 324, 348-50, 550
WILPF 135, 171, 269, 271-4, 278, 281, 283, 297, 317
Wilson, Dagmar 280, 282, 433
Wilson, Diane 297
Wilson, Edith 51
Wilson, Edwin 355
Wilson, Woodrow 28, 33-52, 71-72, 74, 153, 264, 267, 269-70
Wingfield, Charles 215
Winooski 44 344
Witness for Peace 345-7, 522
WMD 443, 467, 468, 473
Wofford, Harris 213
Wojtyla, Karol 372
Wolf, Harold de 220
Wolfowitz, Paul 322, 512
Wolpe, Harold 405
Woman Suffrage Alliance 266
Woman's Peace Congress 266
Woman's Peace Party 265-7, 269

Women for Women International 297
Women Strike for Peace 278, 281-283, 304
Women's Pentagon Action 285, 311, 318
Woods, Donald 412
Woolsey, Lynn 504
Workers Party 168
Working People's Daily 292
World Bank 530
World Council of Churches 320, 328, 428
World Court 32, 271, 340, 447, 461, 463, 469, 529, 548
World Federalists 178, 536
World Food Program 491
World Health Organization 186, 296, 489-90, 493, 517
World Peace Brigade 172
World Peace Council 177
World Peace Movement 536, 549
World Peace Through World Law by Clark and Sohn 178, 181, 191
World Set Free by H. G. Wells 174
World Trade Center 463
World Tribunal on Iraq 512
World War I 8, 32, 34, 39, 84, 118, 133, 142, 152, 166, 176, 178, 181, 258-9, 261, 273, 364-5, 455, 477
World War II 67, 76, 118, 145, 157, 178, 223, 234, 248-9, 252, 261, 263, 270, 276, 308, 350, 356, 366-7, 436, 439, 442, 451, 465-6, 484, 499
WPS 271-2
WPU 271-2
WRI 176
Wright, Jim 341
WRL 171, 242, 272, 279, 303
WSP 278, 281-3, 304
WTO 296, 449, 530
Wylie, David 350
Wyszynski 368-9

Xuma, Albert 393, 395

Yakovlev, Alexander 375, 384
Yanayev 386
Yasko, Stephen 289
Yeltsin, Boris 374, 377, 384, 386, 491
Yeravda Pact 16
Yogi Bhajan 540
Young India 11
Young, Andrew 114, 207
Young, Whitney 207, 218
Youth League 394-6

Yugoslavia War 457

Zalaquett, Jose 425
Zamora, Mario 329
Zapatistas 296, 450
Zellner, Bob 215
Zhou Enlai 163, 238
Zinn, Howard 214-5, 290, 431, 434, 450-7, 465-6, 493
Zionists 370
Zorin, Vasily 189-90
Zulu Rebellion 4
Zumach, Andreas 290

World Peace Communications
Books by Sanderson Beck

ETHICS OF CIVILIZATION:
 Volume 1: Middle East & Africa to 1875
 944 pages ($25)
 Volume 2: India & Southeast Asia to 1875
 775 pages ($25)
 Volume 3: China, Korea & Japan to 1875
 764 pages ($25)
 Volume 4: Greece & Rome to 30 BC
 640 pages ($25)
 Volume 5: Roman Empire 30 BC to 610
 628 pages ($25)
 Volume 6: Medieval Europe 610-1300
 766 pages ($25)

HISTORY OF PEACE:
 **Volume 1: Guides to Peace and Justice
 from Ancient Sages to the Suffragettes**
 616 pages ($25)
 Volume 2: World Peace Efforts Since Gandhi
 624 pages ($25)

Nonviolent Action Handbook
 95 pages ($5)

The Art of Gentle Living
 107 pages ($5)

BEST FOR ALL: How We Can Save the World
 121 pages ($5)

WISDOM BIBLE (Editor)
 920 pages (hardback $45, paperback $25)

Complete texts of all these books and other writings by Sanderson Beck are available on his website at **san.beck.org**. Books can be ordered from **1worldpeace.org**.